# REVOLUTIONARY DREAMS

N. Field

2002

# REVOLUTIONARY DREAMS

## Utopian Vision and Experimental Life in the Russian Revolution

RICHARD STITES

OXFORD UNIVERSITY PRESS

*New York*      *Oxford*

## Oxford University Press

Oxford   New York   Toronto
Delhi   Bombay   Calcutta   Madras   Karachi
Petaling Jaya   Singapore   Hong Kong   Tokyo
Nairobi   Dar es Salaam   Cape Town
Melbourne   Auckland

and associated companies in
Berlin   Ibadan

Library of Congress Cataloging-in-Publication Data
Stites, Richard.
Revolutionary dreams.
Bibliography: p.
Includes index.
1. Soviet Union—Intellectual life—1917–
2. Utopias.   3. Soviet Union—History—Revolution.
1917–1921.   I. Title.
DK266.4.S75   1989   947.084   88-5263
ISBN 0-19-505536-5
ISBN 0-19-505537-3 (pbk)

6 8 9 7 5

Printed in the United States of America
on acid-free paper

*To Helena
and her Country*

# ACKNOWLEDGMENTS

In this work—which might be called history from the side rather than history from above or below—the object of study is often odd: street motion, funerals, science fiction novels, dress styles, parades, the formation of queues, the naming of babies, songs, and many other things—as well as the more familiar categories of historical behavior. The source base, like the subject matter itself, is extremely diverse and eclectic. One can hardly ask a librarian or an archivist for the files on gesture, "revolutionary space," life styles, or images. There is therefore no "main collection" or fond from which I have drawn my information. I have simply read widely in some of the best libraries in the world. To do this, I have accumulated many scholarly debts over the past ten years. For financial support I wish to thank Ohio State University, the Kennan Institute for Advanced Russian Studies of the Wilson International Center for Scholars, the National Endowment for the Humanities, the Graduate School and the Quigley Fund of Georgetown University, the W. Averill Harriman Institute for the Advanced Study of the Soviet Union at Columbia University, the John Simon Guggenheim Foundation, the Fulbright Faculty Research Awards program, and IREX. A bare enumeration of grants cannot convey the intangible assistance that I have gotten from these organizations—a place to study and research, an intellectual environment, a band of friendly well-wishers, letters of support and introduction, and various kinds of material and logistical aid. I thank them all deeply.

Among the many libraries and other study centers I have used, the following were the most important: in Leningrad, the State Public Library, the library of the Philharmonia, the city network of listening-rooms (fonoteki) provided by the public library, the library of the Rimsky-Korsakov Conservatory of Music, the Institute of Theater, Music, and Cinematography, the Museum of Musical Instruments, the Museum of the History of Atheism and Religion, and the Library of the Academy of Sciences; in Moscow, the Lenin Library; in Helsinki, the Slavonic Library, the Finnish Literature Society, the Soviet Institute, the Labor Archives, the Library of the Museum of Finnish Architecture, and the science fiction collection of the Ursu Astronomical Society; in London, the British Library and the library of the School of Slavonic and East European Studies; in Munich, the library of the East European Institute; in Garmisch, the U.S. Army Russian Institute; in New York, the New York Public Library and the libraries of Columbia University—especially the Avery Library of Art and Architecture; in Washington, the Library of Congress, the National Archives, the National Institute of Health (Bethesda) Medical Library, and the American Red Cross.

I thank those who read parts or all of my manuscript and made helpful comments about my research: Joseph Bradley, Jeffrey Brooks, Katerina Clark, Theodore Friedgut,

Ben Hellman, John Hutchinson, Peter Kenez, Louise McReynolds, JoAnn Moran, Daniel Orlovsky, Gennady Ozernoy, Deborah Pearl, Marcus Rediker, Roman Serbyn, Jutta Scherrer, Ronald Suny, Ilmari Susiluoto, Robert C. Tucker, and Peter Weisensel. For conscientious research assistance at Georgetown, the Wilson Center, and Columbia, thanks to Alessandra Schroeder, Dina Birman, Denis McAuley, William Verley, Douglas Blum, Mark Rykoff, Thomas Barrett, and, most of all, Richard Johnson. My warm gratitude for the typing done by Helen Whitlock, William Di Giacomantonio, Karen Shellman, and Kathleen Ruschaupt. For that special combination of intellectual encouragement and warm friendship, I thank Abraham Ascher, Abbott Gleason, David Goldfrank, Leopold Haimson, Lars Kleberg, Marcus Rediker, Priscilla Roosevelt, Charles Rougle, Jonathan Sanders, S. Frederick Starr, and Richard Wortman. Most of all I am grateful for the love and companionship of Helena Järvinen and Andryusha Stites.

Chapter 3 is a reworking, with additional research, of an earlier essay published in Abbott Gleason, et al., eds. *Bolshevik Culture* (Bloomington: Indiana University Press, 1985). I thank Indiana Press for allowing me to use it here.

# CONTENTS

# LIST OF ILLUSTRATIONS
## *(following p. 164)*

# REVOLUTIONARY DREAMS

# Introduction

The present work of history is rooted in the intuitive belief that what large numbers of people want to know about a society of the past is actually what is important about that society. It is rich in illustrative material but simple in design. Its main argument is about the fate of utopianism and social experiment in the Russian revolutionary process, roughly from 1917 to 1930. That argument challenges the view that utopianism in the Revolution was largely or only Marxist and that this Marxism was (depending on one's view) either distorted in the final outcome by Lenin, Stalin, or both; or that it was fulfilled. Without expelling Marxism from the Revolution—an impossible thing—I ground my interpretation on the larger field of the social, intellectual, and cultural history of Russia—before, during, and after 1917. This broader focus has led me to the inevitable conclusion that the Russian Revolution took on its main spiritual, mental, and expressive forms from the collision and collusion of the major utopian traditions in Russian history: those of the people, those of the state, and those of the radical intelligentsia.

Utopianism, social and cultural experimentation, and drastic self-conscious innovation—symbolic and concrete—occur in the midst of all major social revolutions of modern times. They occur because of analogy, infection, and euphoria. The spectacle of falling idols and fallen kings erases the myth of infallible authority—on thrones, in books, in ways of life. The urge to symmetry in cultural instinct impels some people to remake everything, once the binding system has been repudiated and renounced. Revolution opens up new space and discloses endless vistas; it invites rebirth, cleansing, salvation. Revolution is Revelation, an eschatological moment in human experience that announces the New Order, the New World, the New Life. The motifs of release, liberation, and devolving power that infuse the rhetoric and symbolism of the revolutionary moment are invitations to refashion and redesign. The Russian Revolution possessed all of these features, and its pathos was deepened by the confluence of two remarkable facets of its history: the traditions of utopian dreaming and alternative life experiments that marked its past and the intersection of the moment of revolution (1917) with the swelling of the twentieth century technological revolution. Russia's was the first revolution to occur when both politics and technology were seen to be globally interlocked. The political side gave its international messianism a special force; its technological side added tremendous Promethean power to its visions and aspirations, releasing a much greater surge of futuristic fantasy than any previous revolution in history.

This book is about revolutionary dreams, utopianism in fancy, in programs and designs, and in behavior. As a study of revolutionary imagination and innovative action, it deals with the stormy period of history before and after the Great Russian Revolution of 1917. In it I have taken a fresh look at the familiar terrain of revolutionary historiography—high politics, the quest for power, party programs and ideology, and economic policies, all of which have been much written about by eminent scholars. And I have something to say about art and high culture. But my emphasis is on the feelings, words, thoughts, and actions that express, evoke, or symbolize what has been called "the utopian propensity."[1] It has long been a generally accepted, though seldom examined, commonplace that the Russian Revolution was a particularly utopian phenomenon. Writers often employ the word "utopian" to mean wholly unrealistic, harmful, or naive. This study is not an exposé of the "utopianism" of the Bolshevik movement though I will certainly have occasion to comment upon the "utopian" in Bolshevism, both in theory and in practice. My purpose is to uncover and retell in an interpretive framework the story of the rich, colorful, and deep currents of utopianism that swirled around the Russian Revolution.

Few scholars have analyzed the role of utopianism in the Revolution as a device for exciting the fantasy, dismantling an old order, forging a new world, or constructing a New Man. Yet, utopianism in this sense is the key to the emotional force of the Russian Revolution—as it is to any successful revolution. In this study, I deal with the "poetics" of revolution: its adornments, its goals related to the life of people, its forms, ideas, languages, feelings, inventions, temper, action, pathos, experiments, visions, and hopes. In other words, it is about revolutionary culture—as that term is now widely used by historians—about the building of a new civilization, the rich texture of social tradition and habit, and the interplay of material life and intellectual activity. By focusing on the utopian motif in the emerging revolutionary culture (including those currents in the Revolution that were defeated), I hope to advance the study of this remarkable phenomenon and to help humanize the subject which has often been the analysis of an enemy.

Why was utopianism so prominent in the Russian Revolution? What accounts for the blazing color, the luxuriant growth of experiment in the realms of society and culture? Is it simply that Marxism itself is "utopian" (i.e. impossible of realizing) and that the Russian Revolution was simply one among many twentieth century attempts to create a socialist society along Marxist principles of economic life? Even the most superficial glance at communist regimes wherein the Marxist programs have been imported and imposed from above—as in most of Eastern Europe for example—reveals at once that Marxism in and of itself (however defined) does not generate the kind of enthusiastic dreaming, the maximalism, and the euphoric expectation that occurred in Russia—and elsewhere—during its revolutions. The answer is to be found both in the indigenous utopian traditions as well as in the violent and explosive circumstances of its revolution. Utopian dreaming was a psychological mechanism experienced by many different kinds of people and induced by their perception of how to survive—as a state, a nation, a people, a culture—in a geopolitical and material-physical milieu that rendered survival and success questionable. Both social reverie and social design were alternatives to a system that seemed unable to deliver the two things essential to human happiness: a victory over nature to insure material abundance and a victory over egoism and exploitation to insure social justice.

There are many ways of classifying utopia, and scholars have constructed endless schemes of toponymy—without ever exhausting the types or explaining much about the role of utopia in history.[2] We all know that there are utopias, eutopias, eupsychias, and dystopias; that utopias come in pairs of hot and cold, hard and soft, time and space, near and far. The applications of these terms to my material will be perfectly clear to the reader, springing as they do from logic and common sense rather than from "utopiology." More essential to historical understanding than these mechanical devices is the social mentality of utopian dreaming in traditional Russia and in the Revolution. I have summarized these mentalities as popular utopia, administrative utopia, and socialist utopia. It has long been a convention to characterize the major social outlooks in Old

Russia as those of state, people, and intelligentsia. Each of these was enormously complicated and subject to modulation over time.

For the statesmen of the administrative utopian persuasion, Russia seemed difficult to govern and defend, threatened from without, too big, too poor, too weak. A survival mechanism emerged from their training and their perception of Russia's paucity of educated rulers and lack of a self-governable population. They did not wish to impose repressive slavery upon the masses, but to create order and purvey justice. Isolated psychologically from the common people because of Peter the Great's cultural revolution that Westernized an elite and retained a deeply rooted manorial and patrimonial system, they developed a compulsion to organize, shape, and train (not educate) the rural population on the model of an army, to regiment life, symmetricize living space, militarize part of society, and surround it with graphic and living symbols of solidarity, prosperity, obedience, and order.

Peasant utopianism was fed by fear of the state, anxiety about change that periodically led peasants to escape from the unreal Russia to a more "real" one by flight, rebellion, or sectarianism, to a quest for order—their own order. The changes wrought by reform and development in the decades from 1860 to 1917 were not sufficient to obliterate these psychic mechanisms of administrative or popular utopia however much they may have eroded the harsh conditions that gave birth to them in past times. The eruption of dormant forces in the Great Revolution of 1917 proves beyond the shadow of a doubt that subterranean mentalities had migrated down the generations, causing ancient visions to flash again on the screen of consciousness, latent feelings to be driven to the surface, hidden energies to be released. After the Bolshevik Revolution, a saddened and angry moderate socialist, voicing fear and aversion, saw it as a combination of tsarist military utopia (symbolized by Arakcheev) and violent peasant revolt (symbolized by Pugachëv). He was perhaps the first chronicler of this relationship between the events of 1917 to the deep forces and visions in Russian history.[3]

For the intelligentsia of the radical socialist persuasion, social daydreaming was a vocation, almost the only permissible one to a man or woman of culture and conscience. They felt alienated both from the state that they despised and from the *narod* (peasants, poor people, toiling masses) whom they worshipped, and they endured the agonies of repentance and shame at the backwardness and the oppressiveness—as they saw it—of the entire Russian system. Armed with elaborate ideas and intellectual systems partly imported from the West, they built utopias and taught personal revolt and dedication to the reshaping of society along the lines of social justice and a viable economic system. The maximalist cast of their thought, which was extraordinarily informed by passion and feeling, led them to the only "ideology" that fit their "utopia"—socialism, a way of life that overturned autocracy and class oppression, taught equality and justice, and repudiated capitalism—the evil menace that lurked around the corner of the future.

Each of these belief systems sought welfare and justice but through different means. For administrative utopians, the dominant metaphor was parade—marching and laboring under benevolent orderly authority; for peasant utopians it was *volya,* untrammeled freedom combined with village order or religious rule. Among the radical intelligentsia, order and freedom intermixed in their visions, their behavior patterns, and the organizations they created to overthrow the state. The urban and industrio-centric utopians that arose at the dawn of the twentieth century—in particular the Bolsheviks, the Russian Marxists with radical designs and insurgent energies—shifted the intelligentsia's utopia sharply from the country to the city, from the peasantry to the proletariat, from the

pastoral idyll of minimal, healthy consumption to the throbbing dynamo of development, national greatness, and power. Their rosy images of harmony and virtue in the
coming dawn of liberation were set in a frame of control and centralized organization.

The position of the intelligentsia in this history was complicated by the fact that on
the eve of the Revolution, it was undergoing extreme change and fragmentation, and
was achieving new levels of articulation and self-analysis at the very moment that West
European avant-garde culture began flowing into elitist circles at flood volume. Rapidly
assimilated, reinterpreted by the Russian artistic intelligentsia, European modernism in
many forms was introduced onto the stage of Russian revolutionary culture-making and
speculation. Thus even before the outbreak of the Revolution, an avant-garde utopia,
called by some a "revolution of the spirit," coexisted with, though seldom touched,
the utopian visions of the radical intelligentsia. Although the culture of the Silver Age
(roughly 1890–1917) was often at odds with social consciousness in the political sense,
some of its later outgrowths, particularly Futurism, generated extravagant visions of the
total transformation of the world—if not the cosmos—through an aesthetic revolution.
This strand of speculation, proclaimed in a very loud voice, melded in with the social
and technical utopia of the revolutionary years, enriching it, enlivening its mode of
expression, and often enough conflicting with it. My study is not a history of revolutionary high culture—many qualified scholars have written on this. But it does examine
certain key elements of culture in the broad sense to illustrate how people tried to live
the revolution, to express revolutionary feelings through myth, ritual, symbol, cult, or
community; some of these intersect at points with the history of early Soviet architecture, sculpture, ritual design, theater, music, literature, and graphic art.

When the Revolution—accompanied as it was at almost every stage with violence
and rapid change (both contrived and spontaneous)—demolished old authorities and old
alienating forces with the suddenness of a summer storm, the whole structure of utopianism underwent drastic change. Minds, feelings, emotions, gestures, and acts boiled
up in a cauldron of revolutionary speculation and experimentation. The hatred and fear
of power, authority, cities, central government, deference, luxury and wealth, outsiders,
science, technology, and machines—and conversely the exaltation of some of these
things—erupted in a blaze of imaginative metaphor and physical violence. The slum-
bering animosity between State, People, and Intelligentsia, among classes, regions, and
nations, and between town and country produced extravagant dreams and solutions to
the hideous terrors arising out of war, revolution, famine, and collapse. The victorious
branch of the radical intelligentsia—the Bolsheviks—was caught up in the drama of
spontaneous mass behavior and appalled by its "excesses", delighted at the breakup of
familiar forms and symbols but frightened at the prospect of unending destruction,
preaching freedom and demanding order, shattering the power edifices of the old order
and designing new and bigger ones to house the perfect society, applauding Pugachëv
and emulating Arakcheev.

Revolutionary dreamers and fighters now became rulers armed with the Bolshevik
dream of an urban industrial order of modernity and productivity combined with justice
and armed against competing dreams of the "people" and of the old intelligentsia. The
vistas opened up by the chaos of the Civil War allowed peasants and many other kinds
of people to activate old dreams of withdrawal, flight, anti-urbanism, and rural communalism. The war between Populism and Marxism that had accounted for a major
strain in Russian intellectual history now became a more complicated and active war

between dreamers, between the agents and apostles of Bolshevism on the one hand and a whole range of peasants, workers, sailors, and intellectuals formed under the green and black banners of peasant withdrawal and anarchical freedom on the other. The intelligentsia, hopelessly splintered, joined the camp of Bolshevism in order to promote their own visions and timetables of utopia, fought the Bolsheviks by enlisting in the opposition, or—as artists and cultural figures—tried to impose an avant-garde interpretation of revolutionary restructuring on the Bolshevik regime. The result was an extraordinarily lively market-place of ideas and feelings, projects, and experiments that adorned the social and cultural landscape of the next decade. The utopianizing of the nineteenth century now became a broad enterprise, continuing some of the themes of the prerevolutionary period but intermixed with new perspectives and hyperbolized by the atmosphere of reordering that was going on all around. The utopias, projects, and novels that emerged from this frenetic environment sometimes fit the general outline of the Marxist-communist future, sometimes opposed it, and at other times transcended it.

Simultaneously, the rich variety of customs and revolutionary styles of life cultivated in the decades before 1917 were now harnessed into the service of experiments in the remaking of culture and everyday life, experiments conducted in the full gaze of revolutionary society and drawing from the regime attitudes ranging from approval and support through skeptical tolerance to hostility. It is the tentative and hesitant attitude of Bolshevik leaders in the period 1917 to the early 1930s towards utopianism and experiment that marks off so visibly and palpably its political culture from that of the period that follows.

I have given special attention to revolutionary utopian behavior—iconoclasm in all its variants, carnival and ritual, moral practices and quasi-religious experience, egalitarianism, machinism, and communalism, among others. The connection between written utopias and utopian energies unleashed is well established in the history of millenarianism, East and West. The best known historians of utopian thought in the western world have even devised a cunning name for it: "applied utopistics."[4] In the Russian Revolution—as in the English and the French before it—utopian behavior was the living texture and illustration of utopianism itself.

The fresh breezes of revolutionary innovation (as well as its devastating winds) cannot be felt unless one steps from the pages of written utopias to examine the quasi-religious experiments of revolutionary innovators and the interiors of the workshops and laboratories of Revolution. One must make the distinction between a "mental model" or "blueprint" (utopia) on the one hand and the "practical enactment" or "experiment" (utopian community) on the other.[5] But experiment in this sense is to be sought not only in the isolated subcultures of small groups, but in the vast tableau of revolutionary life itself—from the onset of the Revolution in 1917 up into the Stalinist period when it was drastically transformed into something else.

In time of revolution, a utopia is a script for the coming drama of life, a scenario of novel human relations, and a guide to the use of space, time, and technologies. But one must not envision the utopianizing process of the revolution as one where actors scrutinize a text in order to find a guide to action—though this often happened—but rather as a very thick and rich interaction between what is sometimes called life and art, one imitating the other and each reshaping both. The writers, directors, actors, and audiences of the utopian world were part of an entire revolutionary performance inspired by vision and fantasy, driven by daily needs and aspirations—together creating a whole and distinctive epoch of revolutionary remaking. This book is the story of a laboratory of revolution, a theater of future life, and what Moshe Lewin calls "society in the making."[6]

The structure of the book reflects the general argument outlined above. The principal forms of utopian thinking and experimental impulse are established in the first chapter. Chapter 2 shows how the authoritarian elements in the dreams of the victorious intelligentsia—the Bolsheviks—and their surging vision of city, machine, and industrial organization clashed inevitably with their sponsorship of the libertarian behavior of the revolutionary masses and with large segments of the population who saw revolution as a gate thrown open for the escape to localism, freedom, and withdrawal. It was a brief and terrible season (1917–21) of frenzied, unfocused collision between the two views, the urbanite and the pastoral, grandly articulated in the former case, more often expressed in the language of action in the latter. It was in a sense a national performance of that great metaphor of Russian nineteenth century literature wherein the master talks, smiles, offers, and urges and the peasant nods mutely and then proceeds to wreck his lofty plans.

During the 1920s, utopia building proceeded in a more self-conscious and formal way. It took two forms: independent experiments in life and culture building (described in chapters 3 through 7) and the construction of ideal societies of the future and present (in chapters 8 through 10). The experiments and cultural innovations generated behavior patterns and values, the living components of the utopian pictures being constructed by writers, architects, city planners, economists, planners, and sociologists, which were combined into functioning "utopian" communities through the 1920s up into the early 1930s, when the experiments were dissolved and the utopian speculations prohibited.

The utopian visions of the 1920s contain the assembling of dreams, the recapitulation of revolutionary experience as genuine expectations for the future. On a time scale, they fall into visions of the far future, the immediate future, and the present. Science fiction and futurology, dealing with the far future, synthesized speculations in the scientific possibilities of human and material change. Utopian city and building plans were specific blueprints of life in the coming decade rather than in the future millennium. Communalists—the utopians of the present life—went a step further and endeavored—with some astonishing successes and some predictable failures—to begin utopia in the here and now from the bottom up. Their movement was both the ultimate utopia and the ultimate experiment of the revolutionary era, applying to life a whole range of revolutionary dreams.

The concluding chapters explain how revolutionary utopianism was replaced by Stalin's "utopia in power," how the old dreams and their experimental variants in the 1920s were repudiated by those in power in favor of an ideology of bureaucratic state centralism and a theology of the Stalin personality cult. The pathos of the radical idealist rotting away in a revolutionary prison is one of the great themes in the literature of the Stalin purges. How the Bolshevik Revolution, premised as it was on the destruction of class enemies—capitalists, White Guards, Romanov dynasts, high officials—was transformed into a ravenous and thirsty god who devoured its own children has been one of the most compelling intellectual puzzles of the twentieth century. The war against revolutionary utopianism waged in the first decade of Stalin's power (1928–38) provides a key to this puzzle of Russian history. In the very process of negating and attacking the main currents of utopianism of the 1920s, the Stalinists created a structure of force and power designed to transform a nation's economic base overnight, but used also to sweep away the dreams and dreamers that would remind the world of the original goals and ways of revolutionary fantasy. Stalinism was a novel phenomenon, undreamed of either by the dreamers of the nineteenth century or by those of the revolutionary era, a deified mystification of the revolution, a composite of dream and nightmare.

The only book that has previously addressed itself in detail to the subject of the present work is the well known *Mind and Face of Bolshevism* (1926) by the versatile Hungarian philosopher and journalist René Fueloep-Miller. It is unique and indispensable for its first-hand reportage by a learned and sophisticated intellect. But it is seriously flawed as a true record of the utopian impulse because of its pervading irony, its unabashed animosity to revolutionary experimentalism, and most of all its lack of understanding. Fueloep-Miller, though surrounded on all sides by prophets and practitioners of utopian life, relied too readily upon the printed word and took the most extravagant abstractions as a picture of reality in Soviet Russia. This is particularly true of his critique of collectivism and "the mass" which he uses in a sloppy and undifferentiated manner. Yet the book remains, and should remain, a classic of revolutionary reportage from the inside; in vividness of style and colorfulness of subject matter, it surpasses all books ever written about the 1920s.[7]

The nineteenth century Russian radical community had always asked questions about the future: What would be the nature of the new society after the revolution? Would the present culture be preserved or destroyed? What would be the role of religious feeling? What kind of moral code would replace the old one? How equal would people be? How would people live and work together in harmony and productivity? Yet largely because of the artificial professional wall between students of the prerevolutionary and the postrevolutionary periods these old questions, nursed and debated for three generations, have rarely been treated in the standard accounts of Soviet history.

One of my purposes is to connect nineteenth century Russian ideas with their fate in the Revolution itself. In the words of Marshall Shatz: "For all its limitations and shadows, the twenties—roughly from the end of the civil war to the introduction of the first Five Year Plan in 1928–29—can be considered the one time in Russian history when an attempt was made to put into effect some of the intelligentsia's aspirations."[8] I believe it is necessary to break down the barrier of 1917 in the study of Russia's past.

I have written a book about the dream of human liberation and about the pathos of remaking society and mankind in the heat of revolution because I believe it is a process of thought, feeling, and action that is both eternal and relevant to our times. The utopian vision—a surging altruism accompanied by towering confidence and free-flowing social fantasy—was the best thing that nineteenth century Russian intellectual and cultural history bequeathed to the twentieth century, and not the disaster that some critics have called it. Revolutionary utopianism in its broadest sense not only summed up and took into the social laboratory of the 1920s this tradition. It also survived as vestigial idealism all the way through the bitter Stalinist years, even in the camps, even in the hearts of some of Stalin's victims. Most important of all, elements of it survive today, particularly at this moment of extraordinary change taking place in the Soviet Union.

Russian revolutionary utopia contained an abundance of star-gazing—sometimes in a literal sense of cosmic thinking and space fantasy, sometimes in the figurative sense of social daydreaming. Its history allows us to look from the dreamy cloudland of social utopia down into the day-to-day reality of life which, in times of revolution, all too often meant turmoil, confusion, brutality, and civil war. No one should blame revolutionary leaders for not succumbing to all the rosy appeals of utopia as they faced the grueling and exacting tasks of state-building. But neither should one blame utopians for plotting the parameters of the coming age and engaging in futuristic discourse. Their dreams were a major ingredient in the poetics of the revolution, lending it the needed sense of justness and dignity, the human dimension without which reality might be unbearable for all instead of only for the victims. Utopianism hovered like a religious aura over a land that was cutting its ties with the old faiths, a glowing myth in a landscape of darkness and struggle.

But this is only part of the story. Those who took utopia down from the light blue skies of Russian fantasy into living experimentalism enriched the revolutionary process. They invented and contrived, tried and erred, innovated and lived their innovations in what they believed to be the central spirit of the revolution. They attempted to bring the theory alive in a physical setting. The merging of practical need with experimental striving in the revolutionary years is striking in its incidence and density. The practitioners viewed these experiments not as the "impossible dream," the well-known Quixotic leaning of the Russian intelligentsia, but as the only antidote to the impossible reality. The irony of their effort and their fate has brought sarcastic smiles and disapproving shrugs from commentators ever since. Yet what they deserve is empathic laughter, sympathetic tears and an occasional burst of applause for their courageous, outlandish, and at the same time hardheaded view of reality and their determination to affirm what is best in the human condition. The German philosopher Ernst Bloch, the most brilliant and touching commentator on utopia in our century, called this whole tendency the "principle of hope" without which man cannot remain sane and survive in a world beset by the madness of our times.[9]

# PART I

---

## From Dreaming to Awakening

# 1

## Social Daydreaming Before the Revolution

The pinnacle of utopia may rise right up through the clouds but the soles of
its feet rest squarely on solid ground.

P. N. Sakulin, *Iz istorii russkago idealizma: V. F. Odoevskii* (1913)

### Utopian Mentalities

Soviet historians tend to conflate the history of utopianism with the history of socialism.
It is not my intention to obey this convention because they are not the same thing,
though the overlapping is frequent and very important. The history of Russian socialist
thought, programs, and movements has been written many times. But not all of socialism was utopian. Nor was all utopianism socialist; some of it was conservative, reactionary, Slavophile, monarchist, and Christian. It is not easy—or even prudent—to separate out utopian longing from programs, tactics, and behavior to which it is often
attached. Within the same document or statement, one can discern alternating episodes
of concrete political instructions and rosy pictures of a better world to come. But there
is also a sense in which "social daydreaming"—the term used by the Russian intelligentsia to describe the yearning for a new order—springs from a different level of the
consciousness than that which produces the program or manifesto.

The Soviet historian V. F. Zakharina, in her study of populist revolutionary propaganda literature of the 1870s, correctly observed that this literature fell into two main
categories: "pictures of a future ideal society" and "programs."[1] It is clear from reading the programs that they deal in a different order of perception from utopias. They
are demands, appeals, intentions, manuals of strategy and tactics, plans and platforms,
usually concerned with the taking of power and the use of that power to reorder the
state and reshape the economy—and they are often mute on the subject of how people
will live, work, think, feel, and interrelate in a future community. Programs tend to be
tabular, static, flat, dry and singularly unemotional; if emotion is in evidence, it is
usually in the form of hatred or indignation. Programs and plans are of necessity too
brief and schematic to offer lyrical descriptions of a coming life.[2]

Utopian social daydreaming is something else. It is visionary in the extreme. The
dreamer may be a peasant, an emperor, or a revolutionary socialist—the mechanism is
the same, and it may be distinguished from the authorship of programs in two fundamental ways. Sleeping dreams, reveries, daydreams, fantasies, and imagination all de-
tach the dreamer from the immediate environment. But the mode varies. It can be
formless reverie—fortuitous, unstructured, free-associational, and passive. Or it may be
what Chalinder Allen called "constructive imagination," which uses intellectual selec-

tion, control, and classification in order to create "some new form for the expression of the ideas of the Man-thing."[3] If this creation is focused on the self it becomes artistic or scientific creativity; if on the outer world, then it can take the form of utopia or social fantasy. The paradox and the power of social daydreaming is that, though it springs from leisure and fantasy, it leaps to concrete details in its construction of another world. Utopian dreamers wish to describe how the new society looks, lives, and works.

Another difference between the dream and the program is that the former is analogous to a game. Just as chess is an abstraction of battle, utopia is an abstraction of life or society, a game between virtues and vices. The utopian begins with an ideal person and then constructs an ecology, an environment, and institutions as a game board for the optimal development (winning at life) of this person. In the words of Michael Holquist, the utopia, through scenario and detail, dramatizes and humanizes while the manifesto dictates and instructs.[4] The Renaissance scholar Henry Berger goes further: playground, laboratory, theater, battlefield, and ideal society are linked together psychologically as times or places created or cleared "in order to withdraw from the actual environment."[5] The element of play and even of aesthetic enjoyment is strong in certain kinds of utopia building—particularly by those already in power. This is not the leisured and lazy play of the Land of Cockaigne where all is provided and work is abolished, but the playlike manipulation and regulation of other human beings.

Utopianism in the last two centuries of the Russian Empire was extraordinarily rich and variegated, expressing itself in literature, political thought, religious fantasy and practice, revolutionary idealism, personal experimentation, mystical visions, legend and folk wisdom.[6] I shall focus on the themes and motifs of utopia that emerged from the three complex organisms of Russian society whose interaction forms the matrix of Russian history before the Revolution: the people, the state, and the intelligentsia. By doing this I hope to show how the conflict of visions in the revolution was rooted in the diversity and power of social daydreaming in Russian history.

## Popular Utopia: Justice, Community, Rebellion

There is no such thing as a "utopian mentality" *per se*. Mentalities—utopian or otherwise—spring from the social circumstances, culture, and behavior patterns of a given group in the population. There certainly was no single peasant mentality either, but several modes of thought can be identified as peasant, folk, or popular utopia. The peasant village was a world, a system of action, an arena of play, and a unit of moral obligation. Inside the unit, equity, fairness, and charity were supposed to prevail; equality referred to a clear belief that natural resources (water, woodlands, game, meadows) ought to be free for the use of all. Written law and progamatic notions of equality were unknown. When millenarian dreams captured the peasants, they called for brotherhood, leveling, an end to ranks, common property, and sharing. Modern students of peasant "moral economy" have found these dreams to be universal—based as they are upon similarity in the peasant condition as a class and as an occupation—and clouded by perpetual subordination and a precarious life. The picture must be balanced by the undeniable competitive and individualist—even ambitious—aspects of peasant life, the "rational peasant"—as one scholar calls him—often coexisting with the traditional or communal one inside the same person.[7]

In the time of Russian serfdom, c. 1600–1861, peasant relations among themselves and with outsiders were complex.[8] Male peasants perceived themselves as equals, calling each other "brother" or "Orthodox one." Towards their families they behaved like bosses. To outsiders, they were suspicious; to guests, polite, hospitable, and cautious; to lords deferential, dignified, even warm—this pattern giving way to ferocious anger and violence in time of stress. Collective responsibility was partly imposed upon them by authorities and partly a mechanism of survival and gain (as in forcing entire villages into the looting process). In a large percentage of peasant villages, periodic redistribution of the arable strips of land was employed in order to maintain a rough correspondence between holdings and family size. Wandering peasants brought some of their customs with them such as itinerent teams of workers who pooled their labor and their wages. The traditional peasant outlook was rooted in a religious culture, was devoid of Western rationalism (as opposed to simple logic and economic reason), was alien to geometric forms and elegant symmetries, and suspicious of growth *per se* and of central authorities—except for the person of the tsar. Until the emancipation of the serfs in 1861, peasants seem to have been indifferent or hostile to big cities as well.

An outstanding student of the Russian peasant mentality has observed that "Russian peasants were dreamers" and also full of "practical Wisdom."[9] The long Russian winters and deep rural isolation helped to shape their dreams. Some of them were "utopians," creating worlds of great color and richness, the shapes and hues perhaps derived from those of their ever-present religious ceremony. These dream worlds were full of *pravda* and *volya,* terms that were transformed by the Russian intelligentsia—first by the Populists into "Land and Liberty" and then by the Marxists into "socialism" and "democracy." To a peasant, *pravda* did mean "land" and "socialism" in a way: it connoted straightness, justice, truth, and right. Truth had to be just; if not, it was a lie. This explains much of the scepticism of the peasant toward the "truth tellers" from the capital bearing laws. Peasant utopia was a land full of "truth"—that is, justice and fairness. In social terms, this meant land to the tiller, the sacredness of labor, and the virtue of fraternity. Its antipode was *krivda*—crookedness, falsity, an alien force. Utopia meant the supplanting of *krivda* with *pravda*. *Volya* meant "freedom" and "democracy" in a way, also. Not abstract liberty under law and laissez faire, and not parliamentary rule—the freedom implied by *volya* meant escape from the oppressive state, flight if needed, withdrawal from under the yoke of manor lord and policeman.

The bulk of the Russian peasantry rarely voiced or displayed utopian dreams. When they did, myth prevailed over evidence, as in the legends of a "just land" and of a "just tsar." Maxim Gorky gave literary expression to the former in Luka's monologue from *The Lower Depths* (1902): a peasant who believed in a just land asked an intellectual to show it to him on his maps and charts; he refused to believe the empirical "truth" that it was not to be found there. This was four years after the last known expedition in search of one of these legendary lands, *Belovode* (the Kingdom of the White Waters), when three cossacks of the Urals set sail from Odessa to Asia and Siberia and back again, declaring on their return that it did not exist. The first printed account of this legend appeared in 1807. In the 1830s and 1840s, large migrations were mounted to find it. It was said to be located "across the water," perhaps in Japan, and to be inhabited by Russian Old Believers who had been persecuted in the seventeenth century for their schismatic religious beliefs. In *Belovode,* spiritual life reigned supreme, all went barefoot and shared the fruits of the land, which was devoid of oppressive rules, crime, and war. Originating among the sect known as the Wanderers, it was taken up by others. A dozen or so variants appeared in the nineteenth century, according to the foremost student of the phenomenon, but none appeared after 1900. Similar arcadias of popular and religious fantasy were the City of Ignat, the Land of the River Darya, Nutland, and Kitezh—the town beneath the lake.[10]

The dream of a just tsar was the belief in the imminent appearance of a deliverer, although some versions of the White Waters also told of a White Tsar who ruled there justly and who would some day liberate all of Russia in the same way. The tsar-deliverer, in this vision, would give *pravda* and *volya* to the people whom he loved. The image flourished in the sixteenth and seventeenth centuries and was even applied to Ivan the Terrible. False tsars appeared again and again in the seventeenth and eighteenth centuries at the head of popular rebellions promising freedom and justice.[11] In the nineteenth century, "golden charters" with forged signatures of the tsar appeared, "freeing" the peasants and granting them all the land, including the lord's. One such charter, issued in Kharkov Province by peasant pretenders in 1861, gives some notion of the peasant attitudes to work, idleness, and privilege: the lords, like devils, were relegated to meagre swampy land but were also welcome to sow and to reap by their own labor as did the toiling peasants.[12] It was an anticipation of the levelling process that was applied to the upper classes during the Revolution. The peasant utopias did not envision a Cockaigne paradise where no one had to work; rather, all would work and enjoy the fruits thereof.[13]

The lushest environment for popular utopia before the Revolution was among the Old Believers and the Sectarians. The former had broken violently with the Orthodox Church in the seventeenth century over seemingly trivial but pyschologically and culturally important issues of ritual reform. Known as *raskolniki* or schismatics, they were ruthlessly persecuted by the Patriarch Nikon and his successors and by the Muscovite authorities. The Old Believers clung tenaciously to their ancient practices and expressed their separation from the official world of Muscovy and Imperial Russia in flight, collective migration to the fringes of the state, mass suicide by fire, rebellion, and religious communities.

The most famous of these communities, that of Vyg in the furthest reaches of northern Russia, lasted from the 1690s to the 1850s and has been called "a theocratic utopia."[14] Its central ideology was *sobor*, that sense of harmonious spiritual community so beloved by the Slavophiles in the nineteenth century. It was anti-Western, antimilitarist, and anti-expansionist. It provided communal ownership of property, collective labor, and mutual aid in a religious surrounding, far from the center of state power. With its arable lands held and tilled in common, a monastic communism that embraced a network of federated communities, it was "a miniature socialist state based upon a collective economy,"[15] with about 1000 members at its peak. It was also hierarchical and regimented: discipline, obedience, loyalty, and chastity were required (though the last did not always hold up); males held all positions of authority, and the elected chief of the community lived in a cell larger than the others. At various moments in its history—although it engaged in regular economic life and commerce with the outside world and enjoyed the protection of the state—the Vyg community outlawed money, passports, and even sidewalks (see Fig. 1).[16]

The Sectarians—Dukhobors, Molokanes, Wanderers and their offshoots—arose in the wake of the Old Believers and displayed even greater radicalism and a deeper utopianism. Their experiments, shorter lived and invariably repressed by the government, took the form of written documents such as the *Tolling of the Bells* (1794) and *The New World and its Law* (the 1820s) and communal religious sects such as Common Hope (mid-nineteenth century), United Brotherhood (1850s), Love of Brotherhood (1850s), and the Righthanded Brotherhood (1840s). These and similar groups may have attracted thousands of followers in the nineteenth century, and they were joined by individual prophets and preachers who "saw" the outlines of a perfect community.[17]

These experiments varied greatly over time and space, but most of them taught or practiced common landownership in a prosperous economy where everyone worked, social equality (one group even outlawing the words "mother" and "father" as excessively authoritarian),[18] and social relations bound together by religion rather than by oaths, laws, or law enforcers. "In God's capital, there are no gendarmes or police," proclaimed the leader of the Righthanded Brotherhood, a sect that flourished in the Urals.[19] Some of them lived tightly, residing and dining in the same building; and in some of them also there prevailed a rigid discipline and the regulation of sexual activity. There were also instances of abolishing saints' names for infants, the labeling of all children of the community as "ours" by adults, and abolition of deference even between adults and children—all of which were taught and practiced by some people during the Russian Revolution.[20]

In the mid-nineteenth century, government officials, commenting on the "fraternal love" and "universal brotherhood and equality" taught by the Dukhobors, called their aspirations "a kind of Platonic utopia" and even compared the Molokan sect of M. A. Popov to the St. Simonians.[21] Both observations were erroneous; though the religious utopians were often enamored of discipline, their community did not in other ways resemble the philosopher kingdom of Plato; and though they preached a quasi-socialist religion of love as did the St. Simonians, their ethos, social background, and world outlook diverged sharply from those of the French utopian socialists of the 1830's who preached equality of the sexes, the liberation of labor, and global economic development. The Russian sectarian quest was not for a universal heaven so much as it was for a local haven—which would allow for a tsar and his family (but no other ranks or titles), an element of rationalism in some cases, and a serene world possessed of *pravda* and *volya*. In spite of occasional elements of universal messianism and a rhetoric of paradise on earth, the sectarian utopians wanted to withdraw rather than build and develop, were pastoral rather than urban, and religious rather than secular and Promethean.

The most dramatic expression of popular utopianism broke forth in peasant and cossack rebellions, such as those great upheavals of the seventeenth and eighteenth centuries—of Bolotnikov, Razin, Bulavin, and Pugachëv. They possessed certain persistent unities: the tendency of oppression and fear in time of crisis to generate myths of evil boyars and redeeming tsars who would "restore a golden past"; explosions of destructive violence against people, things, and places; temporary coalitions of the lower orders—peasants, townsmen, Cossacks, and ethnic minorities; and social banditry.[22] Stenka Razin became enshrined in legend among the peasantry for his boldness and magic cunning. Pugachëv, to a greater extent, was the darling of the anarchist intelligentsia. Both were surrounded by admiring cults during the Russian Revolution—and their ways were emulated by popular rebels of the Civil War. Pugachëv, whose revolt was the largest in Russian history before 1905, desired a world free of nobles where "each can enjoy tranquillity and a peaceful life which will continue evermore."[23] In the words of Marc Raeff, his ideal was "a static, simple society where a just ruler guaranteed the welfare of all within the framework of a universal obligation to the sovereign."[24] Peasant monarchism was present in most other utopian visions and rebellions in prerevolutionary Russia.[25] The ultimate goals of popular rebellion were touched by what the founder of intelligentsia socialism, Alexander Herzen, called "the moonlight of fantasy" (which he, typically, contrasted with the sunlight of reason).

The utopianism of rebellion ushered in novel modes of behavior that would surface again and again in the coming revolutions of the twentieth century. One was the presence of revolutionary heroes, idealized like Robin Hood for their punishment of the rich and distribution to the poor and immortalized like Christ after their execution. The second was a certain concretizing of goals by means of symbols and images. "Rise, rise, O red sun/And warm us poor people," a motif borrowed from religious imagery, was used in popular songs to summon back Stenka Razin and call up a new dawn.[26] In one minor revolt of 1861, a red flag was carried around the village on a cart.[27] Iconoclasm and vandalism frequently broke loose. Prisons and towns were reduced to ashes; in manor houses, peasants destroyed glass panes, windows, and mantle pieces—symbols of things new and foreign.[28]

Symbolic retribution, an ancient form of punishment, was given an antimodern and anti-intellectual twist when Pugachëv had a German St. Petersburg astronomer lifted on pikes to get him "closer to the heavens."[29] And peasants in the riots of the post-emancipation period talked of *volya* as if it were a material thing wrapped in paper or hidden in a box. Thus utopian visions and popular dreams of community came to be associated during times of violence with a peculiar kind of behavior that is familiar from millenarian movements of medieval and early modern Europe and from the great European, revolutions of the seventeenth and eighteenth centuries: egalitarianism, leveling, anti-urbanism, iconoclasm, symbol building, and the construction of new values.[30]

In his treatment of the Bezdna revolt and massacre of 1861, Klibanov devotes some moving and vivid pages to the funeral panegyric paid to the martyrs by the democratic publicist and radical ethnologist, Afanasy Shchapov.[31] It was one of the first visible links between the aspirations of popular revolt and the radical sensibility of the intelligentsia in Russia, made the more vivid in being perhaps the first public revolutionary funeral in Russian history, giving birth to the well-known revolutionary funeral march, "You Fell Victim."

What happened to these myths, practises, visions, and sensibilities in the dynamic half century between the emancipation of 1861 and the Revolution of 1917? Many forces combined to erode them: the rising flow of peasants into the big cities and factory towns in search of employment, the consequent construction of a Russian proletariat, the demographic upsurge in the countryside which pushed people off the land, the growth of literacy, schooling, and the emergence of a huge body of popular reading materials that projected and reflected "modern" values of national belonging, social mobility, ambition, success, adventure, travel, and a fondness for science over superstition.[32] To this must be added the agrarian reforms of Prime Minister Peter Stolypin in the last years of the Empire which promoted and, in a limited sphere, effected the breakup of the old peasant *mir* and its mechanism of compensatory redistribution. It is all the more extraordinary that all the peasant ways and visions outlined above erupted and fought their way into politics in the middle of the revolutionary cyclone. The peculiarities of that revolution dredged to the surface all kinds of "premodern" and "antimodern" fears and longings among the rural population, re-ruralizing in a sense its outlook, and even re-peasantizing some of the proletariat of the collapsing cities.

Peasants of the 1870s failed to respond to the socialist utopias of the populist intelligentsia; those of the 1900s similarly failed to rise up to (or even understand) concrete

Marxist visions of the future outlined to them by radical workers. Russian peasants were not socialists in any European or intellectual sense; nor were they conservative in the sense attributed to them by the ruling elite—they were peasants. Their dreams and aspirations, however cloudy the formulation, of land and freedom and order (their own order) resurfaced in 1905 with great force. In 1917 the peasants swept away an ancient social system and then stood puzzled and angry at the looming menace of a new order not of their making. The traditions of peasant utopia were based upon deep popular aspirations.[33] How they behaved during the Russian Revolution and what they wanted to create and sustain, before their civilization was destroyed by Stalin's collectivization, is a clear demonstration that the image of *pravda, volya,* and self-rule shone far brighter in the vastness of the Russian skies than the red star of Bolshevism, or any other political idea.

## Administrative Utopia: Parade, Facade, Colony

Administrative utopia is a peculiar kind of dreaming by those holding power. In it, the few arrange the lives of others not necessarily to bring them happiness but to organize them for production (factory), for combat (army), or for detention (prison). The resulting institutions are based upon hierarchy, discipline, regimentation, strict order, rational planning, a geometrical environment (the production line, the cantonment, the cell-block), and a form of welfarism. Certain kinds of utopias, often called by the insulting term "barracks communism," have been attacked for being modelled on those institutions. But the institutions themselves contain a large element of utopia: a desired order, an extreme rationalism, an outlet for the constructive imagination of organizers who wish to build environments and move or control people like men on a chess board. The militarization of the body, as analyzed by Michel Foucault, was designed to abolish a peasant and create a soldier. The body was the object and the target of power; it was trained and shaped to obey—like a machine. Another expression of the Enlightenment's love for rational control through discipline and order was symbolized by Jeremy Bentham's model prison, the Panopticon, built to atomize, control, and surveille. It was not just a "bizarre little utopia" but a central metaphor for what Foucault calls the "technology of subjection" or the massive projection of military methods into production, penology, and other walks of life.[34]

Administrative utopia in Russia was conceived as a rational light beamed into the perceived darkness of the barbarous village world. In all its expressions—"beautiful autocracy" and "well-ordered police state," the militarization of estates, the parado-mania of the Gatchina emperors, panegyric ritual, utopian town planning, and the fanciful hope of regimentalizing all of Russia—the aim and the mode were alien to the deepest dreams of peasant utopianism. That aim was to bestow order and welfare upon an unwilling population, to dress them, schedule them, dragoon them, use them, and sometimes even to reify them into human toys for the enlightened amusement of the toymakers. The mode was military order and discipline, Western reason, geometric shapes and lines to contain and channel people—all in the context of an elaborate and graphic hierarchy of rank, privilege, appearance, and personal style. In the eighteenth century, reason, embodied in the city and the regiment, was proceeding into the green garden of Russia, its wilderness and pasture, its forests and steppes, in much the same way that it was proceeding on the Western reaches of the European continent. But in Russia the currents of administrative utopia were marked by a sincerity and a harshness—a utopian arrogance—that was rooted in ambivalence about national identity, and by the knowledge that in Russia the soil, the human material, and the popular spirit were much more psychologically resistant to the charms of Euclid, Martinet, and Plato than were their European counterparts, and at the same time less able to resist physically. The immediate model for all this in eighteenth century Russia was the Prussian state.

"The discipline of the army gives birth to all discipline" said Max Weber.[35] So believed the Prussian military autocrats of the eighteenth century. Their little state was called at various times "an army with a country" and "an armed camp." The army was said "to stand above the State and [was] also its soul;"[36] it has also been called "a gigantic penal institution."[37] Under a remarkable series of energetic Electors and Kings, particularly Frederick William I (1713–40), "the drillmaster," Prussia promoted the "militarization of society." They built a powerful state in a "collectivist Prussia"[38] in the words of a modern student, where *Disziplinierung* was applied to productivity as well as to war.[39] Government and military were intermixed in personnel and ethos, both subjected to minute rules of discipline, conformity, efficiency, punctuality, and rigid codes of behavior. The economy was partially militarized, soldiers being assigned to farming and factories run by the state. Even the environment was regimented when possible: streets were straightened in the towns, new roads were laid out in ruler-straight lines, town buildings and traffic were planned and regulated from the center in line with the symmetry and harmony of a rationalist age. An attempt was made to cleanse society of messy elements—beggars, vagrants, Gypsies—and to reduce the number of "wasteful" festivals. All this was done out of a deep impulse to turn Prussian society into, in the words of Hans Rosenberg, "a huge human automaton."[40]

The attempt to apply Prussian forms of the militarization of society to the vastness, emptiness, and weakness of the Russian land produced not only tension and conflict but also utopian visions. At the onset of the imperial period of Russian history, we find Peter the Great employing "rationally constructivist" policies to his empire—minute ordering of space, documents, procedures; impersonal and formal bureaucracy; scientific separation of administration from subjects through the physical arrangement of offices; the fixing of the population into full serfdom and the movement of that population for construction and war.[41]

Peter the Great (1682–1725) introduced Western-style military ritual at about the same time as he imported geometry. Prussian *dressage*—formation, parade, drill—came to adorn the squares of the capitals and later the new towns.[42] In the middle of the eighteenth century, it was taken back into the villages and estates by noble former officers released from service. The "militarization of estates" was a vivid example of administrative utopia at the local level. The world of Western rationalism and military symmetry which the gentry servitors lately abandoned was now recreated in miniature. Serfs were organized into military units with timetables, schedules, and planning, accompanied by the flourish of the trumpet and the beat of the drum. Servants were sometimes fitted out in uniform and paraded for the amusement of the landowner and his guests. The theatrical and playlike quality of military command and the graphic shaping of people into squares were here fully on display. For the officer who practised this custom, "it was less a sense of responsibility and awe which he felt than joy and satisfaction that he could now shape the destinies of men according to general, modern principles in the aestheticially pleasing way of rational orderliness and uniformity."[43]

"Paradomania," a quality ascribed to the Emperor Alexander I, was endemic among

Russian tsars in the later eighteenth and early nineteenth century. The "Gatchina school" of rulers took its name from Tsar Paul's estate near St. Petersburg where a Prussian style cantonment was laid out with parade grounds, barracks, sentries—all alive with a continuous round of *dressage* and changing of the guards. Gatchina was the perfect world where Paul (1796–1801), rejected and superfluous in the long years before ascending the throne, could regiment the lives of peasants, release his locked up energy in the tyranny of drill, and create a model welfare state complete with the best hospitals, schools, and buildings.[44]

His son, Alexander I (1801–25), possessed a "passion for order, efficiency, and minute regulations" as well as a "passion for military trivia"—especially the rituals of parade. And Alexander's brother Nicholas I (1825–55) took this passion to the extreme: in the words of a recent biographer, he was "addicted to ceremonial parades." The fixation of Nicholas on things military has often been interpreted as "martial paranoia" or playing at defense. But it was more than that. Nicholas merged the paternal and the military patterns of organizing society in Russia and introduced military principles into the state, with unit designations, commanders, uniforms, and codes. In fact, as an observant contemporary remarked, Nicholas really saw his task as "disciplining the country."[45] The Marquis de Custine, for all his gross exaggeration and hysterical Russophobia, was able to perceive Russia in 1839 as an "empire of military maneuvres" where everything was "regulated as in a barracks or camp." Russian life he saw as a "masterpiece of military mechanics" and the lowly Russian as a "member of a machine, functioning according to a will which is not his own, [living] as much as the movement of a clock."[46]

If military order was the substance of administrative utopia, spatial symmetry and panegyric facade was its form. The early modern town in Russia was a bastion of static order and control rather than a symbol and base of transformation.[47] The new capital, St. Petersburg, "reflected imperial grandeur and monumentality" and the new towns were expected to do the same. Eighteenth century Russian town planning reveals an extraordinarily detailed and uniform design for all new cities of the Empire: radial, rectilinear, or fanlike layouts; grids of straight thoroughfares, to be twice as broad as the height of the tallest buildings; regularly placed squares and plazas, with a central square for military parades, a main avenue, and the administration building at the center; a unified architectural style; and rigidly segregated zones of residence as well as graphically differentiated structures, according to social class, in size, height, material, and facade design. Under Alexander I, especially in the fear-ridden decade of 1810–20, the Scottish architect William Hastie and his Russian colleagues designed model facades to be used in town and home construction all over the Empire. Grid layouts were even decreed for villages in the eighteenth and nineteenth centuries, though not universally enforced.[48] Custine called St. Petersburg a "camp of stone" and "the general staff of an Army, not the capital of a nation." The Russia that he visited reminded him of Prussia under Frederick William I. "The square and the chalk-line," he observed, "accord so well with the point of view of absolute sovereigns that right angles become one of the attributes of a despotic architecture."[49]

From the time of Peter the Great through the eighteenth century at least, a tradition of "panegyric utopia" flourished in court ritual and ceremonies, creating an "iconography of happiness"—prosperity, security, order, virtue, harmony, and calm.[50] Such iconography was an essential element of administrative utopia. The new towns themselves were icons of the imperial order; some planners of St. Petersburg even proposed model facades in the capital, allowing the owners to build anything they wanted to behind them.[51] The famous dream of Prince Grigory Potëmkin to colonize newly conquered lands in the south and to adorn them *ex nihilo* with a network of new and magnificent towns was a perfect example of the rationalism inherent in administrative utopia. The notion of social and environmental transformation by administrative means captivated him, and he longed to "modernize" and "rationalize" the anarchic world around him by planning and mobilization—in the literal sense of that word: to move people around. Kherson, Nikolaev, Taganrog, Mariupol and other towns sprang up under his command on the broad southern steppe and on the coast of the Black Sea. Ekaterinoslav, the ultimate panegyric city, was designed as the "Athens of the Ukraine"— a monumental "ode" to his Empress, Catherine the Great. And he achieved it by the use of serfs, drafted artisans, and all manner of enrolled labor.[52]

Historians have cast some doubt upon the accepted legend of "Potëmkin villages"— whole communities and structures raised overnight to delight the eyes of Catherine and her entourage as she sailed down the Dniepr River in 1787, but there is no doubt that the miniature utopia on the banks of the river was an outgrowth of the larger production design of Potëmkin's utopian dream. His preparations and the voyage of the imperial suite combined all the elements of panegyric utopia: as Catherine's spectacular festivities on shipboard replicated the "iconography of happiness," the ship itself floated serenely past artificially built villages, symmetrical towns, and—to complete the vignette with a graphic summary of obedience—a military parade along the shore.[53]

Panegyric utopia, the geometrization of space, rationalism, and the military ethos of order and obedience were fused in the early nineteenth century in the Military Colonies. The man who helped create them was Alexei Arakcheev, a prominent civil and military servant of Paul and Alexander I. Under Paul he served as commandant of the City of St. Petersburg; his "passion for detail, order, and smartness" led him to clean up the streets and squares of the capital; and his weakness for facades allowed him to store the refuse and filth in the courtyards and side streets. He modelled his estate at Gruzino after Paul's Gatchina, thus in the manner of a Prussian camp. Rows of identical pink two-family houses stood on each side of the straight paved streets. Showplaces were erected near the approaching roads, and the tiny military city was adorned with twelve monuments, and with towers, lookouts, turrets, flags, and an Athenian Acropolis on a rise (see Fig. 2). Arakcheev's soldier peasants were put into uniform, subjected to a rigid daylong routine of drill and work details, given minute instructions on the upkeep of streets and buildings, and cared for by welfare services. Punishment books were maintained for all inhabitants.[54]

On visiting Gruzino, Tsar Alexander I became enamored of "the order which prevails everywhere, the cleanliness . . . the symmetry and elegance." He was converted by the outward appearance of Gruzino, just as his brother Nicholas was later converted to the colonies by their neatness. His vision of a network of Gruzinos across Russia grew into the huge project of Military Colonies, combining field work with army service under a military regimen. They began to appear before the 1812 campaign, reached their peak in the early 1820s with about 750,000 men, women, and children, and were gradually dissolved in the reign of Nicholas because of disorders, corruption, and general unpopularity.[55]

A glimpse of life inside these colonies illustrates vividly their utopian character and their immense debt to a Prussian model that was ill-suited to the social infrastructure of Russia. Isolated and immune from the rest of Russia, they were an artificial state within a state where farming alternated with drilling and meaningless tasks. The population was formed into five separate classes of settlers ruled by military officers. All the houses and buildings were designed according to a master plan hatched in the War Ministry by imperial architects and were symmetrically arranged. Poverty in the familiar sense was eliminated by free housing, health care, and schools, although no one was permitted to own any real property. "Loose elements" were eliminated and the entire community was subjected to collective responsibility. It was as artificial and unrealistic as the communities dreamed of by Cabet, Fourier, and Owen, but imposed from above upon an unwilling and uncomprehending population of peasants whose own dream of the good society was precisely to be left alone. Furthermore, this "planned, rational society" of clocks and schedules, aside from violating the ethos of country folk, failed ultimately even in its stated purpose because of the rampant inefficiency, the resistence to regimentation that flashed into violent revolt, the corruption, and the bungling administration.[56]

The dream of an administrative utopia, military in spirit and symmetrical in shape, was a central motif in the history of early imperial Russia. It achieved its fullest force under Alexander I. In the reign of Nicholas I, what was left of the dream was part of a broader scheme of autocracy.[57] In subsequent reigns, however rigid, the dream began to fade. Alexander II (1855–81) blasted huge holes in the smooth facade of administrative utopia by emancipating the serfs and promoting the reforms—of local government, especially—that would preclude the drum and bugle society of Gatchina. Alexander III, the last of the consistently strongminded autocrats, launched a counterreform after the assassination of his father, but also set in motion a rapid program of industrialization which added industrial cities to the symmetrical garrison towns. And the last of the Romanovs, Nicholas II, while preserving the ceremonial pomp of St. Petersburg, personally nourished an earlier Christian Moscovite society as his model.[58]

Administrative utopia—like popular utopia—springs from specific social and psychological bases. During the period in question, rulers were particularly self-conscious about their almost unlimited personal power to transform and were unusually amenable to borrowing easily assumed models and categories of administrative rule; their sense of power was in fact shaped by a formalistic fetish. They perceived their realm as exceptionally poor and weak and difficult to govern, composed overwhelmingly of illiterate serfs and state peasants. Their vague fear of Europe may have been joined by a sense of insecurity about their thrones in an age dotted with coups and putsches. The Russian tradition of drastic change from above ran deep and it fed the arrogance of administrative utopia. In so-called backward societies, where firmly established communities of political and economic interest are weak or non-existent, utopian vision is an etherealized form of politics where there is no other political life. It is symptomatic of the appeal of this kind of politics that Tsar Alexander I chose the visual "text" of Arakcheev's estate for his model of Russia over the sober and very verbal state reform project of Speransky.

Administrative utopia declined in the late nineteenth century with the desimplification of Russian society and the rise of political and economic life. But the dream of a state power refashioning the land and the people was too alluring to die, and it appealed even to the most radical socialist dreamers who hated the tsarist state and whose ultimate vision was a stateless society. The allure was magnified in the Revolution by the reappearance of those things that had given it shape earlier: fear and insecurity, deep anxiety about how to create order and efficiency, the desire to provide the people with justice and food, and the lack of trust in the masses to create their own forms of rule and ways of life consonant with state survival.

Mentalities, moods, visions, and dreams are not permanent states of mind or feeling. They may pass and then resurge with renewed strength—not only from one generation to another, but within the same generation. Utopianism—popular and administrative— was activated by peculiar events or circumstances. Both forms expressed yearnings that declined in the late nineteenth century. Elements of popular utopia captured peasants again in 1905–6 and in the Revolution of 1917; but some of these elements also passed into the mental makeup of the socialist intelligentsia, which kept them alive in a continuous literary and conversational discourse—what we now call the Russian radical tradition. In the same manner, elements of administrative utopia captured the thinking of certain radicals even before they came into power, mingling with socialist ideology and adopted popular aspirations, and accounting for the utter complexity and richness of revolutionary behavior and thinking in the first decade of Soviet power.

## Populism: Vision and Counterculture

The Russian intelligentsia of the nineteenth century was almost by definition utopian in its cast of mind. European social utopianism of the romantic age escaped into a golden past or a rosy future. In Russia, these trends became absolutized by the social emptiness of Russia, which seemed to offer good soil for reworking: Russia, seen by many to be "youthful," could still be shaped. The rigid social structure of Russia and the alienation felt by educated elites who loved not the state and knew not the people fed dreams of reintegration and community. For the Slavophiles, this meant peering backward into the mists of Slavic tradition; for the left intelligentsia, it meant looking outward to the land and forward to progress and "socialism." Intelligentsia daydreams differed from those of peasants, Sectarians, or the Gatchina emperors; they were beset neither by physical labor and worry about survival nor by the responsibilities of empire. But their lack of a meaningful function, their over-education, and their feeling of superfluousness led to loneliness and social daydreaming of a maximalist variety. It was precisely the psychology of maximalism and the emotional drive to escape the odious reality of their Russia that prompted so many among the intelligentsia to organize—and respond to— dreams of a perfect society, warm-hearted visions of a lovely land, denuded of the oppressive state, graced by justice and prosperity. The anti-capitalist mentality that gripped a large segment of the intelligentsia in the formative years nourished a dream of rural life, with technology, industry, and cities relegated—at best—to the margins of their dream worlds.

Written utopias—novels and stories—flourished in Russian letters for about a century, from A. D. Sumarokov's *The Dream: a Happy Society* (1759) to V. A. Sollogub's *Tarantas* (1848). They were almost all "conservative" in the widest sense of that term: nonradical, panegyric exaltations of official Russia, Slavophile dreams, or apolitical moral diatribes—sometimes idyllic and sometimes laced with the harshness of administration utopia. Preponderantly anti-modern, anti-European, and anti-urban, the nationalist and paternalist genre contained doses of rationalism and technological fantasy. M. M. Shcherbatov's *Journey to the Land of Ophir* (1784) and V. F. Odoevsky's *The Year 4338* (1838) are the best known, but perhaps the most typical was *Tarantas*, the last of them. A Slavophile utopia, Sollogub's dream-land is abundant, enlightened, harmonious, and strong. This condition has been achieved not by Westernization, but by a return to "Slavic" values of mutual (but unequal) obligations, hierarchy, Orthodox brotherhood, family life, and national culture—the cities are now bright and clean, but adorned with ancient Russian motifs, gold domes, and bells. Peasants are still peasants, to be sure, but they live in small brick and iron cabins in symmetrically circular villages, so designed to save labor in reaching the fields.[59]

With the Decembrists, a movement of liberal and radical officers who rose up against the tsar in 1825 only to be crushed, we see a shift to more distinctly rational and Western outlines of the future. But the mix remained a blend of popular tradition (filtered by the elite), administrative urges, and imported thought. The Decembrists were a varied lot—though socially and culturally homogeneous. Like all emerging subgroups in Russian history, they created a personal style—flourishes of defiance, abrupt speech, serious demeanor, heroic and undeferential manners—all interpreted by Yury Lotman as a kind of living literary text or chain of gestures. Their visions tended to the unsentimental and businesslike. Colonel Paul Pestel, leader of the more radical Southern Society, owed much to his military background. He aspired to reduce the cities, move the capital (and rename it), and "unify" certain nationalities in the Empire. A critic in 1909 wrote that "to Pestel, tribes, peoples, finally the entire mass of 'citizens' were imagined as a deck of cards which he shuffled and laid out according to his own judgement."[60]

The movement produced one written utopia, *A Dream* (1819) by A. D. Ulybyshev, describing Petersburg and a new Russia in the year 2119. The tsars are gone, as are their portraits and monuments, replaced by a State Assembly meeting in the Mikhailovsky Castle and a collection of elders who alternate public service with officiation at public rituals. The double headed eagle—symbol of the autocracy—has been decapitated and replaced by the phoenix of peace; fanatical religion, by a kind of cult of the Supreme Being (obviously inspired by Robespierre); churches, by monumental civic temples and museums; the army, by a popular militia. Ulybyshev bestrides the dilemma of westernization by restoring Russian national costume, Russian pride, and Russian consciousness in his land of democracy, legality, charity, property, and even emancipated women.[61]

Of the many schools of European utopian socialist thought that filtered into Russia in the next generation, Fourierism surely made the most lasting impression. It is precisely the spectacular pathos and the grandeur of the vision in Fourier that so appealed to the Russian radical intelligentsia. The utopia of Fourier—communal life in phalansteries of about 1600 people (see Fig. 3), communal meals, work, and play on a globe transformed—certainly linked up with latent notions of community in peasant Russia and with upper class pangs of shame at the backwardness that was so visible at midcentury. But the release of passion and the emancipation of personality—equally prominent in Fourier—accounted for the emotional attachment to a doctrine outwardly so remote from Russian conditions. The Petrashevsky Circle (1845–49) were among the first teachers and pupils of Fourierism in Russia and the first intellectuals to live in urban communes. The leader, Mikhail Butashevich-Petrashevsky, combined a practical bent with outlandish visions. He is said to have built a phalanstery upon his own small estate—a pitiful collection of small buildings on swampy earth at the forest edge, with forty serfs as his experimental subjects. He had them erect a common house with a communal kitchen and rooms for winter work. They burnt it down.

Nikolai Danilevsky, later prophet of Panslavism, envisioned a unified world of rotational labor, higher payment for useful work than for pleasant work, global competitions, and vast worldwide entertainments. V. D. Akhsharumov combined the main elements of the vision in his impassioned speech at the commemoration of Fourier's birthday in 1849. Describing the horrors of the Russian capital—disease, poverty, vice, crowds, dirty and repetitive labor, urban blight—he announced that "we celebrate the future remission of humankind." His hope was to "destroy the capital, the towns, to make new buildings out of their building material, to end this life of torment, poverty, squalor, and shame" to make way for one of wealth, luxury, and joy, and to cover the earth with palaces and fruits, adorned with flowers.[62]

Nicholas Chernyshevsky's *What Is To Be Done?* is the most important radical novel in nineteenth century literature. Its author, the son of a priest, a journalist, critic, and revolutionary publicist, was the chief martyr of the revolutionary tradition and a moral leader of the generation of the 1860s and beyond. *What Is To Be Done?* (1863) was composed in prison before he was shipped off to an exile which lasted most of his life. It deals with the expressive realm of human life—the spiritual, associational, esthetic, ethical, erotic, and recreational life—of the here and now and of the future. It was utopian in two ways: an explicit vision of a future society and a handbook for New People who would build and perhaps inhabit it. These two sides of the novel were combined in Vera Pavlovna—the central character—whose "fourth dream" was the utopian fantasy and whose character was the model of a utopian personality—the starting point for any remodelling of humanity.

Chernyshevsky's social picture of the future is a community of people, without city, state, or central power, living a round of work, leisure, love, equality, and shared lives.[63] The immediate environment is a glass palace, enclosing a communal building, with a winter garden, private rooms, and rooms for communal dining and social intercourse. Field work is assisted by machines beneath a wondrous canopy that shields the communitarians from sun and rain. Joy, song, and the sweat of honest toil punctuate the round of life. In design it recalls at once its original inspirer, Charles Fourier; but it was also a utopian metaphor for all of Russian Populism which preached a moral community, vaguely stateless in political form, localized in activity, mutual in human relations, and religious in spirit—the natural socialist religion of the common people. In this lay its power to illuminate and to inspire generations of radicals.

Chernyshevsky's Northern Commune near the center of Russia does not depend on futurist tecnology for its "eternal happiness." The palace of glass and steel (so hated by Dostoevsky), the light metallic furniture, the farm machinery, and the canopy are clearly marginal adornments to the central vision, which is pastoral. No cities or factories are mentioned or projected. Nature is exalted in graphic terms, and the verdure, the fields, the meadows, the mountains, and the forests are a source of joy and human renewal. Except for domestic chores, performed by children and old folks, all work is done outdoors. Minimum technology, material prosperity, and sanitation (the glass motif representing both cleanliness and enlightenment)[64] were acceptable to a science-worshipping generation of radicals and nihilists. But the dynamic city as such held no charm.

Collective labor and communal life were the concrete modes of organizing behavior. The cooperative artel of Vera Pavlovna—a device for mutual aid and profit-sharing in a semisocialist environment—was modelled on the peasant artel and the student mutual aid groups of the time. The heroine organized the sewing artels into a residential commune where everything was pooled and where the learned uplifted the ignorant by reading to them. The novel culminated in Vera's luminous communitarian dream where everything is arranged to perfection. The environment is secure, clean, and free of outer interference. The communards labor hard in the morning to prepare themselves for leisure. The memory of danger and hardship is expunged. Curtains provide privacy; carpets deaden the sounds of play. A hundred-piece orchestra and a huge chorus provide amusement and dance for playful balls and nightly entertainments. The cycle of work, merriment, love, and rest—taken right out of Fourier—are all accomplished in an aura of what the author calls *polnaya volya, volnaya volya*— "complete freedom, free freedom" for all.

Crucial to the formation of the radical personality, and partly conditioned by such personalities already at large, was Chernyshevsky's appeal for what writers now call "pre-figurative behavior," a social ethos and sensibility that would enable the human race to move from the corrupt world of today to the better world of tomorrow:[65]

> Then say to all [he wrote]: this is what will come to pass in the future, a radiant and beautiful future. Have love for it, strive toward it, work on behalf of it, bring it ever nearer, *bear what you can from it into your present life*. The more you can carry from that future into your present life, the more your life will be radiant and good, the richer it will be in happiness and pleasure.

Anatoly Lunacharsky, the first Bolshevik Commissar of Enlightenment, read this passage from the novel engraved on the walls of the Bolshoi Theater in Moscow in 1928, an agonizing moment in the chronicle of revolutionary morality. He voiced a plaintive wish that the words be a guidebook again for his generation.[66]

Chernyshevsky, in urging—via the powerful idiom of political fiction—that Russian youth adopt a deliberate pattern of life including health, work, sensitivity, and a thirst for merriment as well as serious struggle for a better future, established the critical link between utopian dreams and "utopian" behavior. The religious tone and the moral emphasis, taken together with the golden picture of the future, explains the spontaneous warmth and reverence with which it was received. The substance of Chernyshevsky's "guidebook" on the road to utopia is to be found in its main characters and situations as well as in the dreamy fantasies of Vera Pavlovna. Iconoclasm was one element: a refusal to bow to idols of the establishment—social rank, masculine gender, family authority, organized religion, and (by implication) political and social despotism. In this of course, Chernyshevsky was merely voicing the ethos of a whole generation, already exhibiting its disrespect for the "old" in what is commonly called "nihilism." Chernyshevsky's undisguised moral code taught mutual respect, the emancipation of women, frankness and honesty (to the point of rudeness if need be), the study of "useful" subjects, systematic (not charitable) rescue of the poor by means of cooperatives, social reorganization, and equality in every corner of life.

During the Bolshevik revolutionary epoch, hardly a phase of utopianism and experiment in society was entered without a nod to Chernyshevsky, to Vera Pavlovna, to her glittering dreams. The novel was cited and quoted again and again. Science fiction novels, city planners, and people living in communes invoked or emulated *What Is To Be Done?* Marxism and the urban vision of the early 1900s replaced Populism and the pastorale of the 1860s. But the shimmering specter of the Northern Commune and the life styles of Vera and her friends never lost their luster, their emotional impact, the appeal of their very Russian creator.[67]

Populist utopia of the nineteenth century was a product not of peasants and religious prophets, not of colonels and town planners—but of members of the intelligentsia. Their motivations were complex, mixing personal ambition, religious sensibilities, guilt, shame, pride, willpower, arrogance, towering Promethean faith, and love—as well as occasional self-hatred. The configurations of their utopian reveries, statements, novels, plans, and songs, as well as the pattern of their behavior in the realm of "applied utopistics" defy any effort to encompass them into some unified utopian schematum.[68]

Social daydreaming was very much a part of the mental universe of the Russian intelligentsia. It sometimes arose from a childhood of privilege and superior education in a world of house serfs. This could produce a feeling of solidarity with the weak: children, poor peasants, and servants were in various ways socially powerless. We read time after time—especially in the memoirs of radical women—of daytime reveries of action, liberation, and sacrifice for a better world. Social daydreaming was also fed by a sense of otherness, of not fitting emotionally into a world of ranks and offices, chanceries and regiments, balls and salons. The philosopher Vladimir Soloviev once said that the dream was a window to another world, a world of happiness and right.[69] In contrast to the popular and administrative dreams of a better world, those of the intelligentsia were reinforced and enriched by a constant and intense discourse, overladen with immense metaphysical implications, emotional investment, and a drive to action.

In a social movement, the word is made flesh, and the idea is worked out on the ground of existence. In the 1860s and 1870s the dreamers created a subculture and ethos of innovation and experimental reworking of human relations, attempting to *live* the revolution in attitudes, gestures, manners, modes of dress, mutual relationships, ethical codes, and even residential styles.[70]

Populist men and women by the 1870s had developed a rough and informal code of values, varying from person to person, group to group, and year to year, but sufficiently visible to generalize about. It included an iconoclastic urge to wipe out old values and norms and to challenge the whole array of cultural habits associated with the ruling circles, the upper classes, and (sometimes) the urban middle class; a strong and principled moral standard of behavior which, while allowing for violence and deception against the "enemy," was binding among the revolutionaries themselves, with complete self-sacrifice and loyalty to the underground as its chief elements; equality of gender and ethnic relations within the circles; a sense of hostility to cities and city life as basically corrupting; and communalism—meaning renunciation of most worldly goods, sharing, and living together in supposed emulation of the peasantry's own communal sensibilities.

Populists split and split again in the 1870s mainly on issues of tactics. What of their outline of the future, their sense of a coming order, their relationship to peasant ideas? It is sometimes claimed that Populists were remote from popular aspirations and that this is why they failed when they went out to the countryside in the early 1870s in the famous "To the People" movement. This is only partly true. Their tactics, timetable, style, and mode of propaganda often conflicted with the peasants' world view. But their programs—the future ideal—were partly modeled on peasant myths and traditions. Some Populists insisted on advancing the "rebellious" tradition as central to peasant dynamics. Radical ethnographers of the 1860 believed that the study of Stenka Razin and Emelyan Pugachëv revealed the revolutionary secret of the common folk. The father of Russian anarchism, Michael Bakunin gained fame by declaring that "the brigand in Russia is the true and only revolutionary." Other radicals of the 1860s frightened readers by invoking scenes of a coming total destruction of the present order by a bloody rural uprising. In the later 1870s, urban propagandists of the People's Will pictured Razin and Pugachëv as "good folks" who plundered from the rich and gave to the poor. This motif surfaced again in 1905 and became a virtual cult in the Revolution of 1917. But the radical ethnographers went much deeper than this. By closely studying peasant traditions and the legends of dissident religious movements, they linked up to the main elements of popular utopia. Like the Slavophiles, they looked to Russia's past by examining the lower strata of society still untouched by Western custom; unlike them, they discovered there not a multitude of childlike and deferential people, but rather The People: a dormant revolutionary world.[71]

A Soviet scholar, using a wide array of sources, calculated the peasants' own program in 1861: the end of all private gentry landowning and the division of all its land and property equally to the peasants; an end to the gentry power and to "feudal" obligations; an end to State Peasant obligations, taxes, and liability for army draft; a resulting system of individual peasant communes (*mir* or *obshchina*) independent of landlord and state. Around this core, Populists wove their programs. The other great prophet of anarchism, Prince Peter Kropotkin was among the first to look into the postrevolutionary future. In his *Should We Concern Ourselves with the Ideal Society of the Future?* (1873), he depicted the new Russia as a freely formed federation of self-governing peasant communities in full possession of all the land, commonly held and equally partitioned. All town property has been taken over by workers, including management of factories. The déclassé officers, officials, and former owners of land and buildings have been reduced to a status of workers or peasants. Schools for useful trades have replaced higher learning, and all castes of intellectuals and specialists have been eliminated. Urban housing space has been thoroughly redistributed. Kropotkin, while outlining a probable system of barter and a stateless community of communities, declined to provide more specific details of daily life since the psychology of each future generation would, he believed, modify current views of equitable life and morality. Another major theorist of Populism, Peter Lavrov, went a bit further in *The State Element in the Society of the Future* (1876) by predicting (à la Marx) that the institutionalization and processes of socialist production would gradually induce an altruistic and cooperative morality into the personality of the future. He also urged that the parasitic "losers" in the coming revolution be cared for humanely rather than being forced to work—a clear shift away from the retributive emphasis on universal labor in the peasant utopian dreams.[72]

Populist propaganda brochures of the 1870s designed for peasant consumption reiterated these main themes in the syncretic language of legend, morality tale, and fantasy. The resultant corpus of teaching was often vague and inconsistent, but its content was a merger of Russian intelligentsia socialism (some of it derived from Europe) and genuine peasant aspirations. Tactical fights dealt with ways to link up mentally and physically with the "people" and with ways to fight the threefold foe: landlord property, the menace of capitalism, and the autocracy which promoted the other two.

The Populist vision was overwhelmingly rural. It yielded no fantasies of urban life—with one minor but curious exception: the circular city of L. S. Zlatopolsky. In the long nights of Siberian exile in the 1880s, he sketched out for his prison mates a giant industrial center with a population of thousands "where science, technology, and art of the future provided dwellers with unheard of comfort, a minimum workday, and labor transformed into pleasure." The city had eternally moving panels on its streets, phones, radioscopes, and airships. The phalanstery-like metropolis was designed with wide concentric streets crossed by radials. The author, a former student of the St. Petersburg Technical Institute, had a passion for inventions, and was called "the mechanic" in underground circles. In exile, he also planned an aircraft that would take him and his fellow prisoners out of prison to the moon, or to any planet in the universe—a technical version of the Stenka Razin legend which portrayed the rebel hero as a wizard who could draw a boat on the wall of his cell and sail away in it. Zlatopolsky's fantasies, although they made no impact on the utopianizing of the Populist period, were piquant and pathetic examples of early technologism in Populist revolutionary circles, an anticipation of things to come.[73]

## Marxism: City and Machine

The rapid surge of Russian industrialization in the 1890s amplified the forces—technology, urbanization, and the proletariat—that enlarged the scope of utopian thinking in the last years of the Empire and shaped the utopianism of the Revolution itself. The clogging of industrial neighborhoods with newly migrated peasants, overcrowded housing, the heavy demographic preponderance of males, the noise and smoke of the factories, and the sharp increase in prostitution all combined to produce among social critics a heightened perception of the "urban problem." Organized crime, the "wild disorder of our populated places" in the words of one critic, abandoned children, slums, the lag in municipal reform—all cried out for correction.[74] But urban sprawl, the rise of big buildings, public transport, and what was perceived as the "freer air" of urban life also nourished visions of a new and better urbanized Russia that would allow the application of technology to the comforts of life and where the density of the crowds would promote and make possible a communal order beyond the hazy dreams of phalansteries, isolated peasant communes, and military colonies.

The large-scale introduction of modern industrial technology to Russia, the expansion of technical education, and the growing availability of imported literature, including science fiction, gave rise to a new genre: technical science fiction by popular science journalists. The country was flooded by translated foreign science fiction, especially H. G. Wells and Jules Verne, the latter being perhaps the most widely read foreign author of the age among Russians. In Russian, V. N. Chikolev's *Electric Tale* (1895), A. Rodnykh's *St. Petersburg-Moscow Self-Propelled Underground Railway* (1902) and V. Bakhmetov's *Billionaire's Legacy* (1904) all appeared in the decade of rapid industrial growth—the Witte period. Chikolev's book was the most interesting. An engineer by training and a popularizer of science by avocation, he wrote of a future world transformed by electricity, which performed miracles of production and also graced everyday life with recorded concerts through hidden microphones and speakers. The main message was that technology abolishes war. Mars Field in St. Petersburg—the major parade ground of the Empire—was occupied in Chikolev's fantasy by a gigantic Temple of Technology, a monument to peaceful economic growth.[75]

The onset of rapid industrialization quickened utopian longing. As in Germany and America, it sprang from hopes, questions, and fears as to what industrial civilization would bring to humanity. In Russia, it was sharpened by the persistence of a heavy-handed autocracy, the lingering tradition of dreaming among the intelligentsia, and the appearance of a new social character on the scene: the working class—half peasant and half proletarian, thronged into unhealthy living quarters, and often brutalized at the workplace. The working class produced no proletarian utopia as such, but they did evince behavior patterns of iconoclasm, comradeship, collectivism, egalitarianism, and morality partly brought with them from the countryside and partly adapted from the revolutionary subcultures around them in the cities. Their vision of a just future was more complicated than that of the peasantry, for the village mentality of their origins was enriched by imported ideologies and by the very structure of factory life. They also had to contend with a new kind of relationship: that between themselves—the simple people—and their intellectual mentors who came from another world.

Recent innovative research on the tastes of the "common reader" in this period persuasively argues that the great majority of lower class readers were infatuated with *lubok* and folk tales, and with the adventure and detective stories that appeared in the penny press, particularly after the easing of censorship in 1906–14. The writers and the readers of this genre seemed to share the same vision and values: the vision of mobility, success, and modernization and the values of patriotism and individualism, with a strong taste for the exotic—but not for traditional utopian dreams of pastoral idylls or socialist cities.[76]

But it is also true that a growing stratum of "conscious proletarians"—skilled, literate, and self-consciously radical—began to respond to the "visions" of revolutionary reordering. The culture they received from propagandists of the intelligentsia, from books, and from autodidactic exercises, in Reginald Zelnik's words, "for all its secularized vocabulary and self description . . . offered its adherents a millenarian goal that was essentially religious; nothing less than the permanent liberation of the Russian people from the double yoke of autocracy and capitalism"—and all this without losing their identity as industrial workers and their pride of skill. The conscious worker Semën Kanatchikov was entranced by his reading of the Polish propaganda tract, *What Should Every Worker Know and Remember?*: "Factories, workshops, the land, the forests, the mines—everything would become the common property of the toilers!" One of his comrades, dreaming aloud about the future, predicted that "then everyone on earth shall be equal. There will be neither tsars, nor earthly rulers, nor judges, nor gendarmes, nor priests."[77]

Conscious workers were exposed to popularly written radical propaganda stories—morality tales such as Voynich's *The Gadfly*, a heroic story of the Italian Risorgimento, Giovagnoli's *Spartacus*, and the countless socialist fairy tales that were read to them, or which they themselves read, on the evils of capitalism, autocracy, and religion and the beauties of a coming order of equality under socialism. These tales did not offer concrete details about how things would work in the coming age. This was done in a series of translated "urban utopias" circulated in large numbers, especially after 1905, and dealing with the technologized city as the locus of the future society: August Bebel's *The Society of the Future* (from *Women and Socialism*, 1879), Edward Bellamy's *Looking Backward* (1889), Lili Braun's *Female Labor* (1891), Karl Ballod's (writing under the name Atlanticus) *A Glimpse into the Future State* (1898), and a number of futuristic pictures by the intellectual leader of German Socialism, Karl Kautsky.[78]

As Kautsky explained, in endorsing their publication on a mass scale in Germany, Marxists were not trying to lay out a static order of the future, since that could not be known. But, he argued, there was no harm in looking at "the structure of the future social edifice" since its foundations (the coming revolution and the abolition of capitalism) were already known. Kautsky believed that in the Marxist movement the ultimate goal was important and that the workers had the right to know the outlines of that goal.[79] All of these works focused on the shape of the city, collective living in large residential ensembles, communal dining, and all sorts of community services made possible by a combination of the cooperative organization of life and the massive use of electricity, gas, modern building materials, and rapid transit. An important byproduct of this mode of life was the drastic modification of the nuclear family, the end of individual housekeeping, and the consequent emancipation of women and their release into "productive" work. Lili Braun, a German Marxist feminist, proposed communal apartment houses of 50–60 families with central laundry, kitchen, dining room, and childcare facilities—a graphic three-dimensional transformation of the turn-of-the-century bourgeois apartment building, housing dozens of atomized families, into a collective of working comrades. Russian Marxists interested in the future of the family and the fate of women—Kollontai, Krupskaya, and Lenin—were inspired by this vision of an urban future as were some of the Soviet utopian city planners of the 1920s.[80]

The most elaborate, and probably the most popular in Russia, of the imported utopias was Bellamy's *Looking Backward,* a picture of superindustrial society a hundred years in the future, dotted by huge cities, squares, statues and buildings of "architectural grandeur," and with piped-out music for the entertainment of the masses. Society was hierarchical and militarized, with "festivals of mustering" and compulsory labor. There was no deference and no snobbery, waiters being equal to doctors in social rank. Everyone was to work for society and for the public benefit. It was a well ordered state run like an army, cemented together by discipline and by the religion of solidarity. Bellamy's dream of authoritarian, military, egalitarian, bureaucratic socialism was, by his own admission, inspired by the Prussian values which he greatly admired, and by an anguished rejection of the anarchic competitiveness unfolding in American economic and social life in the late nineteenth century.[81]

In Russia, *Looking Backward* was first published in 1891; by 1918 it had had seven Russian translations and had sold 50,000 copies in Russian, Georgian, Lithuanian, and Hebrew. After the Revolution, a Bolshevik journalist called it the "first novel to give a lifelike depiction of scientific socialism." A Soviet scholar claims that Bellamy's work was virtually devoured by intelligentsia, workers, and students. An underground May Day speaker in 1891 recommended it as a picture of the future. M. I. Tugan-Baranovsky, economist and historian of the Russian factory, thought it the most effective propaganda vehicle in thirty years. Workers in Nizhny Novgorod, on Sakhalin, in Ekaterinoslav, Ivanovo, and Petersburg read it. It was not only attacked by the Russian Right, but even gave birth to a whole genre of Russian anti-Bellamy dystopias.[82] One can feel how the novel's critique of laissez-faire capitalism must have appealed to anyone with socialist sensibility and how its vividness must have fed workers' preference for tales to programs. Its authoritarian cast must also have appealed to layers of the population who were beset by uncertainty, social fear, and puzzlement abut the future of capitalism unleashed in a Russian autocracy.

The only Russian Marxist science fiction utopia published in these years was the two-novel epic of a communist society on Mars by the Bolshevik Alexander Bogdanov: *Red Star* (1908) and *Engineer Menni* (1913).[83] Bogdanov was a trained scientist, physician, economist, and philosopher who worked closely with Lenin in the leadership of the Bolshevik Party from its birth until the two men fell out over philosophical and political issues in 1908. Bogdanov's revolutionary Martian fantasy grew out of his personal experiences during the bloody events of 1905–7—Russia's first nationwide revolution. The setting was suggested to Bogdanov by the popularity of science fiction in

Russia, particularly space travel, and by his still emerging theories of Tectology, a science of systems thinking, the organization of all human knowledge, and an early version of cybernetics. Seized with a desire to present a social sketch of the future to the Russian proletariat, and intrigued by recent publications in Russia concerning the now disproven "canals" on Mars, Bogdanov created a Martian-Marxian society that was about three hundred years in advance of Earth in technology, ideology, and human behavior (see Figs. 4, 29).

On the "red star," peasant, labor, and ethnic questions, which so plagued Russia in 1908, had been eliminated by the mechanizing of agriculture, the deruralization of the planet, the construction of ultramodern cities, the free choice of labor and consumption according to need in the classic canon of Marx's final vision of communism, and a monolingual population. Factories were operated by electric power and fully automated, and the "moving equilibrium" of supply, labor assignment, and production needs were finely calibrated by data-retrieval machinery and protocomputers. Equality, collective work, comradeship, and the full emancipation of women were the binding social values of Martian life. Rules were based on "science" not religion or philosophy; rank and deference did not exist, nor did coercive and authoritarian norms. People wore unisex clothing and had genderless names and related to one another in a comradely and businesslike fashion—without the polite adornment of manners. Superior talent was its own reward. And there were no monuments to the heroes and heroines of the past—to the people described in his second novel, *Engineer Menni,* wherein the foundations of communism were laid on Mars, along with its canals, in the seventeenth century. The role of art was to celebrate the collective efforts of the masses, past and present. Bogdanov's ultimate form of fraternal solidarity on Mars was the "comradely exchange of life," in which mutual blood transfusions were used to prolong life.

Bogdanov's *Red Star* was the first and only full attempt before the Revolution to present a graphic outline of a Marxist future for the planet Earth. A rank-and-file Bolshevik veteran of the 1905 revolution recalled that he and his comrades saw this novel as "the first swallow" of a renewed and victorious revolution.[84] Though Bogdanov was repudiated by Lenin after their break, his book was reprinted many times and enjoyed a huge circulation after the Revolution of 1917. It also served as the foundation stone for Soviet science fiction in the 1920s. Together with Maxim Gorky, the semi-official bard of Bolshevism, and Anatoly Lunacharsky, its first Commissar of Enlightenment after 1917, Bogdanov formed a kind of Marxist counter-movement to Lenin's official Bolshevism in the years before World War I, operating mostly from exile like Lenin himself. Out of this circle came two important intellectual currents that played a major role in the utopianism of the early Soviet years—the Proletarian Culture movement and Godbuilding.

Urbanizing visions of the perfect life by no means accounted for all the utopian currents that pulsed through the population of Russia in the period of industrialization. The gleaming giant cities of the future generated revulsion in some quarters. Tolstoyanism, the Anarchist movement, and anti-socialist dystopias with a dash of anti-modernism provided alternate visions of the coming transformation. The Tolstoyan movement attracted intellectuals who sought the traditional popular utopia of the past. It preached pacifism, withdrawal to the simplicity of rustic life and away from the moral and physical dirt of the cities, a loathing for the state and for public authority in general, an interior mystical religion outside of the bureaucratic state church, opposition to politics in any form and to terroristic violence on the part of state or revolutionary. It was a rejection of passion and anger and even sexual drive—a colossal "no" to the advance of technology, "progress," and modern life as it was understood in Western civilization. Tolstoy's response to the puzzling menace of capitalism, egoism, and productive anarchy was one of the strongest antimodern currents in Russia at the turn of the twentieth century.[85]

Tolstoyanism was a quasi-religious form of anarchism. The Anarchist movement showed greater drama and diversity. Statelessness—the mandatory common denominator—was often a shorthand term for the rejection of the world for some anarchists, but the movement itself was distinctly activist, political, revolutionary, and often violent. Its most systematic ideologue, Kroptkin, offered the vision of a future of "fields, factories, and workshops," composed of federated communes, minus central state power, church, police, and other institutions of coercion—a self-regulated society. It was not only the state, but authority, inequality, and hierarchy that the Anarchists fought with an undimmed passion—sometimes with pen and ink, sometimes with the revolver and the bomb.[86]

The relationship of science fiction and social fantasy to real life, to politics, culture, and revolution has not attracted much attention from serious scholars. Yet the world of fantasy, like the world of myth and legend, reveals and evokes deep layers, archaic dreams and longings that may better describe feelings and anxieties than some conventional acts of political adherence. A study of American utopian novels in the generation before World War I (over a hundred appeared) shows how these reflected malaise in U.S. society in that generation of rapid change. Only about thirty or so science fiction works appeared in Russia at that time, about half of them utopias or dystopias, but their growing frequency and their sociological sharpness attest to a similar malaise in the Russian empire. Russian science fiction on the eve of the Revolution was a dialogue of fantasy and a duel of dreams. Bright and hopeful utopias of progress, with strong urban, technical, and socialist elements, generated counter-utopias of alternate scenarios and dystopias of warning and fear. Their authors were well known names whose ambivalence and talent give their works a mark of literary distinction, political journalists and publicists of the Right, and popular writers who are otherwise almost unknown.[87]

Before the revolution of 1905 a genre of geopolitical novel appeared in Russia with visions of a catastrophic war and hopes for a Pan-Slav victory. The most interesting was A. I. Krasnitsky's *Behind the Raised Curtain: a Fantastic Tale of Future Things— the 20th Century* (1900). The "future things" are submarines, a European holocaust and war, a rebellion in the colonial world, a foiled attempt to create a Jewish State on the site of a ruined Austria in order "to extend Jewish power throughout the world," and the emergence of a regenerated religious, patriotic, monarchic Russia, with its capital renamed Petrograd, ruled by a Russian God of Truth *(pravda)*, Good, and Love, and heading a Pan-Slavic political union.[88]

Throughout this period, some conservatives were longing for what one historian has called a "reactionary utopia"; they identified cities with industry and with Jews, "urban outsiders in an agrarian society," and they lamented the "destructive influence of the city."[89] Some of this was clearly reflected in science fiction. N. N. Shelonsky's *In the World of the Future* (1892) attacked Bellamy and socialism but not technology as such. Television *(telefot)*, tunnels, antigravity machines, and all manner of super-technology appear in the book, but cities have been eliminated and the people of this thirtieth century world have returned to the land, living in individual houses, widely scattered and separated from each other, each family being self-sufficient. Religious and bearded elders are the wise men of Russia's capital (Moscow) and a Temple of All Rus has been erected by a million people. L. B. Afanasiev's *Journey to Mars* (1901) warned against modernization by describing Mars where the rise of cities, roads, and factories has turned the simple, primitive, trusting, rural Martians into greedy, competitive, canni-balistic brutes and egoists—into a "neurotic society." S. F. Sharapov, a gentry land-owner and reactionary publicist, wrote a Slavophile romance called *Fifty Years from Now* (1902) showing Russia in 1951 with Tsar, gentry, peasant *mir*, and Church—but no bicycles or cars or any other kind of unnerving technology.[90]

After the revolution of 1905 appeared the fear-laden dystopia, warning of the perils of urbanism or collectivism. The master of the genre was Valery Bryusov who began his dark search of the future with *Earth* (1904) set in the "city of future times," an underground geometric labyrinth of rooms, passages and machines, unexposed to natu-ral light and air. *Republic of the Southern Cross*, written in 1904–5 at the very onset of the first revolution, is a classic of the dystopian genre. The City Hall of Stellar, capital of the Republic, sits astride the South Pole and all streets with identical buildings radiate from it. In this metropolis of 50 million beneath a glass dome all needs are cared for by the state, though only skilled workers have full rights. But behind the welfare facade, "the directors" enforce a hideous regimentation, uniformity of life, and rigid police control.[91]

A remarkably prophetic dystopia called *An Evening in the Year 2217* appeared in 1906 under the authorship of Nikolai Fëdorov (not the philosopher). Its heroine, Citizeness No. 437–2221 (all citizens wear their work numbers on their arms) resides in a socialist city of the twenty-third century—St. Petersburg—all stone, steel, and glass, bustling in a network of balloon buses and moving sidewalks. Members of society are paid accord-ing to need; and cold, hunger, and disease have been abolished. But each citizen is expected to recompense society by registering for "sex-choosing sessions" and to give themselves impersonally by appointment to those who choose them. Children are par-entless, anonymous, and raised by the state. The heroine and her male friend are thor-oughly alienated from this society; they long for individual love and family and yearn to give up the guaranteed happiness of the state in return for the risks of deprivation and "unhappiness"—like the bygone peasants they have read about in the "old books." Most of all, they want the right to choose.

Fëdorov's book was the closest thing produced in Russia before the revolution to an anticipation of Eugene Zamyatin's famous dystopia *We* (1920). Its author is an other-wise unknown figure—perhaps pseudonymous; the story is not discussed in any of the studies of Russian science fiction. It might have been an answer to some of the foreign works well-known in Russia at the time: *Looking Backward;* "The New Utopia" (1891) by the popular English writer, Jerome K. Jerome; or *L'anno 3000* (1898) by the Italian anthropologist Paolo Mantegazza—all of them translated into Russian. But, as with *We*, the genealogy of the work is not as important as the impulse that created it: the growing fear that all the progressive processes associated with the words modern, urban, indus-trial, rational, harmonious, socially just, equal, and fair were coalescing into a night-mare of future conformity and repression.[92]

Long, detailed, weak on narrative, naive, and philosophically simple, these works were accessible to a rather wide audience of educated readers—but obviously not to the masses of peasants and workers. What did this wealth of predictive detail, prophetic longing, and anticipatory fright in the "utopias of hope and the utopias of fear"[93] mean to their authors? Dire predictions and hopeful dreams can flourish and coexist in any kind of society. But in the Russia of the twilight years, there was a clarity in the discourse and a mirror-like symmetry in the visions that made utopian and anti-utopian speculation more than simply popular entertainment or a minor eddy of a nation's literature. Both kinds of vision possessed a political content and a frantic desperation arising out of the rapid and disconcerting pace of urban life, economic growth, the menace of revolution, and cultural innovation of a sudden radical type. Utopians and anti-utopians were sending out signals across a great and dark divide. The familiar tones and colors of the intelligentsia tradition were there as well, lending vigor and national authenticity to the ideological duel. In a sense, one can read in the pages of these works an outline of the coming civil war in Russia that pitted Reds, Whites, and Greens against each other in a revolution that was more visionary than any previous one in history.

On the eve of revolution, the pillars of the old regime no longer harbored visions of elegant control; they dreamed of holding the empire together against forces of disruption and of transforming the economy and the defense establishment in utterly conventional ways. The peasants' dream of ''general distribution'' of the land—though modified by new political forms and opportunities—continued to haunt the countryside. Intelligentsia writers, prophets, and revolutionaries, faced with vistas of technology and rapid social change, indulged in fantasies of hope and fear while the creative intelligentsia, heavily influenced by *fin-de-siècle* Europe, spun all kinds of apocalyptic webs of mystical anarchism, cultural renewal, ''revolutions of the spirit,'' and religious ecstasy. These reveries, partially paralleled in other societies of the time, did not cause the Russian Revolution and the collapse of the monarchy. That was caused by the travails of war, state mismanagement, dynastic myopia, and a host of social movements and currents whose complexities have been examined by generations of historians. But after the Revolution, utopian visions resurfaced or intensified, generating experiments and social fantasies that flourished for a decade as the ''revolutionary dreams'' that colored and shaped that era.

# 2

# Revolution: Utopias in the Air and on the Ground

New faces. New dreams.
New songs. New visions
New myths are we flinging on,
We are kindling a new eternity . . .
Vladimir Mayakovsky, *150 Million*

## A New World

The fall the Romanov dynasty at the height of the war was occasioned by uncontrollable popular rioting in the streets of the capital. The abdication of Nicholas II, the last tsar in Russian history, was followed by the formation of a Provisional Government dominated by liberal and moderate conservative figures, and of a popular council or Soviet that spoke for the working classes and the men in the ranks. Within five months the Provisional Government had shifted to the left, the moderate socialist leaders of the Soviet had joined it, and all had been left far behind by the growing radicalism and anti-war feelings of the masses. To the right, military elements plotted to end the life of the weakening Government, dissolve the Soviets, and fight the war to victory. To the left, the Bolsheviks led by Lenin, though deeply divided, also eventually vowed to seize power on behalf of the masses who were visibly moving to the left. The continued inefficacy of the Government under Alexander Kerensky, the attempted coup from the right, and the appealing slogans of Bolshevism led to the October Revolution which was a combination of an urban coup in the capital (Petrograd) followed by scores of uprisings of various kinds and dimensions throughout the country, the establishment of a Soviet regime, and the beginnings of an immense social upheaval.

A few weeks after the fall of the tsar, the victims of the street fighting in the February Revolution were buried. A conservative Petrograd journalist solemnly wrote that with the bodies of the martyrs was being buried Russia's past, the long ages of struggle and disharmony. Being born was a "new era" and a "new land." It was a remark typical of the rhetoric that invariably accompanies political change—not only revolution. But judging from myriad similar remarks, and from the behavior of the crowds in the first few weeks who smiled, looked joyful and congratulated each other as free citizens, the sense of euphoria was deep and widespread in the cities and towns of Russia. The popular masses comprehended what had happened. So did intellectuals. A group of Polish Marxists from Moscow, looking outward, proclaimed on April 2 that "Europe and the entire world will be refashioned on new principles by revolution." And the irrepressible bard of the Russian Revolution, Mayakovsky wrote that "today the millennium of 'beforetimes' is broken" and that "we will remake life anew—right down to the last button of your vest." The concrete imagery in Mayakovsky's verse exactly reflected the difference between those who spoke of "new principles" of revolution and those who, like Mayakovsky, wanted precisely to make new buttons and new vests too. The poet Alexander Blok echoed this a year later when he spoke of the purpose of revolution: "to *remake* everything. To organize things so that everything should be new, so that our false, filthy, boring, hideous life should become a just, pure, merry, and beautiful life." [1]

The iconoclasm, utopianism, and experimentalism ushered in by the Revolution of 1917 were frightening to the Provisional Government. The removal of the tsar, the linchpin of the Russian authoritarian tradition, made an aperture through which a torrent of ideas and dreams, accumulated like lava through the ages, poured forth and burst over the landscape of revolutionary Russia. The Provisional Government, lasting from March to October 1917, produced no utopias and created no symbols of the future. In ethos and style, it slid with lightning speed from eclectic and cosmopolitan in the first weeks to national, Russian, religious, and conservative a few months later as it buried its own martyrs of the July Days in Orthodox and military splendor. [2] Its first premier, the gentle Prince G. E. Lvov spoke of the "inexhaustible kindness of the Russian heart," and his successor, Alexander Kerensky, abolished the death penalty. But these leaders tried to make ready for a peaceful and moderate transition to democratic institutions, with a tinge of socialism and welfare, and the retention of a "Russian" spirit—all this in the midst of war. Paul Milyukov, the more conservative leader of the liberal party that dominated the Provisional Government in its early phase, explicitly rejected "utopian schemes;" he believed that "only the war"—that is the manifestation of discipline, patriotism and conventional law and order on a national scale—could bring stability to a disintegrating Russia. The task of the Provisional Government was not to pull asunder and "remake" but rather to hold together what appeared to be flying apart. [3]

Early 1917 was one of those moments of revolutionary explosion that liberates the press, the pen, and the tongue in an outpouring of millennial expectation. The euphoria of radical Petrograd workers—especially the young, the unskilled, and women—was expressed not in visionary statements but in actions and gestures—reversals, the occupation of offices, street movement, and arranging a "new order" in their places of work, all of this inducing, in the words of one historian, a transformation of consciousness in "moral and affective terms." In the midst of this revolution, young Putilov Factory workers were "trying to imagine what a communist society would be like." [4]

But the October Revolution which—ironically enough—bridled the press and tied the tongue within a remarkably short time, created a psychological environment where, in the words of the Manuels, "the utopian appears no madder than other men." The psychic and cultural fetters that had chained the fantasy of Provisional Government leaders were now struck off.

> An epoch, the like of which has never been since the creation of the world, has opened. The pillars propping up old horizons of belief, hope, and beauty have collapsed. Cascades of novel ideas gush forth amid the storms of war and revolution; and trains of new words wind their way through the smoke, the blood, and the joy of the Revolution.

These words were spoken in 1919 by Alexei Gastev, prophet of the mechanized man and poet of the machine. The novelist Ilya Ehrenburg later recalled the period of 1917–21 as "a great time for projects . . . for a heavenly life on earth." Another pro-Bolshevik writer, Fëdor Panfërov, recollected the Civil War as a moment of expectant euphoria.

> If not today then in the very near future we will live in a communist society. Until then the main thing is to defeat the bourgeoisie and extirpate the petty bourgeois routine from our lives: official marriage, weddings, baptisms, curtains (especially tule curtains), carpets, irons and so on. Destroy petty-bourgeois life! In a word: clear away all the old from our path—the army of the young is on the march!

Thousands, perhaps tens of thousands of people like Panfërov, especially young people, believed, not dreamed, just as surely as they believed in the rising and setting of the sun.[5]

The vision, the faith, and the dream of October—the myth of the great Red Dawn with its Rising Sun that grants Heat and Light and Joy—was not the monopoly of Bolsheviks. Isaak Steinberg, a lifelong member of the Socialist Revolutionary Party, and the first Commissar of Justice in the new Soviet coalition regime of Bolsheviks and Left Socialist Revolutionaries, explained that the October Revolution brought a serene sense of relief after eight months of tension, uncertainty, and crisis, and this serenity in turn opened up broad perspectives on a new social horizon:[6]

> All aspects of existence—social, economic, political, spiritual, moral, familial—were opened to purposeful fashioning by human hands. Ideas for social betterment and progress that had been gathering for generations in Russia and elsewhere seemed to wait on the threshold of the revolution ready to pour forth and permeate the life of the Russian people. The issues were not only social and economic reforms and thoroughgoing political changes: with equal zeal the awakened people turned to the fields of justice and education, to art and literature. Everywhere the driving passion was to create something new, to effect a total difference with the "old world" and its civilization. It was one of those uncommon moments of self-perception and self-assertion. The storm passed nobody by: neither those who hailed it as a blessing nor those who spurned it as a curse.

This impassioned fragment of recollection, colored though it might have been by the bittersweet nostalgia of a defeated dreamer, was one of the most eloquent and concise evocations of the euphoric mood of the victors and of their myriad potential supporters—Socialist Revolutionaries of the Left, Anarchists, Maximalists, Tolstoyans, Fëdorovists, and even religious Sectarians.

From the very onset of the Revolution, utopia was fed by millenarianism—dreams suddenly transformed into concerted beliefs, and beliefs into actions. Russian dreamers had achieved the state of awakening; they now possessed the will and, so it seemed, the power to change the world. Optimism, disappointment, and despair alternated and mixed freely to feed the wishes and dreams that Freud has called illusions. Euphoria means "the good light" that would henceforth embrace, envelope, and illuminate the spirit of the world; it gave a feeling of relief, of collective joy, of being rewarded at long last for the patience and suffering of generations of humanity. It meant an opportunity to realize all the beautiful dreams of those who had fought, languished in prison, and died for the sake of freedom, justice, equality, decency and prosperity for the people of Russia and for the world. The compelling faith of the Russian intelligentsia in the power of the will to create the good now seemed justified to many revolutionaries.

When the optimism generated by the Revolution and by the Red victory in the Civil War was shattered by the failure of War Communism and by the turn to a mixture of Old and New Economies in the 1920s, the utopian mechanism did not perish. It was refueled by the powerful belief that if the larger scheme of a new world had to be abandoned for the time being, then there was all the more reason for communists to begin laying its foundations in a culture and mode of life that would prefigure the new order, and by fashioning new people who would be fit to live under such an order. This was the social circumstance and the psychological mechanism that explain why, after the collapse of War Communism, an even intenser culture of utopian behavior, experiment and dreaming flourished in the midst of petty capitalists, bourgeois restaurants, and philistine values—the despised world of the N.E.P.

But beyond the realm of conscious alternation of optimism and disappointment lay the subconscious realm of guilt and despair. Utopian ideas of the revolutionary period were not solely or even mostly responsible for the disastrous condition of the country and for the relentless waves of misery unleashed at the time. It will not do, as Soviet historians are in the habit of doing, to lay everything at the feet of the "imperialist" war of 1914, the White forces in the Civil War, the Allied blockade and intervention in that war—but it must be recognized that the regime was faced with almost insoluble problems and a legacy of harsh conditions from the very beginning: food shortages, economic breakdown, near anarchy in the countryside, and a general brutalization of life. In spite of the frequent arrogance and blindness of Bolshevik leaders and their supporters, it was clear to all of them that their utopian feast was set in a time of famine. The gap between the revolutionary dreams and the conditions for realizing them was simply colossal.

In a novel set at the end of the Civil War, Fëdor Gladkov depicted the dreamers as "possessed with a vision of the future, a glittering romance which for them extinguishes the ruined present." It is likely that some of the most extravagant wish-dreams were driven onward by feelings of doubt and guilt at the ocean of misery outside the walls of the dream chamber. Trotsky's doctrine of "permanent revolution" drawn partly from Marx, is usually understood as a rather mechanical prediction based upon the historical fact of unequal development and the natural solidarity of the European working classes: the arrival of a liberating proletarian army from the West, laden down with goods, equipment, and specialists to help defeat the Whites and build a new socialist order. This notion was formulated at the time of the Revolution of 1905 in the highly intellectual partnership between Trotsky and Alexander Gelfand-Parvus, two brilliant political journalists. But in its popular form, as probably understood, perceived, and felt by workers, it more resembled the millenarian cargo cults that flourished in the Pacific Islands at just about the same time. Gastev lamented in 1921 that the enormous mass of workers suffered from the "expectation" that an outside force from abroad would arrive and "grant unto them"—the phrase used to describe the mythical tsar deliverer who would grant *(dast)* land to the peasants.[7]

In the long perspective of Russian history, the Revolution was one of those times—like the Baptism of Rus in 988 and the reign of Peter the Great—wherein a decisive break with the past is consciously and visibly effected and announced. In referring to the tenth century conversion, the monk Hilarion of Kiev spoke of new land, new people, "new skins" into which new teachings were poured; in the eighteenth century, Feofan Prokopovich—apologist of Peter's reforms—announced that Russia was "reborn in a new form" after the victory at Poltava which he saw as a victory of Peter's radical Europeanization of Russia. In a brilliant semiotic reading of Russian cultural history, Yury Lotman and Boris Uspensky have stressed its dual or "binary" element: the absence in Eastern Orthodoxy of purgatory, the dualities of Heaven or Hell, Right or Left, black or white, orthodox or heretical which have made the dynamics of Russian growth not developmental but transformational and negational—"a process of turning [the old] inside out" and the "radical exchange of 'top' and 'bottom,'" rendering the past in a minus sign and painting it as a dark frame to highlight and dramatize the brightness of the New World.[8]

This notion of dualism helps to explain the utter sincerity and graphic quality of the revolutionary visions, the profusion of utopian speculation and symbols, and the contrived myth of an evil past. The Bolshevik regime was a nation builder, one of the first governments in history to attempt the creation of a new society with new values involving all the population in an elaborate break with the past. The role of utopianism was to summon up archaic memories and ancient dreams, construct new projects, and put on display an "exhibit" about social and spiritual innovation. As in all revolutions, it faced the regulatory mechanism of authorities who had to deal with the retention of power, military victory, territorial survival, economic production, and the continuing organization of life.

Utopianism accompanied every phase of Soviet history up to the early 1930s when Stalin came to power. In outlining the utopian elements in Bolshevism during the Revolution and War Communism, 1917–21, I must remind the reader that a murderous Civil War was raging all round the perimeters of Soviet Russia in this period. The contrasting picture of popular mentality and behavior in the same period demonstrates that the ancient duel between state and people was still very much alive, making the Russian Revolution a utopian war on all fronts, pitting many spirits, emotions and mentalities one against the other.

## The Dreamer in the Kremlin

At the epicenter of the utopian landscape was the sacred site of the Kremlin, and in the Kremlin sat Lenin, described in a by no means jocular way by H. G. Wells, who interviewed him there in 1920, as "the dreamer in the Kremlin (See Fig. 6)."[9] Lenin has often been called in accusatory tones a utopian—a fanatic possessed by extravagant dreams, impossible to realize, a heartless experimenter determined to turn his patrimony into a vast laboratory, and emotionally immune to the human costs. He has also been called an anti-utopian, a grim and power-hungry despot who despised all fantasy and all utopias. One could build a convincing case on either side, but to do so would violate the complexity of Lenin's mind, personality, and vision. Like all great revolutionaries and like most great statesmen of any persuasion, he was both a visionary inspired by outlandish dreams and a man of practical action and ruthless realism. In an oft-quoted 1902 passage on Dmitry Pisarev, Lenin spoke of "the need to dream." Pisarev, a well-known radical of the 1860s, impatient with the sloppy thinking habits of the intelligentsia, had written in 1864:[10]

My dream may run ahead of the natural march of events or may fly off at a tangent in a direction in which no natural march of events will ever proceed. In the first case my dream will not cause any harm; it may even support and augment the energy of the working men. . . . The rift between dreams and reality causes no harm if only the person dreaming believes seriously in his dream, if he attentively observes life, compares his observations with his castles in the air, and if, generally speaking, he works conscientiously for the achievement of his fantasies. If there is some connection between dreams and life then all is well.

Lenin agreed: he favored dreaming that "may run ahead of the natural march of events" as a projection of an ideologically sound program that leads to action—but not the passive reveries of the old intelligentsia or the hazy visions of peasants reclining upon their stoves on a winter day. From Chernyshevsky's *What Is To Be Done?*, Lenin's favorite book as a young man, he got not only the title of his own most famous work (the source of the above quotation from Pisarev) and the tough behavioral model of Rakhmetov, but also the "vision of Utopia"—of happiness, prosperity, technology. But he believed that the realization depended on the active work and physical struggle of "new people"—tough, hard, and determined like himself.[11]

Lenin was capable of romanticizing the masses. "Revolutions are the festival of the oppressed and the exploited," he wrote during the Revolution of 1905. "At no other time are the masses of the people in a position to come forward so actively as creators of a new social order as at a time of revolution. At such times the people are capable of performing miracles."[12] He was also in the habit of letting his fancy take flight, as when he shared his reaction to *The Time Machine* with its author:

Human ideas—he told Wells—are based on the scale of the planet we live in. They are based on the assumption that the technical potentialities, as they develop, will never overstep 'the earthly limit.' If we succeed in making contact with the other planets, all our philosophical, social, and moral ideas will have to be revised, and in this event these potentialities will become limitless and will put an end to violence as a necessary means to progress.

But Lenin was no devotee of space fantasy, as were so many of the literary and artistic attendants of Bolshevism in the early years. The science fiction component in his personal library of 10,000 volumes was sparse. When Bukharin asked Lenin in 1918 for an outline or sketch of the socialist future, he replied: "What socialism will be like when it reaches its final form we do not know; we cannot predict it."[13]

Right before the interview with Wells—at a particularly critical moment in the early history of the Soviet State—Lenin wrote that "those who engage in the formidable task of overcoming capitalism must be prepared to try method after method until they find the one which answers their purpose best."[14] Wells found Lenin prepared for unlimited experiment until the right solutions were found. Lenin had some of the rigid, arithmetic, and self-confident dogmatism often associated with utopia builders, but also the flexibility and realism associated with the experimental method. Revolutionary innovation, like much else in human activity, requires both thought and action. Revolutions produce pure dreamers and pure actors, a whole spectrum between these two extremes, and individuals who possess the entire range of impulses. Lenin was among those individuals who act out certain missions by day and then sit down and write about them by night (or vice versa), glossing the written account with logic and pattern, the people who alternate physical, political, military, or administrative work with revolutionary planning and even dreaming. Lenin's outpouring of projects in the midst of the revolutionary swirl and Trotsky's tireless printing press aboard an armored train in a war zone are simply two examples of this familiar phenomenon. Extravagant visions can be fed as easily by the crush of events and the flash of red banners on the move as they can inside a fortress prison.

Thus Lenin's apparent duality cannot be explained by the notion that he employed utopian speculation in order to gain, retain, or extend his power, nor even by the notion of a man gripped by sincere but naive dreams who then gives way to angry force. It was rather that Lenin combined deliberately what Stalin would later call Russian revolutionary sweep and American practicality and efficiency.

Lenin's most elaborate excursion into future speculation, *State and Revolution*, actually belongs in time and context to the period of urban and anti-urban utopianism of the period 1890–1917. It was composed before either of the revolutions of 1917, begun in 1916, virtually completed in January 1917, and polished and revised only in the late summer of 1917, just before the Bolshevik takeover. Its utopian basis was to be found in Marx's vision of the communist future: universal social ownership and the end of private property; rotation of work and the end of the social division of labor; communalism in work and life and the end of egoism; victory over nature and the end of fatalism; liberation from authority and the end of state, law, and punishment; a single humanity and the end of hostility between classes, races, sexes, and between town and country. This vision was adapted to Russian conditions and embellished with concrete details from the experience of the Paris Commune in 1871.[15]

The time for its projection is sometime in the unspecified future—vague enough not to bind present day activists, vivid enough to provide something concrete for the movement to contemplate. Lenin's document is almost devoid of utopian passion. Though it has been rightly called a utopia, it is also a "program" both in its aridity and its absence of the pictorial element. Though issued eventually in huge numbers and apparently widely read, at least in excerpts, by workers, it is not likely that it would attract the kind of spontaneous interest that other genres of utopia did. It was in fact a political and social prediction of "what will be" rather than fictional projection. Production, now in the hands of all the people, would require labor obligation for all, of both sexes, and the concomitant equality of rights; and it would generate a love for labor as well, since the productive apparatus was now to be everyone's household economy. The diminution of physical labor, made possible by technology, would add leisure and time for the spiritual development of all—apparently in a communal context. Nature would be tamed, and there is no hint of the kind of tragic and continuous war against the elements that is found in Bogdanov's Martian communist society.

Central to *State and Revolution* is the theme of the revolution's victory over the state, which would disappear in the wake of the unleashed energies of the masses—meaning both the spontaneous skills of the people as a whole and the super energies of the New People. Equal and rotating administration would replace the whip of authoritarian bureaucrats and capitalist managers. Lenin, like Marx and Bogdanov, required the special skills of technical experts who would guide enterprises and operations just as a specialized conductor would have to lead an orchestra, though the relationship between superiors and subordinates in the industrial and government processes was left distressingly vague.

*State and Revolution* is written in two tenses, future imperfect and future perfect, so to speak. These are the classic divisions of Marx, called the early and the final stages of communism or, more commonly, socialism and communism. Failure to discern this distinction (sometimes muddled in the text) has led to confused interpretations about Lenin's "one-time" lapse into utopianism. There is "utopianism" enough in the description of statelessness, classlessness, and all the other elements enumerated above in Marx's final vision. But this had been a staple of Marxism since 1875 when first codified in the *Critique of the Gotha Program*. Lenin verbally defends this picture against accusations of utopianism by reminding readers that socialists do not "promise" or plan to "introduce" it as their fearful detractors claim. Unlike utopographers who describe the future world as static and readymade, Lenin shows the process and the mechanism through which "imperfect" socialists may move towards "perfect" communism: not by rocket, space ship, or time machine, but by long economic development under the auspices of socialist organizations.

The future imperfect is the transition period from near future to far future. Until communist society comes into being, people are faced with palpable problems of survival, reconstruction, and development. On the question of authority and the specialization of labor during this period, Lenin was unambiguous. The state could not be abolished at once, everywhere, and completely. The economy could not be maintained, much less amplified, by self-administering workers. Lenin thus resisted workers' control and promoted discipline, organization, the use of specialists, division of labor, and inequality in privilege. Lenin denied that the vision of communism was utopian but he criticized "the utopians" for ignoring the need for a transitional period—and a lengthy one at that.[16]

Thus Lenin could have his utopia and eat it too by retaining the distinct image and picture in vague outline but rejecting a leap toward it. In practice this meant resorting to some very conventional and well-established forms of human organization in the early years of the revolution—taken not only from capitalism but also from Russian "administrative" traditions. For this he has been bitterly castigated by modern Marxists. In 1905 a critic depicted Lenin's view of the party "as an immense factory headed by a director." To Lenin the factory was the highest form of capitalist cooperation uniting and disciplining the proletariat, "a discipline based on collective work united by the conditions of a technologically highly developed form of production." Lenin's technological mystique made him envision society as well as the party as a vast office or factory—an idea that is rooted in St. Simon and Marx. Neo-Marxists ground their critique of Leninism in its failure to develop a pre-revolutionary "anti-commodity fetishist counterculture." Thus Lenin introduced a "reversal" of repressive bureaucracy, not its removal—just as he erected new "hero" statues on the site of old "idols" (see Chapter 4). When such a counterculture did appear in the form of workers' control, anarchism, syndicalism, and various democratic intraparty oppositionists, it was repudiated by the Bolshevik leadership. Lenin, in welcoming the structure of labor relations built up by capital, "sacralized" the productive process.[17]

Lenin believed that there was no other choice in a society like Russia's. In 1919, he said as much:[18]

> The old utopian socialists imagined that socialism could be built with other kinds of people, that they could raise up at once good and decent and well-trained people and that they could build socialism through them. We have always laughed at this and said that this is like playing with dolls—that it is like a diversion from socialism, a pastime of well-bred ladies and not politically serious.

Exegesis of a person's work rarely yields a true picture on any issue—especially in the case of a dynamic and active revolutionary whose career spanned over 30 years of political work and writing. And yet the quality of Lenin's comments on the pre-Marxian utopian socialists and indigenous Russians such as the Populists is remarkably consistent over the years. To Lenin utopianism consists of unreal and impossible programs and visions. The European utopian socialists of the 1830s and 1840s—whom both he and Marx admired for their "titanic" thoughts and the pathos of their critique of capitalism—fall prey to his attack for their static formulas and for their posture of "expectation." "Utopian" are all those who believe that justice will come without socialism, that socialism will come without a struggle, or that a "socialist" state can survive without coercion, harshness, cruelty, and the active recruitment of the leftover human materials of the old regime as specialists. This generally restrained critique occasionally flashes into anger at rosy pictures of the future as a substitute for work and struggle in the here and now.[19] Lenin shaped the official outlook of Bolshevism in the early years: an article on "The Future State" of 1919 praised the good points of More, Babeuf, Fourier, Owen, Cabet, Bebel, Hertzka, and Morris but warned that the ideal society was unattainable without hard work.[20]

Lenin's impatience with "utopian" currents was selective—allowing himself pet projects such as electrification, monumental propaganda, and Taylorism but producing disapproval of other dreamers. These included individuals such as Bogdanov for his Proletarian Culture movement, Mayakovsky for his Futurism, Kollontai for her "new morality," Lunacharsky for his Godbuilding, and Bukharin for his early Left Communism as well as currents such as specialist baiting, iconoclasm, egalitarianism, pedagogical fantasies, avant-garde art, militant atheism, and communal life. Part of this annoyance was rooted in Lenin's cultural and personal style—dress, speech habits, manners, taste in art, sexual life, and self-discipline. At a deeper level it was Lenin's relentless insistence on the centrality of political power, order, and systematic building by means of unleashed energy of the masses through established modes of organization. The state simply had to exist in some real form, teaching and tutoring the coming generations to take it over and eventually dispense with it. In this regard, Lenin was one of the first—along with Sun Yat-sen, who was revising his own "Three Principles of the People" at about the same time—who saw the tutelary state as the only possible mode of survival and transition to social justice in a backward yet revolutionary society.[21]

How then did utopianism function in the Revolution: How was it used by the regime? What was its relation to radical policies? to Marxist ideology? The relationship between Marxism, the regime, and utopianism was conditioned by two circumstances: first, the endemic backwardness of the country and the crises created by war and revolution encouraged sweeping solutions, hopeful vistas, compensatory fantasies, variety in experiment and second, the Russian radical tradition with its vast sweep, plus the newness of the regime, its lack of experience and its success in taking power as the first regime of its kind in the world opened up the doors of Marxism to further elaboration and experiment, and opened wider vistas beyond or outside Marxism for utopian speculation and for actual experimentation. The utopian fantasies were mostly grounded in socialist visions and therefore, when seen as the prediction of a more or less distant future, accepted as harmless at worst or inspiring and useful at best. The experimentalism often intersected with a perceived practical need for innovation by the Bolsheviks:

machinism, militarization, egalitarianism, ritualism, communes, town planning, icono-clasm. When they went "too far," they were curbed and redrawn into acceptable chan-nels. But it was not always easy to define acceptable limits to attractive experiments and ideas, so the relationship remained fluid and complex through the 1920s.

The sheer existence of the dreams, plans, projects, and experiments enumerated above, flourishing in the years of revolution, Civil War, and N.E.P.—before and after the death of Lenin—sets this period off in a stunning way from the years of Stalinism. The utopians were like so many experimental teams in Lenin's gigantic laboratory of revolution, using materials and expending time and exuberant energy on projects that were marginal to the Party leader's own "research design" for building socialism by means of tutelary state power and organization—from the top down. Lenin frowned on some of the experiments, barked at the experimenters, and sometimes even deprived them of their equipment and funds. But, unlike his successor Stalin, he did not destroy this vast laboratory, did not close it all down, did not arrest and exterminate its principle investigators.

## War Communism as Utopia

The term *voennyi kommunizm,* usually translated as War Communism has generated considerable historiographical heat. The battle usually rages over what the Soviet leaders had in mind in launching it. Some argue that it was a conscious and deliberate attempt to jump directly into communism; others, that it was a series of *ad hoc* emergency measures, posthumously elevated to a "historical period" of the revolution. Most of the evidence, as well as common sense, points to the second as being closer to the truth. The writings of Lenin before the Revolution and his actions in the first eight months after it show no intention of leaping over Marxian stages into a state of communism. The relatively moderate nature of the Bolshevik economic order in these months fore-shadows much of what was done under N.E.P. after 1921 and thus indicates that War Communism was at least originally an emergency.

Once it got started—in the summer of 1918—War Communism took on an intellec-tual impetus of its own, feeding "utopian" impulses for the great leap and attracting a wide variety of economic glosses on Marx to justify it. The recent superb study by Silvana Malle transcends the somewhat meaningless either/or debate by shifting the weight of analysis from the texts of the main political leaders to the writings, speeches, policies, and actions of the secondary and tertiary administrators, economists, techni-cians, engineers, and planners (both Mensheviks and Bolsheviks)—and those who had recent close contact with the German wartime economy (nicknamed *Kriegskommunis-mus* at the time). What emerges is a welter of interaction and discourse revealing a heady brew of visionary speculation and hardheaded, desperate measures designed to make the economy work and the Soviet regime survive. One of the many incongruities of War Communism is that self-conscious borrowings from German experience resulted in lifting practical solutions and details from a work that was once considered visionary, Atlanticus's *Glimpse into the Future State,* and in deriving an enthusiastic vision from the eminently practical businessman-statesman, Walther Rathenau. Intrigued by the spectacle of the state—their state—enveloping all of the economy and society, some Soviet leaders looked upon War Communism as a permanent system.[22]

What was it? At various moments in its three year life, the "system" of War Communism entailed the nearly complete nationalization of the economy, the reorganization of industries and other enterprises into state organs arranged according to production type, government control of supply and distribution of all products including food, a continuously changing array of devices to extract food from the countryside to feed the cities by elaborate forms of rationing (a problem that the regime inherited from the World War economy and the Provisional Government), militarization of labor and production, vast centralized bureaucracies bearing such exotic new names as *Glavbum* and *Tsentrotekstil* which attempted to regulate and control output according to the exigencies of war and shifting central plans. The result was the first sustained assault on capitalism on a nation-wide scale in history, an almost fully communist economy—right down to the abolition of money for a time and in some places the use of barter. But it was not the utopia of anyone's dreams. The byproduct of War Communism (and of war, inexperience, and backwardness) was social disaster on a mammoth scale: the emptying of cities, the luxuriant growth of a black market, bagging, speculation, gross inequality, systematic terror, and disease and hunger of such a scope as to create ghost towns and to flood the landscape with whole armies of bewildered refugees who crisscrossed the country on trains in search of food and security.

Yet it was precisely in the atmosphere engendered by battle, heroism, martyrdom, and national resurgence that ideas, plans, fantasies, and utopias arose. The almost total takeover of the economy by the state, the nationalization of most enterprises, the mass distribution of the land to the peasants, and looming conflict between town and country, the mobilization of labor, and the spectacle of a world turned upside down—what an American journalist called "the greatest economic experiment and social adventure in the history of the world"[23]—all gave impetus to ascending dreams of imminent transformation. As memoirists and contemporaries put it again and again in their contrastive metaphors, it was out of the turmoil of a dying civilization and the agonized death throes of an ancient culture that a new life was emerging. It was precisely the violence and the lethal menace of the Civil War—in which prisoners were almost always executed and often tortured—that gave such lustrous promise to the visions of a coming world. And it was the deep radicalism of the economic revolution, unprecedented in human history, that seemed to fling open the portals to unending possibilities for drastic change.[24]

The most elaborate picture of the future to come out of the War Communism period was *The ABC of Communism,* a lengthy gloss on the party program of 1919, written by Nikolai Bukharin and Evgeny Preobrazhensky, two relatively younger economic specialists and members of Left Communist circles in the early period of Revolution. The *ABC* sold a million copies in the few months after it appeared and millions more through the 1920s—to disappear from Soviet print from the late 1920s until this day. It was a popular condensation of classical Marxism, a Marxist precis of recent European social and economic history—with an emphasis on the crises of capitalism, imperialism, and world war—and a codification of Bolshevik experience in revolution and the organization of the Soviet state. The pages dealing with the communist future predicted that full communism would take root fairly soon, bringing with it all the solutions embedded in the classical canon of Marx. In Russia "within a few decades there will be quite a new world, with new people and new customs."[25]

In these pages two motifs stand out with particular clarity: order and mechanics. The discourse on order seems bathed in deep Russian traditions of phobia toward anarchy, chaos, disorder, and panic. The root evil of capitalism in this context—looming even greater than its unfairness—is the unpredictability of competition, the irresponsible flow of market forces, the powerful and destructive egoism of owners and individual firms who can contrive shortages and famine, create unemployment, subvert whole nations, and unleash extravagant wars. The communist future would be one of global order and stasis, of harmony and control, of organization—"one vast people's workshop" where everything "must be precisely calculated." To insure and regulate such an order, a machine is required: accounting offices and statistical bureaux that count, process, compute, and decide what is needed by whom and who is needed where. The imagery is similar to the quasi-cybernetic and proto-computer society on communist Mars outlined by Bogdanov in *Red Star*. "When the social order is like a well-oiled machine, all will work in accordance with the indications of these statistical bureaux." This was a main theme of Soviet utopian science fiction of the 1920s. By comparison, the language of fairness, equity, and justice, and the attacks on exploitation seem lifeless and formulaic in the pages of *The ABC of Communism*. Even if one takes into account the immediate atmosphere in which this document was written—one of appalling uncertainty and hardship—one cannot ignore the deeper layers of fear in the authors, and widely shared by Bolshevik leaders, of colossal and elemental upheaval and breakdown inherent in the forces of Russian history.[26]

During these stormy years, the institutions most concerned about shaping the society and culture of the coming world took form. The Proletcult *(proletkult)* movement, launched in 1917, set out to design and construct a new culture of, for, and by the working class on the bones of the "old" culture. The Futurists and other schools of avant-garde art, born shortly before the Revolution, aspired to shatter the old forms, make new ones, and as revolutionary missionaries and "culture-bearers," take them out to the people. Both the Zhenotdel and the Komsomol came into being in the midst of the war as vehicles for organized women and young people, respectively, to reform and refashion sexual behavior and morality. New kinds of schools and cultural institutions sprang up overnight to shape the values and feelings of the emerging Soviet people. In the cities, intellectuals dreamed of massive projects for the future—clean and bright super-civilizations that would come to replace the darkness and misery of their world. In the countryside, communes were formed in order to introduce the ideologies of the town into the life of the village.

City light and rural darkness came to be the Soviet metaphor for Marx's "the idiocy of rural life" and the "contradiction between town and country" and a major theme of early Soviet intellectual, cultural, and social history. To Soviet authorities the city was identified with civilization, culture, progress, and dynamism—and light was its symbol. Although electric power had come to Russia as early as the 1870s, it remained almost nonexistent in the countryside. Lenin, an enthusiast about technology in general, became almost fixated on the prospect of the rapid electrification of the Soviet Union. The revolutionary pathos and the Promethean arrogance of this dream were put on full display in 1920, when before an assembled audience in the Kremlin, Lenin demonstrated by means of a huge map of the country, studded with bulbs, how electrification would look. During the demonstration, all the electricity in the city of Moscow had to be cut off in order to provide sufficient power for this show.[27]

This did not deter Lenin; he gave full backing to G.O.E.L.R.O.—the State Commission for the Electrification of Russia—and to its leading figure, G. M. Krzhizhanovsky, one of the many technical persons attracted to the Bolshevik movement in the early years. Their hope was to use electricity to integrate the vast village world into the culture of the cities—especially the capitals; to lay the groundwork for industrial production over the entire expanse of the land; and to kindle the light of knowledge by means of literacy campaigns and electric lamps, hitherto virtually unknown. It was a titanic scheme, especially given the time. As Krzhizhanovsky himself put it in 1920:[28]

> How, in view of the enormity of the destruction and ruin we have lived through, can we possibly establish a plan for the widespread electrification of such an economically backward land as Russia has been and still is . . . Doesn't the scheme of electrification in a period of gigantic economic dislocation seem a fantasy, a utopia, a paper project?

It did not to Krzhizhanovsky and Lenin. Lenin called electrification the Party's second program and coined the constantly quoted phrase "communism equals Soviet power plus the electrification of the entire country." In his enthusiasm, he suggested that an electric grid extending to neighboring countries could help replace national prejudice and hatred with fraternal internationalism.[29] The whole scheme became a kind of hobby for Lenin, perhaps a technological compensation for the rapid dissipation of his earlier dreams in the face of hard reality.

Wells, a man who understood the power of technological fantasy, wrote that "Lenin, who like a good orthodox Marxist, denounces all 'utopians,' has succumbed at last to utopia, the utopia of the electricians." Lenin saw electric power stations (and railroads) as binding devices in building a nation; as early as May 1918, he outlined to Raymond Robins vague schemes of the joint development of certain parts of Eastern Siberia in cooperation with the United States—an idea reminiscent of Gastev's Siberian utopia (see Chapter 7). Lenin wanted copies of the electrification plan (a huge document) in every local library and power station and wanted it read. For him, electricity was the bearer of hygiene, sanitation, and a bright, healthy environment in the workplace and a substitute for degrading domestic chores. "Electrification will regenerate Russia," he said in a 1920 interview. "Electrification on the soil of the Soviet system will produce a decisive victory of the principles of communism in our country, the principles of a cultural life without exploiters, capitalists, landowners, and merchants." Lenin seemed to endow electric current with magic power—as did many Russian peasants. His oft-quoted definition of communism really summarized much of his thinking: he saw it as a fusion of social justice, embodied in the policies of the Soviet government headed by the Communist Party, with technical prowess, wealth, progress, and sheer survival. Electricity stood for heat and shelter in a land of arctic climates, light and knowledge in a land of darkness and bigotry, energy and economic growth in a land of poverty and sloth.[30]

Lenin's vision was widely shared. Krzhizhanovsky, invoking Marx and Engels, spoke of how electricity would eliminate the contradictions between town and country and even linked it to the old visions of More, Campanella, Fourier and other utopians of a crystal clean and happy civilization, humming with productivity and beaming with brightness. Like their counterparts in the United States at the same time, agricultural planners rhapsodized about electric power: "the electrification of agriculture will bring not only bodily but also spiritual nourishment. The electric light will serve as a mighty source of political and scientific education for the countryside"—an idea taken up by the godless crusaders in the 1920s. In the Russian Revolution—as in ancient religions—light was a metaphor for everything good, just as darkness was for poverty, evil, and prejudice. A 1921 poster "Electrification and Counter-revolution" depicted a worker holding a light bulb—the updated torch of enlightenment and liberty—to search out the cringing figures of a bourgeois, a minister, a political foe, a White general, and a priest. "We must snatch aways God's thunderbolts," wrote Mayakovsky in *Mystery Bouffe*. "Take 'em/ We can use all those volts/ for electrification." The proletarian poet M. P. Gerasimov portrayed Soviet Russia as a vast power station humming with collectivist energy; the Kremlin, its huge dynamo bristling with antennae, performing magnetic songs—all for the "electrification of the soul" and the triumph over darkness.[31]

There was something warmblooded about the utopia of electrification. When coupled with the invocation of the utopian socialist utopias of the past, it seemed to promise a lightened life eased and enriched by exposure to art and learning. And this is precisely what the promise meant. But another kind of dream reemerged during the Civil War: administrative utopia. Its written expression was a manifesto and future design entitled *Against Civilization* (1918) written by two figures in the world of avant-garde art and letters, Evgeny Poletaev and Nikolai Punin. It was an appeal for the Prussianization of Russian society. Though in form it seemed an isolated literary episode, in fact it resonated with two ideas that were much in the air during World War I and the Russian Civil War: the hopelessly flaccid and degenerate character of Western civilization, and the beauty and utility of harshness.

*Against Civilization* declaimed at length about the egoism, sickly emotionalism, and romanticism of the English and the French with their cult of love, their aversion to pain, and their fear of nature. Poletaev and Punin, both Bolshevik supporters, lashed out at the French utopian socialists whom they saw as sentimental and Christianoid. Against these they opposed Germanic *Kultur:* discipline, bravery, military prowess, solidarity, battlefield camaraderie, and machine-like organization. In nature they saw a cruel and powerful friend, not a mistress or a foe. The "society of *Kultur* is a good machine in the full sense of the word," they wrote. And they wished to replace "the psychosis of individual freedom" by a system of "voluntary slavery organized into creativity in the interest of the whole." Their hope was to see a fusion of German *Kultur* with what they saw to be the virtues of Bolshevism: machine-mindedness, proletarian solidarity, class violence, hierarchy, and revolutionary discipline and obedience. *Against Civilization* was a revival—updated in the light of Darwin, Nietzsche, and Spengler—of that tradition of Russian administrative utopia which found so much to admire in the Prussian model of a military society.[32]

Trotsky's militarization of labor experiment in 1920, though often linked to this tradition by his opponents (who shouted "Arakcheevshchina" at him), was different from it in a number of ways and distinctly divergent from the racist and eugenic fantasies of Poletaev and Punin. But its central elements—the total organization and disciplining of society along military lines and the intermixing of civil and military economies—was a familiar form of applied utopianism and experimentation in human organization, however much Trotsky denied this. In his writings of the early 1920s, Trotsky, in the spirit of the times, sketched humane visions of the future life; but in doing so he was always careful to deny any utopian element in himself (no miracles, no overnight results) and to deplore in it in others (such as Proletarian Military Doctrine and Proletcult). No "bureaucratic fanciful experiments" he warned; the state cannot remake life without people combining "by their own choice and will into a commonwealth." But in 1919 and 1920, Trotsky, in the words of his most admiring biographer, went into "grotesque flights of military-bureaucratic fancy over the field of economic and social policies."[33]

Facing a ring of White armies and accompanying forces of Allied interventionists, the Bolsheviks resorted to mass mobilization of the civilian population to supplement the mass recruitments of soldiers. Every able-bodied person was pressed into service—the housewife, the prisoner of war, the convict laborer, the priest, the member of the former ruling and possessing classes—to sew clothes, dig trenches, and build fortifications. About six million people were mobilized into the timber industry in the first half of 1920! The main agent of all this dragooning and movement of people was Trotsky. In it he was fully supported by Lenin, whose reverence for discipline deepened during this war.[34]

But in his speeches and actions of late 1919 and early 1920, Trotsky went much further than the usual forging of a nation in arms. To fight chaos, he said, the government needed "to view the population of the entire country as a reservoir of labor power," to be harnessed, trained, allocated, or "tied down" when necessary. He spoke of treating economic and social tasks as "problems of military combat." The whole economy was to be redrawn to fit military tables of organization, and the population incorporated into regiments, brigades, and divisions under the command of army officers who were trained in industrial centers. A culture of precision and obedience had to be imposed as well as a fusion of military and industrial psychology. Production orders were to be couched as battle orders; the command "procure firewood" would take on the form of "take that village," and crude reconnaissance would give way to systematic collection of data. Above all, Trotsky stressed, the agrarian sector must be fully subordinated to the industrial centers. The city, the machine, and the army were thus linked together once again to bring order out of chaos. *Every* worker was now to become a soldier.[35]

How did it work? Revolutionary Labor Armies were formed in all the major fronts and in the rear, composed largely of peasants and used for raw manual labor, digging, felling trees or carting lumber supplies. In some places, workers were tied down to their factories like the industrial serfs of tsarist times. Twenty mobilizations were launched in 1920 alone, covering thirty-six provinces. They fell chiefly upon the peasantry who were dragooned to remote districts to cut wood under military guard. Peasant resentment was massive and broke into open rebellion. Trotsky admitted the terrible shortcomings of the system and yet fought to sustain it. It was abolished when the war wound down and N.E.P. was established.[36]

What about the charge of building a utopia worthy of Arakcheev lodged against Trotsky by Menshevik and other critics? Was Trotsky's "flight of military bureaucratic fancy" a utopia? Even at his most lyrical, Trotsky did not revive or emulate the mentality of everyday militarization that characterized officers and landowners of the eighteenth century—the stress on esthetically pleasing troop formations and the movement of people in the geometric gyration known as the parade. No drum and trumpet, no spit and polish, no insane scheduling of daily life. But the charge of Arakcheevism was largely correct. Rafail Abramovich, one of those who made it, was certainly right in comparing Trotsky's methods to those "which the Egyptian Pharoes used in building the pyramids:"[37] forced labor for a "higher" cause, a machine fashioned out of human bodies, and a hierarchy of decision makers, trained overseers, and unfree toilers. This was a major feature of Arakcheev's world at Gruzino and in the Military Colonies, as were the crossing over of civil and military economic activity and the attempt to induce a military culture into the population. Trotsky resembled Arakcheev not because he studied the methods of the tsarist general but because Trotsky perceived the problem in the way Arakcheev did, both of them having a very low opinion of the spontaneous self-organizing capacity of the Russian people as a whole, and because, as he said emphatically and repeatedly at the time, labor obligation, coercion, and "militarization of labor" were the natural and only forms of economic organization on the road to building socialism.[38] This feature of Trotsky led Lenin to render his famous testamentary comment about his excessive love "for the administrative side of things."

Abandoned in 1921, Trotsky's scheme of a militarized society did not die. It surfaced again under his successor as War Commissar, Mikhail Frunze in his now much discussed design for the "militarization of society" *(voennizatsiya obshchestva)* outlined in a 1925 article entitled "Front and Rear in the War of the Future." Struck by the prospect of a war of immense destructive power, by the enormous cost of conducting it, by the staggering backwardness of Russia's infrastructure, and by the growing fear of death from the skies by means of long distance bombing, Frunze concluded that the old difference between front and rear in time of war would disappear and that the entire nation would be living on a military front. The only way to prepare for this, he argued, was the complete militarization of society: discipline, ranks, reorganization of the government, a wartime footing for the economy, and a permanent military posture for the entire population—thus turning the Soviet Union into an armed camp in the most literal sense of the term. Frunze's plan was never realized in peacetime, though there are a number of contemporary Western analysts of Soviet affairs who believed that Soviet society moved that way in the Breznev era.[39]

As a plan of the future, Trotsky's lavish human experiment in the militarization of labor during the Civil War did not have much impact on the utopian imagination. On the other hand, his language concerning the conversion of peasants and workers into robotic servants of the state remained very much alive in the visions and programs of the machine worshippers and Timeists of the 1920s (see Chapter 7) and of some of the industrial planners and political leaders of Stalin's revolution from above.

## Beyond the Green Wall

The central element in the utopian longings of Soviet leaders, cultural figures, and most pro-Bolshevik intellectuals was the exaltation of the urban order over the rural and the triumph of the machine over nature. A major image in avant-garde productions, proletarian poetry, and revolutionary science fiction was a world-city or the world-as-a-city, with urban minds beaming out reason and wisdom into the primeval darkness and city-built machines shaping the tangle of nature into symmetrical forms. "After electricity," Mayakovsky put it bluntly, "I lost interest in nature. Too backward." He longed for great cities, proudly soaring skyscrapers, forests of chimneys and networks of highways covering the earth. The exorbitant taste of Bolshevik leaders for technology, electricity, giant production units, machines, and the human machinery of a disciplined work force and an army, their "large scale theories," and their dominant view of the city as the locus of power and reason as against the lethargic and somnulent countryside—all of this set the stage for what has sometimes been called a war between country and city, reflecting the longstanding dichotomies of consciousness and spontaneity, state and people, leviathan and anarchy, and, in Boris Pilnyak's phrase, "machines and wolves."[40]

"Beyond the green wall," Zamyatin's metaphor for the natural wilderness of forest and countryside untouched by the urban and metallic hand of the United State, the old tensions between peasant and townsman were awakened by the wars and revolutions. Measures taken by the tsarist regime, the Provisional Government, and the Bolsheviks all provoked peasant hostility and suspicion, nourishing an attitude of "what we have we hold." The great agrarian uprising that accompanied the revolutions of 1917 was not simply the seizure of landlords' land; it was also a massive withdrawal of the peasantry from the state, the expulsion of alien elements (urban intruders, intellectuals, outside laborers, and prisoners of war) from active village life, a chorus of rumor, and frequently violence and vandalism. Peasant anti-urbanism was augmented by the fact that pro-Bolshevik elements in the villages tended to migrate to the city or to serve in the army. In the Civil War, the peasants hated and feared the Whites who, they believed, wanted to take back the land, but they also hated and feared the "white hands," city folk who had nothing to offer for the grain they took.[41]

Nestor Makhno, the Ukrainian anarchist leader of peasant background, summed up the anti-urban resentment when he spoke of "the political poison of the cities." The actions of the peasants in the revolution seemed to support this. So did their words, as uttered to Gorky in his travels around Russia during the Civil War. On city life, industrial technology, electricity, and intellectuals, his interlocutors were unambiguous. The city was "a complex organization of cunning people who live off the bread and toil of the countryside, make useless things for the peasants, and who in all ways adroitly try to cheat and deceive them." Great factory complexes were unnecessary and harmful, said a Ryazan peasant. "From them you get only trouble and vice." Better to live on the soil with small mills, scattered so as not to let workers congregate, with each province for itself, full bellies and tranquility. Electricity, they thought, was dangerous, like most technology, since it might easily burn down a village. The villagers to whom Gorky talked harbored no gratitude for intellectuals and their revolutionary suffering and martyrdom—after all, the peasants had not asked the intelligentsia to make a revolution. And in any case, the peasant could not fathom why a person would work so hard and die simply for ideals.[42]

Flight from the city during the hard years of revolution, though directly due to harsh conditions in the towns, was also sometimes an expression of revilement of the big towns where stalked "hunger, syphilis, and death," in the words of a character in Pilnyak. Between 1918 and 1921, Petrograd's population fell from 1,217,000 to 722,000. The insecurity and instability of city life (particularly where towns such as Kiev and Ekaterinoslav changed hands again and again—each occupation attended by executions and depredations) and the lack of food drove thousands to seek out a rural abode as a place to hide and to eat—a haven of survival. Like rebels, deserters, and Sectarians of past centuries, all kinds of people now bade farewell to the two capitals and to their new "tsars," Lenin and Trotsky, to central authority, and to utopian intellectuals in the cities who dreamed of urbanizing, electrifying, militarizing, and mechanizing the ancient land of All the Russias. And since central authority, and often local authority, had ceased to function in vast areas, this was not so difficult to achieve.[43]

A virtual orgy of separatism broke out, giving birth not only to the recessionist states of Finland, Poland, and the Baltic, but to temporary withdrawals in the Ukraine, Belorussia, Siberia, the Caucasus, and the Far East—much of it under White control—and to tiny "republics," or "communes." Sometimes these words were used as pure rhetoric, as with the Don Soviet Republic and the Rostov Commune, which lasted seven days, distributed food equally to the population, put the local bourgeoisie into forced labor gangs, and built public works for the unemployed. The name was inspired by the Paris Commune of 1871. Sometimes they were high sounding names, such as the Karelian Workers' Commune in the immense and thinly populated forests east of Finland or the Union of the Communes of the Northern Region—the Petrograd Commune or *Petrokommuna* being one of these—with its own governing body separate from Moscow. And sometimes it was simply a celebration of local patriotism, as with the Kazan Workers' and Peasants' Republic formed immediately after the October Revolution and the Tsaritsyn Republic, originally a pejorative to denote exceptional radicalism and disobedience to the Provisional Government. Kronstadt was at first one of these "republics within the republic" but then broke away into its own separate identity as a revolutionary commune. The Baku Commune of 1917–18, a tiny workers' democratic socialist state, produced by its very existence "a socialist form of thinking and feeling" among the workers.[44]

The centrifugal forces and the feelings of liberation engendered by the Revolution produced many variants on this kind of behavior. In industry, annoyed Bolshevik officials called it "factory chauvinism;" in the army it was called *atamanshchina* and *partizanshchina,* the widespread tendency for whole units to operate like highly individual "enterprises" run by a charismatic commander who would disobey the center, horde weapons and food, and refuse to coordinate his fighting with other units. They were miniature fighting republics, fighting their own wars and living off the land.[45] The agricultural commune was partially another response both to the unhinging of central power and to the menacing noises from the cities. They were organized and assisted by the regime and adorned with ideology (see Chapter 10). But some communes seem to have been born out of the hideous conditions in the towns. Withdrawal and the quest for security accounted for the motivations of many founders of communes, though some of them also sought a Kingdom of the White Waters and the Dream of Vera Pavlovna as well. Some hostile Bolsheviks, such as Yury Larin, scorned the commune as a "peaceful shelter;" others called it a primitive throwback and a "flight from politics."[46]

Those in outright opposition to the Bolsheviks, but not necessarily affiliated with the Whites, launched various "black" (anarchist) and "green" (peasant) revolutionary withdrawals. Raising the flag of an independent republic during times of insurrection was not new in Russia. The free cossack republic, sometimes called a "Don," was part of the rebel tradition in Russian history. In 1905, Krasnoyarsk was independent for a month; the Chita Republic controlled most of Transbaikalia and ran everything until suppressed; the first Far Eastern Republic, headed by a Polish engineer, lasted for fifty-three days; and almost adjacent to Moscow, the Markovo Republic held the authorities at bay for a year.[47]

This phenomenon reached far greater dimensions in the Civil War period: Samara was ruled by Socialist Revolutionaries, Anarchists, and Maximalists in defiance of Soviet power in 1917–18; the so-called Khrustalëv Republic appeared in South Russia in 1918–19, headed by Trotsky's former rival in the St. Petersburg Soviet of 1905; Cossack republics flourished on Russia's great steppes and river basins; and a Menshevik Republic appeared in the distant wastelands of Central Asia. The Siberian Soviet Republic of 1918 dissolved into a republic of republics. The mystic Ouspensky (Uspensky), wrote that in 1919, "to travel from Mineralnye Vody to Rostov and thence to Novorossisk, you pass through four states, each with different laws, different prices, different sorts of police."[48]

Organized anarchists were especially prominent in creating new communities on the ground. Some of them came back into the capitals during the Revolution in order to "transform the city into an egalitarian commune, patterned after an idealized image of the Paris Commune of 1871," expropriating houses, handing out food, requisitioning buildings and factories, and flying the black flag under the noses of the local Bolshevik authorities. A small group, known as the Immediate Socialists, requisitioned a house and made the following statement:

> Our aim is to reconstruct life completely according to purely socialist principles. Not having the opportunity to apply these principles on a large scale, we are putting them into practice on a small scale, starting the reorganization of society not from above but from below, by creating communities of production.

Anarchist schemes for a new world included a universal language, cosmism or universal humanity, geanthropism (the emancipation of women), pedism (the liberation of children), and Anarcho-Biocosmism, a plan to launch a social revolution "in interplanetary space but not upon Soviet territory."[49] These short-lived Anarchist schemes and experiments—some serious and practical, some eccentric and bizarre—quickly dissolved or were snuffed out by a hostile government.

Vigorous popular anti-Bolshevik movements (often called "green" in rural areas) erupted in the Civil War period. The Kronstadt Commune, called by Paul Avrich "a lost revolutionary utopia," was established at the very outset of the revolution in 1917 on the island maritime base in the Gulf of Finland. Virtually independent from 1917 to 1921 and strongly pro-Bolshevik in the early years, Kronstadt had a population of about 50,000—half of it military personnel (largely sailors of Ukrainian peasant background). Egalitarianism, compensatory justice, equity, and grass-roots democracy took on active meaning in this little republic in the Baltic. Communes of 40–60 people were formed where intellectuals, workers, and sailors of all ages toiled side by side in urban garden plots and were rewarded according to labor or special need. Housing and building space was distributed according to family size. Sailors (who got "special" rations on the mainland) shared their portions equally with all the rest—including Bolshevik prisoners taken during the fighting of 1921!

Kronstadt was one of the most vivid utopian socialist experiments to surface in the Revolution. One striking element of its life was the extreme anti-authoritarianism of the sailors, whose naval experience had taught them to hate shipboard discipline. On their island, they resembled pirates or mutinous crews in control of their own vessel, and like pirates of a bygone day, they made equal sharing and solidarity an operative social ideology. Another element was the peasant-like character of Kronstadt: the democratic arena of Anchor Square where crucial decisions were noisily hammered out in the open air was akin to the traditions of the village *mir,* the Cossack assembly *(krug),* and the ancient town *veche.* In 1921, having supported the Bolsheviks for three years, Kronstadt rose up and declared its independence from the Soviet State. It assailed the Bolsheviks for "Commissarocracy," Taylorism, and dictatorship and called itself the center of a "Third Revolution" for workers' control, democracy, and the independence of partisan units. When this occurred, the Bolsheviks called them "mutineers" and counter-revolutionaries and crushed their commune in a bloody act of repression.[50]

The most spectacular, indeed cinematic, episode of the Russian Revolution was "the Republic on Wheels," the Insurgent Army of the Ukrainian anarchist peasant leader, Nestor Makhno. His arena was the vast prairie of the southern Ukraine, the steppe-land where towns were few and the population mostly peasant. It was the scene of intense fighting between Reds, Whites, Germans, Austrians, troops of the Rada—the Ukrainian nationalist phantom government—and various shades of "green" atamans or local chieftains. Makhno was one of these, though his flag was black, due to his conversion to Anarchism while in prison as a youth. His program was simple regionalism, local self-government, and communal work and life for those of his own home region. No coercion, no state, no outside interference, and death to the agents of these things, Red, White, or Green. Like Emiliano Zapata in Morelos Province in Mexico, Makhno emerged directly from the people and was perhaps the closest thing the Russian Revolution produced to a peasant leader with a utopian vision that seemed to fit the culture of his people.[51]

Armed with anarchist texts and sometimes accompanied by a political writer, Makhno and his Insurgents roamed the huge space between Ekaterinoslav, Alexandrovsk, and his home base at Gulyai-Pole. The army itself was a protean body that could change shape instantly, peasants dissolving into fieldhands and easily reassembled in battle. The symbol of Makhno's great mobility was the *tachanka,* a four-wheeled Ukrainian peasant cart, mounted with a machine gun. The presence of purely peasant commanders and the certainty of local popular support made Makhno's roving bands resemble guerillas and partisans. A heavy drinker and a shrewd fighter, Makhno came to resemble the legendary rebels of the past as he rode in his cart, black flag unfurled at the head of a horse army.

When he occupied Ekaterinoslav, Makhno opened all the prisons, proclaimed self-organization, turned the mills over to the citizens, established "fair" prices, and allowed the use of any kind of currency—of which there was an abundant variety in a town that was taken a dozen times in the course of the revolutionary years. Makhno expressed his venomous hatred of the urban scene by acts of iconoclasm and vandalism (see Chapter 3). In his base at Gulyai-Pole, a country town of 30,000, Makhno placed all factories in the hands of the workers and established communes on the land around his capital, consisting of 100–300 persons and based on Kropotkin's doctrines of anarcho-communism: full equality, work for all, sharing of goods, communal or individual dining according to choice. Though a few imported flourishes were added—such as naming the first of them the Rosa Luxemburg Commune—these communes were overwhelmingly peasant, incorporating only a minority of the region's peasantry but with the moral support, according to Makhno's claim, of the surrounding rural population. Makhno himself spent two days a week toiling in the fields and workshops.[52] Like the Kronstadt experiment, Makhno's communes and his army dissolved at the end of the Civil War as the Red Army moved in. Makhno himself went into exile and died in Paris in poverty in 1934.

The last great peasant revolt against the Bolsheviks took place in Tambov Province. It was "green"—that is, it opposed Reds and Whites, central power, and "city slickers." Its "official" program was a rough variant of the Socialist Revolutionaries' ideology—an end to Bolshevik rule, the summoning of a Constituent Assembly, "equality" for all except members of the Romanov dynasty, land to the tillers, and workers' control in the towns. But a vague traditional mentality clearly predominated over a grafted-on ideology: partisan warfare, home armies and local commanders, a suspicion of all politics and programs, a strong religious element (field churches accompanied the rebellious troops), and a generalized longing for nothing more than peace and quiet, enough food for the stomach, and—summing all this up—*volya,* their major slogan. No communes, no planned anarchism, no schemes or dogmas, and no particular desire to link up with workers. The Bolsheviks called the Tambov rebels bandits (a term often used in history for troublesome rural insurgents). The Tambov rising was crushed in bloody repression and its leaders executed.[53]

The same fate awaited the most curious and the tiniest of all insurgent peasant manifestations of the Civil War: the Tsardom of Ur, known long afterwards as "the empire of the swamps." In a remote village of Ur, in the dense forests of the North between Viatka, Kostroma, and Nizhny Novgorod, a small unit of Bolshevik soldiers arrived to bring a new dream to the pious Old Believers there. Setting up his "main speaker"—a machine gun—and a red flag, an urban Bolshevik outlined a rosy future for the simple forest folk: in the rudest of tones he insulted religion, launched a search for "Hydras" and "Contras," and described a new world without money where all could have what they needed. Lenin would be the tsar of all the world—a huge commune where everyone would speak the same language. The villagers, utterly unmoved by this dream, rose up and chose their own "tsar", Peter Alexeevich, whom they dubbed Tsar Peter I, invoking the great liberation of 1613 as they crowned him. According to the narrator of this episode, after the enthronement of the autocrat of Ur, "then everything was as of yore and even better" because there was a real tsar to preside over ritual and dispense justice in the peasant manner. In due time, when the ice froze over, the Bolsheviks arrived again in force and crushed the Tsardom of Ur, sending the ringleaders to the Solovetsky Prison.

On one side of the Ur campaign, forest people on skis and armed with bear guns and flintlocks, with scouts who knew the terrain of almost impassable swamplands and thick forests, saw the foe as "city folk" and as the "Satanic horde of Lenin" and wished to remain outside a new world coming into being. On the other side, well armed Bolsheviks stormed the village on sleds with red banners in order to desymbolize and desacralize a piece of territory that had no earthly political or military value. It was, in a way, a summary in miniature of the ancient dual between the two major visions—that of the state and that of the people.[54]

# PART II

Living the Revolution

# 3

---

# Revolutionary Iconoclasm

> I've got a feeling we're going to catch up with the Russians. That would be
> beautiful, Europe burning at both ends.
>   Conversation in Barcelona, 1917. From Victor Serge, *Birth of Our Power*

The making of a revolutionary culture and way of life required clearing away old forms
(iconoclasm) and fashioning new myths, rituals, and moral norms through revolutionary
festival and atheist "godbuilding;" a surge to establish social justice through equality;
and the compulsion to transform Russian work habits and revise Russian notions of
time, space, motion, and order with the goal of introducing the Revolution to the culture
of the machine.

Experiment in the Russian Revolution took on flesh in the decade or so after 1917
when various kinds of people, exhibiting varying levels of consciousness, began "living
the revolution" by renouncing the old and trying out the new. All utopias are in a way
texts of negation of the present order, a deep critique of society as a whole as well as
of its constituent parts. Revolutionary iconoclasm was the old impulse, now fed and
reinforced by the Revolution, to expunge the hated past and make way for the future by
means of destroying odious images, idols, icons, and structures and by a sweeping
negation of cultural and social values.[1] It was one of the devices used by revolutionaries
to prepare for the building of an ideal society. Proudhon's motto, "I destroy in order to
create," had enjoyed a great vogue in nineteenth century Russia, especially among the
followers of Bakunin who made it central to his vision of the first stage of any revolution. It has also had resonance in other societies marginal to Western Europe—such as
Spain, China, and Mexico—where tradition was deeply implanted and where symbols
and ritual life were still very much alive and possessed of political overtones. In the
Russian as in other revolutions, the descending fist wielding a hammer against a piece
of statuary and the angry manifestoes of poets and anarchists reflected the same underlying desire to smash, demean, profane, mock, neutralize, and ultimately destroy a
culture that was perceived as deeply offensive and immoral in order to construct a
wholly new one.

## Vandalism: War on Luxury

In the Great French Revolution of 1789, the literal and the metaphorical sides of iconoclasm had unfolded simultaneously: a tempest of burning and defiling of art, books,
icons, and regalia and an anti-art movement in the capital that pronounced "art" cor-

rosive of republican simplicity and virtue. Thus both the "ostentation, prejudice, and tyranny" of the Old Regime monuments and the perceived frivolity, opulence, and uselessness of its culture came under a heavy assault that was fueled by a volatile mixture of hatred, envy, resentment, incomprehension, ignorance, indignation, and moral outrage.[2]

In Russia, the physical "vandal" and the intellectual iconoclast dwelled for a long time in separate worlds. The big peasant rebellions of the seventeenth and eighteenth centries and the less volcanic disturbances of the nineteenth were always accompanied by acts of vandalism, graphic episodes in the periodic war of the peasant to achieve land, to free himself from alien authority, and to negate imported (and to him useless) artifacts of a foreign way of life—Prussian uniforms, window panes, ball gowns, harpsichords, phalansteries, French books. In the middle of the nineteenth century, at the dawn of what is called "nihilism," certain members of the Russian intelligentsia began to give structure to this dissonant popular chorus by denouncing all of art and high culture, created as it was by a privileged elite at the expense of the faceless millions who labored in servitude and who derived absolutely nothing from it. The nihilists, in consigning things like lyrical poetry to the trash heap, were not only echoing a new materialist sensibility of Western Europe, born of emerging technology and of the collapse of the romantic revolutionary dream—they were also, and to a greater degree, paralleling in an only slightly more sophisticated idiom, the mentality of the peasant—the only major difference being an ambivalence on the part of the intelligentsia that the peasants probably did not feel. The parallel but independent currents of thought and feeling flowed together in the revolution of 1905 and then, in a soaring crescendo of verbal and physical violence, in the Great Revolution of 1917–21.

Vandalism in the Russian countryside was never a single-minded or a mono-emotional act. It was practical, symbolic, playful, and spontaneous, often in combination. Practical vandalism could mean burning or gutting the manor house of the lord so that he would never return, destroying records of tenure or debt, wrecking railroad stations and telegraph lines to inhibit the incursion of pacification forces, or demolishing the tavern or school in order to evict an alien force from the village world. Symbolic vandalism could also mean ruination of the manor house, even if empty, as a standing insult, a monument to inequality and foreignness, a concrete reminder of balls, midnight suppers, overwork, and humiliation. Playful vandalism could mean knocking out windows, decapitating statuettes, or pulverizing musical instruments. The shattering of doors and windows is related to insurgent feelings about space and openness, especially among crowds. The smashing of windows and glass panes reflected the xenophobia in eighteenth century peasant revolts—a feeling that was far from dead in 1917. But one can hardly discount the pristine pleasure that can be gotten by some people from the sheer act of annihilation or arson. Peasants sometimes revelled as a manor house went up in flames.[3]

Vandalism can also be spontaneous, random, even accidental—a result of the proximity of an angry mob to a suitable object of wanton hate, as in the destruction of a Russian village near the scene of a strike in the 1890s but wholly unrelated to that strike or the razing of structures that are in the way of a frenzied mob. All of the above motivations and targets of destructive will or fury can and do intermix constantly, one giving way to another in a flash of emotion, and often one giving birth to another. This is hardly surprising since a "mob" is always made up of separate individuals each of whom possesses his or her own set of destructive instincts.[4]

Rural vandalism tends to be directed at social symbols—representing a way of life repugnantly and bewilderingly different from that of peasants. When it was conscious, it included acts of rejection, negation, and withdrawal—rejection of outsiders, negation of their values, and withdrawal into a "natural" peasant world. Vandalism was not utopia-building in the ordinary sense of planning and creating something new—or even deliberately resurrecting the old. But as an accompaniment to the withdrawal movements described in the previous chapter, peasant rampage was a statement, a living "document" of the longing for a world different from that which was dying and that which was being born. When urban iconoclasts completed their work of demolition they began at once erecting new monuments and images. When peasants purged their space of alien ornaments, they erected nothing to replace them.[5]

Well before 1917, the disorders on the land had a furious prelude in Poltava and Kursk Provinces in 1902 and reached a majestic peak in 1905–6. In Kursk, Chernigov, and Orël peasants destroyed the dwelling places of those landlords they hated, leaving those of poorer elements untouched. In one locale, they burned what they called "the raven's nest" so that the owner would no more return. Everywhere records were burned. In some places, the pacification forces of the government burned down the village huts of the ringleaders before the assembled peasants. Peasants also tried to burn down railroad stations, telegraphic lines, schools, teachers' homes, and taverns. In the houses they slashed pictures and chopped up furniture and anything regarded as a sign of comfort and luxury. They vandalized orangeries, orchards, and flower gardens with particular fury; among lower class audiences in St. Petersburg's People's House, the felling of the orchard in Chekhov's *Cherry Orchard* was said invariably to arouse enthusiastic reactions—a sure sign of the lingering resentment among transplanted rural folk of the ostentatious flourishes of their masters and neighbors.[6] The pattern was by no means universal; most peasants throughout Russia did nothing. Outside agitators from the city sometimes had to threaten to burn out the peasants themselves if they declined to take action against the estate. And sometimes, violence seemed unrelated to any revolutionary mood: in 1914, peasant recruits, marching cross country to their units, got out of control, plundered estates, and burned stations, shops, and homes.[7]

Cultural vandalism resurfaced in the great agrarian uprising of 1917 and 1918 and during the Civil War. In a study of the revolution in Saratov Province, Donald Raleigh found that essential equipment was seized and divided, while fancy furniture, books, art works, and parks and orchards were vandalized. John Keep's study of the rural revolution tells how, in Tambov Province, peasants cursed and played the accordion while igniting the mansion of the lord. In Ryazan Province, peasants merely emptied a manor house; but when a sailor arrived, he told them to chop it up and burn it down. Keep found that the great majority of manors were left to rot or turned into schools that were hardly used during the Civil War. Keep and Raleigh use almost identical language in interpreting the events they describe. The former speaks of an archaic joy in destroying "symbols of their former subjection;" the latter of the destruction of "the symbolic reminders of their poverty."[8]

In surveying the devastation of art wrought by the Revolution, a commission for artistic preservation, headed by the noted art historian Igor Grabar and working closely with the Bolshevik government, reported a wave of destruction and arson in the summer of 1918 in which masses of art treasures perished or were stolen. The Revolution and the Civil War, said the report, had brought "manor houses reduced to dust, slashed paintings, demolished statues, gutted palaces, and cathedrals destroyed by shells." Some of this of course was the offshoot of combat; but most of it was vandalism—the wilful destruction or defacement of ornamental objects. The beauty of these objects, lamented the commission, was not appreciated by the peasants who saw in "pictures, sculptures, antique furniture, and musical instruments not works of spiritual value but only characteristic features of landlord life—a life alien to them." The most heartrending example of this, from the perspective of those who revered the glories of Russian high culture, was the sacking of Mikhailovskoe, Alexander Pushkin's summer estate near Pskov.[9]

There was still another side to the destructive behavior of rural people in the Revolution: anti-urbanism. In late December 1918, in the midst of the Civil War, Makhno's peasant army entered the city of Ekaterinoslav. In addition to emptying the prisons, dousing them with kerosene, and keeping them in flames all through the night, they destroyed archives, records, and libraries. But the most spectacular act of destruction took place in the streets adjacent to the railroad station. The shops and bazaars were put to the flame and Makhno himself mounted a three-inch cannon in the middle of the street and fired point blank into the tallest and most beautiful buildings. This was an expression of city-hatred on the part of a peasant army investing an "immoral" city. Makhno hated big cities; Ekaterinoslav had 50,000 people, was a busy port on the Dniepr, and was in fact one of the original creations of Potëmkin's great urban panegyric to Catherine the Great. Makhno was in the tradition of the rebels of an earlier day who had often sacked as well as looted when they occupied towns.[10]

Peasant vandalism was not a monolithic phenomenon. One could claim that peasants were bound together less by class than by their collective sense of their "world." But within this world there erupted a whole range of ravaging acts—some symbolic and some not at all—against many kinds of alien presences. On May Day 1917 in the first flush of freedom, peasants of Tambov Province destroyed the family crypt of General Luzhenovsky, the man who had "pacified" them in 1906. They outraged and burned his corpse. But during the Civil War, peasants (many from the same province) burned down the headquarters of the Bolsheviks and committed acts of symbolic retribution on food collectors—by stuffing their slit-open bellies with grain. And in 1919, in the "Fortress of Communism" commune—nominally a beacon of Bolshevism in the countryside—a peasant covered his face at the first sight of a fearsome tractor; it was later burned by neighbors. Vandalism was an instrument of language in a relatively mute universe; its lexicon of gestures was used to say many things and denote many feelings. Among them, hatred of the artifacts of affluence and idleness played a prominent role. The peasants' war against these helped to reinforce the currents of wholesale iconoclasm in the towns; indeed, it was exalted by urban intellectuals as the truest and deepest expression of the popular Revolution.[11]

## Iconoclasm: War on Signs

In the cities, the vandalistic war on luxury was intermixed with a war on signs. Cities in imperial Russia were replete with images; they were museums of tsarist, Orthodox, and national culture. Their horizontal space, transected by geometrically aligned streets, was itself a symbol of abstract order; and their vertical space was composed of structures that graphically represented inequality, power, and for some, alienation. The juxtapositions and contrasts were dense, blurred only by the tempo of urban life. Symbols, signs, and names were everywhere. Urban iconoclasts hardly needed to take a step in order to begin their work. But the process was complicated: the conscious political symbol smashers had to operate amidst the crowds of more spontaneous "vandals" and against the wishes of the "preservers;" and the rhythm of iconoclasm modulated with the course of political events and social action. The objects of the iconoclastic assault were icons (pictorial and plastic images), indexes (names), symbols (indirect representations of abstract values), and buildings that were both symbols and "practical targets." [12]

During the February Revolution, publicly displayed portraits of the tsar and other offensive figures were defaced or taken down, as they had been during some of the riots in 1905. But "deromanovization" was by no means complete: in Ekaterinoslav, officials quietly removed the tsar's portraits two weeks after the fall of the monarchy and hid them in the attics of their buildings. In 1917, an angry soldier-member of a deputation said to Kerensky: "Very odd that you, an S.R. and a revolutionary minister, give receptions in a hall where the tsar looks down from every side. About time to take them down." The citizens of Kansk-Eniseisk, far out amid the frozen wastes of Eastern Siberia, agreed to a proposal of local exiled revolutionaries to replace the statue of Alexander II with a monument to freedom fighters. On March 18, a statue of Stolypin in Kiev was removed before a great throng of people; and in the capital, rioters demolished all the statues of monarchs inside the Circuit Court Building before setting it on fire. But the Provisional Government, though it discussed the issue, took no general action on the removal of the monuments to tsars, generals, and grand dukes in the two capitals or elsewhere, and the massive ensembles and equestrian monuments continued to tower in lordly manner over the streets, squares, and gardens of the major cities. [13]

The Bolshevik leaders also felt ambivalent about the destruction of monuments, but their ambivalence led to a policy and to action. Perhaps sensing that their revolution would unleash a greater storm of iconoclasm and pillage than had the February Revolution, after a few days in power they demanded the protection of all valuable works of art and prohibited vandalism and looting. A little more than five months later they replaced this negative injuction with Lenin's decree on monuments, to be discussed in the next chapter. Among other things, it required the removal or dismantling of repugnant vestiges of the tsarist past that had no intrinsic historical or esthetic value. This vague formulation opened the way for the "preservers" to intervene and save some important monumental works, and it opened a fierce debate between them and the "destroyers." It also caused friction between the impatient leaders, Lenin foremost among them, and those responsible for dismantling the massive ensembles. These had a minimum of engineering skill and technology at their disposal and the process of denuding the capitals of the Romanovs and their "feudal" retainers resembled much more a prosaic public works operation (complete with unemployed citizens doing the manual labor) than any kind of iconoclastic ritual.

The first major statue in Moscow to go was that of the conqueror General M. D. Skobelev, taken down in time for May Day, 1918. The first replica of a tsar to feel the force of Lenin's decree was that of Alexander II which was uncomfortably close to his offices in the Kremlin. Lenin ordered him removed and, with a trace of irony, replaced by Leo Tolstoy. (This never materialized.) The huge statue of Alexander III was methodically dismembered and hauled away, an act that was cinematically immortalized by Eisenstein in the film *October*. The process was repeated on two statues of Catherine the Great, and those of various Grand Dukes—most of them dating from the late nineteenth and early twentieth centuries. In Petrograd, a commission of art experts and officials appointed by the government decided to eliminate all Romanov statues except for the Bronze Horseman, the magnificent equestrian of Peter I in Senate Square. A debate erupted over this and a compromise was reached. The Horseman was preserved as were the great figures of Nicholas in St. Isaac's Square and Catherine II on present day Lomonosov Square. But even the offensive Alexander III atop a huge pedestal near the Moscow Station stayed on for years—though adorned with a sign saying "Scarecrow"—and was later remanded to the yard of the Russian Museum. Those not taken down at once were often covered during public celebrations—as that of Louis XV had been during a French revolutionary festival and indeed as Russian icons were covered during the act of intercourse.[14]

If icons were visual reminders of a "dark" past, names were both visual and audial reminders. As in previous revolutions, places, things, and people were renamed in order to avoid odious associations or to honor new heroes and commemorate dead ones. One could almost construct a thin outline of Soviet political history by inspecting the renaming of certain places—Tsarytsin-Stalingrad-Volgograd being only the most famous such case. Petrograd—still bearing in Slavonic form the name of its founder—was renamed in 1924 after the death of Lenin. Lenin towns appeared all over Russia and were interspersed with places such as Sverdlovsk, Zinovievsk, Trotsk, Stalingrad, Dnepropetrovsk, Luxemburg, Uritsky, and Pervomaisk (May Day). Catherine the Great had ordered the levelling of Pugachëv's birthplace on the Don, the removal of its villagers across the river, and the renaming of the settlement Potëmkinskaya—in addition to renaming a river and a Cossack community associated with the revolt; now the dozen towns honoring her fell victim to the same impulse. Bolsheviks were not alone in this habit: during the Civil War, Gulyai-Pole was known locally as Makhnograd.[15]

Inside towns, a similar practice prevailed. In Petrograd-Leningrad, for example, the Nevsky Prospect became for a while the Prospect of the 25th of October, a cumbersome name that never caught on (though during the 1920s it was sardonically called "NEPsky Prospect" in droll reference to the commercial elements associated with the New Economic Policy). Names like Bakunin and Marat Streets appeared; and names like "Senate" and "Resurrection" gave way to "Decembrist" and "Insurrection." Millionaya Street, adjacent to the Winter Palace and the locus of royalty, now took on the name of the terrorist who had tried in 1880 to blow up the palace and the royal family. Two short streets north of the Nevsky, near the site of Alexander II's assassination, were rechristened Zhelyabov and Perovskaya in commemoration of their common deed and their mutual love. In Kiev, Vorovsky Street replaced the ancient Kreshchatik and to some, even devoted Communists, "it just [didn't] sound right." Renaming became so common that citizens could hardly learn the new names, and the practice was the frequent butt of jokes in satirical literature. In 1921, a group of poets let by Esenin and Mariengof went around the central streets of Moscow, pulling down nameplates and putting up their own names. Yet Moscow and the Kremlin were never renamed; the Winter Palace was too closely associated with royal power to allow it to be endowed with the name of a virtuous revolutionary; and Smolny was too redolent of the euphoric October days to change it. The Nevsky and the Kreshchatik eventually retrieved their original names.[16]

Tsarist emblems—imperial regalia, arms, and flags—though more abstract than portraits or statues, were nonetheless recognized for their meaning and were more easily removed and exchanged in the symbolic war of 1917. When the February Revolution reached the front, soldiers displayed great anger at the presence of imperial emblems and began wearing red ribbons on their sleeves, weapons, and vehicles. Officers were sometimes arrested for retaining royal signs, for breaches of the new symbolic etiquette, and for calling the red banners "rags" and "babushka's underwear." In the capital a veritable hunt was mounted for imperial emblems: crowns and eagles were torn from gates and fences and even blown out with explosives. Signs were removed from store-fronts and tossed onto the ice of the Neva River. Eagles at the Alexander Theater were defaced; at the Mariinsky Theater all Romanov coats of arms were removed—and as an added touch ushers wore dirty jackets and the imperial box was filled with recent polit-ical prisoners. Piles of imperial arms and regalia from the Court Provenor's shops were made into giant bonfires. In Moscow, fire trucks with ladders and crews went round with iron hooks to pry off the offensive eagles. The Bolsheviks merely continued more systematically this assault on the Romanov symbols. Yet as late as August 1918, Soviet authorities had to order the removal of imperial arms, portraits, and crowns from official buildings.[17]

Buildings were a special problem in the iconoclastic war. A very large number of them in imperial Russia were palaces or official edifices. They therefore bore names and contained icons and symbols considered odious by the revolutionaries. They were also the homes, workplaces, and stations of the enemy. On the other hand, they were much harder to destroy than coats of arms or portraits; they were also of enormous practical value in the struggle for space that accompanied the upheaval, and—to some—they had esthetic worth as well. Practically the only buildings that felt the fury of symbolic destruction in the February Revolution were the jails, and by no means all of them. Schlüsselburg Fortress was considered by some the Russian Bastille. The Populist Morozov, who had languished there for over twenty years, wanted it preserved as a reminder. But the occupying gangs of 1917 destroyed it. After the burning of the hated Litovsky Fortress in St. Petersburg, a postcard was published depicting the conflagration as a revolutionary festive act (see Figs. 9, 10). The invading mobs were usually assisted by the inmates who were then set free. But The Crosses, also in the capital, was left unharmed although its books and records were burned. Jails were burned in Chita, Ekaterinoslav, and Tsaritsyn. The Socialist Revolutionary terrorist, Maria Spiridonova, who had ordered the burning of the Chita prison, returned to Petrograd in a triumphal procession. After the October Revolution, she requested the blowing up of the Peter Paul Fortress. Her hatred of what a Decembrist had called "a hideous monument of absolutism" was immense: it was the central symbol of martydom and oppression. But her request was denied and that edifice stands today as the architectual centerpiece of the majestic former capital.[18]

Most of the destruction and burning of buildings in the February Revolution was of a functional nature: to smoke out police and displace rooftop snipers. But practical incursions sometimes flowed into vandalism. Even during the war, in "food pogroms," mobs broke into shops to take bread but then smashed glass and furniture as well. Trespassing into forbidden space was itself an energizing act of defiance; masses who entered police stations and arsenals to get guns could then use them to smash things. Unauthorized seizures and lawless forced entries generated their own kind of anger which then produced unplanned acts. Plain looting and burglary erupted all during 1917, and the Provisional Government seemed helpless to prevent it. One historian suggests that the citizens of Petrograd were more concerned with security, law and order, and property than they were with the change of regime in October. The buildings taken by political groups were used rather than destroyed. The Tauride, Mariinsky, and Winter Palaces all housed the Provisional Government; the Bolsheviks seized the mansion of the tsar's former mistress, Ksheshinskaya; the Anarchists, the Durnovo dacha. When the Bolsheviks came into power, they took vigorous measures to end random destruction and to curb looting—and with considerable success.[19]

In political art and in the popular imagination, the myth of the flame, the bomb, and the dance is very powerful in modern times. It is based on an image of major revolutions acted out like carnivals of mass destruction. Present-day cover art on books about revolution is one illustration of this. 1789, the Paris Commune, the Mexican Revolution, Barcelona in 1936 have all been pictured as scenes of flames and flame-like crowds enveloping old structures and civilizations. An ancient symbol, the flame evokes elemental force, power and menace, cleansing and searing fire, the punishment of evil, Promethean man, and many other things. Fire and fire imagery have always been important in Russian history. The "Red Cock," a popular name for arson in the countryside, appealed to the imagination of city dwellers. Bakunin evoked it all the time as a mechanism of pan-destructionism. Mystical sects talked of burning down all of Russia. The reality of iconoclasm and vandalism was more limited, more sober, less cinematic. But the myth here is as important as the reality. Minor acts of demolition were transformed into mass surges of monumental annihilation by the mythologists of the Russian Revolution. Physical iconoclasm was more than paying obeisance to the obvious: a change of signs. The very act, and the impulse which drove hating hands to smash and tear, were glorified and associated with other gestures of annihilation that accompanied the Revolution.[20]

## Nihilism: War on Culture

Expunging the symbolic evidence of the old order did not satisfy the revolutionary nihilists who wanted to clear the ground for a new cultural order. Naming streets and hauling down statues was only the beginning: the entire corpus of pre-revolutionary culture had to be emphatically and enthusiastically repudiated. The roots of cultural nihilism go deep into the traditions of the nineteenth century intelligentsia—especially the "nihilism" of the 1860s, an outlook that Berdyaev once defined as a secular version of religious asceticism that held art, thought, and religion in utter revulsion. "What can be smashed should be," Dmitry Pisarev had written in the 1860s. "What stands up under the blows is acceptable, and what flies into a thousand pieces is trash." The earlier nihilists prefered science over faith, artifacts over art ("a pair of boots is worth all of Pushkin"), materialism over idealism, and realism over romanticism.[21]

The historical setting was a repressive regime, a continued separation of the intelligentsia from the peasantry, and a generational revolt against radicals of the 1840s. Unable to command the destruction of culture, the nihilists acted out their desires by innovative dress, simple or coarse manners, and social rebellion. Many of them turned to outright political radicalism of such intensity that there was little energy left for debating the future of culture. But now and then the issues heated up: a group of radical Russian students in Zurich once spent an entire night in a shouting match over the fruits of culture after the revolution: "we'll keep them" said some; "we'll destroy them," said the others.[22] The nihilism of the revolutionary movement of mid-nineteenth century Russia was not only destructive, generationally rebellious, ascetic, and scientistic—it was also utopian in its faith in material progress, its belief in the ease with which culture could be destroyed or refashioned, and its panacea of spreading scientific ideas to the masses of Russia. The cultural nihilists of the Revolution inherited much from this lingering tradition.

The milieu for nihilism in 1917 was very different from that of the 1860s and 1870s. Michael Bakunin, the anarchist prophet of pan-destructionism, had appealed furiously throughout his later career for a revolution of unrestrained annihilating fury and "the destruction of everything"—the temples, the shelters, the forms, and the Gods of the old order, so that not one stone would remain.[23] Now this seemed to be happening all over revolutionary Russia. As monuments and idols were being toppled physically, intellectual movements and theories of unparalleled negativism and reductionism rose up and demanded a serious hearing in a revolution that seemed to hold out the promise of immediate and complete remaking of the psyche. Machinism, robotism, primitive reticence, antiverbalism, nudism, social militarism, revolutionary sublimation, and suicidalism—all of them prewar in origin—reappeared in intense form at various stages of the Revolution, often representing a profound fear of human expression, thought, articulation, art, individual assertion, affective relations, unmeasurable feelings, transcendant longings, play, joy, anguish, elation, religious ecstasy, and spontaneous gestures.

"Sign consciousness," write Yury Lotman and Boris Uspensky, "comes to embody certain social relations and the struggle against various kinds of social evil in cultural history often takes the form of negating individual sign systems, including even such an all-embracing one as natural language, or of negating the very principle of using signs." In the arts, there were movements to negate everything: to replace color and form by a void, sound by silence, fashion by nudity, language by vowell signs, poetry by the blank page. This was part of a prewar European current but took intensified forms in Russia directly as a result of the Revolution. Did the spectacle of unprecedented violence generate fear of unchained human emotions? In 1920, the "nothingists" *(nichevoki)* unveiled their manifesto of "revolutionary hoboism" whose main command was to write, read, speak, and print nothing. In the realm of thought, nihilist spokesmen of the Revolution turned their guns on philosophy, which was seen to be the quintessential expression of the bourgeoisie as religion was of the gentry. The most extreme of these currents, Enchmenism, negated mind, spirit, and psyche altogether. These were to wither away in the future "world commune" of languageless people run by a Revolutionary Scientific Soviet. Two currents of nihilism wished not to destroy expressive culture, but to introduce their own: Futurism and the Proletcult.[24]

During the Civil War, the archetypical iconoclast of early Soviet literature, Vladimir Mayakovsky, was asked to play the role of Bazarov in a film version of Turgenev's *Fathers and Sons.* Unfortunately the film was never produced and we are left to wonder how the great poet might have interpreted the sweeping negation of those angry men and women of the 1860s in the light of his own revolutionary battle against old culture. Nineteenth century cultural nihilism and that of the Revolution were not simply two episodes in the general history of "cultural revolution" in modern times. The link between them was concrete and specifically Russian: it was the permanent tendency of a certain portion of the intelligentsia to look askance at anything "old" or well-established, particularly if it was couched in a romantic idiom or seemed either to celebrate a privileged way of life or to lament its "little" tragedies. In the nineteenth century, this way of life was scorned as "gentry indolence" or Oblomovism; in the twentieth, it was called *meshchanstvo.*

The Russian artistic Left—now enjoying extraordinary revival in the West—were among the most self-conscious and provocative of all the cultural iconoclasts in the Revolution. Sergei Tretyakov captured their mood retrospectively in 1927:

> All for combat.
> Force is best.
> A bullet in the brain
> Of Basil the Blest.
> Smash all the icons
> And the signs They have made.
> Explode the Iverskaya
> With a hand grenade.

The rhetoric of the Futurists was especially provocative and contained more than a modicum of playful hooliganism. Mayakovsky loved to shout down "bourgeois" speakers and, in his verse, to point "Comrade Mauser" at the orators of the world, to put Raphael and Rastrelli against the wall. He and his colleagues rejoiced in mocking the culture of the past. Their archetypical iconoclastic act was painting the trees near the Kremlin in glowing colors for a holiday celebration. As in all avant-garde movements, the element of generational revolt was strong; and in their reverance for technology and machinery, they put themselves in the tradition of nineteenth century science worship.[25]

The Futurists aspired to snatch art from the clutches of bourgeois civilization and move it on to the streets and to the people by means of carnival and show. "Museum junk," and the preservers of this junk were the special targets of Mayakovsky. In the oft-cited poem of December 1918, "It's too Early to Rejoice," he declared that "it's time for bullets to pepper museums." According to Ilya Ehrenburg, Mayakovsky wanted to abolish "those store-rooms and warehouses of human genius, such as palaces, galleries, salons, libraries, and theaters." The Italian Futurist, and later Fascist, Marinetti had said the same thing in 1909: "We want to demolish museums, libraries," and for good measure "fight morality, feminism, and all the opportunist and utilitarian cowardice." In his discussion of Futurism, the Swedish theater critic and dramatist, Lars Kleberg, stresses the movement's struggle to free art from the dual clutches of the market and the museum. The new art belonged on agitation-trains, on posters, in the squares and streets among the masses. What then was the sense of preserving the art of the past in museums—edifices that automatically exalted their own contents? When members of the avant-garde found themselves in policy bodies in the new Commissariat of Enlightenment, they attempted to transform their aggressive views into programs.[26]

The Proletarian Culture movement tried this also on a much larger scale. Its origins lay in the cultural institutions of the European socialist and workers' movement before the war, and particularly in the theoretical and educational work of a group of original and energetic Russian Marxists in exile—most of them at odds with Lenin in the period of their greatest activity, 1908–14. Chief among them were Alexander Bogdanov, whose novel *Engineer Menni* contains a brief but vivid sketch of his notion of culture; Maxim Gorky who edited anthologies of proletarian poets; Alexei Gastev who was one of the most noted of these poets; and Anatoly Lunacharsky, future Commissar. Proletcult was virtually a child of pre-war Russian utopianism, its origin closely connected with the science fiction and Tectology of Bogdanov, the Godbuilding of Gorky and Lunacharsky, and the machine-worship of Gastev (see Chapter 7). At its founding, in September 1917, Proletcult resolved to develop a "new" proletarian culture destined to become universalized. Proletcult became a genuine mass movement during the Civil War, reaching a peak estimated at half a million participants in 1919, with thirty-four journals and about 300 organizations.[27]

Present day Soviet historians give Proletcult some credit for its cultural achievements among the workers, but echo Lenin's hostility to certain leaders, especially Bogdanov, for taking a "nihilist" position. Bogdanov was not a cultural nihilist, as his main writings clearly reveal. But nihilist and iconoclastic strains were strong among some of the leaders. At its first conference, a Proletcultist awash with expectant euphoria argued "that all culture of the past might be called bourgeois, that within it—except for natural science and technical skills . . . there was nothing worthy of life, and that the proletariat would begin the work of destroying the old culture and creating the new immediately after the revolution."[28]

Even the most militant leaders often qualified their destructive designs. Lebedev-Polyansky, one of these, accepted the work of past culture, "not as an obedient pupil, but critically." The theater critic, Sanin, wanted a theater by, for, and of the workers, though he allowed the selective retention of older plays, if properly revised and purified. And the Petrograd chapter of Proletcult—one of the most active—saw no harm in using a sumptuous former Hall of the Nobility as their headquarters—even though they rejected what they called "bourgeois" writers such as Pushkin. But the disclaimers seemed halfhearted, and those parts of their discourse where emotion was manifest seemed more authentic. In December 1917, for example, a Proletcult speaker explained that bourgeois culture (i.e., all previous culture), "though sometimes valuable in form, was nevertheless for the most part vulgar and provocative in content and criminal in origin." Generational struggle and self-affirmation were apparent when Pavel Bessalko, a founding member, announced that proletarian writers did not need the past, particularly their "older brothers" such as Leskov, Chekhov, and Korolenko. In Tambov in 1919, local Proletcultists planned to burn all the books in the libraries in the belief that the shelves would be filled on the first of the new year with nothing but proletarian works! All in all, argued M. Grishin in *The Coming Order,* science and art were class phenomena and "weapons in the class struggle." Proletcult's job was to destroy the arsenal of the enemy.[29]

Proletcult did not stand united with Futurism and other avant-garde currents, however. On the contrary, there was war between them. A study of anti-intellectualism among workers in the 1917 world of journalism revealed that workers were often antagonistic to "pure" intellectuals and artists who were removed from "life;" a particular target were the Futurists "who place the ego above all else." Intellectuals were accused of trying "to fasten onto the proletariat" by infiltrating and trying to control Proletcult and thus poisoning the class purity of the movement. Proletcult wanted to build culture for itself and for the masses in general. It could not fail to be pained or rise in anger at words such as those of Punin that "realists and the ungifted are synonymous" or of Osip Brik that if one can easily understand a work of art, it will be boring. One of the biggest issues dividing Proletcult was professionalism—whether workers could cut their moorings from the factory, become "artists" and still retain their working-class identity. Proletcult fought Futurism on almost every issue: on style, content, vocabulary, method. Futurism was after all another new wave in art—a brilliant one—but one of a cycle of avant-gardes and Bohemias that arise almost every generation or two. Though they fought tradition, they were in fact part of a tradition. Proletcult was a genuinely novel experiment designed to arm and teach an entire class in quick time to construct wholly new culture in a still very much illiterate society and to do so with minimum guidance from the past.[30]

Yet, as recent research has shown, the masses in the Proletcult movement at almost every level continued to do obeisance before the cultural idols of the past. Plays of tradition were intermixed with the machinery evenings of Gastev; collective concerts (without a conductor) performed Beethoven—and not Schönberg. Bogdanov's constant pleas that proletarians must master the culture of the past and not simply taste a sampling of it from time to time certainly did not catch on—but the sampling did, and the more visible and audible of the cultural nihilists at the center were partly defeated on the ground by the tastes of the workers themselves. This is not to say that Proletcult did not innovate: on the contrary, it produced some of the most exciting cultural experiments of that age, and provided an enthusiastic audience, particularly for those who made the machine, technology, and the workplace a prominent motif in their art.[31]

The Proletcult movement, even when it smuggled in productions of former culture, declared war against what it called so often the "old world." The teen-age proletarian poet, V. D. Alexandrovsky summed up this feeling in an 1918 poem.[32]

> Blow up,
> Smash to pieces
> The Old World!
> In the heat of battle of the Universal Struggle
> By the glow of flames
> Show no mercy—
> Strangle
> The bony body of destiny!

Merging the language of iconoclasm and cultural nihilism with the general destructiveness of the Revolution, Alexandrovsky and dozens like him were voicing a deep longing to clear away the past altogether and start all over again with a new civilization.

## Makhaevism: War on Intellectuals

One of the poignant sides of the struggle against the old idols was anti-intellectualism, a familiar feature of modern history that has played a very big role in politics in many places. In any society where there is or seems to be sharply differentiated growth in education from one class to another and where knowledge seems to be self-perpetuated in a limited segment of the population and is identified with power, anti-intellectualism is bound to appear. The poignancy emerges when the non-possessors of specialized learning are told that the new world is now theirs but that they must still defer to holders of knowledge. This is what happened in the Russian Revolution, and the result was confusion, disappointment, bewilderment, and resentful actions directed against intellectuals old and new.

The roots of anti-intellectualism run very deep in Russian history. It was an organic part of the village world's indigenous distrust of thinkers, talkers, and city folk in general and of "new-fangled" ideas, gentry utopias, ultra-energetic schoolteachers, and even agronomy and modern medicine. Evidence of it is everywhere in Russian literature from Tolstoy's "Morning of a Landowner" (1859) to the novels of the 1920s. Peasants were bewildered by the efforts of fine folk to "save" them and by their willingness to labor, "like the sun" without pay on behalf of an ideal.[33] There were many exceptions to this outlook, of course, even in the countryside, and when peasants migrated to the city to become workers, some of these traditional feelings and impulses eroded. But even the more advanced among the emerging proletariat have told of their uneasiness in the presence of "real" intellectuals, their resentment of verbal facility and endless theorizing. The workers who wanted to replace the *intelligent,* a nonworker with a formal education and usually of superior class background, with their own "worker-intelligents" could not help but feel the tension of upward mobility and loss of identity with former comrades. Even intra-class tension in the proletariat was sometimes couched in this idiom as in 1917 when unskilled "black workers" cursed lathe operators and machinists as *"burzhui"* precisely because of their superior skills. If the popular tales that workers read in the cheap prerevolutionary press reflected their outlook on this matter, there is evidence that workers wanted solidarity and equality and were ambivalent about mobility and stratification and that they resented the too ambitious and the high toned.[34]

The intelligentsia itself was often beset by hatred of the intellectual, curious, and cerebral side of themselves, sometimes matched by a love of the peasants who allegedly retained "natural" feelings. Richard Wortman has brilliantly analyzed the disillusionment among Populists, their exaltation of the people, the abasement of self, the desire to immerse that self in the common folk, and the tendency to see feeling and primitive impulse as superior to thought. This was a familiar occurence all through the Western world in the late industrial period—a longing for "real people" and "down home folks" after the spiritual exhaustion of city and mental life. But in Russia it went further. During the period of Populism, many of those who went to the people did so in order to repudiate their own former life as students or intellectuals. Sergei Nechaev, terrorist and failed intellectual, said that "the revolution knows only one science, the science of destruction" and that "he who learns of the revolutionary cause in books will always be a revolutionary do-nothing."[35]

Self-doubt, self-pity, and self-hatred continued to blossom in the early twentieth century with the growing complexities of life and the grievous disappointments with revolution. When the Great Revolution came in 1917, the malaise was still very strong. Gorky predicted that the intelligentsia, the creator of spiritual nourishment, would be swallowed up by the peasantry (as would the proletariat) who would simply take from them what they needed for themselves. At the very beginning of the Revolution, in April 1917, the poet Blok said "If I were they I'd hang the whole lot of us." Sitting on a park bench in the Summer Garden of Petrograd two years later, he told Gorky of his growing hostility to the brain. "If only," he said, "we could stop thinking completely for ten years." The Russian Revolution had brought about a fusion of the separate currents of popular, governmental, and the intelligentsia's own anti-intellectualism.[36]

The most concrete expression of anti-intellectualism before the Revolution was Makhaevism, the teaching of Jan Waclaw Machajski, an adopted Russian of Polish birth who had developed a strong suspicion of political intellectuals in his native land. Drawing partly from Marx, and anticipating such celebrated sociologies of knowledge as those of Roberto Michels and Karl Mannheim, Machajski in *The Mental Worker* (1899) analyzed Marxian Social Democracy and pronounced it the self-interested ideology of the radical intelligentsia. Socialist intellectuals, he said, wished to abolish capitalism and nationalize the means of reproduction, but since knowledge was also a hidden instrument of production, these leaders would then possess a monopoly of power, give themselves privileges, and lord it over the workers who would become slaves in a socialist state. "Educated society" or "the army of mental workers" were not the friends of the proletariat: they were exactly like the bourgeoisie proper, in style of dress and life, with "white hands" engaged in mental labor, and living in comfort. The proletariat must "seize the property of the ruling, educated society, the property of the learned world, in order to wrest the heritage of mankind from the hands of the ruling minority." Machajski's program for the workers was to expropriate property and the means of production, abolish family and personal property and inheritance as well as any means of passing on privilege or knowledge within an elite, to "socialize knowledge," and to equalize all wages by leveling.[37]

The extreme egalitarianism, the angry iconoclasm, and the menace of violence that informed Machajski's work was probably more appealing to his working-class followers than was the theory itself. The only course for the hungry masses, he wrote, would be "to rise up at the first opportunity and destroy and annihilate to the last iota the accursed accumulations of wealth which you have helped to create through the ages and which the masters have always seized entirely for themselves." The intelligentsia and the socialist leaders, he warned, "will not perish under the tsarist bullets but under the knife of a ragged tramp. The people in rags will beat, burn, and cut up the well dressed teachers of the socialist ideal." One of his followers in 1906 summed it up very simply: "All evil can be traced to ideology and to ideals." Another, Evgeny Lozinsky, subjected the entire Russian Revolutionary tradition to "Makhaevist" analysis, mocking the "thinking proletariat" of the 1860s, calling the "To the People" movement a cynical plot and a class struggle *against* the people, and dismissing the martyrdom of Zhelyabov and Perovskaya as hypocrisy and egoism. All history in fact, claimed Lozinsky, was "one endless, uninterrupted chain of violence and fraud."[38]

The learned and sensitive critic, Ivanov-Razumnik (who would feel the force of a late variant of Makhaevism in a Stalinist prison), dismissed Makhaevism as a warmed-over version of the nihilism of the 1860s and the Tolstoyanism of his own time. All were based, he said, on the erroneous belief in the mutual incompatibility between culture and social justice, between the beautiful and the good. This in fact formed a link in Makhaevism between iconoclasm, nihilism, anti-intellectualism and leveling— all bringing down rather than raising up. Bakunin had said in 1869 that "the one who knows more will naturally dominate the one who knows less." The question is: should one decrease the fund of knowledge and the holders of knowledge by persecuting culture and intelligentsia or should one try to produce more culture and more intellectuals? It was a question that carried over into the Revolution. Ivanov-Razumnik claimed that all of Makhaevist literature could be put in one's pocket and all Makhaevists on one couch. But he also admitted that the teaching of Machajski would appeal to "black" or unskilled workers and to bums, hoboes, and hooligans. According to a hostile Bolshevik scholar, it appealed only to unemployed artisans before the revolution of 1905, and then peaked during the years of despair and reaction, especially among unskilled workers.[39]

Makhaevism predicted much about the Russian Revolution. The Bolshevik leaders, mostly members of the journalistic intelligentsia, were ambivalent about intellectuals. On the one hand, they admired the social hatred and spite that the urban masses could sometimes level against the old intelligentsia, and they had their own grievances as well. But they themselves tended to fit the description of Machajski's new coming elite of bureaucrats, scientists, privileged technocrats, and sacerdotal ideologues who lorded it over the workers in the name of a new opiate known as "socialism."

It is impossible to say how strong anti-intellectualism was, where it came from, and what its real shape was. It was already building up under the Provisional Government and had become a storm by December 1917. Makhaevist influence was cited by some intellectuals who could feel that storm brewing. Gorky observed that side by side with the leveling directed against people of wealth and property which could be taken and shared grew a resentment of the learned and the skilled per se. A leading academic complained in a 1918 letter to Lunacharsky about the mob's anti-intellectualism, "that deeply false conception of qualified labour as privileged, undemocratic." Many people in the Revolution tended to lump together old elites, professionals, educated persons, members of the bourgeoisie, gentry, bosses, tsarist officers, technicians, literati, Old Bolshevik journalists, artists, and simply well dressed people. The writer Konstantin Paustovsky recalled the mood in 1919: "everyone treated people in glasses suspiciously in those violent times. They thought them cunning enemies and hated them bitterly." It is no surprise that Bolshevik officials were sometimes shot down by their own people because they looked *burzhui*. Rural teachers came in for widespread abuse during the Civil War—from all sides.[40]

Makhaevism, although it never organized itself around a circle or party, appeared in many arenas. One of these was Proletcult. Bessalko, a major spokesman, was a worker himself and made no secret of his long-time adherence to the ideas of Machajski. Strong echoes of it could be heard everywhere in the Proletcult debates over who had the right to make proletarian culture. Among the proletarian poets, satirical gems such as *Old Intelligent* (1918), *Conversation with a Scholar* (1920) and *Song about a Russian Intelligent* (1918) bristled with anti-intellectual drollery. A brutally frank Proletcultist wrote in 1918 that "the intelligentsia is a bourgeois concept and must vanish along with the bourgeois class." It was precisely a kind of Makhaevism that linked together the major Bolshevik opposition currents, and linked them all to the anarchists. Their targets were privileged specialists. The anarchist Alexander Ge demanded the mass repression of the intelligentsia, conceding that specialists could be allowed to serve the state, but only under guard. Alexander Shlyapnikov, then a Left Communist, accused the party of pampering specialists, people who were after all "from another social world." All through the Civil War and into the 1920s, a Makhaevist undercurrent continued to run and *spetseedstvo*—specialist baiting—remained to harass the specialists, sometimes to the point of suicide. Makhaevism in its conscious, theoretical forms and in independent acts of specialist baiting continued to express a deep feeling that brains had once again outwitted revolutionary virtue.[41]

Makhaevism was always strongest among the anarchists, the guardians of undiluted revolutionary ideals and passions. They may have been on the fringe of politics in terms of specific programs, but they seem to have represented at least a segment of popular mentality in the realm of intellectual-hatred. Their proclamations and manifestos—which virtually shout from the page—combined the swirling currents of vandalism, iconoclasm, and militant atheism in a war against what one of them called "that loathesome culture which divides men into 'ignorant' and 'learned'." Darkness in their metaphor was false and mystified learning—and light, the glow of flame and the flash of the bomb. "Destroy the churches, those nests of gentry lies; destroy the universities, that nest of bourgeois lies. Drive away the priests, drive away the scientists! Destroy the false gentry and bourgeois heavens. Smash their Peruns, gods and idols." The Anarcho-Futurists of Kharkov—a veritable revolutionary cauldron of ideas and experiments— were among those utopians whose main vision of the future was a clarifying and purifying destruction, the creation of a charred landscape of ruined churches and museums and of paintings and books reduced to ashes. For these people, and many like them, the Revolution was to be a long black light of devastation—their black banner signified nothingness, the void, annihilation—in which all old culture, which had become a hated icon, must be wiped out.[42]

## Anti-Iconoclasm

All these currents were closely linked. At various points in time and place, they possessed peasants and workers, soldiers and sailors, journalists and poets who longed to assault the old. In the Revolution, whole classes and institutions were enveloped and vanished into the debris. The remaining purveyors of old values, the men and women who lived mainly on ideas, were beset by the menace of an anti-intellectual storm. Why did this storm which built up great power in the early revolutionary years not blow away all traces of the old culture and its makers? What happened to revolutionary iconoclasm?

Iconoclasm seems so very Russian, so very revolutionary. But so is anti-iconoclasm, the impulse to conserve. One of the major features of Soviet culture and the Soviet way of life and one of the secrets of its survival is its ability to retain certain key elements of the deep Russian past, modified and harnessed to the use of the regime. The urgent grasp at tradition is not an invention of Stalinism in the 1930s. It appeared in the very first days of the Revolution and had its roots in pre-revolutionary times. As early as 1910, a Society for the Protection and Preservation of Monuments of Art and Antiquities had been founded whose members emerged in the Revolution as the "preservers." The artist and set designer Alexander Benois was prominent among these. In the early months of the Provisional Government, he argued for the renaming of Petrograd back to St. Petersburg and contradicted those who wished to destroy "idols of autocracy" by saying that one would have to destroy the entire corpus of Russian art and culture if such a harmful category were to be invoked. The job of the Revolution was systematic preservation of palaces as museums for the people. This impulse was organized under the Gorky Commission—an informal body of the intelligentsia which took up the question of the fate of art in the Revolution. Its brief life was marred by constant reorganizations and fights between, on the one hand, Gorky, Benois, and Nikolai Rerikh, who wanted to protect monuments, and on the other, the "leftists" Mayakovksy, Meyerhold, and Punin, who believed that "over-protection" of the old would inhibit innovative art. The Provisional Government itself possessed no overall cultural policy.[43]

On the very day the Bolsheviks took power, they appointed "commissars" to protect museums and art collections during the fighting. An appeal in *Izvestiya* a few days later informed citizens that they had "inherited enormous cultural riches, buildings of rare beauty, museums full of rare and marvellous objects, things that enlighten and inspire, and libraries containing vast intellectual treasures. All of this now really belongs to the people." In November the masses were invited to tour the Winter Palace—the "den of tyrants." When they looted, this and other buildings were put under guard and their contents carefully catalogued, stored, or removed to safe places. Benois took vigorous measures to inspect and preserve. Preservation commissions were established in other towns, all of this institutionalized eventually under the Commissariat of Enlightenment. In January 1918, it chased local occupiers out of the home of the composer Chaikovsky at Klin; in February, it sandbagged the monuments in expectation of a renewed German assault on Petrograd. Garrison troops and even the sick and wounded were denied the use of premises designated as cultural treasures by the government. The Bolshevik authorities even presented a monastery to a group of Tolstoyans for a commune in order to protect it from the ravages of the local population. Money was levied for repair, and the sale of art treasures abroad was prohibited by a decree in September 1918. Private collections were not immune to the collecting energies of the Bolshevik commissions, and a mass of treasure now flowed from homes and families, through requisition, into the museums and storehouses.[44]

The schism that had wrecked the Gorky Commission now reemerged in the government's Section for Museums and Preservation of Monuments, headed by the indefatigable art historian, Igor Grabar. The "preservers" included himself and Benois and were supported by the Cooperative network whose leaders, Alexander Chayanov and others, stressed the need to keep intact the cultural infrastructure built up in the countryside under the old regime. The "destroyers" or "nihilists" were Shteremberg, Tatlin, Korolëv (the sculptor) and other avant-garde figures. Grabar recalls that he had to fight a two-front war against the vandalism in the countryside in the summer of 1918 and the continuous harassments of the avant-gardists. As in the French Revolution, travelling teams were sent into the country to assess the damage and collect and preserve what was left.[45]

In the government the main force behind preservation was Lunacharsky, with the blessing of Lenin. Lunacharsky is said to have wept and offered to resign when he heard of damage done to St. Basil's during the November 1917 fighting in Moscow. Lenin is also said to have laughed at him. But this episode in personality differences signifies no essential dispute between the two men on the issue of preserving the glories of the past culture. A decree of November 1917 called for the pulling down of odious and worthless monuments to past rulers but for the preservation of those having artistic or historic worth. Lunacharsky suggested to Lenin in 1918 that the best of the past be retained (cleansed of harmful components if needed), that the old and new cultures be allowed to grow together, and that "psychopaths and charlatans"—such as those who want to burn "feudal-bourgeois instruments and sheet music" be rebuffed. Lenin agreed, only adding that the old culture ought not be allowed to overshadow and stunt the growth of new, revolutionary culture. In practice however, Lenin was really more nervous about the new culture—as expressed in Proletcult and Futurism—than he was about the old. He was a man of traditional tastes and thought it essential "to grasp all the culture which capitalism has left and build socialism from it." He opposed the indiscriminate smashing of the artifacts of the past just as he opposed intellectual baiting. Had he lived longer, he would probably have opposed the epidemic of renaming which threatened to turn hundreds of cities into "Lenin" towns and every other theater into "October."[46]

By the end of the Civil War, a network of museums in the Soviet Union was fully operating. Though émigré scholars have rightly criticized the museum work of the Revolution, there is no doubt that the new regime contributed much to the preservation of old culture in Russia and voiced a preservational and conservative attitude toward culture and art. Though there was much looting, much carting of precious art objects abroad, a paucity of museums, and maladministration, the fact remains that the private treasures of the imperial past were opened to the public. Between 1918 and 1920, the museum section registered over 550 old mansions, about a thousand private collections of art and treasure, and almost 200 separate pieces of art. It is difficult to take the moral measure of this termination of the private worlds of splendor that had graced the mansions of the rich and the cultivated when seen against the dazzling of peasants and workers by those splendors assembled in a museum. The people got the art and the private market was replaced by the museum. But the Bolshevik leaders got the big palaces as their workplaces, and the keepers of cultural order got extra wages and rations for their work—a relationship between beauty and inequality that the Makhaevists had feared.[47]

Thus, as in revolutionary France, the museum solved the dilemma posed by the desire to "deromanovize" Russia graphically and to save the esthetic treasures of that dynasty and its supporters. By placing crowns, thrones, and imperial regalia in a people's museum, the regime depoliticized them, neutralized their former symbolic power, and offered them as a gift to the masses who—by means of guides and rituals—were to view them as emblems both of a national genius and of an exploitative order of luxury and oppressive power. Bolshevism was the anti-iconoclasm of order, disarming, demythologizing, and antiquarianism. In their selectivity, the Bolsheviks resembled the anti-iconoclasts of the French Revolution. "The revolutions of barbarous people," said the deputy Barère in 1791, "destroy all monuments, and the very trace of the arts seem to be effaced. The revolutions of an enlightened people conserve the fine arts, and embellish them, while the fruitful concern of the legislator causes the arts to be reborn as an ornament of the empire." This was perfectly illustrated by the famous poster of N. N. Kupreyanov, "Citizens, Preserve Works of Art" (1920; see Fig. 12). The picture, commissioned by Grabar and approved by Lenin, displays the Tauride Palace, the Klodt horses on the Fontanka Bridge, a classical urn, an open book, traditional scrolls, a seventeenth century Russian chest, and a framed oil painting—precisely the "useless junk" hated by Futurists and the needless luxuries hated by village vandals. The poster was mass-produced and sent all across the expanse of Russia.[48]

The war against culture and culture bearers was won by the preservers during the Revolution. In the context of revolutionary vision and utopia, the scope and the fate of iconoclasm is striking. When peasants went beyond "rational" economic destruction in the countryside and indulged in allegedly irrational vandalism, they were clearing the space and purging the scene for a creation and recreation of their own kind of life: a vast symbolic cleansing operation to accompany the raucous expulsion orders they had issued. Urban iconoclasm was far more variegated and complicated in motivation, intellectual inspiration, and sociological basis. But it was also a utopia of negation, of *tabula rasa*, of leveling and denuding as the prelude to the construction of a new world. The congruence of this vision of negation on the part of workers and creative artists allowed the two cultures to collude and connect on occasion, a connection soon shattered over the question of the content of the new. On this issue the state decidedly opposed the sweeping away of past culture as a prerequisite to building the new society. While willing to efface Romanov symbols, it nurtured a striking eclecticism that began to emerge in the 1920s and was fully established in the 1930s. On the metaphorical side, iconoclasm continued to feed militant cultural movements of many kinds down into the early 1930s when—after a final sweep—the negational broom was plucked away by the state for its own exclusive use.[49]

# 4

## Festivals of the People

> There are things about which one can think but about which it is impossible to speak except in symbols and hints.
>
> Shestov, *Dostoevsky and Nietzsche* (1903) (Kline, *Religion,* 76)

> A detachment of troops, their weapons flashing coldly and jangling harshly, cut through the brightly colored crowd. Dark, bloodstained memories flooded over everyone, threatening to drown the beauty of the moment. This time, however, the gray snake-like column was harmless.
>
> Bogdanov, *Engineer Menni* (1913)

Revolutionary festival, ritual, and symbolism, the inseparable companions of every self-conscious revolution, provided in gesture, movement, performance, and art the new cultural apparel of the innovative order that was being born. This experiment in myth-making and adornment generated conflicting visions from the very outset. One was a carnivalesque image of freedom and dance, a boundless perspective of newly opened space on which to fashion a world; it was marked by spontaneous celebration, light-hearted buffoonery in the midst of violent political struggle, constantly self-creating forms of art and entertainment, and the movement of those forms onto the streets and into the villages. Against this rose a vision of order, solemn monumentality, and myth-making, conditioned by a fear—the anti-iconoclastic fear—that the masses, if left to their own ludic and Dionysian impulses, would unleash chaos. There were no simple sides in this confrontation. All kinds of people—artists and workers, officials and soldiers, Proletcultists and Futurists—felt both of these visions successively and often simultaneously. But the conflict caused tense interaction: in the language of Bakhtin, it was the war between the lower and upper regions of the body, the spirit and the mind, *volya* and order, the mocking laugh and the solemn visage.

The Russian Revolution drew on a rich tradition of ritual culture, of forms, traditions, and motifs rooted in the past. Of greatest antiquity were the survivals of pagan festivals—song and dance, lewd carnivals, bear ceremonies, ritual burnings of stylized devils and the like. Also of great antiquity were the Orthodox Church festivals and processions which combined hierarchical order, music, stationary worship, a luxurious array of vestments and ornament, and the popular traditions of feasting and frolic connected with holy days. The military review, established in the eighteenth century, differed strikingly from these. It was power, rationally and geometrically deployed. Its collectivism was impersonal and palpably hierarchical and deferential; its splendor was panegyric art. Its practical purpose was, theoretically, kinetic and psychological preparation (the root of the word parade) for combat; its symbolic purpose was to display strength, organization, and efficiency in a realm where these things were in short supply. The ceremonial parade, embellished with horse, rolling cannon, fancy caparisons, bright uniforms, flags and gonfalons, and glistening bayonets—all moving to a lively martial air—was designed to produce euphoria, loyalty, readiness, and a sense of menace to the enemies of the State. Finally, there was the court culture of the Romanov dynasty, extraordinarily rich in symbols, regalia, and pageantry—an elaborate visual ornament to the sacred and charismatic persona of the emperor-tsar.[1]

All of these celebratory forms were open and legal, if not official. The political frame that surrounded the birth of revolutionary ritual was entirely different: it was illegal. Workers and radicals possessed neither the means nor the freedom to deploy their ranks regularly or display an elaborate set of symbols. Their ritual took shape in two environments: secret meetings and illegal or semi-legal demonstrations. In the former, beginning in the late 1890s, the focus was May Day, the socialist international holiday recently imported from Europe, and the routine utterly simple: radical songs, a show of red and speeches. Demonstrations of protest such as strike marches or funeral processions for fallen comrades began to appear with great frequency around 1905. Since the atmosphere was tense and the space constricted, the marchers were militant trespassers into alien zones, sometimes menaced by police. Their feelings of outrage, anger, indignation, or funerary sadness had to be compressed into taut slogans borne aloft on red banners (often shaped like church gonfalons), molded into shouts, or translated into songs. The principal songs of revolution in that period were either prison laments, funeral dirges (especially the enormously popular "You Fell Victim"), critiques of the autocracy, or visions of a dawning world of freedom. The demonstration thus resembled a parade in form, in its graphic message of solidarity, and in the "tangible impression of its own power," to use the words of Hendrik de Man. But in its emotional shape and show of pathos, it also resembled the religious procession.[2]

## Days of Revolution

What more natural occasion for an emotional people to celebrate than the quick and relatively bloodless overthrow of a despotic government? For three generations, thousands of people had longed for, fought for, and died for the abolition of the autocracy. Suddenly, in March 1917, after a week of rebellion and street fighting in the two capitals, with minor skirmishes elsewhere, Tsar Nicholas had abdicated, removing himself and the heir apparent from the historic line of Russian princes that stretched back for a millenium. On the following day, his brother Michael followed suit and refused the crown. Russians were stunned at this news, some were overjoyed, some were appalled, but no one was indifferent. In the urban festivities that occured in the weeks after the fall of the monarchy, two themes emerge: deliverance and thankfulness. Deliverance was expressed in the carnivalesque and festive side of the celebrations—joyous days of tsarlessness and a euphoric feeling of *volya* exhibited in the liberation of prisoners, acts of burning and iconoclasm, the huge spontaneous crowds, the minimality and speed of the planning, and the atmosphere of fun, play, tolerance, good will, and transcendant solidarity of a free people. The other mood was thanksgiving to those who had worked to bring this about: the iconic prisoners, now paraded and exalted, and the "martyrs" of the Revolution who had fallen in the street fighting. Its tone was solemn, dignified, majestic, and its main expression was the civic-religious public burial ceremonies.

Like the French revolutionary *journées,* the "Days of the Russian Revolution" (so called in some locales) in the towns were massive turnouts of popular celebration, hastily organized by the local Soviet, municipal, or Provisional Government authority— sometimes together.[3] Tsarlessness was shared by all classes of the population, standing or marching together in an eclectic confluence of Russia's ritual traditions: the military parade, the church procession, the workers' demonstration—often inextricably mixed and unnoticed. Ecclesiastic hymns alternated with the "Workers' Marseillaise" while red banners mingled with Orthodox gonfalons and crosses. This accorded with the broadness and generosity of the rhetoric in celebratory speeches and with the social mix of the crowds and organizers—particularly with the novel and thrilling spectacle of revolutionary workers' formations marching side by side with military units.

Neither the intrusion of official solemnity nor the class tensions that might have underlain these events seemed to dampen fun and laughter. Pageantry, gaiety, and good humor were on display. Ethnic and local costumes enlivened the scene as at village festivals, full throated multitudes broke into song again and again. Spontaneous acts interrupted the rhythms of parade and procession. In Odessa, former political prisoners were pulled out of the crowd, exalted, and drawn on carts and carriages for public homage. At the courthouse in Ekaterinoslav crowds cried out "down with the eagle. Tomorrow it won't be there to claw the tormented flesh of a long suffering people." In Kharkov speakers urged outlawing the word *barin* (lord). The color red was apparent everywhere; when flags were in short supply, people brought dresses or waved red dressing gowns from their windows. It was an unrestrained public exhibition of cheer and good feelings, an all-Russian solidarity of joy (see Fig. 13).[4]

Common euphoria and collective emotion were also in evidence in the solemn funeral services arranged in the early days for those killed in the fighting. One of the remarkable features of the February Revolution was its relatively small number of victims—a clear indication that the monarchy was widely hated and that many people welcomed its overthrow. The success, the dignity, the overall unanimity, and the solemnity of the local funerals led the new government in the capital to mount on March 23 its first major public celebration of the Revolution as a funeral—the Burial of the Martyrs.

The ceremonial interment of the 184 people killed during the February Revolution in Petrograd was the perfect vehicle for a physical and iconic exaltation of "Free Russia." The organizers from the Petrograd Soviet and the Provisional Government chose the Field of Mars as the burial site and arranged it as a massive demonstration of columns marching in from the working-class districts through the center of town (as they had done during the February days)—about a million people moving constantly for twelve hours in great order and solemnity. The craze for order and security was matched by the elegant precision of the marchers. Though traditional forms of religious burial techniques were employed, no member of the clergy was permitted to officiate or participate—a drastic break with all past practices of public ceremonial. Columns of workers and soldiers marching together bore the coffins to the graves to the strains of the purely revolutionary hymn "You Fell Victim." Solidarity in freedom was in full display in the mixed participants of all classes, the unconflicting slogans, and the themes of release and gratitude to the martyrs. Conservative commentators were happy with the mood of renewal and the absence of deep class conflict. But strongly revolutionary signs were everywhere: the workers' songs, the draping of the city in red, and the geography of workers occupying the opulent center of town. It was the first secular outdoor ceremony in Russian history, the first major non-oppositional and all-class ceremony in the lifetime of the Provisional Government, and the only one also without a central charismatic figure as focus.[5]

The tableau of domestic peace and social harmony provided by the March celebrations and obsequies crumbled within a few weeks. Society divided bitterly over the linked issues of war and social change. The Provisional Government, the moderate Soviet leaders, and the forces of order continued the war against Germany and delayed the reforms. The Bolsheviks and other oppositional parties and social elements—peasants, soldiers, workers—demanded a deepening of the Revolution and immediate peace at the front. The red flags that had adorned the revolutionary days of good will in March became the symbols of opposition once again as demonstrators took to the streets. The Provisional Government possessed no symbolic culture of its own to set against the seas of red that swirled around the streets of the capital. The tricolor flag of Peter the Great was pronounced politically neutral and retained. "God Save the Tsar" was outlawed. The Government adopted the "Workers' Marseillaise" whose melody was a solid French Bourgeois republican hymn. But it was hated by conservatives because of its association with radical workers. No monuments were erected. City fathers in Ekaterinoslav voted to rename a square after Michael Rodzianko, a prominent political figure in the early days of the Revolution, and put his bust in it; the Government itself had an offer from American businessmen to help finance a monument to the Russian revolutionary movement to be "visible from one end of Russia to another." Nothing came of these or similar schemes.[6]

Most astonishing, in retrospect, was the Provisional Government's approach to remaking the national seal and emblem. These were essential for conducting business in chancery and mint, but the Romanov eagle had obviously become too repugnant for continued use. A juridical council of the Government made the dubious judgment that the Romanov eagle, in and of itself, did not connote monarchy. It commissioned the well-known artist Ivan Bilibin to design a new emblem for seal, money, and stamps with the double-headed eagle now astride the Tauride Palace (home of the Government), but with wings folded down, domesticated, devoid of monarchical ornaments (see Fig. 14). But the two-headed eagle, with its tearing claws and beak, had become virtually a metaphor for tsarist reaction, barbarous cruelty, and aggressive imperialism by the time of the Revolution. Thus armed with a Petrine flag, a still very Byzantine eagle, and a hymn that evoked both solidarity with the Entente and the excitement of street demonstrations, the Provisional Government when it wished to show a symbolic face could only show one that was either traditional or highly ambivalent.[7]

This was vividly illustrated in the Provisional Government's last major attempt to mount a public outdoor ceremony: the July 15 funeral of the seven Cossacks killed in the July Days. The depth of political change since the March 23 mass political burial was enormous: division over the war was sharper than ever, masses in town, country, and garrison were visibly more radicalized, and Lenin had returned to Russia to help mobilize the Bolshevik party in militant actions. One of these was the July Days, an armed demonstration that flowed into a failed attempt to replace the Provisional Government by Soviet power. Among the casualties were seven Cossacks who had defended the Government. The Government, after suppressing the uprising, decided to make the interment of these Cossacks a political statement. They were buried with full military regalia. The service was embellished by all the resources of the Orthodox Church in Petrograd: St. Isaac's Cathedral for the Requiem mass, choirs from the major churches, high prelates of the capital, and the full repertoire of icons, crosses, censers, and vestments—a striking contrast to the secular funeral of March 23. The military-patriotic motif was undiluted: no workers' formations, no "Workers' Marseillaise," no revolutionary or anti-war banners. The all-day ceremony terminated at the sacred Alexander Nevsky cemetery, where the symbols, speeches, and wreaths continued to celebrate the spirit of traditional Orthodox, patriotic Russia.[8]

In the rhetoric of the ceremonies, speakers called for "loyalty to the revolution." But in the symbolic context of the moment, it sounded like a hollow reification of an abstract concept. In fact the ceremony was displaying a powerful impulse of counter-revolutionary revulsion and an upsurge of the spirit of order, discipline, stability, state power, and frontline patriotism. We know from the memoirs of members, former members, and supporters of the Provisional Government that this was precisely their private mood, a mood that was given muted utterance at the Moscow State Conference later that summer. But in the funeral of the Cossacks, we have it on full and open display. It is the sharpest and clearest "document" that we possess on the actual aspirations of the Provisional Government leaders in mid-summer of 1917. Since it possessed no "modern" symbols to express its themes and goals, that Government automatically drew on the symbols and rituals that were rich in the imagery of patriotism and social order: the army and the church. As the Bolsheviks were to do a year or so later, the Provisional Government had moved from celebrating revolution to celebrating itself and its deepest values.[9]

## Early Signs of Bolshevism

There were no "days of revolution" after the Bolshevik seizure of power in October 1917, nothing resembling the festivities that broke out in March of that year after the fall of the monarchy. There was—to put it another way—no joyful celebration of Kerensky-lessness. The reason was only partly seasonal. The main problem was the political frame. The first side of this frame was lack of popular understanding of what this seizure meant and how deep the change would be from the "other" revolutionary regime. The second was the continuation of political war in the capital, including demonstrations of anti-Bolsheviks. The third was the prolonged fighting in Moscow and other cities before Soviet power was visibly established across the heartland of Old Russia—thus adding uncertainty about the longevity of the new government. And the fourth was the emergency nature of this government which was determined to maintain and restore order, defend itself, and make peace. The absence from history of "October days" is upon reflection a striking historical fact. Among other things, it explains why the mythologized "Storming of the Winter Palace" has always remained a truncated narrative lacking the orgiastic release that drama would require and also why the Bolsheviks subsumed and collapsed the drama of the February Revolution into their own.

Although the Bolsheviks were instantaneously and concretely aware of the cultural power of symbols in the new revolutionary order, it took them about a year to put together a new symbolic and ritual system. The main ingredients were the first festival on May 1, 1918 and the adoption of a new anthem, arms, flag, and "Red Calendar."

In regard to festivals of revolution, the Bolsheviks were bound by an ambivalence, faintly apparent at first. They wished to keep alive the élan and the mystique of "October" as a liberating event of profound historical importance—their Foundation Tale in fact—and at the same time wanted to deflect revolutionary energies to state-building, warfighting, and the maintenance of order. Anatoly Lunacharsky, the new People's Commissar of Culture, bestrode this dualism. Although his retrospective theory did not emerge until 1920, Lunacharsky from the outset hoped to keep the flame of revolution alive through symbols and festivals that would celebrate his vision of collective immortality and a new socialist religion. Lunacharsky lacked the status and power of a Jacques-Louis David, the pageant-master of the French Revolution, who had possessed political weight, an artistic reputation of his own, and a ready-made culture to draw from (classical Greece and Rome). Lunacharsky, though responsible for the festival style, was poised between Lenin's conventional taste in art and his preferences for solemn and orderly styles on the one hand and by the avant-garde festival artists on the other, who favored the shock effect, irreverence, and laughter of traditional carnival over stiff and heavy ritual.

May Day, 1918 in Petrograd gave the Bolsheviks their first chance to celebrate the seizure of power. It differed from the March "days" of 1917 in that it came six months after the event and was carefully organized. On the other hand, May 1918 was still a time of relatively good feelings in the Revolution. Although there was working-class and oppositional unrest in the capital, the Civil War was just beginning and the large-scale violence, the universalization of social and political hatred, the assassinations of Bolshevik leaders, the Red Terror, and the extreme rigors of War Communism all lay ahead. May Day was also the onset of spring following the first bleak winter with its mass egress from the city and material deprivation. The explosion of color and movement on May 1 was bound to seem, then and in retrospect, more spontaneous and joyous than those that came later. And it seems clear from contemporary descriptions that some of the spontaneous good will of the March Revolution had survived the crushing events of Year I of the Revolution. And since it preceded the standardization of signs and monuments, the May Day festivities allowed a freer milieu of decor and visual improvisation.[10]

The May Day Parade or demonstration in Petrograd was the main element in the celebrations. Unlike that of March 23, 1917 and unlike those to come in Moscow, there was no central target or objective. It began at Smolny, the Bolshevik headquarters in the October Revolution, marched to the Palace Square, and thence to Mars Field—sparkling and varied. Speakers roved the city in open cars, regaling the public with words—chief among them Volodarsky, soon to be assassinated. The decor was extremely original, having been given over to the talented artists who remained in Petrograd after the movement of the capital to Moscow. K. S. Petrov-Vodkin executed a famous panel to labor in beautiful pastels while ultraleftists did wall frescos in screeching colors, praised by Lunacharsky for their visibility, but later criticized as too provocative by Soviet historians of art and ritual. The military, though prominent, had their horses and weapons adorned with red ribbons and green sprigs—combining revolutionary and pagan motifs. Most affecting were the celebrations after the march: garlanded ships on the Neva River playing music to the masses on shore, bonfires, searchlights, torchlight parades, fireworks, and dancing on the banks of the rivers and canals. Noise, frolic, and good cheer seem to have dominated the daytime hours of this holiday.

The solemn, quasi-religious part of May Day was the natural pendant to rolicking celebration and no more in conflict with it than was Easter service or wedding mass to the feasting that went with it. The Bolshevik solemnities took the form of indoor concerts of mixed genres. The most moving of them was a performance of the Mozart Requiem for the martyrs of the October Revolution, held in the Capella of the Winter Palace—an exceptionally ornate and elegant setting, framing the entire event with the utmost dignity and beauty. Lunacharsky struck a religious note. "I made some general remarks," he reported, "about the Requiem, about Mozart, and about the way we now look at death, at the judgement on the human personality and its victory in the historical triumph of the idea of humanity." During the performance of the Requiem, a small boy fell to his knees and remained kneeling for half an hour, thinking he was in church. The audience was mute and bowed and filed out reverently at the end. It was one of the first opportunities for Lunacharsky to display publicly his old aspiration to combine religion and revolution (see Chapter 5).[11]

One of the reasons for Petrograd's striking success was the fact that most of the major artists and Lunacharsky himself stayed on in the old capital (the latter for over a year). Artists were unleashed to deploy their talents in fantastic graphic decor, imparting to squares, bridges, and broad avenues a religious and carnival quality—Petrograd became a cartoon, a Pleasure Island, a Castle in Spain, and a Land of Cockaigne under their hands; it was adorned with flags, pennons, ample yardage of bunting in fabulous colors, and an almost primitive blaze of imagery controlled by sophisticated design. Carnival emerged in a mock burial of the Autocracy (not of the Provisional Government), circus performers, traditional Russian booth-shows *(balagan)*, fairyland theater sets in the streets, and laughing and shouting decor. The vision of a free and happy world pervaded the holiday, retrieving that euphoria of a year ago and transcending it with more extravagant and deliberate acts of collective rejoicing, despite the official sponsoring and the intrusion of political and military themes. Later a camp of insignia would choke off the flamboyant art, Lenin's frowns would darken the carnival fun, and political statues would cast their shadows over the circus routines. This transformation did not occur all at once but it occurred all the same. Lunacharsky, who witnessed the dampening of revolutionary carnival, was bitter-sweet in 1926 when he nostalgically recalled this day as the happiest national holiday he had ever experienced.

The Bolshevik leaders possessed a strong consciousness of the power of symbols. It is too facile simply to argue that as cynical power-mongers they perceived at once the uses of propaganda and manipulation. They were underground revolutionaries in a land of peasants—thus painfully aware of the problems of communication between leaders and masses and determined to make a fresh start in the matter of symbols, seal, flag, and anthem. Their first symbol, approved April 19, 1918, was the breast badge of the Red Army: a crossed hammer and plough inside a red star (designer unknown). The interior motifs celebrated the alliance of workers and peasants who had allegedly made the Revolution and were now defending it together. The star had no prehistory in the Russian radical tradition. It might have been inspired by Bogdanov's *Red Star*. A contemporary flysheet, couched in fairy-tale language, interpreted the star as the Light of Truth *(pravda*, the people's truth and justice), purloined by the black and evil *krivda*—creature of darkness and enemy of the people. The Red Army man, it explained, was the hero in the battle to win back *pravda* for the people. The resonance of "red star" thus shifted from a rational utopia to a religious-mythic tale of good and evil. This star—devoid of its inner motifs—migrated to the new flag in 1918, to the Kremlin walls, to hundreds of posters and books covers, and to its later central place as the emblem of the Soviet military and of communist movements rising into ascendence. The red star modulated its vocality over the years, designating in various contexts light, power, redness, and a locus of perfection.[12]

The search for a new seal began at once. In the meantime the authorities were forced to use the repugnant tamed eagle in order to curb counterfeiting. Lenin and Lunacharsky opened a contest to artists and designers. It produced a dazzling variety of entries and a wide assortment of curiosities: castles and cornucopias from armorial traditions, crossed axes, zig-zags, triangles, and even exclamation points; motifs from traditional graphics, from Art Nouveau, and from all kinds of ultramodernism. One designer proposed the old eagle, plucked, stripped of regalia, adorned with red stars, wearing a Red Army cap on his head, clutching a stick and stone in his claws.[13]

The jury of artists and officials of Lunacharsky's Commissariat were not interested in comic, abstract, or provocative motifs for the national emblem and seal. The most acceptable entry, designed by an unknown Petrograd artist in early March, contained a crossed hammer and sickle, a wreath of grain, a rising sun, and a sword rising from below. The first known use of crossed hammer and sickle in the Revolution was reported in Saratov some time in 1917. Another contest entry by Chekhonin had a peasant woman holding a sickle against a rustic background beside a male worker with a hammer against a factory background. Independent of these, the Moscow artist Kamzolkin used hammer and sickle crossed in a May Day poster. In Russian traditional armorial art one can find crossed sickles, crossed industrial hammers, and sometimes both as familiar signs of countryside and city respectively. The hammer, often with an anvil, was also widely used in the imagery of nineteenth century European labor and socialist movements. The hammer and sickle was a natural combination to celebrate the Bolshevik belief in the October Revolution as the product of the unified energies and aspirations of workers and peasants. A side effect of Chekhonin's much-copied poster idea which set male-hammer-city against female-sickle-country was subliminally to link women with nurturing and passivity of the rural order and to link men with building, action, and power.[14]

The sword in the winning entry signified no more than the Russian soldier who constituted the third element of the popular trinity of revolution. But Lenin, in an astonishingly persistent and adamant manner, objected to its agressive appearance at a moment when he wished to project the infant Soviet Republic as a peacemaking and peaceloving state (this was right after the Treaty of Brest-Litovsk). "This is not our emblem," he said, "and war is not our policy." A controversy broke out that lasted two months— though its precise issues are not known—with some members of the jury actually suggesting a party conference to decide the matter. Lenin's opinion prevailed. The sword was removed and the sculptor N. A. Andreev embellished the original sketch (not extant) in Lenin's presence, thickening the sheaf of wheat and adding some Grecian designs. The resulting seal was a multivocal ensemble of symbols: the newly arranged but central motif of hammer and sickle suggesting a social alliance of toilers; an international component—the slogan "Proletarians of All Countries, Unite!"; and a reassuring frame of rising sun (the promise of a new day), a wheatsheaf for prosperity, and a classical scroll. Variants appeared in the early months. One of them, the cover of the first constitution of the R.S.F.S.R. in July 1918, contained the antique fasces (in the form of the Third French Republic's medieval fransiques) crossed behind the emblem, a device that was to be used by the emerging fascist movement in Italy (and was then dropped by the Soviets; see Fig. 15). In August 1918, all other seals and emblems were forbidden, and this became the national emblem.[15]

On the Soviet flag, there was apparently no debate. Flags, pennants, and banners of the old regime, including the national tricolor of red, white, and blue and the Romanov family banner, were outlawed. The first Soviet flag issued to foreign legations in 1917 by the new state was a simple red field with the letters R.S.F.S.R. on the canton. In the summer of 1918 a new flag was prepared: the red banner, adorned at the canton with the hammer and sickle from the Soviet emblem surmounted by the red star of the Army. Thus the red flag, which had long ago fluttered from a peasant cart in Kandeevka as a sign of defiance, which had streamed through the cities in 1905 and 1917, and which had a broad following in the European labor movement all through the nineteenth century, for the first time became the central symbol of a state. The redness of the star and the flag not only linked the Russian Revolution to the century-old traditions of the European labor movement, but also lent itself to etymological linking in Russian of *krasnyi* (red) with *krasivyi* (beautiful) and to the new "charismatic center" of Soviet power—Red Square.[16]

The "Internationale" on the other hand had to struggle to become the Soviet anthem. Its popular rival, the "Workers' Marseillaise" was poly-resonant in 1917: it dominated street demonstrations of workers and soldiers; it was hated by the right; but the Provisional Government heard it partly as an invocation of the French Republic, its ally. Lenin, because of this ambiguity, preferred the "Internationale," a specifically socialist song. But this song was not yet widely known in Russian labor circles. Only the band from Kronstadt had played it at the Burial of the Martyrs in 1917. When Lenin arrived in Petrograd in April, he was greeted at both major stops by the "Workers' Marseillaise." When this was played at the Finland Station, he asked for the "Internationale," and all through 1917 the Bolshevik press urged workers to learn it. When they came to power, the Bolsheviks made it their State Hymn. In the summer of 1918, while the Spasskaya Tower in the Kremlin was being repaired from the damage in the October fighting, a mechanic reset the bells to replace "God Save the Tsar" with the new hymn and the liturgical song "Kol Slaven" with "You Fell Victim"—both to be played twice a day and very loud—a musical element of the "talking city" that Lenin was now planning. These two songs—one of triumph, one of sorrow—became standards in the revolutionary repertoire. The former proved to be eminently singable, having been musically "Russianized" in 1907 by replacing the French 2/2 march tempo with the majestic 4/4 maestoso to give it solemnity.[17]

Alphabet and calendar reform were accelerated rather than invented by the Bolsheviks. The former had been accomplished by the previous regime and its simplifying of the Cyrillic alphabet made the mottoes which accompanied all festivals somewhat more legible. The new calendar was decreed in January 4, 1918 making the upcoming February 1 coincide with the Western date. Practicality was the first cause: it was suggested by the foreign minister. But it had anti-religious overtones as well and was advertised as bringing Russia "into line with most civilized peoples." It made the Orthodox Church seem to be always two weeks behind the rest of the "world." The decree removed church holidays with dynastic associations from the register, allowed some to remain, and designated Sundays and Soviet festivals as rest days.[18]

The rapid assembling of a symbolic face and the attention that rulers of the state devoted to this matter (especially compared to their immediate predecessors) reveal a key feature of Bolshevism: its insistence on unambiguous images, its quest for novelty, and its willingness to undergird the novelty with the familiar but unconflicting motifs of old traditions. Part of this was perhaps symbolic overcompensation, graphic, sonic, and gestural counterparts to the insistent rhetoric of the revolutionary intelligentsia designed to persuade the world (and themselves) that they were indeed in power and would stay there. But it was also another stage in the history of the intelligentsia's longing for cultural unity among all Russians by way of culture fashioned at the top and made available to the masses for their moral edification which was now couched in terms of political education. In the prewar years, German Social Democratic leaders had been distressed by the practice of workers singing socialist songs set to tunes of dubious or "bourgeois" origin wherein "the musical tones sent out contrary signals."[19] This attitude, illustrated in Lenin's feelings about the "Workers' Marseillaise," presaged the role of the revolutionary state in officiating over the experimental world that was now opening up.

## Moscow: Talking City

The anniversary celebration in November 1918 of the October Revolution contrasted sharply with May Day in Petrograd. The political frame was of course far more grim. But certain changes in Bolshevik ritual style, independent of the crisis, began to assert themselves visibly: greater planning and control, a sacred center as the target for all movement, a charismatic living symbol (Lenin), and a reinforcing iconography of monuments to the heroes of the past. Together, these elements helped to create the myth of revolutionary prehistory and a religious aura that was both less conscious in its articulation than the "immortality" cult of Lunacharsky and at the same time heavier and more durable. At its center was Lenin's "monumental plan of propaganda." This artistic-political scheme is crucial to understanding the further growth of Soviet ritual—and much else besides. It has been called "utopian" both in the trivial sense of the word (impractical) and because of its original inspiration, Tommaso Campanella's *City of the Sun*. But its true relation to the utopian traditions of Russia may be seen in its underlying vision and the uses to which it was put then and later.

Campanella seems an unlikely spark to Lenin's architectural imagination. "Prometheus in a Naples dungeon," as the Manuels have called him, he was a fanatical seventeenth century Catholic, heretical, religio-political rebel of great complexity, whose ultimate vision was a Papal world-state. But his 1602 utopia, *City of the Sun,* was an ideal city state which turned religion into science and the urban landscape into a museum and outdoor school—both of these ideas appealing mightily to the schoolmaster in Lenin. Campanella's model city had seven concentric walls, adorned on both sides with the rules and laws of the major sciences, alternating with statues of dead heroes in the realm of knowledge, religion, and war. Gorky had brought this book to the attention of Lenin and Lunacharsky before the revolution—during the Capri years. Two Russian translations appeared in 1918.[20]

Lenin was determined to build on Campanella. He told Lunacharsky that he wanted cities decorated with plaques and blocks of stone, inscribed with passages containing the essential principles of Marxism as well as busts, statues, or bas-reliefs of great figures in the history of socialism, revolution, and culture. These would replace the hateful statues that were to be taken down, but there were to be many more of them.

Lenin wanted—in a still illiterate society—cities that talked: engraved solemnities on the walls and unveiling speeches for the new statues placed at strategic places, constant reminders for the pupils of his gigantic new revolutionary school.[21]

Between 1918 and 1921 about 50–60 such monuments were erected, mostly in Moscow, as well as dozens of inscriptions. The list of figures to be honored, after much discussion, included about twenty each of Russian and European radical thinkers and activists and a smaller number of Russian and European artistic and cultural figures. The latter group was eclectic and arbitrary—clearly the fruit of bargaining. The revolutionary figures, however, were subjected to political judgment. The following list will give an immediate sense of the themes and the balance in this, the first public lesson in the pre-history of the Russian Revolution given by the Bolsheviks:[22]

| RUSSIANS | | EUROPEANS | |
|---|---|---|---|
| Bolotnikov | Chernyshevsky | Spartacus | Owen |
| Razin | Dobrolyubov | Gracchus | St. Simon |
| Novikov | Karakozov | Brutus | Garibaldi |
| Radishchev | Lavrov | Voltaire | Blanqui |
| Ryleev | Mikhailovsky | Rousseau | Marx |
| Pestel | Perovskaya | Danton | Engels |
| Herzen | Zhelyabov | Marat | Lassalle |
| Belinsky | Khalturin | Babeuf | Jaurès |
| Bakunin | Kalyaev | Fourier | Luxemburg |
| Shevchenko | Plekhanov | | Liebknecht |
| | Baumann | | |

This display of history-by-monument was a reasonable rendition of the accepted intelligentsia tradition of the Russian revolutionary movement: Radishchev, the Decembrists, the thinkers of the 1840s and the 1860s, and the Populists—including even an assassin from a rival party—Sergei Kalyaev. Missing from the Populists were the still living Morozov, Kropotkin, Figner, Zasulich, Breshkovskaya, Natanson, and Chaikovsky—all neutral or anti-Bolshevik. Plekhanov (a former Populist) was the only Russian Marxist, and also a bitter enemy of the October Revolution. Baumann was the star martyr of the labor movement; he was joined by Volodarsky and Uritsky, murdered in 1918. A fairly high number of regicides, would-be regicides, and assassins were honored by monuments (Ryleev, Pestel, Karakozov, Khalturin, Zhelyabov, Perovskaya, and Kalyaev—all hanged by the autocracy), a signal perhaps that the recent execution of the Tsar and his family was an act imbedded in the revolutionary tradition. The inclusion of the traditional rebels Bolotnikov and Razin joined the Cossack-peasant rebellions of early modern times to the intelligentsia-radical revolt of the nineteenth century in a schema of continuous popular revolution. This scenario was enriched by including an almost equal number of European rebels and socialists. The founding fathers of Marxism were given a special place, but included were rebels of antiquity and of 1789, the "utopian" forerunners of Marx and Engels, and a selection of "internationalist" Marxists such as Jaurès, Luxemburg, and Liebknecht (the latter two after their martyrdom in 1919).

The experiment was not an artistic success. Some revolutionaries looked askance at the whole idea. Bogdanov in *Red Star* had disallowed monuments to people—dead or alive—in his communist utopia on Mars. Avant-gardists such as Vladimir Tatlin and Punin thought heroic statuary undignified and unsuitable to a revolutionary state. The practical difficulties were prodigious. Materials, talent, and labor were in short supply and this caused the delays that so enraged Lenin. The project yielded only temporary busts and figures, poorly executed in plaster or cement. Some were never even unveiled, others crumbled under the elements or were withdrawn as substandard. At least two— Robespierre and Volodarsky—were dynamited by unknown persons. By 1920–21 the unveilings ceased and the experiment was abandoned, incidentally causing Soviet sculpture to decline through the twenties until revived in quite another style under Stalin.[23]

Lenin was not much perturbed by the rapid erosion of the statues. He knew they were temporary. But he badly wanted them up—and fast, perhaps by May Day. When this failed, he became very angry and shrill in his complaints to Lunacharsky and the sculptor N. D. Vinogradov, one of sixty-five working on the project. His angriest moment came at a time of crushing political crisis: the Socialist Revolutionary rebellion in Moscow and the rising of the Czech legions in Siberia—a major episode in the onset of Civil War. How is one to explain this passion for made-to-order monuments of stone? It was, I believe, Lenin's overpowering desire to legitimize the Revolution historically and to communicate rapidly with the urban masses. The teacher in him was straining for expression, and the tone of his political pedagogy was emphatically solemn and pious. He wanted busts and statues that were ''appropriate and accessible to the people'' and was thus angered by the cute, the humorous, and the esthetically trendy productions of some Cubists and abstractionists—particularly the later figure of Bakunin in a Cubo-Futurist style by Boris Korolëv. But neither did he want the sinuous and heroized monumentality that was found on posters and that would mark the Stalinist style in the 1930s. He wanted to show life-like figures of men and women of his own intelligentsia tradition who had talked and acted and written. Lenin may have known that many people who, having envisaged him physically as a muscular giant of revolution, were then puzzled by his ''bourgeois'' stature and then enthralled at last by the power of his thought and speech.[24]

Lenin's monumental propaganda scheme should be read only partly as graphic heroization and the birth of cultic idols. His central compulsion—it was exactly that—was to get out the word. The monuments, he said, should be ''professors' podiums of the street from which fresh words and rousing thoughts and notions must soar straight to the people.'' His Campanellan city was to possess the artifacts of a museum, the teachers of a school, and the reverent milieu of a church. Children were to be taken round the city and told of the exploits and the life meaning of the statues' subjects, relating these stories to the present revolution. Lunacharsky thought that every Sunday should be devoted to an unveiling and an evening celebration of the subject's life. In 1919, he composed the text to the monument for the martyrs of the February Revolution on the Field of Mars—another conflation of February and October. The stone slabs and plaques with text seemed as important to Lenin as the personal monuments. He selected some texts himself and the authorities held a contest to generate more. Lenin's relative indifference to outer form was strikingly illustrated when he was asked what to do with the Romanov Tricentennial Obelisk outside the Kremlin (erected in 1913). His response was to keep the obelisk, erase the tsarist inscription, and replace it with the names More, Campanella, Winstanley, Fourier, and Chernyshevsky.[25]

The November 7 celebrations of 1918 in the new capital illustrate the intrusion of the Lenin style of ritual into the earlier, more spontaneous expressions. The planners—professional revolutionaries turned bureacrats—were asked by the Moscow Committee of the Party to stress the "inner," "intellectual" side (meaning political) over the "external" in the coming festivities. The tsarist regime had almost always projected its image and mystique graphically—in contrast to the intelligentsia who dealt in words and ideas. The Bolsheviks were not ready to adopt an exclusively "subrational" mode of communication. Speech filled the air at almost every point in the three days of celebration. Set texts and explanatory lessons surrounded the unveiling of the revolutionary statues and monuments in a way that would have been unthinkable (and perhaps useless) in tsarist days. But the art of carnival was not rejected—only toned down. Garlands, placards, and red bunting abounded, the red being even more effective against the cold whitened city of early winter in Moscow than it had been in May when it had to compete with colorful flowers and dress. Hunters' Row in the center of town was decked out by avant-garde artists to look like a "wonderland red city," colorful and festive in the extreme and a delight to the eye of witnesses. But the early extravagances of the artistic left were lost in the forest of mass-produced discs emblazoned with the new hammer and sickle. A typical Leninist touch was the order by the planning committee to preserve all the decorative artifacts after the ceremonies as the basic collection of a new Museum of the October Revolution.[26]

The official ceremonies on Red Square and the march past the Kremlin were the main spectacles of the anniversary day, and Lenin was the visible focus of it all. When he walked, always heading a column of government colleagues, the deference to him was palpable. His first act was the unveiling of a statue to Marx and Engels in Revolution Square beside the Bolshoi Theater. His brief speech established, for those who did not yet know it, these two Germans as the ideological and spiritual forefathers of the Russian Revolution. Awaiting his return at the Senate Tower of the Kremlin were assembled delegates of various kinds, military units, foreign communists, a band, a huge chorus from Proletcult studios, and—in one account—great excitement and exultation in the crowd. The second act was the solemn unveiling of a big memorial plaque by Sergei Konenkov symbolic of Liberty and commemorating the fallen martyrs of the Revolution. The revolutionary funeral hymn "You Fell Victim"—by now rich in associative memories—was played. Then, amid triumphant cheers, Lenin mounted the tribune to honor "those who fell in the struggle for peace and the brotherhood of all people." His speech was filled with national pride, international solidarity, emotion, hope, and messianism.[27] As the march past began, the poet Sergei Esenin declaimed solemn verses:

> Sleep, dear brothers, sleep.
> Past you march the people's hosts
> Toward a universal dawn.

The march itself—rolling on for hours before the eyes of Lenin—was a parade, a procession, and a demonstration. On display were the corporate elements of revolutionary society in gild costumes with models of their work tools and products, Committees of the Poor, unions, Futurist floats that "dazzled the eye."[28] Proletcult shows, an allegorical tableau from Red Presnya district, the martyred neighborhood of the 1905 Revolution, showing a chained peasant worker about to be liberated, units of school children, cavalry, cannons, folk music ensembles, and ethnic minorities in full costume filed past the Kremlin and then returned to assembly points for the unveiling of statues in all the main squares.

The ancillary festivities were extremely elaborate. Twenty one theaters were taken over for the various performances between November 6 and 8, and blocks of tickets were assigned to officials, workers, and children of the poor. Musicians were virtually drafted to perform all over town—in concert halls, Proletcult clubs, theaters, and union headquarters, even in the premises of the political police. Among the items performed were the Brutus monologue (again invoking the theme of a just regicide), and the verses of Emile Verhaeren (a favorite of Lunacharsky) and of Gastev (a hero of the Proletcult). Lenin made token appearances and short speeches at many of these events. The main performance of the three day festival was Beethoven's *Fidelio* (renamed *Liberation*)— characteristic of the traditionalism that dominated the operatic stage all through the Civil War.[29] That night, at eleven designated points around Moscow, straw figures of the Entente leaders—Wilson, Clemençeau, and Lloyd George—and those of Russian class foes (kulaks, landowners, barons, and generals) were made to burn for forty minutes, after which fireworks were set off and the new Soviet emblems were raised aloft.[30]

These ceremonies and celebrations accomplished what Petrograd was never able to do: make Moscow the sacred center of the Russian Revolution and identify Lenin clearly as its central charismatic figure. Recently the victim of an attempted assassination, Lenin had recovered to find himself the object of adulation and rejoicing over his survival. The November 7 celebration was an important landmark in the emergence of the cult of Lenin. The Kremlin was the point of convergence of all the processions—the point, in Christian ritual, where man, earth, universe, and God meet; and it resembles the central point of the city from which, in some utopias, radiated all streets, roads, energy, and power. Russian power seemed to have returned at last to its home in the heartland whence it had been artificially removed for two centuries by Peter the Great. Lenin, though a partly Westernized intelligent who had lived abroad many years and was surrounded by Letts, Georgians, Jews, and Poles (as well as Russians) nevertheless seemed to project a Russian persona. What Trotsky later called "the national in Lenin" and what others have seen as the peasant in Lenin harmonized well with the Kremlin Towers, the mood of national regeneration, and the Russianness of the moment. The very cultural geography of the city and the traditional holdovers in the syncretic ritual forms seemed to reinforce the national dimensions of the celebrations, and thus to give legitimation to the regime that occupied the territory of the Kremlin and arranged the festivities.[31]

The utopia of release and reversal which carnival plays at was overlaid by Lenin's utopia of order, historical reverence, and political pedagogy. Krupskaya claimed later that this was the happiest day of Lenin's life, an interesting contrast to Lunacharsky's nostalgia over the previous May Day. Lenin in 1918 was probably unaware of the emerging resonance of Moscow as the Russian center of the Revolution, the eccleciastical and spiritual associations of the Kremlin area, and the growing perception of himself as the personification of the new order. Thus November 7 was a complex blend of carnival, monument, rhetoric, and sacrality which together offered a picture of continuity and change, of mystery and majesty. The irony was that Lunacharsky in Petrograd, who consciously invoked religious idioms and motifs, could not do for that eminently secular-looking city what Lenin and the festival planners did for Moscow without even trying.[32]

## Petrograd: Theater City

The Petrograd festival resembled that of Moscow, but Petrograd had its own local style and its leaders wished to stress that style for reasons of prestige. The political boss of the old capital, Grigory Zinoviev, acted the satrap in his new realm variously known as the Northern Commune or Petrocommune—Petrograd and a huge hinterland. He wanted his city to be redesignated the capital of Soviet Russia after the crisis of the German threat had passed. His house organ, *Red Petrograd,* constantly promoted the special virtues of the city—its maritime flavor, its "historical stones," its role as cradle of three revolutions, its leading proletarian forces. Zinoviev, with the help of Lunacharsky and the artists, displayed the full panoply of Petrograd's physical beauty and its ceremonial powers in the early years. Moscow remained the "sacred center" of Soviet power, but the leaders of Petrograd aspired at least to make it the Revolution's festive center. The distinctive features of its festival style were experimental urban decor, street theater and carnival, and mass spectacle.[33]

The decor for November 7 in Petrograd was brilliant, having been executed by major artists such as Mstislav Dobuzhinsky, Natan Altman, K. S. Petrov-Vodkin, and Boris Kustodiev. Dobuzhinsky retained the classical beauties of Zakharin's Admiralty, augmenting its thematic with maritime pennants, flaglets, and anchors, and hiding the ugly structures that had been erected in the 1880s along the Neva River. Altman, on the other hand, sought to destroy utterly the monumentality of autocratic architecture in Palace Square by obscuring the vast facade of the Winter Palace, the Victory Column, and the chariot atop the Headquarters Arch behind modernist designs. The result was festive richness but also a diminution of Petrograd's appearance as a center of unambiguous power. The eclecticism and cosmopolitanism of the decor stood in vivid contrast to the national mystique that dominated the Kremlin in Moscow. The same held true of the march: it wended its way from Smolny to the Winter Palace and then to Mars Field as if undecided about where the actual "center" of the city was (a question frequently asked by modern visitors). This city had for a long time lacked the unambiguous image of Russia's national capital—for a variety of reasons. The contrast in the two November ceremonies was another event in the long history of the cultural duel between the two cities since 1714. Even after the avant-garde ornament was toned down, and the marchers chose the Winter Palace as the permanent convergence point, this ambiguity did not disappear.[34]

Lenin's iconic festival of statues was not as popular or as effective in Petrograd as in Moscow—even in 1918, in spite of Lunacharsky's endorsement of it and of the rhetoric that went with it. Petrograd had been a great center of Bolshevik orators in 1917–18—Trotsky, Zinoviev, Volodarsky, Kollontai, Lunacharsky—but in the Civil War, the city seemed more inclined to show than to tell. The blossoming of street theater was a sign of this. It was a revival of traditional folk festival with mobile units presenting carnival shows and acts all over the city. A specialist on adult education suggested the street was a natural school and theater for revolutionary people. His pedagogy was not Campanellan but carnivalesque—like that of the Futurists. He wanted to make the streets into a joyful and comradely arena for processions, outdoor movies and museums, concerts and choral performances in order to satisfy the demands of the masses and to evoke their "collective creativity." Street theater became big in the holidays of 1919 with "flying troupes" on platforms pulled by streetcars and trucks, carnival acts and circus shows at designated stops with clowns, skits, and songs lasting about 15–30 minutes. But these shows were overshadowed in 1920 by the mass spectacles of revolutionary myth.[35]

The urban mass spectacle—a single huge performance outdoors with thousands of spectators—grew out of grassroots experimentation in Red Army and Proletcult theater workshops in 1919. On March 12, in the Iron Hall of the People's House in Petrograd, a Red Army theater group put on a version of the "The Fall of the Autocracy," one of the first large-scale historical pageants of the revolution. On red and white platforms at either end of the hall, actor-soldiers representing the autocracy and the Revolution, spoke lines taken from the press, held stylized meetings, sang, and simulated combat, the soldiers playing themselves as heroes and the villains as buffoons. So striking was the effect that it was repeated 250 times in barracks, camps, and squares in and around Petrograd in the next seven months—surely one of the most successful and spontaneous of all revolutionary theatrical events. The first outdoor spectacle in this genre was the Theater and Drama Workshop presentation on May Day 1919 of "The Third International," a staging of slogans about revolution, the end of tyrants, the burial of martyrs, and a world of peace.[36]

In the course of events, theater professionals, already active in civic festivals since the February Revolution, began to take command of this emerging genre. The most famous of these was the Bolshevik actress Mariya Andreeva, former artist at the Moscow Art Theater, wife of Gorky, and friend of Lunacharsky. Another actor, Alexander Mgebrov, moved easily from a prewar theater career, through staging the Provisional Government's Liberty Bond celebrations in 1917, to Proletcult theater, into the grand stagings of Petrograd. None of these people were flaming iconoclasts: Adrian Piotrovsky, S. E. Radlov, and N. N. Evreinov, for example, were trained classicists from scholarly families. Dmitry Tiomkin (later a Hollywood composer) was trained as a classical musician, recently the pupil of Scriabin. Yet they all lent their talents, skills, and fantasy to the task of organizing the masses in performances of a Wagnerian dimension, total works of art embracing many arts, huge numbers of spectators and performers, and ample outdoor space. Spectacle and show of this sort had precedents in Russia, especially during the last reign of the Old Regime. The organizers drew on this and also on foreign notions of civic theater, including those of Wagner and Romain Rolland. All of this was reshaped by the euphoric atmosphere of a revolutionary city in the midst of war, by the means given to the organizers by the new rulers, including the casting of thousands in the giant productions. The ultimate effect was one of state and intelligentsia leading the masses, including and especially the vast audiences, in a kinesthetic exercise of revolution, a massive performance of revolutionary values and myths that were to infuse the new society-in-the-making.[37]

On May Day, 1920 was mounted the first of four mass spectacles that would enliven the city in that year: "The Mystery of Liberated Labor." It was planned and directed by professional artists and theater people. The locale was the spit of land in front of the former Stock Exchange, a huge semicircular plaza overlooking the great fork of the Neva River. On a dais in front of the Exchange were seen carousing emperors, mandarins, planters, and capitalists in an orgy of greed and dancing to cheap Gypsy music and the can-can—stock examples of musical decadence. A huge gate of gold guarded a kingdom of brotherhood and equality—the forbidden land of traditional myths and fairy-tales. Outside toiled the wretched of the earth, shackled and whipped and groaning to the strains of Chopin's "Funeral March." Waves of rebels—Spartacus, Stenka Razin, the sansculottes—assaulted the gates of freedom but were crushed. Then in the East appeared a red star heralding the liberation of mankind. The gates were stormed, the tyrants and idlers scattered, and the Kingdom of Socialism revealed in the form of a rising sun, a red star, a tree of liberty around which the victors reveled, red banners, and a figure of Liberated Labor in front of which the soldiers exchanged their weapons for the implements of peace. In the finale, searchlights from ships on the river shone onto the stage, shots boomed from the nearby fortress, sirens wailed, and four large bands played the "Internationale." The audience seemed to merge with the performers as they crowded the stage and sang the anthem of revolution. Four thousand actors, soldiers, and workers appeared in the cast, and 35,000 spectators watched it.[38]

"Liberated Labor" was the first large-scale display of revolutionary myth to a mass audience. Its high level of abstraction set it off from the rather concrete Red Army productions. Both the masses and the rulers in the play are drawn from all peoples and all epochs. The historical process predominates, and the promised land of utopia is an array of stylized symbols. Unlike in the monumental propaganda of Lenin, the Russian Revolutionary tradition is almost absent. No scenes of Decembrists, no heroic Populists going to their deaths, no mock execution of the Petrashevsky Circle—all of which offer rich material for pageantry and retrospective pathos. On the other hand, the mimetic language of the show was direct and simple. Rich and poor are contrasted visually and audially, with the former displaying utter heartlessness to the latter amid gross flourishes of decadence. The forbidden space captured at the end by the masses added the vital element of mystery and myth.[39] Spartacus, Razin, and the sansculottes were suitable symbols of revolt for workers, peasants, and intelligentsia respectively. And the entire production breathed emotionalism—the mysterious setting, the aura of suspense, the kinetic melodrama, the merciless caricatures of evil men and women, the music and lights, the density of the mass audience were all deployed to generate visceral reaction and to project a historical myth in a union of arts, technology, urban space, and festive occasion.

The second and third Petrograd mass spectacles were held in the summer of 1920. At that moment, the Soviet Republic had passed the biggest crises in the Civil War, but there were still foreign troops on its soil and it was at war with Poland. The two spectacles reflected this by a shift from eternal myths into a theatricalization of immediate political problems. The first, "The Blockade of Russia," was held on June 20 on the summer resort island of Kammeny Ostrov north of the Petrograd Quarter, a huge parkland intersected by rivers. It had been renamed the Island of Rest. This island was staged as a blockaded Russia, assaulted by the Entente, invaded by the Poles, and rescued by the Red Army. There was no text but an abundance of buffoonery, mime, landscaped sets, circus elements, and the usual array of fireworks, light, and sound.

Two themes deserve comment. One was treating the enemy as a hollow clown. The British foreign secretary Lord Curzon was a classic buffoon who emitted loud but empty threats and then fell into the water and drowned (like the effigies in traditional Russian festivals) as his armored car of paper flew into pieces. Curzon a few years later would frighten Soviet officials in the Afghan crisis and then become a minor symbol in Soviet Russia as the man with the "ultimatum" who had to be answered and defied. The "Polish Pan" with an outsized sabre was acted by an acrobatic clown, following the Russian operatic tradition which portrayed Polish lords as foolish, pompous, and slightly effete. The other theme was a clever combination of "Petersburg as a Window to the

West'' and the still vivid Bolshevik dream of worldwide revolution. In the climax of the action, gaily decorated boats bearing "foreign" flags and peoples sailed from the far shores to join Russia in her moment of deliverance.[40]

A similar show was presented to Petrograders and visiting delegates to the Second Congress of the Communist International (founded a year earlier) on the plaza near the Stock Exchange—replicated as beleaguered Soviet Russia. It was called "Toward the Worldwide Commune" (see Fig. 16) and directed by Andreeva and two seasoned festival designers Radlov and Piotrovsky. Lenin was present at this performance that lasted from 1 to 4 a.m. in the few hours of faint light that passes for night during northern summers. The usual pyramid of social exploitation appeared, this time the privileged dancing to Strauss waltzes. The most vivid scene in the cycle of revolt and repression was the 1871 execution of the Paris Communards—a classic, almost mythic, act of counter-revolutionary brutality—and the spiriting away of the red banner for future revolutions. The leaders of the socialist or Second International were depicted as bookish intellectuals who had no interest in real revolution, a timely barb aimed at Karl Kautsky and company. In the finale, the October Revolution in Russia occurs, and the Communist International is ushered in to the accompaniment of fireworks and thousands of red stars illuminated above the audience who sang the "Internationale." Again the young republic is saved from marauding reactionaries by military units deployed around the Neva and on the bridges, thus combining a military manoeuvre with a theatrical spectacle.[41]

The last great mass spectacle of the Civil War period was "The Storming of the Winter Palace" performed on Palace Square, with 6,000 performers—actors, theater students, soldiers, and workers—on November 7, 1920. It began with the playing of Henry Litolphe's *Robespierre Overture*. To the left of the audience was a platform containing dummies of Kerensky and his ministers, with foolishly bobbing heads nodding to the discordant sounds of the French "Marseillaise" and defended by the Women's Batallion. To the right, across a long catwalk, was the platform of the Red Guards who shouted threats and sang revolutionary songs. From its midst rose the gradually louder cadences of the "Internationale" engaged in a musical duel with the faltering "Marseillaise"—a device probably borrowed from Chaikovsky's triumphal overture on the year 1812. As the rival hymn is drowned out, the palace is stormed, the audience joining the attack and melting into the performance.[42]

The Petrograd theater city was a spectacular moment in revolutionary history—analogous in some ways to Paris in the 1790s. But the human limitations in hearing, sight, and organization eventually asserted themselves. The numbers of performers and spectators jumped with each successive show, with as many as 6,000 at the first and 45,000 at the second.[43] The military provided not only the original idea and much of the cast for these productions but also the organizational model: actors were divided into platoons whose leaders were rehearsed by directors according to a detailed score or battle plan and deployed by the use of military signals and field telephones. The result was an ingenious form or urban choreography, but also a distinct division of audience and performers, a massive teacher-pupil format, and a consequent suspension of movement and self-directed activity by the citizens, thus deleting much of the festive from the festival. When the Civil War ended in 1921, mobilized artists and Red Army troops were no longer available in large numbers and the genre came to an end.[44]

What did the spectators think of all this? The sources are contradictory. According to a contemporary, the masses were "electrified" by the finale of "Liberated Labor." A Swedish worker who witnessed it said: "Here a person can better understand socialism in his heart in an hour than he can at home in his head after reading a whole library." From fragments such as this, Soviet commentators argue that an orgiastic moment of "emotional infection" overcame the audiences. Fueloep-Miller, hardly a sympathetic critic, believed that Russians were enthralled by revolutionary theater and spectacles. Yet Emma Goldman thought the "Storming of the Winter Palace" flat and badly done and interpreted the silence of the vast throngs at "Liberation of Labor" as popular disappointment with the Revolution. Victor Serge, another anarchist working for the Bolsheviks, was soured by the thought that his comrades languished in prison while the Revolution was celebrating freedom and brotherhood. Yet, against these sincere observations must be thrown the fact of the extraordinary and ever-growing turnouts for the mass spectacles.[45]

The revolutionary myth presented by these spectacles projected the heroism, sacrifice, courage and nobility of those who made and prepared the Revolution. At the end of a vale of tears lay the forbidden space of utopia conquered at last by the heroes. The magnification of good and evil, aside from its dramatic power, was also the moral justification for the turbulence and violence of the struggle—to set the stage for the absolution of the victors without a trace of nuance or ambiguity. Embedded in this myth was the first text in the genealogy of the Russian Revolution—subsequently elaborated in the historiography of the 1920s. It was a startling picture which obliterated the old regime's virtues, heroes, and values and substituted a stark two-line family tree: a Russian line of peasant rebellion, intellectual radicalism, Populism, the first storm of 1905, War, and the revolutionary year 1917—all seeming to point inexorably toward October; and a European line of slave revolts, the French Revolution, the Paris Commune, and three generations of the socialist family—the grandparents (the utopian socialists), the parents (Marx and Engels), and the children (the Bolsheviks). This mythic history announced Russian solidarity with the world proletariat and invited it to join its "history" to that of a victorious revolution.

The festival shows did not present a snapshot of the future but rather the path to it. As historical fiction it took its readers into utopia and showed them how they got there. Together the revolutionary myth unveiled in the monumental shows of 1918 and theatricalized in the Petrograd spectacles of 1919–20 constituted a fanciful text that wove cultural, psychological, and historical episodes and dramas far removed in time and space from October 1917 into a mythic textbook. Utopian ritual and festival offered a Mosaic glimpse into the Promised Land at the very moment of deliverance—with the promise that everyone would enter. Like most drama, it declined to show·clinical details of the heavens but rather provided the element of sheer suspense for an audience that was energized and euphoric about the nature of the new world about to be made, but in no doubt that this was now possible and indeed imminent. Revolutionary spectacle, emulating religious history and revelation, offered a train of martyrs and a row of messiahs—all marching toward the epiphany of October.[46]

## Ritual and Carnival

Lenin wrote that revolution was "a festival of the oppressed and the exploited." This quotation has often been invoked in modern times when describing carnivalesque dances and the spontaneous joy of liberation in the streets of recently revolutionized capitals. Revolution and festival are both moments of re-birth, freedom, the surge to a new life, boundlessness, euphoria, reversal, and the breakthrough into forbidden passages leading to utopia. In the 1960s, Herbert Marcuse's identification of carnival and revolution and the erasing of the line between barricade and dance floor, erotic play and heroism was very popular among the radicals of the Western world. But Marx himself did not equate revolution with the carnival. Though aware of the street euphoria all over Europe in the Spring of 1848, he associated revolution not with laughter but rather with tragedy— especially for the proletariat. For Lenin, revolution was an awakening of the masses after long slumber into consciousness and action in an arena where people learn—and learn fast. The "festival" element in revolution is the release of political-revolutionary energy that allows marvels of social creativity. For Lenin, refashioning a drastic new order in a land like Russia was serious business and hard work—not euphoric release, wild abandon, and anarchy. Not even for a day. The elements of humor in Bolshevism were dampened by its need to moralize, congratulate itself, teach, speechify, punish, and organize. One could laugh out the old, but one could not laugh in the new. This is true of all religions, all culture-building movements, and thus of all modern revolutions.[47]

Lunacharsky's vision of festival was more capacious and more concrete. He believed that it (and not the movies as Lenin once claimed) was the most important art form of the Revolution. His view of it was essentially religious; he quoted this passage from Robespierre with approval:

> Gather people together and you will improve them because when grouped together, people will aspire to like one another but can only like what they respect. Give this gathering a great moral and political theme—and love for all things worthy will grow together with pleasure in every heart because people will meet each other with pleasure.

As a Godbuilder, Lunacharsky believed that the balance of freedom and order could be achieved through a religious sense of community, periodically exhibited in public festival. His notion of popular self-awareness differed from Lenin's idea of "consciousness." The masses should disport themselves in public with procession, music, and song. Festival for Lunacharsky was "showing the people its own soul." This meant a definite role for "revolutionary cabaret"—the intimate side of the feast, with clowns and carnival, but without the explosive freedoms of Dionysius and Bacchus. Lunacharsky shared Lenin's view of the limits of "spontaneity." The popular mass "lacked its own peculiar instinctive obedience to a higher order and rhythm; it was impossible to expect more from it than joyous clamor and the colorful surging of festively dressed people." The "conscious" element—equivalent to Lenin's vanguard party—were the professionals and artists who provided organization and guidance from outside. From this aspect of the Bolshevik vision sprang the seeds of increasing control.[48]

The process of stiffening was erratic, full of cycles and revivals, complicated by crosscurrents in form as well as content. But a pattern is clearly perceptible of diminishing spontaneity and experiment in the 1920s. The major components of festival— decor, demonstration or march, and related ceremonies and spectacles—had been very fluid and dynamic in the aftermath of the February Revolution. But almost at once, they were taken in hand by authorities—Provisional Government, Soviet, later Bolshevik. Heavy duty (and often heavy-handed) ritual committees managed both the order and the meaning of the celebrations. Written scenarios, as in the French Revolution, were extremely elaborate. In the 1920s, time-motion or "Taylorist" studies were applied to parades and the calendar was strictly regularized. One can read for example a tediously detailed and mathematically charted and mapped analysis of the routes, time, and speed of columns for the eighth anniversary of the October Revolution in Leningrad. Mechanical media began to supplement the speakers at festival time with radio, film, and loudspeakers.[49] In plain terms, the utopian and mythic themes were reduced to the political campaign of the moment.

Artistic decor was the first to feel the stiffening. Futurists, Cubists, ultraleftists of all sorts, and Proletcultists had a relatively free hand in the first year or so of revolution. They aspired not to trim the urban topography but to remake it—at least for the day of festival. Thus the painting of trees, the edificial camouflages, the Cubist projections of every sort, the funny statues, and the mixed symbols. During the revolution, Dobuzhinsky produced a two-headed eagle with a hammer and sickle in its claws; in Saratov an artist adorned a revolutionary funeral tribune with Matisse-like red nude females on a black crepe background. Such things were toned down by the authorities and eventually banned altogether. Decor came to mean an abundance of red cloth, slogans on banners, the perennial red star (sometimes showered from aircraft), and the emblems of revolution. Solid looking bronze plaques with slogans began to replace the earlier linen signs; to a contemporary visitor, they seemed to be saying "we are here and here we will remain forever." The outdoor modern art show had become "parade day." In the 1920s, decor declined even further when workers replaced the artists as festival decorators and (after 1924) busts of Lenin began to proliferate in the cities. The last leftist Proletcults participated in the festivals in 1927.[50]

The marches and demonstrations also felt the heaviness of instrumentalism in the 1920s. Beginning in 1921, the military began leading off the major parades, thus signaling a certain heroic and moral hegemony of the armed forces over civilian society. Although the monument project fell into disuse, iconic representations of leaders began to sprout from the marchers with greater frequency, especially after 1924 with the onrush of the Lenin cult. On May Day 1924 these elements were combined in a vivid display of old-fashioned patriotism as tanks, troops, and guns filed past Lenin's tomb with a squadron of planes overhead. All branches of the service were on hand, including the political police. These were followed by workers' and other organizations, with bands and drummers, each unit bearing aloft banners inscribed with quotations from Lenin—a mobile version of Lenin's talking city.[51]

A major device in the festivals in the 1920s is what the Soviet art critic and festival historian Mazaev calls "political carnival." He believes that revolutionary ridicule is the same as carnival laughter. Indeed at the time, Soviet researchers were examining the power of what they called "the revolutionary laugh" as a weapon that debases a previously awesome object. The tradition of ritualized mockery of political foes—past or present—remains very much alive to this day. The old enemies—Kerensky, the White generals, rival party leaders of 1917—were long stock buffoons in circus, folk ensemble concerts, puppet theater, and other media. The foreign enemies were constantly updated—from the Entente statesmen, the "fascists" and the Social Democrats of the 1920s to the evil Uncle Sams of yesterday. The form of demolition changed from the traditional pagan burnings and drownings of the revolutionary period to the "mechanized" disposal of the 1920s when a mill was used for grinding up capitalists, giant scissors for cutting up speculators, a pan for frying a White Guard, and a hammer for smashing the bourgeoisie. One of the most famous posters of the time shows Lenin with a broom (a carnival motif) sweeping away the filth from the globe—king, priest, banker

*Living the Revolution*

(see Fig. 11). In the mid-1920s, festive ridicule was extended to include shirkers, hooligans, drunks, and substandard workers. Parades began to feature workers holding up graphs and production figures as visual promises to do better in the next quarter. The regime always decided on the targets of this shame and ridicule. But it was unthinkable to mount a carnivalesque demonstration of laughter at the leaders themselves. Since only designated enemies were fair game, Soviet "revolutionary laughter" was actually a panegyric ritual.[52]

True carnival demands freedom of the laugh. One can imagine what would have happened to demonstrators in pre–glasnost Soviet history who held aloft a demeaning effigy of Lenin. It might be funny to watch poor Lord Curzon explode, but it has no interior political bite. Mikhail Bakhtin's study of carnival shows that it is edged with risk and danger of social turmoil. It criticizes and mocks and it chooses its own target, for true carnival is of the people. It is in fact a festival of the people and not merely the political illumination of the oppressed in the class struggle. Carnival can flow into rebellion. Bacchus, Venus, Saturn—feasting, sex, and ironic reversal—are its gods. The world of laughter, writes Bakhtin, is "a completely different, nonofficial, extraecclesiastical and extrapolitical aspect of the world, of man, and of human relations"; it is a "second world and a second life outside officialdom." The official celebration of an "eternal truth," draped in regalia and arranged in ordered ranks, is solemn and thus alien to laughter.[53]

The muting of the carnival laugh in public ritual from 1917 to the end of the 1920s was gradual and never complete. It reflected the persistent pluralism of the social and cultural life of the 1920s, narrowing but still vibrant and tentative, uneasy but experimental. The no-nonsense and quasi-ascetic qualities in Bolshevism, of which the anti-Futurist frown on Lenin's brow is the physiognomical emblem, deepened; but it did not expunge the laughter until Stalin's rise to supremacy. Under him, "fun" would be separated physically and psychologically from the political culture altogether—for himself and for his people.

# 5

## Godless Religion

Lamarck and Darwin have killed God, finally and for all time so that He may never reappear after such blows. These great murderers deserve the gratitude of all mankind.

Vladimir Taneev, *Communist States of the Future*, 1879

The war against God in the Russian Revolution was a long and complicated one. In the end, the Bolsheviks won and they lost: like Jacob, they wrestled with Jehovah through the long night and broke their thighbone. As a culture-changing movement, throbbing with iconoclastic and utopian impulses, Bolshevism looked upon God as the most mighty of the authority symbols to be torn down and upon belief in God as a malady generated by the disease-ridden miasma of the Old Order, shaped by "feudalism," autocracy, and capitalism. The Bolsheviks upon assuming power in 1917 were therefore faced with the problem of "de-Baptism"—of converting religion believers into non-believers. But unlike their ancient predecessors of the tenth century, they came to the task almost unarmed, that is without religion. The question that beset many revolutionaries from the outset was whether or not a movement that possessed a fixed dogma but no elaborated ethic or ritual could command allegiance.

### Godkillers and Godbuilders

This dilemma predated the Revolution, going back at least to the Populists of the early 1870s who had to face the question of religious belief as they prepared to go out and preach to Christian peasants. Their responses varied: to denounce God altogether, to use religious imagery in socialist propaganda, to construct a socialist religion, or to abandon revolution and embrace religion. The first of these is the best known because of the anarchist Bakunin, who proclaimed that "it is now the freethinkers' turn to pillage heaven by their audacious impiety and scientific analysis." To Bakunin the church was a pendant to the tavern—the one designed to drug the mind, the other to intoxicate the body. Mockery and science seemed to vie for the blasphemous energies of the early Godkillers. Ivan Pryzhov, a radical of the 1860s, so hated religion that he would conduct his drinking bouts in a parody of Orthodox ritual, and Nikolai Morozov wrote scientific exposés of sacred texts while in prison. To such revolutionaries, God meant the degradation and enslavement of man.[1]

While not repudiating atheism, a number of Populists saw utility in couching revolutionary ideas in a religious idiom in order to reach the peasantry, turning religious scriptural arguments against authority, property, and inequality or combining the Gospel with notions of socialism. Vilgelm Bervi-Flerovsky in 1873 proclaimed a "religion of equality" but "without God and without saints." A. V. Dolgushin, displayed a cross emblazoned with the words "Liberty, Equality, Fraternity." Another Populist, I. F. Fesenko went among the Sectarians depicting a heavenly future of human brotherhood; they took him for a prophet and lifted him aloft in their arms. Women were often drawn into the revolution by a quasi-religious faith, and the exalted atmosphere of struggle and liberation produced its own kind of moral code, initiation rites, and vocabulary—secular in aim, religious in spirit. A tiny group of radical Russian St. Simonians actually went into ecstasy during their conclaves—in emulation of the French utopian sect.[2]

In the aura of sacrifice and religiosity surrounding revolutionary circles, some found satisfaction in religion itself, and they deserted the cause which ultimately required violence and social hatred. A. A. Komarova went among the poor preaching that "Christ was a great socialist whose teachings had been distorted" and reading out passages from Vera Pavlovna's dream in Chernyshevsky's *What Is To Be Done*? Later she crossed over to Christian religious zealotry. A more complex phenomenon was the "religion of Godmanhood" (*Bogochelovechestvo*) that rejected both revolution and Christian religion in favor of a man-centered faith and a repudiation of violence, politics, and science as modes of salvation. Inner peace, harmony, and brotherly love were the core of God-manhood, the possible nucleus of a religion of socialism, but of a distinctly non-active kind. Its leaders migrated to America to join a religious commune. It was the first parting of the ways between the religious utopianism and the socialist utopianism of the intelligentsia.[3]

The God issue was given the fullest possible publicity in the period between 1905 and 1917, years of extraordinary freedom of expression. The political and social climate in Russia made religion, together with sexual morality, crime, suicide, and decadence in art, a topic of intense discussion among the intelligentsia. Two of the many fruits of this interest were Godseeking and Godbuilding. Godseekers were committed Christians searching for ways to find God within the context of an enlightened intelligentsia. Godbuilding, directly inspired by the Godseeking movement, was an effort to make socialism compatible with religion by "constructing" a new God system.[4] Its real innovator was Lunacharsky, a man of broad learning in European thought, who had ties with the Godseekers and who was temperamentally a "soft" Bolshevik. Godbuilding received its direct inspiration from European thinkers, in this case the philosopher Ernst Mach, the writers Maurice Maeterlinck and Emile Verhaeren, and the socialist Joseph Dietzgen.[5]

Lunacharsky's major statement of belief was *Religion and Socialism* (1908–11) which argued that the essence of religion was its human spiritual bond and that this could be achieved without God (in the usual sense), mysticism, the other world, metaphysics, or superstition. Marxism and modern science alone were not sufficient to produce solidary ecstasy, the psychic cement of common love and struggle. Lunacharsky envisioned a future world of dreams and myths, of sounds, and rituals that would elevate humanity to the status of divinity and bring collective immortality. Light, hope, poetry, beauty, dignity and enthusiasm were to adorn the struggle of the proletariat, first against its human foes in the class war and then against nature in the building of a socialist order. "Religion is enthusiastic, and without enthusiasm, people can create nothing great." These rhapsodies enraged Lenin but set the stage for Lunacharsky's interest in a new "proletarian culture" and deepened his friendly association with Gorky and Bogdanov. Though Lunacharsky would later downplay religious imagery, it remained central to his thinking as Commissar of Enlightenment.[6]

The writer Maxim Gorky joined the quest in *Children of the Sun* (1905), an exceptionally lyrical paen to human solidarity and immortality with its motifs of enlightenment, Prometheanism, and community. "But we," he wrote, "we people are the children of the sun, the bright source of life; we are born of the sun and will vanquish the murky fear of death." To distance himself from Christian notions of life and salvation, Gorky sometimes verged on pagan sun-worship—very popular at the time elsewhere in Europe. In *Confession* (1907), where the terms Godseeking and Godbuilding were coined, the "people" have become God, creators of miracles, possessors of true religious consciousness, and immortal. Gorky envisioned a beautiful future of work for the love of work and of man as "master of all things." His approach to Godbuilding was more rational than that of the warm-blooded and ecstatic Lunacharsky, but they found common ground in the Godbuilding experiment—which consisted mostly of writing books and teaching workers at the party school on the Isle of Capri in association with Bogdanov.[7]

Godbuilding was one of the issues that divided Lenin from his erstwhile colleagues on Capri. He considered religion in any form as "stupefaction" and "stultification" like individual housekeeping and other "wasteful" forms of human activity. Godbuilding, in his view, was dangerously close to traditional religion and mysticism, a useless and even harmful version of daydreaming that could lead to inertia and immobility. He attacked Godbuilding publicly and privately. In a 1913 letter, Lenin rejected the notion that God was "a set of ideas that aroused and organized social feelings." God was always at the center of a world that subjected, impoverished, and oppressed, however well-intentioned and refined was one's definition of it. Though Godbuilding attracted the attention of some Bolsheviks, the construction of the proletarian deity was temporarily abandoned when the circle dissolved. Lenin had triumphed, little suspecting that his own persona after death would provide the missing face of the workers' God.[8]

Godbuilding was a debate of the intelligentsia, not of rank-and-file revolutionaries, party agents, and factory workers. And yet, some of these were doing some Godbuilding of their own through a different mode of expression. The appearance of industry, factories, and Marxist literature in Russia on a large scale did not automatically shed the light of atheism upon the masses and burn away the dark film of belief. Socialist agitators—Menshevik, Bolshevik, Socialist Revolutionary, and Anarchist—turned their attention to religion. Some brought their persuasive energies to bear on unmasking, mocking, and demystifying the Gods by means of anti-religious and anticlerical propaganda, exposure of relics, scoffing, and public "demonstrations" of the nonexistence of an almighty God. "There is no God," shouted a factory worker. "It is all our stupidity. Bring me a thousand icons and Gods of yours and I will smash them and nothing will happen." But in at least one case, a blasphemer in the countryside was put to death by the peasants he was trying to convert.[9]

Others attempted to engrave the imagery of religion upon their propaganda. The Socialist Revolutionaries produced some particularly vivid examples. A May Day broadsheet of 1901 depicted socialism as a religion, a faith in the bright future of mankind and a sacred cause worthy of personal sacrifice for a transcendant ideal: the fraternal harmony of the great human family in communion with nature. May Day was the Holy Day of Festival (*prazdnik*) of this new religion. The May Day message of the Socialist Revolutionaries in 1905, entitled "A New Sermon on the Mount", rejected Christ's exaltation of the meek and conferred its beatitude instead upon the "dissatisfied, the strugglers, and the valiant." Socialist Revolutionaries incorporated the theme of Christ as the first socialist preacher of equality and brotherhood. In the Jewish Pale, Anarchists composed a Passover Hagadah prayerbook for workers that gave the traditional Seder questions a Marxist twist: "Wherefore are we different from Shmuel the factory owner, Meir the banker, Zorekh the money-lender, and Reb Todres the Rabbi?" A radical protest song printed abroad couched its social dream in Christian vocabulary:

> And when our Tale is ended—Glory be!
> Our Song, O brothers, will be another one—Glory be!
> Joyous and free will be that song—Glory be!
> Reverent to the spirit of Light and Truth—Glory be!
> To Mother Truth our protectress—Glory be!
> To freedom of the will, liberty of the People—Glory be!

From yet another source, a peasant Old Believer wrote an agitational parable entitled "Christ Leading the Poor out of Hell and Leaving the Rich Down There."[10]

Bolsheviks and Mensheviks also enlisted such imagery for the purpose of de-faithing the masses. The most striking of many examples was the *Ten Commandments of a Social Democrat* published illegally in 2,000 copies by N. Vasiliev in 1906 and reprinted after the Revolution of 1917.[11] Emelyan Yaroslavsky, the central figure in the history of Soviet atheism, published illegally in 1907 his first work on the subject, *The Catechism of a Soldier*, an attack upon the army's use of the clergy and the name of Christ to promote repression and counterrevolution. Its 15,000 copies were widely distributed. Another Marxist production was a Social Democratic flysheet of 1911 containing a litany that contrasted slavery, hunger, insecurity, prostitution, and subjugation to equality, and the "festival of life" where Humanity would be "the tsar of a liberated and wondrous earth."[12]

What kind of syncretic behavior do we find among the common people? Studies of working-class funerals indicate the fusion of pious forms with revolutionary content in the factory towns, together with a new concern for the welfare of the departed comrade's family. When radical workers returned to the villages in time of revolution, strange things happened. In Poltava Province in 1905, inhabitants of a village (having forsaken God and the tsar in the opinion of the reporter), greeted city agitators with red flags and church bells. At Easter in 1905 in Kaluga Province, peasants returning from Moscow openly agitated at the church service about labor conditions. In Moscow Province in the same year, local peasants bearing icons joined a church procession and sang the "Workers' Marseillaise." In Simbirsk Province, peasants forced a priest to say a memorial mass for Stenka Razin, the seventeenth century rebel. In other places, people invaded the church with red flags and demanded funeral services for fallen comrades.[13]

We also know something about the "deconversion" process of forty-six workers, mostly from the capital, metal workers, hereditary proletarians, and oriented to Bolshevism. For them the abandonment of Christianity was gradual and not a sudden illumination; life experience over-shadowed intellectual study; disbelief in God usually followed disillusionment with the clergy, unavailing prayers, and traumas such as "Bloody Sunday" after which some workers asked: "Where, then is God?" But in abandoning church, workers (and peasants) seemed to want something else to replace it—as they would openly assert in the 1920s. Social Democrats in Europe began to conclude that workers were "genuinely religious" and in love with ideals and that Marxism was "too dry . . . too pseudo-scientific" to inspire those ideals.[14]

In all of this questing after faith there is much fluidity, confusion, and experimentation. The intellectual Godbuilders spoke in literary and philosophical terms, making learned allusions. Those in revolutionary propaganda work juxtaposed socialism and religious categories. And the workers and peasants displayed a mingling of signs and gestures. But behind these expected contrasts in discourse, we see common themes: desertion of the old faith, the search for something new, a vision of the future, pious cadences, exaltation of sacrifice and the virtues of comradeship, and visible forms of celebration. But we can also discern in almost every text—literary or symbolic—a tension between love and hate, peace and war, community and violence: a surge towards brotherhood and the remaking of sensiblities with old materials of emotional love on the one hand; an angry assault on false Gods, on the selfish and greedy sinners of capitalism and autocracy on the other. It was in simplest terms the contrast between Godkilling and Godbuilding—one of the major moral questions facing the Bolsheviks when they came to power in 1917.[15]

## Storming the Heavens

"We didn't mention God," recalled a soldier about the year 1917. "There was no time to concern ourselves with heavenly matters when such an enormous mass of urgent terrestrial problems rose up to confront us." On the other hand, Baltic sailors threw icons overboard and put their priest ashore; and in June a Russian soldier in Helsinki delivered an apostrophic indictment of God:[16]

> Where art thou, then, righteous Lord, that thou seest not how rivers of blood have flowed for thirty three months? . . . Why hast thou been blinded and seest not the tears of woe and hearest not the moans of thy tormented people . . . Why dost thou not visit thy punishment upon those guilty of unleashing this fratricidal war: Wilhelm and Nicholas, Poincaré and the Sultan, the bureaucrats, hypocrites, priests, who in thy name and bearing crosses have forsaken thy commandment: Thou shalt not kill?

Popular anti-clericalism and even atheism certainly flourished during the Revolution and Civil War, but it was episodic. Initially the Bolshevik regime settled for a separation of church and state. But this, with its entailed loss of property and educational scope, plus the visible hostility of the Bolsheviks and their perceived "foreignness," was sufficient to ignite a war between Bolshevism and Russian Orthodoxy. The Russian Civil War— like the Mexican one—was also a religious war, with "Jesus Christ Regiments" marching out from among the Whites and with consecrated red banners being sent from Bolshevik cities to units.[17]

Organized antireligious movements got underway only after the onset of N.E.P.[18] The official view of antireligious work was encased in a Central Committee Resolution of 1921: "To replace religious understanding of the world with a rigorous communist scientific system."[19] This exceedingly vague and dry formula failed to satisfy either those who wished simply to destroy faith in God at once or those who wished to create a new kind of Bolshevik "religion."

The League of the Militant Godless (*Soyuz Voinstvuyushchikh Bezbozhnikov*), 1925– 42, was founded by Minei Izrailovich Gubelman (1878–1943) whose Bolshevik *nom de guerre* was Emelyan Yaroslavsky, generally known also as a favorite and promoter of Stalin in his tendentious popular histories and biographies. Born in Chita of exiled revolutionaries, he spent his youth in the Bolshevik underground and began his atheist mission in 1907. He presided over the commission that decreed the separation of church and state. In 1922 he formed at the Communist University an atheist study circle. He wrote his major works on religion, *Birth, Life, and Death of the Gods* (1923) and *The Bible of Believers and Unbelievers* (1922–25), and founded in 1922 *The Godless* (*Bezbozhnik*), a weekly. Around this formed a circle of "friends of *The Godless*" which held a congress in April 1925 and founded the League in June.[20]

The League of Godless proclaimed that religion was harmful to workers, that science was sufficient to explain all phenomena, and that religiosity was a sign of disloyalty. It set up a central council and launched a number of new journals. An associated group, the Young Godless, was formed out of the newly born Young Pioneers. The League was financed through dues. It remained limp through the 1920s, local areas and organizations defying its bylaws and ignoring its adjurations, particularly in the Ukraine where Godless work was minimal until the five-year plan. Overlapping jurisdiction and organizational rivalry crippled its efforts everywhere. It was composed of party members, Komsomols, and nonparty people—mostly young workers, males, schoolchildren, Civil War veterans and an assortment of *besprizorniki* (homeless orphans) and other recruited elements. Membership was estimated at about 123,000 in 1928 (after which it leaped dramatically), though the nature of "membership" in such organizations during the early revolutionary years is no indication of activity or commitment. Komsomols held a prominent place in the League, but only about ten percent of them actually joined it, having lost interest by the mid-1920s according to a contemporary Soviet commentator. Yaroslavsky's policy was one of noncoercion and nonpersecution of religion. Churches were to be closed only by exception and according to the will of the local people. The main instrument of conversion to atheism was to be agitation.[21]

Through the 1920s, Yaroslavsky fought against two deviations: "liquidationism" and "priest-eating" (*popoedstvo*). Liquidators believed that special anti-religious work was unnecessary outside the regular channels of school and study circles. Invoking Lenin, who occasionally warned against excesses, they demanded that the League be liquidated. The Party upheld Yaroslavsky; but in practice there was much inertia in the struggle against God. The "priest-eaters" had a prominent organ in *The Godless of the Bench*, edited by M. Kostelovskaya, a Moscow party leader, S. Polidorov, a journalist, and Dmitry Moor, the famous poster artist. They opposed the scientific, anthropological, and historical persuasion of the League and preferred simply the immediate obliteration of religion and an "antireligious proletarian dictatorship of the atheist city over the countryside." Illustrations by the talented Moor showed such things as peasants feeding off the innards of an eviscerated Christ or a plump peasant woman combining vermin—priest, chalice, angel, cross, icon—out of her infested hair. Some of these pictures were known to have sent peasants into a frenzy of rage. Kostelevskaya opposed the notion of a moral-atheist code as unnecessary asceticism.[22]

In the years 1922–24, over 300 antireligious titles were published, including Yaroslavsky's *Bible*, tracts opposing anti-Semitism, excerpts from the Marxist masters, and translations of European classics of religious defamation, as well as popular novels such as Sinclair Lewis's *Elmer Gantry*. Most of it was negative assault on the church or scientific arguments against the deity. Typical of a pamphlet aimed at the countryside was Anton Loginov's *The Godless: the Best Friend of the Peasant* (1925). We do not want to take religion away from you, explained Loginov, we just want you to give it up. "And what do you replace it with," he has the peasant ask (quite realistically)? His answer "Evil does not have to be replaced, but simply rooted out. That is our program."[23]

Since the population was low in literacy, preaching the Godless word directly seemed to hold out great promise for the enthusiasts of enlightening atheism. In 1923 big debates were held in every district of Petrograd. In Vladimir, 2,000 listeners heard a six-hour debate between an atheist and a priest on the theme: "Is there a God?" Another in Pereyaslavl lasted two days and was attended by 3000. In both, according to Soviet sources, the priests were defeated and they deserted the cloth. The proletarians of Moscow, in spite of their hostility to religion, jammed the auditoriums to hear speakers like the Archbishop Vvedensky. But the Bolsheviks did not always win these debates. Hindus met a priest who had debated against the Godless, asking his opponent why man, if so powerful, had not invented sunshine, rain, or stars. The answer: nature created them. Question: who made nature? Nature, like a watch or a revolution, had to have a maker. Answer: Nature made itself. Result: public laughter and the victory of the priest. In 1924 "Russia teemed with talk of religion," debates being for a while the chief outdoor diversion, according to Hindus, a native speaker who visited Russia many times. Atheist preachers hit the circuit like American parsons on the Bible Belt; like them, many were sons of rural folk, in their case armed with scientific miracles and blasphemy. A singularly unimaginative atheist sailor tried to keep the faithful out of church by buttonholeing them at the door and reading to them about isoceles triangles.[24]

The country was covered with a network of seminars, study groups, evening and correspondence courses, reference points and home-guides such as "Teach Yourself to Be Godless." Godlessness was a mark of culture among adherents to the regime, and all higher educational institutions included atheist courses. There was even an All-Union Anti-religious University of the Air. Since the majority of schoolteachers were still religious and since the teaching of atheism in school was not required in the 1920s (although the teaching of religion was forbidden of course), the burden of anti-religious propaganda fell very heavily upon the League and its supporters. And since the bulk of its themes were couched in rational, historical, and scientific terms, one must wonder at the effectiveness of the anti-religious propaganda network so acclaimed by its organizers and so defamed by its enemies. But one can hardly doubt the zeal and enthusiasm that went into this quasi-missionary crusade against the faith.[25]

Bolshevik atheist art was not very successful. It possessed no great anti-clerical painters as did the Mexican Revolution. Most anti-religious posters descended to the level of coarseness, such as the one depicting the Virgin Mary with a bulging belly longing for a Soviet abortion. One cannot deny the great emotional effectiveness and even beauty of Russian revolutionary art in general, but it usually turned sour when aimed at the Church. The major exception was Alexander Apsit, who could strike at God and at the same time evoke heroic and mythic grandeur in his works, as in the poster showing a mythological youth on a winged horse above the revolutionary masses who kneel in a posture of reverance as they raise their arms to the red star in heaven; in "To Our Deceived Brothers" of 1918 where a proletarian knight slays the hydra of counterrevolution in the manner of St. George; or in the proletariat storming the Moloch of capital. But Apsit, though an "anti-religious" painter, was not popular with the militant atheists precisely because of his Godbuilding motifs.[26]

Godless theater also foundered. In Moscow a theater called *Atheist* lasted half a year and ran only two plays: *Tarquinius the High Priest* and *Torquemada the Inquisitor.* Godless plays were also put on at meetings and concerts. The Jewish section of the Party in Kiev mounted a theatrical "trial" of the Jewish religion in the very courtroom where the ritual murder trial of Mendel Beilis had been held before the Revolution.

Mayakovsky's *Mystery Bouffe* of 1918 showed Promethean proletarians vanquishing Jehovah. Atheist films followed the same pattern. Atheist theater as such did not catch on as a special genre. But in the "theater of everyday life," red flags flew over church steeples, "merci" was used by some for thank you to replace the God-laden *spasibo* (God save), clergy were designated as *zhretsy* (pagan or civic "priests"), atheist slogans covered the towns, and churches were vandalized or ceremonially closed. The melting down of church bells seemed to herald the growing silence of the Orthodox faith.[27]

Bolshevik exposure of miracles and the unmasking of religious fraud brought two cultures into direct confrontation. Cases of "renewed" icons—old icons that seemed to glow again in the radiance of an apparition—appeared during the stressful years of Civil War and famine and were taken by peasant believers as signs of hope and salvation. When the Bolsheviks uncovered a renewed icon industry in Ekaterinoslav where gold foil was used to make the renewed effect, the icon-makers were shot. Entombed saints were exhumed amid cheers from organized street crowds who guffawed at the "uncorrupted" remains of the saints: rags and bones. "Incorruptable cadavers" were shown to be nothing more than wax effigies (at just the moment when the body of Lenin was being embalmed). Believers were shown how weeping icons were hooked up with rubber squeezers that produced "tears" in return for an offering. Eventually "demystification" work was transferred to permanent museums of religion and atheism. A Soviet historian describes the "strong impression" made on the assembled masses who witnessed the disinterment of saints. But Gorky, an observer, claimed that the atheists often used non-Russians and former members of other religions out of spite in the desecrations and that many peasants simply disbelieved what they saw and were told. Some viewers praised the revelation of monastic frauds and then insisted that those of scientists and physicians should also be exposed![28]

The gap between the Bolshevik belief in the power of science and the peasant distrust of it was not as extraordinary as was the former's failure to appreciate it. "We are going to change all that [superstitious farming]," said a Sovkhoz manager in the years before collectivization and the imposition of authority on the villages. "We are going to free him from the dominance of the priest and the church and superstitions" and get him "to read Marx and Ilyitch and books on science, machinery, electricity, instead of the Bible and the prayer books." School-children demonstrated to their parents that lack of light caused calf-blindness and that insecticide (not prayer) could kill cabbage worms. "Godless acres" were laid out beside "God's acres," the former treated with chemical fertilizer, the latter with holy water—and a competition was held. Contests occurred between "atheist" babies who were raised on "scientific principles" and Christened babies. Godless weather forecasting was shown to be superior to peasant instinct. And everywhere cleanliness, sanitation, and health were linked to Godlessness.[29]

Promethean man and his machines were natural emblems in the conversion process. In a rapturous eulogy of man, the jurist Mikhail Reisner promised that with its "steel beasts, machines," mankind would build a "magnificent garden all over the earth" after declaring war on the gods. Modern vehicles had a particular appeal. The "atheist tractor" appeared in the 1920s, described in a pamphlet called *Prayers on a Tractor* and used in posters showing the tractor fighting the cross. The railroad was another potent symbol. Before the Revolution, the antimodernist Leontiev's parable of a long black train blocking a religious procession had been a metaphor for modern evil. After the Revolution, agit-trains sped into the vastness of Russia with their "good news" of a godless universe. One of them was actually called "The Godless Express." For a touch of menace, agit-planes—remodelled German Junkers bought from the Reichswehr—on Sundays and Holy Days would fly to some village and buzz the church steeple, disrupting the service with their fearful roar. In Siberia in the 1920s, peasants were taken for an airplane ride to show them there were no angels or gods in the heavens.[30]

The most drastic antireligious activity, aside from the arrest and shooting of priests, was blasphemy and mockery. As in the years before the Revolution, but now quite freely, blaspheming Bolsheviks would plant themselves in the middle of a village street, hurl obscene and provocative epithets into the sky, and then stand there, smug and unharmed by the thunderbolts of the Almighty. The shortlived experiment with antireligious carnival opened in 1922, when Skvortsov-Stepanov suggested a Komsomol anti-Christmas with fir trees, red stars, snowmen and a defaming of the gods. On Orthodox Christmas Day, January 6, 1923, in Moscow, processions formed up at noon and paraded until dark. The marchers included students, Komsomols, members of women's organizations, and working class youth, with horsemen holding anti-religious banners. These were followed by trucks bearing clowns who mocked God, a figure of God embracing a nude woman, and rabbis and priests in ridiculous poses chanting parodies of church liturgy set to indecent lyrics. As night fell, effigies of all the gods were burnt on a bonfire while the students danced around it and Komsomol Christmas carols based on the Orthodox Troparion were sung.

In Odessa, a parade ended with the burning of Moses and Jehovah on the main square while the adjacent church was packed to overflowing by Christian worshippers at Christmas mass. In Tsaritsyn the parade included performances of the play *The Liberation of Truth* in front of a church and ended with effigy burning at the grave of the revolutionary martyrs. Scenes like this occured in 417 cities all over Russia.[31]

Public reaction boomeranged. Believers and nonbelievers alike were deeply offended by the cruel public frivolity of the Komsomols in many places. Skvortsov-Stepanov later claimed that his original idea had been a historical-anthropological tableau illustrating the essential similarity of all gods and that the youthful ebullience of the organizers had turned it into carnival instead. Yaroslavsky also recognized that mockery, offensiveness, and insult were useless in trying to build up a new ritual and a new religion. It was partly because of the failure of the antireligious carnival that a movement was launched to elaborate a new ritual culture to replace the ancient rituals of the gods that were being assaulted.

## Rituals of a Counterfaith

The argument for new socialist rituals began to emerge in the Civil War and became more focused after the debacle of Komsomol Christmas. Among the spokesmen for new ritual were Mikhail Kalinin, "peasant" president of the Republic, P. M. Kerzhentsev, a Proletcult theater specialist, Trotsky, Yaroslavsky, and the novelist and physician V. V. Veresaev. Kalinin quoted peasants who were asking him for surrogate rituals. Trotsky observed workers already creating their own forms. Kerzhentsev spoke of theatricalizing life. Yaroslavsky stressed the need to move beyond the mocking carnival. Veresaev, the most thoughtful of them all, tied ritual to the rich and healthy world of emotions. They saw that since religion was being discouraged and taken away from the people, something had to be given back to them.[32]

After a good deal of debate, the party in October 1923 recommended communist public festivals and private rituals. As to the first, Yaroslavsky promoted "revolutionary counter-celebrations," sober and joyous, processions with revolutionary songs and music, lectures and reports, and reasonable games—all timed for the cycles of the seasons to compete with church holidays. These festivals were to eschew all mockery and insult but were to offer fun as well as enlightenment, perhaps embellished by a voluntary act of labor in order to woo youth away from the prayers and drunkeness of the old holy days.

After the misconceived Komsomol Christmas, a Komsomol Easter had been organized in 1923, not a one-day act of carnival, but a kind of unholy week of anti-religious consciousness with speeches replacing the mockery, reports, charades, skits (such as "The Political Trial of the Bible" and "The Komsomol Petrushka"), songs, poems, tales, stories, and legends. In Leningrad in 1924, Pioneers sang "materialist" songs, displayed slogans such as "The Smoke of the Factory is Better than the Smoke of Incense," and performed an atheist play to an audience of a thousand people. Eventually a whole new counter-festival calendar presented "parallel" days opposing Electric Day to Elijah Day, Forest Day to Trinity Sunday, Harvest Day to the Feast of the Intercession, and the Day of Industry to the Feast of Transfiguration.[33]

In the local community the focus for new ritual was the club, envisioned by some as a surrogate church or civic temple. An apologist for the Palace of Workers described it as "a cultural building of a new healthy life of the proletariat."[34] The problem was to make the workers' club into something solemn, joyous, and celebrative of the new order without descending to banality. A barrier to the fulfillment of this ideal was the dichotomy between the designers and the users of the club. The exterior forms and the interior space were in many ways congenial to the utopian speculations that accompanied the Revolution, in spite of their great variety. Architectural experimentation, fueled by self-consciously radical impulses, coincided with the turn toward indoor ritual and a search for the forms of community.

The first clubs were simply the premises of confiscated mansions or public edifices. But almost at once appeared grandiose plans for huge central palaces of labor, followed by local clubs in neighborhoods and enterprises. They varied little in interior design: library, dining room, auditorium for the solemn occasions, music room, theater, and recreational facilities. Variations of the name workers' club (*rabochii klub*) abounded: Worker's Palace, House of Lenin, Proletarian House, House of Workers, Palace of Culture (and of Rest) and so on. The earliest projects bordered on fantasy, with grandiose structures resembling medieval cathedrals, the Hôtel de Ville in Paris, railway stations, and châteaux. In the mid-1920s, especially with the work of the brilliant architect Konstantin Melnikov, they became more functional and more like the places where their users worked. These buildings provided—on paper—a broad range of collective activities, public services, and a grandiose setting, often with imaginative use of partitions for rearranging space.[35] A sense of what went on inside the clubs may be gained from the report of a ritual advisor and specialist, on the basis of "long observations" of a workers' club in the 1920s. The closest thing to a ritual service of a quasi-religious kind was the frequent meeting to honor special people or events. According to his observations, the decor was uniformly artless: red table cover, a bust or portrait of a leader, slogans on the walls, and a dais; and on particularly "festive" occasions, the bric-a-brac of a bygone age—paper lanterns or a fir tree. Music was provided by a brass ensemble which offered "flourishes" to punctuate the proceedings and endless renderings of the "Internationale;" bands that had a funeral march in their repertoire were considered "armed to the teeth."[36]

The meeting itself was always poorly timed, too long, and stilted, consisting of repetitive speeches, the awarding of prizes, and marches of the honored up to the dais. The whole routine was "boring, dreary, and tiresome." The eternal awkwardness of ushers who carried banners up to the front reveals in a flash how the easy grace of the outdoor festival with its stately reverence and its familiar catalogue of movements and gestures became cramped inside the artificial premises of the new "workers' church."[37]

For family rituals, the Bolsheviks made an effort to drape the three main events of human life—birth, marriage, death—in revolutionary clothing. Octobering (*Oktyabrina*), the dedication of newborns, was the most celebrated of these (see Fig. 19). It began haltingly and sporadically in the Civil War but only spread in the early 1920s. Trotsky, learning of a mock ceremony of "inspection" of a newborn child of workers by their comrades in a factory, followed by a feast, saw it as a spontaneous expression of a new workers' ritual culture. No survey of the number of Octoberings was ever published, but it seems to have taken hold in factory towns in the early 1920s. One of the first recorded in detail (November 22, 1923) took place in Kharkov where a baby daughter was Octobered and presented with a gift—a portrait of the infant Lenin. The parents delivered a verbal promise to raise the child in the spirit of communism, the "Internationale" was sung, and choruses performed folk songs.[38]

At a Moscow club, a detachment of pioneers with flag and drum chanted "We are the Young Guard of Workers and Peasants" and escorted the mother to the dais. "The child belongs to me," she declaimed, "only physically. For spiritual upbringing I present it to society." The pioneers then folded the baby in a red banner and vowed to enroll her in their unit. Since Soviet law of 1917 permitted all citizens to change their names at age eighteen, some adults began to follow suit. A group of women workers, hoping to promote Octobering, had themselves renamed at a club ceremony as the "Vanguard of the New Life" amid some muffled guffaws from the menfold. After a few months, they reclaimed their old names, except for one, Avdotiya, who had taken the name Revolution (*Revolyutsiya*) and was ever after known as Auntie Revo (*Tëtya Reva*).[39]

The new names given to Octobered babies offer a startling set of symbols of the values that were officially revered in the early years. The French Revolution had invoked the shades of classical figures (Brutus, Hannibal, Gracchus), and European Social Democrats had tried to popularize socialist names (Lassallo, Marxina, and Primo Maggio in Italy; Bebelina in Germany). The few dozen Russian "revolutionary" names that I have uncovered from the period divide in the following way:

### Revolutionary Heroes and Heroines

Spartak, Marks, Engelina, Libknekht, Lyuksemburg, Roza, Razin, Mara, Robesper, Danton, Bebel; Vladlen, Ninel, Ilich, Ilina (all variants of Lenin); Bukharina, Stalina, Budëna, Melor (Marx, Engels, Lenin, October Revolution).

### Revolutionary Concepts

Pravda, Revmir (revolution and peace), Barrikada, Giotin (Guillotine), Bastil, Tribuna, Revolyutsiya, Krasnyi (Red), Kommuna, Parizhkommuna (Paris Commune), Proletarii, Buntar (rebel), Fevral, Mai, Oktyabrina, Serpina (from sickle), Molot (hammer), Smychka (alliance of workers and peasants), Volya (will or freedom),

Svoboda (freedom), Dinamit, Ateist, Avangarda, Iskra (spark), Marseleza (Marseillaise).

### Industrial, Scientific, and Technical Imagery

Tekstil, Industriya, Traktorina, Dinamo, Donbass, Smena (shift), Radium, Genii (genius), Idea, Elektrifikatsiya.

### Culture, Myth, Nature, Place Names

Traviata, Aida, Les (forest), Luch (light), Okean, Orël (eagle), Solntse (sun), Zvezda (star), Razsvet (dawn), Atlantida, Minevra (*sic*), Monblan (Mont Blanc), Kazbek, Singapur.

There were the usual cases of error, resulting from misunderstanding of words. In 1919, peasants in a commune named their daughter "Markiza" (Marquise) thinking it irreligious and somehow vaguely foreign. Other names chosen included Commentary, Embryo, and Vinaigrette![40]

This particular form of utopianizing seems to have been an expression of the wish to create a new reality by means of imagery, to better the world by populating it with humans called Spark, Joy, Will, Electric, Rebel, and Barricade, and to fashion living monuments to the past. It was a quest for another world by means of imaging what is perhaps the most intimate possession of any human being. As Boris Uspensky points out, a name is a social sign, and thus name changes reflect a new social state.[41] In their variety, color, and rich associative capacities, the revolutionary names of the 1920s represented a sensibility exactly opposite to those who aspired to a collective identity and a reduction of people to "human parts" of a future society. It was also a national and generational revolt against the Greco-Russian Orthodox culture of the past with its ancient and limited repertoire of Tatyanas, Andreis, Sofiyas, Peters, and Nicholases, though some tried to do this by choosing pre-Christian Slavic names such as Mstislav or Sviatopolk that had fallen into disuse in modern times.

Getting married at a Red Wedding—instead of the dry official registration office or in the church—had a dual significance. Its form showed a desire for solemnity, decor, and ritual that were wholly absent at the offices. Its content treated the wife and the husband as legally, politically and symbolically equal. During the French Revolution, the policeman Josephe Fouché had wanted Temples of Love built to stage all weddings. Such edifices did not bloom in the Russian Revolution, and the registry office remained a cramped, crowded bureau where couples got married in twenty minutes. Some people obviously wanted more, as did the prophets of the new ritualism.

Red Weddings appeared at about the same time as the Octobering ceremonies. Critics like Veresaev thought them banal. He described one, of December 1924, in a club of leather workers: a red covered table, a portrait of Lenin, the vows to nuptial fidelity and to communism, reports and speeches, a wedding gift for the new couple—works by Lenin and Zinoviev—and the mandatory "Internationale." Red Weddings in the village added the traditional custom of *chastushka* (witty folk sayings) and *khorovod* (round dance and song). Among the peasants, attempts were made to inject industrial imagery to the feast by employing the new Ford tractor, adorned with red flags, as a wedding carriage. But the custom did not take hold in the countryside—peasants wanted something longer, more solemn and elaborate, followed by a day or two of carousing. In 1925, according to one estimate, 75 percent of peasant weddings were still held in church. And even in the industrial towns, there is no sign that the Red Wedding became a universal or even mass phenomenon.[42]

The revolutionary funeral—it is significant that no neologism was applied to it—was the most problematic of the invented rituals and the most resistant to innovation. At the root of the problem was its origin as a martyr's funeral. Drawing on nineteenth century precedents, the genre had emerged in 1905 with the funeral of Baumann and found artistic stylization in the painting "Red Funeral" by Isaac Brodsky (1906). This was expanded in the first great Bolshevik interment, that of M. S. Uritsky, held in September 1918. With its guard of honor, the lying-in-state in luxurious surroundings, the huge cortège with ornate red catafalque, the carriage escort and lone caparisoned horse, rows of bedecked armored cars, and overflying aircraft, it surpassed the obsequies of the burial of the martyrs in 1917—all for only one man. The city boss, Zinoviev, displayed the full power of Petrograd's ceremonial magnificence and mobilized an entire city for the most elaborate funeral seen there since the interment of Alexander III in 1894—and even more dazzling in that the public was in full presence for the entire day, with dispersed units touching almost every neighborhood in the huge city. It became a model for hero funerals in the Civil War and prefigured most of the elements in the Lenin funeral of 1924, an event of stupendous importance (see below). For the next two years, revolutionary burials became a regular feature of the street life of Russia.[43]

But not all people who die are revolutionary martyrs or heroes. The Orthodox Church *panikhida*, a work of extraordinary textual richness and beauty, continued to attract masses of people, and not only in the countryside. At Kronstadt in the early days of the Revolution, fallen sailors were given an Orthodox requiem on Anchor Square followed by a general singing of the "Worker's Marseillaise." As tension between church and state mounted, people began searching for alternate and politically acceptable ways to bury their dead. A peasant in 1919 asked Kalinin what kind of service the regime had in mind and if it was really necessary for him to bury his son—who was no revolutionary—to the strains of "You Fell Victim." New ways began to appear ad hoc, uneasy blends of old pious forms and political speeches. Veresaev described them in the mid-1920s as arid: a sterile chamber for the wake, mourners with nothing to do, and the customary speeches about the departed—all of it leaving a void instead of an affirmation of life for the survivors. He proposed a wholly new ceremony with original music instead of the eternal Chopin or the revolutionary funeral marches: mournful sounds to evoke tears of genuine emotion followed by triumphant cadences to celebrate continuing life, a choreographed tableau of white-robed young women (recalling the maiden mourners of Orthodox funeral rites), and the mourners' participation in a great catharsis—in other words, unabashed public display of emotions in the company of loved ones. But even Veresaev conceded that a "symphony of scarlet and black banner and a forest of marvellous palms" was suitable for a great national leader—such as Lenin.[44]

Some hoped to achieve the democratization of death by the use of crematoria. The first European crematorium had been built in Milan in 1876, and many major cities of Europe had them, but none had been allowed in tsarist Russia because of the power of the Orthodox Church. As early as 1919, architects began designing ceremonial crematoria, bearing such names as "To the Heavens" and "Phoenix" and taking the shape of civic basilicas, towers, castles, and churches. In some of these, the lying-in-state halls came in different sizes, indicating a hierarchy of importance of the departed. Yet the crematorium seemed to promise a mode of neat standardization. Trotsky urged speedy cremations and simple ceremony with red flags, the funeral march, processions, eulogy, and a rifle salute. The architect Melnikov devised a "crematorium-columbarium" for ordinary people where the "family ritual would be revolutionized in a stroke, transcendent beliefs broken down, and the cause of sound health advanced'' (see Fig. 20). The first Soviet crematorium was built in 1926 and opened the following year in a Moscow cemetery church with a Farewell Hall of 150 seats. By the end of 1928 over 4,000 bodies had been cremated there, most of them by ''administrative'' process (that is, cadavers assigned to it by various institutions, presumably hospitals and morgues). Among the first ''volunteers'' who requested cremation in their testament were I. I. Skvortsov-Stepanov, a major publicist of atheism, and Alexander Bogdanov.[45]

The fiery machines of the crematoria were the perfect emblem for the Bolshevik way of death: clean, rational, and economical. But this particular fire did not spark the emotions of the majority of Russians, who continued to look to the life-giving earth for their place of final rest. The sculptor Konenkov dreamed of new kind of cemetery for the future.[46]

> The very concept of a 'cemetery' will change. They will be parks of good memories. In them, the grateful descendants will 'recall' those who did not spare themselves in the name of the common good. Young life will seethe around magnificent works of sculpture and under the canopies of beauteous trees. These parks will become places of leisure and the pride of every Soviet city.

Except for the seething youth, such places have in fact sprouted up in Soviet Russia: the Mars Field in Leningrad, the Revolutionary Necropolis on Red Square, the various military-revolutionary sections of the Novodevichi in Moscow and the Alexander Nevsky Lavra and Volkovskoe in Leningrad, and the huge memorial grounds containing those fallen in World War II. They are places of immeasurable sadness as well as of national pride and love of homeland—but in this they hardly differ from the overgrown Orthodox churchyards that continue to cover the Russian land.

The communist ritual movement of the 1920s did not become a mass phenomenon. Peasant dislike or indifference to it is easily understood: rural people of the older generation missed the little glasses of vodka and appetizers, the cry of ''it's bitter,'' the priest, and the dancing at weddings; the plates of food for the dead; the mysteries, beauties, joys, and ebullience of country-style ritual. But there was hostility among communists as well. Some distrusted acts of piety and ''beauty'' no matter how Bolshevized. Vitalii Zhemchuzhny, a film-maker and writer for the avant-garde *Novyi Lef*, expressed his malaise in a critique of ritual building in 1927. ''The spreading or propagation of some sort of new, invented ritual,'' he wrote, ''is an absurd utopia.'' Yaroslavsky told of a comrade who, in order to avoid a red funeral which he considered immoral and barbarous had endowed his body to a soap factory.[47]

Deophobia and the repugnance for ''Bolshevik *dvoeverie*''—the coexistence of old (Christian) and new (communist) religions—was part of a general aversion for God-building that many communists, including Lenin, felt deeply. But neither this nor the prodigious indifference of the masses prevented those communists, mostly urban workers and intellectuals, from continuing to invent and adapt rituals. Ritual building was not simply an exotic experiment of the 1920s. It possessed historical roots in proletarian traditions, a psychological value for some kinds of people, and a certain perceived utility for the regime as well—as proven by its revival on a vast scale a few years after the death of Stalin. But with the coming of the Stalin revolution, it was doomed along with all the other experiments.[48]

## Proletarian Morality

The word "orthodoxy" (in Russian, *pravoslavie*) means "the correct way to worship or exalt God": it does not mean the right way to behave. The Russian Orthodox Church had never been particularly enthusiastic about the dissemination of moral codes. Right ritual was its strong suit; the church had split asunder over it in the seventeenth century. Radical critics of religion had often pointed this out, and some Bolsheviks, whether or not they were Godbuilders, raised the problem of building their own code of morality. Those who spoke in general terms about the meaning of "communist morality" said almost nothing that could be fitted into a new religion or related to ritual. Such leaders as Lenin, Kalinin, Bukharin, Lunacharsky, and Trotsky gave weight to political behavior and class allegiance—the ultimate standard for this brand of morality, with occasional references to work attitudes, treatment of women and so on. Although Lunacharsky invoked the notion of Marxism as a religion from to time, he did not enrich the discussion or explore the concrete expressions of such a religion. Kerzhentsev offered in 1927 a suggestive essay on the ideal communist man of the future and gave as models the deceased Lenin, Dzerzhinsky, and Sverdlov. They were, he explained, masters of the correct mode of life in their class fidelity, daring, firmness, solidity, and superhuman energy. Only one sentence dealt with comradely feelings and human relations in other than formulaic terms. His models were mummified robots, tough and efficient, and endowed with an abundance of will power.[49]

A more interesting approach to the ideal comrade of today and of tomorrow was the debate on revolutionary sensibility and tribal mores. The first dealt not with behavior vis-à-vis class enemies, but rather toward one's "own." Even people who later became bitterly opposed to Bolshevism recognized in retrospect that the workers' movement, the revolution, and the Civil War had generated impulses for sharing, bonding, and even mutual love. A more or less complete recapitulation of well-established revolutionary virtues can be found in the first code of the Pioneers, founded in 1922: common decency, fairness, solidarity, and responsibility—in other words virtues that practically all religious, military, and patriotic codes have preached for centuries.[50]

But the concept of solidarity on the level of everyday comradeship posed a problem: how big should one's circle of "friends" be, conceding that everyone in one's class was a comrade? Aristotle had taught that the universalization of love dilutes it. But as early as the 1920s, serious commentators were arguing against small circles of intimate friends (cliques), because they weakened friendship for the entire "collective." Komsomols in Odessa wore badges and swam together in large groups in order to develop corporate identity and solidarity. This was apparently a nostalgic attempt to retrieve the comradeship-in-arms of the Civil War. In student communes of the 1920s, the "communards" often marched off in a body to the theater and frowned upon "bourgeois friendship" groups of two or three based on common likes and interests (see Chapter 10).[51] But many realized that deep differences in gender, ethnicity, and culture required specific measures and concrete bridges of comradeship to break down ancient prejudices. They were not convinced that harmony and mutual respect flowed automatically from class affiliation. The moral experimenters, paralleling the quest for new ritual, endeavored to construct a new morality based on realistic perceptions and with specific devices.

Among these were the campaigns to end racial, ethnic, and national discrimination.

The case of anti-Semitism may serve as an illustration. Like most of the revolutionary parties of the tsarist period (in spite of some well–known exceptions and ambiguities), the Bolsheviks condemned pogroms, opposed anti-Semitism on principle, and often fought it in practice as well, sometimes rescuing Jews during the Civil War from widespread violence. Through the twenties, speeches and laws poured forth in opposition to an impulse seen as diversionary and counterrevolutionary. Books, posters, and rituals identified anti-Semitism with the old order, priests, and brutal counterrevolutionaries. But it persisted among officials, merchants of the N.E.P., students, peasants, and workers. Pogromists were arrested and anti-Semitic students were expelled. The question of how effective the laws and propaganda were against it is still an open one. But after the last great battle against anti-Semitism in the late 1920s, it was abandoned in the 1930s campaign against specific moral causes.[52]

A new approach to urban-rural relations was begun, known as *smychka*—a moral alliance of workers and peasants (see Fig. 22). The Bolsheviks possessed no feeling of debt to the peasants. Yet their early symbols and rhetoric reflected a desire to reach out to the peasant. *Smychka* was an urban idea, elitist and patronizing, and the friendship it envisioned was strictly tutorial. But it also evoked considerable idealism and enthusiasm in the early years when friendship societies were established, when Komsomols went into the countryside to "teach" and organize the peasants in the ways of communism. And though many a peasant may have looked on *smychka* as an organization of city slickers and "Varangians," the element of moral comradeship was clearly on display. It was a kind of "to the people" movement in the context of a revolutionary state— with all the strengths and distortions attendant upon it. In the end, *smychka* gave way to the rule of force and to war against the countryside.[53]

A concept closely related to *smychka* was *sheftsvo*, often translated as "patronage" or "adoption" and thus clearly suggesting a parent-child relationship. It began early in the revolution with certain institutions (factory, army units, Komsomol groups) taking over and helping social units seen as deserving. An offshoot of *smychka*, it widened its scale in 1921 in Western Siberia and then took hold in Euoropean Russia. In 1923, factory, party, trade union, and other groups established cultural and organizational links with particular villages. By 1926, there were millions of members; conferences and publications abounded. Later the technique was used inside cities and industries to allow stronger elements to help weaker ones. The impulse, though always tied to the practical desire to impose city ways on village minds or good work habits on those with poor ones, was idealistic and altruistic in both statement and in deed. Later it degenerated into commandism, urban arrogance, and a humiliating symbiosis between strong and weak.[54]

The repudiation, after a decade of speculative experiment, of the search for a new "proletarian sexual morality" illustrates perfectly the difference between those who were serious about culture building and reshaping from the bottom up through trial and error, persuasion and example, on the one hand, and those who saw only sweeping macro-solutions to social problems and who put national power and wealth before social justice. The most prominent figure in the Bolshevik movement who sought to create a new morality based on what she saw as certain natural impulses of the proletariat was Alexandra Kollontai, who went beyond mechanical liberation, divorce laws, and formal equality into the realm of sexual relations, including carnal and spiritual love. She linked the notion of a "socially affirmed sexual life" to the natural spontaneous creativity of the workers, labor democracy, joy in work, and self-regeneration—all of these in direct contrast to the authoritarian work models of Lenin's state-as-factory-or-office. Influential authorities feared the power of her arguments or misunderstood them, and they correctly lamented the realities of the post-revolutionary sexual culture in Soviet Russia where brutalism, abandonment, crude sexuality and prostitution flourished under the N.E.P.[55]

The other realm of behavior—tribal mores—excited some very vigorous controversy in the 1920s. This was the realm of personal habit, appearance, and style. How such things as the cleanness of one's fingernails could become the subject of "revolutionary" discourse is not hard to understand when we recall the nihilist contempt for orderly array in the nineteenth century, the sociological meaning of dress, the campaigns for neatness and punctuality, and the notion among certain Militant Atheists of the good communist as a model of "atheist" morality. And in a revolution where the word "culture" was on the lips of every articulator of new values, the tango and the foxtrot could hardly escape scrutiny.

At the base of the discussion was a fundamental divergence about what was "revolutionary" or communist—meaning modern, full spirited, humane, rational, and healthy, and what was *meshchanskii* (a prerevolutionary term indicating narrowminded, cramped in spirit, "petty bourgois," and philistine in outlook) or *khuliganskii* (troublemaking, unruly, savage, primitive). To the new moral teachers of Bolshevism, the practitioners of *meshchanstvo* and hooliganism were not only blocking the process of culture building by their unrevolutionary behavior but were clouding the issue by calling their behavior "communist." As a result, whole choruses arose in an effort to explain what was acceptable in the realm of everyday life and mores. The problem lay in the fact that both the hooligans and the moral preachers hated *meshchanstvo* and also what they took to be the effeteness of the upper classes in general. But in their rejection of these, the latter took something like a puritan and businesslike approach and the former a more lyrical, disorderly, and even macho approach.

A common target for all revolutionaries was the perceived falsity of upper class manners, based on inequality and indolence and bathed in social hierarchy—a whole world of footmen, table service, social rank, invitations, small talk, and impeccable gestures. To redblooded workers, veterans, and Bolshevik students the pendant to this image seemed to be "toughness" in everyday life (as it had been on barricade and battlefield): swearing, smoking, hard drinking, and, for men, cavalier use of women. It was in fact a "gang" mentality, bred of the Civil War, of the hardships of urban life, and of the widespread phenomenon of *besprizornichestvo* (abandoned and orphaned children). Swearing has ever been a social lubricant for working people, a theater for themselves as they toil or play, and perhaps for males an affirmation of virility. So has a kind of rudeness to outsiders been an affirmation of internal solidarity. Trotsky, who wrote a mini-treatise on rudeness and manners, did not see this; he detected only the "feudal" rudeness of the old nobility (towards inferiors), the natural and simple rudeness of peasants, and the rudeness of bureaucrats who often succumbed to "communist" imperiousness toward employees and ordinary citizens.[56]

Drink was another divisive issue. Drunkeness, in the words of two Komsomol authors in 1927, "is a violation of our class, proletarian, communist morality. Vodka poisons and destroys the organism, it bears us out of the world of reality into a world of illusion, it deprives us of judgement." Vodka and the tavern, symbols of the enslavement of the masses by the classes, were now counterrevolutionary instruments. Drinking to excess has always been attacked by Soviet regimes, with greater or lesser success. In the 1920s, the literature on it was enormous, connecting liquor with health problems and antisocial activity. But the literature (including the anti-tobacco tracts) was hardly different in tone from that of the prerevolutionary temperence movement, and just about as effective. Alcohol and cigarettes were flatly declared foolish and sinful—like worshipping God.[57]

The leisure pattern of early Soviet youth was also assaulted in about the same terms as in Europe and America. In-groups, evening parties, street lounging, dirty jokes, loose sex, and roughhouse, all befogged by the fumes of *makhorka* (inferior tobacco) and lubricated by wine continued almost unabated after the Revolution. Apologists called it "proletarian." The ready answer of the "cultured" Bolsheviks was better recreation. Lenin appears in hagiography so often as a skier, hiker, swimmer, and chess player that one wonders how he found time to make a revolution. The ideal communist had to be forged within the walls of youth and workers' clubs, designed by architects to trap the energies of uproarious youth and channel them into culture: cinema, sport, theater, reading, and lectures. But these clubs—few in any case—were no more successful in building a new morality than they were in shaping a new ritual life. Meetings, formalism, and games did not suffice—then or now—to woo young people from their own pursuits.[58]

The question of the dance as a healthy way to regulate and sanitize contact between the sexes among youth presented a dilemma. To some Bolsheviks, dancing was associated with upperclass frivolity. "Dancehalls are gathering places for counter-revolutionaries," said the Bolshevik official Zorin to Emma Goldman during the Civil War. A motion at the first Komsomol congress to promote dancing as a means of reaching peasant youth was defeated since dancing was seen as a non-serious diversion—in contrast to theater, excursions, walking, and inspecting experimental factories! To serious Komsomols of the 1920s, the foxtrot was a symbol of affluent nightlife and café society with its "wild passions." *Fokstrotizm* and *tangoizm* were condemned for generating "African passions" and tropical lust. This fear was complicated by the flourishing nightlife during the N.E.P. period and by the appearance of jazz and Black musicians in the clubs of Leningrad and Moscow. All this was associated with wild abandon, illicit money, ugly egoism, and the display of wealth—all accompanied by "decadent" sexual behavior. Dancing was associated with private parties and—even among communist youth—with physical contact, dirty jokes, anti-Semitism (!), Oblomovism, and decadence. As a counter to it, some Komsomols actually arranged for revolutionary evenings, with young men and women marching up and down the dancefloor singing revolutionary songs as a productive and appropriate substitute for the dance.[59]

The "revolt in the dress" which could have been predicted by the sartorial culture of prerevolutionary Russia, by the studied codes of nihilist sloppiness, and by the symbolic use of certain garments in revolutionary posters to indicate corrupt plutocracy, never reached a high level of self-consciousness. The major responses were to dress down, to dress up, to dress equally, and not to dress at all. The last two are treated in the following chapter. Dressing down was the cultivation of "proletarian" simplicity sometimes brought to the level of dishevelment, a visual protest against the fancy attire of the old regime and the conspicuous display of fine apparel by N.E.P. men and their women. The Bolshevik moralists, however, believed that clothes reflected the man and the woman, and that combed hair, clean clothes, and a generally neat appearance betokened a correct and "modern" attitude of decency, respectability, and punctuality.[60]

Bolsheviks were aspiring to *kultura*, one attribute of the old intelligentsia which they admired and identified with civilized behavior in the face of hooligan anarchy and backwardness. This exaltation of *kultura* was the everyday version of their alliance with specialists and tsarist officers against the wave of undisciplined anti-intellectualism of the Civil War period. But it was not the inner *kultura* of the intelligentsia that the Bolsheviks really admired since that included much that was repugnant to them—breadth of view, impetuousness, self-doubt, soulful introspection, and universal humanitarianism. It was really *kulturnost*, the external virtues of cleanliness and punctuality. As Vera Dunham has shown in a brilliant analysis of literature and values in the Stalin period, the reverance for good manners, businesslike behavior, and a clean suit blossomed under Stalin into a thirst for opulence, a showy and vulgar taste, and a certain code of behavior in accordance with one's place in the deeply hierarchical social order of the 1930s and 1940s.[61]

What to do? Some lecturers on communist morality resisted the notion of codifying moral rules or handing out punishment. Others wanted something specific to end the "sins and crimes" and believed that morality had to be built in process, and not postponed until socialism arrived. Life could be regulated, they argued, and a "moral catechism" of proletarian ethics was absolutely essential. They also thought that leaders should enlighten the masses on moral issues, "to show the backward workers and uncivilized peasants how to live according to this new *byt* [everyday life]," especially in manners, dress, and language. Their terminology was, like much of Bolshevism in the 1920s, that of missionaries and anthropologists in a distant colony.[62]

The significance of this whole oral-cultural discourse throughout the 1920s lies in its very existence and not its resolution or lack thereof. It was a nationwide course in anthropology and ethics, carried out largely by amateurs—workers, students, Komsomols, and intellectuals—with regular contributions by representatives of the state, a state-people debate over the nature of man and the shape of man-to-be under socialism and communism. It generated a whole range of research, practice, acrimonious argument, and experiment on a vast scale. As an offshoot of communist Godbuilding, its dialectical opposite, it was an exercise in "manbuilding." Since all utopia building must begin with notions of an ideal humanity, the urge to create that humanity through talk and action in the here and now reflected the fierce desire to achieve the utopia.

The moral and ritualist quest of the 1920s, however crude and contradictory, was the secular equivalent of the devotional preparation of the Christian believer for entry into the Kingdom of Heaven. Arguments over the "new Soviet man" in the pedagogical world—a subject covered ad nauseam in hundreds of books—focused on raising a new generation in a spirit that would allow it or its successors to live virtuously under socialism and eventually, by shedding greed, egoism, and consumerism, under communism. The script for this transformation was largely the scripture according to Marx. But those who set about changing themselves and others in an adult state through discussion, practice, and experiment resembled more the disciples of Chernyshevsky, who had urged his followers to pull the future into the present, to enrich and embellish this life by living the ideals of a "radiant future," by living the Revolution.[63]

## The Missing Faith

There was never anything like a single unified approach to Godbuilding or the making of a religion. Godbuilding elements were on display everywhere, and they clearly shared

the same impulses that gave rise to them before the Revolution: the belief that bread
and politics alone were not enough, that life had to be enriched by emotion, that communism itself was a kind of religious commitment, and that many people needed a
unified set of rituals and symbols to bind their feelings to the goals of the regime. But
anti-Godbuilding was so immanent in Bolshevism that no one ever voiced an open
desire for the construction of a Bolshevik religion as such. Yet something like one was
in fact launched in the mid-1920s, the cult of Lenin—of the man who ironically was
most articulate in his opposition to it.

It began to unfold slowly in Lenin's lifetime; at the time of his death in 1924, it
took on nationwide dimensions. The funeral and lying-in-state were grand and traditional. The theme of revolutionary immortality was very much in the air before and
after 1917. But the immortalization of Lenin went way beyond the old rhetoric in scale
and intensity. Stalin insisted that Lenin not be cremated, that the remains of this "Russian" man not be desecrated, a clear invocation of Orthodox burial traditions. Under
the influence of Leonid Krasin and others, the decision was made to embalm the body
for all time and put it on display in front of the Kremlin. Krasin had been a Godbuilder
before the Revolution, and he was supported by Lunacharsky. Melnikov designed the
sarcophagus as a "sleeping chamber for a sleeping prince." The architect Shchusev,
who had been a specialist in building Orthodox churches in the past, designed a cube-
like structure for the eternal remains of the deceased Lenin. The painter Malevich wanted
a full-scale religious cult of Lenin, with ceremonies and song, and with the cube in
every home as a sacred artifact. The party launched a campaign of oaths, publications,
and ceremonies focusing on the dead leader. His tomb became a shrine for pilgrims.
His life habits were invoked as the norm of a good communist. Institutes, museums,
Lenin Corners, and a flood of toys, mementos, monuments, and even kitchy junk appeared—sometimes cheapening the intended effect of reverance.[64]

The language of the campaign and many of the spontaneous responses clearly outlined Lenin as a saint, a Christ, or an anointed tsar. He was idealized, heroized, and
romanticized beyond recognition. The embalming was opposed by his wife and family;
by Bonch-Bruevich, his secretary and a specialist on religious studies; and by Trotsky,
Kamenev, and Bukharin in line with Lenin's own expressed wishes for a simple burial
or cremation. Lunacharsky, though an old Godbuilder and a keen practitioner of the
language of revolutionary immortality, made it clear that he thought literal personal
immortality to be a naive "peasant" belief.

The promoters of the cult won out, but the cult itself was not an undiluted traditional
religious affair. Elements of science, technology, and modernism insinuated themselves
at many points and at many levels. Airplanes flew over the funeral cortège, and at the
moment of interment, a mass stoppage of work across the entire length of the U.S.S.R.
was made possible only by modern means of communication (radio especially). The
spokesmen for cremation argued on rational and sanitary grounds. The mausoleum was
augmented with modern equipment designed by the engineer Krasin. Full medical and
autopsy reports were published, with minute physiological details not only of Lenin's
death but also of their efforts to embalm and preserve the body against decay. Schemes
of Lenin's crypt included a tower of steel, housing turbines and radio stations, and a
huge structure containing a moving locomotive, a tractor, and a running stream. Monument projects included the erection of a giant screw.

Ambivalence seemed to attend every stage of the cult, although the "traditionalists"
who stressed sober and familiar motifs with religious overtones usually prevailed. But

the same kind of ambivalence appeared in the reception of the cult. Its makers were inspired by both genuine reverance and a political desire to mobilize the masses around a vital symbol and insure the continuity of party rule and the traditions of the October Revolution. In this they were very successful, and large numbers of people exhibited deep emotion—whether based on genuine understanding of Lenin's life, on vestiges of peasant monarchism, or on agreement with Lenin's policies. Contrivance and spontaneity worked together to build the Lenin cult. The cult was tied to Bolshevik morality in various campaigns that linked the building of "Lenin Corners" (related to the old icon corner of Orthodoxy) to correct behavior. It was a fusion of political and religious ritual to mobilize the sentiments of the Russian people—and like all invented cults it occasionally produced tasteless, repetitive, and even comical elements. But the cult of Lenin was transformed drastically by Stalin in the 1930s and did not grow into a widespread civic religion for the population at large. The God Lenin was in fact demoted by the God Stalin—for at least twenty years.

Another movement of the 1920s became—at least for awhile and on a limited scale—a rival "religion of communism." This was sectarian Christianity. The Sectarians were vibrant in their faith and in their conscious emulation of Bolshevik codes and rituals in order to compete with them, a practice that Bolshevik commentators found both engaging and annoying. Party officials observed that the sects were spiritually vital and attracted converts by their sobriety, mutuality, charity, and joyous song—a combination that Bolshevik Godbuilders dreamed of. The Baptists of Kursk Province attracted followers because of their model behavior, genuine brotherhood, relevance to life, and the unabashed prayers to Jesus in time of joy and woe. Perm Evangelists, copying the Bolshevik parallel feasts, launched a Day of Youth, a Festival of Sisters (for women's equality), and religious texts set to revolutionary and church melodies. Novgorod Sectarians held concerts full of spontaneous singing and "love evenings" that fused the revolutionary concept of comradeship with Christian motifs of brotherhood in clean, sober and highly organized settings, avoiding both the wild drunkenness of village feasts and the banality of Bolshevik events.[65]

Commentators were astonished at the frankly modern and syncretic methods of the Sectarians. Socialist imagery was freely adopted in slogans of justice, solidarity, and equality, in agitprop campaigns to enlist youth, and in organizational names such as Bapsomol (or Baptomol) and Christomol to rival the Komsomol. They held meetings and challenged other religions to friendly competitions. On May Day in Saratov Province, Baptists launched a Day of Classless Solidarity with Brothers in Christ and a two-week campaign against biblical illiteracy. Almost every Bolshevik method of reaching the masses was imitated, including *sheftsvo*. Some Sectarians, grateful to the regime for having lifted the onerous persecution by the Orthodox Church, seemed to want some kind of merger between Bolshevik economic forms and a vibrant sectarian Christianity, infused with brotherhood, equality, and harmony.[66]

The Sectarians were more successful than the Bolsheviks in arousing genuine emotion and commitment, and their conversion record was impressive. The Bolsheviks wondered why this was so and urged activists to emulate the methods of the sectarian groups. But the secret of the Sectarians' success was not, of course, the forms of ritual and propaganda. It was their transparent faith and moral power. They preached no hatred against class enemies and opened their doors to people of all ethnic origins, sexes, classes, and nationalities. Their charity was unabashed and unlimited, and most of all uninhibited by ideological and political animosity. Their concept of "comradeship'' was universal and yet encouraged strong cohesion within community and family. Paralleling their stated social faith was a practical religion of genuine brotherhood. This is why their ceremonies, rituals, parades, and campaigns came alive with enthusiasm. Ultimately, the success of their communal life style and their missionary work evoked the hostility of the Bolsheviks, who could not compete with them on moral grounds. This fact, as much as the fundamentalism, anti-scientism, and dogmatism of the sects, brought the wrath of the regime down upon them after a decade of tolerance and puzzled admiration.

There is no way to know how many peasants lost their faith and became atheists in the 1920s, and it may never be understood just what ''religion'' of any sort meant to the peasants' life. But we do know that they had a fantastic ability to absorb new ''faiths'' and rituals when necessary and combine them with their own ways. Peasants who accepted atheism and its forms may have done so as accommodation, just as the Christianized peasants of ancient Russia had retained their old pagan thought forms and modes of worship alongside the new in a culture known as *dvoeverie*—dual faith. There was not only much *dvoeverie* in rural Russia in the 1920s, but *troeverie* and perhaps even *mnogoverie* (multiple faith); we hear of pagan, Christian, and Bolshevik festivals celebrated not only by adjacent villages, but in the same village at the same time. In this context, there was much opportunity for a kind of tactful, syncretic Godbuilding that would be humane, religious, and progressive as well. Whatever chance there might have been, however, was doomed at the end of the twenties by the great transformation in antireligious activity.[67]

Because of certain outward features of Bolshevism—and other communist movements of our century—commentators have often called it a religion. In the 1920s, Fueloep-Miller remarked that Bolshevism taught science but was not a science, that it fought religion while being like one. In our time, Jacques Ellul has said, ''the Russians have gone furthest in creating a 'religion' compatible with Technique.'' These judgements are misleading. Maurice Hindus—writing in the 1920s—was more perceptive. Bolshevism, while containing many of the outward attributes of a faith, he observed, was actually a nonfaith because it was not forgiving, possessed no deity, exalted science and nature, and possessed a ''revolutionary'' system of ethics instead of a humane one. It lacked beauty, dignity, and spirit. Berdyaev in the 1930s emphasized its lack of inward drama and depth, its weakness in religious pshychology, and its pedantry. Mao Zedong, a major communist of our time, put it very succinctly and honestly: ''Marxism-Leninism has no beauty, nor has it any mystical value. It is only extremely useful.''[68]

One of the most striking pictures of the ''Bolshevik God'' is to be found in Andrei Platonov. Mikhail Geller's introduction to Platonov's *Chevengur* contrasts the apparitions of two fictional peasants named Makar. In an 1883 story by V. G. Korolenko, ''Makar's Dream,'' the protagonist, after a lifetime of bitter work, tragedy, and sin, finds a merciful and compassionate God who grants him redemption and salvation. Platonov's Makar, a Soviet worker, also sees God in a dream. But this God is a ''man of science'' who does not even look at the miserable Makar but peers blankly into the distant future with terrible dead eyes—a fat, enormous, and lifeless idol. This is what Bolshevism became to many in the 1930s and to some even earlier. But it was not perceived that way by those who believed that a godless religion, Bolshevism, could still be a religion for the new humanity.[69]

There can be no question that some people found religion in the Russian Revolution. Utopians and experimentalists of all sorts sought to rebuild mankind along essentially religious lines, and their enthusiasm was evangelical and millenarian. Many artists saw themselves as the priesthood of a new "revolution of the spirit." Thousands of communists, Komsomols, workers, and pro-Soviet activists found inspiration in the Revolution itself, in Bolshevism—its myths, heroes, martyrs, and memories. In spite of the power-lust and cynicism that engulfed so many in the party, there always remained dedicated and reverent communists whose vision of the future clearly resembled a religious faith. Red Army men and women, though operating amid inefficiency, apathy, desertion, undiscipline, and brutality, were particularly affected. "They were crusaders for a new idea," writes a major historian of that army:

> They had before their mental eyes the blueprint of a new world, a bonny world, worth living and dying for. There was great dynamism in their fervor, a feeling of being fully and entirely right, of deserving to win because of what they thought the consequences of their victory might be, not only for Russia but for the entire world. This element—call it religious or revolutionary enthusiasm, as you prefer—was undoubtedly the great stimulus, the tremendous force that sustained the Red Army during the Civil War.

The ideals, exalted moral sense, comradeship, the sharing of goods and what one veteran called the "blind faith in a bright future" are acknowledged as hallmarks of the era even by those who became anti-communists. This faith possessed even many inhabitants of political prisons and labor camps in the 1930s. The moral fervor generated by the Revolution, based on an ideology of struggle for justice and modernity through heroism and sacrifice, was so potent for some Bolsheviks that they ended their lives in Stalin's terror still believing not only in the goals of communism, but in the party and in Stalin himself.[70]

# 6

## The Republic of Equals

To the eyes of all the Utopians, with the exception of the very few who for a
good reason had visited foreign countries, all this gay show appeared disgrace-
ful. They therefore bowed to the lowest of the party as to the masters but took
the ambassadors themselves to be slaves because they were wearing gold chains,
and passed them over without any deference whatever.

Thomas More, *Utopia* (1516)

The Russian Revolution of 1917, far more than any previous revolution, was heavily
saturated with concepts of equality. There was no social consensus about equality and
no commonly held egalitarian mentality, yet ideas, words, symbols, and gestures denoting varying forms of equality pervaded revolutionary sensibility. Egalitarianism was
in fact the central element in all utopias and experimental movements of the period. It
was inherent in the standardization and reductionism of cultural nihilists, in vandalism
and iconoclasm, in symbol and festival, in militant atheism, in the machine cult, utopian
science fiction, revolutionary town planning, and communalism. When Stalin attacked
egalitarianism or "equality-mongering" (*uravnilovka*) in the early 1930s, he not only
assaulted wage leveling but gave a signal that the entire movement of revolutionary
utopia was doomed. How deeply and widely did the notion of equality take hold in the
Revolution? What did it mean to those who clamored for it?

### Equality and Justice

I have already touched upon peasant notions of *pravda* in the opening chapter. Here I
wish to explore for a moment some of the implications of lower-class views of justice,
fairness, and equity—what intellectuals called *ravenstvo* (equality)—a word that was
not in the village lexicon. Analyses of peasant life show clearly that the Russian village
embraced the extremities of equality and inequality. The former was expressed by the
common management of village enterprises and equitable land distribution periodically
according to tillers or to "eaters." In dividing up the land, the peasant *skhod* (meeting)
handled the tensions of competition like a theater or encounter group, marked by seemingly immense disorder and chaos, interruptions, and shouting; in fact it achieved businesslike results and then managed to carve up the land with minute refinement. The widespread notion of *pravo truda* also indicated a belief that only tillers—not landlords—
ought to have use of all the land. The source of this aspect of peasant mentality was
probably religious and ethical but not "legal."

But the peasant religion of fairness did not extend much beyond this level. Peasant lore from time to time generated a vague belief in the "universal commune." In practice, neighboring villages were supposed to take care of themselves, not each other—even in time of famine. In the household the explosive relationship of *bolshak* (head-of-household) vs. family, mother-in-law vs. daughter-in-law, and various other tensions based on sexual relations and on territorial rights of table, stove, and living space were rarely egalitarian. And then there was the problematic belief in *pravo na trud*, subtly different from and partly contradictory to *pravo truda*: the right to land for all in the commune—which could work for equality in helping the weak, but could also allow for the emergence of the aquisitive peasant or kulak who justified his wealth on the basis of skill or industrious management.[1]

The artel, which originated in the countryside, was another arena where peasant concepts of sharing and equity were put into practice. Artels were teams of men who pooled resources, hired out for a common task, and shared the wage. There were variants to the pattern. A boatman's artel shared pay equally even though the nature and quantity of the work was not always identical. Among certain Cossacks of the Ukraine, men would disperse in groups of 6–10, elect an ataman, sell and trade for several months on the road, and rendezvous for distribution of the profits: all got equal shares except the ataman, who got a little bit more, and slackers, who were penalized. The custom was widespread among itinerant laborers, craftsmen, and even the porters of St. Petersburg. It migrated to the industrial towns where it took the form of "eating artels"—the pooling of money for the common purchase and consumption of meals. This dwindled in the twentieth century with the growth of family life of industrial workers in some trades but was still very much in evidence in 1914. Other forms of solidary life, such as the *zemlyachestvo*—associations of workers from common geographical origins—supplemented the economically oriented artel. The latter persisted in the army where it was almost institutionalized. An example of the precision to which artel members were dedicated in the matter of sharing is a peculiar episode on the Saloniki front during World War I: each man was issued a tiny ration of wine in a unit commanded by Count Lobanov-Rostovsky; a dozen men immediately formed an artel with the purpose of allowing one man to get drunk every twelve days.[2]

If any summary can be made of such a complex and rich collection of mental attitudes, it would be that peasants (in field or factory) had a strong emotional and moral committment to welfare for all, to the protection of the weak, to some extra reward for the industrious, to a concept of "brotherhood" for one's immediate community (what the Bolsheviks would later term the *kollektiv*), and—in time of strife or absence of restraint—to a dethronement of the "idle rich," and to the practice of equitable apportionment of land, confiscated property, earnings, and even loot. Belief in group involvement in and acceptance of basic economic decisions was deeply ingrained.

The intelligentsia was not ignorant of popular impulses and popular aspirations. Many early revolutionaries of the sixties who laid the foundations for the "populist style" versed themselves in the habits and customs of the peasantry. A clear example of this was Bervi's "religion of equality," discussed in the previous chapter. Another was a document produced in the mid-1860s by radicals associated with Dmitry Karakozov, would-be assassin of the tsar, and found on his person:[3]

> The land will not belong to idle parasites but to artels, societies of the workers themselves. And capital will not be squandered by the tsar, the landlords, and the tsarist magnates, but will belong to the workers' artels themselves. The artels will

produce a profitable return on this capital and the income will be divided equally among all the workers in the artels. . . . everyone will be equal and the Russian working people will live happily and honestly, working only for themselves.

Similar images were invoked in Populist propaganda literature designed for peasants in the nineteenth century. The theme of egalitarianism-as-religion in revolutionary propaganda of the early twentieth century was part of this tradition.

But the Russian intelligentsia was deeply divided over the issue of egalitarianism. Liberals promoted legal, ethnic, and formal political equality (*ravenstvo*)—especially equal rights (*ravnopravie*)—though often on pragmatic rather than exalted moral grounds. The anti-radical intelligentsia of *Vekhi* criticized the leftist intelligentsia for its "anti-cultural" egalitarianism and its desire to "turn all people into workers." Marxists of course denied this. Lenin in 1919, in response to a similar lament of "bourgeois professors," emphatically denied the reductionist ambitions of Bolshevism. It wanted, he said tersely, to abolish capitalism and social classes now, to end the distinction between peasants and workers in the future. Marxist views on the distribution of wealth and goods are well-known: under socialism "to each according to his work" and under communism "to each according to his needs." Marxists often described the first phase as equality in distribution though they did not mean by it identical shares. In their literature and agitation, they tended to focus on the injustices and inequalities of "feudalism" and capitalism in orthodox Marxist language. But in their talk about the future, they tended rather to sketch very vaguely a just society, where people would be equal in some way or another. The precise mechanism of distribution on the day after the revolution, the nature of relations among people, their wage, appearance, manners, their role in life—was left for the most part unexplored. But it was precisely in this realm that some of the biggest questions arose.[4]

## Russian Levellers

The word "levellers" emerged out of a "world turned upside down" in the English Revolution of the seventeenth century, described so eloquently in the book of that name by Christopher Hill. Fueled by religious fervor and social conflict, the English Levellers endeavored to bring down the haughty and to share wealth. A similar current surfaced in the French Revolution, represented at its most extreme by Sylvain Maréchal and Gracchus Babeuf. Leveling has been variously interpreted as a millenial dream of fairness and equality or as a mean-spirited example of social envy and lower-class desire to pull everyone down. In the Russian Revolution, both elements were present. In their war against the privileges, living space, and property of the old upper classes, the masses were generally supported by the Bolshevik regime, which added its own decrees and policies to the movement. On the question of extending the leveling process to the new regime itself, the Bolshevik leaders were at best ambivalent and in most cases hostile.

Leveling on the land displayed many exceptions and local variations. The agrarian revolution broke out in two explosive stages, the spring, summer and autumn of 1917 and, with greater force, in the following summer, spreading like fire across the land. Village *mirs* took the initiative in most cases and required all to participate in a takeover of the landlords' land. Indeed, sometimes peasants were actually dragged by force to the village assembly to share in the pillaged land or the loot from the manor house. In all cases some principle of equality was invoked. But for the vast majority of peasants, equality did not mean creating a common pool of land to be worked collectively—in other words a commune—but rather the division into shares. Parcels were awarded according to family size or "eaters," landless were given shares, and even livestock and other property were divided up. On the other hand, the so-called second revolution of poor peasants against kulaks did not materialize spontaneously but had to be prompted, with little success, by the Committees of the Poor. In the Ukraine, however, Makhno compelled kulaks to give up "surplus wealth," distributed this to the poor, and took a share for his army. Known as social banditry elsewhere, it was a perfect application of the artel principle. The great Black Repartition of the land in 1917 and 1918 fit, in major outlines, the age-old aspirations of the peasants that they alone should have all arable land and work it in accordance with their established traditions. The symbol of peasant-style egalitarianism and justice, the *mir*, came to life with great vigor in 1917 and held onto it until being dissolved by force in the 1930s.[5]

In the towns, the pattern varied also. In some places, exactions from the rich (or the "richer") appeared spontaneously before the coming of the Bolsheviks to power. Bolsheviks in the Ufa region of the southern Urals, for example, established a City Commune and levied a million ruble contribution by diverting apartment rents from landlords to the Commune. Petrograd witnessed all kinds of takeovers ranging from revolutionary acts of parties to outright theft by street marauders (often dressed as revolutionaries or sailors). But in Moscow there was little of this in 1917. After the October Revolution, the Bolsheviks, while attempting to control the uncontrollable, also issued decrees on fortunes, inheritance, rents, and other property. The Petrograd Soviet in December 1917 formed a committee for requisitioning warm clothes from the rich, defined as those living in apartments costing 150 rubles per month or more. Each was to donate one blanket and one item of warm clothing—fur coat, sweater, mittens, or boots. By January 1918, about 900,000 rubles worth of garments were thus taken and given to the men at the front. Eventually this military rationing measure flowed into a general assessment of household property, the confiscation of valuables and treasure, and the reassignment of living space. Some affluent people were taxed by house committees for having a servant or a bathroom (500 rubles) or a piano or a dog (600 rubles). In Ekaterinoslav, a town of great revolutionary violence, the local Bolshevik leader explained that the workers must "wrest from the bourgeoisie those millions taken from the masses and cunningly turned into silken undergarments, furs, carpets, gold, furniture, paintings, china. . . . We have to take it and give it to the proletariat and then force the bourgeoisie to work for their rations for the Soviet regime."[6]

Bukharin in 1918 lamented the fact that some people thought that all wealth should be divided among the poor "according to God's will." The lament was well founded. During the 1917 events in Saratov, the administration of a large factory donated 10,000 rubles to improve the workers' conditions; less conscious workers wanted to divide it up at once in equal shares. Factory committees sometimes measured off the profits to the workers after wheeling out the owner in a barrow. The sailors of insurgent Kronstadt and the Bolsheviks of War Communism both adopted the rough-and-ready policy of food rationing: equal shares for workers, more to heavy labor, less to nonworking people. When the lower class members of an ephemeral Bolshevik government occupied the governor's mansion in Ekaterinoslav, they carved up the huge Turkestan carpet in the reception hall into small equal pieces for themselves! Sharing was extended from loot to honor and guilt: a Petrograd theater held anniversaries for stage hands as well as artists, and stevedores who concealed food during the famine of 1921–2 confessed to equal guilt when one of them was apprehended in the act. The intellectuals of War Communism who, like the Menshevik economist Shefter, wanted full planning and the equal distribution of all consumer goods might have been utopians, but they seemed to have reflected the deep impulse of many ordinary people.[7]

The Russian city before the Revolution was inequality carved in masonry. Housing was extremely expensive in the two capitals, even by European standards. Yet thousands of affluent people maintained enormous apartments, some so immense that after the revolution the new occupants marvelled that they did not get lost in them. For the working classes, available space in big cities was probably declining in the last decade before 1914. They occupied cellars, garrets, rooms or parts thereof in sprawling slums such as the Hay Market in St. Petersburg or the Khitrovka in Moscow, or in urban shanty towns near factories. The overcrowding created the "communal" experience long before the Revolution. St. Petersburg in 1900 had 50,000 one or two room apartments with four persons in each room; in the Empire at large, the average was eleven persons per apartment. In his "Letters from Afar" and *State and Revolution*, Lenin— inspired by Engels—called for the eviction of the "bourgeoisie" from their homes and the installation in them of the proletariat. This does not mean, however, that the urban masses were everywhere seething to occupy the homes of the rich. The workers of Moscow between the two revolutions of 1917 seemed to want lower rents, better housing, and a kind of municipal welfare socialism—not necessarily the wholesale eviction or displacement of the bourgeoisie. Passions were hotter in Petrograd, partly because residential segregation and the visible contrast of rich and poor seemed greater.[8]

The Anarchists took the lead in launching the housing saga right after the February Revolution. In a rash of expropriations and expulsions, they took over public buildings and homes of prominent statesmen now discredited. The Durnovo dacha was a headquarters for a time. On Kronstadt, the Anarcho-Syndicalist-Communists and the Left Socialist Revolutionaries aligned against Bolsheviks and Mensheviks to demand an immediate housing revolution. The former military school director there cried burglary when the Kronstadt authorities "repopulated" the twenty room apartment in which he lived alone. Anarchists also excelled in social hostility toward the bourgeoisie: "Right here is a home," said one of their papers of 1918. "Go in and settle down. Let the owners of the houses and palaces roam the streets and feel their own teeth chatter."[9]

In the absence of detailed and fair-minded studies of the housing revolution of 1917– 20, it is difficult to gauge the relative inputs of masses and regime. The Moscow government began rather slowly with municipalization of larger buildings. In 1918 it began to reassign the city's inhabitants by means of scaled rents and assigned space according to occupation and need (this meant for the most part workers and lower employees sharing or taking the former space of upper employees, businessmen, and *rentiers*). About 20,000 people were moved in the first year of revolution, the figures peaking at the time of Lenin's attempted assassination, when occupants were shoved onto the streets unceremoniously with or without their possessions. In Petrograd, 12,000 were relocated in the winter of 1918–19. The formula was to leave one room per adult or per two children for the "bourgeoisie," the remainder to be redistributed to workers. The Vyborg Quarter, the most radical of Petrograd's neighborhoods, took the lead. In some districts factories took over certain apartment houses directly.

The process was standardized by a government decree of August 1918. From then to the end of War Communism, rehousing became a mass movement, wrapped in confusion and contradiction and bewildering in complexity—balanced as it was in some places (such as Petrograd) by urban outmigration. In the vortex of this revolution within a revolution, the "intelligentsia" were often lumped together with the "bourgeois" exploiters and expelled even though the regime made it clear that certain specialists were exempted from the calculations of the House Committees. Larger buildings in the center of the capitals were made into public offices; suburban mansions were earmarked for workers' clubs. Excess furniture was given to the needy, warm clothes to the army, and art treasures to the museum apparatus.[10]

But what was it like inside the expropriated buildings? In many ways it was like an epic or fairy-tale, a reversal of the normal order of things. The occupancy by the poor of spacious mansions and flats designed for the elegant life style of the gentry and the urban rich brought together in almost daily association two kinds of people who had theretofore been as from two different planets. Former servants, emulating the solemnity of their old masters and displaying the new-won dignity of the rising proletariat, would read out in ungrammatical Russian the rules of comportment to yesterday's arbiters of social life. Revolution touched the fabric of intimate life when servants were given the dining room and the use of fine table service and linen while the former owners were denied their use. Lenin aroused much levity when he told of a professor who complained about being ordered—for reasons of space—to sleep in the same bed with his wife, and a physician was allowed to keep his piano only if he allowed workers' children to practice on it. The grandest lords fell hard: the opulent palaces of the Yusupovs, Shuvalovs, and Stroganovs were taken over for public purposes. The Russian dancer Igor Shvetsov has left a minute description of how his family's twelve-room house, laden with "furniture, pictures, pianos, bronzes, carpets, porcelain, books—everything that goes to furnish a comfortable home" was snatched from him at childhood. All goods were carefully registered and removed, and the family was evicted with three small wagons full of beds and basic furniture. In Saratov, a local order evicted bourgeois families on twenty four hours' notice, warning the evictees not to trouble the authorities with petitions for leniency but to move at once to the outskirts of the city where basements stood ready to receive them. The workers, meanwhile, poured into the vacated flats and homes, sometimes squabbling among themselves for space and facilities, sometimes forced to tear up the floors for firewood—thus giving what some wished to see as a new collective life an emergency quality that dampened the egalitarian triumph.[11]

One of the most enduring socialist teachings of the nineteenth century was that every able-bodied person ought to work—to the best of his or her capacity—thus adding to the general weal and ending idleness. The word idler (*tuneyadets*) became a snarl during the Russian Revolution. A Petrograd Anarchist union in August 1917 called for the mobilization of "all able-bodied elements from the parasitic and intermediary classes of the population." This was one area where Lenin was not outstripped by Anarchists. In his major programatic writings of 1917 he used violent words and leveling imagery against the rich, the idle, and the shirker. In December 1917, the Bolsheviks ordered all citizens out for snow-shovelling duty, with the idlers taking first shifts; at the time of the Brest peace negotiations, Lenin ordered labor battalions of bourgeois men and women to dig defensive trenches on pain of being shot. In August 1918, with the deeper mobilization of the War Communism period, a Committee on the Mobilization of the Bourgeoisie was appointed which added to that nebulous category monks, journalists, professionals, officers, officials of the old regime, and cadets—all males aged eighteen to fifty (the elderly and women were taxed instead of being put to work). In the Civil War, with most able-bodied people at the front, the old privileged classes, were put in charge of house and yard maintenance and sweeping streets and squares. Princess Obolenskaya—once at the pinnacle of Russian aristocracy—was forced to shovel snow from the Fontanka Embankment. Nobles, generals, and prelates of the church felt the agony and humiliation of physical work performed in public.[12]

At the peak of War Communism, in 1920, the entire population was enjoined to turn out for general cleanup and other civic duties; on the site where Skobelev's statue once stood was mounted a big sign: "He Who Does Not Work, Neither Shall He Eat." The general mobilization of labor was tied to egalitarian justice and to national survival. But leveling was as much an expression of social hate as it was of egalitarianism. The World War was partly responsible for this. In 1917 soldiers on the Nevsky were angered by the sight of "dolled up people" with "cars, perfume, lace, gowns, and laughter . . . too much laughter" in time of ubiquitous slaughter at the front. When Civil War broke out, those who had sat out the earlier war were sometimes forced into the ranks and sent to the front. The October Revolution released some deep impulses for reversal and symbolic retribution. There was even a legend abroad in the early days of the Revolution that it was caused by Jews who wanted to ride Cossack horses and make Cossacks walk, that sailors had revolted in order to be able to ride inside the trams (a practice previously forbidden). Such myths are the stuff of major revolutions. But so were the real reversals—jailers jailed, owners sent into the mines, managers evicted from plants on wheelbarrows, generals reduced to privates. In the tiny town of Solvy-chegodsk, a typical scene of reversal was fashioned when, in August 1918, merchants, former Land Captains, and police of various kinds were marched out into work gangs under the watchful eyes of proletarian guards. It happened everywhere.[13]

"Egalitarianism" fell into two basic categories in the Revolution. On the one hand was war, strife, anger, demeaning and insulting behavior, a compulsion to pull down and thus "level"—to extend not the hand of harmony and brotherhood but rather the fist of social envy and spite. On the other was the utopian dream of community through equality, sharing, and fairness in income and privilege. Its drive to overturn, mock, and demean was essentially destructive and not culture building or community building. The Bolsheviks promoted this popular passion that was closely linked to the peasantry's habit of punishing—in stressful circumstance—the perceived agent of its misery past or present. The upper classes, whose mentality was shaped after the social trauma of 1905, did not offer fraternal welcome to the egalitarian and leveling masses—and the masses knew this with a precise instinct. If their word for the hated ones was *burzhui*, the upper classes had their own epithet of contempt: the *tovarishchi*, uppety plebeians who addressed not only each other with this term, but extended it also—as insult—to the former ruling and cultivated classes. It was precisely in this area of human relations that the broad sweep of inconoclasm and anti-intellectualism intersected and melted in with the elemental force of lower class egalitarianism. And it was here also that the more vigorous articulations of class hate among nineteenth century revolutionaries finally merged with the less verbal but gesturally eloquent class hatred of the lower classes toward the upper.[14]

## Dress, Speech, and Deference

Leveling was in a way the negative side of the egalitarian movement, a rude and dismissive blow against the Old Classes (soon to be called the "people of the past" or *byvshie lyudi*), just as iconoclasm was a blow against old culture, symbols, and forms. But egalitarianism had its positive side as well: its symbolic and behavioral reinforcement, demonstration, or celebration. The Bolshevik regime promoted equality in its rituals, symbols, and myths, to say nothing of its rhetoric. One of the most dramatic living "texts" composed by the new regime was the delegation to the peace talks at Brest-Litovsk early in 1918. To face the steel-helmeted and beribboned spokesmen of the Hohenzollern and Habsburg dynasties, the Bolsheviks carefully chose the team of people who would be the first to meet the outer world of dynasts and exploiters in public show. It contained several Russians, an Armenian, two Jews, a revolutionary woman (the assassin of a general at that!), an old soldier, a very large and strong sailor, and a rough looking worker. To complete the sociological mosaic of the worker-peasant state, they picked up on their way to the station in Petrograd a peasant from off the streets and pressed him into service as the embodiment of the People. The old world was duly impressed (though this helped the Bolsheviks not at all in the parlays). But the delegation remained, in function, in style, and in outer appearance an obvious assortment of unequals, and the colorful old muzhik insisted on calling everyone *barin*—master—much to the chagrin of the composers of the delegation.[15] How was one to fight deference and visible inequality?

Deference, in the language of Edward Shils, is the attribution of worth unconnected with moral superiority but with the "entitlements" of occupation, wealth, income, style, education, power, associations, and symbols. Structures of deference do not account for class, as Shils maintained, but they certainly shape and reinforce perceptions of class, particularly in the giving and receiving of deferential signals: salutes, greetings, forms of address, bows, tone of voice, gestures, and demeanor. Old Russia was rich in these, and one could virtually "read" the social text of conversation between two unequals from a distance: soldiers snapped into stiffness and shouted clipped ritual responses to orders; peasants bowed low before their barins and to each other as well; nannys cackled with glee at the approach of their betters; and lower orders moved aside in the presence of visibly powerful or wealthy people.

There was less ambivalence than in more recent times, but there were complexities and nuances. Peasant values of religion and common labor allowed for "superiors" among them in skill to be admired; but the admiring and respectful inferior did not demean himself and expected similar respect from the superior talent. The most extreme form of heraldric behavior was found at the uppermost reaches of society—the court. But elsewhere it was in flux. Workers in the twentieth century began—as the radical intelligentsia had done since the 1860s—to fight the visible forms of deference. Trotsky's worker friend Mukhin explained to him in 1896 that the essence of inequality was form. He lined up a pile of beans on a table in ranked order—and then he scrambled the beans, showing the ultimate equality of all beans and all human beings.[16]

A revolt in the dress seemed a good place to begin fighting the inequality of outward appearance. Clothing and caste went together in prerevolutionary Russia where ermine cape, pince-nez, frock coat, bast shoes, bark boots, sheepskin, and rags had easily decodable social meaning. Uniforms abounded in the military, the civil service, the universities, the church, and at court, and there was a dazzling array of folk, regional, national, and even occupational costumes. In Bogdanov's *Red Star*—as in much science fiction utopia—the psychological equality of the Martian communists was underlined by identical unisex costumes. But in the Russian Revolution, the bulk of the population did not change clothes. Workers continued to dress as they had before the revolution in a partly bourgeoisified combination of boots, stuffed-in pants, plain shirt, jacket, and proletarian cap (with some frills for Sunday best)—except insofar as they sported red ribbons or joined the Red Guard, whose costume, hastily devised in 1917, was a militaroid greatcoat, red armband, and workers' cap. The peasants altered their appearance even less—except insofar as they flaunted the furs and feathers of a looted mansion.[17]

It was the military, the political leaders, and the artists who innovated. In 1917, sailors and soldiers liked to tilt back their caps and open their coats in defiant and euphoric gestures of what Jean Marabini called street theater or carnival, his somewhat exaggerated transfer of the French revolutionary journées into Russian conditions. Kerensky reflected his ambivalent view of democracy in the dress by coming to a diplomatic reception without a tie and by assuming the military tunic when speaking to the troops. When the Revolution deepened it became a "visible revolution" wherein personal appearance became a political statement. In the Civil War, citizens with clean fingernails and smooth hands were shot in Sevastopol by the incoming Reds. In the Omsk region, a White commander surrounded a factory, examined the hands of all the employees, and shot those with calloused hands. In March 1918, the secretary of the Bolshevik committee in Saratov was killed by a Red Army man who took him for an undesirable "bourgeois" on account of the trim fashionable suit he wore.[18]

Remarkably enough, very few history books have pictures; fewer still have good ones. When they do, people rarely study them. Yet it is clear from the iconography of the first Bolshevik commissars that most of them looked like Chekhov—more or less. the pince-nez and the three-piece suit with tie abounded. Stalin, Trotsky and a few others donned the tunic; hundreds of local commissars and officials—emulating Sverdlov—assumed the leather jacket which became a veritable uniform of politics in the eyes of their enemies. Ironically, most of these were obtained from a deserted shipment of clothes left by the British during the war. Among the women leaders, only Kollontai adhered to her fashionable wardrobe; Krupskaya and most others wore the plainest dresses. The Bolshevik leaders certainly avoided the extravagance of upper class raimant, but most would not take off their familiar garb for the sake of egalitarian symbolism. The occasional unkempt and unshaven official was a product of personal carelessness, overwork, or a shortage of blades—rarely of self-conscious show.[19]

The military—ever conscious of the importance of signs—made plainness its chief principle. The red star (see Chapter 4) was for a long time the only embellishment. Gone were the dazzling medals, epaulettes, shoulder boards, chevrons and braiding of the old order. The epaulette was a particularly repugnant symbol of the old uniform: captured White officers sometimes had the epaulettes nailed into their shoulders as symbolic retribution before being executed. But uniformity in the services did not prevail. There was little standardization until the 1920s. A famous photo of 1920 on Red Square shows Muralov in a traditional shirt-tunic (pullover), Sam Brown belt and revolver, jodphurs, and boots; Trotsky in British-style World War I uniform; Antonov-Ovseenko as a Red Guard—the archetypical intellectual commissar, militant and bespectacled; and an unidentified cavalry officer wearing a costume designed in 1918 by the artist Boris Kustodiev. This uniform became symbolic of red forces on the march—especially Budënny's Red Cavalry Army. It was probably inspired by Bilibin's prewar designs for fairy tales, so closely did it resemble his illustrations: a Mongol-type cap with big red star, an antique Slavic coat—vaguely oriental—held together across the front with three pointed tabs (see Fig. 23). Commanders attempted to assume some kind of distinctive garb, but the men in the ranks often had to wear whatever they could scrounge up.[20]

The intelligentsia headed in various directions in a search for socialist dress. Komsomols enveloped their views in a discourse on morality and custom. But to bohemian artists, equality meant wearing anything one wanted. According to Ehrenburg, in the early 1920s, "women with pretensions to smartness wore soldiers' greatcoats and green hats made of billiard table cloth. Dresses were made of wine-colored curtains livened up with Supermatist squares and triangles." The painter Rabinovich wore an emerald colored sheepskin, and Esenin appeared in a shiny top hat. Other avant-gardists believed in functional proletarian costumes for the whole nation. Constructivists such as Stepanova, Popova, Exter, Tatlin, and Rodchenko wanted a style that was vaguely democratic and socialist—uniforms for industry, specialists, work, and sport—in a "democratic style that would replace both the notion of a fashion for the elite and, no less important, the mass eclecticism of the post-Revolutionary period" (see Fig. 24). This was a new kind of equality via a new kind of variety. The most radical idea was "throw-away clothing" made of paper. Almost nothing in this wide range of stylistic sensibilities made any inroads among the Russian masses then or since. These artists, writes Bowlt, "were designing for utopian worlds."[21]

The most spectacular reform proposal came from the "Down with Shame" movement, a well-known but almost undocumented episode of the 1920s. Believing that the only democratic and egalitarian apparel was the human skin itself, members demonstrated this belief by exhibiting their nakedness in public. Evenings of the Denuded Body were held in Moscow in 1922. Later there were marches and processions in Moscow and Kharkov and the occupation of trolley cars by the nudists who wore nothing but scarlet sashes bearing their device—to the amazement of onlookers and to the annoyance of the police who arrested them.[22]

The absence of a consensus—or even much interest—in the question of dress does not mean that there was no revolution. No uniform was devised for the Soviet people along the lines of science fiction dreaming, but the vast gulf in attire diminished visibly and rapidly. Tielessness, tousled hair, and plainness of raiment were the rule for most people high and low—except for the N.E.P. fops—throughout the 1920s. In Stalin's time, the culture of inequality would have its own expression in the outward appearance of the new managerial class.

Aside from dress, titles and language were the main instruments of expressing and receiving deference. The Revolution assaulted these at once in a very deliberate way. On November 11, the new government decreed the elimination of social estates and civilian ranks and titles, to be replaced by the single designation "citizen" (*grazhdanin, grazhdanka*), a clear emulation of the French Revolution. Old terms and linguistic forms now fell out of use. *Gosdpodin* was one such casualty. Strongly hierarchical usages in the army (such as *chelovek,* "my man") disappeared totally, as did plural pronouns and verb forms for a lone exalted person. Officers suddenly found themselves referred to in the singular and as Mister and later Comrade Captain instead of the lengthy designations of the old army. Officers became commanders, sires and madames became citizens or comrades. Words like governor, governess, lord, heir, prince, lycée, chamber-maid, ambassador (*posol*), and minister were abolished (though the last two were later reinstated). Trotsky, in addressing his new staff at the People's Commissariat of Foreign Affairs, said: "Comrades, don't forget, everybody from commissar to watchman is equal now! 'Your worship' doesn't exist anymore."[23]

Of greater significance was the reordering of the personal pronouns "thou" *(ty)* and "you" *(vy)*. Before the Revolution, *ty* was used by superiors to inferiors, adults to children, husbands to wives, bosses to employees, people to animals—the superior expecting *vy* in return (except from the last). The power implied by the *vy-ty* usage was almost palpable—especially in the army. The 1860s radical Yakushkin became enraged when the police addressed him as *ty;* a worker of the 1890s was converted to Marxism partly because his recruiter called him respectfully *vy*. In the 1905 Revolution, workers very often demanded the polite form of address from factory owners; and a radical song about soldiers' dignity said:[24]

> Sure we'd like some tea
> But give us with our tea
> Some polite respect
> And please have officers
> Not slap us in the face

The Lena strikers in 1912 demanded to be addressed as *vy*. For many people, the word *ty* was indeed like a slap in the face. After the fall of the monarchy, some soldiers took revenge by addressing their officers as *ty,* and the soldier-captors of Count Fredericks, Minister of Court and arbiter of social etiquette at the peak of society, deeply offended him by addressing him as *ty*. These were violations of the accepted revolutionary etiquette which was to use *vy* in every situation except among affectionate equals. (But in the family, the inequality of speech prevailed.) In 1922, Trotsky had to warn officers not to revert to the *ty* usage. "Military subordination," he wrote, "must be accompanied by a sense of the civil and moral equality of all and that sense of equality cannot endure if personal dignity is violated."[25]

There was considerable confusion over the words "citizen" and "comrade." The Former was a neutral egalitarian form available for all citizens. *Tovarishch* was an old Russian word which meant "comrade," but the Soviet version had been directly inspired by European Social Democracy—particularly the German *Genossen* which means "party comrade." Russian Marxists and other radicals used it at the turn of the century; during the 1905 Revolution it apparently gained wide currency among workers, and for some possessed great bonding significance. Bolshevik party members were supposed to us it exclusively to each other in public and private address; they did not like the impersonal "citizen." But it was also used in the army ("Comrade Captain") and in everyday life by workers in all kinds of situations. Sometimes it was an ironic taunt: an upperclass woman became hysterical in 1917 when the streetcar conductor called her "comrade." But when Grand Duke Paul was arrested he was called "Comrade Highness" with no apparent disrespect. Delegates to the countryside from Moscow were addressed as "Mister Comrade" by peasants, and in Yaroslav province in the early 1920s, peasants responded to a question about the word "comrade" that it was "what people call each other nowadays." The use of the word was so replete with comic irony that it became well nigh irresistible to Western humorists and film-makers of the 1920s and 1930s. Like so many aspects of leveling in the Russian Revolution, the revolt in the language was bewildering to some, uplifting to others, and menacing to those who felt the social and psychological storms that accompanied it.[26]

For the experimentalist mind, reforming terms of address and titles was not enough. Some wished to revise the Russian language altogether, substituting criminal argot as the true language of the proletariat. During the Civil War, an anarchist busied himself constructing a universal monosyllabic language that he called "Ao." The Commissariat of Culture set up a subsection for new languages. Among these, Esperanto (Hope) became the focus of hope for a new world of language. Invented in the 1880s by a Warsaw physician, L. L. Zamenhof, it was at first called "utopian." But the movement to advance it (to supplement and not replace other languages) spread throughout Europe. In Russia its membership was emphatically middle-class and respectable—cosmopolitan and urban but also patriotic. Its journal, *The Wave of Esperanto,* attracted related kinds of social reformers—vegetarians and garden city enthusiasts. Its main argument was that an artificial language was as good as a natural or historical one and that—with its broad linguistic base (in fact it was almost exclusively European in etymology)—Esperanto could serve the cause of peace and commerce.[27]

In the Summer of 1917, in the very heat of revolutionary events, "a grey-haired lady argued that Esperanto would save the Revolution," Ehrenburg recalled. But no one, he observed, listened to her. He was wrong in his implication. By 1921 Esperanto had become an organized movement once again, now under Bolshevik auspices—the Soviet Esperantist Union. Its leader was Ernst Drezen, a Baltic German and former tsarist officer who served in the Red Army and was for a few years the secretary of President Kalinin. Under his vigorous if abrasive leadership Esperanto linked up with the international "socialist" wing of world Esperanto and fought for domination over it and against the "nonpolitical" and the anarchist branches of the movement. A world congress of Esperanto was held in Leningrad in 1926. A number of works, including Bogdanov's *Red Star,* were translated into Esperanto under official auspices, and a large Esperanto-Russian dictionary was published. Young enthusiasts such as Lev Kopelev were enchanted by the trans-national dream of Esperanto, some of them believing that soon its writers would rival Dante, Shakespeare, and Tolstoy. Under pressure from the regime in the later 1920s, the Soviet Esperantists began breaking their international ties and later were persecuted and destroyed in the 1930s under Stalin.[28]

The patterns of leveling, egalitarianism, and revolt against deference exhibited a widespread feeling of class consciousness and social alienation in Russia at the moment of the Revolution. The variety and intensity of its expression strongly indicate spontaneity and not simply the result of manipulative demagogy by the Bolsheviks. All the revolutionary parties and large portions of the lower classes shared the feeling. Their behavior in the Revolution displayed a sense of participation in the enterprise of social reordering, a surge toward the remodeling of status and its symbolism. Though much of this behavior was ill-humored, it was also a positive program, acted out in all corners of life, for a new society—a society of equals as a prelude to a world of equals.

## Utopian Miniature: The Conductorless Orchestra

A striking instance of how egalitarian and related impulses were woven into the fabric of everyday life—in this case collective labor—was the conductorless orchestra movement of the 1920s. These orchestras raised the banner of equality not only by abolishing conductors as symbols of old style authority but also by organizing their work in a pattern that insured maximum participation and equal voice in the daily routine of rehearsal and in public performance. Early in 1922, concertgoers in Moscow were notified of a concert to be performed "without a conductor." When they arrived at the Hall of Columns in the House of Trade unions in the Kremlin, they witnessed a very unusual sight: the musicians were seated in a semi-circle facing one another, many with backs to the audience. This was the opening demonstration of an experiment in collective labor known as the Persimfans *(Pervyi simfonicheskii ansambl bez dirigera)* or First Symphonic Orchestra without a Conductor. Its ten year existence, 1922–32, was an example of continued belief in unalienated labor, equality, anti-authoritarianism, and—in its date of termination—of the ultimate fate of these things under Stalin. Persimfans and its seventy musicians was a utopia in miniature, a tiny republic, and a model workshop for the communist future. Like many practicing utopias of the 1920s, it was an island in the midst of persistant inequality, a laboratory of communism, a beacon of early idealism, an inspiration for the future, and a graphic demonstration of how egalitarian mechanisms could actually work if given the opportunity.

The musical context of this experiment was a richly innovative and dynamic one. Although Persimfans and its imitators constituted a socially egalitarian experiment rather than musicalogical innovation, its birth was facilitated by an extraordinary atmosphere of musicalizing the Revolution and revolutionizing music. Outdoor concerts and large public performances had been growing in Russia in the years before the fall of the monarchy. Russia's stage traditions, not unique in Europe, tended to mix musical performances of all kinds with poetry reading, drama, and pageant in high-toned civic and artistic evenings and with comic routines, dancing, and other forms in music hall or vaudeville *(estrada)* events. Wartime and revolutionary governments made use of the country's exceptionally large pool (in relation to its educational resources) of musical performing talent. Drawing on the precedents of nineteenth century revolutionary Europe, especially France, the Bolshevik regime was quick to enlist musicians in festivals and other large-scale civic events. The concert-in-the-factory became the radical equivalent of elitist concert halls of the past. Musicians were mobilized and music itself made mobile: agitational trains transported whole ensembles out to the front lines and into distant rural regions to accompany the verbal messages of the Revolution. The avantgarde revolt in music, particularly the Futurists' attempt to capture the sounds of the city and of industry, helped to heat up the atmosphere. "Industrial" or "machine" composers attempted to replicate factory noise with conventional instruments, and the Engineerists used turbines, sirens, and hooters. A whole school of electronic composers and inventors appeared with machines designed to amplify the number of tones, create new music out of them, and transmit it to every home and village in the Soviet Union.[29]

It was in such a setting that Persimfans was born: its founder, Lev Tseitlin, called by Prokofiev "the soul" of Persimfans, was a versatile and indefatigable musician and music worker. Violin soloist, concertmaster, teacher, editor, chamber music leader, the pupil of Leopold Auer (whose progeny direct and indirect included the Oistrakhs, the Kogans, and Nathan Milstein), Tseitlin worked for many years as the concertmaster of Serge Koussevitzky (Sergei Kusevitsky) until the latter emigrated to America. Before the Revolution, Tseitlin had lamented the fact that the modern symphonic orchestra had become the conductor's huge personal instrument which "he played" and whose members were "mechanical keys" that he struck or banged. Indeed, since the time of Berlioz, the conductor had become the dominant figure in the classical musical world, evolving in Central and Eastern Europe into a notoriously tyrannical, temperamental dictator of the podium. An orchestra in Warsaw in 1913 had tried a performance without a conductor. Perhaps Tseitlin knew about it, and perhaps he had also suffered under the brutal baton of Koussevitsky. He may have been partly motivated by the shortage of good conductors after the Revolution (some of the best had emigrated). Whatever the original motivation, his orchestra consciously proclaimed a war on authority figures.[30]

Persimfans was a high quality ensemble. It was staffed with some of the finest instrumentalists of the early twentieth century Russian musical world. It was also remarkably hard-working, performing hundreds of concerts a year, most of them in the factories, workers' clubs, or military units. Tseitlin's orchestra played traditional Russian and European composers as well as contemporary moderns. To make the music palatable and ideologically relevant for their working-class audience, Persimfans employed the "monographic concert" method: an evening of selections by a single composer, preceded by a crude Marxist sociology of the composer and his times and followed by discussions and questionaires. For all its primitive musicology and its foolish political commentary, the monographic approach certainly reached the working-class audience—some of whom were hearing "serious" music for the first time. A spokesman believed that the orchestra was successful in its contact with the workers precisely because of its "collective" structure and the "comradely closeness of the two collectives." The Soviet government, for whom it worked, commended the orchestra not only for its performances but for its "modern" style of work. Following a "production plan," Persimfans adhered to a rigid schedule of concerts and rehearsals and promoted efficiency in everyday life by starting on time and cutting intermissions to a minimum.[31]

Tseitlin's assistant, Arnold Tsukker, was the ideological spokesman for the orchestra: he established its journal and wrote articles, books, and program notes about it. Tsukker elevated "persimfansism" to a revolutionary political issue by calling the practice of the orchestra "musical collective reflexology" and attacking what he saw as "the abolished ones" (conductors) and their sense of "infallibility and monopoly of power," their "absolutism and dictatorship." It was clear to Tsukker that a people who had dethroned its tsar and reviled contemporary dictators in Italy and Spain had no place on its podiums for musical monarchs. The orchestra, he said, was not "a lifeless machine" which the conductor can play like an instrument as a pianist plays a piano. It was a community of players, democratic, socialist, and egalitarian. The conductor had no right to rob and alienate the labor of his players by arrogating to himself alone the mastery of the entire score and having the players know only their "parts." But Tsukker argued on strictly artistic grounds as well. The conductor, he said, provided a superfluous "scenic" element by visually interpreting the music with gesture and body language and by "choreographing" his movement as a dance. This, argued Tsukker, was nonmusical and antimusical, harmful and irrelevant to the appreciation of the music itself, and deeply humiliating to the orchestral players who provided dance music for an ego-oriented conductor. Tsukker and other commentators emphatically rejected the individualism, the unconstrained sovereignty, and the boundless autocratic power of the modern conductor.[32]

What were the "collectivist" principles of the Persimfans? Foremost among them were the dispersion and the diffusion of authority. This meant the equal sharing of important tasks, rather than the division of labor between the conductor who got the "big view," the power, and the creative scope and the players who got only their own parts. "Equal rights for all members of the orchestra" meant equality of pay, of voice in picking the repertoire, and of participation in the artistic performance and interpretation of the music. The orchestra was a "collective performer." Persimfans did not limit itself to short, simple chamber pieces but took on the workhorses of the symphonic repertoire (including such sprawling works as Richard Strauss's *Ein Heldenleben*). The orchestra was seated in an ellipse for maximum mutual eye contact and rhythmic synchronization. Each player learned the entire score—not a common practice in symphonic ensembles. The "director" *(rukovoditel)* ran the players through the score after which each choir would play its parts with running discussion and commentary by the whole orchestra. This of course meant exceptionally lengthy rehearsals for every piece. Joseph Szigeti, who played and rehearsed with Persimfans many times, described in his memoirs its "workshop atmosphere generated by proud artisans bound together in the common task of making good music." He found the orchestra characterized by mutual respect and an absence of temperamental ego and backbiting. Persimfans was a socialist community in miniature—both in ideology and in practice.[33]

But how well did it play? The reviews were mostly favorable, with a few dissonant voices. In the major journals of the 1920s, reviewers were consistently favorable, criticizing particular interpretations, not the principle or structure of the orchestra itself. Prokofiev, who played with this orchestra many times, praised its rendering of his music. And the German conductor, Otto Klemperer, was quoted as saying: "If this kind of thing continues, we conductors will have to find a new trade."[34]

It did continue. In 1923, a conductorless orchestra, modelled on Persimfans, was formed in the Moscow Conservatory. This was followed by Petrosimfans in Petrograd and an Ukrsimfans in Kharkov. By 1928, there were eleven conductorless orchestras: two each in Moscow and Leningrad, one each in Kiev (1926), Kharkov, Odessa, Ekaterinoslav, Voronezh, Tiflis, and Baku. Other orchestras performed conductorless concerts from time to time. These orchestras were short lived. A Soviet music historian in the 1970s claims that this was due to opposition (unspecified) and to the shortage of the big musical names that made Persimfans so successful. In 1928, the conductorless orchestra movement spread to Europe: in direct emulation of Persimfans, with which it corresponded, the Leipzig Symphony Orchestra presented conductorless concerts. This was repeated in Berlin, Munich, Würzburg, and Warsaw. In the same year, the American Symphonic Ensemble was formed on the principles of Persimfans, which it called its older brother. Anti-Bolsheviks apparently came to Carnegie Hall on November 3, 1928 to witness musical chaos and failure. (The *Evening Standard* warned them that they would be "as disillusioned as the White Army after its first encounters with the Red)." *Musical America* offered a favorable review of Amsimfans's Soviet inspired performance of an all Beethoven concert, but felt "the absence of a commanding personality." This orchestra also did not long survive.[35]

Persimfans got through the first five-year plan but dissolved, under circumstances that are still murky, in 1932. Opposition to it had appeared from the very outset. Laughter and abuse greeted the new orchestra as well as malicious gossip about Homeric rehearsal sessions and rumors about a hidden conductor. The "abolished ones" were especially acid. A leading Leningrad critic told his readers that a "headless horseman is galloping around Moscow." The players were definitely overworked and underpaid. A Soviet account of the last years relates that the orchestra declined in the early 1930s, lost the experimental verve of earlier times, and succumbed to economic forces. This is also the opinion of several very old musicians from Soviet conservatories who knew Tseitlin personally. S. Frederick Starr in the 1960s heard stories in Moscow about ideological fights between the string section and the winds that exploded into scandals and brought dissolution to the orchestra.[36]

Modern critics insist on the need for a conductor and dismiss conductorless orchestras as an interesting experiment: big forces and complex scores require a determining will.[37] But it is doubtful if Persimfans could have survived long into the Stalin era even if this were not true and even if there had been no internal strife. Structural disabilities had had ten years in which to unfold. But the experiment ended at just the moment when the Soviet Russian cultural establishment was coming under central ideological control. There is no evidence that Stalin or his people had the orchestra dissolved because of its political symbolism, but it is certainly likely that they would have.

Persimfans, in its organization and its self-conscious statements, promoted everything that Stalinism was repudiating in the early 1930s. It summarized a dozen utopian ideas of the revolution—total democracy in a tiny republic of labor; complete equality of tasks, of decision making, and of wages; workers' control or what is now called workers' management; anarchist—in the strict sense of the word—notions on authority; hatred of personality cult and authoritarian leaders; reintegration with one's labor function and product; and so on. The conductorless orchestra even served as the model for a utopian state in one of the most popular science fiction novels of the 1920s (see Chapter 8). It was, on a reduced scale, what so many of the political opposition groups outlawed by Lenin had wanted for the Soviet Union as a whole.

Persimfans was squarely in the revolutionary tradition, but there were other traditions about orchestras, conductors, and authority in politics. In the 1840s, Gogol wrote that "a state without an absolute ruler is like an orchestra without a conductor." Marx in *Capital* had this to say: "In all kinds of work where there is cooperation of many individuals, the connection and the unity of the process are necessarily represented in a will which commands and in functions which, as for the leader of an orchestra, are not concerned with partial efforts, but the collective activity." And by "function" Marx meant "the work of supervision and of direction." Lenin, in a famous addendum to *What Is To Be Done?*, wrote, in the context of organizing the party on the ground from a central apparatus:

> In order that the center can not only advise, convince, and debate with the orchestra—as has been the case up to now—but really to direct it, we need detailed information: who is playing which violin and where? What instrument is being mastered and has been mastered and where? Who is playing a false note (when the music starts to grate on the ear)—and where and why? Whom to relocate to where and how in order to correct the dissonance.

These quotations illustrate rather strikingly how often the analogy between orchestra and society was made by people who think about such matters and who face the problem of equality, authority, democracy, coordination and efficiency in the work-place.[38]

Stalin could not have looked favorably upon such a symbolic affront to authority. Canetti's analysis of the power symbolism of the orchestral conductor is very apt: he is the center and focus of the audience; all vision radiates toward him and all energies through him. He enters majestically, leads, corrects, and rewards in full view. Only he stands—and he stands on a dais. After the decree on art of 1932, a series of competitions among young conductors was inaugurated. In 1938 an All-Union Competition of Conductors was held in Moscow. This practice established a Soviet "school" of conducting characterized by firm discipline, one-man control, strict division of labor, and the traditional pattern of orchestral and audience deference to the easily recognized central figure. In a post Stalinist comment on the Persimfans, a Soviet music history had this to say: "Notwithstanding the superb complement of musicians, in performance Persimfans nonetheless lacked and felt the absence of a single directing will."[39]

It would be silly to romanticize Persimfans as "a real child of the revolution"[40] and nothing else. We know little of the motivations of the players in joining the ensemble: employment, convenience, the magnetism of Tseitlin, distaste with conductors? There may have even been lurking behind Tseitlin's scheme the fear that the orchestra itself, under open assault by Engineerists and machine-worshippers, might perish unless somehow linked to the Revolution in the spirit and style of its work. Whatever the motivations, the men and women of Persimfans created a genuine laboratory of revolution, an egalitarian and democratic forum, work-place and operating community, all aspects of which were constantly on public display in hundreds of concerts every year for over a decade. They hauled down egalitarianism from the skies of utopia to the practice of everyday life.

## Privilege and Revolution

The visible and audible struggle against deference through dress, language, and work style could only be won if the structure of "entitlements" could be dismantled. The question of who defers to whom was inseparable from the question of who commands and who consumes. As to command, power, authority, and discipline, there is hardly anything to add to the story because historians understandably have focused very closely upon this key issue. The fate of the anti-authoritarian or democratizing movements inside and outside the Communist Party has been exceptionally well documented. The Anarchists of several persuasions, the Military Opposition, the Democratic Centralists, the Workers' Opposition, the Workers' Group (the only true proletarian movement among them), all wanted, in shifting degrees of emphasis, equality in decision making, a weaker central apparatus in state and party (or none at all), more lower-class participation, elections, spontaneous self-management, and an end to authoritarian bosses. Comradely self-discipline and large-scale popular participation were set against elitist, self-selected, and coopted hierarchy. These political currents were successfully resisted and eliminated by the party leadership, with Lenin at its head, in the early 1920s.[41]

The same theme was apparent in the pedagogical experiments of the time with their collective exploration of themes, mutual consultation, equality of teacher and pupil and a general view of the school as a "small republic." Kollontai and other prophets of a free family applied egalitarianism to gender roles, women's rights, the upbringing of children, and love-making and affection. Equality of authority was a central motif in all the experiments and utopias of the 1920s and was the mainspring of "prefigurative communism"—the creation and maintenance of democratic and socialist egalitarian structures and sensibilities in the process of revolution itself in order "to anticipate the future liberated society" instead of postponing them to the dawn of communism.[42]

Side by side with the augmentation of power among revolutionary leaders came the accretion of wealth—goods, services, wages, and privileges—for themselves and for designated "specialists." If elitism in power could be justified on the basis of survival amid war and chaos and the building of socialism in a backward country, what could justify the inequality of wealth that began almost at once? One was Marx's formula that under socialism distribution stems from the principle: "from each according to ability, to each according to work," meaning quantity and quality of work performed. But how does one measure the quality of work? The implicit answer was that it is measured by what it does for the survival and maintenance of the Revolution. The other justification, closely related, was specialization of labor: some people had to run the country, lead troops, and manage the economy—and some were better at it. The hallowed principle of the "rotation of work" was part of the vision of socialists, both utopian and Marxist. Lenin had believed on the eve of the revolution that an entire nation of workers and peasants could be deployed as checkers and administrative watchdogs at once, but only with the retention of capitalists and specialists who possessed expertise. When War Communism dissolved civil society, this became impossible. Even so, during it, workers were drafted into party and administrative work with the vague hope that they would return periodically to the bench, but the process turned into permanent promotion rather than "rotation." The leaders—including the maverick Bogdanov—invoked Marx, who saw rotation as a mechanism of a communist society of the future.[43]

Within the working class as well as between it and the leaders and specialists, stratification of wages continued as of old—with the support of many skilled workers. But the struggle for equal wages continued. Richard Lowenthall has argued that wage egalitarianism appeared only in the Civil War as a result of shortages and not of "utopian dreams." Bolshevik critics later called the egalitarian impulse selfish grabbing. In fact it was all of these, with revolutionary idealism at least as prominent as other things. Workers drew their varying notions of distributive justice from factory or village or artel and from what they knew or understood of radical pamphlet literature. Since the "egalitarian" war of leveling against old privilege was waged with the regime's blessing, many workers could not grasp the nuances of "the stages of communism." The notion of equality was kept alive in every area from Proletcult to political poster and slogan. Through Civil War and N.E.P., workers fought the continuous if erratic growth of wage stratification in small groups and face-to-face contacts with employers. They were joined by opposition groups, intellectuals, and government trade union leaders such as Tomsky who anguished over the growing inequality and wanted more leveling of wages in the name of elementary class justice. But this was unavailing. Party leaders spoke again and again of the impossibility of wage equality in a transitional period and of the need for incentive pay.[44]

The growth of reward and privilege among the leaders outstripped wage stratification among workers. In the Civil War, these were not huge: salaries of top leaders were 100–150 percent of the average wage of their institutions and this principle was invoked all through the 1920s. Lenin became angry when his chancery gave him a raise without consulting him. But when A. D. Tsyurupa, Commissar of Food Supply, fainted of hunger during a cabinet meeting, Lenin ordered the increase of wages and rations for commissars. This was later revoked but revived again. For specialists, Lenin insisted on high wages as well as "comradely consideration"—something that could easily slide into deference. The beneficiaries of this policy were bourgeois specialists, old officials and officers, and cultural figures, with their special ration cards and apartments—all justified on the importance of their work. Alexander Barmine recalls how in the army he balked at getting twenty times the wage of a common soldier. "Wait a few years," he was told. "When we've trained a corps of Communist officers and put the Socialist regime on a firm footing, then we will introduce equality." This melody, sung in all sincerity at the time, has been sung ever since.[45]

How did the Bolshevik leaders live during the Revolution? A rare pamphlet, *Communists on Leave* (1921), instructed Party members how to conduct themselves in their home-towns and villages and made a special point of warding off slander about "rich communists": tell the people back home, it adjured, that in any other place Lenin would be a wealthy and famous man, but in Moscow "he lives worse than a poor tsarist clerk and works harder." About working harder, there can be little doubt. Did he live worse? Like other People's Commissars, Lenin was to receive 500 rubles a month and one room per family member (he of course received no children's allowance). In fact, he possessed four rooms to himself, his wife, and his sister—in the Kremlin. His personal life was simple. Though he dined on leftover imperial table service adorned with the Romanov eagle, rode in a chauffeured car, and possessed a library of 10,000 books, his immediate surroundings were modest and he amassed no personal fortune. He also waited his turn in barber shops and pitched in for a while on voluntary work days, carrying logs for firewood or cleaning up Red Square. This was symbolic. Lenin and other high officials were always fed and fully protected from storm and wind and famine and disease (the Commissar of Health took a personal interest in his medical wellbeing). The symbolism itself of course reflected an egalitarian impulse and a desired image.[46]

In the heady days of October 1917, the Bolshevik leaders often slept at their desks or in a corner of Smolny. Later they moved to hotel space in the new capital and— some of them—into the Kremlin. In 1919, the Kremlin had the best food in town, and in the twenties contained five restaurants. Lenin, Felix Dzerzhinsky, Georgy Chicherin, Lunacharsky, Alexei Rykov, and a few other high officials had a reputation as simple men. Lunacharsky's "modest home" reminded the violinist Joseph Szigeti of a mid-western American professor's. The Czech communist, Ivan Olbracht, proudly described life in the Second House of the Soviets (the Metropol Hotel), the official residence of the Foreign Office Staff, where all lived and ate as equals, from Chicherin down to minor employees and servants, and where self-service was in order when the servants were off. The vignette is revealing: it is of an island of warmth and comfort—however simple—and regular meals in a sea of misery, a place where servants were servants, however often they may have supped with commissars. Zorin, Emma Goldman's host in Petrograd—a powerful man—lived with his pregnant wife on a simple diet of bread, herring, and tea. But Karl Radek and Grigory Zinoviev had reputations as high livers. In 1924, L. B. Kamenev celebrated "Christmas" in his luxurious Moscow flat (in the mansion of the former governor) with a tree, communist trinkets, and skits celebrating the class war.[47]

Even those commissars who allegedly lived simply, such as Lunacharsky, rushed to extend the privileges and living space of famous artists, intellectuals, and scholars. Igor Grabar describes how he wrangled from him permission to keep assigned workers' families out of his flat and on the same page contrasted the "democratic and egalitarian manner" of Lunarcharsky with his tsarist predecessors. In Moscow, lofty academic figures secured the right to extra study space in large pre-revolutionary apartments— which they often used for friends and servants. Many intellectuals suffered torments in the Revolution, but those who made peace with the regime were well rewarded. By 1920 a whole pattern of residential inequality had taken hold in Russian society. During the Civil War, when Kronstadt sailors heard that Smolny had three restaurants, they came over and closed them down. But the process itself was irreversible.[48]

Inequalities in the "little things" began piling up quickly. Less than a year after the abolition of ranks and orders, the Order of the Red Banner appeared, rewarding a moment of bravery with a lifetime of distinction and privilege. In the government, Radek and Zinoviev were known as seekers of privilege and preference. When Zinoviev's maidservant tried to get an extra portion of vinegar for her "master," storms of anger broke out in the waiting line. People who controlled rationing during the hungry years of Civil War often could not resist taking a larger share for themselves and their families. There was some agonizing about all this. In 1920 the government ordered 300 party workers to the bench in order to allay workers' complaints, but most of these "mobilized" men arrived in automobiles dressed in warm garments and slept in the plush Astoria Hotel at the end of the day! In the spring of that year, in planning the welcome of foreign delegations, the Bolshevik hosts debated over whether to serve a Soviet meal or to offer more sumptuous hospitality, including wine. They settled for the superior menu, of which they themselves partook. Gorky—the hero of the lower classes—was enraged to learn that forty-three artists had been mobilized and sent to the front. Tolstoys and Rachmaninovs he said are *not equal* to the Battalion Committees![49]

Housing, food, office space, furnishings—all became subject to gradual, then elaborate, differentiation. Travelling classes were abolished in 1918 and then restored, and soon there appeared special and "fast" trains for busy executives and "delegates' carriages" for honored guests. To a Soviet ear, the work *delegatsiya* (official foreign guests) has spelled enviable privilege ever since. A famous illustration from life that combined these elements was the lavish parlor car of Zinoviev and Radek that took them to Baku in 1920 for the Congress of Eastern Toilers and allowed them to consume their opulent meals amid plush surroundings and "important" foreign visitors. There were always good reasons for granting privilege. For example, after the Revolution, mothers with babies in arms were allowed to move to the front of the line. But pretty soon people began borrowing or renting babies for the purpose. It was not long before "important" people moved routinely to the front of queues, a maddening practice that prevails to this day.[50]

And yet through all these years of visibly growing inequality within the socialist political and economic sector—to say nothing of the free market world of N.E.P.—almost everyone remained ambivalently attached to the spirit of equality. The word was invoked all the time. Some promised it for the future; others claimed its benefits now; still others pretended that it existed. The poster art of the period assiduously avoided juxtaposing rugged workers and sailors with necktied officials. Only the lower classes were symbolized; except for Lenin, a cult figure, the images of leaders were not displayed much because they were not seen to be the embodiments of the egalitarian and populist ethos—as indeed they were not.

The major positions on equality emerged during the Revolution itself. Machajski, who had formulated his outlook in 1905, returned to Russia in 1917 to proclaim that all his fears had been justified. "The intelligentsia," he wrote, "defends its own interests, not those of the workers. . . . After the expropriation of the capitalists, the workers will have to equalize their incomes with those of the intellectuals, otherwise they are doomed to manual labor, ignorance, and inability to manage the life of the country." Entitlements of power, wealth, and education, he believed, were inseparable and had to be abolished together. Bogdanov, on the other hand, thought that unequal emoluments were compatible with egalitarian authority in work:

> The proletarian collective is distinguished and defined by a special organization bond, known as *comradely cooperation*. This is a kind of cooperation in which the roles of organizing and fulfilling are not divided but are combined among the general mass

of workers, so that there is no authority by force or unreasoning subordination but a common will which decides, and a participation of each in the fulfillment of the common task.

But "equalization" *(uravlenie),* he argued a few years later, is impossible since the day of "consciousness of a higher order of mutual interests" would not soon dawn. At least one Bolshevik official of the time had a compensatory view of wages and work. Angelica Balabanova argued that the leaders of the Revolution should have *fewer* physical comforts, privileges, and rewards than the masses because of the psychic joy they got from revolutionary work and because of their responsibility for the sufferings unleashed by the Revolution. She thus endeavored to live austerely as did (she claimed) Lenin, Chicherin, Bukharin, and Trotsky. But the leaders themselves, whatever their own personal style, soon gave in to the operating principle of inequality both in wealth and in power.[51]

Radical leaders and masses agreed that the notion of equality transcended mere legal or political equality, and that it would reshape the economic order and social relations. Before the Revolution, people and intelligentsia—in various ways and to varying degrees—dreamed of a republic of equals. After the Revolution, they demanded a conversion of the dream into reality. The Revolution itself, its social acts, its symbolism and rhetoric, and its promise of utopia fed this demand. Bolshevik leaders were divided among themselves and even within themselves on this important issue—often extolling it in theory and ignoring it in practice. The Bolsheviks were now the state, and state power, survival, and economic recovery and growth were seen as incompatible with an egalitarian revolution of major dimensions. The result was ambivalence and pluralism. The difference between the state's attitude towards equality in the 1920s and that of the 1930s is this: the original Bolsheviks enforced inequality in certain key sectors of life but allowed equality and egalitarian movements to prosper and flourish not only as ideals but also as experimental practices in many corners of Soviet life. Their successors in the 1930s, in vivid contrast, were to pronounce the very idea of egalitarianism in life counterrevolutionary.

# 7

## Man the Machine

Yes, this Taylor was undoubtedly the greatest genius of the ancients. True he did not come to the idea of applying his method to the whole of life, to every step throughout the twenty-four hours of the day; he was unable to integrate his system from one o'clock to twenty four. I cannot understand the ancients. How could they write whole libraries about some Kant and take only slight notice of Taylor, of this prophet who saw ten centuries ahead?

Evgeny Zamyatin, *We*

One of the most remarkable experiments to emerge from the Russian Revolution, fascinating in its vision and menacing in its ambition, was the cult of the machine. It was the culmination of a long process, beginning in seventeenth century Europe, of trying to fit the rhythms, sensibilities, and creative dynamics of the human body to those of the machine—the opposite of the "primitive" habit of investing machinery with a humanoid character. In Soviet Russia during the 1920s, the prophets of this cult, anguished by the backwardness of Russian work styles in the factory, and inspired by the industrial geniuses, Frederick Winslow Taylor and Henry Ford, dreamed of remolding the human psyche and remodeling human society along the lines of machine and workshop.

Although the cult of the machine that produced Soviet Taylorism, the struggle for time, and allied currents of efficiency was not a design for a utopian society as such, it was deeply utopian. Anchored in the fear of backwardness and the thirst for technical and industrial modernity that haunted so many Russian prophets, radicals, and statesmen of the prerevolutionary era, it related to two traditions.[1] One was the administrative utopia of the eighteenth and nineteenth centuries which drove certain people to attempt the "mechanization" of society, or part of society, on the model of the military unit in which human commanders designed drill and motions to refashion the body clock and streets, homes, and schedules to regulate the social clock.

The second was the urbanized utopia of the early twentieth century which replaced the regimental model with that of city, machine, and "computer." In both of them, "social justice" was a goal. In the first, this was defined as a kind of military welfarism, but it was distinctly subordinated to the concerns of defense and control. In the second, it was socialism, a more fully articulated and comprehensive program, but one that also had to compete with the practical, developmental aspects of the vision. Different emphases can be seen in the visions, programs, and models of Bogdanov, Lenin, Bukharin, Punin and others. In embracing and intensifying "Taylorism," the American efficiency system, and applying it to the backwardness of Russia, Alexei Gastev and

Platon Kerzhentsev assumed some of the critical and fearful perspectives of the administrative utopians—the former specializing in the body clock, the latter in the social
clock. As modern urbanists and revolutionaries, they stressed the power of dynamism
and material growth rather than static defensive power. Although they spoke in the
idiom of mobilization, discipline, and control, their aim was to "free' the Russian
population from its enslaving lassitude and to transform it into a spontaneously functioning army of producers who saluted and served under the machine rather than the
colonel.

## The Cult of Ford and Taylor

Frederick Winslow Taylor (1856–1915) of Philadelphia has been described as a "small,
thin, persnickety engineer," a rigid man who mapped out his steps for economy of
movement, a neurotic possessed by a "frenzy for order." An anti-intellectual and a
hater of individualism, Taylor analogized the human body to a machine and the industrial to the military order. For him the factory was not only an arena of production and
an idyll of elegant precision but also a moral gymnasium for the exercise of good
character. The chief virtue of his moral systems was silent obedience. He has been
rightly called a latter-day disciple of Bentham (and his factory order likened to the
Panopticon) by more than one observer. His ideal work force was a crew of ox-like
men who could be trained by means of time-motion study and "scientific management"
to perform precise movements at speeds and qualities set by himself and his managerial
students. In practice, the Taylor time study was "a ritual whose function it was to
validate, by reference to the apparently objective authority of the clock, a subjective
estimate of a job's time." The result was a disruptive revolution that upset familiar
patterns of work and produced anxiety and resentment. But at the time, Taylor was seen
as the harbinger of a new dawn in production by many managers all over the United
States and later of Europe.[2]

Taylorism and its efficiency craze spread across the country, becoming in the words
of a contemporary "a normal American madness." Part of its appeal was the homespun
ethical message it preached. Harrison Emerson, a Taylorist engineer, spoke of the five
great moralities—righteousness, hygiene, education, industrial competence, and adap-
tation; in the workplace, a single director was always necessary whether on shipboard,
in the army, in the church, or in an orchestra. In a climate of moralism, authoritarianism, reform, science, and mastery, Americans began organizing themselves into efficient modules: clubs, societies, and campaigns showed how Taylorism could be applied
to the home, the school, the university, the army, the government, and the library.
(Melville Dewey, inventor of the Dewey Decimal System, reduced his name to Melvil
Dui in order to make the point.) In Europe, Jules Amar opened the Research Laboratory
of Industrial Labor and spoke of the elimination of defective and useless work habits
and attitudes, and the British Taylorist H. L. Gantt suggested, "what we need is not
more laws, but more facts, and the whole question [of labor disputes] will solve itself."
Labor movements everywhere opposed Taylorism as exploitative, and yet it attracted a
large segment of leftist intellectuals, latter day St. Simonians who admired the organization, power, and discipline more than the socialism, equality, and justice of that
tradition. It was exactly this issue that divided Russians over Taylorism in the Revolution.[3]

At least since the 1870s in Russia, a number of individuals and associations had devoted themselves to a study of the labor process in industry. Taylor was translated before the War, and the first Taylor society appeared in 1915, though his methods were already being used in industry. One of the first critiques of Taylor's system—written by the chronicler of the 1917 Revolution Nikolai Sukhanov—exhibited the ambivalence that would mark the Russian reception of Taylorism from that moment onward: it was seen to be positive on the technical side and exploitative on the social side. During the Revolution, numerous Bolsheviks were attracted by Taylorism's exaltation of efficiency and organization.

In 1921, the first conference on Taylorism quickly settled on the name Scientific Organization of Labor (*Nauchnaya organizatsiya truda*, or N.O.T.) in order to expunge the exploitative connotation of the word. It created a network of labor institutes and schools and launched a fistful of journals dealing with efficiency and productivity. A split between Gastev's Central Institute of Labor and Kerzhentsev's League of Time (the subjects of the following pages) preoccupied the movement for the next two years until the second conference, when Gastev was upheld and Kerzhentsev denied. The N.O.T. movement continued, took on a new guise in the 1930s, and then was dissolved.[4]

The schism over Taylorism—like many controversies in Russian history—was a schism within a schism. The larger gulf was between those who, like Semën Frank, Tolstoy, the antimodernists, and the ruralists, feared that "nihilist rationalism" and the faith in human initiative was a Promethean heresy that would bring personal disaster and those who, like Lenin and Peter Struve, believed that steady work, machines, and a disciplined mass was the healthy remedy for Russia's woes. Lenin's views on Taylor have been well documented. One of his best-known statements was made at the time of Brest Litovsk:

> The war taught us much, not only that people suffered, but especially the fact that those who have the best technology, organization, discipline and the best machines emerge on top; it is this the war has taught us. It is essential to learn that without machines, without discipline, it is impossible to live in modern society. It is necessary to master the highest technology or be crushed.

Lenin was explicit about the need to adopt Taylor-like methods of labor organization, piece work, progressive wages, scientific management, and one-man control. In the words of a recent neo-Marxist critic, he accepted "the materialized values of bourgeois society" in the realm of production. Lenin and his numerous followers on this issue tried to claim selectivity in their use of Taylorism—avoiding the "capitalist" or "exploitative" elements—and labelled the anti-Taylorists utopian. Lenin personally adopted Taylorite methods of work during the last years of his life.[5]

The anti-Taylorists charged that N.O.T. was N.E.T.—a Scientific Exploitation of Labor, a practice that divided labor against itself, diminished equality, and turned the worker into an ox or an automation. Self-regulated norms, the rate of the average worker, and human welfare should govern the industrial realm, and not Taylorism. The most articulate spokesman of the anti-Taylorist position, O. A. Ermansky, pointed out that Taylorism—contrary to its touted claims—meant not the optimum use of labor but rather the maximum use. Soviet officials repeated the debate which had been ventilated in America a decade earlier. Zamyatin's novel *We* (1920) was, among other things, an anguished outcry against the excessive dreams of the Soviet Taylorists, depicting the workers of his futuristic nightmare state moving "swiftly and rhythmically like levers of an enormous machine." As elsewhere, labor opposed Taylorist methods and aims. The insurgent sailors and workers of the Kronstradt Commune, observing that the Bolsheviks were "planning to introduce the sweated labor system of Taylor," included it in their bill of indictment of the Soviet regime in 1921.[6]

Between 1895 and 1915, Henry Ford had radically transformed American industry by a revolution in factory procedure that included several engineering innovations, the partial application of Taylorism to management, and a mass production assembly line marked by precision, continuity, coordination, speed, and standardization. In two extraordinary essays of the 1920s, Ford attempted to explain the essence of his work. In "The Meaning of Time," he exalted planning, coordination, timing, precision and the fight against the criminal waste of time, material, and energy. In "Machinery, the New Messiah," he explained the moral dimensions of Fordism: "A clean factory, clean tools, accurate gauges, and precise methods of manufacture produce a smooth working, efficient machine, [just as] clean thinking, clean living, and square dealing" make for a decent home life. But by the 1920s, the reality of the Ford system was being likened by critics to a Prussian regiment with "the rules of an army" whose workers were turned like cogs in a ruthless industrial machine, surveilled, silenced, and punished. "A great business," said Ford in 1929, "is really too big to be human." Brusqueness, friction, and competition were the order of the day. "Pity the poor fellow," said Ford, "who is so soft and flabby that he must always have 'an atmosphere of good feeling' around him before he can do his work." As with Taylorism, Fordism possessed two faces and presented to its disciples in Soviet Russia a dual legacy.[7]

If Fordism as a managerial, intellectual, and technocratic cult in the Europe of the 1920s tended to supersede Taylorism because of its apparently more comprehensive social scope, in Soviet Russia the two were blended as part of "Americanism," the giant emblem of modernity. In the first six years of the decade, the Soviet regime ordered over 24,000 Fordson tractors (about eighty five percent of the total Soviet production), as well as Ford motor cars. During the first five-year plan, a contract between Amtorg and the Ford Motor Plant brought factory layouts, purchase agreements, parts replacement deals, and American specialists from Detroit — one of the largest single technical import deals in Russian history to that time. With the parts, the tractors, and the engineers came also the ideas and values that had made Ford the auto king and the symbol of colossal productivity. Henry Ford's *My Life* appeared in eight Soviet translated editions, four alone in 1924, and other works of his were also published in the 1920s, including the essays cited above. Enthusiastic notices and prefaces accompanied these books, and they became required reading for party members, economists, Taylorites, engineers, managers, and technical students. The words *fordizatsiya* and *teilorizatsiya* were common in Soviet towns and universities in the 1920s—both denoting good work habits. To some, Ford's conveyor belt was not only the model for the factory but for society as well.[8]

This was standard Russian-style enthusiasm for things foreign, especially material things that promised deliverance from backwardness—and also professional admiration for stunning success. But workers and peasants took to this craze in their own way. Workers were seen holding banners bearing Ford's name in parades along with those of Soviet leaders. Peasants called their tractors *fordzonishkas,* and deep in a Volga province village, peasants harnessed a wedding cart to a Fordson decked out in red bunting. Some peasants were unable to pronounce the name Ford (calling him Khord instead), but they saw him as a magical persona, asking the journalist Maurice Hindus if he was richer than the tsars and was the most clever American. They longed to gaze upon him personally. Hindus claims that in the backwoods, Ford's name was better known than those of most communist figures, excepting Lenin and Trotsky. Some peasants named their children after him; others endowed their new "iron horses" with human characteristics. An American business reporter in 1930 observed that Lenin was the Russian God and Ford his St. Peter. There were in fact two cults of Ford: an urban cult of "fordism" among intellectuals and technical personnel that revered a system of efficient production and a rural and lower class cult of Ford himself as a man of magic who could, by means of his "American" technique, release forces otherwise little understood by the peasant, a mechanical genius and an inventor rather than a master of large scale organization and a manager of space, people, and time.[9]

The rediscovery of America by Soviet Russia in the 1920s is in some ways reminiscent of what happened to Russian intellectuals in the 1860s, with their cults of Moleschott and Büchner, their science worship, their naive faith in materialism, and their fetishism of Western intellectual styles. Literature and journalism in the 1920s are full of debates and parodies that are as funny and pathetic as those long-gone discussions of Oblomov, Stolz, and Bazarov. If the Bunsen Burner was the totem of progress in the ironies of Turgenev, then the American automobile and the Taylorized worker were in the 1920s. Expressions of this ran from the bitter potrait by Zamyatin to the jocular parodies by Marietta Shaginian and Ilya Ehrenburg. "An American," observed Hindus in 1926, "is considered a superior being, accurate, punctual, clever, daring, persistent, gloriously successful in everything he undertakes, a worker of prodigious miracles, an unconquerable modern Don Quixote." Shall we have the "American Automobile or Russian Cart?" asked Valerian Osinsky in an emotional appeal for technological progress that was as full of shame for the "Asiatic" streets of Moscow as it was a vision of new civilization. *Amerikanizatsiya* was a metaphor of the time for speedy industrial tempo, high growth, productivity, and efficiency. Stalin's well-known juxtaposition of American efficiency and Russian revolutionary sweep was rooted in Bolshevism from the very beginning. It both fitted and fed the surge toward superurbanism *(chikagoizm)* and the belief that a proletarian culture was only possible as a culture of the machine and the factory. From this vision came the extraordinary dreams of Alexei Gastev and Platon Kerzhentsev.[10]

## Utopian Robotry

Alexei Gastev spent the first part of his adult life in industry, as a lathe-operator, a skilled metal worker, and a tram repairman, recording the rhythms and pictures of this life in a body of factory poems (See Figs. 25-28). The last part he spent as an industrial trainer of workers and a prophet of efficiency. As an educated man (his father was a Suzdal school teacher) turned worker and as a poet turned manager, Gastev experienced precisely the kind of contrived reversals in life that he wished a whole nation to undergo in his experimental laboratory of human robotry known as the Central Institute of Labor (1920–38).

Gastev had been a student radical in the 1890s, became a Bolshevik organizer, and was arrested and exiled several times in the first decade of the twentieth century. In Paris and in the factory towns of Yaroslavl, Kostroma, Ivanovo, Kharkov, Sormovo, and Nikolaevsk, he breathed the smoke of big industry, absorbed the crashing noises of machines. He marvelled at the vastness of the Siemens-Halske Plant in St. Petersburg. In his version of "going to the people" the attraction clearly was not only the proletarian who dwelt in the dark world of manufacture but the technology and machinery of that world. The peak years of his poetic output (1910–13) were spent in Paris, where he continued to toil among the toilers and also to work with Lunacharsky, Fëdor Kalinin, and Pavel Bessalko in a League of Proletarian Culture, an offshoot of the movement hatched on Capri by Gorky, Lunacharsky, Bogdanov and others. Gastev left the Party in 1908. In 1913 he returned to Russia to continue his double life as man of the bench and man of the pen.[11]

Fascination with the machine was nothing new in European literature—as Maxime du Camp and Emile Veraheren, among many others, had shown. But Gastev raised it to a religion of "iron messiah" and "machine paradise" (the titles of poems by two other factory poets during the revolution). In Gastev, "stone, metal, and workers are all mixed up in a vortex." His vision of "machinism"—a term borrowed from the French—speaks of "the iron demon of the age with the soul of a man, nerves of steel, and rails for muscles," of "my iron friends," and of man growing "out of iron" and becoming a machine. The animation of machinery and the mechanization of man are the two faces of his vision. Like a character in Gladkov's *Cement*, Gastev was possessed by a sensual "yearning for machines" and a distinctly romantic vision of the factory as a "festival," a camp of solidarity (three of his poems have the word "we" in their titles). Whistles, dynamos, gates, towers, cranes, hammers, and rails—the future musculature of a transformed globe—produce simultaneity and uniformity in the rhythm of work and life which denotes not only Promethean power over nature but a prodigious grandeur of its own. This, the obvious aspect of his poetry, was part of what drove Zamyatin to such ferocious satirical flights in *We*.[12]

But these poems, along with his prose fiction and journalism, reveal something else as well. The romance of the machine was tempered by pain in stories and essays that dealt with hunger and overwork, with the raw village youth who came pouring into the factories after 1905, with strikebreakers, with the "backward," neurotic, and vicious elements in the Russian working class, and with workers who beat and mistreated their wives. Passion and control are at war in these pieces that depict a chiaroscuro picture of bright, powerful, invincibly progressive metallic equipment set against a still dark and sluggish human workforce.

His longest work, written in Siberian exile right before the Revolution, "Express—a Siberian Fantasy," is a utopia about the future shape of the vast and sleepy land. Its form is the voyage of the express train "Panorama," a hurtling monster of steel symbolizing speed, power, and constricted space. Siberia has become enmeshed in a dense network of factories, tunnels, roads, canals, stations, and towns. Cities such as Energy and Steel City are enormous concentrations of life and production, with buildings towering to the sky and plunging for miles beneath the earth, linked together by other linear cities that give no berth to rural space. In this ungreened land, a struggle between Americanoid trusts, Siberian peasant socialists, and the international proletariat is being mooted at conferences in the huge metropolis of Irkutsk and the language of their intercourse is a Russo-American pidgin tongue.

"Express" contains many of the themes taken up by early Soviet science fiction and is a summary of Gastev's proletarian exaltation of the machine and a hint at the coming utopian robotry. The soft values of Old Europe—dreamy songs, passive prayers and reveries—are brutally rejected in the dynamism of Siberia. Nature is assaulted not only by the physical upheaval of the environment but by a symbolic assault on natural shapes, lines, and curves which are now replaced or concealed by geometric forms and symmetrical lines, by cubes, parallels, magistrals of agonizing straightness and squares. Man is reforged by his environment. Like the River Ob, now fettered in granite, and like the land itself, strangled in muscle-like rails, man is molded by the symbolic train which aspires "to drown man in metal, melt all the souls and out of them create one great one." The purpose? To realize grandiose Promethean schemes resonating with motifs from Fourier, Jules Verne, and H. G. Wells: to melt the Arctic ice cap, to join America with Russia, and to forge the two continents into a roaring, raging machine shop of productivity and industrial might. Though the poem may be read as an indictment of capitalist inhumanity, the exalted tone adopted toward technological achievements and the dismissive treatment of their myriad victims suggests that Gastev had passed into the realm of a full technical utopia, devoid of humanist sentiment.[13]

Gastev returned to Petrograd when the Revolution broke out. During the first years of Soviet power, the influence of his machine literature was immense in the burgeoning Proletcult movement. His poems were performed in factories. But he turned his own energies to labor problems. His dream was to put the entire unified economy in the hands of the trade unions and the factory committees under the leadership of advanced unions such as the metal workers (of which he was a leader). His views partly resembled Bogdanov's who called for a threefold division of authority—the party for political matters, the unions for the economy, and the Proletcult for cultural life. But Gastev's syndicalism was rejected by the party. In any case, Gastev was not a grass-roots syndicalist; he believed firmly in control, authority over the workers, discipline, labor draft, compulsion, rationing, piece rates—in short, the Taylor system.

In 1918, Gastev envisioned the triumph of the machine throughout the world, the emergence of "machine cities," and a culture of "engineerism" wherein life was run by machines, where workers' rhythms were geared to machine tempos, and where technicians wore uniforms and punched in like anyone else. It was a leveling collectivism under the authority not of the party but of machinery itself, in the literal sense of the word. Gastev gave new meaning to the American term "machine politics" when he predicted that "future society will be managed by special 'production complexes' wherein the will of machinism and the force of human consciousness will be fused in an unbreakable weld."[14]

> The debates between the majority and the minority, all the stormy polemics of the democratic order will be pushed aside as the 'all too human' passion of a past age and replaced by competing production complexes. . . . The method of solving social problems by 'vote' and by finding the majority or minority must be seen as old fashioned hand production; the essence of the new industry will be to end this and to create new means of revealing the general will.

In retrospect, this lyrical fantasy may be viewed as the ultimate version of the technocratic society, transferring decision making not to experts but to an expert computer, dissolving traditional politics not into committees of technocrats but into programmed data centers. It was another example of the dream of self-regulation—akin to Lenin's commune state of the future and to Bogdanov's Tectology—a dream that had enormous attraction in a land where human efficiency and dispassionate managers were in short supply and where severe economic backwardness seemed to demand dialectically the most wondrous of mechanized solutions.

In 1919, Gastev reached the limit of his utopian vision: he described a mechanized, standardized world, in a literal sense, with production ruled by self-regulating and self-correcting machines, joined throughout the world in a machine city—that is, a single unbroken mechanized civilization stretching around the globe. All production people (not workers now) are reduced to a single level of skill—the middle range—and the machines are transformed into managers and decision makers, with production people adapting themselves to the rhythm of the machine. With this reduction and standardization of the work force and production space comes the uniformization of gestures, language, and thoughts—a human geography of symbols and movements copied from the machine, a single mode of speech, a standardized catalog of thoughts, and a unified collection of meals, of housing, and of sexual and spiritual life. Man is to become an anonymous production unit, an A, B, C, a 324, or a 075, "soulless and devoid of personality, emotion, and lyricism—no longer expressing himself through screams of pain or joyful laughter, but rather through a manometer or taxometer. Mass engineering will make man a social automation."[15]

Zamyatin's masterful parodic treatment of this dream in *We* is well known (see Chapter 8). A whole genre of Soviet science fiction was built upon it. Bogdanov, to whose Martian computerized planet in *Red Star* Gastev's visions was uncomfortably close, was quick to attack it as excessive, inhuman, and in violation of the true comradely collective in which man mastered the machine and created his own proletarian culture. To Bogdanov, Gastev's machines seem to have replaced the Gods and the tsars that Bolshevism had so painfully and at such great human cost cast down. A major challenge for science fiction was to confront the visions of Bogdanov, Gastev, and Zamyatin and to combine the wonders of mechanized modernity with the warm-blooded visions of egalitarianism and comradeship that were also born of the Revolution.[16]

Gastev discovered the essence of the new proletarian culture—what he called "a culture insurgent." It was a culture not of Proletcult studios and workers' theater and art but one of routinized life and work. In 1919 he was still straddling two worlds: as Commissar of the Arts in Bolshevik Kharkov, a particularly radical and innovative city in the Civil War years, and as head of an institute of labor where he taught "social engineering," the name he gave to the new culture. Without a backward glance, he left the world of art and literature altogether and devoted the rest of his life to the training of workers in a newly created Central Institute of Labor in Moscow. Gastev was galvanized and shocked during the Civil War by the unbelievable backwardness of Russian labor. It was thus a combination of his worship of the potential of the machine, his perception of the workers as spontaneously wandering peasants, and his understanding of culture as the remaking of the psyche rather than the teaching of the arts that pushed Gastev into his obsession with making human robots.[17]

At the first conference on Taylorism, Gastev was a prominent voice in favor of adopting it. But a debate erupted over its exploitative aspect. An uneasy compromise was reached by proclaiming its socialist and pro-labor aspirations. The movement remained weak, resisted by union leaders and workers and attacked by intellectuals within, who focused on Gastev's elitist Institute of Labor. But Gastev was upheld, as was N.O.T. itself, which then began to spread unevenly but steadily throughout industry. It was, in one historian's phrase, "a remarkable act of faith," a desire to "cut short the birth pangs of the emergence of the new socialist technostructure"—in other words, to substitute millions of Taylorized workers and efficient organizational technique for what it lacked in engineers and technology.[18]

At the dawn of the Taylorist movement in Soviet Russia, Gastev laid out the psychic dimensions of "social engineering." The main foes of the worker, he wrote in pedantic and imperious tones, were laziness, panic, and "wildness" in work style. Workers must refrain from smoking, eating, and drinking on the job and restrain childlike enthusiasm on successfully completing a production task. Fantasy and dreaming—"the gentle idyllic fantasy that feeds dreams of the land of milk and honey"—must give way to hard analysis of the task at hand, and "eastern heroism" must give way to a worship of detail—the minute of time and the inch of space. The "insurgent culture" was a taste for work, an internalization of continuous success and efficiency, a constant posture of awareness, attentiveness, and alertness, careful preparation of tools, timing, order of tasks, and organization of workspace. The sources of this mentality, he explained, were modern industry, the military, and the revolutionary movement, whose cult of punctuality and coordination had turned over an empire. Down with passivity, with vagueness of gestures and speech, and with the "lyrical disorder" of the Russian, cried Gastev. Walk and move like city people with precision in the gait, like marching troops alert to every inch of the surrounding terrain. And like the revolutionaries of the bygone days, urged Gastev, "go to the people," invade the countryside with battalions of labor, armed with ideas of work, citify and colonize our own country. "The Hour Has Come," wrote Gastev, to launch the Russian troika of Gogol's metaphor and to destroy Oblomovism, "maybeism" and the dreadful Russian attitude of *nichevo*.[19]

Gastev's image of "man the machine" was certainly not new. La Mettrie in 1747 had described humans as "perpendicular moving machines" in order to promote his materialist outlook. His *L'homme machine* appeared in Russian in 1911, and Jules Amar's Taylorist rhapsody of the body, *Le moteur humain,* was published in Soviet Russia. The expression, and variants of it, were widely used in the discourse over work in the 1920s. But what did Gastev really mean by it? Was it simply the soldier, that "stereometric figure," in the words of Elias Canetti, who "lives in a permanent state of expectation of commands," the raw target of drill and the "sting of command?"[20] Or was it a robot? The word "robot," from the Czech for unfree peasant toiler (and whose root means "work" in most Slavic languages) appeared in Europe just at the moment Gastev began his work. The robots were the machine-men who came to life in Karel Čapek's *Rossums Universal Robots* (1920). In an earlier work of 1908, Čapek depicted the factory owner's ideal worker as "a machine, able only to move, not to think or feel." "The worker must become a machine. We need movement from him. Nothing more. Any idea is a breach of discipline." A few years later, Čapek, observing the apparently inert and lifeless workers who rode the trams of Prague, applied the word "robot" to them—human beings who worked without thinking.[21]

Gastev's ideal worker of the 1920s was neither pure soldier nor pure robot. Gastev had descended from the extravagances of 1918–19, when the elemental industrial chaos had driven him to the vision of a machine world of anonymous creatures. His speeches and writings of the 1920s, though hyperbolic, more often spoke of practical needs in the current workforce than of future scenarios. Gastev's ideal worker is neither the oxen brute of Taylor's dreams, nor the lifeless robot of Čapek's nightmare. He is rather an active, sentient, and creative part of the productive process who behaves like a seasoned, conscious, and well-trained warrior. Armed with sharpness of vision, acute hearing, attentiveness to environment and detail, precision and even grace of movement, and "scoutlike" inquisitiveness about the relationship and locations of things and people, he enters the factory as though it were a battle-field with commander-like briskness,

regimental routine, and a martial strut. For him, no romance, no heroic individual deeds—
only a relentless battle waged scientifically for production.

But the robot is present in Gastev's vision nonetheless: it is the machine itself, not
the man. For Gastev, the machine also takes on a life that gives it not only the power
to produce and enrich, but also to train, to inspire, to organize. His wildest visions of
1918–19 are previsions of Čapek and Zamyatin and celebrations of a coming event often
warned about in science fiction: the takeover by machines. Gastev could never quite
decide whether the machine was to be the master or the servant of man. Since he
continued to use the machine metaphor, he eventually opened himself to attack by those
who opposed his policies on other grounds. But Gastevism differed from administrative
utopia—the heavy-handed martialing and mobilization of raw labor in a palpably unequal hierarchy. Gastev's man-machine meant a symbiosis of the two, interacting in a
way never wholly understood even by himself. It clearly contained fearful elements.
But Gastev himself, by all accounts, was not a cold-hearted machine-like fanatic but a
warm and engaging person. He did not fear the power of the machine. He feared backwardness, passivity, and sloth.[22]

The public arena of Gastev's theories in practice was the Central Institute of Labor,
what he called his "latest work of art," founded on August 24, 1920 with nothing more
than a pencil and a plan in Gastev's mind. It soon expanded into offices and a network
of training centers in which workers were taught to think, act, and work in the Gastev
manner. The German Expressionist writer Ernst Toller, who visited one in the 1920s,
described a hundred identical gray benches, with a hundred men and women trainees in
identical costumes obeying instructions conveyed by electronic beeps of machine. They
approached the work benches in columns, performed tests in unison, graduated in dif-
ficulty. Their hammer-teacher was a machine to which their arm was strapped until they
were able to work independently. A "cyclogram" photographed their work and recorded their progress by means of moving lights. There were no books, no theories, no
meetings—only practical work, from simple to complex, in a course lasting three to six
months. The purpose: to study "the human machine' and to create new people by means
of social engineering. From simple functions such as striking and pressing, workers
proceeded to more complex factory operations. Between 1921 and 1938, 1,700 Institute
stations were set up which trained a half million workers and 20,000 instructors in 200
different skills. The Institute was twice awarded major Soviet decorations for its efforts.[23]

Gastev publicly praised Taylor and Ford as his models, and apparently recognized
the Ford plant—a huge American training center which turned rural people and unskilled
immigrants into skilled operatives—as a model for a cultural transformation. And like
Ford managers of the late 1920s and early 1930s, he constantly invoked "iron discipline," piece work, intensity, and organization. He looked upon his trained instructor
cadre as an army of "civilizers," modern *Kulturträgers* who would spread their skills
and "postures" of body and mind into the dark countryside of unskilled labor. Gastev's
quest for "new people" in fact resembled a vision of the "superman" who would
master nature, death, and time by a new work culture. He may even have been influenced in some of his fanciful visions by Valerian Muraviëv (a follower of Nikolai
Fëdorov), who worked in the secretariat of the Institute all through the 1920s and who
linked up these themes in his book *Mastery by Means of Time* (see Chapter 8). Thus
the search for "new people" whose image was early connected to science and technology in the "nihilist" characters of the 1860s had ultimately led to "scientized" workers

in the millions—a massive human link between creative intelligentsia and material transformation.[24] There is no indication that within the Central Institute of Labor and its branches there reigned any attempt to reduce all workers to the mindless creatures described in Gastev's fantasies of 1918–19. It is tempting to view Gastev as a smaller Stalin, a fanatical hard utopian who desired to reduce, standardize, and enslave. Zamyatin's immortal parody of Gastevism in *We* invites the notion that Gastev, who invented the term "social engineering," envisioned something like the hideous United State of that novel. In fact, as a recent scholar has argued, his vision was of equality, decent and effective work habits, and community.[25] He believed that a machine culture would democratize and modernize the work force and lead it into the longed for world of dignity and strength—for workers and for the nation as a whole. It was neither the heartless arrogance of Arakcheev and his imitators nor the vastly more magnified mobilization and brutalization of raw labor and exploitation of slave labor that emerged with Stalin.

Gastev's sparkling and kinetic vision of a vast continent unified by steel, electricity, and asphalt, of bright and throbbing machinery glinting in the sunlight as it labored to refashion a world, and of workers trained by industrial metronomes into something resembling a huge and elegant *corps de ballet* tending that machinery and deriving its graceful precision from it was a romantic dream. It sprang from his life in the bleak world of Russian industry in a particularly painful and ugly moment of its history and from the spectacle of anarchy and paralysis that he witnessed in the Revolution. His "robots"—animated machines and mechanized humans—were an exceptionally extreme and one-sided response to this experience and to the permanent menace of Russian backwardness. But from the perspective of the 1930s, Gastevism—for all its apparent harshness—was a vision of hope.

## The Struggle for Time

Kerzhentsev's contribution to the cult of man-the-machine shifted the emphasis from the body and the consciousness of the individual worker to society at large. Kerzhentsev yielded nothing to Gastev as a fanatic of efficiency in life, but his conception of life was broader. Like the popularizers of Taylorism in the United States who created a "normal American madness," Kerzhentsev took Gastevism out of the factory and into the realm of everyday life.

Platon Mikhailovich Kerzhentsev (real name Lebedev) came from a loftier social and cultural background than Gastev's, and he never tried to be a factory worker. His father, a physician, had been a liberal member of the First Duma. Kerzhentsev's studies of peasant economy at Moscow University led him into Marxism and to the well-worn path of underground agitation, prison, and emigration in Europe. In 1904 he became a Bolshevik. After the failed 1905 revolution, Kerzhentsev blossomed into a minor journalist and traveled through Europe, America, and Japan. He acquired considerably more cosmopolitanism and culture than most of his colleagues in the N.O.T. movement. But this made him an extreme iconoclast during the Revolution and Civil War, when he gained notoriety as a theater critic who urged the complete overhaul of theatrical life. The iconoclastic impulse and the enthusiasm for the theatricalization of everyday life informed his brief excursion into the world of social management in the early 1920s.

Both before and after this parenthetical episode, Kerzhentsev served in a number of
minor diplomatic missions. The brevity of Kerzhentsev's infatuation with Taylorism was
characteristic of his tendency to jump from one cause to another.[26]

Kerzhentsev's regular movement back and forth from the world of the theater—
where precision always counts—to the bureaucratic world of early Bolshevism—where
order and punctuality were very hard to enforce—led him into his angry war against
inefficiency. In the midst of his writings on theater, he composed a short manual on
*How to Conduct a Meeting* in 1919. He then joined the burgeoning N.O.T. movement
and produced his first Taylorist work, *The Principles of Organization.* Kerzhentsev opposed Gastev's excessive emphasis on worker training, but what made him cut out a
new path was an episode that he described with great vividness. In July 1923, a meeting
of some 3,500 workers was kept waiting for two hours before the speakers arrived to
open it. An American journalist present (unidentified) calculated on the spot for Kerzhentsev that the 7,000 man hours lost could have been used to build one or two airplanes. Kerzhentsev was electrified by this revelation. Within a few weeks he had written an impassioned article in *Pravda* entitled "Time Builds Airplanes," founded the
League of Time, and produced his two major works on the subject, *The Struggle for
Time* and *The Scientific Organization of Labor.*[27]

Like Gastev and other Taylorists, Kerzhentsev expostulated on the value of time—a
commodity, he said, that foreigners instinctively revered due to their industrial environment, but that Russians ignore, misuse, and kill. Like Gastev, he also preached the
gospel of personal time-keeping, thorough planning, alertness, and a "feeling for time."
He advocated the use of a "chronocard," a permanent record of the daily round that
should be scrutinized every half hour with the aim of inducing "spontaneous self-discipline." But his main stress was on "social time," the coordination of all "personal
times" in a given community or organization. In plain terms this meant a struggle
against tardiness at work and at meetings, long repetitive speeches, avoidable lines and
bottlenecks, and excessive paperwork and red tape. He reserved special venom for those
speakers who introduced every report with a history of mankind from the time of creation.[28]

Kerzhentsev's main concern was to "introduce scientific principles not only into
man's economic activity or production but into all organized activity or work"—the
army, the school, all of social life. Kerzhentsev echoed Gastev's belief that the sources
of efficient behavior were Western industry, the military life, and the revolutionary
movement. But he wished to borrow not only psychic patterns from these social forms
but the forms themselves, to organize militant groups—soldiers of efficiency—who would
go out into the world to preach and practice and wage a war for time. "A struggle for
the correct utilization and economizing of time in all aspects of public and private life
is the basic precondition for the realization of the principles of N.O.T. in the U.S.S.R.,"
he wrote. In fact, he envisioned a revolution in time, a revolution from below—differing
from Gastev's robotry in its grass-roots organization and its comprehensive social sweep.
The League of Time was an experiment in human refashioning that would bring a utopia
of efficiency and productivity to the Russian land.[29]

The League of Time was founded at Kerzhentsev's initiative in July 1923 as "The
League 'Time'" (later renamed "League-N.O.T."). Though technically independent of
government and party, its intimate relationship to the N.O.T. movement was clearly
reflected in its board members: Kerzhentsev, Gastev, and other Taylorists, including the
theater director Meyerhold, with Lenin and Trotsky as honorary officers. It launched a

journal, *Time*, and started its first cell in a military academy. Within a month there were 44 cells with a hundred members; by October there were 100 cells with 2,500 in thirty-three cities; and by the end of 1924, there were 800 cells—20 percent in enterprises, 35 percent in government bodies, and 25 percent in schools—and 25,000 members, 40 percent of them party or Komsomol members. The documents of the period indicate that local bodies were pretty independent of the center. The Kazan chapter—a big one—had sixty-two members; at its inaugural meeting it vowed to limit meeting time to seventy minutes and to apply a scale of mild punishments to latecomers. At the grass-roots appeared spontaneous cells or circles called "Time" or "Productivity." Members (called *elvisty* after the initials L.V., *Liga* and *"Vremya,"* and sometimes *Notisty*), wore L.V. buttons and carried chronocards; some of them displayed oversized wristwatches as the emblem of their struggle—a poignant symbol in a land where less than a million watches and clocks were produced in 1928.[30]

The League was more a police force than an army. It eagerly feretted out "tardy embezzlers of time," including respected workers and officials, who were reprimanded and fined. A storm of criticism was unleashed against lateness and bad organization. Timeists poked their faces into every conceivable kind of enterprise and operation to uncover inefficiency and sloth as well as to reorganize and teach. Brigades marched into railroad stations to rearrange the furniture (at the Kazan Station in Moscow, for example, a passenger had to walk the entire length of the terminal three times in order to buy a ticket, check bags, and board train). At a Moscow factory, a time team reduced the period for distributing wages to 337 workers from thirty-nine hours to one hour and ten minutes. Speeches and articles pleaded with workers and managers to save time, conserve energy, and use space rationally. Worker's clubs held court trials of machines, workbenches, and forges in order to prove that these were "innocent" in work stoppages and that poor work habits were guilty. Even in the country, cows were "tried" to determined who was responsible for low yields of milk. A virtual craze for efficiency erupted in the economy.[31]

In a very Russian fashion, the campaign for efficiency migrated from the realm of production into the larger arena of everyday life and took on an unreal dimension that was often comical. In a hilarious scene in Ilf and Petrov's *The Twelve Chairs*, the opening of a Soviet town's first tram line is preceded by an elaborate festival whose main speaker begins with an interminable survey of the present international situation, a jab at the common habit of politicizing the most trivial event of life. This Kerzhentsev and the Timeists-N.O.T.ists hated above all. Much of their activity in the mid-twenties was devoted to eliminating needless meetings and streamlining necessary ones. One Komsomol group banned all meetings prior to 2:00 P.M., enforced the practice of getting to the point, and expelled people for inefficient behavior. At a medical school in the Don region, a local cell of N.O.T. leveled fines against tardy students and locked classroom doors the minute a lecture began, forcing (as in a theater) latecomers to stand outside until break time. Amoeba-like lines were straightened out in shops and cafeterias, and an effort was made to unclog the service and distribution process—to this day a major psychic scourge to foreign residents in the Soviet Union. In dormitories and communes fanatics of time, called "models" or "leftists," attempted to regulate the lives of their comrades by schedules, time boards, and minute accounting of all activities day and night, an aspiration that was also taken up by town planners in the late 1920s.[32]

The Young Pioneers were founded at about the same time as the League of Time, and their earliest exercises and games were infected with the compulsions of time and space assessment. Pioneer manuals were replete with methods for sharpening the children's sense of time, space, coordination, memory, and powers of orientation on the local terrain. Their games were drawn from military experience (though played without weapons or simulated violence)—excercises in escape and evasion, capture, the liberation of a comrade, sabotaging "fascist" telegraph lines and so on. All of them put great stress on precision of thought and movement. One of them was actually called "League of Time." In it Pioneers drew a slip of paper with a given number of minutes written on it. They were then to disperse without wristwatches and return at the time given them, with a twenty percent margin of error. The most accurate team in the sensing of time was the winner of the contest.[33]

Enthusiasts in the Red Army coopted the League of Time into their own pet theories of organizing society. The first of the time-cells appeared in the army, and they spread widely with the full support of the High Command. Frunze addressed a League conference. In fact "Taylorization" had been suggested in the military as early as 1920, and Trotsky's militarization of labor had overtones of it. But in 1923–25, it became a virtual craze. Going beyond applying Time League methods to army life, it sought really to apply the forms of army life to society at large. *Po voennomu* (the army way) was a synonym for efficiency in civilian life for military writers. The army was seen as the basic training ground for life—as opposed to the weak and inefficient schools—and "a cultural force" in reshaping the nation. A manual of discipline compared the army to a factory, and people began agitating for the "militarization" (meaning standardization) of consumer goods, tools, and equipment. All of this was to make the civilian and the military population—its habits, outlook, physical plant, and equipment—more or less interchangeable in time of war. Here again was the convergence of factory, regiment, and life.[34]

The League of Time was rather suddenly dissolved in February 1926 while Kerzhentsev was on a diplomatic mission, the Workers' and Peasants' Inspectorate having declared its work accomplished. Like the Workers' Correspondents and the Zhenotdel (women's section) activists, the Timeists were considered a nuisance by administrators. Komsomols who lived by League principles were often criticized by their comrades as "red-tapeists," egoists, violators of the collective spirit, and super bureaucrats. Technical, managerial, and government people accused them of dilettantism, excessive and uninformed demands, and of being a menace to competent professionals. In any case, the League was not very successful in realizing Kerzhentsev's dream: to teach all Soviet citizens "spontaneous self-discipline." Instead it pitted a legion of enthusiasts and busybodies against uninterested citizens. The N.O.T. movement itself was preserved in the economic sphere, and Gastev's Institute was wholly unaffected by the dissolution of the Time League. But Kerzhentsev's vision of a mass nationwide movement to make Russia efficient and to rationalize space, time, order, and movement in a short time collapsed.[35]

Art and life were constantly imitating each other in the Russian Revolution. This happens in all great upheavals where the impetus to reshape humanity takes hold. Although Kerzhentsev and Gastev liked to invoke military and industrial metaphors and models, they were both copying the art they knew the best. Gastev, who had created an animated world of machines and machine-like workers out of the buzzing universe he had inhabited for a decade, transferred his imagery—not the known reality—into social engineering and robotry. Kerzhentsev, a specialist on the theater, really wanted to theatricalize life. His surge towards "economizing" seemed like the soul of common sense to a regime of technicists and a land groping for organizational culture. But behind this impulse was the esthetic impulse to stage everything, to develop acting skills among the population, to join audience and cast in a great social "performance" of his utopian real-life play, which he might have entitled, had he succeeded, the Land of Time.

## The Art of Production

The world of art in the Russian Revolution returned the compliment by borrowing for its own uses the imagery, themes, and mental styles of the Taylorists and the Timeists. This borrowing expressed itself in three general ways: the exaltation of the machine in the arts, the rhythmic revolution, and the scientization of artistic production. These were not the fruit of Gastevism and Kerzhentsevism. They all arose before the Revolution and blossomed independently, though in some cases artists felt obliged to invoke Taylor or Gastev directly and to legitimize their innovation by linking it to pure proletarian thematics and the modernizing thrust of Bolshevism. It was precisely in the realm of technology and its physical celebration that Bolshevism and the avant-garde were closest in spirit. A broad range of artistic innovation—often lumped under the rubric Constructivism has been well documented in recent studies. Painting, sculpture, poster art, book design, furniture styles, costume, theater, music, the dance, architecture, and poetry were all infected with the magic of machine, of geometrism, and of functionalism. Though all of it was traceable to European prewar currents, the October Revolution lent the frenetic energy and official support that allowed its exponents to couch their experiments in political discourse.[36]

Speech was called "word chemistry of the scientifically enlightened proletariat" and poetry made not only to glamorize the machine, but composed in the manner of a machine product. Osip Brik, a leading avant garde theorist, writing in *Art and Production,* said that "by artistic production we mean simply the conscious creative relationship to the productive process. We would like every worker who gives an object a particular form and color to understand why that form and color is necessary." The theater critic Fevralsky in 1922 wanted to "establish a science of art which will help to achieve the transformation of art into scientifically organized production." That this notion was not simply a fad of eccentric artists is clear from the almost universal presence of "art production" machines in the visions of science fiction of the 1920s (see Chapter 8).[37]

The history of machine worship in the visual and literary arts of the 1920s is well known. But it also embraced music. Music-as-machinery-noise and urban-sound-as-music received their first notable currency among the Italian Futurists in the immediate prewar years. Balilla Pratella and his "ideologist" Luigi Russolo yearned for a music that not only celebrated the city in some programmatic way but that reproduced it. Russolo's "Art of Noises" glorified urban sound—shouting throngs, motors, machines, valves, pumps, pistons, streetcars rattling on rails. In revolutionary Russia, this idea was quickly taken up in Proletcult circles. A Soviet critic in 1919 urged musicians to "listen carefully to the new tempo and sonorities in the revolutionary life of the proletariat, work out new instruments and instrumentation to express the sounds of contemporary life" to capture its "might and titanic oscillations," its "rhythm of iron and granite," and the thunderous sounds that herald "the establishment of communism on earth." Since, as one of the Taylorist theoreticians noted, the sounds of modern machines had drowned out the old "songs of work" among the masses, it was now thought possible to enlist that very noise as the music of the future.[38]

This vision—or aural premonition—took two main forms during the Revolution: the symphony of factory sirens and the noise orchestra. The first was a series of "concerts" of factory whistles, first attempted in Petrograd in 1918, repeated in other towns during the Civil War, and culminating in the "symphony of factory whistles" in Baku in 1922. The arena of performance was the entire city. Industrial sirens and whistles around Baku were tuned and conducted from rooftops by flagwaving "conductors" who attempted to produce the cadences of the "Internationale" while percussive and sonoric effects were added by foghorns of the Caspian fleet, two batteries of cannon, a machine gun section, and hydroplanes. The result was, according to Fueloep-Miller (who did not witness it), a deafening cacophony.[39]

The "noise orchestra" was launched by a sect of machine worshippers called Engineerists. At their concerts, technicians "played" engines, turbines, dynamos, sirens, hooters, and belts of all kinds on the premises of the factory itself, producing what Fueloep-Miller called a "whole world of noise which deafened the ear." They were sometimes accompanied by a ballet of mechanical gymnastics choreographed to the machine noise and performed on the workshop floor. Fueloep-Miller's irony is thickest when describing these sonoric flights into technicist utopia. He saw them as arrogant or insane attempts to celebrate the mass man of the factory by the solipsistic deployment of his own work tools as art. But what they illustrated so vividly and with such pathos—more than did a hundred posters of smokestacks and steel—was an aspiration to worship the present and the future, to deny the pastoral past, and to affirm the magical power of technique. For only these would transform Russia into a land of abundance and social justice and simultaneously shape the political and aesthetic realm of the proletariat. "Rational music," wrote the avant-garde critic Kashnitsky a few years later, "is the chronicle of contemporary sounds and noise that must be captured and transmitted by radio out into the countryside and thus bring the life of the city to the darkness of the rural areas." As a representative expression of the Proletarian Culture movement, noise music resounded with the hope of the working class to create its very own culture.[40]

Conventional composers, perhaps alerted to the danger of a movement that would substitute sirens for woodwinds, attempted to fasten the cult of the machine to their own art. This was already being done in Europe by Henri Kling (a 1918 piece for fire irons, dish pans, a cow bell, plus conventional instruments), Arthur Honneger (*Pacific 231*, imitating the sound of a train), and others. The raging polemics in the 1920s over what was revolutionary music could not go unfazed by a current such as this. Leonid Polovinkin's *Teleskop II* and Vladimir Deshevov's *Rails* (both of the mid-1920s) tried to suggest the noise and clatter of industry and transport. Even Dmitry Shostakovich in his Second Symphony *(The October Revolution)* felt compelled to add to the massed chorus and proletarian program of his work a factory whistle. The most notable—at one time world famous—contribution to this genre was Alexander Mosolov's *The Factory (Zavod, 1928, known in the West as The Iron Foundry)* scored for conventional brass, woodwinds, and strings but with the addition of brittle percussion and sheets of iron that are struck persistently as the machine-like rhythm reaches crescendo and finale.[41]

The machine—its shape, its power, its shrill song, and its roaring menace—were central to the Constructivist vision in art and music. Vsevelod Meyerhold, the world famous and supremely influential champion of an "October in the Theatre," employed in his revolutionary theater both the Constructivist art of machine-like settings and Constructivist gesture which he called Biomechanics *(biomekhanika)* or the mechanics of the human body, a term he borrowed from Gastev. Meyerhold, long before the Revolution, wished to exalt the rhythmic generation of stage action and reject the more cerebral modes of Stanislavsky, and he drew deeply on prewar styles of theatrical rhythmics (Georg Fuchs) and the Eurhythmic movement of Dalcroze. But he also drew directly and self-consciously from Taylorism. Meyerhold was a leading member of the League of Time and a friend of Gastev and Kerzhentsev for years. In 1921, a year after the founding of Gastev's Central Institute of Labor, Meyerhold set up his own training workshop as a school of body motion, strikingly similar to Gastev's (they were both closed in 1938, the year these three men fell from grace).[42]

A recently translated archival record shows how similar Meyerhold's regime was to that of Gastev: alertness, rhythmic motion, scientific control over the body, exercises and gymnastics, rigorous physical lessons in precision movement and coordination—in short "organized movement" designed to create the "new high-velocity man." Meyerhold cites Gastev as his inspiration. In explaining Biomechanics to the public in 1922 as an openly admitted application of Taylorism to the theater, he claimed to be trying "to discover those movements in work which facilitate the maximum use of work time"— no superfluous motions, good rhythm, poise, stability, precision, economizing of production time. He hoped by this not only to enhance the true acting ability of his troupe but also to reduce productions from four hours to one hour, without lessening aesthetic content or form. "Taylorization," he promised, would create that physical state needed for the appropriate emotion which was "excitation" and not "ecstasy."[43]

In all these Constructivist and Taylorist art movements, one discerns, as in Futurism and related genres, the desire for speed, efficiency, angularity, and "industrialness" not only for their own sake—as fashionable European fads—but as psychic weapons leveled against the bodily, the mental, and the social "lyricism" and pastoral grace that the new generation associated with utter weakness, pallid gentility, and sloth. It was a revolution in gestures deeply related to the militarist and gymnastic movements that swept over the world at the beginning of our century—the high stepping and straight armed saluting that promised a needed assault on a dying world. Meyerhold not only staged marching sailors as a pendant to foxtrotting bourgeois couples of decadent Europe, he also had his audiences march around the foyer before assaulting them inside the theater with his *Gesamtkunstwerk* of movement and kinetic power.[44] In the opinion of his best biographer, Meyerhold's Biomechanics was an offspring of the poetization and exaltation of machinery that ruled in those days: a dream of the mechanization of man. "This idea," he writes, "like many others akin to it, of a thorough-going Americanization of life, remained a touching and unrealizable utopia, arising out of conditions of a poor and badly organized everyday existence of the early 1920s."[45] And here, above all, is the true source of the Soviet madness called Taylorism.

## Time, Space, Motion, Order

The Taylorist movement in revolutionary Russia had risen beyond the prosaic task of making workers better and faster. It aspired to introduce scientifically rational order into every corner of life: family, school, art, war, government, and even friendship and leisure. In a nation where industrialization had hardly begun to breathe, where skilled labor was in pitifully short supply, where peasant traditions of time, space, motion, and order were arrayed against the Taylorist canon of optimum efficiency, the Soviet variety of Taylorism was quickly transformed into a utopian movement. It was perhaps one of the most poignant cases in the Revolution of the romantic ideal outstripping the human reality. But it was not simply another example of the fate of imported ideas, twisted into an unrecognizable parody of the original, and not only another example of the enormous capacity of the Russian mind to engage in social dreams of transformation. At its deepest level, robotry and the struggle for time were part of a widespread current in Western history: the process (still very much unfinished in Soviet Russia) of eliminating the social, psychological, and cultural forms of a huge peasant population and to make them into "modern" people.

Being modern in our world means, among other things, being able to measure time and distance accurately, to calculate the dimensions of a problem, and to act accordingly. Time, space, motion, and order in the mind of man are prime ways by which we distinguish—as we like to see it—the primitive from the advanced. The contemporary psychic and social urban landscape is dense with shapes, paths, people, events, processes that are vital to survival. A knowledge of this topography is as important as is a map to a traveller. It is not in the realm of aesthetic fashion, or in the soaring of extravagant fantasy, or in the arrogance of intellectuals suddenly endowed with power that we find the underlying root of the revolutionary "madness" of Taylorism. It is rather in the baffling spectacle of an overwhelmingly peasant population, gripped in its own internalized system, who are about to inhabit the factories, streets, and edifices, and to ride and operate the conveyances and machines of the future city.[46]

The mechanization of awareness as a means of survival in an urban industrial society is one of the most far-reaching phenomena in the history of human culture. Few historians, until recently, have paid it much attention. In an eloquent study of time and discipline in the early modern era, Edward Thompson has shown how organizers of capitalist life perceived nature's time to be wasteful and immoral and how they fought it. The watch became an emblem of loyalty through prudent work culture, and the machine, in the words of an early nineteenth century preacher, meant "discipline in industrial operations" and "habits of calculation." Beginning around 1700, bells, clocks, timesheets, incentives, punishments, supervision, preaching and the suppressing of fairs and sports were the machinery of creating new labor habits. This was not a capitalist plot to exploit labor (though it did that); the socialist Robert Owen in 1813 also asserted openly that "habits of attention, celerity, and order" were the best means to "remoralize the lower orders." The metropolis itself demanded a reworking of "social time" and a "frame of temporal reference different from that of the small village" because of the vastness and density of the field of interaction.[47]

This revolution in cultural outlook came very late to Russia. At the start of the twentieth century, the workforce was still peasant, and even though the "hereditary proletarian" element in it steadily grew, it was frequently deluged by an influx of raw rural labor from the villages. From the village also came traditional modes of time. Social time in the Russian village—as in villages elsewhere—was task-oriented and locked into the agricultural cycle. Long winters of enforced idleness (at least for the men) were interrupted by frantic bursts of fieldwork. Habits of efficient distribution of energy were lacking. Observers lamented this before and after the Revolution; Preobrazhensky, an economist, thought it to be a Russian national characteristic. Hours and minutes had no meaning to the peasant, only days and seasons. There were no watches and clocks in the villages (thus the emblematic use of the watch by the League of Time) and the word *seichas* (right away) could mean anything at all. Work and rest, mealtime and slumber, family rites and church feasts were the timesheets of the Russian peasant. Peasants were concrete in their thinking, weak on future time and planning. As in some other peasant communities, haste meant loss of dignity or excessive ambitiousness. Workers brought some of these habits to the city, and not only workers. In a land that was so overwhelmingly rural for so long a time, and where gentry sat out their summers on idyllic estates, multiple systems of social time coexisted.[48]

Space and motion, in the peasant culture, were related to the concept of time. Rhythm after all is merely movement in space over time. Though their land always seemed insufficient, the peasants' space was immense—the vaulted sky, the vast plains, the endless forest. Peasants wasted space prodigiously, in spite of their meticulousness in dividing what they owned in common. The scattered strips were a case in point, families sometimes possessing 50–60 strips flung far and wide and divided by little walls of soil. In a village in the Valdai Hills above Moscow, a peasant would walk 1,200 miles per season to make his rounds. Peasant estimates of distances were as imprecise as those of time: *dva shaga* (two steps away) could mean a few feet or a mile (as it can today). The peasant knew his own space and tried to organize it, but he knew little of land outside his own ken—and cared less. In the 1920s, Maurice Hindus noted a peasant genius for taking three, five, or ten steps instead of the needed one. A peasant, unitiated to the science of Taylorist striding, would just as soon wind around a vast arc to get from one place to another as to march a straight line. In 1932, an American businessman was astonished at Moscow pedestrians jaywalking among the vehicles like peasants in country lanes. Ropes were needed to keep them on the pavements! Lateness, the tortoise-like torpor of waiters, *seichasism,* and *nichevoism* (the Russian equivalent of mañana, "it doesn't matter," "it can wait"), irregularity, asymmetry, inefficiency, and unnecessary queues—which to this day resemble blobs, not lines—were all the result, not only of socialism, but of the sudden and massive juxtaposition of two cultural frames— the village and the city.[49]

The apparent aimlessness and the untimed milling of the Russian was related to a weak capacity to "calculate," to look ahead, plan, size up, check out the environment, the time, and the job. The ballet of street movement with its headlong rushes, unseeing pedestrians, constant collisions, lurches and sudden halts, all mingled with stately rustic meandering, seemed to betoken a massive condition of sleepwalking. It was a lack of concern for the time and the space beyond the present moment—a weakness in everyday futures. The same mentality accounted for the oft-lamented "factory chauvinism," the *partizanshchina* during the Civil War, and the weakness of lateral coordination between government agencies in what was supposed to be an "integrated" national economy. People from a world with a limited field of vision, few contacts (mostly emotional and face to face), direct communication (speech), and concrete semantic expressiveness found it difficult to adjust to the abstractions, mechanisms, and schedules of the modern city. The very language of peasants' gesture—particularly the broad sweep of the arm (suggesting and no doubt derived from the wielding of the scythe)—seemed to reject the angular world around them.[50]

The peasant, transported to the urban world, still seemed to be dreaming. It was not the fantasy of construction or the reverie of reshaping man and the outer world. It was the old dream: of surviving. Kerzhentsev, in a revealing vignette, retold the fable of the peasant and the hare in his *Agitator's Notebook* (1925). In it the peasant sees a rabbit. At once he begins to dream about how he will catch the rabbit, sell it, buy a shoat, watch it grow and breed it, then buy a cow. He screams for joy. And the rabbit runs away. This is Kerzhentsev's frustrated parable on dreaming and planning.[51] And it was this perception of the bumbling, daydreaming peasant that sent him, Gastev, and people like them into rapturous dreams of their own about reshaping the timeless, open-ended and stubborn peasant into a modern person who would save the revolution and save Russia and the world.

These dreams did not survive in any recognizable form the great Stalinist revolution. Gastev, Kerzhentsev, and Meyerhold were all purged and killed at about the same time (see Chapter 11). Only the crudest and harshest elements of Taylorism were retained, but stripped of all dreamlike qualities and aspirations and made into tools of labor exploitation. But the phenomenon must be judged on its own ground and in its own time. Machinery loomed up after the Revolution as a God to be revered, a model of the new art, an engine of escape into fantasy, an emblem of modernity and happiness, and a teacher of the new gestural culture. Soviet devotees of the machine in the 1920s sacralized it because of its power to create and its potential for reshaping thought, work, and gesture. The *contraposto* of the peasant body culture and a machine world brought tensions—and the fantasy was designed to resolve that tension. Russian "sloth" (as they saw it) was an agony to Bolsheviks, or at least to those who were not themselves infected with it. It was the curse, the disease, the affliction of the nation. The cult of the machine was a response to this curse: an assault on "backwardness," on aristocratic lassitude among the elite and apathy and inertia among the masses, a war on romanticism, pathos, pity, and the lyrical—while being replete itself with all of these. It also meant "moral collectivism" in the dream of Gastev even though this dream was to degenerate into the collective moral subordination to the machine and its "owners"— the technical elite of the new order.

Since the Russian revolutionary movement was, from its very inception, a struggle not only for a new culture and for social justice and equality but also for modernity and productivity, it was perhaps inevitable that experiments designed to create an efficient and machine-disciplined population overnight should have taken on an extravagant and utopian character. Machine utopia stands in contrast to the more spontaneous currents of culture building, egalitarianism, and communalism. It was nonetheless an independent response, generated by the Revolution, and wildly embraced by many kinds of people, to an age old problem of Russian society: the lack of spontaneous self-motivation among the population at large. Had it been able to survive, in all its variant forms, it would have had to fight constantly to win over the psyches and the bodies of the Russian people. That it was not simply the hysterical fancy of an arrogant minority is borne out clearly in the way that machinism and timeism in a wide array of guises, took their places beside culture building and social justice in the main visionary genres of the 1920s: science fiction, architectural utopia, and the communal experiment.

1. *Religious utopia: the Vyg Old Believer Community (18th century)*

Gruzino

2. *Gruzino: the Militarized Estate of Arakcheev (c. 1800)*

Фаланстер
С литографии, принадлежавшей П. М. Дебу
(из коллекции Дебу)

3. Phalanstery: from the Collection of a Petrashevskian (1840s)

4. Utopian Landscape on Mars: Bogdanov's Red Star (1908)

5. *Euphoric Vision: ''A Year of Proletarian Dictator-ship'' (1918)*

6. *Dreamers in the Kremlin (1920) Lenin and H. G Wells*

7. *Trotsky and the Train: The Intellectual Militarized (c.1919)*

8. *Pugachev Redivivus: "The Ukraine Insurgent" (c. 1918)*

9. *The Gutted Litovsky Fortress:*
*A Photograph (1917)*

*The Litovsky prison in flames. The postcard is enscribed: "Hurrah! Greetings to Freedom!"*

10. *The Gutted Litovsky Fortress:*
*A Romanticized Postcard (1917)*

*11. Lenin Sweeps Away the Old Order (1920)*

*12. Citizens, Preserve Monuments of Art (1920)*

13. *February Days, Moscow (1917)*

14. *The Two-Headed Eagle of the Provisional Government (1917)*

15. *The Soviet Hammer and Sickle (1918)*

16. *Toward the Worldwide Commune, Petrograd (1920)*

17. *Fighting God with Religious Imagery:
a Banner of the Agit-Train Red Cossack
(1920)*

18. *Fighting God with Technical Imagery: the Anti-Religious Express of the Five Year Plan (c.
1930)*

19. *New Ritual: Octobering a Communist Baby (1920)*

20. *New Ritual: Melnikov's Crematorium and Columbarium (1919)*

*21. Woman and Man Are Equal:*
*Chekhonin's Medallion (1918)*

*22. Country and Town Are Equal:*
*A Smychka Poster (1925)*

23. *Simplicity in the Dress: Kustodiev's Design (1918)*

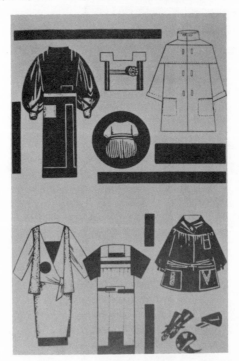

24. *Equality in the Dress: Exter's Designs (1920s).*

25. *Gastev: Prophet of the Machine (c. 1923)*

26. *Man as Clock: Advertisement suggesting that "A Human Being Is Only Human with a Watch."*

27. *"Take the Blizzard of the Revolution in the USSR, add the American Pulse of Life, and We'll Regulate Work with the Precision a Chronometer."* (1920s)

Модель «социально-инженерной машины»

28. *Model of Gastev's Social Engineering Machine (1920s)*

29. *Map of Mars: Bogdanov's* Engineer Menni *(1913)*

30. *Model of a Martian City by I. Rabinovich for the film* Aelita *(1923)*

31. *Cityroad in the Year 2927: Nikolsky,* In a Thousand Years *(1927)*

32. *Ritual in Utopia. Nikolsky* In A Thousand Years *(1927)*

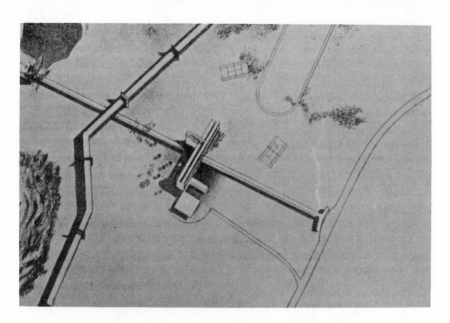

33. *Disurbanist Vision: A Ginzburg Project (1929)*

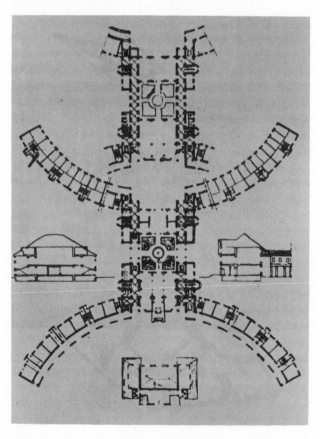

34. *Soviet Phalanstery: Tverskoi and Buryshkin, designers (1921)*

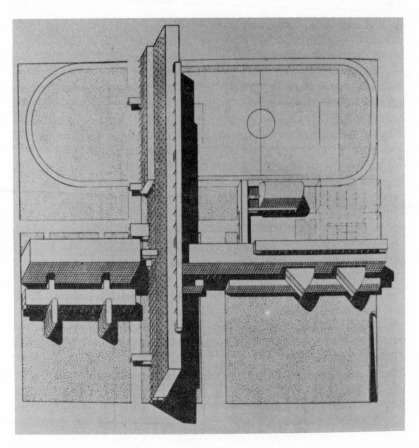

35. *House Commune: Barshch and Vladimirov, designers (1929)*

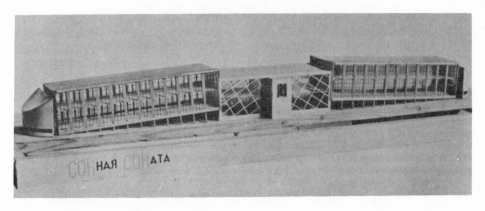

36. *Laboratory of Sleep: Melnikov (1929)*

37. *Commune of the 133: Epoch of Storm and Strife (1920s)*

38. *Women Communards of the Urals (early 1930s)*

39. *The Stalin Team (early 1930s)*

40. *Stalin and the Twelve Apostles*

# PART III

---

We: The Community of the Future

# 8

# Utopia in Time: Futurology
# and Science Fiction

A map of the world that does not include utopia is not even worth glancing
at, for it leaves out the one country at which humanity is always landing.
Oscar Wilde

## Time Forward

Radical dreamers and experimentalists of the first revolutionary decade lived their
dreamworlds apart from each other. Cultural nihilists, utopian festival creators, Godless
believers, levellers, and machine worshippers did not combine to create an interflow of
their visions and projects. There was no Department of Utopia in the Russian Revolution, no Dream Commissar to function as a clearing manager and coordinator of all the
life experiments cast up in the wake of the great upheaval. And yet scenarists, designers, and actors appeared on the social horizon in the midst of the imaginative turmoil
who tried to project and even act out utopia—in the grander, integrated sense of the
word. The scenarists were the writers of science fiction utopias, the designers were the
architects and city planners of the imminent future, and the actors were the "communards" who tried to shape the revolutionary dream by living in it. In their various ways,
these utopian creators embraced experimental ideals and values and embedded them in
a larger context—pictures, structures, narratives, fantasies, blueprints, surrogate families, and miniature experimental worlds. Lacking communication among themselves,
they peered off in different directions: into the future, into the cosmos, across the spacious land, or at their immediate environment.

Soviet science fiction of the 1920s continued the dialogue of the old regime and
expressed the utopian fantasy born of the Revolution itself. The old elements were on
full display: a gloriously tinted portrait of the communist heaven, framed in wondrous
technology, and inhabited by happy and virtuous people; dystopian forebodings about
the likely outcome of such a paradise; and counter-utopias of rustic joy and traditional
structures. The new ingredient was a hideous "map of hell" in which Marxist anti-
capitalism and the old Slavophile and Russian nationalist fears were condensed and
synthesized into a picture of an evil empire of the West. The entire corpus of revolutionary utopian science fiction, which disappeared with the emergence of Stalin,
parallels on levels at once fantastic and concrete the debate over the Revolution and
the nature of communism. Science fiction was a striking example of revolutionary discourse because of its total vision of communist life and its treatment of "revolution-

ary dreams" and life experiments in culture, ritual, religion, egalitarianism, and technology.

Revolutionary science fiction was the utopia of time. Its practitioners donned scarlet colored glasses to see what a communist society might, should, or would look like across a widely variant stretch of the ages. Their dream of a communist heaven created on earth and in the skies beyond by human hands—workers' and revolutionaries' hands—was informed by a vision of a unitary globe, adorned by imaginable technological perfection and humane social justice and equity, a vision that was implicit both in Marx and in the native dreaming of Russian radical traditions—and is still implicit in the latest program of the Communist Party of the Soviet Union and its many imitators.

## Utopia, Science, and Futurology

Bolsheviks—like other Marxists—had always been ambivalent toward Marxism's utopianism. In the aftermath of revolution, the ambivalence remained but the concept attracted enormous attention. Vladimir Svyatlovsky, in the earliest history (1922) of the Russian utopian novel, called the Russian Revolution itself "the first great utopia in modern history." Utopian classics began pouring off the presses. B. I. Gorev, an ex-Menshevik, wrote a long history, *From Thomas More to Lenin* (1922), placing the father of Bolshevism within the utopian socialist tradition (More's *Utopia* had already appeared in Russian translation in 1903). Campanella's *City of the Sun* appeared in 1918. Ten editions of Fourier's works appeared between 1917 and 1926 and many books about his ideas. Owen, Cabet, Buchez, Blanc, St. Simon and others enjoyed new translations in the 1920s. Their influence on the science fiction of the period is apparent, though never acknowledged. These classics were praised and scolded in the Leninist manner, but pilfered freely for ideas about community, housing, work styles, equality and all sorts of other things not easily available in the Marxist canon.[1]

Far more interesting was the mini-utopia or capsule projection of a world under communism in the final pages of Trotsky's *Literature and Revolution* (1923). In a tone of controlled lyricism, Trotsky envisions the disappearance of "ant-like piling up of quarters and streets" and decayed old cities and the emergence of "architectural democracy," with masses of ordinary people, compass in hand, forming factions of opinion and "true people's parties" to decide on the nature of new titanic "city-villages." Man would rebuild the earth to his own taste by re-registering mountains, rivers, meadows, fields, and steppes through technology and a "general industrial and artistic plan." The city, he continues, would not dissolve into the village. "On the contrary, the village will rise in fundamentals to the plane of the city. Here lies the principal task. The city is transient, but it points to the future, and indicates the road. The present village is entirely of the past." Trotsky's dream suggested richness, variety, and drama. "The shell of life will hardly have time to form before it will burst open again under the pressure of new technical and cultural inventions and achievements. Life in the future will not be monotonous." Physiological experiments of science would transform the body, balance metabolic growth, and reduce the morbid fear of death. The resultant "superman" would "rise to the heights of an Aristotle, a Goethe, or a Marx. And above this ridge new peaks will rise."[2]

This is an extraordinary endorsement of the experimental utopianism that characterized the 1920s. Trotsky encouraged and predicted "competing pedagogical systems and experiments" and displayed the breadth of his fantasy. Like many other members of the intelligentsia—in and out of power—he was enchanted by the enterprise of predicting the future and suggesting the manifold forms it might take.

Science and technology provided a very compelling inspiration for speculative fiction. Although levels of scientific research and applied technology remained below those in the developed West during the golden age of science fiction, the volume of discussion and the temperature of hopefulness was very high. Fascination with the possibilities of science for transforming society is endemic in revolutionary backward societies in the twentieth century. Soviet Russia glorified science and worshipped machines. Ford and Taylor, Einstein and Edison were shorthand terms in the student world, and the engineer was a hero of popular culture. The cult of the machine and the image of an electrified nation saturated the arts as well as the political discourse of the age. The wedding of scientific and technological achievement to science fiction was a natural one in this milieu, in that both, in a way, were futurological.

An example of this was an attempt to elicit futurological projections through a questionnaire published in the late 1920s in the periodical *Thirty Days*. Writers and publicists were quizzed on their visions of Russia "a hundred years hence." The replies were laconic but revealing. The economist Yury Larin talked of a stateless world without classes or exploitation, an upsurge of technology, and a "happy future." Gladkov the novelist saw a "joyful globe of progress" with no war, no churchbells, no crime, and no kitchens. The satirist Efim Zozulya's "Moscow of the Future" possessed a House of Herzen in which 50,000 writers lived and worked in a population composed exclusively of people in their early twenties (children having been consigned to healthier zones). The popular novelist Pantaleimon Romanov's "Citizen of the Future (the year 2027)" was (in contrast to the Soviet citizens of his own day) courteous, service-minded, responsible, full of initiative and attentiveness to consumers. Most of the contributors, though differing on their vision of the urban-rural mix of tomorrow's world, saw world peace and world unity as absolutely inseparable.[3]

A massive volume published in 1929 provided a more technological thrust: projections about the future world by an assortment of distinguished scientists on topics ranging from physiology and astronomy to land use, agriculture, anthropology, and psychology. The contributions dealing with science, technology, and society predicted commune-cities, personal flight, skyscrapers of huge dimensions linked by bridges and air stations, and healthier and longer lives. Aron Zalkind, a very influential physchoneurologist of the time, combined some of them into a vague picture of a coming world commune inhabited by people with new organs, new minds, and new sensibilities—a world where the major problem of humanity would not be relations among people but rather relations between humanity and nature—a direct borrowing from Bogdanov, who incidentally died in that year.[4]

Two aspects of science and technology deserve a special comment: immortality and space travel. Both illustrate vividly the relationship between the futuristic speculation and pathos of the period and the reality from which it arose: immortality yearned for in a land still groaning from a decade of holocaust; space flight, in a land where wooden plow and urban horse-cart were everyday sights. The former was inspired by the curious and influential Russian recluse, Nikolai Fëdorov (1829–1903), a librarian and speculative theologian who never published a book. He combined certain features of Russian Orthodoxy and tsarist ideology with an extravagant belief in cosmic possibilities. The world of his vision, converted to Orthodoxy under the tsar in Moscow, spoke a single language (recovered from pre-Babel times by a congress of scientific linguists) and lived in rural communes, working in factories in winter and fields in summer. The social bond was faith and fraternity, not materialism or equality, since Fëdorov opposed both socialism and capitalism. Each commune was situated around a cemetery with a model of the Moscow Kremlin at the center. The rule of communal life was Psychocracy: mind control, open diaries, public confession and penance, and the regulation of sexuality. Global security was provided by a Godloving Army and a Pacification Fleet.[5]

Fëdorov's vague scientific-mystical utopia was designed for a specific set of tasks which he called "the common mission" of mankind: victory over death, resurrection of all the dead, and the settlement of outer space. The syncretic quality of Fëdorov's dream generated a school of disciples in the Soviet period, loosely know as the Biocosmists, whose slogan was "Immortalism and Interplanetism." Beyond their study and discussion circles, figures as diverse as Konstantin Tsiolkovsky (the rocket scientist), Leonid Krasin (who designed Lenin's mausoleum), and V. K. Vernadsky, the earth scientist, were said to have been in Fëdorov's orbit at one time or another. The most consistent of the Fëdorovites was Valerian Muraviëv, a man with an extraordinarily checkered career even for those times, a fanatical Bolshevik, and a devout Fëdorov adept. He combined the ideas of his master with those of Frederick Taylor—he was in fact editor of Gastev's journal at the Central Institute of Labor for a time, though it is not clear how his influence might have seeped into the Soviet Taylorist movement. The cult of Fëdorov in the Russian Revolution, a seemingly impossible idea, illustrates precisely a vagrant mentality that some have chosen to call the "crankish" side of the Revolution but which was really a millenarianism and a utopianism fed by serious erudition of a special sort and by the unbounded Promethean belief in man's ability to transform nature and reverse its laws.[6]

A far more popular craze of the 1920s that fed into science fiction was aviation. Russian fascination with aeronautics has been immense in our time—a kind of fear of not flying, of remaining earthbound and thus immobile. Flying—as in the archetypical dream—is a kinetic metaphor for liberation. The literary obsession with it in Europe, America, and Russia is well-known. Figures such as Tatlin and Mayakovsky are inconceivable without the airplane image. Vasily Kamensky—like d'Annunzio—was an aviator poet. Alexander Lavinsky in 1923 designed a plan for an "airborne city." And Georgy Krutikov in 1928 envisaged a "Flying City Apartment Building" moored to dirigibles when at anchor. Taking off into a better world was semantically and psychologically linked to taking flight. The revolutionary terrorist Nikolai Kibalchich, waiting for his execution in 1881, designed a flying machine that was based on rocket principles. The father of Soviet rocket design, Konstantin Tsiolkovsky, hatched most of his ideas while living in an obscure little Russian town. N. A. Rynin, professor and popularizer of space literature in the 1920s, began his work on the cosmic age during the dark years of the Civil War. "I was hungry," he recalled, "I was cold, but one good thing about it—nobody came to see me."[7]

Russia's first airplane flight occurred in 1894, but it took another ten years for aviation to take hold in society. On the eve of World War I, a modest network of clubs and societies had emerged. During the war itself, Russia's air arm was tiny, but out of it came the legendary four-engine bomber of Igor Sikorski (later a well-known plane builder in the United States). The bomber was called Ilya Muromets after the Russian fairy-tale giant who slept forty years and then awoke in possession of colossal strength. During the Civil War, the Soviets created their own air arm and established schools and journals to promote it. The air age became a social fact in the 1920s. It was partly inspired by the fearful debate over strategic bombing. But the greater impulse was the vision of an integrated nation. An air transport network for the new Soviet state was a way of constricting time and space, promoting social communication and health, supplying a far-flung population, and educating the people of that vast republic. Gastev's Siberian utopia, "Express," had been the poetical expression of this dream, but in 1929, it still took thirty-six hours to fly from Moscow to Irkutsk. As a civil air fleet (later called Aeroflot) took shape in 1921, government and semi-public bodies launched a campaign to popularize air study and travel with clubs, sport and parachute societies, journals, and all-purpose patriotic leagues. Air, space, the stratosphere, the cosmos seemed to represent spatial freedom for crowded terrestrials, and slogans such as "Workers, take to the air!" were used in campaigns to finance new aircraft.[8]

Rocketry and space travel, the very stuff of early science fiction in the West, had a similar appeal—however distant and unrealizable it must have seemed. Long before the Revolution, Tsiolkovsky had explored its possibilities and had made discoveries which were later incorporated into practical research by the first generation of Soviet rocket scientists—N. E. Zhukovsky, F. A. Tsander, Yu. V. Kondratyuk, and N. N. Kovalëv (the developer of Sputnik). Tsiolkovsky's work first became widely known in scientific circles in 1911, and he became a public figure in the 1920s. Rynin unearthed Kibalchich's rocket scheme from the police archives after the Revolution, and he began teaching and agitating on behalf of space travel; at the end of the 1920s he wrote a nine volume collection on interplanetary flight. Societies and public bodies mushroomed, and popular journals took up the theme with great enthusiasm. In 1925, Moscow University staged a forum on the subject of "Flight to Other Worlds." Kondratyuk's *The Conquest of Interplanetary Space* (1929) was a summary of much of this ferment in learning and discussion and a scientific undergirding to the literary speculation of the first decade of revolutionary science fiction.[9]

All of these themes turned up in science fiction, and it seems clear that people who thought about the matter at all saw a future for Russia as one that enshrined the opposite of the circumstances in which they then lived. The 1920s was a period of dreadful poverty and social misery, a backward and illiterate rural morass, an urban world of crime and unemployment, of dirty dorms and crude interchange, swarming orphans, open prostitution, vulgar displays of wealth and corruption, and a suspicious, authoritarian government still locked in ideological war with surrounding civilizations. The optimism inherent in Marxism, the heady euphoria of the still fresh revolutionary years, the traditions of hope that ran through the old intelligentsia, and the realities of the dark landscape at hand all combined to infuse science fiction with what seems now to be a towering faith.

## Maps of Heaven and Hell

Utopian science fiction works of this decade chronicle and document an ascending surge in the revolutionary imagination, a fictionalized assessment of the October Revolution, an almost xenophobic view of foreign capitalist states, and a composite picture of the "coming world" of harmony and perfection. Science fiction in these years established itself as a major genre of popular art. The main categories, though sharpened and reshaped in a revolutionary milieu, drew upon the past. The "capitalist hells" added a

Marxist and Soviet edge to the anti-Western war fantasies of the 1890s. The "communist heavens," drawing freely from Bogdanov's *Red Star* but surpassing it in optimism, explored the outer reaches of technical innovation, with a strong emphasis on dynamism, the power of the machine, the limitless capacity of man to harness and exploit nature and the stratosphere, and the ultimate triumph of the shining *pravda* of social justice over the dark *krivda* of greed and power hunger.

Between 100 and 200 native works of science fiction appeared (depending on what is counted)—novels, stories, poems, plays, and movies. In the peak year, 1927, almost fifty came out, an unprecedented figure in Russian publishing history, though modest by Western standards. Although the cheap commercial popular press of pre-revolutionary Russia which might have taken up these themes with or without a revolution was now gone, the fact remains that the Revolution was the launching pad for utopian science fiction. Beyond this, about 200 foreign translations appeared—particularly the still immensely popular Jules Verne and H. G. Wells. In the context of world science fiction, Soviet fantasy in the 1920s was unique. Some scholars have called the period, c. 1890–1930 the Age of Wells—future oriented, highly technological, and deeply pessimistic. On the latter count, the Soviets stand out in their towering optimism about the shape of things to come. Science fiction in England, Germany, and the United States was strong on technology, adventure, and exoticism, but not on positive utopia. It did not possess the kind of ideological and sociological projection about the future world that dominates the Bolshevik genre. And although technology, streamlining, and modernism infected the arts of the 1920s in the West, as it did in Russia, no culture matched the Soviet avant-garde in the scope and depth of radical experimentation with a social dimension and a future orientation.

It is no exaggeration to say that almost the entire culture of the Revolution in the early years was "utopian." All the arts were suffused with technological fantasy and future speculation: Constructivist art, experimental film, "rationalist" architecture, Biomechanics, machine music, Engineerism, and many other currents. Had the artists of these schools possessed power, resources, and consensus, they would have tried to transform Soviet Russia immediately into a physical utopia of modern cities of glass and steel, inhabited by functionally dressed citizens who would be treated to Constructivist and Futurist culture. In literature, the avant-garde as a whole and important elements of the Proletarian culture movement, though differing greatly in style and tone, created works that paralleled science fiction texts. A number of major novelists of the period who worked in a more traditional canon, felt impelled to write one or two works that fit the science fiction genre—Alexei Tolstoy, Ilya Ehrenburg, Viktor Shklovsky, Valentin Kataev, the dystopian writers Zamyatin and Platonov, and a few others. Tolstoy's *Aelita* (1923), a romantic, symbolic and theosophic adventure story set on Mars, although often named the chief science fiction work of the period, was actually the end of a tradition (dating from 1905) rather than a model for the new genre.

Many lesser known writers engaged in the very popular "red detective" *(krasnyi pinkerton)* form in which fantasy, science, and future pictures were often interwoven. The authors of the utopian novels were usually not "writers" at all, but pro-Soviet publicists, agitators, popular science practitioners, engineers, or simply revolutionary adventurers who turned to the pen. The first professional science fiction writer in Soviet history, Alexander Belyaev, dealt mostly in inventions, technological suspense, and warfare rather than descriptions of future society.[10]

Every genre and all the major themes of the science fiction *ouvre* were represented in the Soviet offering: further and nearer anticipation, planetary tales, adventure, political intrigue, utopianism, dystopianism, technological projection, romance, ethical discourse, automation, "value-free" science, critique of capitalism, and galactic wars. Recent interdisciplinary scholarship on science fiction argues that since man is constantly enticed by the unknown, he must possess a "mindscape," an imagined "geography of the unknown" space and time. As vision, it stems from fantasy; as hypothesis, it is rooted in science and empirical observation. Literary, scientific, and political speculation about the future in the Soviet Russia of the 1920s tried to create a mindscape of the future, grounding it in "scientific" Marxism, linking it to revolutionary society, and poeticizing it in fantasy.[11]

How did Soviet revolutionary science fiction differ from that of the West? First of all, the war scare novel that had flourished in prewar Europe and then declined remained still very strong in Soviet Russia. This was both because of Russia's relative weakness and because the horrors of the Great War in Europe diminished the impact of "awful warnings." Secondly, the output of science fiction in the West was much greater, especially after the American Hugo Gernsback launched the mass magazine of "scientifiction," *Amazing Stories,* in 1926. The utopian dream, so strong in the Soviet corpus, had only one major spokesman in the West—H. G. Wells—whose socialist utopias with a technical elite appeared from about 1905 to the late 1920s and were flanked by periods of pessimism. The West, like Russia had its mainstream science fiction (that written by conventional writers)—Karel Čapek, G. K. Chesterton, A. Conan Doyle, E. M. Forster, Rudyard Kipling, Kurd Lasswitz, Jack London, Saki, Thea Von Harbou, and others. But in the mid-1920s, "genre science fiction" (the kind written by specialists) broke away from mainstream themes and degenerated into space opera. In the USSR, the clear break came for ideological-political reasons, in 1931. Audiences in the United States, now emerging as the world leader in science fiction production, were judged to be teenaged boys, and therefore the product stressed simplicity and adventure with strong taboos on sex and religion. The range of Soviet readers was probably broader (though smaller in numbers); Soviet works shared the sexual taboo (though without sexist leanings), were antireligious, and supremely political.

Who read science fiction utopia in the 1920s? This is difficult to measure. The printings were not huge, though some of the novels appeared as supplements to mass circulation journals. By the standard of the market, none could compare in popularity with the adventure-detective serials of the last years of the monarchy. Contemporaries and later commentators speak of the "popularity" of science fiction of the period, but without documentation. But one can speak confidently of the intended audience. The repetition of certain themes indicates that writers in the 1920s had discovered a popular formula; they were not constrained to produce potted propaganda. The simplicity of language and certain other key features show—to the extent that one can imagine the reader from the text itself—that these books were directed towards a big part of "revolutionary society," that is, workers, party members, some of the urban intelligentsia, rural youth, students—all mostly male—the same audience incidentally that consumes science fiction today in the U.S.S.R. Conversely, they were not written for N.E.P. men, capitalists, political dissidents, members of the former upper class, or the bulk of the peasantry. Peasants had no time for fantasy of this sort and could barely comprehend it—one peasant reader taking Wells's *War of the Worlds* for an actual historical event, as did American radio listeners a decade later under different circumstances. Until the late 1920s and early 1930s, no one seemed to object to the genre, although the Kom-

somol did come out from time to time against the "red detective" which pitted proletarian heroes against capitalist warmongers and spies.[12]

"In Russia," writes Darko Suvin of the early revolutionary years, "this was one of
those epochs when new Heavens touch the old Earth, when the future actively over-
powers the present."[13] As in a mirage, space-time was compressed as dreamers reached
out to touch the future, and the rainbow hues of that future inspired the warmth of
human brotherhood in the experiments of the time. Utopian science fiction of the 1920s
as a genre summarized the experiments of the Revolution—or from long before
it—and synthesized them into larger pictures of the future. Like slogans, posters, and
agitational literature, these stories were signposts and guidebooks for the current
march.

In analyzing the social and political significance of fiction, the method of topical or
thematic analysis of a large number of works has much to commend it. Jeffrey Brooks
has brilliantly demonstrated how much richness of insight can be conveyed in this way.[14]
But for this study, the number of works would hardly justify such rigorous quantifica-
tion. Out of two dozen or so science fiction works that contain the utopian portrayal of
the future world, I have chosen about a dozen on the basis of their representativeness,
their relative obscurity in literary history, their stylistic and lexical accessibility, and
their themes: capitalist hells, communist heavens, alternative "antimodern" utopias,
and dystopia. They make certain assumptions about Russian realities, offer a critique of
Soviet society, and indicate a path into the future via a fictional historic scenario, and a
projection of wishes about the future of technology, nature, city-country relations, social
justice, culture, and globality.

One of the earliest of these was *The Land of Gonguri* (1922) by Vivian Itin (1893–
1945). Itin was one of those revolutionary adventurers of the period who wandered and
fought the length and breadth of the huge republic in the Civil War. In Siberia, Itin
passed death sentences in Bolshevik tribunals, closed churches and took away their
bells, preserved ancient monuments, and wrote poems to exalt Siberian aviation. He
was one of the few utopian writers who was a party member. The initial core of his
story came to him in 1917, a fantasy dream of other worlds which he folded into a
revolutionary plot and published in the obscure town of Kansk on the Enisei River. One
of the ironies of *Gonguri* was that it cost 20,000 rubles in the inflated currency of the
moment and that the peasants who bought it used it for cigarette paper. The other was
that its author, the first post-revolutionary reconnoiterer of the socialist heaven, was
purged under Stalin.

"Gonguri" is a land—seen in the dream of a Red partisan—of oversized fruit,
machines that work better than people, cities inside buildings holding tens of thousands
of people and erected at astonishing speed. Work is conducted as a festival and the
fruits of this labor are public squares of mirrored glass, continuous gardens, and palaces
of dreams where writers create their works. Murder, war, intrigue, hungry children,
terror, and the state have disappeared. The pathos of the story is provided when the
sixteen-year old hero-dreamer is awakened at dawn by White soldiers who take him out
to be shot. The brightly colored vision of tomorrow is thus limned by the dreadful
cruelties of class war in the bloody Siberian campaigns.[15]

In Yakov Okunev's *The Coming World* (1923) we have a fleshed out picture of a
world, 200 years in the future, containing an interconnected global environment, an
eco-technical complex, and a new culture of human relations. In this, as in some specific matters, Okunev was the student of Bogdanov as well as of the Western science

fiction masters. The author was a publicist and active figure in the Godless movement of the 1920s, known for his debates with Orthodox prelates wherein he insisted on the proletarian character of the first Christians. The premise of the novel—"sleepers wake"— is a tour by a Russian man and woman from the world of 1923 of the world of 2123. It is an almost completely urbanized Earth right out of Gastev, an "all-world city" of endless streets, squares, tunnels and bridges which permit one literally to walk on city streets around the world from Australia to Central Russia. The Paris-London sector is a mega-city running right across the filled in channel. All continents and islands are joined. The houses made of steel-strength cardboard are joined at the rooftops by bridges and terraces. Public buildings are topped—like the churches of ancient Russia—by gold-in-azure domes and spires. There are no states, nations, or frontiers.[16]

I call the vestigial administrative apparatus of this new land an eco-technical complex because of the almost total absence of government or political life. But something other than the Russian idyll or Kropotkin's anarchy has emerged: it is a self-administered economy run by machines, a crude version of Bogdanov's Tectology. Organs of accounting, checking, and administration (so dear to Lenin) have replaced force and wealth as the sinews of rule. People work two or three hours a day. The machines do the rest, and machines are designed to oversee the productive machines as well. Statistics have replaced the state. The Supreme Statistical Bureau of the Federation of the World Communes is the closest thing to a human polity on the planet. It is elected and rotated every three months. Bogdanovesque computers do the real work. The author argued that this was a realistic projection of present reality and not merely a techno-fantasy.

Human society, liberated from alienating labor and power, is also freed permanently—as in almost all of the 1920s utopias—from the familiar historic problems and social cancers: war, prostitution, crime, exploitation, famine, specialization of labor, sorrow, tragedy, and shame. People are equalized to a high degree through unisex clothing, hairlessness, rotation of work according to desire, identical housing (but with individualized interiors and furniture), collective bathing, harmony, order, and gracious comradeship: a single communist family struggling to master nature. There is but one law in this world: freedom. Its meaning? "All citizens of the World City," explains the host, an elder named Stern, "live as they please—but each desires what all the rest desire." No one sleeps, lies, or keeps secrets in 2123. "You will want to work" Stern lectures to the wakers with a smile. Since there are no ungifted people, there are no school teachers; people learn from life and labor. Men and women are free to couple without marriage or family or jealous ownership. Love blooms as in any human environment, but when one partner leaves, the deserted is automatically "cured" of love. Children live on the Mountain Terraces of the Alps, Pyrenees, Appenines, Himalayas, and Pamirs in special health resort colonies and palaces. Idiots and the "hopelessly deformed" are painlessly put to death.[17]

Here was the big picture with the small details embodying all the hopes and dreams, the naïveté and the ignorance, the technical answers, the "equitable" solutions to the eternal human problems—and all the monumental avoidance of reality and of human nature that had been part of utopian science fiction of the past and was now endowed with revolutionary credentials. Okunev reversed Bogdanov's premise and situated the communist heaven on Earth, not Mars, and removed as well the entropy, the ambivalence, the nuances, and the contradictions required in any major fiction.

Where was one to go from here? A minor tale of 1924, also inspired by Bogdanov (even in its title), provided a few additional curiosities: Innokenty Zhukov's *Voyage into the Wonderland of the Pioneer Detachment 'Red Star.'* The setting is 1957, not 2123, but Zhukovsky's utopia is hardly different from Okunev's. It does contain a historical explanation of how the new world emerged: a simple class-and-revolutionary war, beginning in 1924 and ending in the victory of world communism with all people living in a "peaceful world laboring commune." And there are a few technical fetishes repeated in many science fiction tales of the period: personal flight—practically central in this children's tale; symphonic music beamed by radio sets throughout the world; and revolutionary names such as Red Kim, Krasarm (Red Army), Yul (Young Leninist), Revmir, Spartacus, Vladlen, and October. This was also the first Soviet utopia in which Esperanto was the language of the planet.[18]

The engineer V. D. Nikolsky's *In a Thousand Years* (1927) was one of the most popular renditions of the future produced in those years—and it is still widely read in the Soviet Union. The secret of its success is perhaps its startling prediction of the first atomic explosion in 1945, its shattering description of a global atomic war of utter destruction, and its detailed mosaic of the coming life under communism. No Marxist utopia has ever provided as rich and cluttered a picture of what it might be like in the next millennium. The time-travellers are a Russian engineer and a German professor—both caricatures and stereotypes—a classic coupling (à la Jules Verne and Alexei Tolstoy) of the vigorous, simple, practical man who touches the real world and the cerebral inventor-scientist-academic who peers at the abstractions. They journey in a chronomobile or timeship to the thirtieth century where they learn the history of the millennium, 1927–2927. Atomic experiments in Paris had resulted in an explosion that destroyed half of Europe. This was followed by the "last world war" started by a monopolist-capitalist Pan-American Empire but won by the Union of European Socialist States. The war was global and total: no neutrals, no protected "rear areas," no immunity for women, children, and civilians. In the succeeding fifty year period of peace, the losers had imposed a repressive regime upon their workers in the manner—as Nikolsky put it—of Jack London's "iron heel." The war had resumed for a century and a half until 2155 when a peace congress at Berlin created a World Union of Fraternal Republics—socialist all. The globe was now freed of international strife, thus ready to reconstruct the fabric of man's life. Implicit here, as in many of the tales of the 1920s, is that the ultimate collision between capitalist and socialist multinational superpowers and the defeat of the former must occur in order to usher in the new order.[19]

Nikolsky-land is bound by a single language similar to Esperanto but with a greater infusion from Asian languages. It is administered by a Central Learned Council whose election and composition are left utterly unexplained. The mechanism of rule at the local level is a system of self-regulating independent communes, each with its own council (soviet) that coordinates with its neighbors. The entire structure is overseen from Mechanopolis, the ceremonial capital. But there are no real cities as such. Huge green forests give way periodically to buildings, glassed-in communities, museums, and theaters; people link up through speedy transport rather than urban proximity. Variants of the garden and linear city (see next chapter) have triumphed over the old city, only remnants of which may be seen—as antique ruins—amid the forests and the modern settlements. Pure air and country life are available to all. The whole complex is meshed together by Cityroads—mulitstoried and many-laned arched highways whose piers double as residential buildings—punctuated periodically by town-like "hubs" in the manner of Le Corbusier's Radiant City (see Fig. 31). The urbanography of Nikolsky, like his political science, was lyrical but awesomely vague and confusing. On the other hand, it echoed perfectly the urbanizing poetry and the architectural planning of the time.

In the midst of describing the "economy," Nikolsky flashes back to the dismal Moabit section of Berlin of 1927 with a grim industrial imagery reminiscent of that used in Fritz Lang's film *Metropolis* (1925). In 2927, there are very few workers as such and no grimy underground slave pens or machine hells. Man-made satellites *(sputniks)* gather data about global food and resource supplies; using these data, computers activate electromagnetic vacuum-tube railways that suck goods at 1,000 kilometers per hour—vegetables from India and grain from South America move to Europe in 5–6 hours. Heavy industries are concentrated, centralized, and run by sophisticated machines. Most human labor is therefore engaged in pleasurable, nonalienating crafts. Like walking or exercise, work is a health-giving pleasure; no one shuns it and the productivity is high. All of life is embellished with time-saving and rational technology: talking books in mechanized libraries, automated shops and cafeterias, energy produced by sun, wind, tides, and atomic power (now peacefully harnessed), medical and scientific research that has eliminated disease and extended life to 200–300 years, and applied eugenics that allows only the best to multiply. Personal flight is used by all citizens; the Earth is fully engaged in interplanetary exploration.

What could be interesting about the inhabitants of such a world? All the predictable things are in place: "a single laboring family" of equals, of nondeferential relations (a point is made about the absence of majestic bows or elaborate gestures) where beauty and brains are never in opposition. The author tries throughout to present a population of joyful, warmhearted human beings who break into full-throated song and revel in production and its festivals. It is a non-Zamyatin image of liberated humanity that excels over the "noisy, quarrelsome, faceless mass of people" of the past. But the climactic celebratory scene of the novel—its end in fact—is a session of the Central Council in a classical marble amphitheater of colossal size, presided over by a grey-bearded patriarch who leads a hymn of victory (over nature) and happiness to the accompaniment of organ music, followed by speeches and reports (see Fig. 32). As in so much utopian science fiction, the projection of technology (though extravagant) is more believable than the dawning of equality and social justice. The virtues of the coming species are established by authorial fiat and not by plot, organic development, or convincing mechanisms of change; the human machinery of political interrelationships is replaced, literally, by a Political Machine; and the moment of greatest communal bliss is housed in a wholly traditional monumental structure, orchestrated and led by an iconic male father figure, while its symbolic and ritual actions and songs give way to the prosy dross of "speeches and reports"—an almost incredible capitulation to the revolutionary idiom of political discourse.[20]

The last science fiction utopian novel to appear in Soviet Russia until after Stalin's death was Yan (Jan) Larri's *The Land of the Happy* (1931). It is interesting precisely because it was the last of its era and because of the fate of its author. It seems to have been written as a reply to the fearful picture summoned up in Zamyatin's *We* (see below) of a future nightmare state. Larri was born in Riga, in the Latvian lands of the Russian Empire in 1900, but became known as a Russian writer. His youth was a Gorky-like odyssey of labor and wandering, of underground conspiracy, of journalism, and the study of biology at Kharkov University. In the 1920s he became well-known as a children's writer (and is still read in the U.S.S.R.). A terse entry in a Soviet source tells us that "in 1941 he was illegally repressed." Then in 1956, he was rehabilitated and released from a camp. The novel, if not responsible for his own purge, certainly floated the themes that would result in the purging of the genre in the 1930s under Stalin.[21]

The arresting thing about *The Land of the Happy* is that it is set not in a future world of global unity but in the U.S.S.R. itself—sometime in the 1980s. In Magnito-gorsk (nearing completion at the time of writing), the skyscrapers of the Statistical Directorates (again the techno-state) occupy the very center from which radiate streets connected by concentric rings and criss-crossing boulevards graced by blue and white science buildings. Beyond these open up the forests and parks interspersed with sixty-story hotels holding deep green gardens on their rooftops. Further on are the giant factories—all interlinked by pneumatic trains, autos, cycles, and a metro. Silent eleva-tors and body wings keep the citizens moving safely. Yet another zone of cultural institutions lies further on. At mealtime, all dwellers speed to the "communal meals section" in outdoor lakeside dining facilities with piped-in music, plenty of laughter, and conversation. All Soviet cities are like this one, whether in Kamchatka or in the Murmansk region, and the tundra is now covered with concrete, rail, and electrical installations.[22]

Larri's telescreens, aeropters (strap-on flying sets), electro-membranes and teleboxes (that open doors, move vehicles, tell time, and prevent accidents) are old-fashioned in science fiction by 1931. But the use of music as a pervading medium of community and joy is exceptionally prominent and shows a perspective on this art that is peculiar to the Russian Revolution: music everywhere as proof of the power and breadth of future electrification, a nonverbal binding of huge multilingual populations over vast expanses, the marriage of color and sound, and the identification of ubiquitous music with a cult of the young. The major "performance" moment in the novel is a staging of "Youth," a "symphony of color and sound." Social relations are also set in the standard utopian mode of equality—the universal use of *ty* and the studied comradeship of all the main personages. The sartorial ethos is at least original: the youngsters—bearing names like Neon, Nefelin, and Shtorm—work five hours a week at "socially necessary work" and wear standardized work clothes; in their hobbies, called "socially useful work" they dress according to individual whim. What is both novel in this work and also reflective of its time (at the very end of the generationally combative cultural revolution of 1928–31) is the constant tension and debate between the young (dynamic and explorative) and the old (stuffy and prudent). A bubbly atmosphere of laughter, good fun, and antics of the young pervades its pages from beginning to end.

The editor reveals the motivation and spirit of *Land of the Happy* and defends utopia as a society within reach. Larri's work, he argues, is not the usual depiction of the demise of the old world and the sudden appearance of a perfected planet. It is the projection of "what we have now" in a believable direction. He cites Bogdanov's *Red Star* as a prototype of *The Land*. The editor sees Larri's picture as the Soviet answer to Zamyatin's *We*. Larri's technology is set in Russia, a real Russia-in-the-making—and it is benign, controlled by humanity, and conducive to joy: a land run by a Council of One Hundred and not a Well-Doer.[23] It is inconceivable that Larri himself did not read Zamyatin, and just as *We* was in one sense a reply to *Red Star*, *Land* is a counter reply. *Land of the Happy* builds on Bogdanov (one of its main themes is a debate on space exploration) but it populates its glassy surfaces with noisy and laughing people who in many ways actually resemble Russians, who go beyond the big-eyed Martians of Bog-danov and the faceless "numbers" of Zamyatin as well, racing off to the resort hotels—

Sun City, The Happy Fisherman, Calabria, The Gay Pilot, Land of the Soviets, Evening Stars, Future, and The Bronze Horseman. It was an attempt, however flawed in literary merit, to pull time closer, to look the dream in the face, to show a more direct blueprint of the coming world.

Was Larri silenced because of this novel? There was provocation enough in *The Land of the Happy* to anger an exceptionally short-tempered and defensive dictator like Stalin. First was the overall attitude of irreverence by the young heroes towards elders and authorities and the formers' assertion of experimental innovation (in this case space travel) and freedom to explore new horizons. Ossified and conservative leaders were opposed by an organized campaign of "public opinion" in the newspapers—organs that have replaced political parties. This meant that they have in fact revived political parties (which were totally dead at the time of writing). The leaders of the authoritarian faction and the opponents of the hero are called Molybdenum and Kogan. Molybdenum (*Molybden* in Russian) is a hard mineral used to make a steel-like alloy. Like Stalin (from the word for steel), the character Molybdenum is hard, direct, "simple," and unyielding. His crony, Aron Kogan, is nervous, obviously Jewish, brash, and short-tempered— a fair picture of Lazar Kaganovich, at that moment widely seen as Stalin's principle henchman and a major force in the campaigns against utopia and experiment (see Chapter 11). They lose their struggle against the adventurous heroes. There is an added touch of disrespect: one of the more ebullient characters proposes to "launch a bloody revolution in the libraries" to save space by reducing the content of all books and printed materials into shorthand summaries and then pulping the works themselves, including Marx and Lenin. "And Stalin? He too will have to suffer" (p. 29). After 1931, there would be no room for this kind of impiety.

## Decoding Revolutionary Fantasy

How did Soviet science fiction "fit" the ideology of early Bolshevism? In asking the question I wish to distance myself from those who dissect Marxist texts in order to show—through exegesis—a Soviet plan for total global conquest.[24] Such a method is in my mind unproductive. Bolshevism meant different things to various people in the 1920s, and early Bolshevism gave way on important issues to later, Stalinist versions of Marx and Lenin. "Ideology" in any case has not been a fixed body of ideas to which leaders are ever bound.[25] Science fiction of the early years was an elaboration and a popularization of the vague and programmatic nods at the future given in the Marxist texts. The classics of Marxism offer glimpses rather than visions of a unified world. Engels, for example (echoing many previous thinkers of a non-Marxist persuasion), spoke of a "world republic." Lenin (at a moment of supreme darkness for Europe) spoke of a "United States of Europe" in 1915, and Trotsky independently of a "united world economy," both inspired as much by the holocaust of war as by Marxism.[26]

In the Revolution and Civil War, such pronouncements took on more immediate relevance. Upon the publication of the first Soviet constitution (of the R.S.F.S.R.) in the summer of 1918, when revolutionary expectations were at a fever pitch, Lenin saw a "world socialist republic" emerging out of the constitution of the first socialist state; Bukharin called the coming order an "International Republic of Soviets;" and the 1919 statement of the newly born Communist International spoke of an "International Soviet Republic" defined as "one cooperative commonwealth"—that is to say, a community of socialist nations or states. When the next constitution (of 1922) forming the U.S.S.R. was issued, Stalin glossed it as a step to a "World Soviet Socialist Republic." The rhetoric and the hope behind it continued into the 1920s and then was muted under Stalin in the 1930s as nationalism and socialism-in-one-country took a tighter hold on Soviet imagery.[27]

Science fiction writers were the mediators between official ambitions and popular conceptions, and their filled-in image of the unified globe reveals a layer of hope beneath the political veneer of language. The global unity of science fiction was not a Russianized world but a cosmopolitan one where the capital was more often London or Paris than Moscow, where Russia was part of a United States of Socialist Europe or Eurasia—or simply an undifferentiated sector of the planet. Implicit is the hoped for acceptance of the Russians into an egalitarian world order, a world where Russia is finally greeted and assisted on equal terms in a new community of peoples, a world where the language is usually Esperanto-like and not Russian. As Jerome Gilison has pointed out, utopians need a unified globe because islands of utopia can be corrupted or invaded.[28]

The imminence of war is a dark and heavy theme in the anti-capitalist dystopias of science fiction in the 1920s. Some were separate novels dwelling on the evils of Taylorist exploitation, death weapons, and mad scientists; some were the infernal antechambers to a communist heaven. For mankind to reach the heavenly gates, the hellish world had to be vanquished in a decisive war—usually launched by the capitalists, personified by a captain of industry, a dictator, a plutocrat, or a fascoid anti-socialist leader. These wars possess a standard scenario: a fiendish plot to dominate the globe and destroy the "eastern" half. Socialist heroes (not always Russian) enlist their own technology in the struggle against injustice and enslaving warfare, and they are aided by the insurgent proletariat or mutinying crews and armies—a potent combination of international war and interior revolution. More and more often in the novels, the United States came to personify the "shark of capitalism" and the menace to world peace, and its leaders emerged from the pages of Soviet science fiction as an ugly array of bloody butchers, cynical prelates, and frenzied proletariophobic industrialists.

The "capitalist hells" were partly inspired by Jack London's *Iron Heel* (1908), translated into Russian before the Revolution and made into a film in 1919, and partly by Emile Verhaeren's *Les Aubes* (1898). But the probable direct model was the masterplot for a wartopia outlined in Eugene Preobrazhensky's "glance into the future of Russia and Europe." Writing in 1921–22, he predicted that Europe, devastated by the catastrophes of late capitalism, dispirited by Spenglerian pessimism, and rotting with decadence and religious revivalism, would burst into revolution and war, producing in one camp a Soviet Germany allied with Austria, Hungary, Northern Italy, Bulgaria and Soviet Russia against a coalition of France, Poland, and Romania, supported by a reactionary United States. Out of this war would emerge victorious the Federation of the Soviet Republics of Europe; in it "Soviet Russia, which previously had outstripped Europe politically, now modestly took its place as an economically backward country behind the advanced industrial countries of the proletarian dictatorship." It is a scenario echoing with Slavophilism, Populism, early Bolshevism, and Trotsky's "permanent revolution," all of these bound in a way by the common notion that Russia's moral-political superiority and messianic power would save it from economic backwardness.[29]

One of the first science fiction versions of this was Yakov Okunev's *Tomorrow* (1924) which reverses the dismal conclusion of *Iron Heel:* the Wheat King and other millionaires who support a racist and chauvinist regime in the West provoke strikes in order to liquidate workers and set up a militarist, capitalist, clerical order, but they are overthrown when the Atlantic fleet goes red, the German workers' army attacks Paris, and the Soviet army liberates India, setting the stage for a world-wide federation of soviets with its capital in London. A. R. Palei's *Gulfstream* (1928) is both more elaborate and more subtle. His "capitalist hell" is the United States where large machines, short hours, high wages, safe working conditions, and welfare are undercut by extreme specialization of labor, mind-blunting routine, regimented family and homelife, mandatory TV, and a gradual reduction of human speech—in short a Zamyatin kind of nightmare in the land of capital. But the Union of Soviet Republics of the Old World (Russia, China, and Japan)—where children have names like Rem, Roza, Elektra— sends its techno-knights against the foe with orange-colored rays to help the workers liberate themselves. A similar theme, with U.S. workers made into robots of the Taylor System, unfolds in Alexander Belyaev's *Struggle in the Atmosphere.*[30]

In spite of their Marxist rhetorical flourishes and invocations of decency and harmony for the future, these geopolitical fantasies anticipate the Manichean nationalism and xenophobia of the Stalin years. Ironic also is how the Bolshevik ambivalence toward Taylorism in the 1920s was treated. In the utopias of communism, rationalism, symmetry, and mathematical efficiency in work were seen as liberating virtues. In the dystopias of capitalism, the darker side of mechanized labor—mindless robotization—were emphasized.[31]

The political vision—more accurately the anti-political vision—of the Soviet utopia in the 1920s drew its central premise from Marx's theory of class and state, namely that once private property and classes disappeared, so would the state, a coercive instrument of the dominant economic class. Under communism, government by persons would give way to the administration of things. This potent image had inspired Bogdanov, Lenin, and Bukharin, who envisioned a gigantic centralized economy, state or no state—not only a single polity but also a single, enormous workshop.[32] If governance consisted solely in economic problem-solving of the most mechanical sort, this implied an issue-less world, a world without questions, or a world where questions had only one answer. This arose partly from Marxian class analysis but it was partly indigenous also.

In the science fiction of the time, the aversion for authority and friction is palpable. In Belyaev's utopia, for example, "all worked in close harmony, like so many musicians in a conductorless orchestra."[33] When there is a government, the apolitical population is happy to turn over the coordination of the economy to specialists, technocrats, Councils of a Hundred and even bearded patriarchs or elders. The rulers in these novels are faceless and interchangeable—the real political foundation is the consensual attitude of the people. Everybody wants to work; everybody wants what everyone else does. This is the vaunted collectivism or "collective will" of the masses of which the Bolsheviks talked so often. In fact, it was the revolutionary version of *sobornost.*

Russian *sobornost* (celebrated widely by Orthodox theologians and Slavophiles before the Revolution) and Soviet collectivism—for all their vagueness and obvious differences in origin—possessed a common element: concern for and control of the group by the group. Concern in the Soviet context was expressed in many ways: welfare, communalism, sharing, cooperation—all the features connected with harmony and brotherhood. In Soviet science fiction this was extended to everyone on the globe precisely as a universal moral perspective. But the impulse to control had the same force: a strong desire to check the egoistic and individualistic impulses of others—meaning all.

In this view—translated into political language—both democracy and capitalism meant collision, conflict, competition, and thus anarchy and chaos. It need not be repeated that the Russian Revolution destroyed not only the old autocracy but also the Liberals and the Anarchists. In many ways, the elemental drive for a consensus that would shorten or eliminate divisive debate, avoid conflict, provide justice, and exert control with a minimum of machinery resembles more the ancient Russian *veche* or the village *mir* than it does Western Marxist political views. Thus when we do glimpse on occasion the vestigial organs or persons who deal with "politics" in Soviet science fiction, they resemble peasant elders, church fathers, ecclesiastical councils, or tsars presiding over ultra-modern machinery of production, distribution, accounting and control.

Perhaps science fiction as a genre should really be called "technical fiction" because in it science often only means technical innovation in a finished form. The level of scientific literacy is not very high in the Soviet works. Pure theory and explanatory processes are rarely offered. With a few exceptions (usually not in the utopias), the technology is ready-made and reasonably convincing as futuristic projection. Several areas of technical development stand out: transportation, electricity, communications, and weaponry. The first—a transport system and range of vehicles sufficient to bind a planet together—was as prominent in the Soviet science fiction as it was in American, in that it broke down distances in these two huge countries, eliminated the backward *tachanka* image of Russia by putting the population into speeding and flying conveyances of every sort. Communications networks performed the same function at a more intimate level: dense cultural bonding via telescreen, TV, radio, and phone. Electricity, as in Lenin's vision, was the source of great power. A single, invisible, clean, and "modern" energy source, it was also the emblem of triumph over the dark forces of ignorance, superstition, religion, and disease. The use of architectural glass and the brightly colored worldscape are the almost inescapable fantasy features reminding us that Light means Right.

The weapons deployed in the science fiction war were more frightening and devastating than those of the previous epoch. Not only had an entire generation of physics intervened, but also the Great War had ordered, reshaped, and used destructive weapons and thus partly reorientated scientific research and practical production. Russia in the 1920s, with its weak economic base, its fresh memory of the intervention, its scars from the great bloodletting of 1914–21, felt defenseless and vulnerable in a world of advancing nations and sinuous hardware. One almost feels the terror of things to come—of the 1941 skies blackened with German aircraft, of the huge herds of machine-powered vehicles and tanks rolling across the flat landscape, of millions of civilians perishing in a war without well defined rear areas. These phobias reflected the discussions of strategic bombing, the militarization of society, and the need for universal mobilization of the Soviet citizenry. They helped to fuel the "air-topias" and "scaretopias" of Soviet science fiction. The culmination of these themes in the literature was Alexander Belyaev's *Struggle in the Atmosphere* (or *War in the Air*) of 1928, an epic of—for that time—frightening prospects in a total war between the United States and Soviet Russia. So famous did this novel become that the U.S. Air Force discovered it and had it translated into English in 1965.[34]

What of speculation about the nature and quality of human life and personal relations—power, culture, leisure, and love? A major feature of fictitious societies is the pervading egalitarianism. In all the utopias, work (what remains of it) is rationed equally or according to ability, hand and brain labor alternate for all, the city-country contradiction has dissolved, women are equal to men, children possess more independence than they did in the old worlds, and dress codes make everyone look alike. Deference has given way to egalitarian systems of communication and gestural behavior.[35] The remnant of administrative decision-making not handled by self-governing "systems" is rotated by election and its holders made pallid and undistinguished. This was a perfect rendition of revolutionary iconoclasm—the abolition of authority, authority figures, and symbols. Nowhere in the literature, however, is there a description of how human beings got themselves into a mode of egalitarian life.

The moral question has in a sense been "solved" by the prevailing culture of harmony and equality. Soviet utopias are lands of peace, affluence, sharing, cooperation, integration, altruism, non-alienation, and community—exactly the formula that can be pieced together from the various Marxist speculations about life in the future.[36] As Okunev remarked, there is only one law: freedom, the freedom to do as all others do. Labor, the prime necessity of life, is desired by everyone. Struggle is no longer interspecific but against the forces of nature. Thus a New Morality is possible only under communism. But none of the scenarios that detail the military and geopolitical stages of the path to future perfection talk at all about the process of human transformation. Yet, although the science fiction utopias offer results rather than processes, and therefore suffer as guides to building communism in daily life, the values they celebrate—especially the unpatronizing treatment of women characters, the hostility to deference, and the stress on altruism and cooperation—were probably given more widespread publicity in the society of the 1920s than if they had merely remained on the pages of Komsomol and party handbooks or on posters.

Machine worship, on the other hand, comes out in an unexpected way. There are traces of Taylor-like movements in the lives of utopian citizens, but not on the industrial front where Taylorism began. Gastev's ultimate dream was of a new humanity, transformed by the clock and the machine, through a "revolution in time," reorganized in its diet, housing, clothing, transport, leisure, and work into a community of kinetic-minded units, running around on schedule, organizing themselves, their work, and each other and producing in abundance. Kerzhentsev added to this picture what workers should do with themselves and the goods they produce after work. The utopias of Soviet science fiction were more serene than the frenetic visions of the Taylorists and Timeists, their stress being more on humanoid machines than on human robots. The treatment of festival and ritual in Soviet science fiction is also interesting. There is hardly a utopian work from this period that does not describe scenes of ritual celebration: to accompany labor, to glorify construction, to grace the leisure hours, to bring large numbers of people together. It becomes a surrogate for ordinary community life which is hardly ever described. One can learn almost nothing about family relations, friendship patterns or communal life as it was being planned by architects and city planners at exactly the same moment or lived out in Soviet communes. The celebrations are both solemn and joyous—but again only at the command of the author's pen. However much the authors may paint smiles of bliss upon the faces of their participants—they resemble more the herd-like marches and cheers of Zamyatin's *We* (and their real-life equivalents of the 1930s) than they do the early spontaneities of revolutionary festival.

The content of the ritual is harmony, unity, solidarity—freely and collectively expressed in massed formation and communal song. Reverence and celebration on the public squares or in the coliseums of fantasy is a fictive shorthand for writers who are trying to persuade readers that their recipes for social perfection actually work.

The arts, which are supposed to embellish life and fill the leisure time of workers in a communist society, are surprisingly neglected, with one striking exception: music. But it is a music transposed from art form into therapeutic instrument. Utopian writers favored proletarian mass song or machine-music. A whole array of electronic music inventions appeared in Soviet Russia in the 1920s designed to broaden the range of sonority and to broadcast on radio the wonders of urban noise, electricity, and revolutionary music.

The sonic compulsion resounds in the science fiction novels of the 1920s. In Efim Zozulya's *Grammophone of the Ages* (set in 1954), "the sunrise is greeted by musical factory whistles and orchestras." Every building contains musical equipment that drones mighty music. It "greets the sunrise, wakes up the workers, accompanies them to their work, to dinner, and home again." One can hardly finish reading a science fiction work of the period without hearing a buzzing in one's ear—music dazzles at festivals, ennobles and enriches, entertains at lunch, enhances labor, soothes one's sleep, and invests one's dreams. In the vision of the Komfut (Communist-Futurist) movement, a tiny sect of the avant-garde, "in the future communist society all should eat, work, sleep, and listen to music at the same time." The musical utopia comes close to being a nightmare for those who cherish silence.[37]

The peculiar quality of Soviet science fiction lies in the fact that it was the first such body of writing to emerge directly out of a revolutionary experiment raging around it and so intimately tied to it. Science fiction utopia in the 1920s gave self-conscious articulation to revolutionary dreams. A scholarly conference on futuristics—of the kind so abundant today—including authors and readers of this literature, party and economic leaders and planners, and ordinary revolutionary citizens might have done much to clarify the relationship between dreams and reality, fantasy and possibility. Out of it might even have emerged an institutionalization of "futurology"—as it has in the U.S.S.R. in recent years—the study of what is called *globalistika,* organized speculation on the prospects of global life in the near and not so near future.[38]

## Back to the Future: Nostalgic Utopia

In the years 1920–22 four extraordinary Russian science fiction works appeared that challenged the world vision of Bolshevism: Zamyatin's dystopia, *We* (1920), and three counter-utopias exalting the peasant world. These were not answers to Soviet science fiction, since they largely preceded it, but answers to Bolshevism and its visions. The peasant utopias—two of socialist persuasion and one monarchist—launched their fantasies from the Civil War period. Though strikingly different from each other in emphasis and vision—anarchist, populist, and monarchist—they represent a strand of Russian thought and feeling that paralleled a genre of early Soviet literature known as *muzhik* socialism—a lyrical assertion of the beauties of a disappearing world.

Apollon Karelin (1863–1926), an Anarchist-Communist disciple of Kropotkin, was an enthusiastic foe of parliamentary democracy and all other measures short of stateless anarchy. During the Civil War, he collaborated with the Bolshevik regime in the hopes that it would evolve into his ideal. Karelin was the epitome of the dreamer, weakly bobbing in a revolutionary maelstrom. In projecting his last major utopian sketch, *Russia in 1930* (1921), only a decade into the future, the author set himself a relatively modest imaginative task.[39]

His hero, S. P. Voronov (a symbolically anarchist name),[40] possessed the power once a year, on the Feast of Ivan Kupala, to dream the future. What he sees is that, gradually, after the "great peoples' uprising" of 1917, the Bolshevik order has given way to anarchism in free elections. By 1930, Russia is stateless. Two English Fabian socialists pay a visit in order to compare it with the poverty stricken land they had known in 1900. The Russia of 1930 is a world in flux. All urbanites live in city communes; practically all peasants, in village communes. The city "teaches" the countryside by achievement and example what communism is all about. The village, already highly communalized, is really a foyer, a social preparatory school for the higher system of agro-towns.

Karelin does not explain how the stateless communal federation would defend itself against the outside, which is never described. The visitors inspect a rural commune that is fifteen miles by horse from the train station—there are no cars in this region. In the commune there is no money, but free housing for visitors, good roads, a paved central street, clean cabins, nice furniture, and metal bedsteads and roofs. Every house has a clock. Beyond this, technology seems nonexistent except in the machines that help process the crops and fields. The author presents a culture of flowing words at festival time—speeches, readings, debates—and of icons of revolutionary heroes. Mutual trust is that of "a very close-knit family." The library has replaced the tavern; shaming and ostracism have replaced physical punishment or incarceration. Crime is really no problem: "Who would oppose the common good?" asks the host. "The *mir* is Man writ large." Karelin's rural ideal is hardly different from the utopian *sobornost* of the urban fantasists. Communal dining has become the norm and wages in kind are equal for all.[41]

Nothing is told of urban life: the town is a center of production, a coordinator of distribution, and a storehouse of goods. Quite incidentally it is described as a locus of higher schools and railroad stations. It was all very much Kropotkin's world of "fields, factories, and workshops," freely contracting into mutual arrangements without the coercive power of a state. It was also the last full statement of nineteenth century Russia's anarchist and Populist dreams.

Chayanov's Russia of 1984 is considerably more bizarre. An economist whose theories of peasant economy have captured world attention in recent years, a specialist in cooperative movements, a preserver of monuments, and a genuinely versatile and learned man of the old regime, Alexander Chayanov (1888–193?) held various posts in Soviet economic life before being arrested in 1931 and then disappearing in Stalin's camp system.[42] His *Journey* was published in Russia in 1920 under the pseudonym Ivan Kremnev. The traveler-to-the-future, laborer number 37413, Alexei Kremnev, leaves his office one night in 1921, disgusted at the mechanical extremism of the socialist regime in which he lives, muses over the works of More, Fourier, Morris, and Bellamy, and falls into a dreamy sleep, awakening in the Russia of 1984. He learns that after a global war of the mid-1920s, the world was divided among the rival systems, each of whom received a share of the earth's good land and climate—exactly as in the strip system of the peasant *mir*. In Russia, the Bolsheviks were overthrown by the Socialist Revolutionaries and a peasant regime came into being by 1932, after which factories were dismantled and whole populations relocated away from the capitals along distant rail junctions and smaller towns—exactly as happened in real life during World War II. This was completed by 1944.[43]

The land Kremnev discovers forty years later is remarkable for its anti-urban character, its peasant nature, and its apolitical politics. All towns of 20,000 or over are eliminated and Moscow's hundreds of buildings are demolished by dynamite. Towns are now market places, festival centers, and clusters of transient hotels—places to shop, gather, celebrate—but not to live in. The culture centers are the villages and the smaller townlets. Moscow has been almost wholly reforested. Russia is a peasant republic— somewhat reminiscent of the little peasant kingdom of Bulgaria under Alexander Stamboliisky (1918–23) that flourished at the very moment this book was written.[44] Unalienated from his product by either capitalism or collective farms, the Russian peasant has become king at last. Gone is the "enlightened absolutism" of the proletariat and the centralized state. This peasant regime is based on the cooperative movement with— astoundingly—one tiny monarchist enclave at Uglich (the appanage used by heirs to the Moscow throne in the sixteenth century)! Eclecticism and tolerance are emblematized by a national monument containing the statues of Lenin, Kerensky, and Milyukov.

The culture of Chayanov's Russia was drawn largely from the past—village life, peasant izba, traditional songs, games, and festivals, the bells of Moscow's churches (to ring out Scriabin's *Prometheus* as the national anthem!), musketeers, Moscovite costumes and customs—antiquity frozen into a tableau of bygone times as static as those of the twenty-first or thirtieth century. Yet amid the rustic toil of the muzhik and the aroma of cabbage soup intrudes the inevitable bow to modernity—weather control by electronics, a wind machine that sweeps invading armies away, and a system of national service resembling Bellamy's scheme and Stamboliisky's civilian army of universal service. That well-known combination of rural nostalgia and reverence for military power that often accompanied fascism between the wars is faintly present, but hardly any of its other usual components.

Chayanov shared the anti-capitalism, anti-Bolshevism, and antiurbanism of the Socialist Revolutionaries but he was clearly more conservative in his exaltation of cooperatives and individual peasant plots, his allowance for inequality, and his cultural nostalgia. "The improvement of morals," he wrote, "moves with the speed of geological processes." His book generated little resonance. It was published by the State Publishing House, an absolute impossibility ten years later. The dissenting preface by V. V. Vorovsky—a well-known Marxist critic and diplomat—poked fun at the futility and utter unreality of an arcadia of individual peasants run by "cooperative-type" intellectuals. This gentle chiding was tolerance itself compared to the suppression and arrest that awaited Chayanov and people like him in the early 1930s. The *Journey* has not yet been republished in the Soviet Union although Chayanov has recently been rehabilitated. His novel was once characterized by one of the Soviet Union's most influential contemporary historians as "the counter-revolutionary program of the kulaks."[45]

With Peter Krasnov's *Beyond the Thistle* (1922), we swing sharply to the right. Although in no sense a product of Soviet utopianism, it deserves treatment precisely because it presented an "alternative future." Krasnov, a White cossack general who fought in the Civil War against the Bolsheviks, emigrated to Germany, where he wrote his neo-Romanov fantasy in late 1921—when the idea of restoring the monarchy was still in the air. His Russia of the 1960s displays on its banner restored autocracy, Great Russian chauvinism, anti-Semitism ("Jews do not rule us any more"), Eurasianism, anti-communism, anti-democracy, and anti-decadence. The story tells of the misrule of the Bolsheviks and their dethronement. In the meantime, Russia has disappeared from the sight of Europe, lost "beyond the thistle" wall that now grows around it. Into the void marches Michael II Vsevolodovich, the last Romanov, who has been hiding in

Tibet. The fifteen year-old heir makes the long march to the capital dressed as a "white tsar" with an entourage of 3,000 cossacks on white stallions to reclaim his throne.[46]

*Beyond the Thistle* speaks to us down through the years as a dream of the losers and as hopeful consolation for the monarchist emigration. Krasnov's Russian Empire, including Poland and Finland, is ironically called a "one-party state"—the party of the Brothers and Sisters in Christ. The tsar rules as autocrat with the assistance of *voevodas* and a hierarchy arranged in tens down to elders and male family heads. Punishment and censorship are nonexistent (as is political news in the papers); the people have rejected socialism on their own. The church is supreme in the realm of the mind and spirit, and man is supreme in the home—whether peasant hut, urban apartment, or mansion (distinct classes of bygone days are revived). The Domostroi—a sixteenth century document of extreme domestic despotism—has been revived to guide family life and keep women in their place. The chief goal of schooling is to teach love of faith, fatherland, and tsar. Russia has retrieved its simple peasant face in a harmonious monarchy only dreamed of by the Slavophiles a hundred years earlier.

The contrast between these rustic idyllic visions and the urbanism of mainstream Soviet science fiction hardly needs comment. The communal anarchist peasant of Karelin, the secular but traditional farmer of Chayanov, and the Orthodox monarchist *muzhik* of Krasnov emerge from the pages of this fiction as living icons symbolizing different layers of Russian history. Yet they all coexisted in real life during the 1920s—down to the devastating moment of collectivization when the dreams, the dreamers, and the civilization out of which the dreams were woven were utterly annihilated. In couching their model societies no more than 50 years into the future, these writers seemed to be asking for a respite; begging for their own right to revolutionary experiment (even if seen as counterrevolutionary by the Bolsheviks); perceiving the great upheaval of 1917 as a passage into an alternate world where city is not king, globe is not united, United remains Russia, and peasant may walk his horse and cart across the land in resplendent indifference to the buzzing, destructive, and subversive world that surrounds him.

Zamyatin's antiurban dystopia, *We,* has a different emphasis from the peasant utopias. Before composing it, he wrote that "life in big cities is like that in factories: it de-individualizes, makes people somehow all the same, machine-like." Armed with this central idea, Zamyatin in 1920 composed the most chilling of all dystopias and to some, the greatest science fiction work ever written (Ursula Le Guin). It is often forgotten that Zamyatin despised capitalism: his earlier anti-utopian novel about Britain is a satire on the minute regulations of life. In *We,* the city has blossomed monstrously into the United State, a giant urban mass of blue cubic buildings, straight lines and exclusively geometric forms—a visual parody of all utopian symmetry. The year is 2920, a thousand years in the future, after dreadful wars and revolutions. The countryside no longer exists as agrarian landscape; it has been reclaimed by a savage forest and lies "beyond the green wall." Nature, body hair, foliage, sexual passion, and fantasy are the unsubdued remnants of evil. Life inside the wall is not the teeming urban life of Yan Larri but one of robots, moving in work and at leisure to the rhythms of the Taylor system, marching together like an Assyrian bas relief, and chewing their food in unison at standardized mealtimes. The jabs at Gastev and the emerging N.O.T. movement were obvious to any reader living in Soviet Russia in 1920.[47]

Technology in *We* is ever present but never discussed. Except for the Taylorist motions aboard the Integral, a rocket ship that will allow the colonization of space, the labor process is not indicated; except for scenes of sexual contact, neither is life. The reason is clear: life, work, and love have been denuded of color, passion, and conflict among ordinary Numbers (citizens) of the United State. The "musical factory" provides the tunes that lead them to work and play; their rituals are purely passive and deferential. Freedom means unity of thought: the only self is embedded in the collective "we." Human relations in the United State seem like an answer to the prayers of those nihilist reductionists of the Russian Revolution who wanted to break all forms of human expression and "equalize" all humans into faceless and expressionless units. This Zamyatin deftly and unforgettably accomplishes by using numbers for his citizens, dressing them in identical uniforms, and having them function according to an elaborate mathematical table based on the Taylor system—in short turning them into machines without passion or fantasy. When these traits are exhibited illegally among some of the Numbers, the drama begins—and it ends with fantasectomy.

Zamyatin is more explicit about the political system than any other Russian science fiction writer up to that time. *We* has a real dictator as large as life. The Well-Doer or benefactor *(blagodetel)*, assisted by Guardians *(khraniteli)*, deliver to the Numbers "mathematically flawless happiness." Those who resist are physically liquidated under the gas bell. As Zamyatin said elsewhere, "the religion of the modern city is exact science." The dictator in *We* is knowable, expressive, palpably evil and powerful, and simultaneously benevolent to those who understand the laws of uniform thinking. He has been called a copy of Lenin, a premonition of Stalin, and—by Soviet critics—a Fascist. Zamyatin meant him as an embodiment of the twin spirits of despotism in the modern world: the freedom-hating Grand Inquisitors and the unthinking designers of technologies that strip man of freedom. Zamyatin's novel took shape under a whole range of conditions: his abiding fear of loss of freedom; the popularity of works that he knew so well by H. G. Wells and Bogdanov; the forces of modernization, industrialism, and the city that he saw in England and in Russia; the power of machine fantasy that was seizing revolutionary poets and ideologues during the Civil War; and the recent wars that, he noted, turned human beings into digits. Zamyatin's masterpiece towers high above all other science fiction of that age in Russia—and it grew out of the density of revolutionary discourse and action.[48]

Zamyatin's book has never been published in the U.S.S.R. although plans are now being made to do so. It is rarely mentioned in Soviet discussions of science fiction. When it is discussed, its picture of the future is compared to Nazi Germany—not to any period in Soviet history. But Zamyatin was confronted head-on in the 1920s. The critic A. K. Voronsky wrote an essay on the author in 1922. Noting that the themes of *We* had already been mooted in the anti-British *The Islanders* (1918), Voronsky viewed the anti-socialist elements of the novel as part of an older dystopian tradition. But the Bolsheviks, he argued, did not strive to subjugate people under the "heel" of the State. *We*, he said, resembled the reactionary "state socialism" of a Bismarck(!). Bolshevism stood for a synthesis of the "we" and the "I" and not "we" over "I." Machine-like life, he said, is not our goal, but machine-lightened life. There would be no dual world of nightmare city and wild forest in the future, but a humane combination of urban and rural elements.[49]

When Zamyatin's book was revived and reissued in the early 1950s in the West—coinciding with late Stalinism, the publication of Orwell's *1984* (which was indebted to it), and the emergence of the theory of totalitarianism, many took Zamyatin's nightmare to be simply an accurate rendition of Soviet reality from the very beginning. Few people then—and not many more now—were aware of those utopian experimenters and vision-aries of the 1920s whose main mission was in fact to avert a rising menace of the United State of Guardians, mathematical conformity, odious authoritarianism, and a malevolent Well-Doer.[50]

The death of utopian science fiction in the early 1930s is the perfect metaphor of the death of the utopian revolution of the 1920s. The prose was primitive and the characters forgettable. Perceptions of the West were filled with neuroses, phobias, and stereotypes. There were no loveable heroes, no genuinely funny episodes, no believable villains—and hardly a paragraph of genuinely lyrical description. And yet, Soviet science fiction lies before us like archeological rubble, traces and clues about values held or expressed in an era of drastic and willful change, verbal witness to the ideas and feelings that the Revolution suggested to fertile brains and facile wordsmiths. It is popular culture of a bygone age, taking its place in the museum of visions and fantasies and perceptions along with American comic strips, pulp magazines, and war cards of the 1920s and 1930s, a rich tapestry of crude color and cartoon figures, relaying to us both the stretch-ing power of Soviet imagination and its severe limitations. It shouted to its readers: escape through Revolution into the vast unknown towards a better world.

"To try raising the curtain of the future is an admirable task," wrote Lunacharsky in 1930 on the very eve of the moment when that curtain would be pulled down.[51] The decade of revolutionary science fiction, with no interference by the state, indicates once again that in the 1920s the intelligentsia was still free to explore new worlds and ask questions about the future—and even suggest answers. Science fiction reflected not only Bolshevism but also anarchism, neo-Populism, messianism, Godbuilding, and a dozen other currents. Fantasy was a mode of political discourse in a non-parliamentary society. And in the realm of visionary town planning and utopian architecture, some of the imagery created in the battle between urban and anti-urban futures was reflected in uncanny detail.

# 9

## Utopia in Space: City and Building

If there is truly a proletarian concept, it is the word "We."
Anatoly Lunacharsky

The Soviet government in the 1920s was the first in modern history to possess such mammoth power to design living quarters for its population; to determine the number, size, and style of buildings; to plot the density of the population on the land and within each structure; to decide where to place such structures; to plan future cities and variants of the city; to shape the balance of the population between town and countryside—in other words to proclaim the layout and location of all human services—factories, offices, schools, hospitals, and homes. Town planning in a planning state—which is what Soviet Russia became in 1928—was not simply a minor occupation; it was in fact "nation planning," macro-community design—in other words, utopia building on the ground and on the grandest possible scale. Faced with such possibilities for the expression of their talents and imaginations, what planner, architect, economist, sociologist, or geographer would not have become breathless with anticipation?

City planning and the design of future living space requires a mentality and an imagination closely resembling the concoction of science fiction and utopia. As S. Frederick Starr has written, "the architect could leap into the future even more easily than the novelist. Sitting at his drafting table, he could simply obliterate present reality with a few strokes of the pen and create a new world with a few more strokes."[1] Even in "normal" times and in developed nonrevolutionary milieux, city planning is a blueprint for living in the very near future. In the Russian Revolution, architects and town planners had visions of reshaping an entire nation, of aligning the structures and anti-structures with high-speed economic development plans, of providing "social condensers" for the nurturing of a new socialist race of people. Soviet architects, bound by material limitations and political considerations, could not match the global fantasies of the all-world cities of science fiction. They had to design for real people and for the imminent future. Yet the architectural imagination in Soviet Russia in the late 1920s and early 1930s often verged upon the fantastic, and its treatment of space, privacy, interaction, mobility, social harmony and community, work, family life, and domestic labor intersected continuously with the major themes and issues of utopian speculation of the revolutionary period.

Since socialism in all its variants, including the Marxist one, implies community—some sense of sharing life, residence, and work in a spirit of harmonious and fraternal interaction—socialist architects and town planners had to pose certain questions. What measure of social distance or popular density is required to achieve it? How far apart can people live and still be called a community? How much private space (and time within that space) does the individual require without violating a sense of community? These questions remain pressing ones in the contemporary world of development, dispersion, town and regional planning, and ordinary edificial architecture, and they shaped the vivid debates, blueprints, and presentations made by Soviet architects of the Russian Revolution.

## The Antiurban Impulse

The history of the Russian city as a social organism and as a public concept reveals that many Russians were possessed of a vague "antiurban" sense. The fear of what the Germans called the menace of "civilization" or "Kultur" lay at the heart of intellectual and moralizing anxiety over the steady growth of urbanization. Since the Bolshevik Revolution was suffused by an urban mystique—unmistakable in the force of its rhetoric and its poetics—conflict was inevitable. Indeed the birth of utopian town planning in the 1920s grew directly and self-consciously out of a strong distaste for the current city, a distaste with a long tradition and deep roots in Russian society.[2]

Marx's comment about "the idiocy of rural life" was not sufficiently potent to resolve such an issue as the future of cities. Against it, town planners of the 1920s often cited Engels's equally suggestive remark on "the disappearance of the big cities" and Lenin's comment to H. G. Wells that "the towns will get very much smaller" and that "they will be different." These feelings resembled the recurrent malaise among Western intellectuals and statesmen of the nineteenth century—Jefferson, Schiller, Carlyle, the French romantics among them—who saw the city as the home base of industry, crime, capitalism, and glut. The city became a metaphor of the discomfort with noise, "the fever of the world," ugliness, machine-like rhythms of life, clocks, railroads, hustle and bustle, mobility, and restless change—in short, a naked menace to a real or fanciful pastoral world. In the nineteenth century, the big city no longer remained a spatial concept, but an emblem for immense transformational, subversive, and destructive power.[3]

Like some early American urbophobes, Russian public figures were pulled into antiurbanism not by hatred of towns or industry as such—but by repugnance for such foreign cities as Lyons and Manchester, perceived as festering centers of vice and crime, populous headquarters of dangerous ideas, and flashpoints of social disorder. The attitude of Nicholas I to industrial growth was ambivalent. Russian officials who pondered the agglomeration of the proletariat in the West worried about its appearance in Russia. Because of this, the tsar sought to "halt the further aggregation of factory people in Moscow."[4]

Nicholas's finance minister, E. F. Kankrin, on the other hand, believed that even with urban and industrial growth (which he by no means pushed) the Russian worker would not become a proletarian of the European type because of his strong and permanent roots in the village and his habit of returning there periodically. This keen comment by Kankrin is highly suggestive of things to come: it was a vision of the city as a shell, not a living organism. He wished not to destroy Russian cities but rather to retain them as static places that workers *visited* seasonally in order to work and to keep them from becoming those dreadful sewers of anarchy that festered in the West and bred a "spirit of coalition."[5] The odd-sounding concept of a "part-time" city was central to many science fiction utopias and—in variant form—to the Disurbanist school of Soviet city planning.

Conservative anti-urbanism acquired another dimension in the years of industrialization (c. 1890–1914): rightwing anti-modernism. Economic motivations certainly drove the mechanism of the Russian Right, and its main social focus was the Jews. But its geographical target was the city. As in many societies of that time—Germany in particular—industry, city, and Jew were blended into a dreamy and myopic vision contrasted to a pure pastorale of Russia-of-the-Russians, a fairyland disrupted by the energies and schemes of urban interlopers. This was a kind of perverted Slavophilism and "Muscovite nostalgia."[6]

In the radical response to the city, we detect another kind of repugnance. The "first Russian radical," Alexander Radishchev, in the *Journey from St. Petersburg to Moscow* (1790) displayed frank hostility to urban life as unhealthy and immoral. Mid-century Russian Populism, as we have seen, emerged with a strong anti-urban sensibility. To extremists like Bakunin, modern cities deserved nothing less than violent destruction in an act of sweeping vandalism. More moderate Populists were ambivalent about cities in their futuristic programs and utopias. Most of them believed that the new society would grow out of village communes. The theorist of Populism, Nikolai Mikhailovsky, taught that only rural life allowed for full and free development of human faculties since capitalist cities required the dehumanizing division of labor. Sofia Perovskaya, a major terrorist figure in the People's Will, complained that the premature sexuality of the young (before the age of thirty) was attributable "to the artificial stimuli of urban life," and a later Populist writer, N. N. Zlatovratsky, called the city "the incarnation of sinister forces." A curious anticipation of things to come was the little known utopian tract, *Communist States of the Future* (1879) by the leftist but non-revolutionary lawyer, V. I. Taneev (1840–1921), brother of the composer Sergei. In his sketch of a future Europe, Taneev depicts self-governing agrarian communes organized into states and federations, each commune composed of 2,000 adults and covering one square mile. In this semi-socialist and semi-technocratic world, cities—capitals, administrative centers, and ports—contained no permanent residents, the population continuously rotating in and out. As in many Soviet science fiction works of the 1920s, children were kept out of the cities altogether.[7]

In the generation before the collapse of the monarchy, a whole chorus of liberal, socialist, neo-populist, and Tolstoyan publicists joined the Right in a moral assault on cities as bastions of decadence, prostitution, faceless anomie, and raging vice. The Russian flood of "sin city" literature was of course a local version of the antiurban moral crusading that appeared in many places at the turn of the century, but its edge was very sharp. The outcry over "decadence" (anything from free love to sex clubs and perversion through violence and child seduction) was a major thread in the intelligentsia's discourse in the years after the 1905 Revolution. Its connection with general culture and political climate has never been fully explored. Elements of city hatred sometimes combined with a latent and tortured sexual envy as in the anguished book by P. Dneprov, *The Cruel City* (1907), portraying Petersburg as a mass of icy stone and at the same time an inferno of lust. A revealing piece of evidence from the world of popular culture is the fact that urban song as a genre was widely known as *zhestokii romans* (cruel song). A wide variety of opinions, divergent and even mutually contradictory, seemed to reflect a readiness to change drastically, at the very least, the character of Russian cities.[8]

The wars and revolutions of 1914–21 uncovered new levels of antiurbanism: peasant hostility to towns and urban flight from the cities in search of security and survival.

Odious depictions of the city as such found expression in two literary schools that arose early in the Revolution: the muzhik socialists and the Scythian poets. The former were a half-dozen or so peasant-born poets who spoke with an urbanized voice in the Prolet-cult movement and other forums, decried (and confounded) the city, the West, and government and reached out for a romanticized idyll of the countryside. Among them, though not quite of them, Sergei Esenin called the city "a labyrynth where men lose their souls," a familiar graphic demonology of city space itself. The Scythians and others (Blok, Bely, Pilnyak, and Ivanov-Razumnik) projected a negative image of the city—a chillingly rational world of atomization, lack of community, and isolation (all in spite of the supposed density of population).[9]

Literary currents and the peasant utopias provided a vivid link between the deep layers of city fear and the architects' practical concerns about what to do with existing cities. In literary works, towns were destroyed, abandoned, emptied, gutted, or trans-formed in various ways into administrative centers or temporary camps or visiting sites. In the urbanist science fiction of the twenties, where big cities did exist independent of a single world-city complex or a megacity, the old ones had been torn down, allowed to rot, blown up in the wars, or—in part—preserved as picturesque ruins and archeo-logical sites. Rare was the literary visionary who remained content to reform Moscow or Leningrad, or simply let them grow organically. The revolutionary city planners, educated, well-trained, and socially alert people, were alive to the utopian traditions of Europe and Russia, to the deep anti-urban currents of its past, to the German Marxist urban schemes of the turn-of-the-century, and to Russia's own pre-revolutionary garden city movement. The question was: what would they do with these legacies?

## The Greening of Russia: The Disurbanists

The major schools of utopian city planning came to be known as the Urbanists and the Disurbanists, yet both grew out of anti-urban sentiments and traditions. Both the Euro-pean socialist movement and the international garden city movement—with occasional but not extensive overlap—fed revolutionary Russian town planning. Socialists glorified the city and its productive capacities but lamented its capitalist social evils; they scorned the countryside, but envisioned a world without the contradiction between town and county—a vague formula. In Spain where the linear city was conceived (in the 1880s) and in England where a spate of novels and utopias preceded the garden city movement of 1900–14, social reformers and architects sought to create new communities to illus-trate the possibility of planned living in defiance of the historical growth of medieval towns, fortuitous anarchic industrial patterns, and the resultant nexus with the surround-ing hinterland. E. P. Howard's *Tomorrow* (1898)—a scheme for an anti-city town in the midst of natural greenery (variously called "green city" and "garden city") domi-nated this tradition for about twenty years. Russian "gardenists" were discussing these town plans in the years before the Revolution, and their ideas attracted socialists, Tol-stoyans, religious groups, and even vegetarians who linked healthy diet with healthy environment, open space, and modified residence patterns.[10]

The Soviet Disurbanists and Urbanists of the 1920s took Marxist writings as their avowed texts but were clearly touched by deeper currents. Some had direct links with the garden city movement of the pre-revolutionary period. But their models were also shaped by social concerns, plans for "organizing the psyche of the masses," technical limitations, esthetic impulses, the need for personal expression, professionalism, and ideological considerations. Since "ideology"—though Marxist in name—was in a state of flux and still uncodified, this allowed considerable latitude in urban planning for the future. The Disurbanists in particular disdained modern cities as museums of eclectic styles, haphazard reminders of uneven growth, "irrational" accretions created by ignorant power, and clusters of concretized social evil. Their anti-urbanism went beyond Marxism. They believed that Moscow was a dying city and they wanted to hasten the process; they believed in their "utopian" schemes for creating a new spatial world of work and residence. And in the brief era of their prominence (c. 1928–32), they believed in and worked for the immediate and complete realization of their designs. In this they were for a time supported by the authorities.[11]

Who were the Disurbanists? Not all were architects; their ranks included sociologists, social theorists, journalists, political figures, economists, and professional planners from the Soviet central planning organ *(Gosplan)*. The "ideologist" of the group, Mikhail Okhitovich (1896–1937; died of natural causes), a sociologist, wrote regularly for the main Disurbanist organ, *Contemporary Architecture,* the journal of the Society of Contemporary Architects to which most Disurbanist architects belonged. His associate Mikhail Barshch was a practicing architect and a member of that organization. Moisei Ginzburg, (1892–1946), one of the most influential builders and theorists of the late 1920s, joined them in 1928. Leonid Puzis of Gosplan added his own designs to the main Disurbanist schemes, and the independent and fertile Nikolai Milyutin (1889–1942), though not properly speaking a Disurbanist, provided a "linear" variant to their visions. According to Puzis, they enjoyed wide support in Soviet official circles, including the Commissar of Health Semashko, the housing specialist N. L. Meshcheryakov, and the influential party figure, Yury Larin.[12]

In its most irreducible form, Disurbanism meant the nonurban redistribution of the population. Okhitovich conjured up "a destationed world" meaning a land not only without cities but also without capitals, without a "center," that magic word which then and now in Russian denoted not only geographical situation but also concentration of power, communication, and culture. To Okhitovich, the converse was openness, motion, freedom. In arguing against the Urbanist notion of big cities and buildings as the pathway to communal life, he asserted the then not-so-obvious fact that form did not guarantee content; that a dormitory remained a dormitory whether in a barracks, in a sector of an apartment building, or in a separate communal dwelling; and that a patriarchal *izba* (peasant family home), with all its sociological overtones, could be found in a skyscraper as well as in a village—an acute observation whose truth would become apparent in the communal apartments of the Stalin era.[13]

Okhitovich opposed oppressive and unnatural "collectivism" as much as he did excessive individualism. "Personal property, personal needs, personal initiative, personal development, personal hands, feet, head, and brain not only do not disappear [under socialism] but will be for the first time accessible." Economy of scale, he argued, becomes dysfunctional in life as well as in production when taken to extremes. In a graphic refutation of some classical utopian formulations, he made it quite clear that twenty-five laundries serving about a thousand people apiece were superior to a single laundry for 25,000 people. Collective services, therefore, had to be reasonable and manageable in scale—and not the product of a mathematical mentality. By engaging in oblique debate with Urbanists and science fiction writers, Okhitovich was exhibiting the utility of utopian discourse once again. Unnatural or "social" division of labor—between capital and labor, between men and women, between town and country, between mental and physical labor, between nation and nation (or metropolis and colony) must be abolished—but not the natural and functional division of labor essential to all human life.[14]

Under the slogan "down with the city," Okhitovich called for the depopulation of Moscow and other cities and their regreening as parks. The new locus of population was to be linear—an endless road of habitation flanked by individual dwelling places. His own preference was for prefabricated, portable or mobile, collapsible homes that could be set up anywhere along the "magistral," or line of communication and service points. Some of his colleagues preferred homes on stilts, or adjoining rows of what we would now call "town homes," consisting of one spacious room per person. The service points, easily accessible to residents, were the key element of communalism: shopping, culture centers, and communal gathering points. Their mechanism and administration did not come under Okhitovich's scrutiny, a curious lapse for a professional sociologist interested in human dynamics and not just employment of space.

There are diagrams (see Fig. 33) suggesting what the Disurbanists had in mind. But they are aerial views—often misleading to the layman attempting "real" visualization. If we wish to transport ourselves to the Disurbanists' world, we must look in our minds down a broad and straight paved road heading into spatial infinity (the Russian milieu certainly allowing for such a perspective). Instead of towns or super-cities every 40–50 miles, we see an endless and uninterrupted stretch of dwellings on either side of the road—rows of individual apartment cells, mobile homes on wheels, or boxes on sturdy columns stuck in the ground. Beyond the roads are fields and forests, perhaps farms, industrial sites hidden away along the route. We stop and plant our house; in time we acquire a spouse and plant another box beside our own and attach it; with the coming of children comes the attachment of more boxes. Work and goods are within easy distance (public transport, personal auto, or foot, depending on the scheme). The world beyond the roadside boxes is organized (in a vaguely specified way) along socialist economic lines. At the service points and the workplace occur the moments of communal interaction or spiritual community so important to other prophets of utopian experiment in these years. But it is never described, much less analyzed: space and structure alone seem to possess the power to "communalize" people, an implication quite at odds with Okhitovich's original point.

Other scenarios simply altered the details of the major vision. The "Green City" of Barshch and Ginzburg, for example, stressed row houses as the ideal (not the separate boxes or little houses). They are flanked front and rear by a green world but on the sides by neighbors—endlessly in both directions. Only in the collective of space, argue the architects, can the individual come into full play. The nearby "bases" enrich this semi-private, semi-communal life: bus stops that are also reading stations, autoparks, cafeterias serving 250 citizens, and nearby centers of sport, culture, education, and communal utilities (kindergarten, laundries, etc.). The world is brought in via nearby production centers, radio, T.V., and telephone. As with Okhitovich, marriage, divorce, and family growth are made possible by the constant switching of adjoining rooms with lockable doors. All the planners were extraordinarily sensitive to personal quarters for women and the possibility of divorce, a sensible notion at a moment in Soviet history when divorce was reaching mammoth proportions after the 1926–27 family reforms.

Barshch and Ginzburg put more emphasis on air, light, drenching sunshine, and green-ery than did Okhitovich, but no more on the actual problems and dynamics of residential interaction or communal living.[15]

In later years, Barshch called Disurbanism "our futurological fantasy," based on a perception of the decay and self-destruction of the then existing cities and a vision of the reign of the automobile.[16] In retrospect the Disurbanist planners occupied a peculiar place in utopian thinking. They did not share the basically "rural" sensibilities of the Russian anti-urbanists in poetry or science fiction or of the peasants themselves. But they are akin to those utopian writers such as Shelonsky (see Chapter 1) before the Revolution and Belyaev at the end of the 1920s who saw privacy as the only means to true community. The characters in Belyaev's *Struggle in the Atmosphere* are constantly on the move, almost permanently separated from each other. Parents, relatives, friends, and loved ones never actually visit each other, yet they converse constantly by means of what we might someday call "conference video" (or satellite interview)—a device that apparently provided the same kind of satisfaction for Belyaev's people as does ordinary close-up "company" for present-day mortals in Russia and elsewhere on the globe. The proximity of housing and "service points" are pathetic attempts to compen-sate for the missing "street life" of the old city. Today's dwellers in and visitors to suburban "communities," forest condominiums, town home developments, and the gal-lerias and malls that "service" them might offer a different testimony about the com-munal utility of such visions.

Apparently no one noticed at the time that Disurbanism seemed to herald the end of architecture as a profession—or at least a major branch of it: residential design. The portable boxes or adjoining cells were standardized, leaving the ensembles of service center or communal points as the only foci of constructive genius. Some of the existing designs remind us of present day American shopping centers along the major strips, or "modern" universities built on podiums and pods. In some sense Disurbanism resem-bles Frank Lloyd Wright's scheme for a Broad Acres—a dispersionist design for Amer-ica that would individualize living by blending the structures into the contours of na-ture.[17] What we have gotten instead in Russia is the continuation of the cubic block of apartments marching outward from the city lines.

Disurbanism highlighted in a very dramatic way the eternal conflict in modern, ur-ban society between the yearning for community, sociability, conviviality, the animation of crowds, and neighborliness on the one hand and the need for privacy, family life, individual space on the other. The Disurbanists, for all their claims about synthesizing and reconciling these needs, clearly leaned in the direction of individualism. The ex-treme dispersionism, the yearning to cover all the Russian land with criss-crossing mag-istrals of residence, the insistence on separate living units, and the hollowness and blandness of their visions of communitarian interaction at loosely conceived bus stops and cultural-shopping points all point to this and underline their highly developed aver-sion to the city life they knew as well as to the massive and grandiose schemes of their rivals, the Urbanists and Superurbanists, whose dream would cluster millions of people together in unheard of communal density.

## Supercity: The Urbanists

Although both Urbanists and Disurbanists were inspired by the antiurban impulse in Russian history and fueled by hostility to the "rotting" cities they saw around them, they divided on whether cities as such would replace the current ones or be wholly eliminated from the socialist landscape. Lenin in 1913 had written that "cities are the centers of economic, political, and intellectual or spiritual life of a people and constitute the chief promoters of progress." The notion of the city remained very strong in the Bolshevik vision of the future. Trotsky in the 1920s was quite emphatic: "The city lives and leads. If you give up the city, that is if you let it be torn to pieces economically by the *kulak* and artistically by Pilnyak, there will remain no Revolution, but a violent and bloody process of retrogression. Peasant Russia, deprived of the leadership of the city, not only will never get to Socialism, but will not be able to maintain itself for two months, and will become the manure and peat of world imperialism." A Bolshevik economist, arguing with leftover "Populists" of the 1920s, wrote in 1927 of "the leading role of the city in modern history" as "the bearer of the most advanced economic forms." Men and women of power, culture, and economic weight—however much they allowed for "reshaping" the city—seemed unable to dispense with it altogether. It was their base, their camp, their headquarters—as well as the locus of putative progress.[18]

This explains why there was so much furor in the discussion of the city, so much fear and hostility to an antiurbanism that threatened to become a reality and make Chayanov's dream of detonation come true. It also explains the eventual decisiveness of the Stalinists in reaffirming the city—even in its present form. For ruling circles and responsible administrators, the city was a practical necessity—without it they might float through the void of a vast countryside without power and influence, their voices echoless. For some intellectuals, however, the attraction of the city was positive—like that of the machine. A humble rank-and-file communist, Lev Kopelev, used to dream that Moscow, Kharkov, and Kiev would be as big and as well built as Berlin, Hamburg, and New York, with giant skyscrapers, autos, bikes, fine clothes, and lots of watches, planes and dirigibles. Mayakovsky, Meyerhold, the Futurists, and the factory poets made a regular fetish out of the shape and dynamic quality of the big city. One ought not to see this as a Marxist-urban vs. Russian-rural dichotomy. Superurban fantasy was just as "Russian" in its appeal as was antiurbanism. Architects, science fiction writers, poets, and artists of every sort dreamed up numerous visions of futuristic cities before and after the Revolution. The Anarchists, who were viscerally opposed to most Bolshevik programs and style, projected more than their share of "Free Cities" and "Giant Urban Communes" filled with millions of workers. "We shall build," wrote the Anarcho-Syndicalist Grachev, "as yet unheard of giants from concrete, glass, and steel."[19]

The earliest years of the Revolution evoked a strange mix of architectural fantasy and social vision. The school sketches and projects of the period—especially in the famous avant-garde academy V.Kh.U.T.E.M.A.S—show a variety of abstract, Constructivist projections of hanging, floating, flying, and jutting structures, fantastic temples, mausoleums, crematoria, and monuments. Out of it emerged the victorious principle of "rationalism" in architecture whose main spokesman, Ginzburg, drew on the ideas of the father of modern psychology, Wilhelm Wundt, to prove that the correct appearance of buildings had a healthy civic-minded effect upon the viewer and that simple geometric forms required less physical energy to perceive. Apparently influenced by Ford, Taylor, and Gastev, he stressed symmetry and geometric precision, and the honesty of showing the function of the structure openly. A major Constructivist architect, Alexei Gan, designed a kiosk that would speak to the peasants and help mold in them an urban mentality. A still minor current was early monumentalism. The competition for a Palace of Labor (unrealized) in 1922 brought forth an oft-quoted reverie of Sergei Kirov:

> On this new, magnificent, splendid and revolutionary earth, we the workers born in miserable hovels, will leave those hovels in comradely ranks to enter our enchanted palaces to the strain of the great 'Internationale' . . . [We] are capable of embellishing this wretched earth with monuments such as our enemies could never imagine, even in their dreams.

This was another rhetorical link between fantasy, architectural discourse, and prominent policymakers. The various "Red City" projects of the early 1920s encased both these tendencies, but were almost never built.[20]

Like the Disurbanists, the Urbanist school of town planning was a child of the Society of Contemporary Architects—O.S.A. It adhered to the view, voiced by R. Khiger in 1928, that the city was a "social condenser," and that the architect's mission was to "alter radically the structure of human life—productive, social, and personal." By merging Western technology with Russian revolutionary notions of cooperation and communalism, O.S.A. designers hoped to change the texture of life in the U.S.S.R. and create the New Soviet Person. Furthermore, O.S.A. believed—and said so openly—that this was the responsibility of professional planners and designers, not party officials, and that it should be done not by dogmatic fiat or administrative order, but by a process of experience and experiment—building, inhabiting, testing, and revising. It was the perfect example of the fusion of utopia and experiment directly inspired by the October Revolution.[21]

The O.S.A. planners' decision that big new urban formations would replace the towns of the present produced two ironies: they were widely imitated by other schools, of town planning—including some of their enemies—and, after several years of Urbanist speculation, some of them shifted suddenly to Disurbanism. As early as 1926, B. Korsunov printed in O.S.A.'s journal a project for a city of skyscrapers surrounded by open space and green parks (in the manner of Le Corbusier) and ringed by seven-story workers' dwellings in the form of House Communes. Grounding their argument on cost as well as sociability, O.S.A. writers promoted concentration, density, planning, and mammoth city-forms. In 1928, N. Krasilnikov's city plan required a population density of three quarters of a million persons per square mile—more than double that of Manhattan's Lower East Side in the 1890s! Cities would contain clusters of half-million people housed vertically in tall buildings with helicopters serving as elevators. Varentsov's "City of the Future" was a dream of immense Y-shaped communal buildings linked to a circular community service center—all surrounded by greenery. N. Ladovsky's 1929 "Dynamic City" plan placed a giant arrow-shaped residence building (with administrative offices at one wing) inside a horseshoe of industrial establishments—for density and ease of access to workplace. The group of proletarian architects who came out to assault O.S.A. in the late twenties hardly differed from its opponents in proposing huge house commune cities—with enormous residential structures resembling airplanes and ocean liners.[22]

The ultimate Urbanist scheme was launched dramatically by L. M. Sabsovich, a high official of Soviet Russia's central state planning organ (Gosplan), in the very heat of the first five-year plan. In a burst of arrogant optimism, he called his prospectus *The U.S.S.R. in Ten Years*. In comprehensiveness, detail, and ambitiousness it outstripped all previous urban plans and openly invoked "the great projects" of Bogdanov's *Red Star*. It was widely circulated and discussed in the Soviet Union and translated into foreign languages. Though written by an economist, it was the most extravagant of all city planning exercises produced in the Revolution and a codification of major themes from the whole realm of utopianism and experimental life.

The Soviet Union in 1939—and one must recall the actual condition of the country in that fateful year in order to appreciate the irony—will be a land where the "material and social base of socialism" is already laid down by the complete abolition of private property in the means of production, the disappearance of classes, and the industrial and agricultural transformation of the economy. There will be no great cities, unnatural and inhuman hazards to physical and mental health. Industries and citizens will have been dispersed across the length and breadth of the nation into "agglomerations" of 50,000–75,000 people, the optimum for sane and comfortable living. Creation of new enterprises in the old cities will have ceased, small operations will have been combined into complexes, and both will have been transplanted. The village world will have been eliminated, together with the muzhik mentality (in 5–8 years!); collective and state farms will have been unified around agro-towns on geographically and demographically equal territorial units. Eventually the new industrial cities and the agro-towns would combine into Industrial-Agrarian Cities serving a given geographical unit. This would "drastically change the face" of Russia, destroy "rural barbarism and isolation," and end abnormal urban concentration.[23]

In Sabsovich's vision, communal life replaces the wasteful and deadening private household, a "scourge that deforms the lives of adults and children alike" (p. 123). The aims of communalism? To free all workers (especially women) from responsibility for the provision of daily needs and from the private obligation of childrearing and education, to make woman equal to man by opening the doors of her domestic jail, to release energies for the fulfillment of individual needs and collective life, to enhance the health of children, to raise the cultural level of all people, and to end the distinction between hand and brain labor. The means? The "industrialization" of all tasks previously performed, separately and wastefully, inside the "petty bourgeois" home.

Building on the whole tradition of socialist dreams of household collectivisim, Sabsovich imagined the coordination of all food producing operations in order to transform raw food products into complete meals, deliverable to the population in urban cafeterias, communal dining rooms, and the workplace in ready-to-eat form by means of thermos containers. No food shopping, no cooking, no home meals, no kitchens. Similar industrialization of laundering, tailoring, repair, and even house cleaning (with electrical appliances) would allow each person a sleeping-living room, free of all maintenance cares. Russia would in fact become a vast free-of-charge hotel chain. In his cities of 50,000–70,000, Sabsovich suggested that 25–50 large residence buildings would accomodate the entire population—meaning 1,400–2,000 persons per building (children being housed nearby)—or about the size of Fourier's phalanstery (1,700).

Sabsovich's New City would service its inhabitants culturally at three levels: reading rooms, halls, and galleries within each building; larger and more elaborate culture centers in the city; and higher courses, studios, and laboratories in every workplace and factory. The work week would fall to three days (two of work, one of rest) and then to five days (three of work, two of rest)—and all workers would retire at age forty-nine. The nation's health would be protected by athletic and medical facilities, the short work regime, and acres of greenery surrounding the cities. Sabsovich's mammoth "social condenser" would serve as the physical shell of social being which in turn would shape consciousness. Thus the cultural and spiritual level of all would actually be transformed in a few years.

One is left breathless by the scope and grandeur of Sabsovich's predictions. So outlandish did they seem that he revised his schedule a bit later to project fifteen instead of ten years into the future and reduced some of his exorbitant figures. But if one stands back from any version of the scheme and adds other technological details contained in it (transport, efficiency, sheer output levels), one gazes upon a land utterly refashioned, enveloped in utopian themes—a land of ultramodern medium-sized cities whose population is bursting with productivity and at the same time speeding across the land in large passenger planes or personal aviettes and living happy communal lives in the midst of utmost comfort and convenience. One could cut away the statistical tables and economic prognostications, add some laughter, a few characters, and any feeble plot to build from it a typical science fiction novel of the 1920s. Larri's *Land of the Happy*, written at about the same time, though projecting several decades further, hardly differs from it in the majestic scope of its fantasy.

## Socialism in One Building: The House Commune

The word "commune" *(kommuna)* became a regular part of the Soviet lexicon right after the October Revolution. "House Commune" or Communal Dwelling *(dom-kommuna)* designated a structure or cluster of them designed for collective and communal life. Radical architects freely and often uncritically plundered the works of the nineteenth century utopian socialists, especially Fourier, though often without discussion of social meaning. The earliest on record, called "Phalanstery" and designed by the architect Venderov in 1918, was exactly that: a Fourierist project for thirty-eight families—never built. Indeed very few were ever built; most remained on paper, and the bulk of communal experimentation was done in already existing houses, apartments, or dormitories. Yet the communal house was one of the most crucial elements in architectural experimentation for a new life: the concretized rendering of a hundred utopian dreams.[24]

In the relatively serene years after the Civil War, designers began to combine their colorful fantasies with practical considerations about buildings and their future occupants. The first examples were extremely eclectic and much too lavish to be the models for a general pattern of construction. The 1921 Phalanstery of Tverskoi and Buryshkin, for example, looked like a classical palace from one angle—although its modern outward curving wings place it in the tradition of the American motel also (see Fig. 34). It was a prize-winning entry for a project to be built in the suburbs of Petrograd for thirty proletarian families with common dining room, kitchen, reading room, and day-care center built around a courtyard, and with residence rooms above and in the wings. Leonid Vesnin's Moscow housing ensemble of 1922 was more ambitious: a dozen buildings, including club, bath-house, technical shack, daycare and kindergartens, and residential buildings, with a large play area between them. It was in fact what we call a "garden court apartment complex," spacious and self-sufficient, with common services including a place for socializing. Other projects from this period display the same attractiveness and common sense—but without elaboration on how the inhabitants would achieve communal sensibilities. Though strikingly modern in form, the projects had little ideological content. They seemed to reflect the comfort level of professionals rather than factory workers.[25]

With the formation of O.S.A. and its doctrine of "social condenser," the House Commune came into its own as the central ingredient in town planning of the future among the Urbanists. Recognizing the indisputable fact of overcrowding in Moscow, invoking the wastefulness of repetitive individual living units (homes or separate, fully equipped apartments), O.S.A. leaders saw the House Commune as the only solution: it would cut costs by communalizing services, release women (and men) from repetitive domestic housework and thereby raise national labor productivity, promote a spirit of communism through collective living, and allow some privacy as well. The ideological portion of the campaign announced a "collectivist-social" psychology and the elimination of the "petty bourgeois" and "individualistic" habits of the past—meaning the excessive privatization, hoarding, inwardness, egoism, and coziness that some foes of the family accused it of. The first big O.S.A. scheme for a house commune within the supercity was that of Barshch and V. M. Vladimirov in 1929: two intersecting buildings with 1,000 adults in one, 360 preschoolers in the left intersector, and 320 schoolchildren in the right (see Fig. 35). The adult wing had four communal and six sleeping floors and a communal dining room equipped with a conveyor-belt table. Adults dined with the older children and paid regular visits via a corridor to the little ones. Similar schemes sprouted in 1928–29, with a crossed nest of boxes, a tooth-roofed H-shaped house for students, and an eight-spoked wheel of buildings—the essential combination of communal buildings easily accessible to sleeping space, the separation of adults and children, and available privacy of single rooms for all.[26]

The most interesting social issue to emerge out of these plans was that of the kitchen and the family. It is a singular fact that to this day the individual kitchen is the strongest symbol of a nuclear family (as it once was its main meeting place). Classical House Commune theory had always made the collectivized kitchen its central tenet: to save costs, promote eating together, and rescue housewives from the slavery of kitchen life. The "women question" and the family, hotly debated in the first decade of the Revolution, had informed home planning discourse from the beginning. All Bolsheviks were verbally committed to ending the drudgery of housework for wives, though the question of separation of children from parents—even in a nearby building—evoked considerable division.[27] The most extreme advocate of "de-familization" within the House Commune by means of mandatory communal dining and separation of children from parents, V. Kuzmin, codified his appeals in 1930 in a famous piece entitled "Problems of the Scientific Organization of Everyday Life." To his rigid arguments on the abolition of the known family within the precincts of the commune, he added more than a touch of Gastevism: organized and scheduled efficiency for every moment of the day. Kuzmin's system of "supercollectivism" (his own term) deserves comment precisely because it has sometimes been seen to epitomize the architectural utopianism of the 1920s, even though in fact the opposite is true.

Kuzmin believed that the architect's mission was to frame the expressive side of people's life, how they "suffer, enjoy, rejoice, and lament" as well as work and eat. This could not be done, he argued, by the "hammer and sickle"—in other words by symbol and ritual. Here Kuzmin seems to be filling the void left in science fiction utopias about the nature and quality of communal life, recognizing that symbolic and ritual assemblies of masses did not provide this. It must arise where men and women live, through the "scientific organization of material life"—living space, light, color, ventilation, and the total environment in inner space. The main realms of life—rest, eating, sex, parenting, sanitation, decent medical and cultural levels—were too rich to be satisfied within the realm of the sleeping space alone. Kuzmin offered a "graph of life"—not as an enforceable regulation ("man is not an automaton") but as a guide for joining architectural design with the daily life in a communal situation.[28]

|  |  |
|---|---|
| 1. Lights out. | 10:00 P.M. |
| 2. Eight hours of sleep. Reveille. | 6:00 A.M. |
| 3. Calisthenics—5 min. | 6:05 A.M. |
| 4. Toilet—10 min. | 6:15 A.M. |
| 5. Shower (optional—5 min.) | 6:20 A.M. |
| 6. Dress—5 min. | 6:25 A.M. |
| 7. To the dining room—3 min. | 6:28 A.M. |
| 8. Breakfast—15 min. | 6:43 A.M. |
| 9. To the cloakrooms—2 min. | 6:45 A.M. |
| 10. Put on outdoor clothing—5 min. | 6:50 A.M. |
| 11. To the mine—10 min. | 7:00 A.M. |
| 12. Work in the mine—8 hours. | 3:00 P.M. |
| 13. To the commune—10 min. | 3:10 P.M. |
| 14. Take off outdoor clothing—7 min. | 3:17 P.M. |
| 15. Wash—8 min. | 3:25 P.M. |
| 16. Dinner—30 min. | 3:55 P.M. |
| 17. To the rest room for free hour—3 min. | 3:58 P.M. |
| 18. Free time. Those who wish may nap. In this case they retire to the bedrooms. | 4:58 P.M. |
| 19. Toilet and change—10 min. | 5:08 P.M. |
| 20. To the dining room—2 min. | 5:10 P.M. |
| 21. Tea—15 min. | 5:25 P.M. |
| 22. To the club. Recreation. Cultural development. Gymnastics. Perhaps a bath or swim. Here it is life itself that will determine how time is spent, that will draw up the plan. Alloted time: four hours | 9:25 P.M. |
| 23. To dining room, supper, eat, and to bedrooms—25 min. | 9:50 P.M. |
| 24. Prepare to retire (a shower may be taken)—10 min. | 10:00 P.M. |

Kuzmin—in a way that reminds us of Gastev and the Table of Hours in *We*—is meticulous in timing and arranging the "normal," repetitive and noncontroversial side of the daily round right down to electrified cloakrooms for outer garments (a very crucial aspect of Russian life—thus the many minutes allowed for it). Radio is enlisted to assist the communards in keeping to this suggested rhythm. But sex and leisure remain in a mist. Kuzmin hopes to sleep the unmarried, by gender, in rooms of six (without describing how their sex lives will operate) and "couples" in adjoining rooms whose connecting door is locked when divorce occurs. The family as such evaporates, since the children are housed apart, though, as always, parents have access to them. Everything else in life is assumed to be communal—work, motion, dining, leisure. But the big block of playtime at night is left vacant so that "life itself" will decide what kind of things will be done, and at what level of participation. As in many such projects, a familiar aspect of life is taken away—sitting around the kitchen table, talking, eating with one's own family, lounging with them or tinkering in the evening. Yet the new conviviality is not plotted. The big leisure room of public space remains an empty church.

Most of the O.S.A. architects winced at the prospect of designing away the family at once and forever. They reached compromise instead. Although opposing the oppression of women and the old family that enslaved her, O.S.A. leaders designed a so-called F-Unit of one-room efficiency apartments for couples, complete with kitchens that could be removed in the future when occupants advanced to the level of full communal life and began to cook and eat in common rooms. Children would, however, be segregated. Thus, from the old family hearth was preserved at least a companionate couple with ample arrangement for dining together in privacy. It was far more than many real couples could ever enjoy in the crowded buildings of Moscow and other big cities. It was, in a way, a prelude to the system of small "separate" apartments *(otdelnye kvartiry)* that have replaced the "communal" flats of Stalin's time in the last thirty years. The reasonableness of the O.S.A. architects was apparently conditioned by the response they received to a 1926 questionnaire sent out to workers about their preferences in matters of communal life. Important independent architects such as Milyutin and Leonidov also opted for transitional stages from family unit to family-less communes.[29]

But, aside from the organization of space, time, and daily life, how was one to achieve "socialism in one building" or communalism in the social and spiritual sense that everyone spoke of so glibly and sincerely? The most common answers were through the mechanism of common space and passageways to encourage interaction, communal dining—a mode of enlarging a family custom—and variants of the workers' club. A typical example was Leonidov's 1929 project for a club that contained labs, lecture halls, sports facilities, game rooms, space for military drill, a museum, gardens, playgrounds, libraries, parks, a gymnasium, rooms for radio, T.V. and film, and a planetarium—in other words, a city within a city.[30] Obviously not all communal dwellings could afford such facilities. And where they would exist, their very vastness and variety would hardly make for community—but rather for much specialization and pluralism. Indeed the more one examines architectural notions of community, the more one sees a replication of already existing urban life, but on a smaller scale in a place called communal. Judging from the kinds of rituals and ceremonies conducted in workers' clubs in the 1920s, not much in the way of developing an emotional sense of community could be accomplished by such activity.

The most outlandish communitarian project to come out of the architectural experimentalism of this era was Konstantin Melnikov's 1929 entry in a competition for a Green City (the winner was Ladovsky, but the city was never built). Although meant as a rest town or resort for workers, Melnikov's Green City vividly illustrates how much a practical and talented architect was drawn into the utopian atmosphere that dominated town planning and community design in those years. The main buildings were commodious transient hotels with private rooms. And what did Melnikov offer by way of communal intercourse? A mammoth railroad station to welcome the travelers and surround them by spacious arenas for interaction, galleries and pathways and recreational opportunity—mostly nature trails. Crowning the establishment was the famous Laboratory of Sleep—a double winged structure with sloping floors, multiple sleep chambers, and an elaborate set of controls by which the sleep-inducers could bathe the resting workers in delicious aromas, sweet fresh air, soothing sounds of nature and music, and gently rocking beds (see Fig. 36). Inspired by discussions of sleep therapy that were in the air at the time, Melnikov was also indirectly indebted to science fiction: not, ironically, Soviet works but a 1911 story by the father of American science fiction, Hugo Gernsback, called *Ralph-124-C41 +*.[31]


Architectural utopia, like science fiction utopia, was clearly a product of the intelligentsia—that element in Russian history which had always displayed the greatest extravagance, variety, and richness of fantasy. In the case of science fiction, the state had played a negligible role, the peasants were oblivious to it, and its urban readership consumed it. Town planning and architecture possessed an altogether different political dimension. Its impact was immediate, it made claims on labor resources, it pointed to radical changes in the social landscape, it demanded power and freedom to destroy and rebuild—on the ground and in the present or near future. The state could not be indifferent to such pretensions. But the state, embodied in the party, was ambivalent. Prior to 1928, it paid little attention to the emerging schemes. During the five-year plan, especially 1928–30, the utopian town visions seemed to mesh with the economic designs of the plan. Frederick Starr has shown in meticulous detail how the combination of haste, euphoria, partial delusion, and lack of clarity led both sides to see convergence and compatibility between visionary dispersion and the new projected industrial complexes already underway, between visionary house communes and barracks-like collectives already sprouting up all over the industrial sites, between Okhitovich's Disurbanism and the extreme mobility of the population in these years, and between the social-familial dimensions of house commune schemes and the realities of an immense upsurge in female labor.[32]

The fragile symbiosis of visions collapsed in 1931 in the face of economic realities, revival plans for the older cities, competing transportation networks, the sudden deluge of peasants into already established towns, and the painful realization of Russia's backwardness in the midst of transformation. Reinforcing this collapse were the attitudes and behavior patterns of the rural population who flooded the towns, of workers who were expected to occupy the planned towns and ideal buildings, a people thoroughly unprepared psychologically and culturally for the kind of communal living—Urbanist or Disurbanist—that the utopian blueprints had conjured up as an imminent possibility. Science fiction and visionary town planning both offered visions of a new world. Ironically their convergence came in the year 1931, when both were repudiated.

# 10

## Utopia in Life: The Communal Movement

> Work together, Eate together, Declare this all abroad.
> Gerrard Winstanley

> Communism: it's not only on the land,
> in the mill, in the sweat of your toil.
> It's at home, at table, in family life and daily round.
> Vladimir Mayakovsky

### Native Traditions

Soviet Russia was the first nation in history to witness the birth across its land of thousands of communal organizations spontaneously engaging in collective life. It was the first society to provide a supportive environment—for the "little islets of socialism"[1] that had previously sprouted up in isolation like an experimental archipelago surrounded by an ocean of hostility. The commune was the advanced laboratory of future communism. In its very nomenclature and programs, its slogans and symbols, the new regime was the first to exalt the commune and give it state support. When the atmosphere changed drastically in the early 1930s, that environment collapsed and communalism disappeared.

Many aspects of Marxism were alien to the population—the heavy emphasis on economic modernization and on the town as organizer of human behavior and culture, the centralized economy, and intra-peasant class hostility. But Marx's "from each according to his or her abilities" was compatible with the peasant belief that all residents of the village *mir* should pull their weight in accordance with "nature" or abilities—men, women, small children, old people in their various ways, according to physical condition. Marx's "to each according to his work" was given loose expression (long before Marx was born) by the land partition system described earlier, and by mechanisms allowing the ambitious and hardworking to earn more than others. In the communes of the religious groups of the nineteenth century and then of the revolutionary period, Marx's final vision—"to each according to need"—was enshrined in various combinations of pooling, cooperative labor, and sharing of daily life to assure—within a limited framework of production—that there were no needy, even those unable to work.

The word "commune" *(kommuna)* offers special problems in Russian history in that it is related to the word "communism" which—aside from its various nineteenth century meanings—has two major uses in our own time: the political and social system associated with Soviet-type regimes and the Marxist vision of future society and its productive and distributive process. Also, the Russian words *mir* and *obshchina* are often translated as "commune" or "peasant land commune." These Slavic words indicate the organization of village life in most of the Russian lands before 1930 when the *mir* was dissolved. In the Revolution, *kommuna* meant a place or agreement whereby people lived or worked together voluntarily and shared various important aspects of their lives—labor, property, leisure, mealtimes. This idea is related to "communism" but not coterminous with it, and the peasant *mir* was based on limited cooperation, private dwelling, family land use, and individual household meals.[2]

A distinction must also be made among communalism (in Russian usually rendered as "communal life"—*kommunalnaya zhizn* or *kommunalnyi byt),* collectivism, and cooperation or cooperativism. The word "collectivism" is often used to embrace the other two and to indicate any activity that links or binds people together. "Cooperation" indicates working together or collaborating in some mutually advantageous way, short of living in a commune. Cooperation showed two related but distinct faces in prerevolutionary Russia. One was the organized cooperative movement lasting from about 1860 to about 1930 in rural areas (especially Siberia), and subdividing into producers', consumers', and credit coops—hardly differing from its counterparts in Denmark or Iowa. This was an extraordinarily important movement in Russian history, but had more to do—as Tugan-Baranovsky put it—with surviving in a wicked world than with changing it, and it had no necessary relation to the communal movement. The other—the artel tradition—was very much tied to communalism.[3]

The oldest and most successful communes were the peasant religious ones of Old Believers and Sectarians. But religious dissidents were not the only ones to try communal life. Intelligentsia of various persuasions went out on to the land to set up communal experiments. Most were Populists. The people-worshipper Alexander Engelhardt and his pupils created communes and collective artels. Ex-revolutionaries in the "Godmanhood" movement and followers of Tolstoy in Russia and elsewhere created rural communes designed to share lives in a religious milieu and to cut themselves off from the sinfulness of civilization. In this they resembled the monastic hermits of the middle ages and the sectarian communalists of their own time, the difference being the apparently eternal difficulties of city-raised and educated people in keeping such communities going. Illustrating most of these currents was the Krinitsa Commune founded in the 1870s by a princess who wished to live the code of the intelligentsia (a vague socialism and nihilism) but avoid radicalism. She wanted "an enormous commune covering all the earth and to bring contentment to all." She and her friends sold their jewels and created a community of manual and mental labor, mutual readings, and sharing of property and life. Within a generation, the commune had peaked in membership (to about 75) and then declined radically by 1913 (to 16 full members)—the decline attributed to greed, intrigue, and isolation.[4]

City life proved more amenable to a wide variety of communes for the intelligentsia. Urban communalism had a continuous life from the 1850s among students of St. Petersburg University. Like many such institutions, they got started in a combination of need, mutual advantage, and moral-ideological considerations—usually indivisible. Students from the provinces tended to bring a lexicon and a vaguely understood sense of peasant life with them and named their own organizations accordingly (student protest meetings were named after *obshchina* assemblies, for example). Their communes and artels were hardly more than pooled money for food and rent.

The communes of the Petrashevtsy of the 1840s and the nihilist and radical communes of the 1860s were more self-consciously institutional: they offered shelter from a hostile world, a laboratory for egalitarian sharing, a sense of community, and later, a useful locus for conspiratorial work. They became incubators of revolution and drew in provincial youth, especially women, to a new kind of life. The influence of Chernyshevsky on this development in the 1860s and beyond was strong—"nihilists" were known to have looked to the pages of *What Is To Be Done?* for clues as to how to organize self-help artels and residential communes. Some of the most important radicals of the 1870s came out of a communal environment. When arrested, revolutionaries often carried the communal idea to prison. The men and women of the Kara Penal Colony shared all goods, read to each other, and lived according to a strictly written constitution. Artists and other intellectuals emulated this form in the 1860s for non-radical purposes.[5]

Urban workers eventually surpassed all these little experiments in sheer numbers— but in a very indirect way. The Russian artel had a wide variety of forms in old Russia, but usually denominated a small band of like-minded people of the lower classes— workers, peasants, thieves, musicians, Cossacks, soldiers—who hired themselves out for temporary work and then shared the proceeds equally. When rapid industrialization brought laborers into the towns, they retained the artel tradition which was applied not only to jobbing and dining but also to residential patterns. The so-called *artelnaya kvartira* or cooperative-communal apartment was the fruit of this custom; it sprang from need, the housing shortage, and a clinging sense of community. Groups of workers would hire a communal apartment, share the rent, buy food and dine together, and even attend leisure events in groups. The worker Semën Kanatchikov eloquently describes such a commune of fifteen workers in one large room, with their beds ringing a table. At mealtime they ate from a common bowl (as in the village cabin) and ritually fought for the meat at the bottom. Not dozens, but hundreds of thousands of workers lived in this way in the generation or so before the Revolution.[6]

In smaller towns, peasants often set up agrarian enclaves where the rural traditions of sharing were perpetuated. These customs were a major background factor in the growth of communal experimentation after 1917. Thus when Bolshevik intellectuals uttered a "philosophy" of collectivism, they were drawing upon an authentic tradition quite independent of Marxism. In Lunacharsky's words, "communal life is based not on compulsion and the need to herd together for mere self-preservation, as it had in the past, but on a free and natural merging of personalities into superpersonal entities."[7] This piece of ministerial rhetoric is rich in hope and throbbing with vision but weak in sociology, history, and psychology. It ignored the importance of survival and practicality in the communalism of the pre-revolutionary period as well as that of the Revolution. It was precisely the combination of perceived need in a world of shortage with a utopian hope to reshape the human psyche that accounted for those successes registered in the revolutionary communal experiment of 1917–30.[8]

## Communes on the Land

New communes were organized spontaneously in 1917—before the government decrees of 1918–19—by returning veterans suffused with "trench brotherhood," poor peasants, landless laborers, and urban workers availing themselves of the land and the manor houses being freed up by the peasant revolution. They were diverse enterprises of collective labor, pooled resources (including tools), and shared produce quite unlike the peasant *obshchinas* but very much like the artels—marking a migration of the artel from the countryside to the town and then back to the village again. Nor did they resemble the Soviet "agricultural artel," the direct predecessor of the *kolkhoz,* or collective farm. Terminology varied—sometimes the use of the word *kommuna* was avoided in order not to antagonize neighboring peasants or prospective joiners who were naturally suspicious of Latin root words imported from regiments and cities.[9]

In the Civil War, these grew apace, attracting a large number of returning veterans and landless peasants. I. Kataev, writing a decade later, tried to explain the movement:[10]

> Sometimes middle or poor peasants argue for the commune (and consequently against the artel) in a daze of Russian extremism, radicalism of a kind, 'Well, put everything in one pile, if that's the way it's to be. . . .' This urge to general equality is very strong, especially in the mind of the most backward, poor peasants, partisan fighters, farm laborers. However, on the upturned, agitated soil of half-conscious economic aspirations, there easily take root and grow up the seeds of the old dream of brotherhood—equality, seeds drifting, it may be, even from flaming times of égalité, fraternité, in any case from booklets and preachings of Populists, legends of migrations and fairy-tales of rivers of milk, from partisan dreams of 1919.

This remark has been cited in the literature on communes as somehow definitive. One may discount deep deposited memories of 1789 or even of Populist teaching. The Revolution certainly summoned the familiar rural dreams of *volya* and community because it made them possible. But the sources indicate that the main motivation was survival under new and menacing circumstances. Landless people—as many cynics have pointed out—have no problem in sharing land. The vast majority of the peasants did not form communes or join them; instead they expressed their natural aspirations by reviving and strengthening the peasant *mir* or *obshchina* as they had known it, though in many cases "revolutionizing" it—i.e. making it somewhat fairer and more egalitarian than before.[11]

The Bolshevik government took a hand in the communal movement almost immediately. As part of its effort to promote collective and cooperative agriculture during the Civil War, it exalted the commune as the highest form of rural production and life. Inside the Commissariat of Land, a Commune Section *(otdel kommun)* began organizing, counting, naming, recording, and financing communes, taking already existing ones under its wing, and giving lands and estate property out for new ones. Not only did the landless and landpoor, the front soldiers, and the hungry workers reach out for communal assistance, but also more prosperous peasants and even former landowners—all seeking security and subsidy for survival from the state. By 1921 communes constituted about twenty percent of all collective forms in the countryside. When the war ended and N.E.P. made the cities somewhat more livable, many communards deserted and the commune declined—though still supported by the state right up to the moment of collectivization.[12]

Government spokesmen lost no time in adopting the communes as one of the emerging forms of communism. Vladimir Meshcheryakov of the Land Commissariat of the Northern Oblast (around Petrograd), a specialist on communes, sensibly emphasized the balance between economic utility and moral righteousness in the communal way, warning his readers that most peasants were hostile to the idea and had to be won over slowly through gradualism and intermediate forms of communal work and life. P. V.

Pyatnitsky of the Petrograd Soviet lauded their economies of scale—the famous one kitchen vs. 100 kitchens of the Fourierist tradition. He also stressed the leveling function of the commune.[13]

Most interesting of all was the folksy sermon of M. Sumatokhin of the Central Executive of the Soviets called *Come on, Live Communally!* In it, a returned political exile tells his fellow villagers of the virtues of the commune which was to replace the family through the brotherhood of all members and the parenthood of Soviet power. This tale reflects the looseness of the terminology at that time: equality is equated with need, says the speaker, in that "everyone wears shoes" and there is no need for elaborate measurement of work or need—an idea that was widely accepted. The narrator requires that homes, though varying in size according to family needs, be rebuilt according to a single design. On a note of administrative impatience, he also wants to plan the commune rationally and introduce bells for mealtimes and the divisions of the workday.[14]

Much of this was simply exhortation, the government's attempt to encounter and direct communal forms. The commune section of the Commissariat of Land issued a statute in July 1918 defining the commune as an enterprise where everything was held in common except objects of personal use, where labor was done collectively, and where each received according to needs—as far as was possible. Communards were supposed to combine cooking and eating facilities to conserve fuel and food and domestic labor and to attend regular meetings. Further statements of 1919, 1926, and 1930 gradually reduced the extent of communal activity and life, apparently adjusting to realities. Periodic conferences of commune delegates discussed ways to improve communal forms of life. Some Bolsheviks, notably Yury Larin, opposed the commune as an ideal form of agricultural organization and preferred instead the *Sovkhoz* or State Farm—essentially an attempt to industrialize or urbanize farming. In the popular *ABC of Communism*, Bukharin and Preobrazhensky delivered a qualified endorsement of the commune as both progressive and practical. The major Bolshevik leaders remained ambivalent, though not hostile, to the commune idea until the end of the 1920s.[15]

The commune movement grew rapidly during the Civil War, taking on a broad range of forms. At an early count (1918) there were already about 500–600 communes with over 13,000 members. Figures compiled by Robert Wesson in the 1960s show a steady rise of over 3,000 communes in 1921, a fluctuation between about 1,200 and 1,900 in the 1920s, a sharp rise during collectivization, reaching the peak of 7,600 in 1931. The growth was heavy in the Urals, the Northern Caucasus, and Siberia where partisan veterans played a big role.[16] The above figures suggest a massive social movement, yet it has never found a historian. Wesson's pioneering work is statistical and episodic, with little attention to the interior life of the communes. Soviet historical treatments are dry, critical, and demeaning—as they are to almost all of the experiments of the Revolution that did not survive into the 1930s.

Several levels of motivation were operating: voluntarism, economic need, and coercion. To the first level belonged religious communes and those of intellectuals, some workers, and committed ideologues, including foreigners. The purely intelligentsian communes were—like the sectarian ones—strongly motivated by lofty ideals but apparently not as well equipped to survive the rigors of remote rural life. Economic need seems to have been a major force for poor peasants, workers who fled the towns during the Civil War, and special groups of detached and floating elements: veterans, old people, children, widows, and unmarried mothers. Those subjected to coercion or semi-coercion were orphans, abandoned children, juvenile delinquents, and correctable criminals.[17]

What set communalism off from other cooperative forms of agriculture in those years was the sharing of all nonpersonal property, distribution according to need, communal housing and dining, and symbolic or ideological statements. Common housing and services were virtually identified with the word "commune." According to Wesson's figure, eighty percent of the communes were so arranged, although the physical shape and nature of the living space is not indicated. Scraps of evidence show that when communes were established in abandoned or confiscated manor houses, a communal living arrangement was introduced. When villages were transformed into (or renamed as) communes, this was less likely. Communal residence—so essential to utopian dreamers—seemed less central in rural areas where space, after all, was plentiful. From one-fifth to about one-third of the rural communes possessed preschool institutions where mothers rotated as nurses and teachers. Only two percent had collective laundries. Contemporary commentators observed that communal dwelling tended to reinforce other forms of cooperation and that living in individual cabins and households tended toward the opposite—family egoism, local despotism, and a low communal consciousness.[18]

Communal dining could and did take place in the absence of communal dwelling. It was the official ideal, but only about half the communes had it in 1925, and it declined further on in the decade in spite of constant appeals such as one for "the collectivization of everyday life and the liquidation of the domestic hearth and housekeeping which sustains and feeds a backward mentality" as well as oppressing women. In peasant traditional households, the family supped from a common bowl in the middle of the table—but daughters-in-law cleaned off their "own sector" of the table. Family community thus mingled with atomism. When communal kitchens were set up, big fights exploded among the women over functions and territory. And in most peasant communes, only women performed this work. Some communes achieved a clever solution by communalizing meals in the growing season when almost everything was done outdoors—in other words, picnic meals transported to the field. In winter the individual kitchen came back into play.[19]

Unlike peasants in the ordinary *obshchina,* rural communards pooled their land and worked it together instead of dividing it into roughly equal sets of strips. Shame and social pressure were applied to shirkers. In one case, a lazy member was forbidden to work for three days and constantly greeted with the words, "How did you sleep?" The Red Lighthouse Commune on a barren steppe in Southern Russia, composed of poor and landless peasants, began their commune's distribution with complete "need communism" and an open storehouse for all to take from. This was also a complete residential and dining commune. Later, the wage was tied to labor performed. This seems to have been a pattern: need (often meaning equal shares to each "eater") in the early years giving way to pay according to workdays later on.[20]

Commentators noted that rural communal consciousness was distinctly lower than urban. When it was high, it took the form of self-conscious statements such as those of interviewees in the remote Down with Fraud Commune in the Altai District of Southern Siberia who said: "I see in [the commune] the future happiness of workers and peasants" and its goal to "eliminate egoism and set up equality." In Wheatsheaf Number 1 Commune in the Yamburg District (near the Baltic), the words "my" and "mine" were abolished. In the Proletarian Will Commune, all surnames were abolished, all were known as Proletwill *(Proletvolya),* and everyone wore identical straw hats and clothes.

Although such instances were rare, the naming of communes was not. Commune signs bearing such designations as Brotherhood, Will, Hope, Paradise, Proletarian, Karl Marx, Lenin, Rosa Luxemburg, Hammer, Red Orphan, Paris Commune, Anthill, and Free World began to adorn a countryside that was unused to signs or names—especially alien, urban ones. The names themselves hardly differed from those of city streets and factories—but their presence was another physical symbol of the urbanist presence in the rural world.[21]

Communal life in the countryside was fraught with insecurity, tensions, and hardship. Withdrawal and emigration mark the chronicles of rural communes in Russia as they do in other societies. Sometimes this arose from initial misunderstanding by the joiners about what life in a commune entailed (compulsory work for all, the divestment of all one's goods) and sometimes from an overly authoritarian leader—though a strong and charismatic leader was noted as the mark of a successful commune—again, as in many other societies. Urban workers sometimes suffered from the isolation and boredom of country life. Perils from the outer world compounded the inner malaise: during the Civil War, communes were attacked by Whites, Greens, and "bandits" or kulaks. Sometimes whole communes were wiped out by hostile elements. Even in peacetime, peasant enmity could be evoked simply by the proximity of a *kommuna* with an outlandish name, strange rites of Octobering, agricultural successes, the receipt of coveted land from the government for communal use, or the spectacle of city types and emancipated women.[22]

High motivation helped the growth of foreigners' communes—about 25–30 of them in the 1920s. They were founded by returned radicals and sympathizers, settling mostly on the Don and in the Ukraine. Americans formed the largest number: they clustered according to geographic origins and gave their communes such names as Labor (Boston), Harold (Chicago), Proletarian Life (Cleveland), California-on-the-Don, Seattle (composed of Finnish-American immigrants), New World, and John Reed. Others were formed by radicals or P.O.W.s from among Czechs, Austrians, Canadians, Australians, and Estonians. Lenin hoped to plant an American commune in each district of rural Russia as a model—a tribute to their zeal and apparent efficiency. But many of them ran aground over poor supply, lack of land and other hardships. A French commune, settled in the far Ladoga territory by Victor Serge and a handful of friends, started out with hundreds of acres of land, some cattle, and a manor house. Local peasants called them "Jews" and "Anti-Christs," and after three months the commune collapsed.[23]

Two groups prominent among the non-peasant communal population were veterans and women. If the example of Weimar Germany is a guide, many veterans of that time seemed to wish a prolongation if not of military experience then of the bonding attachments they had made in service. German veterans signed up in private Freikorps armies and many also went in teams into industry or to the vast Junker estates of the East. The *partizanshchina* of the Civil War in Russia generated a similar myth and emotional bond—particularly in the new urban atmosphere introduced by private capitalism in 1921 as the war ended. Commune life was a way of continuing the struggle and a way to make a living after the return of unemployment in Soviet Russia. The Red Lighthouse, made up of veterans of Budënny's cavalry army, was a successful example of this mentality: it grew from 50 to 2,000 members and from tents to buildings by the end of the 1920s. Single or widowed women similarly found solace and refuge in each others' company and set up all-female independent communes for themselves. In all these cases, there is no way to draw the line of motivation among economic hardship—

which was prodigious throughout the whole period—personal and emotional bonding, and utopian ideology.[24]

A group that has received much attention in specialized literature on penology and pedagogy were the orphans, abandoned children *(besprizorniki)*, and young criminals. Colonies of them were fashioned into little "republics" by imaginative teachers. The internal structure of the lives of inmates resembled ordinary communalism: absence of property, rotating and collective labor, the sharing and pooling of all goods and services, and communal sleeping and dining. The differences were also obvious: control and discipline imposed from above, non-voluntary entry, and sometimes rigid scheduling of lives as in an army or prison. Some colonies nonetheless achieved notable success in introducing self-government to unruly members, a sense of community and pride, and preparation for the world outside.[25]

The most successful communes on the land were not so much products of the Revolution as byproducts. These were the religious communes—the old ones that were given new life and the new ones formed after 1917. Although the main historical source for them is apologetic, some of it is confirmed by contemporary Soviet sources who praised the diligence and enthusiasm of sectarian communes. They were the most consistently communalist, resisting the growing tendency to reward according to labor days. Run by various sects, including Theosophists, Anthroposophists, Tolstoyans and an assortment of Christian denominations, their motivation was religious devotion. They opposed accounting, bureaucracy, and outside interference—often shutting themselves off from the world. All goods were held in common except clothing. Families were kept intact—though some were ascetic and segregated the sexes, and at least one was described as sharing women and children. Some of them showed an authoritarian, even theocratic streak, with rigid codes of behavior under a stern leader (who in one case was a woman). In the White Vestries Commune everyone used the word *ty* for personal address and all wore white. In the Stranden Commune which, like most of them, was named after its leader, its intelligentsia members—Theosophists and gnostics—elected officers, maintained separate homes for families and dormitories for singles, mandated religious freedom, practiced vegetarianism, and opposed the use of machines and money.[26]

Some religious communes looked to the Soviet regime as one that would allow them to practice their own brand of confessional communard life—in contrast to the persecuting Old Regime. Some called themselves true communists, identified their ultimate goal with that of the Bolsheviks, and engaged in social mimicry (see Chapter 5). The Bolsheviks, especially Lenin, were surprisingly friendly towards these institutions, often seeing them as admirable experiments in communism and willing to give them free berth. During the five-year plan, however, the collectivization campaign brought an end to all communes, replacing them eventually with the Collective Farm that was more directly administered by the state and based upon wholly different principles of ownership, control, and internal life. The anti-God campaigns that accompanied this drive in the countryside also meant the forceful, sometimes brutal, dispersion and closing of all the religious communes as well—with no consideration given either to motivating ideals or level of performance and success.

## Communes in the Town

In 1931, physicians at the Institute of Sanitary Culture published a study of youth communes in Soviet cities. In a rather rigid typology, they spoke of three kinds: the production commune in which members worked together and shared their wages with varying degrees of equity (equal, or according to "need"), the production-residence commune wherein members both worked and lived together, and the residential commune whose members worked in various places (or if in the same place not on communal terms) but lived together communally. On the basis of a wide sampling of living styles, their study showed that the communards were drawn together by material need, the housing shortage in the towns, the chance to secure better meals, the desire for family-like companionship and the warmth of intimacy with friends, and an enthusiasm for the experimental remaking of man.[27] There is of course no way of knowing how the weight of these motivations was assorted. Clearly some members saw communes as a concrete life experiment that would blossom into the communalization of all society. The most successful urban communes were usually the result of careful planning by a close-knit group of people, and the successes they enjoyed were money management, hygiene, collective habits, and dietary planning. Some of them adopted rough and ready methods of group therapy in order to "open up" shy members. The history of urban communes corresponded almost exactly with that of other experimental movements—from soon after the Revolution to the early 1930s when they dissolved.

Communalism in the cities and towns unfolded in three main phases: a rash of House Communes in the Civil War period, a more deliberate and self-conscious movement of students and workers in the 1920s, and a big wave of communal production teams during the first five-year plan. The first stage was marked by sporadic and unplanned occupation of vacated and confiscated houses during the Revolution. Between 1918 and 1924, 500,000 people in Moscow and 300,000 in Petrograd were rehoused. There are no figures for House Communes in Petrograd, but in 1921 there were 865 in Moscow and 242 in Kharkov. According to an architectural historian, they had common kitchens, dining rooms, kindergartens, nurseries, red corners, reading rooms, and laundries. A Petrograd commune in 1919 had 230 members, and a commune of workers at the Kiev Arsenal Works, 80—though these were atypically large. Under War Communism, even those who did not live in communes could avail themselves of public (and often free) feeding in a network of cafeterias opened by the state. Sources are silent about life inside these early House Communes, but a western observer in 1921 noted that when the masses took over a thirty room house in Moscow, they divided themselves into separate rooms, with their own cooking and heating arrangements on an each-for-himself basis. The communalism that grew out of the sudden housing revolution was not a massive ideological phenomenon.[28]

The student and worker communes began appearing after the Civil War as voluntary experiments in collective living. One of the most interesting and well-documented was the Leningrad Commune of 133, founded in 1924 by students of the Electrotechnical Institute inside their dormitory on Red Dawn Street in the Petrograd Quarter (See Fig. 37). The idea was born in the drama of a shared experience: emergency work during the great Leningrad flood of 1924. The intensity of this episode (like the camaraderie of war and revolution) cemented relations among many of the students, who then vowed to continue the epic of their friendship by sharing their lives in a commune. This illuminating genesis explains not only the initial cohesiveness of the communards but also the "generational" gap that arose when new members were drawn in. The flood episode was in a way a miniature version of the larger psycho-social schism in Soviet society between those who had lived through "October" and those who had not. Beneath the spiritual impulse that created the commune lay the eternal poverty of students—low incomes, low stipends—who saw bonding as a way to economize in the tradition of the older student communes and workers' artels. The members were heavily proletarian in background, and intermixed with poor peasants, veterans, orphans, and a minority of young women and non-Russian ethnic groups. The commune's chronicler, M. Yankovsky, frankly admitted that the founders saw communalism as a *phase of life,* not a blueprint for society; at the same time they wanted it to serve as an incubator for communists if not a model for communism.[29]

Occupying several floors of their dormitory, the 60 or so original communards (later expanding to 133) used the enlarged family as their model, embellished with general notions of fairness and equity rather than classical theory. Decisions were reached collectively, the majority ruling and coordinators periodically elected. Housework was rotated equally by duty roster. Space—as in a family—was proclaimed open, except for couples and females. To this initial plan, a fiery "leftist" woman objected and her view prevailed: saws and hammer were put to the walls creating a spatially open commune, without privacy. Collectivism within this communal space was further enhanced by three institutions. The Shop Without a Clerk was a table full of study supplies and minor notions available to members on the honor system (they would help themselves, leave some money, or sign their names). The Customs Commission inspected all incoming parcels—particularly the food packages sent from the village—and divided their contents among the communards (how a single smoked fish could be shared among 60 or 133 eaters is not made clear). The Underwear (or Bedlinen) Trust was a collective laundry basket to which all contributed at the weekly bath and drew from when it was laundered.[30]

Communal life was accompanied by a continuous democratic talkfest, erupting occasionally into major issues—some of them admittedly insoluble. The "Battle of the Budget" was the first of these. Some members, receiving higher stipends, claimed to have more expenses and greater "needs" and were disinclined to put all their assets into the common fund. A division arose between the "masses" and "the privileged" (the debates were always couched in a semi-ironic revolutionary idiom), the former proclaiming the principle "from each according to ability—to each according to needs," but (in violation of the classic canon) disallowing "special needs." A compromise was forged by confiscating seventy-five percent of net stipends (after deductions for communal expenses). This was later revised downward—thus allowing a reasonable degree of flexibility and inequality.[31]

A second controversy was introduced by the N.O.T.ists *(notovtsy),* also called Models or Leftists, the Soviet Taylorists who wanted the regulation of all communal life according to a strict timetable and who insisted that members account for every minute of the day by hanging time talons on a public schedule in the living room. The surrendering of private time was thus added to the sacrifice of private space. The N.O.T.ists also wanted all personal property collectivized—right down to underwear. They further insisted on the indivisibility of love, friendship and comradeship—no couples, no cliques, no bilateral friendships, only the "general comradeship" of the entire commune to be reflected not only in daily personal behavior but also in leisure time activities in which the entire group should engage collectively (for example, group attendance at movies and theater). The N.O.T.ist despotism of norms became so oppressive that the majority called it a "reign of terror," a "sword of N.O.T." suspended over the commune. The annoying movement apparently faded after the dissolution of its mother organization, the League of Time, in 1925 and we hear no more about it.[32]

The problem that defied solution in this commune—and in most others—was sexual relations. Women were a minority in the Commune of the 133, though one served as president for a time. Equality of sexes was the declared norm, and to some men this included the legitimization of foul language in the presence of females. Sexual life was difficult and varied in scope. Some married—within the commune or outside of it. Some took their sex life outside; some abstained altogether. Few were satisified with their sexual lives. The open door policy interfered with sexual activity and the commune clearly preferred "order" and celibacy to the rampant hooliganism that prevailed in most student dorms of the time. Marriages and babies were permitted but regretted by some as divisive. According to an internal poll, sixty five percent engaged in short-term affairs (though preferring longer ones or even marriage), some were celibate, and most believed that the "sexual question" was insoluble inside the commune. In practice this meant a considerable level (there are no figures) of migration and turnover.[33]

How did the communards view their experiment after the first half decade? Yankovsky and other candid critics believed that the routine of their lives was improved in the realm of work habits, order, political and technical education and a certain amount of "collective spirit." Comradeship and brotherhood as such, however, fell below the original goals due to persistent privatism, egoism, and the divisive issues outlined above. Study habits (as opposed to work habits) and sexual life were not improved by life in the commune. The moral tone did not ascend to the desired level—which was perhaps unrealistically high; students periodically "confessed" to feelings of xenophobia, hostility to other members, and even (in a single case) anti-Semitism. Yet this commune caught the attention of commentators at the end of the decade, and other communes in Leningrad were modeled on it. Its subsequent history is not known, though one must assume that it shared the fate of all commune-like organisms in the early thirties.[34]

Built on a similar pattern, the smaller Moscow youth commune (1924–32) described by the eyewitness Klaus Mehnert originated also in the desire to prolong a network of friendship (of ten male and five female recently graduated schoolmates) in the more structured setting of a commune. Its political system was the open meeting recorded in a journal, with committees handling finance, shopping, domestic order, and academic matters. All property, including personal, was held "in fee" and thus returnable to the commune upon departure. The question of work produced some novel arrangements. After an era of "chaos" with rotational and collective housekeeping, the commune hired a peasant woman as a fulltime housekeeper, justifying this as specialization of labor. Work details were employed as punishments. Although equality of sexes in duties was in force, men were not trusted with delicate domestic tasks and a female "laundry commissar" policed the amateur ironing of the males. Space was very limited (two bedrooms, a living room, a "clubroom," and a kitchen) and no privacy was available.

For the first two years, sex was simply outlawed. But nature asserted itself, and soon marriages bloomed and children appeared against the opposition of a communard who said that "marriage would mean the formation of a group within the commune and a still further shock to the unity of the commune." Sex, marriage, and divorce, however, continued to come under collective scrutiny. In one divorce case, when a husband left his wife, an angry female communard commented: "Vladimir is a swine." As in the Commune of the 133, the Moscow commune suffered from sexual tension, arguments over shared incomes, and turnover (one who moved out simply explained, "I want to be alone"). On the credit side, Mehnert recorded a visible advance among members in subordinating private ego to communal need and a marked improvement in personal hygiene (a weekly bath) over that of other students of the time.[35]

In the second half of the twenties, the student commune movement began to catch on—at least in Moscow and Leningrad. The Komsomol promoted the commune idea and thus helped it to spread. In Leningrad, one of the biggest (275 students) appeared at the Herzen Pedagogical Institute. In Moscow a small group at the Timiryazev Agricultural Academy, hearing about another commune, formed its own in 1928, rotating the preparation of breakfast every morning. From a 1929 commune at the Central Medical Technicum in Moscow, the example spread to almost all the other students. And at the Moscow Mining Academy, communards set out to fashion a new man—"a genuine communard"—by means of ordered life, collective sensibility, and shared tasks and property—even though these particular communards were dispersed in separate rooms all over the dormitory. Collectives and communes of all sorts appeared, often created for special purposes—dining, residence, pooling resources, or sharing duties. And they fell apart just as quickly, according to an observer of the mid-1920s.[36]

The pattern that emerges is that of practical need, deep Russian traditions of artels and student organizations, the hard conditions of student life, the appeal of friendship and solidarity, the natural and built-in "collective" nature of the student dormitory (obshchezhitie) of any type, and the possibility of adorning all of this with an ideological and idealistic flourish. But beyond this was the deeply held belief that some sort of equality or equity in everyday life was part of the revolution that the students or their elders had fought for on the barricades and on the battlefields of the Civil War.

Urban workers' residential communes appeared at about the same time as those of students. The first recorded was the Bakhmetevskaya Commune, so named after a street in Moscow. Workers of three factories joined together in 1924 in a residential commune resembling in form those of students: regular schedules, pooling of wealth, the hiring of a cook. With its seventeen workers living in two large rooms, the Bakhmetevskaya Commune strikingly resembled the workers' residential and eating artels of the early 1900s, right down to "collective" leisure activity. But the revolutionary cultural overlay shone through in the way the communards shared their leisure: they marched everywhere together in ranks of four "as in a demonstration [revolutionary parade]," with a leader at the front and the entire formation singing as they moved along, a show of solidarity for public consumption and an outward mark of pride in the community they were building inside the walls of their rooms. And yet this commune, after only a year and a half, collapsed over an embezzlement episode and the influx of newer members. A similar artel-like commune in Moscow made a point of total pooling and equality of incomes and also insisted on maintaining outer links to Soviet society—as against the isolation and withdrawal it apparently saw in other communes. It was still functioning in 1930.[37]

The best-known of the workers' communes of this era and the most remarkable in its ambition and its record was the so-called A.M.O. Commune, officially the "Residential Commune of the Proletarian District," founded in 1928. It originated at a summer dacha on the Volga where a group of coworkers in a Moscow factory rented a vacation house. A distinctive "camplife" style—familiar to scouts, church groups, the military, and all sorts of young vacationers—put its mark on this emerging urban commune. A close knit group of comrades, an easy and informal friendship unit, group activities and games, campfire singing, semi-organized marching and the constant assertion of moral purity and healthiness characterized Komsomol summer camps in the 1920s.[38] The experience of the six young men and four young women from Moscow led them to plan a permanent way of life modelled on their camp experience and enriched with large-scale ideological ambitions to develop a "collectivist" mentality and drive out the egoist strivings of their personalities. With the approval of the Komsomol organization and their factory—A.M.O. or Automotive Works of Moscow—the *amovtsy* amplified their number to twenty-four and secured half a floor (later two whole floors) of an apartment building for their communal experiment.[39]

Like many other communes, A.M.O. pooled only a portion of the members' incomes at first and then moved into full sharing of wealth—even though the range of wages ran from 25 to 200 rubles per month. A doctrine of total equality became operative and a "People's Commissar of Finance" regulated all expenditures. At first there was no provision for marriages among communards, but eventually those who married outside were permitted to bring in their spouses, thus solving at least part of the eternally vexing sexual problem—although the sources are mute on its other aspects. Since hiring a domestic (or any kind of labor) was designated as "shameful," the communards took their turns at housework. A time budget study reveals the average amount of time spent on daily activities.[40] Leisure time was filled with group attendance at theater, meetings, and concerts and with collective reading and discussion. A special combination of work and entertainment was arranged by having a string ensemble (from among the communards) perform while other members did the ironing—an exceptionally graphic demonstration of solidarity, fear of wasted minutes, and striving for cultural enhancement.

The apparent order and harmony that prevailed in this commune was doubtless the product of very careful preparation, an established sense of kinship, and a heavy commitment to ideological goals. The members' vision of the near future was to occupy the entire building in which they lived (their number had grown to sixty by 1930), and build a central cafeteria, "factory kitchen," children's town, reading room, gymnasium, laundry, repair room, and theater—in other words a full House Commune of the kind fashioned so often on their drawing boards by the architects of the 1920s. Beyond that, the communards of A.M.O. aspired to be a prototype for the communal order of the future, to replace the God-given family with a self-chosen family, and to "reorder the mode of life"[41] by acting as a conscious and visible model for collective living. In pursuit of this, they performed missionary work among their fellow workers and residents who lived in a noncommunal world.

A half dozen other workers' communes in the capitals are named in the sources. A few deserve comment. One imaginative group of workers—doubtless inspired by artel principles—consisted of five workers who held down four jobs while one of them rotated in the housework. A Leningrad commune of workers from three famous factories (Skorokhod, Red Triangle, and Red Putilov) set up their commune in a closed synagogue. A commune of library employees in Moscow created an "extreme" commune in which all clothing—including undergarments—was collectivized. According to Mehnert, if a communard preferred to wear his or her own underclothes "it would be characterized as a backslide into darkest capitalism; as prejudice originating in a petit-bourgeois ideology."[42]

Workers' urban residential communes were by no means confined to the two capitals (incomplete data record sixty of them in 1930), though the material on them elsewhere is less abundant. In far-away Nizhny Tagil in the Urals, two young Komsomols founded a commune with ten families in 1930 in a two story house formerly belonging to a merchant (see Fig. 38). Every member was required to participate in public activity in town or workplace. A common dining room, laundry, kitchen, and children's room provided the communal framework. Each family had its own room, but no food was allowed to be taken to it. All the women worked, but a nanny and cook were hired for domestic work. Guests were permitted to stay free of charge. Communards pooled their wages, gathered together at mealtime and in the evenings for discussions. This commune suffered the blows of massive reassignment of workers in 1932 and did not survive.[43] It was one of many that disappeared in the frenzy of the five-year plan.

Communalism in the workplace in the 1920s has only recently been given serious historical study—and there is little data on how many and what kinds of institutions employed wage-pooling techniques or leveling. Soviet historians consider the practice retrograde and even "parasitical," and Western historians have largely ignored it. But with the coming of the tremendous industrial drive of the first five-year plan, egalitarianism in general and communal or collective applications of it in production ascended into visible prominence from mid-1929 to mid-1930. Research has shown how the principles operated in production and how they related to the overall context of the industrialization process in the Soviet Union during those frantic years. The background was one of immense turmoil, unrealistic planning, arbitrary production norms, spontaneous enthusiasm of many workers, massive inflow of new labor recruits, the consequent dilution of skill level, high rates of vertical and horizontal labor mobility and turnover, a haze of utopianizing rhetoric, and a desperate emergency atmosphere—very much like the resumption of a war or revolution.

One of its byproducts was the birth of production collectives and communes—both related to the traditional artel, which also took on new life in this period. The production collective called for equal wages for equal skill levels or differentiated wages for varying skill levels—in other words the "socialist" principle of distribution according to the work performed. Production communes pooled equally and compensated according to family need. Ranging in membership from a half-dozen or less to hundreds of members, these production arrangements reached a probable peak of 134,030 collectives and communes (the former far outweighing the latter numerically). Bearing such names as Spark, Four-in-Five (i.e. the plan in four years), Our Frenzy, and Labor Front, they drew primarily from the ranks of shockworkers, especially in the metalworking and textile branches of industry. Personal statements and charters employed ideological language to depict their outlook. "We, sharing wages equally, bring ourselves closer to our comrades," said one of these. "Our aim . . . is a common life based on communist principles." In stressing their style of distribution according to need, the communards were forcefully expressing a desire to introduce the "communist form of labor" thus hoping to bypass the socialist phase.[44]

A few examples from the period may give a sense of the kind of motivation and activity displayed in these wage-sharing organisms (the terminology was fluid and often contradictory). The Mosstroi Commune in Dubrovka (near Moscow) was a labor gang converted to communalism by the A.M.O. commune: nine men and three women—skilled and unskilled—who shared only 70 percent of their earnings, recognizing in an illuminating admission, that *as recent peasants,* they could not be expected to reach fullscale pooling on an equal basis. The Sorokin Commune, made up of twenty technical students from the North Caucasus who migrated to an auto works in Nizhny Novgorod, achieved high norms, were mobile, young and healthy, and treated the work process as a game or a challenge to their energy. Their stress was on high productivity rather than the amenities of communal residence—indeed they worked twenty hours a day and ate and slept in two tents. At the Steel and Tractor City, north of Stalingrad, Anna Louise Strong visited a commune of young workers—twenty boys and twelve girls—living in two barracks where she was told that the communards engaged in "none of the petting and love-making." Like similar groups elsewhere, this one maintained an elitist identity and was accused by fellow workers of snobbery.[45]

Both the communes and collectives of production were rated high by observers for their "mutual responsibility, self-discipline, and organization," their "skill improving and consciousness raising activities," and "impressive productivity records." Their idealism can hardly be doubted, but—as in many utopian experiments of the time—a heavy admixture of practicality was in evidence. In the arena of struggle between workers, management, and state, productive collectives and communes and the artels helped spread the risk of lowered rates due to accident, inefficiency, poor coordination, or arbitrary measures of the bosses. Equality was not only noble, but, in the words of an artel member, it was "simply more advantageous." For a time, managers saw the utility of such formations in recruiting reliable and productive labor, and the regime gave qualified praise to their work. But eventually, a whole series of forces and circumstances (related in Chapter 11) brought them to an end; communalism and collectivism in the job were identified with harmful egalitarianism and autonomy, and by 1932 they had all but disappeared.[46]

## The Laboratory of the Revolution

What is the historical meaning of this remarkable movement of people into a life together and a sharing of its basic elements? Never in history did a society or a revolution produce such mass communalism. Hundreds of urban, thousands of rural, and tens of thousands of work communes sprouted across the vastness of the Russian land—in the form of phalansteries, apartments carved into open space, tents and barracks planted beside great steel works and power stations. Communalism was the major locus of revolutionary utopianism, the point where many other streams converged, where the banner of equality was flown most visibly and most honestly. Communards did not inhabit a fixed and static world of chilling stone and faceless robots, but a constantly moving and changing current of human beings. In the most difficult of physical circumstances in one of the poorest of the major countries of the world, they sought to construct through their own mental and moral toil the embryo and model of a better world. The communal movement of the Russian Revolution, for all its idiosyncracies and endless flaws, was a monument to the power of human hope and will.

Workers who visited an urban commune in the 1920s are reported to have said: "they live just like rich folks or like dwellers from another planet."[47] This was truth and irony. Although it was but a few steps from a conventional dormitory room to a commune located in the same building or on the same floor, the world of communards was indeed alien—repulsive and funny to some and appealing to others. The irony is in the contrast between the environments of science fiction utopias and architectural fantasies on the one hand and every day communal life on the other. The world of the former was one of sunlight, symmetrical design, and good order—even when skewed by lyrical curves and fanciful schemes; it was light, dry, clean, and cool. The world of real-life communards in town and country was bubbling with life, full of contrast and tension, electric with experimentation, noisy with debate, sometimes dirty and disorderly, often darkened by poverty and disappointment, heated by anger, and moistened with tears.

As a social incubator or condenser—that is, an environment for reshaping consciousness—the living commune was both more ambitious and more realistic than the House Commune. The latter was a shell built to contain a collection of families with additional space for the growth of community; the former aspired to build a surrogate family and not an assembly of nuclear families. "We saw the commune as a family and not a dormitory," said a communard of the 1920s.[48] The N.O.T.ists, on the extreme wing of the movement, wanted to insure this permanently by banning interior families, marriages, and friendships for the sake of the big collective comradeship. This attempt to subordinate primary intimacy to larger group loyalty went hand in hand with their rigid scheduling, segregation, and "scientific organization of life," as it did with dogmatic architects such as Kuzmin and the social architects of Zamyatin's United State. Most of the communards were less rigid and allowed marriage and coupling within the communes—though fearing that this would dilute communal love. Bowing to reality with troubled consciences, they made a blend of the pure commune and the House Commune—a communal family giving birth to biological families.

From this point, communards divided into those who wanted the commune to be a collective parent by having the children around, and those who dreamed of evolving into a House Commune, with special rooms, floors, or "towns" for the little ones. Resistance to the conventional family was weakly based: it did not account for the fact that family relations are ordinarily built around "irrational" and unqualified love; and that artificially built human organisms require contract and calculation—as did all the communes. Communes that most closely resembled "families" were those founded on a shared experience which—like a courtship and marriage—generated a kind of mutual affection and trust approaching that of connubial relations. Given the complexities (not all of them clearly visible to the participants), the very fact that communes combining family and community survived is something of a social miracle.

Participants in communal life constantly spoke in terms of creating a "new personality . . . new comradely relations, new forms of friendship" and of the commune as "the prototype of future socialist life" or as a "factory for the refashioning of psychology."[49] In the nineteenth century, the Slavophile Konstantin Aksakov had described the peasant *mir* as "a union of the people who have renounced their egoism, their individuality, and who express their common accord."[50] He called it a religious act of love. In the absence of a conventional religious impulse, the more idealistic of the Soviet communards were attempting to achieve a life of "common accord" that would bring the ideal of communism down into everyday life where—they thought—it belonged. Schools, the army, and even prisons taught varying degrees of brotherhood and solidarity—but the commune was the only place where it was a central concern, the chief pedagogical product of its classroom. For the many who saw communal life as a temporary stage (until graduation or marriage), communalism was a curriculum for life and a new secular religion. This is why communards were so prominent in the fight against conventional religion and in missionary work among their non-communal comrades and fellow workers or students.[51]

The role of egalitarianism in communal life illustrates once again the importance of flexibility and synthesis in utopian experimentation in this period. Equality was not only a stated goal; it was applied with great thoroughness in all kinds of situations. But when human resistance gained force, communal groups sensibly if reluctantly bent their ideological heads to the human condition. Again and again we read of heated debates followed by compromises on space, privacy, sexual life, the use of time, super-efficiency, and friendship patterns. There was no uniformity among the communes—urban or rural, residential or labor—but rather a kaleidoscopic variety testifying to a kind of revolutionary pragmatism. The commune movement is the most vivid illustration of revolutionaries surging into the realm of communism and backing off into socialism—sometimes contriving a workable fusion of the two. Even the briefest comparison of communal life in the 1920s with that of the prerevolutionary past exhibits the obvious similarity between the two, made more interesting by the way innovations were grafted onto traditions by means of rhetoric and symbol. Most important, and most visible of all, was the demonstration in communal experiments of the "utility of utopianism," the combination under certain circumstances—especially tolerance by the authorities—of morally idealistic and perfectionist schemes with modes of convenience and survival. Paradoxical as it may sound, utopianism's offensive against reality was at the same time a defensive mechanism for living in that reality.

There was apparently a high correlation between ideological commitment or level of spirit in the commune and its material success. The religious communes of Sectarians, it was widely observed, had no trouble with initiative and hard work: their binding principle was faith. According to the fullest source on urban communes, the unselfish principles of the communards correlated with outstanding production records. Thus, he claimed, there was no conflict between "utopian" distributive principles of the commune and incentive. The evidence for production collectives and communes of the five-year plan points in the same direction.[52] In a larger sense, the commune movement was part of the current of grass-roots Soviet and party democracy, workers' control, group autonomy, localism, and self-administration that swept through the Revolution and was eventually defeated by it. The major "opposition" forces within the party had made claims about the power of workers' creativity from below, and their claims were denied by the party leadership. Communalism in all its forms illustrated that workers, students, and peasants could manage their own affairs under the banner of equity in small groups and still deliver both unyielding loyalty to the regime and an adequate social surplus.

The chronicles of communal life—town and country—are full of failure. But those that survived into the 1930s must be counted a success. Under a multitude of circumstances and in myriad ways, communes produced enough to stay alive in the villages and sometimes outstripped their neighbors in productivity and material standards of living. Even in instances where the motivation was almost purely economic, communes offered a haven in the midst of furious revolutionary turmoil and war. The fact that communes were often the last resort for the social detritus of the times does not diminish their positive role. Joiners who openly voiced a utopian culture building motive for entering the communal life occasionally agitated for a nationwide network of communes as the sole path to imminent communist society. But this was by no means a general agenda for communalism. "We must keep in mind," wrote Naishtat, "that new human relations are not created outside time and space. In order to create them we must have a corresponding technical and productive base''[53]—a cautionary note eminently suitable for the time when it was written (1931).

The founders of urban communes envisaged them as a kind of school or training camp—or perhaps therapy center—where communards would learn about the joys and perils of communal life by actually living it. In this sense they belonged to those innovators who wanted to act out the meaning of revolution rather than merely writing, speaking, or dreaming about it. As difficult and problematic as their lives in the commune may have been, we find there an exhilaration and a moral level higher than in the surrounding milieu. In this regard, the worker and student communards of the 1920s were the true descendents of the first generation of the revolutionary movement, the radicals of the 1860s who were inspired by Chernyshevsky's utopia and by his characters who acted out their values in their everyday lives and in the collective institutions they founded. Chernyshevsky had urged his readers that the only way to ascend from the depths of a corrupt reality to the kingdom of tomorrow is to live the values of the future today. After 1917, utopians in general and communards in particular were often told that the Revolution was not yet ready for them, that society would have to wait for the dawning of a new day to see their ideals realized. But these utopians knew what the wise and prudent realists did not know: that the best way to begin a revolution in the human spirit was in the everyday.

How popular was communalism? Among the peasantry, it clearly appealed to a minority—as had the popular social utopia in the past. The dream of most peasants had always been and still remained in the 1920s to be left alone by the state, with all the land managed and rotated in their own tradition of the *mir-obshchina*. Nevertheless thousands of peasants chose the commune, as they understood it, as an alternate way of life, as did dedicated urban elements. Urban communalism, more visible and ideological, was also a minority movement, though the evidence seems to suggest that it was growing—especially in the productive life—in the midst of the five-year plan. The intelligentsia, ironically enough, played a small role in this: a handful of intelligentsia communes in the countryside and the occasional commune of avant-garde figures. The vast majority of practicing communards, town and country, were of the lower classes: peasants, workers, and proletarian students.

*Kommuna* was not an exotic word in the 1920s; it was becoming part of everyday discourse, an increasingly familiar form of life. This does not mean that it would ever have succeeded in winning over the bulk of the population, but only that it was an acceptable and familiar life alternative of the time, a legitimate locus for the voluntary study and testing of communism. Until 1931–32, the state, though sometimes ambivalent and selective, took a positive view of this activity. It financed rural communes, gave them land and preferential treatment, saw them as models for the distant future or as present modes of easing the housing crisis in the towns. When the state turned against communalism as a utopia, it invoked all of its weaknesses, ignored its successes, and cast it into the abyss of historical oblivion along with almost all of the culture building and visionary schemes of the revolutionary era.

# PART IV

---

## Dreams and Nightmares

# 11

---

## War on the Dreamers

The revolution is merciless not only toward those who lag behind it but also toward those who run ahead of it.                          N. V. Ustryalov

### The End of Revolutionary Utopia

Revolutions are often merciless to those who run ahead of them, as Ustryalov suggests in the quotation cited above. An anti-Bolshevik émigré living in Manchuria, he was arguing for a "normalization" of the Revolution and a return to certain traditional Russian values. But this clever truism raises further questions: who speaks for the "revolution" and has the power to do so? When do they begin reining in and punishing those who are running ahead? In the 1920s, some Bolshevik leaders wanted to and tried to rein in the "utopian" elements, but they had limited success. Around the end of the decade, the new leader Stalin emerged and began an emphatic repudiation of all utopian currents and humanistic experiments. Future speculation and living experimentation had been able to flourish for about a decade for two reasons: during the Civil War, many of its impulses simply corresponded with the mood of War Communism; and the N.E.P. period of 1921–28 provided a hospitable political, social, and cultural context. Until 1924, Lenin was in power (though incapacitated a few years earlier) and his relative tolerance and ambivalence about the movements outlined in this book guaranteed their survival. After his death, the internal struggle for the succession (1924–28) and the economic and foreign policy crises of the late 1920s diverted the leadership away from what were always considered marginal matters. The N.E.P. system played a dual role in sustaining utopianism: the relative laxity and pluralism on the social landscape protected it; the more loathsome features of a revived bourgeois culture in the cities helped to fuel it as a counterweight to "Soviet capitalism." The emergence of Stalinist system put an end to N.E.P. and its social pluralism.

But could these experiments have survived even under an alternate form of Soviet power—one headed by Trotsky or Bukharin, for instance? There is no way of answering this question because we cannot know what problems they would have faced or created for themselves. Trotsky's program of "superindustrialization" and his militarization of society seem ominous, yet he favored many of the moods and experiments of his time. Bukharin's insistence on gradualism and a prolongation of the N.E.P. and private peasant agriculture indicates a strong sense of moderation. Neither seemed to augur the savage butchery of Stalin's political style or his despotic self-deification. On the other hand, it is by no means clear that the various notions and movements of experimental life in the 1920s would have survived under any regime. The harshness of economic realities and backwardness might have created a sharply negative attitude toward egalitarianism and thus undercut other schemes. Realpolitik, social pragmatism, exhaustion, or even cynicism had coexisted with utopianism all through the revolutionary decade. They may well have grown in the 1930s even without the special and hostile anti-utopian edge of Stalinism.

Euphoria, culture building, and visionary idealism are human attitudes that are hard to sustain over a long period—whether or not the environment is hostile or sympathetic. Russian revolutionary utopianism was a discrete historical phenomenon lasting a little more than a decade. All its currents flowed from a widely held belief by people of many social classes that human nature could be transformed by the spontaneous action of people acting out the good and the rational inside themselves. Beyond this was the familiar belief, shared by all kinds of optimists and idealists, that mankind was fundamentally good, that bad institutions and evil political and economic systems inhibited that goodness from expressing itself in the "natural" state of brotherhood. In intellectual content, the Russian utopia did not greatly diverge from the European enlightenment tradition. However, its forms and styles were specifically Russian, for it drew its inspiration from a whole array of indigenous traditions, customs, myths, and aspirations. What made the moment so extraordinary was the interaction among divergent currents flowing from common people, radical intelligentsia, cultural figures, and state functionaries in a kaleidoscopic and eclectic panorama of Russian life. The continuous coexistence of utopian speculation about the future and the life experiments on the ground is what sets this period off so drastically from what was to come. Utopianism, like religion, ambition, and ideology, is a vision, a plan, a blueprint for things to come— in distant times or in a foreseeable future. It implies deferment of any fundamental reorganization of human behavior for the moment. Social experimentation, though aroused by utopian longings, is in a temporal sense its opposite; it operates in the present tense in the realm of moral life, culture building, and even the spiritual enjoyment of social creativity.

Stalinism was not simply a negation of utopianism. It was a rejection of "revolutionary" utopianism in favor of a single utopian vision and plan, drawn up at the pinnacle of power and imposed on an entire society without allowance for autonomous life experiments. Stalinism did not aspire to transform human values; it accepted them as they were—and in the peculiar way that Stalin himself perceived them to be. There would be no pluralism and spontaneity, no separate experiments, and no belief in the inner goodness of man. Stalin's utopian design, reinforced by many elements of Russian society and culture, was a crueler mode of thinking based on a view of a man as sinful, evil, potentially criminal, lazy, or stupid; it suggested, therefore, the arts of coercion, authoritarianism, brutality.

The utopian experimenters of the 1920s attempted to build a socialist counterculture from the inside out and the hot-headed "anti-dreamers" wanted a comprehensive leap into modernization and socialism. In the early 1930s, the latter came into power. Their goals were the subordination of all other "socialist" currents and physical energies to the tasks defined by the regime: the rapid industrialization of the country, the abolition of private economy and civil society, and the collectivization of the peasantry. Their means were centralized organization, a command economy, a militarization of work, and a supremely authoritarian political culture. The first five-year plan and its immediate aftermath witnessed constantly changing and extravagant goals, a headlong pace called "Bolshevik tempo," and *sturmovshchina* or assault methods of production, in short the abandonment of all the varied, autonomous revolutionary utopian strivings in favor of the single utopia of Stalinism.

Stalin's revolution from above launched two forces that turned out to be ephemeral, and it laid the base of a more permanent system. The two forces, both fueled by emotion, were spontaneous euphoria and terror. The first, a burst of enthusiasm for construction and transformation, lasted from 1928 into the mid-thirties. It resembled the revolutionary euphoria of 1917 in the number of people it infected; for those who experienced it, it was part of the golden age of the Revolution. The terror, triggered by the murder of Sergei Kirov in 1934, remained in place right up to the death of Stalin, though it peaked in 1936–38. The two were often joined—as in the semi-military occupation of villages by urban forces during the collectivization campaign. The euphoric and millenarian wave affected utopianism by renewing the spirit of imminent transformation and by pitting utopian currents against the state and against each other. The terror, by hanging over society like a sword, rendered the de-utopianizing of the Revolution swift and final. But it was the economic and political system that arose during and after the plan and its social and cultural values that sentenced revolutionary utopia to death. This system erected the new utopia of Stalinism and surrounded it with many traditional elements of the past. The partial "traditionalizing" of the Stalin revolution was a complex amalgam of Stalin's whim and taste, the new ruling class's longing for order and familiarity, and the lingering habits and values of the masses.

## Iconoclasm, Festival, Godbuilding

In the storm of physical destruction and psychological assault that marked the cultural revolution of 1928–31, the old tensions were present but under new conditions. Now the state itself took a more active part in vandalizing treasures of old Russian culture, especially religious buildings. This "offensive" possessed both a physical and a symbolic side; it was largely managed by the authorities—though in a confused and uncoordinated way. Under the ruthless fist of Lazar Kaganovich, the city boss, Moscow witnessed the wholesale destruction of churches and antiquities and the abolition of various preservation societies. The "demonumentalization" of the 1930s far surpassed that of the revolutionary period. A contemporary émigré reported indiscriminate demolition often based on ignorance. Whole cities were altered and the centers of others completely redone under the varying influences of Russophobia, a desire to anticipate Moscow's vandalistic wishes, anticlericalism, Stalinolatry (which led local officials to sweep away the old in order to erect monuments to the Leader), and constructomania. Ironically, some godless writers actually tried to preserve churches of extraordinary beauty or historical interest. Kopelev recalls a wave of "militant antinational nihilism" in 1930, an urge to exterminate the old way of life by blowing up churches and palaces, burning icons and old books, and purging libraries.[1]

Anti-intellectualism, still smoldering during the 1920s, erupted in full force during the five-year plan. It was an inherent component of the government's policies of social mobility, rapid promotion, and affirmative action on behalf of the lower classes, sharpened by the military tone of the entire epoch. During the Shakhty Trial of engineers in 1928, when specialists were accused of sabotage, suspicion toward them deepened in the population. This easily broadened into hostility towards intellectuals in general, professionals in particular, and established or successful people as a whole. The party leadership approved the zeal and tone of the anti-intellectual campaigns of this period for a while, then fell into ambivalence, and finally decided to curb it, punish some of its adherents, and protect its would-be victims on a selective basis—all of this reflecting the arbitrary judgments of the leaders. A Soviet writer in 1931 condemned Makhaevism as an expression of the "backward," "selfish," and "unproletarian" elements of the working class resulting from the alien social origin of most workers, the petty-bourgeoisie, and the peasantry. In 1938, *Pravda* condemned Makhaevism as "savage, hooligan, and dangerous to the Soviet State." Stalin was using the mechanics of social hatred and social prophylaxis of the time of Civil War, channeling the revolutionary energies of the masses into violence against the old privileged classes and thus away from the newly privileged. The Stalinist style of controlled anti-intellectualism was more conscious, contrived, and cynical than that of earlier years.[2]

In the realm of formal culture, some of the old battles were reenacted. The major figures of avant-garde and Proletcult were no longer on the scene. Bogdanov died (possibly of suicide) in 1928 during one of his utopian medical experiments, and Mayakovsky—for a variety of motives—shot himself in 1930. The moderating influence of Lunacharsky was also now absent: the Commissar of Enlightenment had become virtually inactive, had lost much of his influence over cultural policy, and died abroad in 1933—a more than likely target of Stalin's murderous purge had he survived into the late 1930s.

In the wake of the five-year plan, a new cohort of "proletarian" cultural advocates appeared in the form of organizations of proletarian writers, musicians and composers, architects, and others. With the apparent blessing of the authorities, the new "proletarians" waged a bitter war against alleged guardians of an old and hated cultural order. Using battlefield lexicon of assault, ambush, light-cavalry attack, siege and so on, they launched a scurrilous offensive against their enemies, exaggerating their flaws, using guilt by association, and employing every form of calumny. But the assault was stopped by the regime: the assailants were penalized; some of their victims were allowed to feel lashes and blows; others were gathered behind the protective wall of the party. And the entire scene was redefined in a context of the political control of cultural output, a fearful censorship, and a mobilization of art and culture for the stated purposes of the regime. In this, Stalin and his advisers went far beyond any of the controls created by Lenin and his successors in the 1920s. Artists who had been passive obeyers of a censorial system in the 1920s now became active servants of the state.

The transformation of Soviet public holiday celebration from a festival of revolution to a panegyric ritual of power and solidarity was the public emblem of the changing nature of the system and its supporting myths. Already present in the 1920s, the stiffening elements of ritual tightened from 1928 onward. The parade in Moscow and other cities became more rigidly organized, politicized, militarized, and standardized. Carnival was banished to other walks of life or eliminated altogether, and the content of the celebrations bristled with hostility to foreign foes, shaming of inferior workers, and hatred of traitors within. The November 7 holiday in Moscow in particular was organized as a cultic service to a semidivine leader, Stalin. This style migrated to other forms of public show, making Soviet Russia a kind of political spectacle state.

Foreign eyewitness accounts of the November 7 ceremonies on Red Square in the 1930s clearly indicate a steady militarization of the demonstration. The number of troops and variety of units deployed in front of the Kremlin rose steadily each year (falling off only in 1934 in consonance with a diplomatic peace and security campaign) and reached a peak in 1939. The number of overflying aircraft increased each year, darkening the early winter sky above the capital. A parade of tanks was added, and new hardware was introduced regularly to give metallic force to the human show of might. Spontaneity and local input to the urban parades gave way altogether to a single, carefully calibrated plan of march in which the armed forces were given pride of place but supplemented with immense marching units of the civilian population. Canned speeches delivered from a citywide network of loudspeakers replaced the lively oratory of the revolutionary years.[3]

In the content of Soviet national ritual, the dark frown of anger and hate replaced the carnival laugh. Some traces of buffoonery persisted in the ridicule of old-style enemies, but a new venom was brewed for the visual and aural attacks on the "enemies of the people" of the mid 1930s. Trotsky and his alleged internal collaborators (most of them purged, tried, and shot in 1936–38) were depicted as spiders and creeping vermin, friends of Fascism and of Japanese militarism. To guard against them, a huge mockup called "The Hedgehog's Mitten" (a play on the word "ëzh" or "hedgehog" and the name N. I. Ezhov, the principal agent of the purges in 1937) was borne across Red Square, a spiny fist to smite the vermin of treason. Every important political issue, productive campaign, or foreign event was given graphic publicity in the holiday parades and shows. Furthermore, the workers themselves were targeted by the festival managers: with signs and shouts they swore to their leaders to fulfill their plans, held up evidence of their recent achievements in the form of reproduction graphs, repeated work ethic oaths, displayed shame boards, and endorsed competition in the argot of combat. Festival was now a ritualized war against the lazy. Miniature repetitions of these themes of the Red Square parades were held on the Kreshchatik in Kiev, on Uritsky Square in Leningrad, and on Lenin Square in Minsk, resembling the mother ritual right down to format, scheduling, themes, slogans and songs, varying only in costume and in the promotion of certain local themes.[4]

One of the notable features of Soviet ritual in the 1930s was the separation of jollity from public ceremony, the latter being exclusively solemn and political. The rulers, while attending to the ritual performances as to a church service, separated their fun from public ritual, and thus from the people, in the form of Kremlin banquets, Stalin's all-night suppers, and dacha parties of the elite. The masses acted out the frolicking side of their lives in other arenas. A remarkable instance of popular carousing took place on the night of August 5–6, 1937. A Garden Carnival Party for 100,000 people was held in a Moscow park. Dressed in costumes and masks, the public danced to the waltz, the tango, and the fast and slow foxtrot; listened to the music of some 34–40 orchestras; and attended circus acts, plays, concerts, dance clinics, and other amusements. It was an event of pure entertainment drawing on the middlebrow culture of the tsarist past (a Gypsy dance) and of the West (a "big-band" playing "Rio Rita").[5]

Claude Lévi-Strauss has called ritual an "organically integral expression of myth and cult."[6] The ritual of the 1930s was precisely the expression of the cult of Stalin and the myths it comprised. While films, plays, poems, songs, and paintings glorified him as Leader *(vozhd)* and Boss *(khozyain)*, the public show on Red Square each year was the ultimate theatricalization of the Stalin cult.

On November 7, 1938, Stalin—like the high priest of an antique religion or dynastic despot of the age of absolutism—stood atop the tomb of Lenin, above the waxed cadaver of his hero and supported by it. He was flanked symmetrically by four leaders on each side. The veteran cavalry commander Semën Budënny brought his troops into the square for inspection by War Commissar Kliment Voroshilov. Speeches, salutes, and a review of military hardware followed. A whole panoply of weapons and armored vehicles swung by to a solemn march as 360 fighters and bombers flew over the square, the last of them forming the letters L E N I N in the skies. Civilian marchers flowed right behind the army to show the seamless solidarity of the civil and the military population. Workers bearing portraits of Lenin, Stalin and other leaders broke out in cheers for Stalin. The march was estimated at one and a half million people. On the previous evening at the Bolshoi Theater meeting of party notables, the very mention of Stalin's name brought the assembly to their feet shouting "Hurrah for our father and teacher, the Great Stalin" and "Long may he flourish—Our Stalin who has given us a happy life."[7]

From the perspective of the 1930s, the antireligious campaigns of the previous decade seem tame. The new war was launched during the first five-year plan and brought an end to the Godbuilding movement of the revolutionary period—the attempt to find new symbols and rituals of communist belief and a new moral code. A five year antireligious campaign was announced in 1928 and the League of the Godless—militant and resurgent after some quiescent years—met in congress in 1929 and deployed a network of agents to reach peasants, women, and Red Army men—special targets seen as vulnerable to traditional beliefs. Hostile literature and poster art again flooded the country. The assault on church buildings was intensified: thousands were closed or converted into parking lots, barber shops, and museums. Priests were arrested. The Godbuilding experiments of the 1920s, always weak in social roots and government support, fell as casualties along the way.[8]

To Lenin, Godbuilding had always been an odious utopia. At the end of his life he had asked Skvortsov-Stepanov, a leading atheist writer, to compose a little history of religion, exposing along the way the subtly-idealist and subtly-agnostic Kantian religions (he meant Godbuilding). Skvortsov himself had written in 1917 that "no artificial bond is needed for communist society; [it] is inherent in communist relations themselves." Many Bolsheviks apparently confused spirituality and emotional religiosity with the supernatural. Some Bolsheviks who admired the Dukhobors said to them: "We'll build communism on earth without 'spirit.'" Yaroslavsky, in a remarkable 1928 debate with an American philosophy professor who was urging the Soviets to join a universal movement of "moral and religious leadership" to replace the old religions, dryly remarked that the Bolsheviks did not need it since they were already morally superior to the West. Lunacharsky made it clear where he stood on the issue during a public debate in 1927 with the Renovationist clergyman Alexander Vvedensky (such debates being then still possible). He spoke of his "sins of youth" when, in *Religion and Socialism*, he had tried wrongly to read socialism into Christianity.[9]

At the end of the 1920s, the invented ceremonies of family and community fell into disuse. Club members seemed more intent on "closing all centers of these black, demoniacal forces" (i.e. churches) than on building a surrogate religious life in communism. Atheist symbols and rituals were aggressively deployed: in one school, children were made to practice labor skills by dismantling the iconostasis of a church; the seven day week was abolished partly in order to break the venerable sense of social time that had linked work, leisure, and religious life; Christmas trees were banned in 1928 and Santa Claus (Grandfather Frost in Russia) was unmasked as an ally of the priest and kulak. Decks of playing cards appeared illustrating in each suit the blemishes of Orthodoxy, Catholicism, Judaism, and Buddhism. To complete the cycle, anti-religious Carnivals were again unleashed on Christian holidays, attended by mockery and burning of icons. The sale of Christmas trees was again permitted in 1935, but these were now called New Years' trees.[10]

The debate on proletarian morality was abandoned around 1930. Some Communists called it "utopian" to lay the foundations of morality so early. The five-year plan left no time or energy for the exploration of the nuances of everyday conduct. Party leaders began to sneer at the whole enterprise. Kaganovich told Komsomols that it was silly to spend so much time arguing over whether or not communists should smoke. By that time, the Komsomol, the major body exploring these issues, had considerably narrowed its earlier broad vision of a humane society and brought it into line with the party to which it was now almost wholly subordinated.[11]

During the plan, issues of morality, private behavior, and leisure were emphatically downplayed in favor of a work ethic of inequality and incentive. On the construction sites, leaders perceived "culture" and morality wholly in terms of production. Cleanup, hygiene, and anti-racist propaganda continued but seemed ineffective. The reality of power, work, and survival helped to diminish the force of moral crusading. The Volunteer Saturdays and Shockwork, though couched in uplifting terms, were unpopular because of their manipulative use. The harsh military tone of the times discouraged "soft" values. To some Stalinist managers, the only culture was punctuality and the only morality was hard work. Since almost all Militant Atheist work was confined to assault operations and since the cult of Lenin was quickly fading behind the shadow of a new cult figure, there was no one left to promote the feeble experiments in ritual and Godbuilding that had begun in the 1920s.[12]

The original iconoclastic, festive, and Godbuilding currents of the Russian Revolution, taken together, were an expression of the mythic consciousness of the Bolshevik Revolution. They were in fact the main cultural product of the alliance that had been forged between the working class and the radical intellectuals of Russia in the generation or so before 1917. The urge to sweep away the ugliness of the past, to demonstrate and celebrate solidarity in struggle and victory over darkness, and to institutionalize these feelings in the quotidian of post-revolutionary society constituted one of the strongest subconscious bonds between these two variegated but identifiable elements in the revolutionary process. They represent a mentality of partnership that went beyond—or beneath—class consciousness and ideology. The vivid color and rich variety of their manifestations in acts and gestures of revolution and in culture-building discourse should not obscure the psychological function they possessed. However radically the rhetorical modes of the radical intelligentsia differed from the "simpler" and more gestural expressions of the workers, a common spirit can be discerned: a utopian spirit of hope and humanism that required affirmation and votive energy to keep it alive. Like all social innovations and invented traditions, they required experimental scope. When Stalin closed down the utopian laboratories in the early 1930s, part of the original spirit of the Revolution was denied and distorted.

## Anti-Egalitarianism

David Dallin, a Menshevik leader in the Revolution, recalled that in the 1920s "there still remained a good deal of simplicity and emphasized novelty in human relations between superiors and subordinates, between officers and men, between chiefs and employees." The economic inequalities, present from the outset, were still seen by many to be temporary in nature. In fact, when the first five-year plan began, a mood spread among the party rank-and-file that the revolution from above portended imminent equality. This was observed first-hand by the American journalist William Chamberlin in 1929–30. The liquidation of private enterprise in those two years seemed a forecast of renewed War Communism and egalitarian distribution. Civil War veterans saw the next step as leveling of living standards, and some communist officials in the village tried to promote the rural communes as the main instrument of collectivized agriculture. Instead, the opposite happened. Egalitarianism was assaulted head on by the leaders, Stalin first among them, and the structure of privilege and inequality was greatly amplified. The struggle against equality and "leveling" in the years of industrialization and the consolidation of Stalin's power were in fact critical to the emerging social system and a manifestation of the victory of Stalinism over revolutionary utopianism.[13]

Stalin was the most audible and powerful spokesman in the campaign against what he contemptuously called *uravnilovka* (leveling). His hostility—voiced in sarcastic and dismissive terms—was so deep and so clearly enunciated that it rapidly became state policy and social doctrine. He believed in productive results, not through spontaneity or persuasion, but through force, hierarchy, reward, punishment, and above all differential wages. He applied this view to the whole of society.[14] Stalin's anti-egalitarianism was not born of the five-year plan era. He was offended by the very notion and used contemptuous terms such as "fashionable leftists," "blockheads," "petty bourgeois nonsense," and "silly chatter," thus reducing the discussion to a sweeping dismissal of childish, unrealistic, and unserious promoters of equality. The toughness of the delivery evoked laughter of approval from his audiences.[15]

The first major assault came in 1931 at a gathering of economic leaders and enterprise managers. Stalin enumerated four repulsive phenomena that menaced industrial growth: labor turnover, refusal to take responsibility for one's work *(obezlichka)*, leveling, and specialist-baiting. The practice of paying the same wages to skilled and unskilled, manual and intellectual, and heavy and light labor was scandalous, he said. It killed initiative and spurred the harmful process of labor turnover and the whimsical migration of the unskilled "in search of happiness" and of the skilled in search of recognition and reward. Workers acted like vacationers at the factory, visiting until they tired of a particular place or job, feeling no incentive to improve skills or help improve the productivity of a particular enterprise. Leveling of wages fed the process of turnover, and these led to irresponsibility and inattention to work. Stalin mocked managerial speechifying as useless; pleading and persuading were not, after all, a part of Stalin's structure of dignity.[16]

In his most quoted remarks on equality, the Report to the XVII Party Congress in January 1934, Stalin was even more emphatic, as well as insulting and threatening. He referred to the "leftish chatter" on the part of some communists about the imminent disappearance of classes, the diminution of the class struggle, and the passing away of the state. Such people, said Stalin, wished "to sleep while awaiting the advent of the classless society." He called the notion of the "leveling of needs and of personal life reactionary petty-bourgeois nonsense worthy of some sort of primitive ascetic sect," a striking juxtaposition of historical mentalities. Stalin also tied the alleged striving for equality with nineteenth century utopian socialism, a rather more apt comparison.[17] Stalin's sporadic soliloquies on egalitarianism in the formative years of his system were correct readings of Marxist texts and were rooted in practical economic policies. But by couching them in such a sharp, comprehensive, and authoritative manner, Stalin left no room for flexibility, experiment, or exception, dismissed without comment the deep and persistent Russian traditions of egalitarianism, and opened the way for a wide-ranging assault against the revolutionary utopianism of the previous decade.

It did not take long for Stalin's pronouncements to filter downward into the press and into political styles and values. In 1931, a comprehensive attack on egalitarianism was made in the pages of a book devoted to Machajski. Among the major sins of Makhaevism, said the author, was its "ultra-egalitarianism," *rvach* or "grabbing" for oneself in an act of greedy egoism, specialist baiting based on envy, and the substitution of "proletarian instinct" in favor of "revolutionary" (meaning correct) theory—all of it adding up to a historically pessimistic, reactionary, and petty-bourgeois effusion of déclassé elements, unskilled workers, the unemployed, and the Lumpenproletariat. A more shocking combination of vices in a land of Marxism would be difficult to find. To a rising class of skilled workers, managers and technicians, anti-egalitarianism had wide appeal. A young engineer and former communard of the late 1920s told Klaus Mehnert why in the early 1930s he now thought equality was wrong. Without any pseudo-Marxist vocabulary, he explained that salary maximums had been lifted from party members and that engineers and good workers could earn more. This was "only right" in that after years of study, work, and sacrifice he should get a new flat and enjoy the special shops.[18]

Wage inequality shot upward during the first five-year plan. In 1928 there was more equality in wages of industry than in 1914; in 1934 wages were still more egalitarian than in 1914 but less so than in 1928, and the differentials rose in the 1930s. The difference between the average wage-earner and the trained engineers also opened widely in the early thirties: in 1932, the peak year of this differential, the latter earned 263 percent of the average worker's wage. In the same year, the party maximum of 250–300 rubles per month was abolished. Professionals, specialists, and administrators were given high guaranteed salaries. In 1929 came the introduction of devices for extra earnings: bonuses, special money packs, expense accounts, and second jobs or sinecures for certain privileged groups. On the construction sites of Dnepropetrovsk, engineers' salaries towered above those of even the best workers, and they had their own cafeterias, stores, clubs, and travel privileges. Workers were heavily stratified according to occupation and category of skill, and even within a skill level, further arabesques of stratification were woven by piece-work rates. Women there were routinely paid less than men for the same work. Devices of emulation and socialist competition did not alleviate the visible pattern of inequality and its effects upon morale.[19]

Upon the edifice of wage stratification and income differences arose a superstructure of augmented privilege. When the official dismissal of egalitarianism surfaced in public policy, the old pattern of privilege building grew with force. Entire new styles of life appeared for the elite. They were given bigger and better flats, now rigidly classified into four grades according to location, size, and condition. New blocks of high prestige flats with ornamental facades were put under construction in the capital in 1935. Ghettos of privilege inhabited by foreign ministry officials, ballet dancers, officials of the new subway system, highly placed academics, police and party leaders began to sprout. At the first congress of Soviet architects, these groups clamored for more beautiful buildings for themselves. A whole world of inequality and privilege dawned in the 1930s— persisting of course up to this day—in food, service, medical care, travel at home and abroad, contact with foreigners, and even special parks. The new rulers, earning ten to thirty times more than a worker, enjoyed free furniture, beach houses, dachas, cars, concert tickets, and special seating. Stratified and differential feeding and housing could be found everywhere at every level. For a French worker in Moscow all this was symbolized by Stalin's banquet for 1,700 officers and shockworkers on May Day 1935; for an American businessman, it was the sight of waiters in tuxedos at the big Moscow hotels.[20]

Although the Soviet elite did not flaunt its wealth in an orgy of conspicuous consumption, the extreme and growing differentiation of classes in the Soviet Union could be seen in the heraldry of everyday symbolism. In 1934, the term "meritorious artist" was introduced, academic degrees restored, and the order of Hero of the Soviet Union created. In the next year military ranks, abolished in the Revolution, were reintroduced, together with saluting. By 1937 there were sixteen places named after Stalin. A certain amount of unpretentious similarity in the dress still prevailed (and prevails) through the Stalin period. But government officials and other "successful" people began to sprout ties, white shirts, and black shiny shoes. Women's fashions were exalted, beauty parlors and makeup became the accepted norm. The sartorial experiments of the 1920s were dead. As John Bowlt has put it in severely ironic but very accurate terms[21]

> The heroines of the revolution arose from the divans upholstered in material carrying industrial motifs in rococo settings, donned kerchiefs recording complicated episodes from the Civil War, they drank tea from cups depicting Slavic fairy tales, entered Baroque subway stations, and went to work in Neo-Palladian office buildings. Such was the 'haze of fantasy' which clouded the pure visions of the 1920s; such was the monstrous mixture that liquidated Constructivist design.

Visible and audible signs of deference returned with a vengeance. The cult of personality—a near deification of Stalin—required extreme forms of reverence towards the leader, his images, his written and spoken words, his entire persona. "Little Stalins" appeared all over the Soviet landscape, requiring deference in speech and manner of address and even gestures. Stalin addressed almost everybody as *ty* and expected *vy* in return (like a parent, husband, ruler, superior, or lord of the old regime). He was called *ty* only in ritual poems and songs (as had been the tsars). Authority figures in other walks of life resuscitated this pattern of speech—a constant reminder of status in the workaday world.[22]

Gender roles were redefined in the mid 1930s, partially repudiating the revolutionary settlement of the 1920s. Women were promoted, put into technical schools, and afforded wide opportunities to enter and rise in economic life, to establish their own identify through personal earnings, and even gain a certain sense of self-respect and public respect as well. On the other hand, women were saddled with a triple burden: of wage earning in the economy, of principal responsibility for domestic work and child care, and of public or voluntary work. This stripped them of their ability to use economic opportunity to advance along paths to power equal to men. The Stalinist image of woman was patriarchal: the ideal woman was a matronly mother of many children and not the thin and tough barricade fighter of the revolutionary poster. V. I. Mukhina's famous statue of "Worker and Collective Farm Woman" once again and emphatically linked the female with the peasantry, the countryside, passivity, nurturing, and fertility.[23]

The end of equality and the creation of a super-privileged elite arose from the same fundamental circumstances and motivation as did most of Stalin's social policies in the

1930s: an economic imperative that was perceived to respond to "hard" stimuli of incentive (punishment and reward) rather than to altruistic incentives or self-activity and spontaneous productivity. Stalin in this respect resembled Henry Ford, who believed that the workplace was an arena of harshness. Stalin's political machine, with himself at the controls, required varied inputs of energy, motors, large functioning parts, and tiny cogs. Both purposes meshed nicely: by ending the egalitarian surge, Stalin gained stability in the work force and probably greater production records, and he also won the gratitude and support—of such a magnitude and longevity that could never be achieved by fear alone—of a loyal elite stratum. On top of all this, Stalin managed to place in the remote distance the Marxist vision of ending the separation of manual and mental work and of the city from the countryside.[24]

## Fantasectomy: Utopia, City, Commune

Science fiction utopia—like visionary town planning, communalism, and egalitarian-ism—was initially congruent with the general mood of the five-year plan. In 1928 Gleb Krzhizhanovsky, the nation's chief planner, at a Young Pioneer conference compared the coming gigantic projects of the plan to the fantasies of Jules Verne—but on a more grandiose scale, with advanced technology, expanded means of travel and exploration, and super-heroes of scientific achievement and invention. And Lunacharsky in 1930 made a plea for more utopias tied to the planning perspectives, novels showing a world of new cities, new technics, and new people. But science fiction's future speculation had its enemies as well. In 1928–29, the Russian Association of Proletarian Writers, a late and deformed offspring of the lingering proletarian culture movement, attacked science fiction in general, utopias in particular, and most other "entertainment" writing as "useless literature" and a "harmful distraction." The "proletarian" critics, aside from their political and careerist aims, were displaying hostility to "dreamers," to ro-manticism, to fantasy, and to a quasi-religious obsession with the nonexistent. Chil-dren's stories and fairy tales they likened to superstition and prejudice. Extravagant imagination and fancy they saw as a kind of flight from reality akin to spiritual treason. Against it, they promoted empirical study, hardheaded "realism," and a focus on the plan, on work, and on building socialism.[25]

This campaign possessed a moralistic streak, a hostility to pure pleasure, light lei-sure pursuits, "non-serious" behavior, and popular culture. Science fiction, then and later in the Stalin period, was, like jazz and associated activities, linked to Western influences and thus somehow unpatriotic, decadent, or bourgeois. Congress speeches and articles poured out into public discourse in the late 1920s. This alone was probably enough to silence some science fiction writers. Assisting in the anti-fantasy process was the rapid nationalization of publishing firms and the consequent disappearance of jour-nals and publishing houses which had specialized in light adventure literature and sci-ence fiction. *Thirty Days* and *Worldwide Sleuth,* whose circulation had reached 45,000 and 100,000 respectively by 1929, went out of business. Science fiction books or long stories had peaked in number to thirty-nine in 1928, falling off to twenty-seven in 1929, twenty-one in 1930 and seven in 1931 (the bottom was reached in 1934 with four titles). Larri's book was the last to contain a genuine utopian picture. Four of the well known science fiction writers of the twenties were eventually repressed in the 1930s—Rynin, Itin, Nikolsky, and Larri—though it is not clear how their addiction to fantasy contributed to their fate. At the 1934 congress of writers, a landmark in the history of Soviet literary control, the novelist Konstantin Fedin pronounced science fiction "dead and buried," and the very word utopia was outlawed and ridiculed in the 1930s. Soviet historians have conceded openly that science fiction "fell under the shadow of the cult of personality," in other words, was repressed by the Stalinist system.[26]

Was this merely an episode in literary history, or was it related to larger questions of politics and power? The answer is very clear. Visions of utopians, idealists, fantasists—except for those who inhabited the Politburo and Gosplan—could have no place in the political culture that emerged triumphant with Stalin's victory as party leader in 1928–29. Soviet science fiction in the 1920s functioned as what one critic has called "a revolutionary critique of the old world, the pathos of the revolutionary reordering of life, the affirmation of the communist ideal."[27] This kind of critique could not coexist with the power-world of Stalin's regime. Fantasists—the intellectual frontline troops of a revolution—became freaks in a world of courtiers, party functionaries, bureaucrats, smalltime officials, factory managers, and even rapidly advancing skilled workers who wished to see the next day dawn and the quarter's quota fulfilled. The technical, economic, and material urgency of the planning era undermined the humane visions of social justice implicit in the science fiction of the previous decade. The building of a domestic economy on an intensive scale overshadowed world revolutionary and cosmic adventure just as the motto "socialism in one country" drowned out "world revolution."

There were compelling practical reasons for the Stalinist hostility to utopias—of any kind. The "utopias of fear and the utopias of hope" as well as peasant counter-utopias were extinguished. Dystopias such as *We* that pictured a communist hell could not be tolerated for obvious reasons, nor could rural arcadias and monarchist visions of a restored, antimodern Russia. Zamyatin at least was fortunate in being able to leave the U.S.S.R. in 1931 to settle in France. Chayanov was arrested in 1931 and died in Stalin's camps. (Krasnov, who lived in Germany from 1921 to 1945, was taken by the Soviets at the end of World War II to Moscow and executed.) In these cases, of course, the repression was rooted in causes other than utopian authorship. Fantasies about capitalist hells were also curbed because graphic pictures of oppressive elites, privileged rulers, capitalist oligarchies, nationalist dictators, and "iron heels" could easily be turned against Stalinist Russia. Bukharin in fact invoked Jack London's *Iron Heel* to warn against the looming evil of the Stalinist state.[28] Maps of communist heaven, on the other hand, were even more repugnant, since the fictional heavens (of, for example, Larri) were as distant from Soviet reality in the 1930s as the Earth was from Mars. Bright utopias could always be compared to current realities; indeed, that was a major function of utopia. Stalin would not allow such comparisons or brook such implied criticism. A crucial element in the cult of Stalin was his alleged ability to see far across the land and into the future. How could mere writers dare to rival his vision?

"Dreaming is a serious mental disease," said one of the characters in Zamyatin's *We*. At the and of the novel the major characters are subjected to a kind of lobotomy that destroys the capacity to fantasize. Stalin performed a similar "fantasectomy" upon the revolutionary imagination in the 1930s, taking away the habit of dreaming. From 1931 to 1957 (with the appearance of Ivan Efremov's *The Mists of Andromeda*) not one genuine science fiction utopia (or any other kind) was published in the Soviet Union. Science fiction as a whole was greatly reduced in output, narrowed in focus, and lowered in quality. Discussion of utopia, robots, cybernetics, time travel, extrasensory perception, and alien creatures became taboo; replacing them were military, technological, patriotic, and espionage themes, exploring only the most pragmatic sorts of projection such as new weapons and inventions or the application of science to the economy. Thus the lens into the future was refocused from the distant to the immediate, from social analysis to scientific prediction, from global to detailed visions. Spies and wreckers became the main villains in the Stalinist science fiction genre and paranoia the main psychological ingredient. German science fiction went through an almost identical transformation under the Nazis at the very same moment. Although Soviet Stalinist science fiction lacked the open racism, occultism, and irrationalism of the Nazi product, it resembled it strongly in its manicheanism, authoritarianism, hero types, exaltation of "national" science, and military tone. In both countries, science fiction lost the verve and richness it had possessed earlier in the century.[29]

Visionary town planning was also spurred initially by the frenzied aura of rapid industrialization—indeed future speculation about new cities peaked in the very middle of the first five-year plan. Some of the Urbanist schemes were actually adopted, though greatly modified in the process of building them on or near the new industrial sites. The tumult of collectivization and the creation of new industrial towns converged in some of these plans. The Fortress of Communism Commune on the lower Volga, for example, was to be a "socialist farm city" of some 60,000 displaced peasants and new workers who would staff a single huge farm and work in the adjacent processing and auto factories, while living in giant apartment houses and traveling to work by car or bus. Stalingrad was originally redesigned as an immense commune in 1930 with a kitchen capable of feeding a half-million people and apartment blocks of 2,500 each. The Worker's City of the Nizhny-Novgorod Austin Plant was designed by Americans and approved by the Soviets, with centralized schooling, clubs, hospitals, bakeries, kitchens, baths, laundries, and other services for its 18,000 employees in communal blocks of 200 residents each—a symmetrical phalanstery on a modern industrial site. An entire village of 3,000 people was moved to make way for its construction. Yet as late as 1932 there were not enough beds and the premises had no water. These sites were parodies of the bright dreams of clean, rational, community-building homes envisioned by the architects and planners of the 1920s.[30]

O.S.A. and the modernist and visionary planners of the late 1920s came under attack from two fronts. The first was from the "left"—the group of proletarian architects called V.O.P.R.A. who, beginning in the late 1920s, accused O.S.A. of utopianism and "westernism." In 1930, the Party and the regime swung into assault position. The storm broke in mid-May when the Central Committee of the Party called all the utopian planners' dreams "semi-fanatical" leaps over real and impassible barriers. It was one of the regime's first clear signs of anti-utopianism and an admission that the economic backwardness of the nation and the priorities of the rulers were at the base of its hostility to extravagant schemes about remaking everyday life. In June, Disurbanists were vaguely associated with "Chayanovism" a clear reference to that writer's vision of destroying Moscow and all other larger cities.[31]

At the June plenum of the committee a year later, Lazar Kaganovich appeared as the official voice of anti-utopianism. He had visited Vienna in the late 1920s and was struck by what Austrian Social Democrats had done in their capital (retaining the grandeur of historical Vieanna while producing cheap housing for workers—the famous Karl Marx Hof). He announced that since the October Revolution, all Soviet Russia had become socialist, including all its cities. There was thus no need to speculate about abandoning them or to dream up fantasies for new ones. In the next few years, the assaults mounted and charges of Trotskyism, Menshevism, and even Social Fascism continued to be hurled at the planners who—a few years ago—had seemed on the verge of transforming a world physically and psychologically. Many fell from prominence, though very few were politically harassed or arrested. By 1934, all the visions of the future cities had evaporated.[32]

Looking back on the great turnabout, the architect Mikhail Barshch saw its primary cause as the "cult of personality"—in other words, Stalin's megalomania: henceforth, architecture had to sing of victories and achievements (not, he implied, serve the needs of dwellers). His colleague Rozenfeld believed that most people simply did not like the modernism of visionary architecture. G. B. Barkhin thought that people were also exhausted by the constant novelty and the frenetic atmosphere of root-and-branch experimentation and change. And Hans Blumenfeld, a German architect who worked in Russia at the time, thought that the critics found modern planning "not emotional enough." All of them seemed to recognize also that most of the plans were economically unrealizable—given the labor shortage and the absence of certain kinds of key materials.[33]

What followed was an erratic but steady "monumentalization" of Soviet architecture, especially in Moscow which, said Blumenthal, had to look like a great capital, an attitude that he accurately enough called "Haussmannism" after the great reconstruction plan of Paris under the Second Empire. Moscow became a town of broad boulevards, huge buildings, and big apartment blocks. Mammoth but unbuilt projects symbolized the new sensibility: the Stadium of Izmailov, a grandiose festive hall, and Boris Iofan's notorious Palace of Soviets designed to be the largest building in the world, a skyscraper temple topped by a gargantuan statue of Lenin. So did the built structures that came to typify the Stalinesque style: the Council of Ministers building (1932–35), the Hotel Moscow (1935), the star-shaped Red Army Theater (1935–40), and the heavily adorned Moscow metro—known as the Subway of the Revolution—as well as later entries such as Moscow State University and the big wedding cake hotels. Statues, entablatures, columns (functional or otherwise) restored the old respect for hugeness, order, symmetry—all associated with solemn and unchallenged authority.[34]

Kaganovich, an exceptionally important figure in the Soviet power structure at that moment, had punctuated his remark on the contemporary Soviet city with the forceful comment that there was no need for research into future cities. This was more than an offhand remark. It was the enunciation of a central principle of the new order: futurology and speculation were dead. They were outlawed—not only as superfluous but genuinely harmful as such. It was the charter statement of the Stalinist anti-utopian utopia. The graphic dreams of revolutionary cities evaporated in the daily round of urban life in the 1930s and beyond.[35]

Communalism, like egalitarianism of which it was a social expression, felt the direct blows of Stalin's words and policies. He claimed that communes had been a failure and were few in number. In an oft-quoted statement, Stalin said that "blockheads" *(golovotyapy)* admired rural communalism so much that they were introducing it into factories—he was apparently unaware that the communal idea in production had spread from urban student and worker residential communes. All such "infantile leveling practices" Stalin considered harmful and deleterious to production.[36]

During collectivization, enthusiasts who saw the commune as the coming and immediate form of collectivized agriculture were disabused by the regime, which chose instead the "lower" form of cooperative labor, the collective farm *(kolkhoz)*, an arrangement wherein the peasants retained their homes, personal property, and private garden plots but were compelled to labor in teams on the collectivized fields and be paid according to number of days worked. The *kolkhoz* system was a massive violation of the old peasant way of life, a compulsive yoke, and an artificial aggregation of mostly unwilling farmers into state-administered units. On the other hand, it allowed much more privacy than the commune, to which most peasants remained hostile. Yet, those who were living voluntarily in communes were forced to abandon their lives of sharing and enter the *kolkhoz*—or in some cases migrate into industry or be shipped off to labor camps. Communes were disbanded with the same rudeness and brutishness used against the traditional peasant households and private plots.[37]

Religious communes, among the most successful examples of this social experiment, were subjected to special abuse. The collectivization movement of 1928 turned sporadic attacks on communalism into full-scale annihilation. Urban elements rolled into the countryside—workers, Komsomols, party officials, military units—armed with angry and militant atheism, anti-egalitarianism, and sharp hostility to autonomous enclaves on the Russian land. Columns marched into religious communes, demanded space for Red Corners, made threats, and closed down the communes. Thus the last shreds and remnants of an old peasant utopia, represented partially and eclectically by these communes, were wiped away.[38]

Student communes, which had little economic significance, also crumbled. Naishtat reported that by 1930, non-communard students displayed enormous "conservatism" in the face of communards' efforts to enlist them into communal life. Communards teaching the virtue of sharing, mutual aid, and cultural betterment were called "a sect" by other students. A journalist for the Komsomol daily wrote that residential communes were sectarian. When, in the fall of 1932, Klaus Mehnert visited communards he had known earlier, the sign "Youth Commune" was gone, each couple had a room, and the community of students called itself a "collective." The commune, a friend told him, "was all wrong. Tell me—isn't it really a contradiction, when we in the Soviet Union are trying by every means, even with piece-rates and premiums, to increase production, and at the same time are living in a commune, where every one has to chuck what he's earned into the common pot?" Stalin could hardly have put it better. The urban communes that had flourished in the 1920s and seemed on the verge of spreading at the end of the decade now disappeared.[39]

The House Commune never caught on and very few were built. This was partly because the way they were introduced made them unpopular. It was one thing for a group of like-minded students or workers to form a commune based on mutual interests and trust and then occupy a given space; it was quite another to fill a communal shell with hundreds of people and families who had never seen each other before. House Communes were eventually converted by their dwellers into more conventional home units—separate apartments, dorms, or a combination. Some were never occupied. Many decayed through lack of maintenance and were abandoned. Kerzhentsev tells of huge blocks near industrial sites designed as House Communes but actually built with no central or communal facilities—or else a tiny laundry for thousands of workers, dark Red Corners, and worthless basements for the housing and schooling of children.

The House Commune was defeated by its utopian associations, by lack of resources, by suspicion of the regime, and by countless practical considerations. But it was also defeated by the dwellers for whom it was planned. Rapid demographic movement led to overcrowding, stuffing the communes with excessive numbers and turning them into barracks. The pace of urbanization suddenly threw together people of such diverse origins—generational, regional, ethnic, urban and rural, cultural—that communalism would have been difficult even under the best physical conditions. According to Komsomol social critics, when House Communes of proper dimensions were built, workers refused to live in them. Peasant women recalled the fights in the kitchen over appliances and space. Workers also observed that party members did not live collectively and that many of them, having lived next to neighbors for years, did not know them![40]

Years later, Barshch, a prominent designer of communal housing in the late twenties, told Anatole Kopp that "the house commune forgets the problem of the development of the individual personality"—a fact he apparently forgot himself in 1929. Another Soviet architect said that people refused to live in a building with rooms and apartments opening along hallways. "After a hard day's work," he said, "workers wanted privacy and rest." He also believed that families actually like to sit around the table together to eat and talk. And that is why traditional family and housing patterns survived and persisted in the face of experimental and utopian plans and buildings. Hans Blumenfeld admitted that he and his colleagues favored the House Commune. But an official of the Workers' and Peasants' Inspectorate told him in a private talk that every family had a *babushka* to release the wife from domestic chores and allow her to work.[41]

The actual housing system of the 1930s, still persisting in the center of large Soviet towns, was a parody of communalism. The *kommuna* gave way to the so-called communal apartment *(kommunalnaya kvartira* or *kommunalka)*. And between the *kommuna* and the *kommunalka,* the social and psychological gap was enormous. An Englishman in Moscow in 1936 observed a typical example of a communal apartment: a former one-family flat of 8–10 rooms now housing one family in each room, holding 1–5 persons. The "communal" kitchen was a small room shared by all the families, usually at different times, with eight cupboards and eight gas ranges where eight different family meals were separately prepared every night. All the dwellers shared the lavatory and the bath. The only communal services were a playground, a crèche, and a small clubroom. So it was throughout the great metropolis for the masses of citizens; so it remains for millions to this day.[42]

The communes of the workplace—production collectives and communes—were a direct casualty in the assault on leveling. Yet many of these productive associations were in fact successful. A system of screening, recommendations, probation, fines, and expulsions was employed by some to enhance effectiveness and productivity. Until 1930, the regime was cautious in its comment on their achievements and their utility. But at the XVI Congress of the party, Kaganovich warned against the spread of communal labor practices throughout all industry that some enthusiasts were promoting. Managers began to pile on criticism, and later in the year the Central Committee of the party spoke against them. Stalin's anti-leveling speech of 1931 was followed by a press campaign against the production communes and collectives and against artels also. A combination of visceral hostility to any autonomous work group, anti-egalitarianism, authoritarian patterns in management, and the emergence of a host of new labor techniques ranging from shockwork to "cost accounting brigades" all militated against the community spirit and the independent face of production communalism. By 1932, almost all of them were gone from the industrial scene.[43]

Modern studies of industrial psychology have argued that "associational" groupings in the workplace, identification with overall production, the ability to express oneself, participation, decentralization, fewer levels of authority, and a structure of friendship augment the efficiency and the happiness of producers.[44] These things are not easy to provide even in small work sites with a stable and skilled labor force. Under the volcanic conditions of the five-year plan, they were alien notions to managers raised and trained in Russian traditions, working in a revolutionary milieu, and dealing with an extraordinarily volatile, fluid, and untrained body of workers. The air was charged with emergency, panic, and enthusiasm, and it tended to choke off notions of communal or fraternal production styles that emerged from below. The free flowering of artels and productive associations could not alone have solved this problem, but it might have humanized the environment by reminding everyone that the goals of industrialization were not only measured in control figures but also in terms of emotional sustenance for the working man and woman.

By derailing this original impulse of the Revolution, and by dividing the workforce into automized units, the Stalin regime repudiated one of the enduring goals of all socialist ideologies: community. Friendship, banter, and natural teamwork of course continued to assert themselves in the workplace all through the years of industrialization, but the official view promoted labor heroes and faceless production.

Klaus Mehnert's young Soviet friend told him in 1932 that the commune was "a great and beautiful idea" but had now become not only utopian, but petty-bourgeois and Trotskyist at that. Critics of communalism misread its meaning. A Komsomol writer in 1927 had warned against communes as a mode of reordering human life; this had to be done by the "Soviet state as a whole." Stalin said it another way: the commune, he conceded, was the correct model for a future way of life, but not for now. Only under conditions of full technical development and affluence could it flourish—"not soon, of course." Stalin was supported by critics of communalism as a springboard for the leap into communism. The very popular dramatist Nikolai Pogodin described accurately and with gentle irony a student commune in his play *Boldness* (1930). In it, a factory party official says to a young communard: "Ilya, your commune is boldness. But is it a good thing? No—it's bad. Communes are the product of the carefully planned socialist reorganization of society, of daily life. But you people . . . without any plan, you somehow just came up with it: bingo—a commune!"[45]

Communalism in work and life as an experiment in nurturing a new personality or even as a form of survival was abandoned in the early thirties for the sake of a single "collective" goal—as defined by the leaders: building the state and the economy at all costs. The communalism of the experimental era was spontaneous, small in scale, manageable, flexible, eclectic, democratic, and sometimes temporary. The collectivism which descended in the 1930s was imposed from above, total, cumbersome, rigid, monolithic, authoritarian, and eternal in spirit. Stalinist collectivism resembled the belief of Zamyatin's anti-hero that only the collective "we" has rights—not the little "we's" of experimental life, but the total "we" of a single state ruled by a deified "I."[46]

# 12

## Conclusion

Ein Wasserdröpfchen macht sich in den härtesten Stein eine Höhle, wenn er oft darauf fällt; und ein gutes Wort findet, wo nicht heute, so doch morgen einen guten Platz.                                   Theodor von Hippel (1741–1796)

### Lunar Economics and Social Revolution

The "great change" or "great break" that resulted from the frenetic industrial campaign was not only unprecedented in history but also unanticipated. Prudent economists like V. G. Groman used the word "fantasy" to describe the bacchanalia of planning and the speed of the tempo. The great plan, with its arbitrary goals, unpredictable results, and its ragged and continuous pace, transformed the economy and the social landscape and affected the entire national psychology. In the words of Moshe Lewin, "quantitative madness," haste, and shock were the key features of this traumatic experience which changed the face of revolutionary Russia.[1]

The political sinew of forced industrialization under a central plan was—and had to be—administrative coercion and command, rule by whim, and a harsh authoritarian style adapted to the tensions of the industrialization drive. New terms emerged to signify the culture of bossism: *glavokratiya* or rule by heavy bureaucratic methods, *apparatnym putëm* or administrative command, *nakachka* or pumping out orders to underlings, and *davai!*, the harsh and crude word for "do it now!", couched in the arrogantly familiar *ty* form of address—a form of linguistical expression that many in the Revolution had fought to abolish forever.[2]

War or its psychological surrogate, a war atmosphere, generates a need for iron discipline and social control. The Civil War had witnessed the merging of "total" social organization and the waging of war. Stalin recreated the warlike atmosphere and invoked the martial virtues of the revolution and civil war. In doing so, he not only copied and far surpassed Trotsky's "militarization of labor," but also unconsciously adopted the psychology and vision of traditional Russian administrative utopia: the combination of military dragooning and regimentation with defensive needs, economic activity, and putative welfare. As in the case of all such utopias, its organizers described it in rational, symmetrical terms, in the mathematical language of planning, control figures, statistics, projections, and precise commands. As in the vision of military colonies, which the utopian plan faintly resembled, its rational facade hardly obscured the oceans of misery, disorder, chaos, corruption, and whimsicality that went with it.

The ideology of the Russian Revolution had been an amalgam of Marxism (as applied to Russian conditions) and native Russian revolutionary values and visions that often went beyond the schemata of Marx and were expressed by human "texts"—myths, behavior patterns, symbols, visions, gestures, and dreams. Stalinism—a wholly appropriate name for the new political culture born in the 1930s—was also an amalgam: of the ever present authoritarian elements in Bolshevism, of the military zeal generated to control and orchestrate the transformation, of Stalin's personal despotism, of the persistent Russian state bureaucratic heritage, and of the social authoritarianism of the Russian people themselves. It was an extremely potent and violent revolution which altered the spirit of the Revolution of a decade earlier.

Stalin's colossal thirst for power led him to create one of the vastest and most sophisticated political machines in history, founded on principles of information collection and retrieval, secrecy and paranoia, the cynical use of people, moral corruption, gratuitous violence, and a fantasmagoric belief in the potential treachery of everyone. Stalin despised idealists and prophets of moral revolution. The "utopian" character of the system he built must be distinguished clearly from the utopianism of the revolutionary period. His vision was of a unified and tightly controlled political economy run by authoritarian methods, by live men—not machines or computers—and backed by force. "Socialism," he remarked in September 1938, "is converted from a dream of a better future for humanity into a science." Stalin neither understood nor respected the efforts of culture-building utopians and speculative minds to create or generate new ways of life.[3]

Stalin was not alone at the center of this formidable organizational machine. He was assisted by more or less like-minded power-oriented people. At the time of the great transformation, the early 1930s, his principle agent and spokesman for the new order was Lazar Kaganovich, an unyielding purger and a despotic administrator who shared the belief of his brother—also an economic administrator—that "the earth should tremble when the director walks around the plant." The party needed "efficient, powerful, harsh, impetuous" leaders.[4] Kaganovich was the main voice in the war against many experiments of the 1920s: the woman's movement, the visionary town planners, communist moral teaching, communes, equality, and virtually everything else that smacked of autonomous culture building, independent social experimentation, and "useless" speculation about the future.

There can be no doubt that he spoke for Stalin, and Kaganovich's disdain for revolutionary utopia was palpable in his speeches and writings. As boss of Moscow, Kaganovich had ancient churches near the Kremlin torn down over the protest of Lunacharsky and several architects to whom he contemptuously replied: "And *my* aesthetics demands that the demonstration processions from the six districts of Moscow should all pour into Red Square at the same time"—a vivid illustration of the new Stalinist iconoclasm and the exaltation of mechanized precision in ritual over the beauty of decor. In 1932, Kaganovich became furious when egalitarian officials refused to enjoy the privileges of their own "special stores" in Ivanovo-Voznesensk and insisted on queuing up with everyone else. His rude, harsh, ill-mannered style was widely emulated.[5]

The economic revolution, the upsurge of authoritarian management, and the peasant influx into the factories put Gastev's machine utopia among the first casualties in the anti-utopian war. Ironically, Gastevism, seen by many critics as a "hard" utopia contrasting harshly to the more humanistic experiments and visions of the 1920s, was incompatible with the new Stalinist industrial order. The five-year plan altered the structure of the Soviet labor force as millions of unskilled peasants migrated to the towns, factories, and construction sites. Chaos erupted from the failure to foresee the social, demographic, and psychological consequences of the industrialization drive. One response to it was labor discipline, control, and punishment. Another was dramatized—even "theatricalized"—shockwork, spurts of heroic labor performed in headlong fashion by enthusiasts awash with adrenalin and productive frenzy. Order, efficient management, and detailed training were among the casualties of the massive drive. Technological worship and technical voluntarism won out over proletarian rights; intensification of labor was chosen over sophisticated training; in other words, the boss won out over the machine as the "teacher" of workers.[6]

Gastev had constantly endorsed a program of meticulous preparation of workers and lengthy exercises, and he hoped to reduce exhaustion and accidents on the job. He envisioned the entire work force gradually raising its skills as equal parts of an elegant machine, and he downplayed individual "exploits," uneven surges, and storms of productivity. The five-year plan increased the accident rate and injured workers' health by matching untrained labor with complicated machinery and impossible output quotas; it broke the steady pace and rhythms of the line by sudden changes. Later it introduced the Superworker into the system: the Stakhanovite. When Stakhanovism appeared during the second five-year plan, Gastev endorsed it and rhetorically coopted it as a logical outcome of his system. Both were based on common sense, alertness, good work habits, prior planning of the task, and so on. But Stakhanovism was an artificial creation combining highly advertised labor heroes and heroines with teams of assistants who organized their tools and helped them achieve the vaunted colossal norms of work. Gastev's dream was replaced by elitist prodigies of production at the top and low skilled village recruits at the bottom.[7] Gastev, the N.O.T. movement, and the Central Institute of Labor survived the industrial shockwaves until 1938, though with great trauma and many compromises. In that year the Institute was closed and Gastev was arrested for reasons yet unknown; surviving family members believe he was shot in the Solovetsky camp complex in 1941.[8]

A massive social upheaval accompanied Stalin's economic revolution. Between 1926 and 1939, Soviet cities grew by some thirty million people; during the first five-year plan, the urban population swelled by forty-four percent. Moscow and Leningrad regions grew by three-and-a-half million each. This produced a giant urban trauma, raging social tensions, and the misery of overcrowding, crime, and anomie. At the same time, the working class swelled rapidly between 1930 and 1933. The machinery of affirmative action, rapid promotion, and geographic and social mobility brought the reshaping of peasants, freshly arrived from the villages, into unskilled workers, of unskilled into skilled workers, and of high-performing workers into technical or managerial courses and then into positions of power in the economy and in politics. This brought about the "proletarianization" of the party and the corps of managers, a prime goal of the Bolshevik Revolution and of Lenin. But the suddenness of the change and the speedy technicization of millions without the balance of a humanistic education created a generation of ambitious, career-oriented workers-turned-bosses—practical people who were opposed to "disruptive" experiments. The upwardly mobile segments of the population wanted, in the words of Sheila Fitzpatrick, structure, permanence, traditional ladders of advancement, easily apprehended symbols of success and performance, security, and rewards in the coin of familiar goods that were both consumable and showable. They became correspondingly more apolitical, deferential to authority, and conservative.[9]

The "ruralization" of Soviet cities in the 1930s deeply affected Soviet civilization.

The primitive work habits of the newly arrived peasantry, their laxness and drift, their urge to wander in search of better jobs—all led the regime to full-scale compulsion and the imposition of discipline. The general influx of poorly educated masses led to an overall narrowing of culture and to a spread of "irrational and obscurantist tendencies" in the workplace and in all walks of life. Peasants were unable to leave their values behind in the villages. To the extent that the Russian peasants were still culturally isolated, suspicious, dogmatic, superstitious, or even "primitive" in cultural outlook— even though graced with humor, color, and generosity—to that extent the cities become more deeply imbued with peasant values—at home, on the streets, and at work. Urban civilization did not efface rural mentalities; rather, the opposite occurred. In Pilnyak's image, the wolf (a metaphor for the peasant instinct), when captured by civilized man and caged, runs around the cage "like a machine" but remains, nevertheless, a wolf. The Socialist Revolutionary leader Victor Chernov once said that "the peasant is the true autocrat of Russia." This became true, in a figurative way, in the 1930s, when for the first time a Russian political culture became peasantized.[10]

Much of the old political and some of the cultural intelligentsia was annihilated in the 1930s or reduced to impotence. This loss, together with the mass exodus of educated elements in the Civil War, meant that Russia was culturally decapitated. The flooding of the cities by peasants and the simultaneous rise of the proletariat into the ranks of power changed drastically the whole cultural face of that huge country. Old Russian traditions, mostly rural, helped to shape Soviet practices.

The cultural revolution of 1928–31 was marked by a rapid and frenetic ascendance of utopian speculation, millenarian enthusiasm, and amplified experimentation all aimed at building a new world in the near future as an accompaniment to the economic and social changes launched by the five-year plan, by a strong social and generational revolt of young Communists and workers to displace the old established professionals and specialists entrenched in academia and administration, and by a shifting and confused policy of the victorious Stalinists to channel this revolt into an assault against class and ideological enemies and intraparty opponents and then—when it threatened to get out of hand or set off unexpected and uncontrolled forces—to curb it and to retreat into the more familiar ruts of economic realism and ambition.[11]

How did the social and the cultural revolutions of early Stalinism link up? On the one hand, some of the less attractive features of the Russian working class—social resentment of oldtime experts, suspicion of intellectuals and (often) of ideas in the abstract, xenophobia, class pride, and lingering anti-Semitism (related to the above traits by a complex of circumstances)—were unleashed by the generalized anti-intellectualism of the cultural revolution. On the other hand, ambition, technical mindedness, and "seriousness" in the sense of material practicality made them indifferent or hostile to the experimentation, the utopia, the creative fantasies and the daring schemes that emerged at the very time when they were entering a path of social mobility. It was not simply the anger of Stalin and his cohorts at utopianizing—though that was perfectly clear— but also the emergence of a new kind of population in power and in production that helped bring about the end of the age of revolutionary dreams.[12]

## Stalin and the Fantasy State

The political victory of Stalin in the party and the state, the achievements of the first five-year plan, and the cultural revolution of 1928–31, with all their complexities and contradictions, had realized an important part of the Bolshevik program—the continuing ascendancy of the tutorial state led exclusively by the Communist Party, the advancement of the proletariat and other elements of the working classes into positions of authority and privilege, and the modernization of the country, including of course the building of an infrastructure of military security. But upon this achievement, Stalin erected what Robert Tucker has called a "fantasy state"[13] with himself as the unassailable chief. By the mid-1930s, Soviet society had assumed a new form and a new tone. Social mobility was reduced, geographic movement halted for some, and authoritarian traditions reintroduced into all walks of life. The school, embattled during the cultural revolution, was reinvested with familiar components: examinations, uniforms, rigid scheduling, homework, the power of the teacher in the classroom, and pedagogical discipline. The family was strengthened by a change in divorce and abortion laws and the exaltation of family life, motherhood, parental care of children, and solid home life. Throughout society, rank and privilege spoke the message of solidity and seriousness in work, and the utopianism of the revolutionary dreamers was abandoned for Stalin's fantasy of a joyful solidarity.

The culture of this society was an extraordinary mixture of tradition and novelty, an eclectic mélange of styles. As Nicholas Timasheff pointed out many years ago, Stalinism was a museum of Russian historical styles drawn from various periods: architecture of the 1820s endowed with the political monumentalism of the 1930s, concert music of the mid-nineteenth century, and educational disciplines of the late nineteenth century. Stalinist culture was not merely a reactionary form, nor even a weld of tradition and revolution, but a wholly new thing, drawing deeply on peasant mores and values, enmeshed in technological aspirations, adorned with nineteenth century Marxism, and mythologized under the banner of a falsified and distorted reading of October. Like eighteenth century Russia after the drastic but superficial reforms of Peter the Great, Russia was a socio-technical mosaic and a product of extreme telescoped development. In the realm of popular culture, authentic urges kept surfacing. After several years of banning during the cultural revolution, suddenly in 1932 Harold Lloyd movies, Gypsy music, the strains of Sergei Rachmaninov, and other well-liked forms appeared. In the 1930s, War Minister Voroshilov set up dancing schools for Red Army officers. About some modes of popular culture—such as American-born Jazz music—the regime simply could not make up its mind.[14]

In the words of Jerry Hough, "an abhorrence of experimentation" characterized the new mood of the 1930s. This was caused partly by a special form of political paranoia, endemic in all insecure revolutionary regimes but raised to an unprecedented level by Stalin himself, who longed for wholeness and clarity, the capacity to control, check, and surveille everything. Conversely, he detested disorder, freedom of expression, experimentation for its own sake, and especially experimentation in building autonomous communities and promoting equality. Thus Stalin's intense hatred of revolutionary utopianism and his emerging totalitarian system were not simply two independent ingredients of Stalinism but inextricably related. The state machinery of control over Soviet society went far beyond the range of ordinary authoritarian politics. It was in fact an anti-utopian utopia—a fantasy state, wrapped in myth and embellished by the cult of a god-like leader.[15]

Stalin's Soviet Union, a "panegyric utopia," consisted of a myth of well-being, an "iconography of happiness," and a cult of the benevolent ruler. If the reality of the Soviet Union contrasted dramatically with the visions of the revolutionary dreamers and utopians, the myths and images constructed by the regime promoted the fiction that the Soviet people were already living in a kind of utopia, that the conservative stability of the social system and the rigidity of the political structure were "revolutionary." Such notorious Stalinist phrases as "life has become more joyous" and the claim that the Constitution of 1936 was "the only thoroughly democratic constitution in the world" were in fact only fragments of a rich semiotic system of signs, language forms, icons, and other visual expressions of the fantasy state.[16]

Myths of righteousness, omnipotence, and legitimacy were essential to Stalin for his role in a fantasy state. As Max Weber has written: "The charismatic leader gains and maintains authority solely by proving his strength in life. If he wants to be a prophet, he must perform miracles, if he wants to be a warlord, he must perform heroic deeds." Such a ruler must not be bound by abstract codes, the rule of law, or moral norms. He must instead by the exclusive object of glorification. Stalin established his revolutionary legitimacy by associating himself with the founding father of Bolshevism, Lenin, by falsifying the story of the Revolution, and by rapidly creating a "historical memory" by means of the constant repetition in the media of stock phrases, by the display of symbols, and by the rituals that celebrated his historical supremacy in the October Revolution. The purge trials of the later 1930s were not only devices to rid Stalin of real and suspected enemies, but also dramatic rituals familiar from revolutionary experience. In the Civil War, the authorities had staged trials in absentia of the White generals, of the killers of Karl Liebknecht and Rosa Luxemburg, of illiteracy, the louse, drunkenness, kulaks, landlords, Mensheviks, Christian and Jewish gods, and venereal disease. In the mock trial of the White leader Baron Wrangel, the actor was made to confess, tell conflicting stories, and help convict himself in the presence of 10,000 veterans of the Red Army.[17]

Stalin's prophylactic system of security combined with ritual and symbolic deployment on national holidays is reminiscent of, though in no direct way connected to, the widespread Russian and Ukrainian ritual of "ploughing around" the village to protect it from epidemic. In it, only the "pure" members of the village society (maidens and widows) participated while the rest of the village slept. As the women walked around the village in a procession, they ploughed a furrow of protection, while one of them held an icon to invoke and display the presence of God and another cracked a whip to frighten away the devil-disease. The iconic show of power, the menace to the foe, the cutting off of the village from the outside world of danger and infection in this ritual were all reflected in the practices and images of the secret police and the frontier troops of the U.S.S.R., with their unassailable furrow against the diseased and decadent outer world, their show of force on ritual occasions, and their invocation of the divine leader, Stalin. In an artfully contrived atmosphere of alleged conspiracy, secret dealings, devious factionalism, and treason, it was natural for large numbers of people to exhibit solidarity and national will through anger towards dissent, disobedience, breakers of solidarity, and "wreckers" of the system, and natural for the agents of Stalin's terror to demand "transparency" through confession (even if induced by torture) and "unmasking" of enemies of the state. The trials and mass arrests, especially those of 1937, were among the most fantasy-laden elements of the entire Stalin period.[18]

At the pinnacle of the fantasy state was its creator: Joseph Stalin, a legendary poor boy from Georgia who, against all odds, reversed the evil structures of his world, drove out the monsters of injustice, and delivered to the people the justice they had sought for ages past. Understanding completely the essence of "charisma," Stalin invoked the universe, the gods, the past, and the race in the construction of his image, drawing upon Christian imagery of the Orthodox past, the history of the Russian state, and the magical elements of Russian paganism, transforming himself into a hero, a prince, a father, and a god. The official biographies of Stalin in the 1930s made him a hero of the Civil War and extolled his virtues as a "modest man" of courage, boldness, and wisdom. But revolutionary biography was not enough for Stalin; he wanted something with greater resonance and deeper roots—a major role in the entire sweep of Russian history. To get this he had to legitimize Russia's great personalities and heroes, imperial and military, particularly Ivan the Terrible and Peter the Great, who were depicted, like himself, as heroic strugglers against blindly egoistic or evil boyars and opponents of historically necessary modernization.[19]

Stalin saw himself and was seen by many people as a prince—endowed with full power, wrapped in majesty, and revered by the masses. Up until 1934, it had been customary to call heads of local party organizations, "leader" *(vozhd)* or even "beloved leader." After that year, the epithet became Stalin's alone. This trivial detail of history shows not only the strongly grassroots nature of "Stalinism," but also how thousands of people easily cooperated in the building of the Stalin cult.[20] Stalin did not openly demand this particular side of symbolic deference, but he encouraged it, simultaneously describing himself as a simple man. Yet the iconic display of his picture, of his name, and his books as Truth-bearing scripture all pointed to royal or imperial status (see Fig. 40).

Stalin's self-image of father-ruler, converted into a public myth by the media, corresponded with traditional Russian notions of collectivism or community as concern and control. Stalin aspired to make his control over Soviet society complete, but he wished to be seen and loved as a father, the elder of the collective who worked diligently for its safety and well-being. This magnified father cult was a remake of Russian patrimonialism and peasant monarchism. The Soviet state was the household of the party with Stalin at its head, with elaborate ranks and obligatory service for every member in highly specialized roles and with unequal remuneration. Stalin was depicted as the great father of the Soviet family, united in labor under socialism. As in the past, disasters and misdeeds of the government were interpreted by many as the work of "bureaucrats" and not the leader himself. Even in the camps, many prisoners refused to believe that Stalin had a hand in the terrible purges and incarcerations. Peasants, workers, intellectuals, revolutionaries of every sort held to the belief that Stalin's mercy and paternal wisdom would prevail over the evil doers of the purge; some literally regarded him as a benevolent tsar. This bizarre fiction, the belief that Stalin the *tsar-batyushka* would actually deliver the innocent people from oppression, was one of the most typical features of the fantasy state.[21]

As an atheist leader of a Godless state, Stalin of course could not openly proclaim his deification. But something very close to it actually occurred in the mythmaking process of the cult. He was given the ancient religious epithet of "Joseph-Bright," compared to the sun in a folk legend idiom, and associated with immortality. Mothers sang of his omniscience in cradle songs:

> Go to sleep my Kazakh babe
> Knowing hands will care for you.
> Stalin peers from out his window—
> And keeps our vast land in his view.

Local color and folk-religious motifs were woven skillfully into panegyric odes to his power, greatness, and goodness. A Kazakh poem of 1936 by the folksinger Bek described him thus:

> He took unto himself the tears of the ages,
> He took unto himself the woe of the ages,
> He took unto himself the joy of the ages,
> He took unto himself the wisdom of the ages,
> He took unto himself the strength of the ages,
> He burst into the world like morning,
> And the world calls him Stalin.

Dagestani, Lazhinsk, Carelian, Russian, Ukrainian, Mordovian, Georgian, Kurdish, and Kirgiz singers followed suit. To honor him and claim this god for themselves, painters portrayed Stalin with the ethnic features of their own people. During the war, the acting Metropolitan of Moscow called him "the anointed of God," chosen to lead the historical and cultural forces of the Russian people against the Fascist invader.[22]

"Such a man," said Nikita Khrushchëv about Stalin in his 1956 de-Stalinization speech, "supposedly knows everything, sees everything, thinks for everyone, can do anything, is infallible in his behavior. Such a belief about a man, and specifically about Stalin, was cultivated among us for many years." How the myth was presented is illustrated in the account by the worker hero Alexei Stakhanov of his first visit to the Kremlin on November 6–8, 1935. The sight of Marshal Voroshilov cavorting on his horse before the troops on Red Square and the spectacle of new weapons and overflying planes filled Stakhanov with pride and a sense of security. Hundreds of portraits of Stalin were held aloft by the demonstrators. In the evenings, Stakhanov and his associates were taken to see Chaikovsky's *Eugene Onegin,* a monument of nineteenth century tsarist culture, the palaces and cathedrals of the Kremlin, the Armory, and the Tsar-Cannon and the Tsar-Bell. By chance they came upon Stalin and Sergo Ordzhonikidze in the Kremlin yard. Ordzhonikidze, a close associate of Stalin, was addressing an old women with the *"ty"* form of address. Stalin on the other hand called her *"vy"* and described himself as the "most ordinary of men." The company of workers observed that the old woman—a veritable embodiment of the Russian land—revered Stalin. And so, recalls Stakhanov, did they revere him.[23]

Surrounding Stalin was the apparatus of administrative utopia: change by fiat, militarization of society, discipline and welfare, and a facade of universal happiness. Stalinism was not simply a revival of state utopian traditions, mentalities, and practices at the expense of people and intelligentsia; the Stalinist revolutionary settlement also included in its social recesses large vestiges of intelligentsia idealism, arrogance, and dogmatism and, from the lower classes, strong vestiges of what Leo Tolstoy called the "power of darkness"—superstition, paganism, brutality, and a susceptibility to magic—even the magic of rationality, technology, ritual, and myth. The similarity of Stalinism to the administrative utopia of the tsarist past lay in form and method, not in content and purpose. The dream of Arakcheev and the Gatchina emperors was a static one. Stalin, in contrast, launched a radical and dynamic revolution from above which was joined and shaped by a revolution from below. Stalin delivered not only industrial and technological modernization but also social mobility.

Stalinism was a confluence of historical outcomes and a partial merging of tradition with revolution. Stalin's personal role in this system magnified the natural elements of fantasy that accompanies all rapid change. His state differed drastically from the one dreamed about, in fragments or in whole visions, by the utopian dreamers of the pre-Stalinist period of the Revolution. The immense shadow that Stalin cast upon the U.S.S.R. in the 1930s and upon the entire world after 1945 has understandably obscured these differences.


## The Fate of Revolutionary Utopia

"A revolution," wrote Engels, "is certainly the most authoritarian thing there is." In the official communist view of Soviet history, it was the Bolsheviks and the Soviet system that saved the Russian Revolution from precisely the kind of authoritarianism of which Engels had warned: "barracks communism," the ordering of things in perfect symmetry and discipline, and the prohibition of individual differences. Thus Soviet discussions of utopianism almost always defend "common sense" against fanciful and harmful flights of utopianism and its constant handmaiden, egalitarianism. After the Cultural Revolution in China, this argument became particularly sharp.[24] Some prominent figures in the utopian and experimental waves of the 1920s, unmentionable in the late Stalin years, were rehabilitated after his death: Gastev, Kerzhentsev, Meyerhold, Bogdanov (who died before the purges), Vivian Itin, Yan Larri, Okhitivoch, Lunacharsky, and this year Zamyatin and Chayanov. The rehabilitation of some major voices of utopianism ought not to be exaggerated: their fall may have been unrelated to their revolutionary idealism or their commitment to a particular experiment. The various currents I have described in this book were primarily borne on the shoulders of large numbers of unidentified people—crowds, organizations, communities, groups of workers, students, creative artists of various types and many others. The present Soviet view on the utopian currents in the Revolution remains in flux.

The word "utopia" did become a term of bitter derision among Soviet dissidents and émigrés. A song from a Moscow underground youth journal, *The Phoenix*, offers a parody of a well-known official Soviet "March of the Enthusiasts":

> We cannot travel through Europa
> We can't enlarge our views.
> We get our knowledge from utopia
> From gossip and the news.

This example of a very widespread use of the word "utopia" in anti-Soviet anecdotes and ironic comments about the system illustrates its use as a synonym for an outdated and rickety system that is seen as false, hypocritical, and repressive. It is so used in the recent work of two Soviet émigré scholars, *Utopia in Power*.[25]

In the West the word and the concept have come to possess very negative connotations, especially among conservatives—but also among liberals and democratic socialist anti-communists. This reflects a fear that people will still be attracted by sweeping visions of perfection, initiate radical measures to bring them about, and then—through violence and the inability to change human nature—create a terrorist totalitarian state and thus menace the peace of the world and incarcerate new victims in a system of oppression. Utopia in this usage is almost exclusively identified with the goals of a communist revolution. Thus, the anti-utopians of the communist and the anti-communist camps converge in their distaste for utopianism while defining it in different ways.[26]

Partly because of historiographical politics, a whole age of revolutionary dreamers has for the most part been consigned to the margins of history: seen by Western scholars as passing eccentricities in the winds of historical change and by Soviets as harmful cranks, successfully disarmed by hardheaded Soviet power. The revolutionary dreamers of the early years were not a handful of cranks, but whole communities of intellectuals, political figures, economic planners, architects, musicians, writers and artists, publicists of every sort, scholars, journalists, physicians, workers, and peasants—some of them carrying on a continuing interior discourse within fixed circles, other engaged actively in experimental life and work, and all of them signifying to society at large by their words, actions, gestures, and songs that they wished to construct a new world inside the storm of the Revolution and not simply fight for the economic or military substructure of that new world. The utopians were in many ways anthropologists and social workers engaged actively in a vast framework of revolutionary inquiry—field work, data collection, hypothesizing, criticism and self-criticism, a movement that was rooted in the fatal gulf between intelligentsia and people in the nineteenth century, in Populism, in the statistics seminars of pre-revolutionary universities, and in the cultural missionaries of the rural *zemstvos*. This framework of inquiry, based upon freedom of experiment, was dismantled under Stalin, only slightly revived in the post-Stalin decades, and at the present moment promises to reconstitute itself in the context of *perestroika* and *glasnost*.

There was of course no uniformity in the utopian experiments of the 1920s. Every version of utopian speculation as established in the Western world over the course of three millenia could be found expressed in the Russian Revolution: hard and soft, rural and urban, near and far, authoritarian and libertarian, collectivist and nihilist, and all the others. But it is precisely the variety and plurality of this experimental environment that sets it off so dramatically and so definitively from the time of Stalin. There were sweeping, even totalitarian visions of a static world, locked into machine-like processes and inhabited by look-alike lotus eaters. But many others built their utopian vision from the bottom up or from the experience of life outward; their ideas of community, organization, or human improvement came out of collective student life, the comradeship of the barricade and the battlefront, the sharpened sense among professionals of creative urge and social command combining in an act—such as the design of livable and sociable cities—at once satisfying and socially responsible. In the process of utopian design or social experimentation, some were carried away on the winds of arrogant fancy, but others remained on the ground, testing their ideas and themselves in the continuous and delicate work of living the Revolution as devout people had once tried to live their religious faiths.

The period of the Revolution and the 1920s was one of those rare moments in history when a large number of people actually tried to break the mold of social thinking that sets limits to mankind's aspirations, that defines "human nature" in a certain unchangeable way, that speaks in realistic, prudent, and ultimately pessimistic tones to the enthusiasts of this world in order to curb their energies and their fancies. After Stalin died, as Lev Kopelev recalls the time, "rosy memories of the twenties as a time of 'real' soviet power kept bobbing to the surface." In sad but proud remembrance, he writes:

> There was a time when we spoke of the twenties as a 'golden age.' But all too often the gold proved to be only tinsel or 'fool's gold.' Today we know that the romantic revolutionary passions which we recalled so many times with such sweet sorrow degenerated in some men into a fervent desire to serve as executioners, and condemned other men to life at hard labor, to an ignominious end. Today we know how our dreams and ideas of that time turned gradually into dismal doctrine or shameless falsification. But I still think that the time was alive and bursting with youth. Not only with my own tender youth and that of people my own age, but with the youth of the century. The morning of an era we are now living out.

This remarkable testimony by a once dedicated communist, a dweller in the euphoric Soviet world of the 1920s, exhibits both the bitter disappointment over the fate of that dreamworld and the persistent faith in the ideals themselves. It is a view widely shared by many of those Soviet citizens old enough to recall the 1920s, seeing that decade, as Robert Tucker says, as a "retrospective utopia."[27]

Bogdanov, the founder of the Bolshevik utopian genre, defined utopia in the words of one of his characters: "Utopias are an expression of aspirations that cannot be realized, of efforts that are not equal to the resistance they encounter."[28] Bogdanov advocated the ideals embodied in his novels, but was also conscious of the problem of timing in history. All revolutions experience ultraleftist or utopian surges that try to outrun the "natural" course of the revolution (as defined by its leaders), and then fail and are discredited from many sides. This does not stop certain kinds of teaching, once defined as utopian, from becoming commonplace a few generations after they are announced in the midst of revolutionary turmoil and long after their advocates might have been guillotined or sent to death camps. At the present moment of great ferment in the Soviet Union—fueled by Mikhail Gorbachëv's advocacy of openness and renovation—there are signs of a renewed interest among some young intellectuals in utopian socialism, Kropotkin, the Populists, communes, and cities of the future.[29]

Utopianism was a motive force of the Russian Revolution, a major voice of the revolutionary epoch. It is both a product of the revolutionary upheaval and a part of its force and emotional content. The social and cultural variety of this force stemmed from the complexity of Russian civilization in 1917, containing as it did manifold layers of previous history. Rooted traditions of popular and religious utopia resurfaced and made themselves manifest in a welter of expressions—withdrawal, communalism, active sectarian experimentation, revolt against town, center, machine, and alien "power." State traditions of administrative utopia with its peculiar blend of symmetry, brute force, and benevolence, captured the imagination of Bolshevik leaders and dreamers—in and out of the Kremlin—and led them into various forms of militarizing labor, dragooning, and ultimately under Stalin, sweeping integrated plans, "lunar economics," tight control, and forced mobilization. The socialist intelligentsia—Bolsheviks, Mensheviks, Anarchists, Neo-Populists, and others—spun their own fantasies and voiced their own dreams, like ancient oracles, believing in the rightness and the justice of their vision. The resultant cacophony of declamation sounded to some like the gibberish of speaking in tongues, to others like the trumpet blare of liberation and the choirs of angels.

It may be natural in the second half of the twentieth century—the most self-consciously brutal in the history of mankind—to scorn utopian ideals, ideals of perfection, widespread social justice, community, harmony and peace, world-wide cooperation, and a planetary campaign to clean, modernize, preserve and protect the earth from social, military, technical, and natural devastation; visions of an Earthworld of equal people joined in equitable relations and partaking of a universal culture; models of a new way to work, to interact, to play, to study, to love, to live. Soviet programs continue to proclaim some of these ideas, but in the vaguest and most banal of terms. Western leaders and their publics are inclined to be skeptical of such formulations altogether, identifying them either with pro-Soviet propaganda, crypto-communism, or simply idiotic and criminal naïveté. In such a climate, it is hard to imagine these ideas or any combination of them attracting a large number of people. Mutual fear among nations and the relative comfort of the privileged in all societies are the most potent barriers against them. And yet, paradoxical as it may sound, the "utopian propensity" is the only mechanism through which humankind will—if it dares to—protect and preserve all of the realities it so cherishes, including the most cherished of all: the holy and sacred life of mankind and the culture it has created down through the ages.

Utopianism is often naïve, innocent, and childlike. But what virtue is more admired in the whole catalogue of human art and sensibility than childlike enthusiasm, innocence, and spontaneous love and acceptance? What is more lamented than our loss of youth, romance, openness to change, thirst for adventure, and the absence of refined callousness and cold sense of "reality?" These characteristics of the utopian imagination appeal to every generation that discovers it; it is the recurring vision and hope for the "good place" even if it is "no place"—for the better world or even for the one world. The warming springtime of human hope does not give in to the wintry smiles of the cynic and the realist; it blossoms and it perishes in the sad autumnal winds. And then it is born again—for ever and ever.

# A NOTE ON SOURCES AND ABBREVIATIONS

Russian names ending in -skii are so rendered in the notes as authors; and as -sky when discussed in text and notes. I have not used archives for this study except for a few special collections of posters, theater bills, concert programs, recordings and other materials in the Soviet Union (see "Acknowledgments") and a few collections in Washington, D.C. Each of my chapters invites—indeed begs for—archival research; but this would yield ten books instead of one. I believe and hope that these subjects will soon become the object of deeper investigations. My study is a synthesis of source materials and secondary works of many kinds, all of them indicated in the notes. To enumerate them in a bibliography would be pedantic. Below is a list of abbreviations used in the notes.

ARR   *Arkhiv russkoi revolyutsii*
ASEER   *American Slavic and East European Review*
BSE   *Bolshaya Sovetskaya entsiklopediya*
BV   *Birzhevyye vedomosti*
BVSNKh   *Byulleteni Vysshago Soveta Narodnago Khozyaistva*
BVSNTMP   *Byulleten Vserossiiskogo Soveta normirovaniya truda v metallicheskoi promyshlennosti*
BVTsSP   *Byulleten Vsesoyuznogo Tsentralnogo Soyuza Profsoyuz*
CASS   *Canadian-American Slavic Studies*
CSSH   *Comparative Studies in Society and History*
EMIRA   *Ezhegodnik Muzei Istorii Religii i Ateizma*
ES (Granat)   *Entsiklopedicheskii slovar* (Granat)
ESF   *Encyclopedia of Science Fiction*, ed. P. Nicholls (London, 1981)
ISSR   *Istoriya SSSR*
JGO   *Jahrbücher für Geschichte Osteuropas*
JMH   *Journal of Modern History*
JHI   *Journal of the History of Ideas*
JSH   *Journal of Social History*
KA   *Krasnyi arkhiv*
KG   *Krasnaya gazeta*
KLE   *Kratkaya Literaturnaya Entsiklopediya*
KL   *Krasnaya letopis*
KM   *Krasnaya molodëzh*
LC   Library of Congress
MERSH   *Modern Encyclopedia of Russian and Soviet History*
MLR   *Modern Language Review*
PK   *Proletarskaya kultura*
POC   *Problems of Communism*
PR   *Proletarskaya revolyutsiya*
PVRK   *Petrogradskii Voenno-Revolyutsionnyi Komitet: dokumenty i materialy*
OT   *Organizatsiya truda*
RES   *Revue des études slaves*
RG   *Rabochaya gazeta*
RH   *Russian History*
RK   *Revolyutsiya i kultura*

RLT  *Russian Literature Triquarterly*
RR  *Russian Review*
SA  *Sovetskaya arkhitektura*
SAP  *St. Antony's Papers*
SEEJ  *Slavic and East European Journal*
SEER  *Slavic and East European Review*
SR  *Slavic Review*
SS  *Soviet Studies*
Trudy NOT  *Trudy Pervoi Vserossiiskoi Initsiativnoi Konferentsii po Nauchnoi Organizatsii Truda i Proizvodstva, 20–27 yanvarya 1921 goda*
VE  *Vestnik Evropy*
VIRA  *Voprosy istorii religii i ateizma*
VKR (Prague)  *Vestnik krestyanskoi Rossii*
VKVD  *Vestnik Kommissariata Vnutrennykh Del*
VOKVD  *Vestnik Oblastnogo Kommissariata Vnutrennykh Del (Soyuza Kommun Severnoi Oblasti)*
VOKZ  *Vestnik Oblastnogo Kommissariata Zemledeliya*
VOMU  *Vestnik Otdela Mestnago Upravleniya*
VRNK (Paris)  *Vestnik Russkago Narodnago Komiteta*
VT  *Vestnik truda*

# NOTES

## Introduction

1. Frank and Fritzie Manuel, *Utopian Thought in the Western World* (Oxford: Blackwell, 1979) 1–29.

2. Lars Kleberg, "Utopia and its Negations" in *Utopia in Russian History, Culture, and Thought*, eds. Kleberg and Richard Stites (special issue of *Russian History* 11/2–3 (Summer–Fall, 1984) 209–19, describes how scholars have tried to type literaty utopias. See also the Manuels' *Utopian Thought*.

3. Quoted in Jane Burbank, *Intelligentsia and Revolution: Russian Views of Bolshevism, 1917–1922* (New York: Oxford University Press, 1986) 19. The commentator was the Menshevik leader, Yu. O. Martov.

4. Manual and Manuel, *Utopian Thought*, 9.

5. Henrik Infield, *Utopia and Experiment* (Kennikat, 1971), 18–25.

6. Moshe Lewin, *The Making of the Soviet System* (New York: Pantheon, 1985).

7. Harper edition, revised with an epilogue (New York, 1965).

8. *Soviet Dissidence in Historical Perspective* (Cambridge: Cambridge University Press, 1980) 77.

9. Ernst Bloch, *The Principle of Hope* (1938–47), tr. N. Plaice, S. Plaice, and P. Knight, 3 v. (Oxford: Blackwell, 1986).

## Chapter 1: Social Daydreaming Before the Revolution

1. "Revolyutsionnaya propagandistskaya literatura 70-kh godov XIX v.," *Istoricheskie zapiski*, 71 (1962) 74–112 (p. 97).

2. See Manuel and Manuel, *Utopian Thought*, 7.

3. Chalinder Allen, *The Tyranny of Time* (New York: Philosophical Library, 1947), 97, 190–91.

4. James Michael Holquist, "How to Play Utopia: Some Brief Notes on the Distinctiveness of Utopian Fiction," in Mark Rose, ed., *Science Fiction* (Englewood Cliffs: Prentice Hall, 1976).

5. Henry Berger, Jr., "The Renaissance Imagination: Second World and Green World," *Centennial Review*, IX (1965) 36–78 (p. 46).

6. Kleberg and Stites, *Utopia*.

7. For these contrasting perspectives, see James C. Scott, "Protest and Profanation: Agrarian Revolt and the Little Tradition," *Theory and Society*, 4/1 (Spring 1977) 1–38 and 4/2 (Summer 1977) 211–47; and Samuel Popkin, *The Rational Peasant* (Berkeley: University of California Press, 1979).

8. For a fine study of real life in a serf village, see Steven Hoch, *Serfdom and Social Control* (Chicago: University of Chicago Press, 1987).

9. Wada Haruki, "The Inner World of Russian Peasants," *Annals of the Institute of Social Science (Tokyo)*, 20 (1979) 61–65. On folkloric evidence for peasant visions, see Elena Hellberg, "Folklore, Might, and Glory," in *Nordic Journal of Soviet and East European Studies*, 3/2 (1986).

10. K. V. Chistov, *Russkie narodyne sotsialno-utopicheskie legendy XVII–XIX vv.* (Moscow: Nauka, 1967), see esp. 251–53; Luka's dream with commentary in *Vechnoe solntse: russkaya sotsialnaya utopiya i nauchnaya fantastika (vtoraya polovina XIX-nachalo XX veka)*, Moscow, Molodaya Gvardiya, 1979, pp. 5, 27, 218; Darko Suvin, *Metamorphoses of Science Fiction* (New Haven: Yale University Press, 1979), 250.

11. Haruki, "Inner World," 66; Michael Cherniavsky, *Tsar and People* (New Haven: Yale University Press, 1961) 47–49 and *passim;* Paul Avrich, *Russian Rebels, 1600–1800* (New York: Schocken, 1972); Daniel Field, *Rebels in the Name of the Tsar* (Boston: Houghton Mifflin, 1976).

12. Terence Emmons, "The Peasant and the Emancipation" in Wayne Vucinich, ed., *The Peasant in Nineteenth Century Russia* (Stanford: Stanford University Press, 1968) p. 60. See Field, *Rebels*.

13. Field, "A Far-off Abode of Work and Pure Pleasure," *Russian Review*, 39 (July 1980) 348–58.

14. Serge Zenkovsky, "The Ideological World of the Denisov Brothers," *Harvard Slavic Studies*, III (1957) 57.

15. *Ibid.*, 56.

16. Robert Crummey, *The Old Believers and the World of Anti-Christ: the Vyg Community and the Russian State, 1694–1855* (Madison: University of Wisconsin Press, 1970); Frederick Conybeare, *Russian Dissenters* (Cambridge, Mass.: Harvard University Press, 1921).

17. A. I. Klibanov, *Narodnaya sotsialnaya utopiya v Rossii: XIX vek* (Moscow: Nauka, 1978) (to be cited as *NSU*). For a translated excerpt, see Kleberg and Stites, *Utopia*, 168–208. See also D. S. Babkin "Russkaya potaennaya sotsialnaya utopiya XVIII veka," *Russkaya literatura*, XI/4 (1968) 92–106.

18. Klibanov, *NSU*, 12.

19. *Ibid.*, 22.

20. Conybeare, *Russian Dissenters*, 281–84.

21. Klibanov, *NSU*, 12.

22. Avrich, *Russian Rebels, passim.*

23. John T. Alexander, *Emperor of the Cossacks: Pugachev and the Frontier Jacquerie of 1773–1775* (Lawrence: Coronado, 1973) 210.

24. Raeff, "Pugachev's Rebellion," in Robert Forster and Jack Greene, eds., *Preconditions of Revolution in Early Modern Europe* (Baltimore: Johns Hopkins University Press, 1970) 198.

25. Klibanov, *NSU*, 25–33. Field, *Rebels*.

26. Philip Longworth, "The Subversive Legend of Stenka Razin," *Rossiya/Russia*, 2 (1975) 17–40.

27. Klibanov, *NSU*, 32.

28. Raeff, "Pugachev's Rebellion," 198.

29. Avrich, *Russian Rebels*, 238.

30. Norman Cohn, *The Pursuit of the Millenium* (New York: Oxford University Press, 1970); David Goldfrank, "Pre-Enlightenment Utopianism in Russian History," in Kleberg and Stites, *Utopia*, 123–47.

31. Klibanov, *NSU*, 28–30.

32. Jeffrey Brooks, *When Russia Learned to Read* (Princeton: Princeton University Press, 1986).

33. Teodor Shanin, "The Peasant Dream," in *The Roots of Otherness*, 2 v. (New Haven: Yale University Press, 1986) II, 120–38.

34. Michel Foucault, *Discipline and Punish: the Birth of the Prison*, tr. A. Sheridan (New York: Pantheon, 1977) 135–37, 195–228 (225, 221).

35. H. Gerth and C. Wright Mills, eds, *From Max Weber* (New York: Oxford University Press, 1958) 261.

36. Gustav Schmoller, *Deutsches Städtewesen in älterer Zeit* (Bonn: Schroeder, 1922) 417.

37. Sidney B. Fay and Klaus Epstein, *The Rise of Brandenburg-Prussia to 1786* (New York: Holt, 1964) 88–100.

38. Hans Rosenberg, *Bureaucracy, Aristocracy, and Autocracy: the Prussian Experience* (1958; Boston: Beacon, 1966) 89.

39. Marc Raeff, *The Well-Ordered Police State: Social and Institutional Change Through Law in the Germanies and Russia, 1600–1800* (Yale University Press, 1983) 87 and *passim.*

40. Rosenberg, *Bureaucracy*, 38.

41. Raeff, *Well-Ordered Police State*, 181–250.

42. For the introduction of the new ritual, see V. D. Sedykh, *Voinskie ritualy* (Moscow: Voennoe Izd., 1981) 14–18.

43. Raeff, "Home, School, and Service in the Life of the Russian Nobleman," in M. Cherniavsky, ed., *The Structure of Russian History* (New York: Random House, 1970) 212–223 (220); *idem., Origins of the Russian Intelligentsia* (New York: Harbinger, 1966) 78–79.

44. Michael Jenkins, *Arakcheev* (New York: Dial, 1969) 39–46; Christopher Duffy, *Russia's Military Way to the West* (London: Routledge, 1981) 200–201, 235.

45. Allen McConnell, *Tsar Alexander I* (New York: Crowell, 1970) 138–42; W. Bruce Lincoln, *Nicholas I* (Bloomington: Indiana University Press, 1978) 58, 69, 192–94, and *passim;* Nicholas Riasanovsky, *Nicholas I and Official Nationality in Russia, 1825–1855* (Berkeley: University of California Press, 1959) *passim.*

46. Marquis de Custine, *Journey for our Time*, ed. P. Kohler (Chicago: Regnery, 1951) 53, 58, 79, 80.

47. See Chapter 9.

48. Albert Schmidt, "Architecture in Nineteenth Century Russia," in Theofanis Stavrou, ed., *Art and Culture in Nineteenth-Century Russia* (Bloomington: Indiana University Press, 1983) 172–93; *idem,* "William Hastie, Scottish Planner of Russian Cities," *Proceedings of the American Philosophical Society,* CXIV/3 (June 1970) 226–43; *idem,* "The Restoration of Moscow after 1812," *Slavic Review,* XL/1 (Spring 1981) 38–48 (38); Hans Blumenfeld, "Russian City Planning of the 18th and Early 19th Centuries," *Journal of the Society of Architectural Historians* 4/1–4 (Jan.–Oct. 1944) 22–33; E. Beletskaya *et al., "Obraztsovye" proekty v zhiloi zastroike russkikh gorodov XVIII–XIX vv.* (Moscow: Gosstroiizdat, 1961); and Mary Matossian on the village grids in Vucinich, *Peasant*, 2.

49. Custine, *Journey*, 92, 141–42, 148.

50. Stephen Baehr, "Fortuna Redux: the Iconography of Happiness in Eighteenth-Century Russian Courtly Spectacles," in A. G. Cross, ed., *Russia and England in the Eighteenth Century* (Newtonville: Oriental Research Partners, 1979) 109–21.

51. Blumenfeld, "Russian City Planning," 31.

52. Raeff, *Catherine the Great: a Profile* (New York: Hill and Wang, 1972) 197–246; Roger Bartlett, *Human Capital* (Cambridge: Cambridge University Press, 1979) 124–34.

53. For a vivid description, see Gina Kaus, *Catherine*, tr. J. Head (New York: Literary Guild, 1935) 334–43. See George Soloveytchik, *Potemkin* (New York: Norton, 1947) pp. 187–193, 267–88 and George Munro's articles in *Modern Encyclopedia of Russian and Soviet History* (to be cited as MERSH), XXIX, 123–28 and 134–36. The idea of the Panopticon was hatched by Jeremy Bentham while visiting his brother in the employ of Potëmkin: *Vestnik Evropy* (Feb. 1869) 784–819.

54. Jenkins, *Arakcheev*, 62–92; *Russkii arkhiv*, VII/7–8 (1869) 1462–84.

55. Jenkins, *Arakcheev*, 140–7, 171–203; McConnell, *Tsar Alexander*, 138–42 (139); Richard Pipes, "The Russian Military Colonies, 1810–1831," *Journal of Modern History*, XXII/3 (Sept. 1950) 205–19.

56. *Ibid.* The striking similarity between life in the Russian military colonies and in the "militarized" cantonments of eighteenth century Prussia can be seen in Otto Busch, *Militärsystem and Sozialleben im älten Preussen* (Berlin: de Gruyter, 1962). For a detailed history, see Alan Ferguson, *The Russian Military Settlements, 1810–1866* (Ann Arbor: University Microfilms, 1966; Yale Ph.D. thesis, 1954).

57. Riasanovsky, *Nicholas I.*

58. The cultural outlook of Nicholas II is explored by Richard Wortman in his forthcoming volume on the Romanovs and their court.

59. This is one of the many neglected topics in Russian intellectual history. For a beginning, the reader should see: S. Baehr, "Utopian Literature (Sumarokov through Odoevsky, c. 1750–c. 1850)," *Yale Handbook of Russian Literature* (New Haven: Yale University Press, 1984); V. Svyatlovskii, *Russkii utopicheskii roman* (Petrograd: Gosizdat, 1922). For individual writers: A. A. Kizevetter, "Russkaya utopiya XVIII st. (kn. M. M. Shcherbatov)," *Istoricheskie ocherki* (Moscow, 1912) 29–56 (written, 1900); N. P. Vaslef, "Bulgarin and the Development of the Russian Utopian Genre," *SEEJ*, XII/1 (1968) 35–43; D. Čyževsky (Chizhevskii), "Die ältesten russischen technischen Utopien," *Zeitschrift für slavische Philologie*, XXV (1952) 322–24. For texts: Leland Fetzer, ed., *Pre-Revolutionary Russian Science Fiction: an Anthology* (Ann Arbor: Ardis, 1982); *Vzglyad skvoz stoletiya: russkaya fantastika XVIII i pervoi poloviny XIX veka* (Moscow: Molodaya Gvardiya, 1977); and *Russkaya fantasticheskaya proza XIX-nachala XX veka* (Moscow: Pravda, 1986).

60. Quoted in Anatole Mazour, *The First Russian Revolution, 1825: the Decembrist Movement* (Stanford: Stanford University Press, 1937) 104; Yu. Lotman, "The Decembrist in Daily Life," in *The Semiotics of Russian Cultural History*, ed. A. D. and A. S. Nakhimovksy (Ithaca: Cornell University Press, 1985) 94–149; Marc Raeff, *The Decembrist Movement* (Englewood Cliffs: Prentice Hall, 1956) 119–56 and *passim*.

61. Full text and analysis in M. V. Nechkina, "Dekabristskaya 'utopiya'," in *Iz istorii sotsialno-politicheskikh idei* (Moscow: ANSSSR, 1955) 376–84. Abridged text in *Vzglyad*, 91–99; English translation in Raeff, *Decembrist*, 60–66 (with a minor error: the Nevsky Lavra is confused with the Smolny).

62. *Delo Petrashevtsev*, III (Moscow: ANSSSR, 1951) 113. Nicholas Riasanovsky, "Fourierism in Russia," *ASEER*, XI/3 (1953) 289–302; I. I. Zilberfarb, *Sotsialnaya filosofiya Sharlya Fure* (Moscow, 1964) 330–82; J. L. Evans, *The Petraševskij Circle, 1845–1849* (The Hague: Mouton, 1974); and J. H. Seddon, *The Petrashevtsy: a Study of the Russian Revolutionaries of 1848* (Manchester: Manchester University Press, 1985), the best study in English to date.

63. N. G. Chernyshevskii, *Chto delat?; iz rasskazov o novykh lyudakh—roman* (1863; Moscow, 1963) 391–411.

64. H. Lenczyc explores the glass motif in European futurist literature in "Zamjatins glassymbol i den europeiska literaturen," *Rysk Kulturrevy*, IX/2 (1977) 11–15.

65. Chernyshevskii, *Chto delat*, 411 (italics added).

66. A. F. Britikov, "A. V. Lunacharskii ob utopicheskom romane," *Russkaya literatura*, 4 (1957) 52.

67. See V. Revich, "Ne byl, no i ne vydumka," *Fantastika 71* (Moscow: Molodaya gvardiya, 1971). Two recent perspectives are: Irina Paperno, "The Structure of What Is to Be Done? the Novel-Myth as a New Gospel" and Yoshi Imai, "N. G. Chernyshevsky: Pioneer of the Russian Cooperative Movement," both presented at the Third World Slavic Congress, Washington, D.C. 1985.

68. For introductions to the subject: Nicholas Berdyaev, *The Origin of Russian Communism* (London: Bles, 1937); Richard Pipes, ed., *The Russian Intelligentsia* (New York: Columbia University Press, 1961); James Billington, *The Icon and the Axe* (New York: Knopf, 1966).

69. Cited in *Vechnoe solntse*, 17.

70. Abbott Gleason, *Young Russia: the Genesis of Russian Radicalism in the 1860s* (Chicago: University of Chicago Press, 1985) and Daniel Brower, *Training the Nihilists: Education and Radicalism in Tsarist Russia* (Ithaca: Cornell University Press, 1975).

71. Gleason, *Young Russia*, 43, 65, 171–72, 185, *passim*.

72. V. A. Fëdorov, "Trebovaniya krestyanskogo dvizheniya v nachale revolyutionnoi sitsuatsii do 19 fevralya 1861 g.," *Revolyutsionnaya situatsiya v Rossii, 1859–1861 gg.* (Moscow: A.N.S.S.S.R., 1960) 133–48; Zakharina, "Rev. prop. lit."; Kropotkin's text in S. N. Valk *et*

*al.*, eds., *Revolyutsionnoe narodnichestvo 70-kh godov XIX veka*, 2 vols. (Moscow: Nauka, 1964–65) I, 55–118. Trans. in P. A. Kropotkin, *Selected Writings on Anarchism and Revolution*, ed. Martin Miller (Cambridge, Mass.: M.I.T. Press, 1970) 47–116. For Lavrov: Philip Pomper, *Peter Lavrov and the Russian Revolutionary Movement* (Chicago: University of Chicago Press, 1972) 188–91.

73. A. V. Pribylev, *Zapiski narodovoltsa* (Moscow, 1930) 125–28. The subject of utopian socialism in Russia has not been adequately treated by Soviet historians. For texts, see *Utopicheskii sotsializm v Rossi*, ed. A. I. Volodin *et al.* (Moscow: Politizdat, 1985).

74. Quotation from Michael Hamm, ed., *The City in Russian History* (Lexington: University of Kentucky Press, 1976) 198. R. E. Johnson, *Peasant and Proletarian: the Working Class of Moscow in the Late Nineteenth Century* (New Brunswick: Rutgers University Press, 1979); Laura Engelstein, *Moscow, 1905: Working Class Organization and Political Conflict* (Stanford: Stanford University Press, 1982); Joseph Bradley, *Muzhik and Muscovite: Urbanization in Late Imperial Russia* (Berkeley: University of California Press, 1982); Stites, "Prostitution and Society in Pre-Revolutionary Russia," *Jahrbücher für Geschichte Osteuropas*, 31 (1983) 348–64.

75. Soviet libraries contain dozens of editions and translations of Wells and Verne from before the Revolution. On Verne, see Jurij Striedter, "Journey through Utopia," *Poetics Today*, 3/1 (Winter, 1982) 33–60. The Chikolev work is *Ne byl, no i ne vydumka—elektricheskii razskaz* (S.Pb.: Babkin, 1895). Revich, "Ne byl," 294–98 and Suvin, *Metamorphoses*, 251–52.

76. Brooks, *When Russia Learned to Read*.

77. Reginald Zelnik, *A Radical Worker in Tsarist Russia: the Autobiography of Semën Ivanovich Kanatchikov* (Stanford: Stanford University Press, 1986), xxv, 34, 67 and *passim*.

78. On the function of "utopian pictures" among European workers, see Hendrik de Man, *The Psychology of Socialism*, 2 ed. (London: Allen and Unwin, 1928) 165. Kautsky, *Klassovye interesy* (Geneva: Kuklin, 1903) 28–29; *idem, Tomas Mor i ego Utopiya* trans. M. and A. Genkel (S.Pb.: Pirozhkov, 1905). The other works in translation, are: A. Bebel, *Zhenshchina i sotsializm*, tr. from 34th German ed. V. A. Posse (Geneva: Kuklin, 1904), one of many; *idem, Budushchee obshchestvo* (Moscow: Kolokol, 1905); L. Braun, *Zhenskii vopros* (S.Pb.: Volf, 1903); *idem, Polozhenie zhenshchiny v nastoyashchem i budushchem sotsialnoi stroe* (Odessa, 1905); Atlanticus [Karl Ballod], *Gosudarstvo budushchago*, trans. V. Desnitskii (S.Pb.: Znanie, 1906).

79. Kautsky, preface to Atlanticus.

80. Stites, "Future of the Family" in *Women's Liberation*, 258–69.

81. Edward Bellamy, *Looking Backward, 2000–1887* (New York: Grosset and Dunlap, 1888); *idem, Equality* (London: Heinemann, 1897). John Thomas, *Alternative America* (Cambridge: Harvard University Press, 1983) 237–61; Arthur Lipow, *Authoritarian Socialism in America: Edward Bellamy and the Nationalist Movement* (Berkeley: University of California Press, 1982) 16–57.

82. A. N. Nikolzhukin [Nikoljukin], "A Little Known Story: Bellamy in Russia," in Sylvia Bowen, ed., *Edward Bellamy Abroad* (New York: Twayne, 1967) and Svyatlovskii, *Russ. utop. roman*, 50. For editions and printings up to 1898 (almost 20,000), see *Russkie Knigi*, III (1898), 179–80.

83. For background, texts, and publication history, see Alexander Bogdanov, *Red Star: the First Bolshevik Utopia*, ed. L. Graham and R. Stites, tr. Charles Rougle (Bloomington: Indiana University Press, 1984). Its initial tirage was 6,000 copies in Russian and 3,000 in Latvian: *Knizhnaya letopis*, 20 (Nov. 24, 1907) 3 and 18 (May 3, 1908) 21.

84. S. D. [S. Dinamov] in PK, 3 (August 1918) 33–34.

85. A standard older work is A. S. Prugavin, *O Lve Tolstom i o tolstovtsakh*, 2 ed. (Moscow: Sytin, 1911). On anti-urbanism, see Chapter 9.

86. Avrich, *The Russian Anarchists* (Princeton: Princeton University Press, 1967).

87. The most complete bibliography is: V. Bugrov and I. Khalymbadzha, "Fantastika v dorevolyutsionnoi russkoi literature," *Poisk-83* (Sverdlovsk: Sredne-Uralskoe knizh. izd., 1983) 328–52. I have discussed some of the novels in "Hopes and Fears of Things to Come: the Foreshadowing of Totalitarianism in Russian Fantasy and Utopia," *Nordic Journal of Soviet and East*

*European Studies,* 3/1 (1986) 1–20. For the American works, see Neil Harris, "Utopian Fiction and its Discontents," in Richard Bushman *et al.,* eds., *Uprooted Americans* (Boston: Little Brown, 1979) 209–44.

88. A. I. Kransnitskii, *Za pripodnyatoyu zavesoi: fantasticheskaya povest o delakh budush-chago (XX vek),* (S.Pb.: Trei, 1900).

89. H. D. Löwe, *Antisemitismus und reactionäre Utopie: russischer Konservatismus im Kampf gegen den Wandel von Staat und Gesellschaft 1890–1917* (Hamburg: Hoffman und Campe, 1978) 17–23, 30–9, 56–57, 126, and *passim.*

90. N. N. Shelonskii, *V mire budushchego: fantasticheskii roman* (Moscow: Sytin, 1892); L. B. Afanasiev, "Puteshestvie na Mars: fantasticheskaya povest." *Niva,* 1 (January 1901) 275–330 and 3 (March 1901) 483–534; S. F. Sharapov, *Cherez polveka: fantasticheskii politiko-sotsialnyi roman* (Moscow: Vasilev, 1902).

91. V. Ya. Bryusov, "Zemlya" in *Zemnaya Os,* 2 ed. (Moscow: Skorpion, 1910) 114–59 and "Respublika Yuzhnogo Kresta," in *ibid.* 62–82.

92. Nikolai Fëdorov, *Vecher v 2217 godu* (S.Pb.: Gerold, 1906). The postface reveals the author to be a Christian anti-socialist—but little else. For Jerome, see E. Stenbok-Fermor, "A Neglected Source of Zamiatin's novel 'We'," *RR,* 32/2 (April 1972) 187–88. Mantegazza's book appeared in Russian as *Budushchee chelovechestvo (3000-i god)* (S.Pb.: Pavlenkov, 1898). Both works feature harsh, repressive, uniform, regimented societies.

93. The title of a popular Finnish book on the subject: Raoul Palmgren, *Pelon ja toivon utopiat* (Tampere, 1963).

## Chapter 2: Revolution: Utopias in the Air and on the Ground

1. BV, March 25, 1917. Claude Anet [pseud. of Jean Schopfer], *Through the Russian Revolution* (London: Hutchinson, 1918) 72–75; Mayakovsky and the Poles quoted in V. F. Shishkin, *Velikii Oktyabr i proletarskaya moral* (Moscow: Mysl, 1976) 20–21; Blok in Avril Pyman, *The Life of Alexandr Blok,* II (Oxford: the Clarendon Press, 1980) 282.

2. See Chapter 4.

3. Lvov quoted in Anet, *Through,* 82; P. N. Milyukov, *The Russian Revolution,* ed. R. Stites (Gulf Breeze: Academic International Press, 1978), I, xiv.

4. S. A. Smith, *Spontaneity and Organization in the Petrograd Labour Movement in 1917* (Colchester: University of Essex, 1984) 7, 9, 23, 31 and *Red Petrograd* (Cambridge: Cambridge University Press, 1983), chapter 8. David Mandel, *Petrograd Workers and the Seizure of Power,* 2 Vols. (London: Macmillan, 1985), I, 230. Moscow workers before October were euphoric but non-millenarian, and their "maximalism" was caused by fear of capitalists and by political events: Diane Koenker, *Moscow Workers and the 1917 Revolution* (Princeton: Princeton University Press, 1981).

5. Manuels, *Utopian Thought,* 14; A. K. Gastev, *Poeziya rabochego udara* (1918: Moscow: Sovetskii Pisatel, 1964) 7; Ehrenburg, *First Years of Revolution, 1918–1921* (London: Mac-Gibbon and Kee, 1962) 84 (qu.) and 152–58; Panfërov, "Chto takoe kommunizm?," *Oktyabr* 37 (January 1960) 103.

6. Steinberg, *In the Workshop of the Revolution* (New York: Rinehart, 1953) 44–45.

7. Gladkov, *Cement* (New York: Ungar, n.d.) 98; Cargo cults: Hans Toch, *The Social Psychology of Social Movements* (Indianapolis: Bobbs-Merrill, 1965) 41; Gastev, *Poeziya,* 234.

8. Lotman and Uspensky, "Binary Models in the Dynamics of Russian Culture," in *Semiotics of Russian Cultural History,* 31–34, 52–53.

9. H. G. Wells, "The Dreamer in the Kremlin," in *Russia in the Shadows* (New York: Doran, 1921) 145–68.

10. D. I. Pisarev, *Sochineniya,* 4 vols. (Moscow: Gos. Izd. Khud. Lit., 1955–56), III, 147–

48, 149; Lenin, *Polnoe sobranie sochinenii* (hereafter referred to as *PSS*) VI, 172. I cite it from Robert C. Tucker, ed., *The Lenin Anthology* (New York: Norton, 1975) 106.

11. On Lenin as visionary: Tucker, "Lenin's Bolshevism as a Culture in the Making," in Abbott Gleason *et al.*, eds., *Bolshevik Culture: Experiment and Order in the Russian Revolution* (Bloomington: Indiana University Press, 1985) 25–38 and Leopold Haimson, *Russian Marxists and the Origin of Bolshevism* (Cambridge Mass.: Harvard University Press, 1955) 98–99. Lenin's "dream" quotation was constantly invoked in the way he meant it: "The revolutionary must know how to dream. In order to present young laboring people with the correct ideological position, it is necessary to teach youth how to dream and to organize it to fight for the realization of its dreams." V. Dmitriev and B. Galin, *Na putyakh k novomu bytu* (Moscow: Novaya Moskva, 1927) 8–10.

12. Lenin, PSS, XI, 103 (*Two Tactics of Social Democracy*, 1905) in Tucker, *Lenin Anthology*, 140.

13. The first quotation is from Patrick McGuire, *Red Stars: Political Aspects of Soviet Science Fiction* (Ann Arbor: UMI, 1985) 122, n. 39; the second from Striedter, "Journeys," 36. Lenin's library contained Bogdanov's *Engineer Menni* and many of his nonfiction works, the works of Bryusev, Mayakovsky, and Klyuev (see Chapter 9); Nikolai Morozov's *Star Songs*, Ilya Ehrenburg's *Julio Jurenito* and *Trust DE* (two anti-capitalist political fantasies), and the monarchist utopian novel *Beyond the Thistle* by Peter Krasnov (see Chapter 8): *Biblioteka V. I. Lenina v Kremle: katalog* (Moscow: Vsesoyuznaya palata, 1961). Absent from the collection are Chernyshevsky's *What Is To Be Done?* and Bogdanov's *Red Star* (both of which he had read). Lenin must have read Wells's *Time Machine* just prior to the interview since he told the sculptress Clare Sheridan in 1920 that regretfully he had read none of Wells's science fiction: *Russian Portraits* (London: Cape, 1921) 108.

14. Wells, *Russia*, 157.

15. Translation in Tucker, *Lenin Anthology*, 311–98 (*State and Revolution*, 1916–1917). For its composition, see Rodney Barfield, "Lenin's Utopianism: *State and Revolution*," SR, XXI/1 (March 1971) 45–56. Marx's communist stage discussed by Bert Ollman, in Seweryn Bialer and Sophie Sluzar, eds., *Radical Visions of the Future* (Boulder: Westview, 1977) 34–83.

16. Tucker, *Lenin Anthology*, 370–1, 374, 380.

17. François George, "Forgetting Lenin," *Telos*, 18 (Winter, 1973–74) 53–88 (53); Frederick Hayek, *Counterrevolution of Science*, 2 ed. (Indianapolis: Liberty Press, 1979) 173–74, 220–2; Frederic Fleron, "Administrative Theory as Repressive Political Theory: the Communist Experience," *Telos*, 27 (Spring 1976) 79–96 (esp. 88, 93). On problems of authority in Marxism, see also Jeremy Azrael, *Managerial Power and Soviet Politics* (Cambridge Mass.: Harvard University Press, 1966) 16–19.

18. Lenin, PSS, XXXVIII, 39–73 (quote 53–54). The work is "Successes and Difficulties of Soviet Power" (1919).

19. This summary is based on a reading of all Lenin's remarks on utopia and utopian socialism in PSS.

20. Petr Yu [P. M. Solyanyi], "Gosudarstvo budushchego," *Plamya*, 66 (October 12, 1919) 9–10.

21. One can get a good sense of both the restraining and the visionary elements in Lenin's scheme of a Soviet democratic tutelary state in Tucker, "Lenin's Bolshevism" and in Sheila Fitzpatrick's "The Civil War as a Formative Experience," both in Gleason, *Bolshevik Culture*, 25–38 and 57–76 respectively.

22. Silvana Malle, *The Economic Organization of War Communism, 1918–1921* (Cambridge: Cambridge University Press, 1985); E. G. Gimpelson, *"Voennyi Kommunizm:" politika, praktika, ideologiya* (Moscow: Mysl, 1973); Heiko Haumann, "Die russische Revolution und ihre ersten Versuche sozialistischer Wirtschaftspolitik," *Das Argument*, 15 (1973) 768–803; *idem*, " 'Kriegskommunismus' oder unmittelbarer Aufbau des Sozialismus?," *JGO*, 23 (1975) 98–104. An interesting personal perspective from the inside is Victor Serge, *Memoirs of a Revolutionary*,

tr. P. Sedgwick (London: Oxford University Press, 1963) 115–17. L. N. Kritsman, active partic-
ipant, heroizer, and mythmaker of War Communism saw it as an "anticipation of the future"
(Malle, *Economic Organization*, 9) in his well known *Heroic Period of the Great Russian Revolution* (1924). The best analysis of it is Haumann's introduction to the recent German edition in
*Arkhiv sozialistischer Literatur*, 24 (Frankfurt, 1971), v–lxi.

23. Harold Stearns of *Dial* in 1919, quoted in Peter Filene, *Americans and the Soviet Experiment, 1917–1933* (Cambridge Mass.: Harvard University Press, 1967) 131.

24. On the relationship of the Civil War to cultural innovation, an interesting Soviet view is
V. T. Ermakov, " 'Voennyi kommunizm' i kulturnoe stroitelstvo v vtoroi polovina 1918–nachale
1921 goda," ISSSR, 6 (Nov.–Dec. 1974) 136–49.

25. Bukharin and Preobrazhenskii, *The ABC of Communism*, intro. S. Heitman (Ann Arbor:
University of Michigan Press, 1966) 75; Pethybridge, *Social Prelude*, 31–33.

26. *ABC of Communism*, qu. 70, 74. For Bogdanov and Bukharin on systems thinking, see
Ilmari Susiluoto, *The Origins and Development of Systems Thinking in the Soviet Union* (Helsinki:
Tiedenakatemia, 1982). For Bukharin's intellectual formation, the best work is Stephen F. Cohen,
*Bukharin and the Bolshevik Revolution* (New York: Vintage, 1971).

27. Pethybridge, *Social Prelude*, 35–36.

28. *Byulleteni Gosudarstvennoi Komissii po Elektrifikatsii Rossii*, 5 (August 15, 1920) 13.

29. Pethybridge, *Social Prelude*, 37, 165.

30. Wells, *Russia*, 135; Adam Ulam, *Expansion and Coexistence*, 2 ed. (New York: Praeger,
1974) 87; I. I. [Skvortsov-] Stepanov, *Elektrifikatsiya R.S.F.S.R. v svyazi s perekhodnoi fazoi
mirogo khozyaistva* (Moscow: Gosizd., 1922), Lenin's preface; *Plan elektrifikatsii R.S.F.S.R.*
(1920; 2 ed. Moscow: Gos. Izd. Pol. Lit., 1955) 11–14 (qu. from interview, p. 14).

31. Krzhizhanovskii: *Plan*, 11–15, 33; "Elektrifikatsiya selskogo khozyaistva," *Izvestiya Narodnogo Kommissariata po Prodovolstviya*, 1–2 (Jan–Feb. 1920) 30–31. B. S. Butnik-Siverskii,
*Sovetskii plakat epokhi grazhdanskoi voiny 1918–1921* (Moscow: Vsesoyuznaya knizh. palata,
1960) poster No. 2496 (Simakov); Mayakovsky, *The Complete Plays*, tr. Guy Daniels (New
York: Clarion, 1971) 114. On Gerasimov see: Haumann, *Beginn der Planwirtschaft: Elektrifizi-
erung, Wirtschaftplanung, und gesellschaftliche Entwicklung Sowjetrusslands, 1917–1921* (Düs-
seldorf, 1974), esp. 109–17.

32. Poletaev and Punin, *Protiv tsivilizatsii* (S.Pb: Gos. tip., 1918), qu. 41, 42. The work was
obviously inspired by the war, but it also shows strong traces of Bogdanov's prewar teaching,
including the word "Tectology." Punin, "Dnevnik, 1915–1917," N 21, Sept. 16, 1916, ms. in
the Humanities Research Center, University of Texas, Austin. For background see Fitzpatrick,
*Commissariat of Enlightenment* (Cambridge: Cambridge University Press, 1970) 121.

33. L. D. Trotsky, *Problems of Everyday Life* (1923; New York: Monad, 1973) 188–200,
43, 61; Isaac Deutscher, *The Prophet Armed* (New York: Vintage, 1965) 500.

34. E. H. Carr, *The Bolshevik Revolution*, 3 vols. (Harmondsworth: Penguin, 1966) II, 208–
20; Malle, *Economic Organization*, 466–94.

35. James Bunyan, *The Origin of Forced Labor in the Soviet State, 1917–1921* (Baltimore:
Johns Hopkins University Press, 1967), 93–94, 99, 102–104.

36. Carr. *loc. cit.*; Bunyan, *Origins*, 136, 139, 146, 151–53, 255.

37. *Ibid.* 136.

38. Trotsky, *Terrorisme et communisme* (1920; Paris: 10/18, 1963) 208–26.

39. M. V. Frunze, "Front i tyl v voine budushchego," (1925) in *Izbrannye proizvedeniya*
(Moscow: Partizd., 1934) 192–201. For a modern comment by one of the U.S. Army's most
influential generals, see William Odom, "The 'Militarization of Soviet Society,' " POC, XXV
(Sept.–Oct., 1976) 34–51.

40. Mayakovsky quoted in E. J. Brown, *Mayakovsky: Poet in the Revolution* (Princeton:
Princeton University Press, 1973) 28, 88–89; Pethybridge, *Social Prelude*, chapter 5 on "large
scale theories"; Peter Kenez, *Civil War in South Russia*, 2 v. (Berkeley: University of California
Press, 1971–77) II, *passim.*; Jan Meijer, "Town and Country in the Civil War," in R. Pipes,

ed., *Revolutionary Russia* (New York: Anchor, 1969) 331–54; Peter Albjerg Jensen, *Nature as Code: the Achievement of Boris Pilnjak* (Copenhagen: Gyldendal, 1979) *passim.*

41. John Keep, *The Russian Revolution: a Study in Mass Mobilization* (New York: Norton, 1976), 28–29, 31, 33, 540 n. 13, *passim;* Launcelot Owen, *The Russian Peasant Movement, 1905–1917* (1937; New York: Russell and Russell, 1963), 151–63, 193, *passim;* Graeme Gill, *Peasant and Government in the Russian Revolution* (London: Macmillan, 1979) 10–71, *passim.*

42. Paul Avrich, ed., *The Anarchists in the Russian Revolution* (London: Thames and Hudson, 1973) 131–32; M. Gorky, *O russkom krestyanstve* (Berlin: Ladyzhnikov, 1922) 31–33, 36–37, 39, *passim.*

43. Jensen, *Nature,* 147; Peter Juviler, *Revolutionary Law and Order* (New York: Free Press, 1976) 26 (depopulation figure); Z. Yu. Arbatov, "Ekaterinoslav, 1917–1922 gg.," ARR, XII (1923) 83–148.

44. On federalist and centrifugal tendencies in the Civil War, see R. Pipes, *The Formation of the Soviet Union: Communism and Nationalism, 1917–1923,* rev. ed. (New York: Atheneum, 1974). William Chamberlin, *The Russian Revolution,* 2 v. (1935; New York: Grosset and Dunlap, 1965) I, 307; V. Povolzhskii, "Pered Oktyabrëm i v Oktyabre (po Kazani i Kazanskoi Gubernii," PR, 10 (1922) 337–48; Donald Raleigh, *Revolution on the Volga; 1917 in Saratov* (Ithaca: Cornell University Press, 1986), *passim;. idem.,* "Revolutionary Politics in Provincial Russia: The Tsaritsyn 'Republic' in 1917," SR 40/2 (1981) 194–209. Ronald Gregor Suny, *The Baku Commune, 1917–1918* (Princeton: Princeton University Press, 1972) 353–62, *passim.* See his very useful analysis of Lenin and the "commune state" in the appendix.

45. *Voennaya mysl,* 4 (June 30, 1919) 24–28, a detailed critique of the *partizanshchina;* D. Fedotoff White, *The Growth of the Red Army* (Princeton: Princeton University Press, 1944), 64–65. Alexei Tolstoy drew on familiar contexts when he cast his galactic hero as a Civil War veteran who had "founded four republics" in *Aelita: zakat Marsa* (Berlin: Ladyzhnikov, 1923), 22.

46. I. A. Konyukov, *Kollektivnoe zemledelie,* 3 ed. (Moscow: Novaya Derevnya, 1927) 36–37.

47. Avrich, *Russian Rebels,* 57, 80, 88, 158, *passim;* Alan Wildman, *The End of the Russian Imperial Army* (Princeton: Princeton University Press, 1980) 55–58; Ferdinand Ossendowski, *From President to Prison* (London: Allen and Unwin, 1925); I. I. Smirnov, *"Markovskaya Respublika"* (Moscow: Moskovskii Rabochii, 1975) 5.

48. Avrich, *Russian Anarchists,* 396–404; Deutscher, *Prophet Armed,* 131 n. 4; Richard Ullman, *Britain and the Russian Civil War* (Princeton: Princeton University Press, 1967) 46, *passim;* Paul Dotsenko, *The Struggle for a Democracy in Siberia* (Stanford: Hoover, 1983); David Footman, "Siberian Partisans in the Civil War," SAP, 1 (1956) 24–53. On "partisan republics" in Siberia, see V. G. Yakovenko, *Zapiski partizana* (Moscow, 1925) 13 and *Za vlast Sovetov* (Novosibirsk, 1947) 210. P. D. Ouspensky, *Letters from Russia, 1919* (London: Routledge, 1978), 4.

49. Avrich, *Russian Anarchists,* 112, 125–26 (qu.), 130, 177, 231 (qu.); *idem., Anarchists in the Russian Revolution, passim;* Etienne Antonelli, *Bolshevik Russia,* tr. C. Carroll (New York: Knopf, 1920) 237–39 (qu. 239).

50. Avrich, *Kronstadt, 1921* (Princeton: Princeton University Press, 1970), 3, 53–54, 57–59, 64–65, 73, 89, 93, 213, *passim* (qu. 59); *idem., Russian Anarchists,* 229; Israel Getzler, *Kronstadt, 1917–1921: the Fate of a Soviet Domocracy* (Cambridge: Cambridge University Press), vii, 240–41, 249, 251, *passim;* E. [Kh. A., but nicknamed "Efim"] Yarchuk, *Kronstadt v russkoi revolyutsii* (New York: Ispol Kom. Prof. Soyuzov, 1923) 5, 21–24, 37, *passim.* For a penetrating analysis of shipboard radicalism, see Marcus Rediker, *Between the Devil and the Deep Blue Sea* (Cambridge: Cambridge University Press, 1987).

51. Basic works are: Avrich: *Russian Anarchists* and *Anarchists in the Russian Revolution;* Footman, "Nestor Makhno," SAP, 2 (1959) 75–127; Michael Palij, *The Anarchism of Nestor Makhno, 1918–1921* (Seattle: University of Washington Press, 1976); Eberhard Müller, "Autonome Bewegungen des Volkskrieges in Sowjetrussland nach der Revolution von 1917," in Gerhard

Schulz ed., *Partisanen und Volkskrieg* (Göttingen: Vandenhoeck und Ruprecht, 1985) 36–56. Two basic sources: Peter Arshinov, *History of the Makhnovist Movement, 1918–1921* (1923), tr. L. and F. Perlman (Detroit: Black and Red, 1974) and Makhno, *Russkaya Revolyutsiya na Ukraine*, 3 v. (Paris, 1929–31). For the Mexican comparison, see Dittmar Dahlmann, *Land und Freiheit: Machnovščina und Zapatismo als Beispiele revolutionärer Bauernbewegung* (Stuttgart: Steiner, 1986). See also Eric Wolf, *Peasant Wars of the Twentieth Century* (New York: Harper, 1969) 95–97.

52. Documents in Avrich, *Anarchists in the Russian Revolution*, 128–37.

53. Seth Singleton, "The Tambov Revolt (1920–1921)," SR, XXV/3 (September 1966) 496–512; Oliver Radkey, *The Unknown Civil War: a Study of the Green Movement in the Tambov Region, 1920–1921* (Stanford: Hoover, 1976), 2, 70, 72–76, 90, 93, *passim*. Two Soviet accounts of Tambov and other "greens" and legendary steppe heroes are T. D. Korushin, *Dni revolyutsii i Sovetskogo stroitelstva v Ishimskom i v Saratovskoi Gubernii* (Saratov: Saratovskii Gos. Obl. Muzei, 1928) and E. Vasina, *Banditizm v Saratovskoi Gubernii* (Saratov: Gos. Obl. Muzei, 1928). That there were many green utopias, many Makhnos, and many Kronstadts (as observed by Getzler in the preface to *Kronstadt*) becomes clear as research begins to extend into the grass-roots history of the Civil War.

54. Boris Shiryaev, *Neugasimaya lampada* (New York: Chekhov, 1954) 149–225 (186); Negley Farson, *Black Bread and Red Coffins* (New York: Century, 1930) 193–94.


# Chapter 3: Revolutionary Iconoclasm

1. V. K. Myuller's *Anglo-russkii slovar*, 7th ed. (Moscow, 1960) defines "iconoclast" *(ikonoborets)* as (1) one who struggles with icons, and (2) one who fights traditional beliefs and prejudices.

2. Stanley Idzerda, "Iconoclasm During the French Revolution," *American Historical Review*, LX/1 (October 1954) 16, 25, *passim*.

3. Elias Canetti, *Crowds and Power* trans. C. Stewart (New York: Viking, 1962) 19–20; Raeff, "Pugachëv's Rebellion," 161–202.

4. Daniel Brower, "Labor Violence in Russia in the Late Nineteenth Century," SR, XLI/3 (Fall 1982) 419–31 and discussion, 432–53.

5. See Chapter 4.

6. *Agrarnoe dvizhenie v Rossii v 1905–1906 gg.* (Trudy Imperatorskago Volnago Ekonomicheskago Obshchestva, Number 3, 1908) St. Petersburg, 1908, 49, 52, *passim;* S. M. Dubrovskii and B. Grave, *1905: agrarnoe dvizhenie v 1906–1907 gg.*, I (Moscow, 1925) 44, 59, 74–75, 127–28, 134, 141–42, 144, 149, 151–54, 156, 166, 172, and *passim;* Dubrovskii, *Krestyanskoe dvizhenie v revolyutsii 1905–1907 gg.* (Moscow: A.N.S.S.S.R., 1956) 40, 46–49, 67–69; Raoul Labry, *Autour du moujik* (Paris, 1923) cited in E.J. Hobsbawm, *Primitive Rebels* (New York: Norton, 1959) 187. On the *Cherry Orchard* performance see: Gary Thurston, "The Impact of Russian Popular Theater, 1886–1915," *JMH*, 55/2 (June 1983) 236–67 (p. 264).

7. *Agrarnoe dvizhenie*, 49; Wildman, *End*, 78.

8. Raleigh, *Revolution on the Volga*, 184–85, 221, 259 (qu.), and *passim;* Keep, *Russian Revolution*, 210, 212, 214, (qu.).

9. I. E. Grabar, A. A. Chayanov, *et al.*, *Kooperatsiya i iskusstvo* (Moscow, 1919) 1–27 (qu., 27, 17). P. N. Savitskii, *Razrushayushchie svoyu rodinu* (Berlin, 1937) 38. Savitsky was an émigré economist,

10. Arbatov, "Ekaterinoslav," 85–86, 97, 101; Makhno, *Russ. Rev.* I, 116–18, 138. Palij, *Anarchism of Nestor Makhno*, 69, 146; Avrich, *Russian Rebels, passim*.

11. *Delo naroda* (May 2, 1917) 4 (on Luzhenovsky); Alexander Kozlov, *The Poor Peasant Committees in Soviet Russia, 1918* (M.A. Thesis, Georgetown University, 1983); Anna Louise Strong, *The Soviets Conquer Wheat* (New York: Holt, 1931) 124. For peasant mentalities in other

settings, see Edward H. Thompson, "The Moral Economy of the English Crowd in the 18th Century," *Past and Present*, 50 (1971) 76–136 and Eric Hobsbawm and George Rudé, *Captain Swing* (New York: Norton, 1975).

12. Adapted from the American philosopher Charles Peirce: Firth, *Symbols*, 61. See Teddy Uldrichs, "The 'Crowd' in the Russian Revolution," *Politics and Society*, 4/3 (1974) 397–413.

13. A. N. Naumov, *Iz utselëvshikh vospominanii, 1868–1917*, 2 vols. (New York, 1954–55), II, 324. A. Tarasov-Rodionov, *February, 1917* (New York: Covici, 1931) 96, *passim;* Arbatov, "Ekaterinoslav," 84; Al. Khokhryakova (S. Bonner),"Iz zhizni Petrogradskogo garizona v 1917 g.," KL, 17 (1926) 32; *Pravda* (March 23, 1917) 11; *Rabochaya gazeta* (March 21, 1917) 4; *Rech* (March 7, 1917) 3; Jean Marabini, *La vie quotidienne en Russie sous la Révolution d'Octobre* (Paris: Hachette, 1965) 74–75, 107.

14. Fitzpatrick, *Commissariat*, 115; V. Voinov, "Zhivopis," in *Oktyabr v iskusstve i literature, 1917–1927* (Leningrad: Krasnaya Gazeta, 1928) 64; V. D. Bonch-Bruevich, *Izbrannye sochineniya*, 3 vols. (Moscow: A.N.S.S.S.R., 1959–63), III, 361–62; N. A. Vinogradov, "Vospominaniya o monumentalnoi propagande v Moskve," *Iskusstvo*, 1 (Jan–Feb., 1939) 32–49; G. I. Ilina, *Kulturnoe stroitelstvo v Petrograde: Oktyabr 1917–1920 gg.* (Leningrad: Nauka, 1982) 39; *Iz istorii stroitelstva Sovetskoi kultury: Moskva, 1917–1918 gg., dokumenty i vospominaniya* (Moscow: Iskusstvo, 1964) 15; VRNK (Paris), 8 (Dec. 1923) 23; Fueloep-Miller, *Mind and Face*, 91; D. L. Dowd, *Pageant-Master of the Republic: Jaques-Louis David and the French Revolution* (Lincoln: University of Nebraska Press, 1948) 60.

15. A. M. Selishchev, *Yazyk revolyutsionnoi epokhi* (Moscow: Rabotnik Prosveshcheniya, 1928) 189; Alexander, *Emperor of the Cossacks*, 198–99; Victor Peters, *Nestor Makhno* (Winnepeg: Echo, 1970) 19.

16. *Krasnyi Petrograd* (1919) 16–17; Lev Uspenskii, *Zapiski starogo Peterburzhtsa* (Leningrad: Lenizdat, 1970) 510–11; Lev Kopelev, *Education of a True Believer*, tr. G. Kern. (New York: Harper and Row, 1978) 82; M. Roizman, *Vse, chto pomnyu o Esenine* (Moscow: Sovetskaya Rossiya, 1973) 143–44. The Tauride Palace and the (Winter) Palace Square bore the murdered Uritsky's name for a while. For satire, see Ilf and Petrov, *Twelve Chairs*. For prerevolutionary examples, see Yu. Lotman and B. Uspensky, "Myth-Name-Culture" in D. Lucid, ed. *Soviet Semiotics* (Baltimore: Johns Hopkins University Press, 1977) 251.

17. Wildman, *End*, 223–25, 242; Douglas Brown, *Doomsday 1917: the Destruction of Russia's Ruling Class* (London: Sidgwick, 1975) 88; Marabini, *Vie*, 74–75, 107; Anet, *Through*, 56, 64, 86; A. L. Fraiman, *Forpost sotsialisticheskoi revolyutsii* (Leningrad: Nauka, 1969) 351; *Dlya narodnogo uchitelya* (Moscow: 1917) 9, 16; Vinogradov, "Vospomimaniya," 47, n. 5.

18. Tsuyoshi Hasegawa, *The February Revolution: Petrograd, 1917* (Seattle: University of Washington Press, 1981) 81–82, 224, 248, 284, 299, 303, *passim;* E. N. Burdzhalov, *Vtoraya russkaya revolyutsiya: vostanie v Petrograde* (Moscow: Nauka, 1967); Tarasov-Rodionov, *February, 1917, passim;* N. G. Morozov, "Kammennyi grob" (Shlisselburgskaya Krepost)," *Argus* (April 1917) 7–17; Raleigh, "Revolutionary Politics"; I. Steinberg, *Spiridonova*, (1935; New York: Books for Libraries, 1971), 158; *idem, In the Workshop*, 66. The Decembrist quotation is from Raeff, *Decembrist Movement*, 163.

19. Hasegawa, *February Revolution*, 81–82, 224; *idem.*, "Crime and Revolution in Petrograd," unpublished paper. Mackenzie, *Russia*, 274.

20. Canetti, *Crowds and Power*, 75–80; Billington, *Icon and the Axe*, 23–26 and *passim;* Bernice Rosenthal, "The Transmutation of the Symbolist Ethos: Mystical Anarchism and the Revolution of 1905," SR, XXXVI/4 (Dec. 1977) 608–27.

21. Berdyaev, *Origins;* 45–47. Gleason, *Young Russia, passim*. Brower, *Training the Nihilists*, 15 (quoting Pisarev).

22. Vera Figner, *Zapechatlënnyi trud: vospominaniya*, 2 vols. (Moscow: Mysl, 1964), I, 116–19. For background, see Stites, *Women's Liberation*, 133.

23. E. Pyziur, *The Doctrine of Anarchism of Michael A. Bakunin* (Chicago: Regnery, 1968) 101–4.

24. Lotman and Uspensky, "Myth", 242. On the arts, see: Fueloep-Miller, *Mind and Face*,

96; Bowlt, "The Old New Wave," *New York Review of Books* (Feb. 16, 1984) 27–30; *Sobachii yashchik, ili Trudy tvorchestva byuro Nichevokov v techenie 1920–21 g.g.*, ed. S. V. Sadukov (Moscow: Khobo, 1921). On thought, see David Joravasky, *Soviet Marxism and Natural Science, 1917–1932* (New York: Columbia University Press, 1961) 93–94; S. A. Fedyukin, *Borba s burzhuaznoi ideologiei* (Moscow: Nauka, 1977) 150–51, 199; and Fitzpatrick, *Education and Social Mobility in the Soviet Union 1921–1934,* (Cambridge: Cambridge University Press, 1979) 7, 9, 24, 26, 30, 94.

25. Tretyakov in *Novy Lef,* 10 (Oct. 1927) 3. E. J. Brown, *Mayakovsky, passim;* Fitzpatrick, *Commissariat,* 124–28, 148–49; *Lef,* 4 (Aug.–Dec., 1924) 16–21. The best collection of their iconoclastic rhetoric is Anna Lawton, ed., *Russian Futurism through its Manifestoes* (Ithaca: Cornell University Press, 1988).

26. Fitzpatrick, *Commissariat,* 124–28; Brown, *Mayakovsky,* 193 (qu.); Schwarz, *Music and Musical Culture,* 14 (quoting Ehrenburg); James Joll, *Intellectuals in Politics* (London: Weidenfeld, 1960) 140; Kleberg, "Om avantgardets sociologi," in B. Englund, *et al.,* eds., *Material om den Ryska avantgarde-literaturen* (Stockholm: Institutionen for slaviska och baltiska sprok, 1978) 12–31; *idem, Teatern som Handling* (Stockholm: Almqvist and Wiksell, 1980); V. Markov, *Russian Futurism* (Los Angeles: University of California Press, 1968).

27. Lynn Mally, *Blueprint for a New Culture: a Social History of the Proletkult 1917–1921* (forthcoming). McCelland, "Utopianism", 411–18; Kate Betz, "Drommen om proletarkultur," in Englund, *Material,* 47–56; P. Gorsen and E. Knödler-Bunte, eds., *Proletkult,* 2 vols. (Stuttgart: Bad Connstatt, 1974–75), documents; Richard Lorenz, *Proletarische Kulturrevolution in Sowjetrussland (1917–1921): Dokumente des "Proletkult"* (Munich: Deutscher Taschenbuch, 1969).

28. *Sovetskaya intelligentsiya* (Moscow: Izd. Polit. Lit., 1977) 45; Fitzpatrick *Commissariat,* 92 (qu.).

29. G. S. Ignatev, *Moskva v pervyi god proletarskoi diktatury* (Moscow: Nauka, 1975) 333; Sanin, "Teatr dlya rabochykh," *Vestnik truda,* 4–5 (Apr.–May 1921) 81–84; Fraiman, *Forpost,* 344–45; Yu. I. Ovtsyn, *Bolsheviki i kultura proshlogo* (Moscow: Mysl, 1969) 86–89; "2-ya Tambovskaya gubernskaya konferentsiya proletkultov i kulturno-prosvetitelnykh organizatsii," December 2, 1919 (TsIGALI, 1,230–11,519). I am indebted to Bengt Jangfeldt for this document; M. Grishin, "Proletarskaya kultura," *Gryadushchee,* 1 (1919) 11, 20.

30. Kleinbort, "Rukopisnye zhurnaly" 292; Fitzpatrick, *Commissariat,* 123, 239; B. V. Pavlovsky, *V.I. Lenin i izobrazitelnoe iskusstvo* (Leningrad: Khudozhnik R.S.F.S.R., 1974) 56–57; Jangfeldt, *Majakovski and Futurism, 1917–1921* (Stockholm: Almqvist and Wiksell, 1977) 72–91.

31. Mally, *Blueprint, passim;* Bogdanov, "Religion, Art, and Marxism," *The Labour Monthly,* VI/8 (Aug, 1924) 489–97 and "The Workers' Artistic Inheritance," *ibid,* VI/9 (Sept. 1924) 549–56. A striking but typical instance of the contrast between outer form and inner reality was a concert on December 3, 1918 of Debussy's music at a Proletcult Club called "The Red Cock." *Muzykalnaya zhizn Moskvy v pervye gody posle Oktyabrya* (Moscow: Sovetskii Kompozitor, 1972) 113.

32. *Proletarskie poety pervykh let Sovetskoi epokhi* (Leningrad: Sovetskii Pisatel, 1959) 79.

33. Gorky, *O russkom krestyanstve,* 36–43.

34. Wildman, *Making of a Worker's Revolution* (Chicago: University of Chicago Press, 1967), *passim;* Zelnik, "Russian Bebels," *R.R.,* 35/4 (Oct. 1976) 424, 429–30, 433; Gorky, *Revolyutsiya i Kultura* (Berlin: n.d.) 77; J. Brooks, "The Kopeck Novels of Early Twentieth Century Russia," *Journal of Popular Culture,* XIII 1 (Summer 1979) 85–97; *idem, When Russia Learned to Read.*

35. Wortman, *Crisis of Russian Populism;* Gleason, *Young Russia,* 359 (qu.). For an interesting treatment of Nechaev, see Philip Pomper, *Sergei Nechaev* (New Brunswick: Rutgers University Press, 1979).

36. Gorky, *O russkom krestyanstve,* 43; Pyman, *Blok,* II, 257 n. 4, 343.

37. Jan Waclaw Machajski [pseud. A. Ch. Volskii], *Umstvennyi rabochii* (S.Pb.: Yakovenko,

1906), 56, 74 (quotes); R. V. Ivanov-Razumnik: *Chto takoe 'makhaevshchina'* (S.P.b.: Bunin, 1908) 8, 43–50.

38. Another work of Machajski is here quoted from Ivanov-Razumnik; *Chto takoe*, 8 and 7; the quote from Lozinsky p. 90; *Buntar* (Dec. 1906) quoted in I. I. Genkin, "Sredi preemnikov Bakunina," KL, 1/22 (1927) 187–88; E. Yu. Lozinskii, *Chto zhe takoe, nakonets, intelligentsiya?* (S.Pb.: Muller, 1907) 88–89.

39. Ivanov-Razumnik, *Chto takoe*, 22, 85, 90–91; Genkin, "Sredi preemnikov" 186–90; Bakunin quoted in Avrich, *Russian Anarchists*, 94. Two good commentaries: Avrich, "What is 'Makhaevism'?" SS, XVII (July 1965) 66–75 and A. D'Agostino, "Intelligentsia Socialism and the Workers' Revolution: the Views of J. W. Machajski," *International Review of Social History*, XIV/1 (1969) 54–89.

40. Charles Rougle, "The Intelligentsia Debate in Russia, 1917–1918," in N. A. Nilsson, ed., *Art, Society, Revolution: Russia, 1917–1921* (Stockholm: Almqvist and Wiksell, 1979) 54–105 (esp. 79–80); Gorky, *Fragments from My Diary* (London: Allen and Unwin, 1924) 297–99; Konstantin Paustovsky, *The Story of My Life* (New York: Vintage, 1967) 615; Fitzpatrick, *Commissariat*, 70; *idem.*, "The 'Soft' Line on Culture and its Enemies: Soviet Cultural Policy, 1922–1927," SR, XXXIII/2 (June 1974) 274–78.

41. Lunacharskii, *Revolutionary Silhouettes*, tr. M. Glenny (New York: Hill and Wang, 1967) 149; *Gryadushchaya kultura*, 1 (1918) 20; *Proletarskie poety*, 106, 244–45, 268–69; *K.P.S.S. vo glave kulturnoi revolyutsii v S.S.S.R.* (Moscow: Izd. Politlit, 1972) 46; Fedukin, *Velikii Oktyabr i intelligentsiya* (Moscow: Nauka, 1972) 82; Kendall Bailes, *Technology and Society under Lenin and Stalin* (Princeton: Princeton University Press, 1978), 59–60; Fitzpatrick, "Civil War"; *idem.*, *Education*, 114–15.

42. Quotations from Avrich, *Anarchists in the Russian Revolution*, 43, 48, 52–53.

43. Kathleen Berton, *Moscow: an Architectural History* (London: Studio Vista, 1977) 198–201; Benois in *Rech* (Mar 25, 1917) 2 and in *Aleksandr Benua razmyshlyaet*, ed. I. S. Zilbershtein and A. N. Savinov (Moscow: Sovetskii Khudozhnik, 1968) 62–70; Rougle, "Intelligentsia Debate," 59–62; Daniel Orlovsky, "The Provisional Government and its Cultural Work," Gleason, *Bolshevik Culture*, 39–56.

44. Fraiman, *Forpost*, 337–49; *idem.*, *Revolyutsionnaya zashchita Petrograda* (Moscow: Nauka, 1964) 175–77; Ignatev, *Moskva*, 283, 318–28; Petrus, *Religious Communes*, 62; Ovtsyn, *Bolsheviki*, 64–66; Ilina, *Kulturnoe stroitelstvo*, 24; "Kak dalshe stroit Moskvu," *Moskva*, 3 (March, 1962) 148; VOKD, 1 (Sept, 1918) 174; Marabini, *Vie*, 145, 177; Fitzpatrick, *Commissariat*, 17, 127–29.

45. I. E. Grabar, *Moya zhizn* (Moscow: Iskusstvo, 1937) 274–76; *Kooperatsiya i iskusstvo*, 1–27. The prerevolutionary cooperative cultural network in the countryside still awaits an historian.

46. On Lunacharsky: Fitzpatrick, *Commissariat*, 13–14, *passim; Novyi mir*, 3 (Mar 1963) 19—Khrushchëv's version of the St. Basil incident; *V. I. Lenin o literature* (Moscow: Khudozhestvennaya literatura, 1976) 668–69. On Lenin (there is a mammoth literature): the last work cited above; Ovtsyn, *Bolsheviki*, 55; Pavlovsky, *V. I. Lenin;* Shklovsky, "Lenin,"; Ignatev, *Moskva*, 317–18; Bailes, *Technology*, 52 (qu.).

47. *Moskva*, 3 (March 1962); M. Yu. Braichevskii, "Sokhranit pamyatniki istorii," ISSSR, 2 (Mar.–Apr. 1966) 205–26; Martin Conway, *Art Treasures in Soviet Russia*, (London: Arnold, 1925) 23, *passim;* Ovtsyn, *Bolsheviki*, 66–67; Pavlovsky, *V. I. Lenin*, 49; *Iz istorii ustroitelstva*, 5; *K.P.S.S. vo glave*, 39.

48. Stanley Mellon, "Alexandre Lenoir: the Museum verses the Revolution," Consortium on Revolutionary Europe, *Proceedings*, (1979) 75–88, with commentary by Emmet Kennedy, pp. 89–91; Kennedy, "Vandalism and Conservation," in his *Culture in the Crucible: France at the Time of the Revolution*, ch. 9, forthcoming (I thank the author); Idzerda, "Iconoclasm" 15 (qu.); N. Pomerantsev, "Revolyutsionnyi narod khranit pamyatniki kultury," *Iskusstvo*, 5 (1960) p. 38.

49. Fitzpatrick, " 'Soft' Line", 279; Bailes, *Technology*, 47–48, 52.

## Chapter 4: Festivals of the People

1. We have as yet no serious synthetic treatment of Russian religious or military ritual before the Revolution. A major study of dynastic-monarchical ritual and imagery is in progress by Richard Wortman. I thank him for sharing his knowledge and insights with me.

2. E. Hobsbawm and T. Ranger, eds., *The Invention of Tradition* (Cambridge: Cambridge University Press, 1983); de Man, *Psychology of Socialism;* P. G. Shiryaeva, "Iz istorii stanovleniya revolyutsionnykh proletarskikh traditsii," *Sovetskaya etnografiya,* 3 (May–June 1970) 17–27; *idem,* "Iz istorii razvitii nekotorykh revolyutionnykh traditsii," *Sov. etnografiya,* 6 (1975) 63–70; S. Dreiden, *Muzyka-revolyutsii* (Moscow: Sovetskii kompozitor, 1970); and Susanne Ament, *To the Last and Decisive Battle: the Role of Songs in the Russian Revolution* (M.A. Thesis, Georgetown U., 1984).

3. See Hasegawa, *February Revolution* 248–53, 283–92, 309; and "Vozstanie 1.-gv. Volynskago Polka v fevrale 1917 g.," *Byloe,* 5–6/27–28 (Nov.–Dec. 1917) 5–16, for anticipations.

4. *Rech,* the files of March 1917, for the general pattern in many locales; Raleigh, *Revolution on the Volga,* 85; *Rabochaya gazeta,* March 14, 18, 22; BV (March 4, 1917) 3; *Den* (March 22 1917) 2; *Dlya narodnago uchitelya,* 7 (April 1917) 2–5 (eyewitness accounts by schoolchildren); Wildman, *End,* 224 (at the front); Getzler, *Kronstadt,* 28.

5. A sampling of contemporary sources: *Izvestiya* of the Petrograd Soviet, March 21–24; *Rech,* March 25; RG, March 10–11, 16, 25; *Den,* March 25; *Delo naroda,* March 25; *Pravda,* March 23—all 1917.

6. E. M. C. Barraclough and W. G. Crompton, *Flags of the World* (London: Warne, 1978) 142–47; Dreiden, *Muzyka,* 144, argues that the Provisional Government tried to capitalize on the mass popularity of the "Workers' Marseillaise," a doubtful proposition. Monuments: *Rech* (March 7, 1917) 5 and RG (March 17, 1917).

7. G. F. Kiselëv and V. A. Lyubisheva, "V. I. Lenin i rozhdenie gosudarstvennoi pechati i gerba R.S.F.S.R.," ISSSR, 5 (Sept–Oct 1966) 21; M. Yu. Lyashchenko, *Rasskazy o Sovetskom gerbe* (Moscow: Detgiz, 1963) 29–30.

8. Alexander Rabinowitch, *The Bolsheviks Come to Power* (New York: Norton, 1977) 39–43. For pictures, see *Niva,* 29 (July 22, 1917).

9. For a superb study of those values, see William Rosenberg, *Liberals in the Russian Revolution* (Princeton: Princeton University Press, 1974); Milyukov, *Russian Revolution,* I, *passim;* and Orlovsky, "Provisional Government."

10. My account is drawn from: Lunacharskii, "Pervoe Maya 1918 goda," (1918) in *Vospominaniya i vpechatleniya* (Moscow: Sovetskaya Rossiya, 1968) 208–12; *idem,* "Pervyi pervomaiskii prazdnik posle pobedy," *Krasnaya niva,* 18 (May 12, 1926) 8; E. A. Speranskaya, ed., *Agitatsionno-massovoe iskusstvo pervyikh let Oktyabrya* (Moscow: Iskusstvo, 1971) 32–33, 96–97; A. I. Mazaev, *Prazdnik kak sotsialno-khudozhestvennoe yavlenie* (Moscow: Nauka, 1978) 245–53; G. I. Ilina, *Kulturnoe stroitseltsvo,* 215–17. James Von Geldern, who has made the most detailed analyses of these festivals and has generously shared his work with me, makes much of the oppositional tension in the city on May Day but concedes that the ceremonies were successful.

11. Lunacharskii, *Vospom.,* 210–11.

12. E. I. Kamentsova and A. N. Luppol, "Kak sozdavalsya sovetskii gerb," *Voprosy istorii* (Dec. 1962) 194–95; Mazaev, *Prazdnik,* 264 n. 14; Lyashchenko, *Rasskazy,* 82–83; Bogdanov's *Red Star* was republished in both capitals in 1918. A picture of the original red star design can be seen on a 1922 dinner plate in *Art into Production: Soviet Textiles, Fashion, and Ceramics, 1917–1935* (Oxford: Museum of Modern Art, 1984) 37. The fairy-tale gloss on the red star is translated in full in Nina Tumarkin, *Lenin Lives!* (Cambridge Mass.: Harvard University Press, 1983), 70–72.

13. Kamentsova and Luppol, "Kak," 195; Lyashchenko, *Rasskazy,* 34–35.

14. Speranskaya, *Agit.-Mass. iskusstvo,* 144 (illust.); Kiselëv and Lyubisheva, "V. I. Lenin," 21–23; *Izobrazitelnoe iskusstvo,* 1 (1919) 63 (Chekhonin's design; illust.); Mazaev, *Prazdnik,* 263–64; S. Gerasimov, "Pervoe prazdnestvo Oktyabrskoi Revolyutsii," *Iskusstvo,* 7 (1957) 44–45; Lyashchenko, *Rasskazy,* 40; P. P. fon-Vinkler (von Winckler), ed., *Gerby gorodov, gubernii, oblastei i posadov Rossisskoi Imperii . . . 1649 po 1900 god* (S.Pb.: Ivanov, 1899) *passim.*

15. Kamentsova and Luppol, "Kak," 196; Kiselëv and Lyubisheva, "V. I. Lenin," 23–26; Pavlovskii, *V. I. Lenin,* 33; I. S. Smirnov, *Lenin i Sovetskaya kultura* (Moscow: A.N.S.S.S.R., 1960) 388; BES, 2 ed., X (1952) 602–3 for pictures and variations.

16. Barraclough, *Flags,* 142–47; Yu. M. Steklov, *Poeziya revolyutsionnago sotsializma: pevtsy trudogo tsarstva vo Frantsii* (Petrograd, 1918).

17. Dreiden, *Muzyka-revolyutsii,* 137–44.

18. Christopher Binns, "The Changing Face of Power: Revolution and Accommodation in the Development of the Soviet Ceremonial System," *Man,* 14 (Dec. 1979) 588; Mazaev, *Prazdnik,* 235–37; Gerald Janecek, *The Look of Russian Literature* (Princeton: Princeton University Press, 1984) 12–18.

19. Vernon Lidtke, *The Alternative Culture* (New York: Oxford University Press, 1985) 127.

20. Tomasso Campanella, *La Città del Sole* (1602) ed. D. Donno (Berkeley: University of California Press, 1981); Manuels, *Utopian Thought,* 261–88; Nilsson, *Art,* 42.

21. Smirnov, *Lenin,* 347–72; John Bowlt, "Russian Sculpture and Lenin's Plan of Monumental Propaganda," in H. A. Millon and L. Nochlin, eds., *Art and Architecture in the Service of Politics* (Cambridge Mass.: M.I.T. Press, 1978) 182–93; *Istoriko-revolyutsionnye pamyatniki S.S.S.R.* (Moscow: Politlit, 1972) 4–6; A. Mikhailov, "Programma monumentalnoi propagandy," *Iskusstvo,* 4 (1968) 31–34; and 5 (1968) 39–42 (illust.).

22. *Iz istorii stroitelstva Sovetskoi kultury: Moskva, 1917–1918 gg.: dokumenty i vospominaniya* (Moscow: Iskusstvo, 1964) 38–44; Guerman, *Art,* 6, 7, 12–13, 6–7, 12–16, 227–78, 284–85, 299 (illust.) for both capitals. For statues in Leningrad: Ilina, *Kulturnoe,* 203–26; for Saratov: Speranskaya, *Agit. mass. iskusstvo,* 141–43.

23. For comment on the failure of the monuments: Bowlt, "Russian Sculpture", 189, 192; Nilsson, *Art,* 44, 48; L. Shervud, "Vospominaniya o monumentalnoi propagande v Leningrade," *Iskusstvo,* 1 (Jan.–Feb., 1939) 50–53; *Oktyabr v iskusstve i literature, 1917–27* (Leningrad: Krasnaya Gazeta, 1928) 64.

24. Mikhailov, "Programma," 31–33; Pavlovsky, *V. I. Lenin,* 52–53. For two examples (of many) on what people imagined Lenin looked like before seeing him, see L. Stupochenko "V Brestskie dni," PR, 16 (1923) 102 and Robert Tucker, *Stalin as Revolutionary 1879–1929* (New York: Norton, 1974) 134.

25. Ilina, *Kulturnoe,* 209; *Istoriko-rev. pamyatniki,* 15, 16, 120–21 (illust.); Lunacharskii, *Ob izobrazitelnom iskusstve,* 2 vols. (Moscow: Sovetskii khudozhnik, 1967) II, 29–30.

26. *Izvestiya,* November 3 through 9, 1918; Mikhailov, "Programma," 39–41; A. Strigalev, "Proizvedeniya agitatsionnogo iskusstva 20-kh godov," *Iskusstvo,* 5 (1968) 44; Masaev, *Prazdnik,* 262–70; Pavlovsky, *V. I. Lenin,* 14–15; Guerman, *Art,* 282. Wortman, "Moscow and Petersburg: the Problem of Political Center in Tsarist Russia, 1881–1914," in Sean Wilentz, ed., *Rites of Power: Symbolism, Ritual, and Politics Since the Middle Ages* (Philadelphia: University of Pennsylvania Press, 1985) 244–71.

27. Lenin's speeches, PSS, XXXVII, 169–82.

28. *Izvestiya* (Nov. 9, 1918) 5.

29. *Ibid.* For musical performances see *Krasnaya Moskva* (1920) 543–48 and *Muzykalnaya zhizn Moskvy v pervye gody posle Oktyabrya* (Moscow: Sovetskii kompozitor, 1972) 104–5.

30. *Izvestiya* (November 9, 1918) 6.

31. For the long duel between the capitals, see: Wortman, "Moscow and Petersburg"; S. Monas, "St. Petersburg and Moscow as Cultural Symbols," in Stavrou, *Art and Culture,* 26–39. For notions of an "animating center of society," see Clifford Geertz, "Centers, Kings, and Cha-

risma," in J. Ben David, *et al.*, eds. *Culture and its Creators* (Chicago: University of Chicago Press, 1977) 150–53; for the emerging cult: Tumarkin, *Lenin Lives!*, 66–68. For a contrasting picture of Kerensky, see Orlovsky, "Provisional Government" 44.

32. Christel Lane, *Rites of Rulers* (Cambridge: Cambridge University Press 1981) 203; Krupskaya, *Reminiscences of Lenin*, 489; Fedotoff White, in *Growth of the Red Army*, 124, reminds us that having Moscow as their capital in the Civil War—in contrast to such "new fangled 'capitals' " as Omsk, Ekaterinodar, and Archangel—gave the Bolsheviks great prestige.

33. Samples of Petrograd civic myth: see *Krasnyi Petrograd*, 11 (1919) esp. 13–19, 45–48, III (1920), and IV (1921).

34. *Izvestiya* (Nov. 9, 1918) 5; Strigalev, "Proizvedeniya," 44–46; Mikhailov, "Programma," 41–42; Masaev, *Prazdnik*, 270–77; *Plamya*, 28 (Nov. 17, 1918); Wortman, "Moscow and Petersburg".

35. P. Grigoriev "Ulitsa i vneshkolnoe obrazovanie," *Vneshkolnoe obrazovanie*, 2–3 (Feb.–Mar. 1919) 10–24; Masaev, *Prazdnik*, 277–79.

36. A. I. Piotrovsky, *Teatr, kino, zhizn* (Leningrad: Len. Gos. Institut Teatra, Muzyki i Kinomatografii, 1969) 73–76 (by one of the organizers); N. A. Gorchakov, *Istoriya Sovetskoi teatra* (New York: Chekhov, 1956) 77–78, a frankly hostile account; Genkin, *Mass. prazd.*, 37–38; Mazaev, *Prazdnik*, 316–18.

37. Von Geldern, ms.; Kleberg, *Teatern;* Bernice Rosenthal, "Wagner and Wagnerian Ideas in Russia," in *Wagnerism in European Culture and Politics*, ed. D. Large and W. Weber (Ithaca: Cornell University Press, 1984) 199–245. A. Talanov, *Bolshaya sudba* (Moscow: Izd. politlit., 1967), on Andreeva; Katerina Clark, "The Urban Intelligentsia During N.E.P.," ms.

38. Genkin, *Mass. prazd.*, 38–40; Mazaev, *Prazdnik*, 318–21; Gorchakov, *Istoriya*, 91; Fueloep-Miller, *Mind*, 142–44.

39. Lotman and Uspensky, "Myth-Name-Culture," 237.

40. Mazaev, *Prazdnik*, 306–11.

41. *Ibid.*, 318, 321–24; Gorchakov, *Istoriya*, 92; Fueloep-Miller, *Mind*, 145–46; Ivan Olbracht, "Puteshestvie za poznaniem," *Inostrannaya literatura*, 5 (1967) 83–85 (a Czech Communist eyewitness).

42. Gorchakov, *Istoriya*, 92–93; Mazaev, *Prazdnik*, 319, 339–42; Fueloep-Miller, *Mind*, 147–48.

43. I have taken Gorchakov's figure, though undocumented, as more realistic than that of Olbracht (and followed by Mazaev) of a quarter million spectators at "Toward the World-Wide Commune".

44. Binns, "Changing Face," 591–92; Gorchakov, *Istoriya*, 92. Julien Thierseau's *Fêtes et chansons de la Révolution française* was translated into Russian as *Pesni i prazdnestva frantsuzskoi revolyutsii* (Petrograd: Parus, 1917) and reviewed in PK, 3 (Aug. 1918) 34–35.

45. Genkin, *Mass. prazd.*, 40; Mazaev, *Prazdnik*, 327; Fueloep-Miller, *Mind*, 135–36; Emma Goldman, *My Disillusionment in Russia* (1922; New York: Crowell, 1970) pp. 48–50, 176; Victor Serge, *Memoirs* 109–10.

46. For some interesting perspectives on revolutionary mythmaking, see Hunt, *Politics*, chs. 1–3 and Hobsbawm, *Invention*.

47. Marcuse, Marx, and Lenin are discussed in Mazaev, *Prazdnik*, 209–30. On "defestivalization" in revolution, see André Découflé, *Sociologie des révolutions* (Paris: Presses Universitaires, 1968) 88–92.

48. Lunacharskii, *Sobranie sochinenii*, 8 vols. (Moscow: Khudozhestvennaya literatura, 1963–67), III, 562–63, quoting Robespierre's report on popular festivals of May 7, 1794; Mazaev, *Prazdnik*, 230–34 (Lunacharsky quoted, 231–32). See Robert C. Williams, *Artists in Revolution* (Bloomington: Indiana University Press, 1977) 45–46 for the roots of Lunacharsky's festival vision.

49. Binns, "Changing Face," 592, 597; *Massovye prazdnestva: sbornik komiteta sotsiologicheskogo izucheniya iskusstv* (Leningrad: Academia, 1926) 149–61; S. Tretyakov, "Kak desyati-

letit," *Novyi lef,* 4 (Apr. 1927) 35–37; I. T. Bobryshev, *Melkoburzhuaznye vliyaniya sredi molodëzhi,* 2 ed. (Moscow: Molodaya Gvardiya, 1928) 51–52.

50. Ilina, *Kulturnoe,* 219; Speranskaya, *Agit.-mass. iskusstvo,* 139; Lane, *Rites,* 163–73. The quotation is from Georgii Popov, *Stremyashchimsya v Rossiyu* (Berlin: Nashi Problemy, 1924) 14–15 (from observations made in November, 1922).

51. Lane, *Rites,* 156; E. E. Kish [Kisch], "Tsari, popy, Bolsheviki," *Inostrannaya literatura,* 5 (1967) 94–111.

52. Mazaev, *Prazdnik,* 356–64; Fueloep-Miller, *Mind,* 91–92, 137–39; V. Ya. Propp, "The Historical Roots of Some Russian Religious Festivals," in S. and E. Dunn, eds., *Introduction to Soviet Ethnography,* 2 vols. (Berkeley: Highgate Road Social Science Research Station, 1974) 367–410.

53. Mikhail Bakhtin, *Rabelais and his World,* tr. Helene Iswolsky (Cambridge, Mass.: M.I.T. Press, 1968) 6 (qu.), 9–10, 16, 73, 79, 200, 213, 217, *passim.*

## Chapter 5: Godless Religion

1. A history of Russian atheism remains to be written, but see two fine introductions in English: Berdyaev, *Origins* and George Kline, *Religious and Antireligious Thought in Russia* (Chicago: University of Chicago Press, 1968). For specifics: B. Itenberg, "Revolyutsionnye Narodniki i vopros religii," VIRA, XI (1963) 293–305; Bakunin, *God and the State* (New York: Dover, 1970), 17, 40, *passim* (qu. 36); Gleason, *Young Russia,* 336; Adam Ulam, *In the Name of the People* (New York: Viking, 1977), 398; *Revolyutsionnoe Narodnichestvo,* I, 170–71. A peasant baker of the 1870s even denied the value of any propaganda until religion had been completely wiped out:. A. I. Ivanchin-Pisarev, *Khozhdenie v narod* (Moscow: Molodaya Gvardiya, 1929) 14–16.

2. A. A. Kunkl, *Dolgushintsy* (Moscow, 1931) 206–12; Itenberg, "Rev. Narod.," 298–301; Ulam, *In the Name,* 210–13, 291, 463; Zakharina, "Rev. prop. lit."; Klibanov, *Istoriya religioznogo sektantstva v Rossii (60-e gody XIX v.-1917 g.),* Moscow: Nauka, 1965, 22. On the religious sensibilities of women see Barbara Engel, *Mothers and Daughters* (Cambridge: Cambridge University Press, 1983) and Stites, *Women's Liberation,* 115–54.

3. Stites, *Women's Liberation,* 118–19; M. Frolenko, "Chaikovskii i ego bogochelovechestvo," *Katorga i ssylka,* XXVI (1926) 217–23; T. Polner, "N. V. Chaikovskii i 'Bogochelovechestvo'," in A. A. Titov, ed., *Nikolai Vasilevich Chaikovskii* (Paris, 1929) 97–160; A. Faresov, "Odin iz 'semidesyatnikov'," VE, XXXIV/V (May 1904) 245–60; *idem.,* "Religioznye utopisty semidesyatykh godov," *Slovo,* 165 (June 1, 1905) 6; Itenberg, "Rev. Narod.," 304–4.

4. Jutta Scherrer, *Die petersburger religiös-philosophischen Vereinungen* (Berlin: Harrassowitz, 1973); Kline, *Religious;* Christopher Read, *Religion, Revolution, and the Russian Intelligentsia, 1900–1912* (New York: Harper, 1980), and George Putnam, *Russian Alternatives to Marxism* (Knoxville: University of Tennessee Press, 1977).

5. Williams, *Artists* 23–58; *idem.* "Collective Immortality: the Syndicalist Origins of Proletarian Culture," *Slavic Review,* 39/3 (Sept. 1980) 389–402. Scherrer, "Culture prolétarienne et religion socialiste entre deux révolutions: les Bolschéviks de gauche," *Europa,* II/2 (Spring 1979) 67–90.

6. Kline, *Religious,* 118–20; Read, *Religion,* 78–85; D. Grille, *Lenins Rivale* (Cologne: Wissenschaft und Politik, 1966), 37; Fitzpatrick, *Commissariat,* 3–4; M. Laskovaya, *Bogoiskatelstvo i bogostroitelstvo prezhde i teper,* 2 ed. (Moscow: Moskovskii Rabochii, 1976) 67 (qu.).

7. See notes 5 and 6. A. M. Gorky, *Deti solntsa* (Stuttgart: Dietz, 1905) 53, 99. 100, *passim;* Read, *Religion,* 85–87; Kline, *Religious,* 110–13.

8. Lenin: *O religii* (Moscow: Gosizdpolit, 1954) 43 and *Sochineniya,* XLVIII, 246 (cited in Read, *Religion,* 91–92).

9. M. M. Persits, "Avtobiografiya rabochikh kak istochnik izucheniya ateizma v rabochem dvizhenii," VIRA, VIII (1960) 101–27 (quotes 122, n. 56); Maurice Baring, *What I Saw in Russia* (London: Nelson, 1927) 350–53. For examples of mockery and exposure, see: N. A. Lebedev, "Antitserkovnye i antireligioznye nastroeniya sredi krestyan nizhegorodskoi gubernii v nachale XX v.," VIRA, VII (1959) 116–27; cf. Zelnik, *A Radical Worker*.

10. *Krasnoe Znamya: pervomaiskii sbornik* (S.Pb.: Tip. Eserov, 1901) 25–27; *Krasnoe Znamya: sbornik na 1 maya 1905 goda* (N.d., n. p.. [1905] with an SR imprint) 14–21; A. P. Barykova, *Skazka pro to kak Tsar Akhreyan khodil Bogu zhalovatsya* (Geneva: Ukrainskaya tip., [c. 1900–1905]) 24. *Grazhdane! segodnya Novyi God* (Socialist Revolutionary flysheet). All are in the pamphlet collection of the Helsinki Slavonic Library. The Hagadah: Avrich, *Anarchists*, 40; the Old Believer: L. I. Emelyakh, *Antiklerikalnoe dvizhenie krestyan v period pervoi russkoi revolyutsii* (Moscow: Nauka, 1965) 109–11.

11. *Desyat Zapovedei Sotsial-Demokrata*, 2 ed. (Helsinki: Khelsingforskaya gruppa R.S.D.R.P., 1917) 7–8; commentary in V. F. Shishkin, *Tak skladyvalas revolyutsionnaya moral* (Moscow: Mysl, 1967) 285–86.

12. S. N. Savelev, *Emelyan Yaroslavskii—propagandist marskistskogo ateizma* (Leningrad: Izd. Leningrad. U., 1976) 13–15; M. M. Sheinman, "Propagandist ateizma, Em. M. Yaroslavskii," VIRA, VI (1958) 75–103; *Pervoe Maya!* flysheet attached to *Solsial-demokrat*, 23 [1911] in the Helsinki collection.

13. Shiryaeva, "Iz istorii stanovleniya"; Emelyakh, *Antiklerikalnoe*, 105–15; *idem.* "Iz istorii antiklerikalizma i ateizma russkikh krestyan v 1905–1907 gg.," EMIRA, III (1959) 283–85.

14. Persits, "Avtobiografiya"; Putnam, *Russian Alternatives*, 98–99.

15. See also on this subject the flawed but interesting Shishkin, *Tak skladyvalas*. For other aspects: Stephen and Ethel Dunn, *The Peasants of Great Russia* (New York: Holt, 1967) 29; Ezra Mendelsohn, *Class Struggle in the Pale* (Cambridge: Cambridge University Press, 1970) 109, 153–55; de Man, *Psychology of Socialism*, 146–48. For Orthodox missionary methods that the Bolsheviks would later use, see N. A. Smirnov, "Missionerskaya deyatelnost tserkvi (vtoraya polovina XIX v.-1917 g.)," *Tserkov v istorii Rossii* (Moscow: Nauka, 1967) 279–97.

16. E. S. Osipova "Vremennoe Pravitelstvo i tserkov," *Tserkov v istorii Rossii*, 315–22 (qu., 322); D. A. Garkavenko, "Rost ateistskikh i antiklerikalnykh nastroenii v armii i flote v 1917 godu," VIRA, VIII (1960) 206–7.

17. V. Bonch-Bruevich, "Rol dukhovenstva v pervye dni Oktyabrya", *Deyateli Oktyabrya o religii i tserkvi* (Moscow: Mysl, 1958) 14–24; *Krasnyi Petrograd* (1920) 8 (photo). In the Civil War, church bells were feared by the Bolsheviks as signals to the Whites; ringing them was in some places punishable by death: Arbatov, "Ekaterinoslav", 90.

18. A good, though outdated, introduction is J. S. Curtiss, *The Russian Church and the Soviet State, 1917–1950* (Boston: Little Brown, 1950). A newer treatment is Dimitry Pospielovsky, *The Russian Church under the Soviet Regime, 1917–1982*, 2 v. (Crestwood: St. Vladimir's Seminary Press, 1984).

19. *O religii i tserkvi* (Moscow, 1965) 59.

20. BSE, 2 ed., XLIX (1957) 652–53; Savelev, *Emelyan Yaroslavskii; idem.*, "Em. Yaroslavskii v prepodlenie anarkistskikh vliyanii v antireligioznoi rabote v S.S.S.R.," EMIRA, VII (1964) 36–50. One of the fullest collections of his early writings is *Protiv religii i tserkvi*, 3 vols. (Moscow: OGIZ, 1932–35). The word "militant" was added later.

21. Curtiss, *Russian Church*, 206–46; Yaroslavskii, *Religiya i R.K.P.* (Moscow: Bezbozhnik, 1925) 41–44; Bobryshev, *Melkoburzhuaznye vliyaniya* 54. For local styles, see *Tseli i zadachi Soyuza Bezbozhnikov* (Ulyanovsk: Ulyanovskii Gorod. Sov. Soyuz Bezbozhnikov, 1928); and Merle Fainsod, *Smolensk under Soviet Rule* (New York: Vintage, 1963) 430–45.

22. Savelev, "Em. Yaroslavskii," 38–39; Yaroslavskii, *Protiv religii*, III, 102–21; *Bezbozhnik u stanka* Nos. 5–10 (1923); S. G. Rutenburg, "D. Moor—khudozhnik-ateist," EMIRA, V (1961) 168–87.

23. N. A. Krylov, "Iz istorii propagandy ateizma v S.S.S.R. (1923–1925 gg.)," VIRA, VIII (1960) 166–92; M. Gorev (a former priest), *Protiv antisemitov* (Moscow: Gosizd., 1928); A. Loginov, *Bezbozhnik: luchshii drug muzhika* (Moscow: Bezbozhnik, 1923) 11. See also N. Lukin, *Revolyutsiya i tserkov* (Moscow: Krasnaya Nov, 1923). For weakness of the atheist press, see Bezbozhnyi knizhnik (The Godless Bibliophile), "Ob antireligioznoi literature," *Knigonosha,* 29/110 (Aug. 31, 1925) 8–9 and Brooks, in Gleason, *Bolshevik Culture,* 156.

24. Krylov, "Iz istorii," 177, 181; M. Hindus, *Broken Earth* (New York: International Press, 1926) 30; *idem, Red Bread* (New York: Cape, 1931) 169 (qu.), 273–76; Fainsod, *Smolensk,* 433; Fueloep-Miller, *Mind,* 189–90.

25. Curtiss, *Russian Church,* 209–10, 239–55; *K.P.S.S. vo glave kulturnoi revolyutsii v S.S.S.R.* (Moscow: Izdpolit, 1972) 121; Fitzpatrick, *Education,* 18, 22–23.

26. David Powell, *Antireligious Propaganda in the Soviet Union* (Cambridge Mass.: Harvard University Press, 1975) 37, describing the Virgin Mary cartoon. For a sampling of the art: *Bezbozhnik u stanka,* covers and cartoons Nos. 5–10 (1923). For contrasting views of Apsit, see Rutenburg, "D. Moor", 173–74 and Stephen White, "The Political Poster in Bolshevik Russia," *Sbornik,* 8 (Leeds, 1982) 24–37.

27. Krylov, "Iz istorii," 181–82; Zvi Gitelman, *Jewish Nationalism and Soviet Politics: the Jewish Sections of the C.P.S.U., 1917–1930* (Princeton: Princeton University Press, 1972) 301; Fueloep-Miller, *Mind,* 186, 197; VRNK (Paris), 7 (Dec. 1923) 21.

28. Arbatov, "Ekaterinoslav," 130–31; Curtiss, *Russian Church,* 85; Fueloep-Miller, *Mind,* 186–87; M. Sheinman, *Bog sluzhit bogatym* (Moscow: Molodaya Gvardiya, 1925) 11–15; Yu. A. Polyakov, *Perekhod k NEPu i Sovetskoe krestyanstvo* (Moscow: Nauka, 1967) 191–92; Tumarkin, *Lenin Lives!* 174–89, on the embalming; Gorky, *O russkom krestyanstve* 30–31; M. I. Shakhnovich, "Dvadtsatpyatiletie muzeya istorii religii i ateizma Akademii Nauk S.S.S.R.," VIRA, V (1958) 410–24.

29. Hindus, *Broken Earth,* 227 (qu.); Curtiss, *Russian Church,* 212; I. V. Stepanov, *Kak vesti antireligioznuyu progagandu v derevne,* 2 ed. (Leningrad: Priboi, 1930); I. D. Strashun, *Borba za zdorove—borba s religiei* (Moscow: Bezbozhnik, 1925).

30. M. Reisner, *Nuzhna li vera v boga?* 3 ed. (Moscow: Krasnaya nov, 1923) 128; Leontiev cited in Kline, *Religious,* 46; F. Ph. Ingold, *Literatur und Aviatik: europäische Flugdichtung, 1909–27* (Basel, 1978) 58; Walter Kolarz, *Religion in the Soviet Union* (London: Macmillan, 1962) 19–21.

31. Skvortsov-Stepanov, *Osnovye techeniya v antireligioznoi propagande* (Moscow: Bezbozhnik, 1925) 8–9; S. Gorodetskii, *Komsomolskoe Rozhdestvo* (Moscow: Izd. M.K.R.K.S.M., 1923); "Komsomolskoe Rozhdestvo", *Nov* (Paris) 4 (Feb. 1923) 23–24; F. A. Mackenzie, *Russia Before Dawn* (London: Adelphi, 1923) 262; P. Scheffer, *Seven Years in Soviet Russia* (London: Putnam, 1932) 33. Odessa: U.S. National Archives Record Group 38, O.N.I., C-10-N, 1680S, Box 661, pp. 2–3; Tsaritsyn: Curtiss, *Russian Church,* 203. Krylov, "Iz istorii," 183–84; B. N. Konovalov, *K massovomu ateizmu* (Moscow: Nauk, 1974) 74; Binns, "Changing Face," 594; and Jennifer McDowell, "Soviet Civil Ceremonies," *Journal for the Scientific Study of Religion,* XIII/3 (1974) 265–79.

32. M. K. [M.I. Kalinin], "Novyi byt," *Krasnyi pakhar,* 1 (1919) 13–15; *Deyateli Oktyabrya,* 6–7; V. [P.M.] Kerzhentsev, "Teatr kak vneshkolnoe obrazovanie," *Vneshkolnoe obrazovanie,* 2–3 (Feb.–Mar. 1919) 23–28; Trotsky, *Problems of Everyday Life;* Yaroslavskii, *Protiv religii,* III, 220–24; V. V. Veresaev, *Ob obryadakh starykh i novykh* (Moscow: Novaya Moskva, 1926) 5–8; Binns, "Changing Face," 594–95.

33. *Ibid.,* 595; Yaroslavskii, *Religiya,* 47; *idem., Protiv religii,* III, 61–63; *Komsomolskaya Paskha* (Moscow: Novaya Moskva, 1924); Ya. Rezvushkin, *Sud na bogom* (Moscow: Gosizd., 1924); Scheffer, *Seven Years,* 34–39; F. Kovalëv, *Kalendar religioznykh prazdnikov* (Kharkov: Proletarii, 1930).

34. V. E. Khazanova, ed., *Iz istorii Sovetskoi arkhitektury,* 2 vols. (Moscow: A.N.S.S.R., 1963–70), I, 134–35.

35. *Ibid.* I, 134–43, 150–55, and II, 7 (illust.); Berton, *Moscow*, 211–12; Vittorio de Feo, *U.R.S.S.: architettura, 1917–1936* (Rome: Reuniti, 1963) 112; S. F. Starr, *Melnikov* (Princeton: Princeton University Press, 1978) 107–47.

36. M. Danilevskii, *Prazdniki obschestvennogo byta* (Moscow: Doloi Negramatnost, 1927) 3–13.

37. *Ibid,;* F. F. Korolëv, *et al., Ocherki po istorii Sovetskoi shkoly i pedagogiki, 1921–1931* (Moscow: Izd. Ak. Ped. Nauk R.S.F.S.R., 1961) 294.

38. Trotsky, *Problems,* 45–47; Ivan Sukhoplyuev, *Oktyabriny* (Kharkov: Gosizd. Ukrainy, 1925); Selishchev, *Yazyk,* 179–80; McDowell, "Soviet Civil", 267–68 for examples of obscure places where these rituals were performed.

39. Veresaev, *Ob obryadakh,* 22–26; Danilevskii, *Prazdniki,* 4.

40. Comrie, *Russ. Lang.,* 187–89; Selishcehv, *Yazyk,* 190; M. E. Koltsov, *Izbrannye proizvedeniya,* 3 vols. (Moscow: Khud. Lit., 1957), I, 574; Fueloep-Miller, *Mind,* 193–94; Sukhoplyuev, *Oktyabriny,* 20–30; M. K. "Novyi Byt"; personal information. For comparisons, see de Man, *Psychology of Socialism,* 156–64 and Thompson, *Making of the English Working Class,* 407.

41. B. A. Uspensky, "Name Changes in Russia from a Historical and Semiotic Point of View," translated in *Soviet Anthropology and Archaeology,* XVII/4 (Spring, 1979) 26.

42. Veresaev, *Ob obryadakh;* Vadim Bayan [VI. Sidorov], *Kumachevye gulyanki: khorovodnye igry* (Moscow: Mol. Gvardiya, 1927) 16–25; G. B. Zhirnova, "Nekotorye problemy i itogi izucheniya svadebnogo rituala v russkom gorode serediny XIX-nachala XX v.," in K. V. Chistov and T. A. Bernshtam, eds., *Russkii narodnyi svadebnyi obryad* (Leningrad, 1978) 32–47; Hindus, *Red Bread,* 197; Trotsky, *Problems,* 46; Pethybridge, *Social Prelude,* 55 (wedding figures). Fouché cited in Henderson, *Symbol and Satire in the French Revolution* (New York: Putnam, 1912), 409.

43. VKVD, 2 (Sept 1918) 64–71 (Uritsky's funeral, illust.). See also *Plamya,* 67 (Oct 19, 1979) 1–2 for the funeral of General A. P. Nikolaev, who was hanged by the Whites. The motifs of his and Uritsky's funerals are similar to those of a funeral of the 1860s depicted in *Sergei Vasilevich Gerasimov* (Moscow, 1951) 11. For another Bolshevik martyr-funeral (that of Volodarsky), see Lunacharskii, *Revolutionary Silhouettes,* tr. M. Glenny (New York: Hill and Wang, 1967) 117.

44. Avrich, *Kronstadt,* 173; M. K. "Novyi byt"; Fueloep-Miller, *Mind,* 196; Veresaev, *Ob obryadakh,* 9.

45. Khazanova, *Iz istorii,* I, 214–15; Trotsky, *Problems,* 46; Starr, *Melnikov,* 35; Gvido Bartel, "Istoriya i statistika Moskovskogo Krematoriya," *Zdravookhranenie,* (1929) 106–8. B. G. Kaplun, "Sozhiganie chelovecheskikh trunov," *Plamya,* July 13, 1919, pp. 7–9.

46. Quoted in Vasily Komar and Alexander Melamid, "In Search of Religion," *Artforum,* XVIII/9 (May 1980) no pagination.

47. *Tseli i zadachi,* 41–42; Vit. Zhemchuzhnii, "Protiv obryadov," *Novyi Lef,* 1 (Jan 1927) 43–47; Yaroslavsky, *Protiv religii,* III, 223.

48. For European parallels, see Hobsbawm, *Invention of Tradition.*

49. For some general treatments: Herbert Marcuse, *Soviet Marxism,* (New York: Columbia University Press, 1958), pt. II; *Marksistkaya etika—khrestomatiya,* ed. A. F. Shishkin (Moscow: Inst: Mezhdu. Otnosh., 1961); Richard de George, *Soviet Ethics and Morality* (Ann Arbor: University of Michigan Press, 1969). For a sampling from the 1920s: Lenin, *O morale* (Moscow: Gosizd., 1926); Bukharin, *Leninizm i problemy kulturnoi revolyutsii* (Moscow: Gosizd., 1928); Lunacharskii, *Kultura na zapade i u nas* (Moscow: Gosizd., 1928); *idem.,* "Moral i svoboda," *Krasnaya Nov,* 7 (Dec. 1923) 130–36; Trotsky, *Problems;* Kerzhentsev, "Chelovek novoi epokhi," *Revolyutsiya i kultura,* 2 (Dec. 5, 1927) 17–20.

50. As a small sample, see: *Tovarishchi, ne izmenyai!* Rostov-na-Donu [pre-1914]), Helsinki Collection; Shishkin, *Velikii Oktyabr; Komsomol: sbornik statei* (Munich: Izd. Tsentr. Obed. Polit, Emig. iz S.S.S.R., 1960) 33–43 and *passim; Tovarishch Komsomol: dokumenty sezdov,*

*konferentsii, i TsK V.L.K.S.M., 1918–1969,* 2 vols. (Moscow: Molodaya Gvardiya, 1969), I, 96–97.

51. N. Kanin, *O druzhbe i tovarishchestve v Komsomole* (Leningrad: Krasnaya Gvardiya, 1927). Aristotle cited in the Manuels, *Utopian Thought,* 288.

52. L. Kleinbort, "Rukopisnye zhurnaly rabochikh," VE, 7–8 (Jul.–Aug., 1917) 288; B. Weinryb, "Antisemitism in Soviet Russia," in L. Kochan, ed., *The Jews in Soviet Russia Since 1917* (Oxford: Oxford University Press, 1978) 300–332.

53. The *smychka* still awaits a cultural historian. See *Krasnaya zvezda* (Moscow, 1918), a pamphlet in the Helsinki Collection, for the symbolic beginnings of it. See Meijer, "Town and Country," 347 and Osinsky, *Amerikanskii avtomobil ili rossiiskaya telega?* (Moscow, 1930) 14–24.

54. I. Trifonov, *Ocherki istorii klassovoi borby v S.S.S.R. v gody N.E.P. (1921–1927)* Moscow: Politlit, 1960, 46–48 (must be used with care); Marcuse, *Soviet Marxism,* 228–67; Ralph Fischer, *Pattern for Soviet Youth* (New York: Columbia University Press, 1959) 99–100, 161.

55. This issue has received much recent attention. B. Clements, *Bolshevik Feminist* (Bloomington: Indiana University Press, 1979); B. Farnsworth, *Aleksandra Kollontai* (Stanford: Stanford University Press, 1980); Stites, *Women's Liberation,* 346–91. Also the older work, Wilhelm Reich, *The Mass Psychology of Fascism* (New York: Farrar; reprint, 1970) 285–309.

56. G. Grigorov and S. Shkotov, *Staryi i novyi byt* (Moscow, 1927) 144–45; Fitzpatrick, *Education,* 26; Stites, *Women's Liberation,* 358–76; Keith Thomas, "Work and Leisure in Pre-Industrial Society," *Past and Present,* 29 (1964) 54; Trotsky, *Problems,* 49–56; *Zhizn bez kontrolya* (Moscow, 1929); Jennie Stevens, "Children of the Revolution," *Russian History,* 9/2–3 (1982) 242–64. The novels of N. Ognëv and P. S. Romanov are especially apropos.

57. Grigorov, *Staryi,* 134 (qu.); *Krasnye zori* (Kazan) 1 (1919) 18 (a cartoon identifying alcoholism with Tsar Nicholas II); M. K. Mikhailov, *Vodku pit—vse gubit* (Moscow: Doloi Negramotnost, 1927); I. M. Vavushkin, *Pochemu vreden tabak* (Moscow: Gosizd., 1926).

58. Griogorov, *Staryi,* 103–6; Trotsky, *Problems,* 35; *Byt i molodëzh* (Leningrad: Izd. Len. Obl. Sov. Prof., 1928) 21–28.

59. Goldman, *My Disillusionment,* 232; Fischer, *Patterns,* 69; Grigorov, *Staryi,* 44–46; *Obyvatelshchina na pritseli* (Leningrad: Krasnaya Gvardiya, 1928); S. Frederick Starr, *Red and Hot: the Fate of Jazz in the Soviet Union* (Oxford: New York: Oxford University Press, 1982), 54–106.

60. Lunacharskii, *O byte* (Moscow: Gosizd., 1927) 41–45 and Grigorov, *Staryi,* 50, 110–14.

61. *Ibid.,* 139–40. Vera Dunham, *In Stalin's Time* (Cambridge: Cambridge University Press, 1976) 19–23 and *passim.*

62. Trotsky, *Problems,* 70, 76; M. N. Lyadov, *Voprosy byta* (Moscow: Kom. Akademiya, 1925) 120–26; Grigorov, *Staryi,* 23–25, 120–26.

63. For a sense of the richness and scope of this debate, see, among numerous other publications: *Komsololskii byt* and A. Milchakov, *Komsomol v borbe za kulturnyi byt,* both published in Moscow by Molodaya Gvardiya, 1927; B. Dmitriev, *et al., Na putkyakh k novomu bytu* (Moscow: Novaya Moskva, 1927); V. Slepkov, *Na bytovye temy* (Leningrad: Krasnaya Gazeta, 1927); and A. Oborin, *Protiv grubost i samodurstva* (Moscow: Gosizdat, 1928). A good brief analysis of the Leningrad Komsomol on this issue is Peter Gooderham's paper, "The Komsomol and Worker Youth" (1981). Isabel Tirado is completing a book on the Komsomol in the Revolution.

64. Tumarkin, *Lenin Lives!; idem.,* "Religion, Bolshevism, and the Origins of the Lenin Cult," *Russian Review,* 40/1 (Jan. 1981) 35–46; Komar and Melamid, "In Search" ; Williams, *Artists,* 124–25, 180; Starr, *Melnikov,* 79–84; Khazanova, *Iz istorii,* I, 224–29.

65. Fainsod, *Smolensk,* 430–31; Ya. A. Yakovlev, *Derevnya kak ona est* (Moscow: Krasnaya Nov, 1923) 89–94; Korolëv, *Ocherki,* 286; F. Oleshchuk, *Shkola i vospitanie aktivnykh ateistov* (Moscow: Moskovskii Rabochii, 1928) 58 ff.

66. Bobryshev, *Melkoburzhuaznye vliyaniya,* 45; Hindus, *Red Bread,* 186–87; *idem., The Great Offensive* (New York: Harrison Smith, 1933) 169–81; Fitzpatrick, *Education,* 174, 303n.

67. For examples of folk "understanding," see "In Search"; Comrie, *Russian Language,* 137; and Selishchev, *Yazyk,* 215. Anon. ("Sovetskii starozhil"), "V derevne," VKR (Prague) 1/13 (June 1928) 22–25; Fueloep-Miller, *Mind,* 71–89.

68. Fueloep-Miller, *Mind,* 72; Ellul, "The Technological Order," in C. Stover, ed., *The Technological Order* (Detroit: Wayne State University Press, 1963) 38; Hindus, *Great Offensive,* 182–89; *Humanity Uprooted,* 41; Berdyaev, *Origin,* 158–78. Mao is quoted in W. Rosenberg and M. Young, *Transforming Russia and China* (New York: Oxford University Press, 1982) 82.

69. V. G. Korolenko, *Korolenko's Siberia,* tr. R. F. Christian (Liverpool: Liverpool University Press, 1954) 31–74; Andrei Platonov, *Chevengur,* ed. M. Geller (Paris: Y.M.C.A. Press, 1972) 14–15.

70. Fedotoff White, *Growth of the Red Army,* 124–25; Nikolai Lunev, "Blind Faith in a Bright Future," *Soviet Youth: Twelve Komsomol Histories* (Munich: Institute for the Study of the U.S.S.R., 1959) 31, 34.

# Chapter 6: The Republic of Equals

1. Moshe Lewin, *The Making of the Soviet System* (New York: Pantheon, 1985) 72–87; Teodor Shanin, *The Awkward Class* (Oxford: Clarendon Press, 1972) 29, 34–37, 41; H. D. Löwe, "Traditionelle and neue Rollen der Frau in Zeitalten sozialer Umbruche: Russland, 1860–1917," unpublished paper, 1984; John Maynard, *Russia in Flux* (New York: Macmillan, 1959) 127–28; Brooks, *When Russia,* 285–86.

2. F. Terner, *O rabochem klasse* (S.Pb., 1860) 302–18; Yu. I. Kipryanov, *Zhiznennyi uroven rabochikh Rossii (konets XIX-nachalo XX v.),* Moscow, Nauka, 1979, pp. 161–64; Koenker, *Moscow Workers,* 55–56; Andrei Lobanov-Rostovsky, *The Grinding Mill: Reminiscences of War and Revolution in Russia, 1913–1920* (New York: Macmillan, 1935) 274; Zelnik, *Radical Worker,* 7–13. See chapter 10 for artel communes.

3. Quoted in Gleason, *Young Russia,* 328. See Zakharina, "Rev. prop., 91–92.

4. Linda Edmundson, "Civil Rights in Russia: the 1905 Revolution," unpublished paper; Brooks, "Vekhi", 28; Lenin cited in *Marksistskaya etika,* 290–93; Mikhail Gernet, *Ravenstvo* (Petrograd, 1917).

5. Hill, *The World Turned Upside Down* (New York: Viking, 1972); Keep, *Russian Revolution,* 215, 400, *passim;* Goldman, *My Disillusionment,* 149; Gill, *Peasants and Government;* Shanin, *Awkward Class,* 150–60; Atkinson, *End of the Russian Village Commune.*

6. P.R., 10 (Oct. 1922) 357; Mehnert, *Youth,* 220; Koenker, *Moscow Workers, passim;* Krasnikova, *My novyi mir,* 43–44; VOMU, 1 (Dec. 27, 1918) 14; Potekhin, *Pervyi Soviet,* 161–72; Robien, *Diary,* 218; Marabini, *Vie,* 169; Arbatov, "Ekaterinoslav," 117 (qu.).

7. Kopp, *Changer,* 122 (quoting Bukharin); Raleigh, *Revolution,* 161; Avrich, *Kronstadt,* 73; Anet, *Through,* 108; Arbatov, "Ekaterinoslav," 86; Fisher, *Famine,* 81; Keep, *Russian Revolution,* 427 (Shefter's proposal).

8. Hamm, "The Breakdown of Urban Modernization: a Prelude to the Revolution of 1917", in Hamm, *City in Russian History,* 182–200; *idem.,* "Kharkov's Progressive Duma, 1910–1914: a Study in Russian Municipal Reform," SR, 40/1 (Spring 1981) 422–36; Daniel Brower, "Urban Russia on the Eve of World War One: a Social Profile," *Journal of Social History,* 13/3 (Spring, 1980) 422–36; Bradley, *Muzhik;* Engelstein, *Moscow, 1905,* 41; Lenin in Potekhin, *Pervyi Sovet,* 168; Koenker, *Moscow Workers,* 54–57; Farson, *Black Bread,* 3. For comparison, see John Gillis, *The Development of European Society* (Boston: Houghton Mifflin, 1977) 179.

9. Avrich, *Anarchists,* 80, 48 (qu.); Hasegawa, "Crime and Revolution"; Yarchuk, *Kronshtadt,* 22–23, 38–39.

10. *Krasnaya Moskva, 1917–1920 gg.* (Moscow: Izd. Mosk. Sov., 1920) 334–50; Ignatiev, *Moskva,* 280–85; Kulyshev, *Partiinaya organizatsiya,* 261–63; Potekhin, *Pervyi Sovet,* 169–71; Robien, *Diary,* 220; Khan-Magomedov, *Pionere,* 342.

11. For a full sense of the impact of this drama, one must see it also from the perspective of the dispossessed: N.A.R.S./ Record Group 20, Red Cross Records, Box 866, folder 948 (diary of Royal Kelly); L.C., Babine Papers, Section 1 (1917–1919), box 1; Igor Schwezoff [Shvetsov], *Russian Somersault* (New York: Harper, 1936) 80–83, *passim;* N. Wrangel, *From Serfdom to Bolshevism* (London: Benn, 1927) 293–307; Brown, *Doomsday,* 95. See also Conway, *Art Treasures,* 135–39; Kopp, *Town and Revolution,* 102; *Nemerknushchie gody: ocherki vospominaniya o Krasnom Petrograde, 1917–1919* (Leningrad: Sov. Pisatel, 1957) 289; Shklovsky, "Lenin," 56; and Mackenzie, *Russia Before Dawn,* 179.

12. Avrich, *Anarchists,* 71; Potekhin, *Pervyi Sovet,* 161–65; Ignatev, *Moskva,* 297–98; Robien, *Diary,* 186, 218; Fedotoff White, *Growth of the Red Army,* 107–8.

13. Olbracht, "Puteshestvie," 74–75; A. Khokhryakov, "Iz zhizni petrogradskogo garizona v 1917 g," KL, 17 (1926) 30; Brown, *Doomsday,* 155; Marabini, *Vie,* 52–53; Makhno, *Russ. Rev.,* I, 127 (the incarceration of Makhno's jailer in his own former cell); Robien, *Diary,* 186; Keep, *Russian Revolution, passim;* Krasnikova, *My novyi mir,* 105–6; VOKVD, 1 (Sept. 1918) 178.

14. Soviet historians make no secret of Bolshevik punitive policies in the Revolution. On some of these, see Fraiman, *Forpost,* 351 and *idem., Revolyutsionnaya zashchita,* 178. PVRK, I, 205.

15. John Wheeler-Bennett, *Brest-Litovsk: the Forgotten Peace, March 1918* (London: Macmillan, 1939) 84–88.

16. Edward Shils, "Deference," in J. A. Jackson, ed., *Social Stratification* (Cambridge: Cambridge University Press, 1968) 104–32; Wright Miller, *The Russians as People* (New York: Dutton, 1960) 116–21; Trotsky, *My Life* (New York: Scribners, 1930) 105.

17. For photographic sources, see Harrison Salisbury, *Russia in Revolution, 1900–1930* (New York: Holt, Rinehart, Winston, 1978); Chloe Obolensky, *The Russian Empire: a Portrait in Photographs* (New York: Random House, 1979); Marvin Lyons, *Russia in Original Photographs* ed. Andrew Wheatcroft (New York: Scribner's, 1977). See also Brooks, *When Russia,* 279, on dress.

18. Marabini, *Vie,* 63–64; Brown, *Doomsday,* 103. Uldricks, "The Crowd," 405; Mackenzie, *Russia Before Dawn,* 176; Babine Papers, Sect. 1 (1917–1919), Box 1, Jan. 22, 1918.

19. Lunacharsky believed that Sverdlov dressed from head to toe in black glistening leather partly to lend "stature, gravity, and solidity" to his small unprepossessing figure: *Revolutionary Silhouettes,* 106–7. On the resonance of the leather jacket, see Yury Trifonov, *The Old Man* (New York: Simon and Schuster, 1984).

20. The photo is in Salisbury, *Russia in Revolution,* 176–77. Kustodiev's designs in *Art into Production,* 2–3; Tatyana Strizhenova, *Iz istorii sovetskogo kostyuma* (Moscow: Sov. Khudozhnik, 1972) 24–26. See also *Ivan Yakovlevich Bilibin* (Leningrad: Khudozhnik R.S.F.S.R., 1970).

21. Ehrenburg, *First Years,* 143; *Lef,* 2 (April–May, 1923) 65–68 (illustr.); Bowlt, "Constructivism and Early Soviet Fashion Design" in Gleason, *Bolshevik Culture,* 203–19 (qu. 206, 203); Strizhenova, *Iz istorii,* 81–110; Christina Lodder, *Russian Constructivism* (New Haven: Yale University Press, 1983) 145–53.

22. Bowlt, "Constructivism"; Roizman, *Vse,* 16–19, 123, 136; personal conversations.

23. *Dekrety Sovetskoi vlasti,* 3 vols. (Moscow: Gosizdpolit, 1957–64), I, 71–72; Keep, ed., *The Debate on Soviet Power* (Oxford: Clarendon Press, 1979), 187–88, 319 (the vote for this decree was unanimous); Comrie, *Russian Language,* 142, 193–97; Selishchev, *Yazyk,* 74, 193; Barrington Moore, *Soviet Politics—the Dilemma of Power* (New York: Harper, 1965) 160 (quoting Trotsky).

24. Comrie, *Russian Language,* 173–74; Gleason, *Young Russia,* 260; Persits, "Avtobiografiya," 121; Engelstein, *Moscow,* 74; *Soldatskaya mysl,* 4 (April 1907) 4, quote.

25. Wildman, *End,* 28, 35, 49, 233; Anet, *Through the Russian Revolution,* 107. Brown, *Doomsday,* 66. Trotsky, *Problems,* 77–78 (qu., 78).

26. For prerevolutionary use, see Shishkin, *Tak skladyvalas,* 270–71; Hindus, *Broken Earth,*

31–32; Comrie, *Russian Language*, 195–97; Brown, *Doomsday*, 132, 154; Selishchev, *Yazyk*, 214.

27. Comrie, *Russian Language*, 156; Serge, *Memoirs*, 120; Fitzpatrick, *Commissariat*, 23; *La Ondo de Esperanto* (Moscow, 1908–17) a monthly, *passim* and 4/52 (April 1913) 62–63; V. G. Sutkovoi, *Esperanto-Russkii slovar* (Moscow: Ts.K.S.E.S.R., 1927) 4–8.

28. Ehrenburg, *First Years*, 9–10; Peter Forster, *The Esperanto Movement* (The Hague: Mouton, 1982) 188–203. Ivo Lapenna, ed., *Esperanto en perspektivo* (London: Universala Esperanto-Asocio, 1974); Kopelev, *Education*, 96–124.

29. For an introduction to these matters, see: B. Schwarz, *Music*, 11–37; K. Kuznetsov, "Betkhoven i Sen-Simon," *Muzyka i revolyutsiya*, 3 (1927) 12–16; Dreiden, *Muzyka–revolyutsii; V pervye gody sovetskogo muzykalnogo stroitelstva* (Leningrad, 1959); Dreiden, "Lenin znakomitsya s terminovoksom," *Muzykalnaya zhizn*, 7/489 (April 1978) 2–3; A. A. Ivanov, *Sovetskii elektricheskii muzykalnyi instrument Emiriton (Melodin)* Moscow, 1953; V. D. Kirpichnikov, "Elektrifikatsiya muzykalnykh instrumentov," *Persimfans*, (program for 9–16, May, 1927). Kenez, *Birth*.

30. Arnold Tsukker, *Pyat let Persimfansa* (Moscow: Izd; Pervogo Simfonicheskogo Ansmblya Mossoveta, 1927). *Persimfans: zhurnal pervogo simfonicheskogo ansamblya* (Moscow, 1926 ff.); Persimfans programs, irregular, 1922 ff; S. S. Prokoviev: materialy, dokumenty, vospominaniya, 2 ed. (Moscow, 1961) 179; *Muzykalnoe obrazovanie*, 4–5 (1925) 109; S. Ponyatovsky, "Persimfans," *Muzykalnaya zhizn*, 23/481 (Dec. 1977) 15–16; Schwarz, *Music*, 33; M. S. Blok, "O Lve Moiseeviche Tseitline," in *Vospominaniya o Moskovskoi Konservatorii* (Moscow, 1966) 329–55; I. Yampolskii, "K 66-letniya L. M. Tseitlina," *Sovetskaya muzyka*, 5 (1941) 71–72. Moses Smith, *Koussevitzky* (New York: Allen, Town, and Heath, 1947) 73–86, 102. *Muzykalnaya zhizn Moskvy*, 201.

31. Persimfans was under the authority of the Moscow Soviet. For information on many of its players, see *Vosp. o Mosk. Konserv.*, *passim* and assorted programs of Persimfans, 1922–27. *Persimfans: zhurnal*, 1 (1927–28) 3–4, 6–7, 9–12; 2 (1927–28) 3–7; 7 (1928–29) 3–5, plus supplement.

32. Tsukker, *O simfonicheskom ansamble*, (Moscow: Obshchestvo druzei Simfonicheskoi Ansmablya, 1924) 1–30; *idem, Pyat let persimfansa*, 180–200.

33. *Persimfans: zhurnal*, 2 (1927–28) 15–16 and 7 (1928–29) 56. Szigeti, *With Strings Attached*, 2 ed. (New York: Knopf, 1967) 233–34. Tsukker, *O simfonicheskom ansamble*, 26.

34. For a sampling, see: *Muzykalnaya nov*, 5 (Feb. 29, 1924); *Rabochii i teatr*, 6/229 (Feb. 3, 1929). *Muzyka i revolyutsiya*, 1 (1927) 4,7, 28–29; 2 (1927) 30; and 3 (1927) 31; *Krasnaya niva*, 9 (1927); S. S. Prokoviev, 179 on his first meeting with Persimfans. A slightly different account is given in *ibid.*, 426–31. *Persimfans: zhurnal*, 7 (1928–29) on Klemperer's remark.

35. Ponyatovskii, "Persimfans," 15–16; Yu. V. Keldysh, *100 let Moskovskoi Konservatorii* (Moscow, 1966) 116; Yampolskii, "K 66-letniya", 72; *Proletarskii muzykant*, 4 (1929) 41; "Unconducted Symphonies," *Musical America* (November 10, 1928) 135.

36. *Persimfans: zhurnal*, 7 (1928–29) 8; Tsukker, *O simfonicheskom ansamble*, 8; Shwarz, *Music*, 46–47. Starr's sources are mostly from Moscow, mine from Leningrad. Ponyatovskii, "Persimfans," 15–16. Blok gives the year of dissolution as 1934 ("O Lve").

37. For two examples, see: L. Slonimsky, *Music of Our Day*, new ed. (Freeport: 1970) 329–30; Percy Scholes, *Oxford Companion to Music*, 10th ed. (London: Oxford University Press, 1970) 243, 903.

38. Gogol: Lincoln, *Nicholas I*, 246. Marx quoted by Ollman in Bialer and Sluzar, eds., *Radical Visions of the Future*, 67; Lenin, PSS, VII, 22.

39. Canetti, *Crowds and Power*, 394–96. V. Bogdanov-Berëzovsky, *Dorogi iskusstva: kniga pervaya (1903–1945)*, Leningrad: Muzyka, 1971, pp. 184–86. Quotation from *Istoriya russkoi sovetskoi muzyki*, 4 vols in 5 (Moscow: Gos. muz. izd., 1956–1963), I, 46, n. 1. For a good treatment of a "traditional" Soviet conductor of the time—and a pupil of Nikisch—see: G. G. Tigranov, ed., *K. S. Saradzhev* (Moscow: Sovetskii kompozitor, 1962) 7–55.

40. *Persimfans: zhurnal,* 2 (1927–28) 3.

41. Basic works on these matters are: Robert V. Daniels, *Consience of the Revolution* (Cambridge, Mass.: Harvard University Press, 1960); Leonard Schapiro, *The Origin of the Communist Autocracy* (New York: Praeger, 1965): Avrich, *Russian Anarchists; idem.,* "Bolshevik Opposition to Lenin: G. T. Miasnikov and the Workers' Group," *Russian Review,* XLIII (1984) 1–29.

42. Fitzpatrick, *Commissariat;* Clements, *Bolshevik Feminist;* and Farnsworth, *Aleksandra Kollontai.* See Carl Boggs, "Marxism, Prefigurative Communism, and the Problem of Workers' Control," *Radical America,* 4–6 (November, 1977) 99–122.

43. The rotation of jobs has been a frequent feature of utopian literature since Thomas More. See also Fitzpatrick, "The Civil War as a Formative Experience," 69. Susiluoto, *Origins and Development,* 61–62.

44. Richard Lowenthal, "Beyond Totalitarianism?" in Irving Howe, *1984 Revisited,* (New York: Harper, 1983) 218–19; Abram Bergson, *The Structure of Soviet Wages* (Cambridge, Mass.: Harvard University Press, 1944, *passim* (p. 187 for Tomsky); Moore, *Soviet Politics,* 183–86; Smith, *Red Petrograd,* ch. 8. For vivid examples of early wage stratification, see BVSNTMP, 2–3 (Nov. 23, 1918) 11–28 and 4 (Nov. 30, 1918) 9–12.

45. Mervyn Matthews, *Privilege in the Soviet Union* (London: Allen and Unwin, 1978) 60–70; Stephen Sternheimer, "Administration for Development: the Emerging Bureaucratic Elite, 1920–1930," in W. Pintner and D. K. Rowney, eds., *Russian Officialdom* (Chapel Hill: University of North Carolina Press, 1980) 316–54; Fitzpatrick, *Education,* 79–83; Bailes, *Technology,* 46, 51; Alexander Barmine, *One Who Survived* (New York: Putnam, 1945) 58.

46. Baratov (no first name), *Kommunisty-otpuskniki: nakaz* (Moscow: Gosizdat, 1921), 13 (Helsinki Collection): Robert McNeale, *The Bolshevik Tradition* (Englewood Cliffs: Prentice-Hall, 1963) 46–47; Tumarkin, *Lenin Lives!,* 130, 179–81.

47. Chamberlin, *Russian Revolution,* I, 360; Szigeti, *With Strings Attached,* 221; Olbracht, "Puteshestvie," 72, 78–79; Goldman, *My Disillusionment,* 10; VRNK (Paris) 8 (Feb. 1, 1924) 50; W. Reswick, *I Dreamt Revolution* (Chicago: Regnery, 1952) 75–76.

48. Grabar, *Moya zhizn,* 273; Joravsky, "Cultural Revolution and the Fortress Mentality," in Gleason, *Bolshevik Culture,* 102; Fitzpatrick, *Education,* 80; Matthews, *Privilege,* 75–78; Goldman, *My Disillusionment,* 174.

49. *Krasnyi offitser,* 1 (Oct. 1918) 4; Matthews, *Privilege,* 85–90; Balabanova, *My Life,* 248; Goldman, *My Disillusionment,* 15–21, 176; Alfred Rosmer, *Lenin's Moscow* (1953; London: Pluto, 1971) 167–68; Gorky, *Revolyutsiya i kultura,* 16–17.

50. Matthews, *Privilege,* 80–82; Farson, *Black Bread,* 10–11.

51. Max Nomad, "The Saga of Waclaw Machajski," in his *Aspects of Revolt* (New York: Bookman, 1959) 96–117 (quote 115). Bogdanov in Kendall Bailes, "Alexei Gastev and the Soviet Controversy over Taylorism," SS, 29/3 (July 1977) 380 and in *Trudy NOT,* 6; Balabanova, *My Life,* 200–203.

## Chapter 7: Man the Machine

1. See Chapter 1.

2. Samuel Haber, *Efficiency and Uplift: Scientific Management in the Progressive Era, 1890–1920* (Chicago: University of Chicago Press, 1964); Daniel Bell, *The End of Ideology,* rev. ed. (New York: Free Press, 1965) 227–72; H. Aitken, *Taylorism at Watertown Arsenal* (Cambridge, Mass.: Harvard University Press, 1960).

3. Haber, *Efficiency, passim;* Harrison Emerson, "Principles of Efficient Organization," Emerson Engineers Efficiency Organization, *Staff Bulletin,* 53 (1919); Robert Hoxie, *Scientific Management and Labor* (New York: Appleton, 1921); Chales Maier, "Between Taylorism and Technocracy: European Ideology and the Vision of Industrial Production in the 1920s," *Journal*

282                                    *Notes*
*of Contemporary History,* 5/2 (1970) 27–61; Jules Amar, *Le moteur humain* (Paris, 1914). Lenin owned the Russian translation of this book: *Chelovecheskaya mashina* (Moscow, 1922).

4. L. Pamilla and V. Chukovich, *NOT—velenie vremeni* (Minsk: Belarus, 1973); Steve Smith, "Taylorism Rules OK? Bolshevism, Taylorism and the Technical Intelligentsia in the Soviet Union 1917–41," *Radical Science Journal,* 13 (1983) 3–27; N. Sukhanov, "O 'sisteme' Teilora," *Russkoe bogatstvo,* 11 (Nov. 1913) 132–54; Zenovia Sochor, "Soviet Taylorism Revisited," SS, XXXIII/2 (Apr. 1981) 246–64 and Bailes, "Alexei Gastev," 373–94.

5. Frank and Struve: Victor Terras, "Mayakovsky and Time," SEEJ, XIII/2 (1969) 155 and Jeffrey Brooks, "Vekhi," 21–50; Bailes, *Technology,* 49–50 (Lenin quote, 49); Fleron, "Administrative Theory." On Lenin's "American style" of work see: L. Fotieva, *Iz zhizni Lenina* (Moscow: Gosizdat, 1959) 46; P. M. Kerzhentsev, *Zhizn Lenina* (Moscow, 1937) 251–8; and V. Klyukin, "Komsomol i NOT v dvadtsatye gody," *Pozyvnye istorii,* I (1969) 236–62.

6. *Vestnik professionalnykh soyuzov,* 2 (June 15, 1918) 4–6; *Organizatsiya truda,* 1 (Mar 1921) 87–88; O. Ermansky, *Nauchnaya Organizatsiya Truda i Proizvodstva i sistema Teilora* (Moscow: Gosizdat, 1923); *Vestnik truda,* 6 (June 1921) 36–40. On Kronstadt: *Pravda o Kronshtadte* (Prague: Volya Rossii, 1921) 173 and Avrich, *Kronstadt,* 245.

7. Allan Nevins, *Ford,* 2 vols. (New York: 1954–57), I, 20 and II, 514–25 591–93; Henry Ford and Samuel Crowther, *Today and Tomorrow* (New York: Doubleday, 1926) 108–19; Ford, *My Philosophy of Industry* (New York: Coward-McCann, 1929) 37.

8. Maier, "Between Taylorism and Technocracy," 54; Nevins, *Ford,* II, 255, 673–84. The Ford biography, *Moya zhizn,* 3d ed. was issued by the journal *Time (Vremya),* see below, in 1924. For a rhapsodic appreciation of Fordism, see: I. M. Burdyanskii, *Nauchnaya Organizatsiya Truda* (Leningrad: Priboi, 1925) 23–27, On "fordism" in language: Selishchev, *Yazyk, passim;* and N. A. Milyutin, *Sotsgorod: the Problem of Building Socialist Cities* (1930), trans. A. Sprague (Cambridge, Mass.: M.I.T. Press, 1974) 21. Edward Phillips, *American Technical Assistance to the Nizhni-Novgorod Automobile Plant, 1929–1932* (M. A. Thesis, Georgetown University, 1981).

9. Hindus, "Henry Ford Conquers Russia," *The Outlook,* 146/9 (June 29, 1927) 280–83 (illus.); Peter Filene, *Americans and the Soviet Experiment, 1917–33* (Cambridge, Mass.: Harvard University Press, 1967) 120–24; Bailes, "The American Connection: Ideology and the Transfer of Technology to the Soviet Union," CSSH, 23/3 (July 1981) 421–48.

10. Hans Rogger, "*Amerikanizm* and the Economic Development of Russia," CSSH, 23/3 (July 1981) 382–420; Hindus, *Broken Earth* (New York: International, 1926) 41, 182; Osinsky, *Amerikanskii avtomobil;* Fuelop-Miller, *Mind,* 22; and Charles Rougle, *Three Russians Look at America* (Stockholm: Almqvist and Wiksell, 1976). The best study of Russian-Soviet popular attitudes toward America is J. Brooks, "Russia's American Dream," paper, N.E.P. conference, November, 1986. My thanks to the author.

11. There is no exhaustive study of Gastev. Kurt Johansson, *Aleksej Gastev: Proletarian Bard of the Machine Age* (Stockholm: Almqvist and Wiksell, 1983) is an analysis of his poetry. Gastev's son, Yuri Alekseevich, is currently completing a major study. I thank him deeply for his lengthy conversations with me about his father.

12. For earlier European currents of machinism in literature, see Elliott Grant, *French Poetry and Modern Industry, 1830–1870* (Cambridge, Mass.: Harvard University Press, 1927). Gastev's poetry is in *Poeziya rabochego udara* (Moscow: Sovetskii Pisatel, 1964). See also: *Proletarskie poety.* Gladkov, *Cement* (New York: Ungar, n.d.) 115.

13. Gastev, *Poeziya,* 135–52. Analysis by Rougle, " 'Express': the Future According to Gastev," in Kleberg and Stites, *Utopia,* 258–68.

14. See *Proletarskaya Kultura,* 3 (Aug 1918) 1–18; Gastev's poetry was issued in six Russian editions and translated into four languages (including Esperanto). "Novaya Industriya" in *Vestnik metallista,* 2 (Jan 1918) 5–27 (qu., 26–27).

15. *Proletarskaya kultura,* 9/10 (1919) 35–45. This quotation is translated from Lorenz, *Proletarische Kulturrevolution,* 62–63.

16. For particulars, see Lewis and Weber, "Zamyatin's *We.*" Bogdanov's critique: Bailes, "Alexei Gastev," 379–82.

———

17. Gastev, *Industrialnyi mir* (Kharkov, 1919).

18. Gastev, *Poeziya*, 1–20; *Trudy NOT*, I, 120–24; Samuel Lieberstein, "Technology, Work, and Sociology in the U.S.S.R.: the N.O.T. Movement," *Technology and Culture*, 16/1 (Jan. 1975) 52–53.

19. Aside from *Poeziya*, Gastev's major statements can be found in the pages of his journal, *Organizatsiya truda* and in two later collections: *Kak nado rabotat* (1966) and *Trudovye ustanovki* (1973), both republished by Ekonomika in Moscow.

20. J. O. de la Mettrie (De-la Metri), *Chelovek-mashina* (S.Pb.: Obshchaya polza, 1911). The term *zhivaya mashina* (living machine) was in currency among Taylorists: Burdyansky, *N.O.T.*, 36. Canetti, *Crowds and Power*, 315–16.

21. S. N. Nikolskii, *Karel Chapek: fantast i satirik* (Moscow: Nauka, 1973) 35–55; Karel Čapek, *R.U.R.* (Prague: Československý Spisovatel, 1966), 105.

22. See the memoir by E. A. Petrov in Gastev, *Trudovye*, 339–42. Yury Alexeevich Gastev: personal reminiscences about his father.

23. No history of the Central Institute of Labor has ever been written. See the previously cited works of Sochor, Bailes, Smith, Lieberstein, the files of *Org. truda*, the works of Gastev, and Ernest Toller, *Which World—Which Way?* tr. M. Ould (London: Sampson Low, 1931) 114–16.

24. Bailes, "American Connection", 25; Gastev, *Kak nado rabotat*, 262. 286. 309; Michael Hagemeister's introduction to Valerian Muraviëv, *Ovladenie vremenem* (1924; Munich: Sagner, 1983) 1–27.

25. Patricia Carden, "The Case for the Future: the Life and Work of Aleksei Gastev," ms.

26. V. Kerzhentsev was his principal pseudonym. He has attracted even less attention than Gastev. Biographical data in *ES* (Granat) XI/1, 185–86; additional fragments in Fitzpatrick, *Commissariat*, 96, 146–47, 153 and from the bibliographer of the State Public Library in Leningrad.

27. Modern editions of the major collections are *Borba za vremya* (1965) and *Printsipy organizatsii* (1968), both published by Ekonomika in Moscow and both containing the title works. See also *Kak vesti sorbraniya* (Petrograd, 1919), apparently Kerzhentsev's first word on the subject.

28. Kerzhentsev, *Borba*, 61–73, 81, 91–94, *passim* and his other works of the period.

29. Kerzhentsev, *Printsipy*, 272–332 (quotes, 275, 302); *Pamyatka organizatora* (Ekaterinburg: Uralkniga, 1925).

30. Two documentary collections are: *Nauchnaya organizatsiya truda dvadtsatykh godov: sbornik dokumentov i materialov* (Kazan, 1965)—see 192 (photo), 256–72, 191–92, 405–19 for some examples of its work (and *passim*), and *Nauchnaya Organizatsiya Truda, Proizvodstva i Upravleniya: sbornik dokumentov i materialov, 1918–1930 gg.* (Moscow: Ekonomika, 1969) 224–26 and *passim*. Klyukin, "Komsomol i N.O.T.", and Pamilla and Chukovich, *N.O.T.*, have sketchy information on the League. Sochor, "Soviet Taylorism" is useful. On clocks and watches: *Promyshlennost S.S.S.R.: statisticheskii sbornik* (Moscow, 1957) 362, kindly supplied by Sheila Fitzpatrick.

31. Kerzhentsev, *Borba*, 84–85, 134 (quote, 85); *N.O.T. Sbornik* (1969), 226–34; Burdyanskii, *N.O.T.* 33–35 (diagram of Kazan Station); *Pravda*, 287 (Dec. 17, 1924) 7; Klyukin, "Komsomol", 259.

32. *Ibid.*, 248–52; V. Byaltseva, "Nachinaniya kruzhka po N.O.T.," *Krasnaya molodëzh*, 3–4 (7–8) Mar.–Apr., 1925, p. 156–7; M. Yankovsky, *Kommuna sta tridtsati trëkh* (Leningrad: Priboi, 1929) 43–46; Klaus Mehnert, *Youth in Soviet Russia* (New York: Harcourt, 1933) 183.

33. *Yunyi pioner (posobie dlya instruktora)*, Moscow: Novaya Moskva, 1924, *passim*, see p. 145 for the "League of Time" game.

34. Mark von Hagen, *School of the Revolution: Bolsheviks and Peasants in the Red Army* (forthcoming).

35. For various perspectives on the fall of the League: Klyukin, "Komsomol," 247–48, 254; Sochor, "Soviet Taylorism," n. 53; Melanie Tatur, *"Wissenschaftliche Arbeitsorganisation"*: *Arbeitswissenschaft und Arbeits-organization in der Sowjetunion, 1921–33* (Berlin: Harassowitz,

1979) 63–70. A nice piece of satire of Gastev and Kerzhentsev can be found in a popular "red detective" novel of the period, in which a character teaches drill to people on stilts to increase the efficient use of space and time: Jim Dollar [Marietta Shaginian], *Mess-Mend, ili Yanki v Petrograde* (1923: Moscow: Gosiz., 1952) 160–61.

36. The literature on production art in the Russian Revolution is huge. For some good recent examples, see: Lodder, *Russian Constructivism;* John Bowlt, ed. *Russian Art of the Avant-garde* (New York: Viking, 1976); *Art into Production;* Starr, *Melnikov;* Guerman, *Art of the October Revolution; Soviet Union,* 111/2 (1976), a special issue on Constructivism; Williams, *Artist;* John Milner, *Vladimir Tatlin and the Russian Avant-Garde* (New Haven: Yale University Press, 1983); and Mazaev, *Kontseptsiya 'proizvodstvennogo iskusstva' 20-kh godov* (Moscow: Nauka, 1975).

37. Brik discussed in *Organizatsiya truda,* 1 (Mar 1921) 130; Fevralsky in Ya. S. Tubin, *Lunacharskii i stanovlenie sovetskogo muzykalnogo teatra* (Moscow: Muzyka, 1975) 35; Janecek, *The Look, passim.*

38. Russolo and Pratella translated in *Maski,* 7–8 (1912–13) 39–48. The Proletcult article is in *Gryaduschchee,* 5–6 (1919) 28. Ermansky, *Nauchnaya,* 282. For the Italian background and the Russian reception, respectively, see: James Joll, *Three Intellectuals in Politics* (London: Weidenfeld, 1960) 147–48 and Brown, *Mayakovsky,* 90.

39. Fueloep-Miller, *Mind,* 183–84.

40. *Ibid.,* 182–83; V. Kashnitskii, "Umnaya muzyka," *Novyi Lef,* 10 (Oct. 1928) 36–39.

41. Schwartz, *Music,* 53, 85–86; A. Mosolov, *Zavod: muzyka mashiny dlya orkestra (partitura)* Moscow: Gos. Muz. Izd. R.S.F.S.R., 1934). Soviet music critics and historians are almost universally hostile or ironic to this kind of music: see, e.g. *Istoriya russkoi Sovetskoi muzyki,* I, 37, 41, 254–55, 287.

42. Margarie Hoover, *Meyerhold: the Art of Conscious Theater* (Amherst: University of Massachusetts Press, 1974); V. E. Meyerhold, *Meyerhold on Theater,* ed. Edward Braun (New York: Hill and Wang, 1969); K. L. Rudnitskii, *Regissër Meierkhold* (Moscow: Nauka, 1969). See also Williams, *Artists,* 81–100; Lodder, *Constructivism,* 170 and *passim* (for the construction of sets); and Fueloep-Miller, *Mind,* 122.

43. Hoover, *Meyerhold,* 91–92, 311–15 for the training program; Meyerhold, *Meyerhold,* 197–202 for his Biomechanical manifesto, with comment by Braun, pp. 183–204, 193–94.

44. Fueloep-Miller, *Mind,* 126.

45. Rudnitskii, *Regissër,* 265–66.

46. See Alex Inkeles and David H. Smith, *Becoming Modern* (Cambridge, Mass.: Harvard University Press, 1974), esp. 22, 160–62; Pitirim Sorokin and Robert Merton, "Social Time," *American Journal of Sociology,* XIII/5 (Mar 1937) 615–29; A. L. Kroeber, *Anthropology* (New York, 1948) 91–92, 156.

47. E. P. Thompson, "Time, Work-Discipline and Industrial Capitalism," *Past and Present,* 38 (1967) 56–97 (quotes, 75, 78); Sorokin and Merton, "Social Time", 620–21.

48. Pipes, *Russia,* 142, 157 (citing Klyuchevsky); Preobrazhensky cited in Sochor, "Soviet Taylorism," 257; Hindus, *Broken,* 123; For comparisons, see: Thompson, "Time," 56–75; Keith Thomas, "Work and Leisure in Pre-Industrial Society," *Past and Present,* 29 (1964) 50–66; Eugene Genovese, *Roll, Jordan, Roll! the World the Slaves Made* (New York: Vintage, 1976) 385–94.

49. Lewin, *Russian Peasants,* 29–32; Maynard, *Russia,* 27; Hindus, "Henry Ford"; Elisha Friedman, *Russia in Transition: a Businessman's Appraisal* (New York: Viking, 1932) 51–53, 172, 214–16.

50. Vakar, *Taproot,* 115 and *passim;* Selishchev, *Yazyk,* 214–17 (on concreteness of language); Sorokin, *A Systematic Source Book in Rural Sociology,* 3 vols. (Minneapolis: Minnesota University Press, 1930–32,), I, 186–259, III, 338–39, 345–46 (especially interesting are Georg Simmel's "Great Cities and Spiritual Life" and Arnošt Blaha's comment on the scythe gesture).

51. Kerzhentsev, *Pamyatka,* 15.

## Chapter 8: Utopia in Time: Futurology and Science Fiction

1. Svyatlovsky cited in Tamarchenko, "Nauchnaya fantastika i model revolyutsii," in Suvin, ed., *Twentieth-Century Science Fiction in Warsaw Pact Countries*, special issue of *Canadian-American Slavic Studies*, 18/1–2 (Spring-Summer, 1984) 43. B. I. Gorev, *Ot Tomasa Mora do Lenina, 1516–1917* (Moscow: Frenkel, 1922), a long but rather thin work. Publication data on the translations from Helsinki and Leningrad libraries; some are cited in Khazanova, *Sov. arkh.*, 135, n. 26 and pp. 20–42. Academician V. P. Volgin was the most active scholar of classic utopias: see his editions of: Tomas Mor [Thomas More], *Zolotaya kniga . . . utopiya* (Moscow: Academia, 1935); Foma Kampanella [Tomasso Campanella], *Gorod solntsa* (Moscow, 1934), 2nd ed., 1947, an earlier ed. of which is Tomas Kampanella, *Gosudarstvo solntsa*, 2 ed. (Petrograd, 1918); Robert Ouen [Owen], *Izbrannye sochineniya*, I (Moscow, 1950). Volgin's major work of the 1920s was *Sen-Simon i Sen-Simonizm* (1924; 2 ed. Moscow: Kommunisticheskaya Akademiya, 1925).

2. Trotsky, *Literature and Revolution* (New York: Russell and Russell, n.d.) 252–53, 256.

3. *30 dnei*, (1927) 76–92 (esp. 76–77, 80, 82–84).

4. *Zhizn i teknhika budushchego (sotsialnye i nauchno-tekhnicheskie utopii)*, ed. Ar A—n [pseud. for Arkadii Arkan] and E. Kolman (Moscow: Moskovskii Rabochii, 1928).

5. Stephen Lukashevich, *N. F. Fedorov (1828–1903): a Study in Russian Eupsychian and Utopian Thought* (Newark, Del: University of Delaware Press, 1977); N. Berdyaev, "N. F. Fëdorov," RR, 9/2 (April 1950) 124–30; V. V. Zenkovsky, *History of Russian Philosophy*, 2v., trans. by George Kline (London: Routledge, 1953) II, 588–604.

6. Muraviëv, *Ovladenie vremenem;* Michael Hagemeister, "Valerian Nikolaevič Muraviev (1883–1931) und das 'Prometheische Denken' der frühen Sowjetzeit," in the German reissue (in Russian) of the above (Munich: Sagner, 1983) 1–27; *idem.*, "Die 'Biokosmisten'—Anarchismus and Maximalismus in der frühen Sowjetzeit," in G. Freidhof *et al.*, eds., *Studia slavica in Honorem viri doctissimi Olexa Horbatsch* (Munich: Sagner, 1983), pt. i, pp. 61–76. Peter Scheibert, "Der Ubermensch in den russischen Revolution," in Ernst Benz, ed., *Der Ubermensh* (Stuttgart: Rhein, 1961) 179–96; *idem.*, "Revolution und Utopie: die Gestalt der Zukunft in Denken der russischen revolutionären Intelligenz," in H. Barion *et al.*, eds., *Epirrhosis: Festgabe fur Carl Schmitt*, 2 v. (Berlin: Dunker und Humblat, 1968) 633–49.

For the application of Fëdorovism to science fiction, see Konstantin Tsiolkovskii, *Vne zemli: nauchno-fantasticheskaya povest* (1896; revised, 1917; Moscow, A.N.S.S.S.R., 1958). English tr. in *The Science Fiction of Konstantin Tsiolkovsky*, ed. Adam Starchild (Seattle: University Press of the Pacific, 1979) 161–332; A. B. Yaroslavskii, *Argonauts of the Universe* (Argonavty veselennoi, 1926), discussed in Hagemeister, " 'Biokosmisten'," 76; and Leonid Geller, *Vselennaya za predelom dogmy: Sovetskaya nauchnaya fantastika* (London: Overseas, 1985) 63. The Biocosmists were interested in burial rites for revolutionary heroes, climate control, electrification, and citizen armies.

7. Ingold, *Literatur und Aviatik,* with fascinating insights on Russian culture *(passim);* Elizabeth Beaujour, "Architectural Discourse and Early Soviet Literature," JHI (July 1983) 477–95; Bowlt, "The Old New Wave;" Nicholas Daniloff, *The Kremlin and the Cosmos* (New York: Knopf, 1972) 14, 40 (qu.). Kibalchich's drawings were locked in the police archives until 1918, when they were published by Rynin.

8. Robin Higham and Jacob Kipp, eds., *Soviet Aviation and Air Power* (London: Brassey's, 1977); A. Boyd, *The Soviet Air Force since 1918* (New York: Stein and Day, 1977) 13–14.

9. N. A. Rynin, *Mechty, legendy, i pervye fantasii* (Leningrad: Pechatnaya, 1928); idem., *Luchistaya energiya v fantaziyakh romanistov i v proektakh uchënykh* (Leningrad: Profintern, 1930). Both volumes are from his encyclopedic and vividly illustrated *Mezhduplanetnye soobshcheniya*. When these volumes appeared, Bogdanov's name was already taboo, explaining the otherwise unimaginable absence of any discussion of his novels. The entire set of Rynin's vol-

umes was translated on contract from the U.S. National Aeronautics and Space Administration and the National Science Foundation in 1970: *Interplanetary Flight and Communication,* 9 v. (Jerusalem: Israel Program of Scientific Translation). See also Daniloff, *Kremlin,* 1–65 and Suvin, *Metamorphoses,* 260.

10. A. F. Britikov, *Russkii Sovetskii nauchno-fantasticheskii roman* (Leningrad: Nauka, 1970), the standard work, lists only 87 titles, mostly full-length novels, for 1917–1931 (see its bibliography). For the higher count, see Suvin "The Utopian Tradition of Russian Science Fiction," MLR, 66 (1979) 139–59, with a short but useful bibliography, and Robert Maguire, *Red Virgin Soil: Soviet Literature in the 1920s* (Princeton: Princeton University Press, 1968) 28–29, 32. For further coverage of Soviet science fiction see: A. Palei, "Nauchno-fantasticheskaya literatura," *Literaturnaya ucheba,* 7/8 (1935) 122–47 and 2 (1936) 118–32; P. Yershov [Ershov], *Science Fiction and Utopian Fantasy in Soviet Literature* (New York 1954), Research Program on the U.S.S.R. Mimeographed Series, 62; R. Nudelman, "Fantastika, rozhdënnaya revolyutsiei," *Fantastika 1966* (Moscow, 1967) III, 330–69; Berdt Rullkötter, *Die wissenschaftliche Phantastik der Sowietunion* (Frankfurt, 1974); McGuire, *Red Stars;* Suvin, ed., *Twentieth-Century Science Fiction];* Stites, "Fantasy and Revolution: Alexander Bogdanov and the Origins of Bolshevik Science Fiction," in Bogdanov, *Red Star,* 1–16; and Geller, *Vselennaya,* 49–84.

11. Prospectus to "Mindscapes: the Geographies of Imagined Worlds," a conference at the University of California, Riverside, 1987.

12. Suvin, "Utopian"; Brooks, "Studies of the Reader in the 1920s" in Stites, ed., *N.E.P.* 187–202; *idem.,* "Breakdown in Production and Distribution;" Gooderham, "Komsomol". For Western science fiction, see Graff Conklin, *The Golden Age of Science Fiction* (New York: Bonanza, 1946/1980); Nicholls, *Encyclopedia of Science Fiction.*

13. Suvin, *Metamorphoses,* 253.

14. Brooks, *When Russia.*

15. V. A. Itin, *Strana Gonguri* (Kansk: Gos. izd., 1922). Reprinted in his *Strana Gonguri: sbornik povestei* (Novosibirsk: Zapadno-Sibirskoe knizhnoe izd., 1983) 20–84. For Itin's life, see *ibid.,* introduction, pp. 3–14; KLE, III; Britikov, *Russ. Sov.,* 98–101; and the introduction to Itin, *Kaan Kered* (Novosibirsk, 1961) 5–28. On his aviation tales, see *Aviatsiya i Khimiya,* 1 (1928) 39.

16. Ya. M. Okunev, *Gryadushchii mir: utopicheskii roman, 1923–2123* (Petrograd: Priboi, 1923). The printing was 10,000 copies. See also the author's *Kommunizm i religiya: sbornik po voprosam antireligioznoi propagandy* (Moscow: Moskovskii Rabochii, 1922) 252–54.

17. Okunev, *Gryadushchii,* 50, 44 (quotes).

18. I. Zhukov, *Puteshestvie zvena 'Krasnoi Zvezdy' v stranu chudes: povest* (Kharkov: Izd. Vseukr. O-va. Sodeistviya Yunomu Lenintsu, 1924).

19. V. D. Nikolskii, *Cherez tysyachu let: nauchno-fantasticheskii roman* (Leningrad: Soikin, 1927). It appeared in 15,000 copies as a supplement to *Vestnik znaniya.*

20. *Ibid.,* 3, 106 (quotes).

21. KLE, IV.

22. Ya. L. Larri, *Strana schastlivykh (publitsistskaya povest)* Leningrad: Leningrad. Obl. izd., 1931).

23. *Ibid.,* 1–14. I have not identified the editor, Glebov-Putilovskii, apparently a Leningrad worker (judging from the factory that forms part of his name).

24. Eliot Goodman, *Soviet Design for a World State* (New York: Columbia University Press, 1960) is an example.

25. A convincing exposition of this position, to which I adhere, is Stephen F. Cohen, *Rethinking the Soviet Experience: Politics and History Since 1917* (New York: Oxford University Press, 1985) 38–70 and *passim.*

26. See the treatment and quotations in Goodman, *Soviet Design,* 28–29.

27. *Ibid.,* 31, 37, quotations and discussion.

28. *The Soviet Image of Utopia* (Baltimore: Johns Hopkins University Press, 1975) 31.

29. Preobrazhensky, *From New Economic Policy to Socialism: A Glance into the future of Russia and Europe,* tr. Brian Pearce (London: New Park, 1962) 98–116.

30. Okunev, *Zavtrashnii den: fantasticheskii roman* (Moscow: Novaya Moskva, 1924); A. R. Palei, *Golfshtrem* (Moscow: Ogonek, 1928); A. R. Belyaev, *Borba v efire* (Moscow: Molodaya Gvardiya, 1928). On the film *Iron Heel,* co-authored by Lunacharsky, see McGuire, *Red Virgin Soil,* 28 and Suvin "Utopian" 151.

31. For the Russian mixture of cosmopolitanism and xenophobia, see Brooks, *When Russia,* 238–39.

32. On Bukharin's vision, see Goodman, *Soviet Design,* 427, 429 for examples of non-contextual citation. For more illuminating analyses, see Cohen, *Bukharin* and Susiluoto, *Origins.*

33. *Struggle in Space,* 60 (see next note).

34. Belyaev, *Borba.* Belyaev (1884–1942), who died during the blockade of Leningrad—and thus lived to see his fantasy nightmares come true—had training in science and technology. His novel also contains a scenario of combat resembling what is now called "star wars." The English translation is *Struggle in Space: Red Dream—Soviet American War* (Washington: Arfor, 1965) Arfor Classics in Astronautics, III. The preface by the translator Albert Parry is a classic of misinformed Cold War rhetoric.

35. For the images, theories, and realities of women's equality in the 1920s, see Stites, *Women's Liberation* and Lapidus, *Women in Soviet Society.* Soviet female characters in science fiction reflected both the image and the reality. They are never the main characters, but play a far more dignified and active role than do those of Western science fiction at that time: see Marlene Barr, ed., *Future Females* (Bowling Green: Bowling Green University Press, 1981).

36. See the intelligent comments in Gilison, *Soviet Image,* 24–41, *passim.*

37. Fueloep-Miller, *Mind,* 182–84; *Gryadushchee,* 5–6 (1919) 28; OT, 1 (March 1921), 129; V. Kashnitskii, "Umnaya muzyka"; Efim Zozulya, *Grammofon vekov* (1919; Moscow: Avrora, 1923) 13–14. Komfut quoted in Lodder, *Russian Constructivism,* 247.

38. Walter C. Clemens, "Globalistika: The Soviet Union and Global Issues" (Kennan Institute for Advanced Russian Studies Meeting Report, May 8, 1985).

39. Apollon Karelin, *Rossiya v 1930 godu* (Moscow: Vserossiskaya Federatsiya Anarkhistov, 1921). Although Anarchists were being arrested at this time, Karelin's book was legally printed in 5,000 copies. For more on Karelin, see Avrich, *Russian Anarchists,* 113–15, 154–55, 165, 174–76, 201–2, 230, 236; Serge, *Memoirs,* 120.

40. *Voron,* raven; *vorona* crow—the blackest of birds.

41. Karelin, *Rossiya,* 15, 19 (quotes).

42. For background, see Naum Jasny, *Soviet Economists of the 1920s: Names to be Remembered* (Cambridge: Cambridge University Press, 1972) 200 ff.; Boris Smirenskii, *Pero i maska* (Moscow: Moskovskii Rabochii, 1967) 66–68; O. Losunskii, "Chayanovskie izdaniya," *Podëm,* 3 (May-June 1968) 135–39. For commentary on the novel: Katerina Clark, "The City versus the Countryside in Soviet Peasant Literature of the Twenties: a Duel of Utopias," in Gleason, *Bolshevik Culture,* 175–89; and Nonna Shaw, "The Only Soviet Literary Peasant Utopia," SEEJ, VII/3 (1963) 279–83.

43. Iv. Kremnev [A. V. Chayanov], *Puteshestvie moego brata Alekseya v stranu krestyanskoi utopii,* pt. I (and only), Moscow: Gos. Izd., 1920. Pref. by V. Orlovskii [V. V. Vorovskii]. Reprinted in Russian (New York: Silver Age, 1981) with preface by Gleb Struve, 5–13. English trans. in R. E. F. Smith, ed., *The Russian Peasant in 1920 and 1984* (London: Frank Cass, 1977) 63–107. The 1984 dating of the action had no connection to Orwell, who chose the title for his *1984* by reversing 1948 (Struve's preface to Chayanov).

44. On this important episode in East European history, see John Bell, *Peasants in Power: Alexander Stamboliiski and the Bulgarian Agrarian National Union, 1899–1923* (Princeton: Princeton University Press, 1977).

45. Chayanov, *Puteshestvie,* 45 (qu.). Yu. A. Polyakov, *Perekhod k NEPu i Sovetskoe krestyanstvo* (Moscow: Nauka, 1967) 346. The rehabilitation occurred in August, 1987.

46. P. N. Krasnov, *Za chertopolokhom: fantasticheskii roman* (Berlin: Dyakov, 1922).

47. Evgenii Zamyatin, *My* (1920; New York: Interlanguage Literary Associates, 1967). English trans.: by G. Zilborg (1924: New York: Dutton, 1952); by B. G. Guerney (London: Cape, 1970); and by Mirra Ginsburg (New York: Bantam, 1972). Important related works by Zamyatin: *Ostrovityane* (1918; Berlin: Grzhebin, 1923), written in England in 1917; *Gerbert Uells* (Petersburg: Epokha, 1922); *Litsa* (New York: Inter-Language Literary Associates, 1967, esp. 139–46 and 173–74; *A Soviet Heretic: Essays by Yevgeny Zamyatin,* ed. Mirra Ginsburg (Chicago: University of Chicago Press).

Among the more useful of the endless commentaries on Zamyatin and his novel, see: E. J. Brown, *Brave New World, 1984, and We: an Essay on Anti-Utopia (Zamyatin and English Literature),* Ann Arbor: Ardis, 1976, qu., 34; *idem., "*Zamyatin's *We* and *Nineteen Eighty Four,"* in P. Stansky, ed., *On Nineteen Eighty Four* (Stanford: Stanford Alumni Association, 1983) 159–69; Suvin, "Utopian," 147, 150; Lewis and Weber, "Zamyatin, *We*"; D. Richards, "Four Utopias," SEER, XL (1961–62) 220–28; Patrick Parrinder, "Imagining the Future: Zamyatin and Wells," *Science-Fiction Studies,* I/1 (Spring 1973) 17–26; Josephine Woll, "Mixed Media, Mixed Messages: Evgenii Zamiatin, *We,* and Fritz Lang's *Metropolis,"* ms. 1984 (I thank the author for access to it); William Hutchins, "Structure and Design in a Soviet Utopia: H. G. Wells, Constructivism, and Yevgenii Zamyatin's *We," Journal of Modern Literature,* IX/1 (1981–82) 81–102; Ingold, *Literatur und Aviatik,* 159; Lenczyc, "Zamjatins glassymbol".

On the dystopian background in Russia, see chapter 1. For Europe and America, see Eugen Weber, "The Anti-Utopia of the Twentieth Century," *South Atlantic Quarterly,* LVIII/3 (Summer 1959) 440–47.

48. The first quotation is from Zamyatin, *My,* 5; the second from *Soviet Heretic,* 261 (I have changed the translation slightly).

49. A. K. Voronskii, "Evgenii Zamyatin," (1922), reprinted in his *Na styke* (Moscow: Gosizd., 1923) 49–75. English trans. by P. Mitchell in RLT, 3 (May 1972) 152–74. For rare references to *We,* see Yu. Ryurikov, *Cherez 100 i 1000 let* (Moscow, 1961) 92–93 and Britikov, *Russ. Sov.,* 94–95, 141 (where he compares Zamyatin's with Larri's novel).

50. The above novels certainly do not exhaust the anti-utopian and counter-utopian works of the period. See, for example: L. N. Lunz, [Lunts], *The City of Truth* (1924) trans J. Silver (London: O'Dempsey, 1929); Andrei Platonov, *Chevengur* (Paris: Y.M.C.A., 1972), with an interesting preface by Mikhail Geller; and *Rossiya i Inoniya* (Berlin: Skify, 1920), with works by Esenin, Bely, and Ivanov-Razumnik.

51. Lunacharsky, *Sob. soch.,* II, 452.

# Chapter 9: Utopia in Space: City and Building

1. Starr, *Melnikov,* 149.

2. See Hamm, *City;* Bater, *St. Petersburg;* Bradley, *Muzhik.* For an interesting parallel, see Andrew Lees, "Critics of Urban Society in Germany, 1854–1914," JHL, XL/1 (January–March 1979) 61–83.

3. Engels, *Herr Eugen Dühring's Revolution in Science (Anti-Dühring)* (Chicago: Kerr, 1935), p. 311; Wells, *Russia,* 158. Lenin's words came out under prodding and seem terse and perhaps unreflecting. Leo Marx, *The Marching in the Garden* (New York: Oxford University Press, 1964) 156, 169, 248, *passim;* Morton and Lucia White, *The Intellectual versus the City* (Cambridge, Mass.: Harvard University Press, 1962) 12, 30, 32, *passim.*

4. Blackwell, *The Beginnings of Russian Industrialization, 1800–1860* (Princeton: Princeton University Press, 1968) 99–119; Walter Pintner, *Russian Economic Policy Under Nicholas I* (Ithaca: Cornell University Press, 1967) 101–2; Zelnik, *Labor and Society in Tsarist Russia* (Stanford: Stanford University Press, 1971) 23–30 (qu. 24).

5. *Ibid.*

6. See Chapter 1. For the German case, see Lees, "Critics," and Fritz Stern, *The Politics of Cultural Despair* (New York: Anchor, 1965).

7. Radishchev, *Journey, passim:* Perovskaya quoted in Engel, *Mothers,* 113; Zlatovratsky in Wortman, *Crisis,* 109. B. P. Kozmin, "Sotsialno-politicheskie i filosofskie vzglyady V. I. Taneeva," in *Iz istorii sotsialno-polit. idei,* 664–73. On anti-urbanism as an important part of "Provincialism" in the nineteenth century, see Starr, *Decentralization and Self-Government in Russia, 1830–1870* (Princeton: Princeton University Press, 1972) 90–106.

8. Documentation on the sexual question in Stites, *Women's Liberation,* 178–90. On songs, see Rothstein, "The Quiet Rehabilitation of the Brick Factory," SR, 39/3 (September 1980) 373–88.

9. On these currents, see Clark, "The City;" Stefani Hoffman, "Scythian Theory and Literature, 1917–1924," in Nilsson, ed., *Art,* 138–64; Jensen, *Nature as Code, passim;* Trotsky, "The Rustic or Peasant-Singing Writers," in *Literature and Revolution,* 90–104, a scornfully dismissive but brilliant essay on the Revolution. The Esenin quotation is from Brown, *Mayakovsky,* 312.

10. Robert Fishman, *Urban Utopias in the Twentieth Century: Ebenezer Howerd, Frank Lloyd Wright, and Le Corbusier* (New York: Basic Books, 1977) 21–88; Gordon Cherry, *Town Planning in its Social Context* (Ayleberry: Leonard Hill, 1973) 1–36; Starr, "Writings from the 1960s on the Modern Movement in Russia," *Journal of the Society of Architectural Historians,* XXX/2 (May 1971) 170–78; *Vegetarianskoe obozrenie* (SPb., monthly, 1914-).

11. Starr, "Visionary Town Planning During the Cultural Revolution," in Sheila Fitzpatrick, *Cultural Revolution,* 207–40 (qu., 208).

12. General information on the Society (Obshchestvo Sovremennykh Arkhitektorov or O.S.A.) and the Disurbanists is drawn from: Starr, "Visionary;" *idem., Melnikov;* Anatole Kopp, *Town and Revolution: Soviet Architechture and Town Planning, 1917–1935,* trans. T. Burton (New York: Braziller, 1970); *idem., Changer la vie; idem., L'architecture de la periode stalinienne* (Grenoble: Presses universitaires, 1978), especially the interviews with surviving architects of the 1920s, pp. 367–405; Hugh Hudson, Jr., " 'The Social Condenser of Our Epoch': the Association of Contemporary Architects and the Creation of a New Way of Life in Revolutionary Russia," JGO (forthcoming).

13. M. Okhitovich, "Zametki po teorii rasseleniya," SA, 1–2 (1930) 7–16 and another piece in SA, 4 (1929). Discussion in Starr, "Visionary" 212–17 and Kopp, *Town,* 171–79.

14. Okhitovich, "Zametki," 13–15 (qu., 13).

15. M. O. Barshch and M. Ya. Ginzburg, "Zelënyi gorod," SA, 1–2 (1930) 19–36. See also N. A. Milyutin, *Sotsgorod: the Problem of Building Socialist Cities* (1930), trans. A. Sprague (Cambridge, Mass.: M.I.T. Press, 1974).

16. Barshch interview in Kopp, *Architecture,* 372-78 (qu., 374).

17. Fishman, *Urban Utopias,* 89–160.

18. Lenin, PSS, XXII, 34; Trotsky, *Literature and Revolution,* 92; Kruglikov, "Borba sotsializma i kapitalizma v derevne," *Bolshevik,* 23–24 (December 31, 1927) 55.

19. Lev Kopelev, *Education,* 90; Brown, *Mayakovsky,* 88–89; Fueloep-Miller, *Mind,* 148–49, 108; Rougle, " 'Express' "; *idem., Three Russians, passim;* Beaujour, "Architectural Discourse"; Clark, "City"; Dmitrii Maznin, "Gorod budushchego," *Yunii Proletarii,* 18–19 (September 29, 1919) 10–11, a fantasy tale; Boris Arvatov, "Oveshchestvlennaya utopiya," *Lef,* 1 (March 1923) 61–64; N. Aseev, "Zavtra," (1923) in *Sobranie sochinenii,* V (Moscow, 1964) 75–84, which features "the first moving city in the history of mankind" called "Aeroplane I" and composed of 6,000 glass buildings with portable apartment modules that fit into them; Avrich, *Anarchists,* 61–66.

20. Selim Chan-Magomedow [Khan-Magomedov], *Pionere der sowjetischen Architecture* (Vienna: Locker, 1983). This huge, magnificently illustrated translation of a Soviet work is indispensable for the projects of the 1920s and early 1930s dealing with cities and homes; Kopp,

*Town*, 861; Claes Caldenby, "The Vision of a Rational Architechture," in Kleberg and Stites, eds., *Utopia*, 269–82 (quote from Ginzburg, 272), illustrated; Moisei Ginzburg, *Style and Epoch* (1924; Cambridge, Mass.: M.I.T. Press, 1982) 96–97; Lodder, *Russian Constructivism*, 169; Berton. *Moscow* (Kirov qu., 205); Khazanova, ed., *Iz istorii Sovetskoi arkhitektury, 1917–1925: dokumenty i materialy* (Moscow: A.N.S.S.S.R., 1963) 67–76, richly illustrated projects for workers' settlements.

21. Hudson, " 'Social Condenser'," 3–5 (qu., 3).

22. *Ibid.*, 15–16; Fishman, *Urban Utopias*, 161–256; Kenneth Frampton, "Notes on Soviet Urbanism, 1917–1932," *Architects' Yearbook*, XII (London, 1968) 242–45; Khazanova, *Iz istorii Sovetskoi arkhitektury, 1926–1932 gg.: dokumenty i materialy; tvorcheskie obedineniya* (Moscow: Nauka, 1970), 128, 132, 140–43.

23. L. Sabsovitch [L. M. Sabsovich], *L'U.R.S.S. dans dix ans: plan général de la construction du socialisme: hypothèse* (Paris: Bureau d'Editions, 1930), 116–34, 158–62, *passim*, (qu., 159, 116, 121), all subsequent qu. from this source. Commentary and discussion on this and other works in Starr, "Visionary," 210–11, 231, 233; Khazanova, *Sovetskaya arkhitektura pervoi pyatiletki: problema goroda budushchego* (Moscow: Nauka, 1980). See also M. Ilin, *New Russia's Primer: the Story of the Five Year Plan*, trans. G. Counts and N. Lodge (Boston: Houghton-Mifflin, 1932) which contains a version of Sabsovich for children.

24. Khazanova, *Iz istorii* (1963), *passim; idem., Sovetskaya arkhitektura pervykh let Oktyabrya, 1917–1925 gg.* (Moscow: Nauka, 1970); Caldenby and Asa Walden, *Kollektivhus: Sovjet och Sverige omkring 1930* (Stockholm: Almquist & Wiksell, 1979) 44, 42–44. See also Kopp, *Town*, 39.

25. Caldenby, "Vision," 276 (illustr.); *idem, Kollektivhus*, 44; Khazanova, *Iz istorii* (1963) 51–52, 54, 56–57, 60–61, 81–83; Milyutin, *Sotsgorod*, 5; Kopp, *Town*, 144; on the Vesnin brothers, see *Arkkitehtuurin vallankumous: Naytelly/Revolution in Architecture: Exhibition* (Helsinki: Museum of Finnish Architecture, 1985).

26. Hudson, " 'Social Condenser'," 8, 13; Caldenby, "Vision," 280 (illustr.); Khazanova, *Iz istorii* (1970) 98, 126; Milyutin, *Sotsgorod*, 63 ff.

27. For the debates and the literature, see Stites, *Women's Liberation*, 346–76.

28. V. Kuzmin, "Problema nauchnoi organizatsii byta," S.A., 1–3 (1930) 14–17. Schedule trans. in Kopp, *Town*, 153–55. Discussion in Caldenby, *Kollektivhus*, 85–88.

29. Hudson, " 'Social Condenser'," 10–12; S.A., 4 (1926) 109 (questionnaire, whose replies have not been recorded); Khan-Magomedov, *Pionere*, 343–98 (illustr.); Kopp, *Town*, 106–9, 141–42, 172, 184–86, 198; Caldenby, *Kollektivhus*, 118–19, a chart showing how major projects divided (about 50/50) on individual kitchens.

30. *Ivan Leonidov* (New York: Rizzoli, 1981) 52–55, *passim*. For further products of his fertile architectural imaginatioon: Kopp, *Town*, 123–26.

31. Starr, *Melnikov*, 172–83. See also David Joravsky in Fitzpatrick, *Cultural Revolution*, 114, on "therapeutic phalansteries."

32. Starr, "Visionary," 227–34.

# Chapter 10: Utopia in Life: The Communal Movement

1. A. Naishtat, *et al., Kommuny molodëzhi* (Moscow: Molodaya Gvardiya, 1931), 60.

2. The best study of the *mir* in the revolution is Atkinson, *End*.

3. M. I. Tugan-Baranovskii, *V poiskakh novago mira: sotsialisticheskiya obshchiny nashego vremeni* (S.Pb.: Nash Vek, 1913) 96–97; *idem., "Russkaya revolyutsiya, sotsializm, i kooperatwiya," Vestnik kooperatsii*, 2–3 (February–March, 1917) 3–15.

4. Wortman, *Crisis*, 52–53; Tugan-Baranovskii, *V poiskakh*, 85–99.

5. For the European background of revolutionary communes, see Billington, *Fire*, 389–402.

For the 1860s in Russia see Chapter 1; Brower, *Training;* Gleason, *Young Russia;* Stites, *Women's Liberation*, 105–11; Miller, "Ideology"; Zelnik, "Populists", 261–63. For prison camp communes, see A. V. Pribylev, *V dinamitnoi masterskoi i Kariiskaya politicheskaya tyurma* (Leningrad: Gosizdat, 1924) 42–78; Engel, *Mothers*, 139; Lunacharskii, *Revol. Silhouettes*, 123. For art communes, N. N. Punina, *Peterburgskaya artel khudozhikov* (Leningrad: Khudozhnik, 1966) 20–34.

6. Wesson, *Soviet Communes*, 46–47; Alexander, *Emperor*, 31; Zelnik, "Russian Bebels," *RR*, 35–43 (July 1976) 259–60 ; *idem.*, *Radical Worker*, 7–13; Bradley, *Muzhik*, 27, 196–211.

7. L. A. Anokhina and M. N. Smheleva, *Byt gorodskogo naseleniya srednei polosy R.S.F.S.R. v proshlom i nastoyashcem* (Moscow: Nauka, 1977). Lunacharsky quoted in Peter Juviler, "Contradictions of Revolution: Juvenile Crime and Rehabilitation," in Gleason, *Bolshevik Culture*, 267.

8. See a brief treatment of this point in Stites, "Kommuunikokeilut ja niiden loppu Venäjän vallankummouksessa (1917–1934)," *Tiede ja edistys*, 10/1 (1985) 7–21.

9. Basile Kerblay, "Les utopies communautaires: au banc de la Russie des années vingt," *RES*, 56/1 (1984) 97–103; Wesson, *Soviet Communes*, 110–13; Atkinson, *End*, 219–21; V. P. Danilov, *Sovetskaya dokolkhoznaya derevnya* (Moscow: Nauka, 1967) 106–53; A. F. Chmyga, *Kolkhoznoe dvizhenie na Ukraine (1917–1929 gg.): ocherki istorii* (Moscow: Izd. Mosk. U., 1974) 76–79, 90.

10. Cited in Wesson, *Soviet Communes*, 209–10.

11. Confino, "Russian Customary," 42–43.

12. T. Zelënov, "K istorii vozniknoveniya selsko-khozyaistvennykh kommun i arteli v S.S.S.R. (1918 g.)," *KA*, 101 (1940) 122–47; Moshe Lewin, *Russian Peasants and Soviet Power* (New York: Norton, 1975) 107–10.

13. V. N. Meshcheryakov in VOKZ, 4 (December 15, 1918) 121–24; *idem.*, *O selsko-khozyaistvennykh kommunakh* (Moscow: Izd. VTsIK, 1918); Kii [P. V. Pyatnitskii], *Selskaya kommuna* (Petrograd, 1918); Ya. Zhigur, *Organizatsiya kommunisticheskikh khozyaistv v zemledelii* (Moscow: VTsIK, 1918); S. S. Kislyanskii, *Komu vygodna kommuna i kto eë boitsya* (Moscow: Gosizd., 1921).

14. M. Sumatokhin, *Davaite zhit Kommunoi!* (Moscow: VTsIK, 1918).

15. Wesson, *Soviet Communes*, 85, 100, 105, 108–9, 126–27; Meshcheryakov, *Derevenskaya bednota i put k sotsializmu*, 2 ed. (Petrograd: Petro. Sov., 1918); VOKZ, 10–11 (February 9, 1919) 305; Bukharin, *ABC*, 306, Chmyga, *Kolkhoznoe*, 80, 96, 98.

16. Wesson, *Soviet Communes*, 115, 119–21; I. A. Konyukov, *Kollektivnoe zemledelie*, 3 ed. (Moscow: Novaya Derevnya, 1927) 65, 68, 72, 76; KA, 89–90 (1938) document from October 5, 1918, p. 95–97.

17. Konyukov, *Kollektivnoe*, 76–79, contains a brief discussion of motives, as do most of the other sources cited here.

18. Wesson, *Soviet Communes*, 142–45; VOKVD, 2 (September 1918) 171–72 (account of a landless peasants' commune in a manor house); KA, 89–90 (1938) 95–97.

19. Wesson, *Soviet Communes*, 142; V. Tselliarius, *Kooperatisiya i borba za sotsializm*, 2 ed. (Kharkov: Knigospilka, 1925) 53–54 (qu.); Konyukov, *Kollektivnoe*, 190.

20. Wesson, *Soviet Communes*, 148–53; Farson, *Black Bread*, 175–80.

21. I. P. Yarkov, "Pervye kolkhozy Sibiri (1918–1926 gg.)," *Trudy Novosibirskogo Instituta Inzhenerov Vodnogo Transporta*, 8 (Novosibirsk: Min. Rechnogo Flota R.S.F.S.R., 1960) 37–79 (qu. 52); Fëdor Panfërov, "Chto takoe kommunizm," *Oktyabr*, XXXVII/1 (January 1960) 103–22 (esp. 104–5).

22. For a few examples, see A. A. Bitsenko, *Selsko-khozyaistvennaya kommuna imeni Zinovieva* (Moscow: Novaya Derevnya 1924) 3–6, 8–13, *passim;* Kerblay, "Les utopies"; Scheffer, *Seven*, 80.

23. Anthony Sutton, *Western Technology and Soviet Economic Development*, 3 vols., (Stanford: Hoover, 1968–700) I, 26 ff; Serge, *Memoirs*, 148–49.

24. Robert Waite, *Vanguard of Nazism: The Free Corps Movement in Postwar Germany*,

*1918–123* (New York: Norton, 1969) 138; Wesson, *Soviet Communes,* 192–93; Stites, *Women's Liberation,* 407, 409.

25. V. L. Shveitser and S. M. Shabalova, eds., *Besprizornye v trudovykh kommunakh* (Moscow: Glavstosvos, 1926); E. Batova, "Bolshevskaya Trudovaya Kommuna i eë organizator," *Yunost,* 3 (March 1966) 91–93; G. Belykh and L. Pantaleev, *Respublika Shk.I.D.* (Moscow: Molodaya Gvardiya, 1932); Stevens, "Children"; Juviler, "Contradictions." The literature on children's colonies is enormous but has never received a satisfactory synthesis.

26. Petrus, *Religious Communes, passim;* Wesson, *Soviet Communes,* 208; Klibanov, *Relig. sekt.,* 219–47; Dunn, *Peasants;* Christel Lane, *The Christian Religion in the Soviet Union* (Albany: SUNY, 1970).

27. Naishtat, *Kommuny,* 14, 17, 21, 80.

28. Khan-Magomedov, *Pionere,* 342–43; Kulyshev, *Part. org.,* 258; Fisher, *Famine,* 75.

29. M. Yankovskii, *Kommuna sta tridtsati trëkh* (Leningrad: Priboi, 1929) 31–32, 177, *passim.*

30. *Ibid.,* 65–68.

31. *Ibid.,* 70–82.

32. *Ibid.,* 43–50, 11, 125.

33. *Ibid.,* 32, 132–38.

34. *Ibid.,* 84–85, 182, *passim;* review of Yankovskii in RK, 23–34 (December 31, 1929) 58–62.

35. Mehnert, *Youth,* 163–86 (quotes, 175, 177, 170).

36. Gooderham, "Komsomol"; Naishtat, *Kommuny,* 18–19, 52–53, 65; M. Buchel, "O kollektivakh," KM, 3–4 (March–April 1925) 132–34.

37. Dmitriev and Galin, *Na putyakh,* 14–25; Naishtat, *Kommuny,* 39, 43, 70.

38. See for example A. Kagan, *45 dnei sredi molodëzhi* (Leningrad: Priboi, 1929), the summer diary of a physician.

39. Naishtat, *Kommuny,* 17–18, 40, 54; A. Grigorovich, Zhivëm (bytovye kommuny), Moscow: Izd. VTsSPS, 1930, 3–12, 29; Kopp, *Changer,* 164–73.

40. Naishtat, *Kommuny,* 54.

41. Kopp, *Changer,* 164.

42. Kopp, *Town and Revolution,* 109; Grigorovich, *Zhivëm,* 20; Kopp, *Changer,* 184; Mehnert, *Youth,* 182–83 (quote).

43. Grigorovich, *Zhivëm,* 33; V. Yu. Krupyanskaya, *et al., Kultura i byt gornyakov i metallurgov Nizhnego Tagila (1917–1970),* Moscow: Nauka, 1974, 113–14.

44. This account is drawn almost wholly from the excellent article by Lewis Siegelbaum, "Production Collectives and Communes and the 'Imperatives' of Soviet Industrialization, 1929–1931," SR, 45/1 (Spring 1986) 65–84 (qu., 68).

45. Grigorovich, *Zhivëm,* 3, 18, 23, 25; Mehnert, *Youth,* 179; Kopp, *Changer,* 176; A. L. Strong, *The Soviets Conquer Wheat* (New York: Holt, 1931) 150–53 (qu., 153); Naishtat, *Kommuny,* 3–8; Kerzhentsev, *Bolshevism,* 50–52; Wesson, *Soviet Communes,* 205.

46. Siegelbaum, "Production Collectives," quotes, 65, 73. Hiroaki Kuromiya of Cambridge University has written a fascinating study of the artel in this period: "The Artel and Social Relations in Soviet Industry in the 1920s." ms.

47. Grigorovich, *Zhivëm,* 12.

48. Naishtat, *Kommuny,* 26.

49. *Ibid.,* 83, 58 and Grigorovich, *Zhivëm,* 13 (quotes).

50. Quoted by Nicholas Riasanovsky in "The Problem of the Peasant" in Vucinich, *Peasant,* 272.

51. Grigorovich, *Zhivëm,* 21.

52. Naishtat, *Kommuny,* 69–75; Siegelbaum, "Productive Collectives."

53. Naishtat, *Kommuny,* 88.

## Chapter 11: War on the Dreamers

1. Berton, *Moscow*, 202; Savitskii, *Razrushayushchie svoyu rodinu; Bezbozhnik u stanka*, 24 (1929) 8; Kopelev, *Education*, 114.

2. See the informed discussion in Fitzpatrick, *Education*, 140–45; Mehnert, *Youth*, 25; L. Syrkin, *Makhaevshchina* (Moscow: Gos. sots.-ek. izd., 1931) 69–76; Avrich, "What is 'Makhaevism?'," 66.

3. For the details, I have looked at party and government press coverage of the November 7 celebrations, 1930–1945, supplemented by research on the same events by Mary Jo Brooks in the London *Times*, the New York *Times*, *Time Magazine*, and *Literary Digest*.

4. Lane, *Rites*, 173–80; *Pravda* (November 9, 1938) 4–6. See Raymond Robbins's comment of May 13, 1935 contrasting May Day 1918 with that of 1932: Stalin, *Soch.*, XIII, 261.

5. Mazaev, *Prazdnik*, 365; Binns, "Changing Face," 602.

6. Cited in Conrad Donakowski, *Muse for the Masses: Ritual and Music in an Age of Democratic Revolution, 1770–1870*, (Chicago: University of Chicago Press, 1977) 2.

7. *Pravda* (November 9, 1938) 1–3. Lane, *Rites*, 173–74.

8. Pospielovsky, *Russian Church*, I, 163–91; Curtiss, *Russian Church*, 239–55; Fainsod, *Smolensk*, 436.

9. Skvortsov-Stepanov, *Izbrannye*, 26 (quote), 28; *Deyateli*, 8–9; Petrus, *Religious Communes*, 58; Yaroslavskii, *Protiv religii*, II, 449–50; Lunacharskii, *Lichnost Khrista v sovremennoi nauke i literature* (Moscow: Bezbozhnik, 1928) 18.

10. Curtiss, *Russian Church*, 239–55, Fainsod, *Smolensk*, 436; Fitzpatrick, *Education*, 152; Binns, "Changing Face," 601–2; Kopp, *Changer la ville*, 86; W. Chamberlin, *Russia's Iron Age* (Boston: Little Brown, 1934) 316; VKR (Prague) 5/17 (May 1930) 9–12.

11. Curtiss, *Russian Church*, 252; Gooderham "Komsomol;" *Tovarishch Komsomol*, I, 425–28.

12. Ann Rassweiler, "Party and Worker: Dneprostroi Experience, 1927–32," paper given at A.A.A.S.S. meeting, 1980. See also Siegelbaum, *Stakhanovism*, ch. 6.

13. Dallin, "The Return of Inequality," in Robert V. Daniels, ed., *The Stalin Revolution*, 2nd ed. (Lexington, Mass.: Heath, 1972) 109; Chamberlin, *Russia's Iron Age*, 267–73.

14. Walter Connor, *Socialism, Politics, and Equality*, 71 (qu.). See also Yanowitch, *Social and Economic Inequality*, 23–24 and Matthews, *Privilege*, 91–130.

15. I. V. Stalin, *Sochineniya*, 13 v. (Moscow: OGIZ, 1946–51) and 3 v., ed. R. McNeal (Stanford: Hoover, 1967), VII, 375–76; XII, 108–11.

16. *Ibid.*, XIII, 51–80 (qu., 57), 118–19.

17. *Ibid.*, XIII, 350–56 (qu., 350, 351, 354).

18. Syrkin, *Makaevshchina;* Mehnert, *Youth*, 234–54 (qu., 254).

19. Maurice Dobb, *Soviet Economic Development*, 426; Fitzpatrick, *Education*, 216, 316 n.; Lewin in Fitzpatrick, *Cultural Revolution*, 73; Rassweiler, "Party and Worker," 15–18.

20. Simon, *Moscow, passim;* Matthews, *Privilege*, 93–99, 113–26; Kopp, *Changer*, 47; Juviler, *Revolutionary Law and Order*, 41; Yvon [sic], *L.U.R.S.S. telle qu'elle est* (Paris: Gallimard, 1938) 162–72, 199–205; Alcan Hirsch, *Industrialized Russia* (New York: Chemical Catalog, 1934) 40–41, 47–48, 50, 54, 180–81.

21. Matthews, *Privilege*, 126; Timasheff, *Great Retreat*, 317–19; Albert Seaton, *The Russo-German War, 1941–45* (New York: Praeger, 1971) 88; Bowlt, "Constructivism," 218.

22. Vakar, *Taproot*, 80. Although the Esperanto movement meant much more than linguistic egalitarianism, it is characteristic of the anti-utopian war that it liquidated the Esperantists: Ulrich Lins, "Lingvo de cionistoj kaj kosmopolitoj," in Lapenna, *Esperanto*, 720–47.

23. Fitzpatrick, *Education, passim;* Lapidus, *Women;* Stites, *Women's Liberation*, chs. 11–12.

24. See the interesting comments on this in Nicholas Lampert, *The Technical Intelligentsia*

*and the Soviet State* (London: Macmillan, 1979) 135–48; Bailes, *Technology and Society;* and Dunham, *In Stalin's Time.*

25. Krzhizhanovskii in *Pioner,* 20 (October, 1929) 7–9; Nudelman, "Fantastika," 357–58; Lunacharskii, *Sob. soch.,* II, 444–47, 448–52; Britikov, "A. V. Lunacharskii," 46–51; A. P. Palei, "Sovetskaya nauchno-fantasticheskaya literatura," RK, 23–24 (December 31, 1929) 63–68.

26. Ershov, "Science Fiction," 35–43; McGuire, *Red Stars,* 12–15; Suvin, *Metamorphoses,* 264; KLE, VII ("Utopiya"); Brooks, "Breakdown;" Suvin, *Twentieth Century,* 39 (Tamarchenko) and 43–44 (Heuser).

27. Nudelman, "Fantastika," 358.

28. Cohen, Bukharin, 31, 100, 362, 364.

29. Geller, *Vselennaya,* 68–69, 71, 77; Zamyatin, *We,* 31; ESF, 512. Some writers were able to lament openly the narrow scope of science fiction in the 1930s: *Detskaya literatura,* 4 (April, 1940), but this had no visible effect. For Nazi science fiction, see: Manfred Nagel, "Nazistika myter," *Science Fiction nytt* (Stockholm), 67 (February, 1982) 8–30 and the exchange of letters on the subject in *S-F Studies,* VI/I (March, 1979) 114–17.

30. Anna Louise Strong, *The Soviets Conquer Wheat* (New York: Holt, 1931) 119–44; Wesson, *Soviet Communes,* 204–5; Edward Phillips, *American Technical Assistance,* 74–84, 152, based on research in the Ford Company archives.

31. Kopp, "Housing and Revolution," unpublished paper, Kennan Institute, May, 1981; Hudson, " 'Social Condenser',"; Star, "Visionary."

32. *Ibid.;* Hudson, " 'Social Condenser'." For an account of Social Democratic housing in Vienna at the time, see *Traum und Wirklichkeit: Wien, 1870–1930,* 2 ed. (Vienna: Historical Museum, 1985) 640–57.

33. Kopp, *Architecture,* 376, 380, 401–4.

34. *Ibid.,* 403; Berton, *Moscow,* 219–30; Mazaev, *Prazdnik,* 375; Beaujour, "Architectural Discourse," 494.

35. Kopp, "Housing".

36. Stalin, *Soch.,* XIII, 352–57.

37. For various kinds of hostility to communes, see: Konyukov, *Kollektivnoe,* 35–37, 70–71; Mehnert, *Youth,* 152; Wesson, *Soviet Communes.*

38. Klibanov, *Religioznoe sektantsvo i sovremennost* (Moscow: Nauka, 1969) 219–59. Robert Conquest tells of a group of Old Believers who found undisturbed isolation in a remote settlement until discovered in 1950: *Harvest of Sorrow: Soviet Collectivization and the Terror-Famine* (New York: Oxford University Press, 1986), 141–42.

39. Naishtat, *Kommuny,* 22–23; Mehnert, *Youth,* 66, 249–57.

40. Kopp, *Town,* 111, 155, 184, 207; Naishtat, *Kommuny,* 86; Kerzhentsev, *Bolshevism for Beginners.* trans. I. Low (Moscow: Tsentrizdat, 1931) 81–82; Grigorov, *Stary,* 77. El Lissitzky [L. M. Lisitskii], *Russia: an Architecture for World Revolution,* tr. E. Dluhosch (1930; Cambridge, Mass.: M.I.T. Press, 1970) 184–87.

41. Interviews in Kopp, *Architecture,* 375 (Barshch), 380–82 (Rozenfeld), and 398, 399 (Blumenfeld).

42. Simon, *Moscow,* 143–72.

43. Siegelbaum, "Production"; Kaganovich in Stalin and Kaganovich, *Otchët tsentralnogo komiteta XVI sezda VKP (b)* (Moscow: Gos. izd., 1930), 107. Kaganovich, a practitioner of harsh irony, evoked laughter from his audience at the congress by telling of a factory manager joining a production commune. See also Kuromiya, "Artel."

44. J. A. C. Brown, *The Social Psychology of Industry* (Harmondsworth: Penguin, 1954) *passim.*

45. Mehnert, *Youth,* 253; Grigorov, *Stary,* 83–84; Stalin, *Soch.,* XIII, 352–53; Nikolai Pogodin, "Derzost," *Sobranie dramaticheskikh proizvedenii,* 5 vols. (Moscow: Iskusstvo, 1960–61), I, 105–198 (117).

46. Zamyatin, *We,* 109.

# Chapter 12: Conclusion

1. Jasny, *Soviet Economists*, 135; Moshe Lewin, *Political Undercurrents in Soviet Economic Debates* (Princeton: Princeton University Press, 1974) 97–124.

2. *Ibid.* and 357–65; Tucker, "Stalinism as Revolution from Above," in Tucker, ed., *Stalinism*, (New York: Norton, 1977) 91–92; Mehnert, *Youth*, 67, 191; Fitzpatrick, *Education*, 161–62.

3. Stalin, *Problems of Leninism* (Peking: Foreign Languages Press, 1976) 849, 851.

4. Lewin, "Society, State, and Ideology," 62, 64, 74.

5. Roy Medvedev, *All Stalin's Men*, trans. H. Shukman (New York: Anchor, 1985) 113, 118, 120, 124 (qu.).

6. Lieberstein, "Technology," 53–55; Richard Vidmer, "Soviet Studies of Organization and Management," SR 40/3 (Fall, 1981) 404–22; Bailes, "American Connection".

7. Tatur, *Wissenschaft. Arbeitsorg.*, 34–51; Lieberstein, "Technology," 56–58; William Chase and Lewis Siegelbaum, "Worktime and Industrialization in the U.S.S.R., 1917–1941," ms.; John Littlepage, *In Search of Soviet Gold* (New York: Harcourt, 1937) 238–52—one of the most vivid accounts of Stakhanovism as a social frenzy in 1935; Maurice Dobb, *Soviet Economic Development Since 1917* (New York: International Publishers, 1948) 429–32; Simon, *Moscow*, 179–90; and Gastev, *Kak nado rabotat*, 316–471. The complexities and nuances of Stakhanovism are exposed with great clarity by Siegelbaum in *Stakhanovism and the Politics of Productivity in the USSR, 1935–41* (Cambridge: Cambridge University Press, 1988).

8. Smith "Taylorism," 20–21; Susiluoto, *Origins*, 147; and information from Yuri Gastev.

9. Lewin, "Society, State, and Ideology," 44, 54; Fitzpatrick, *Education*, 8, 59, 158, 249–52, *passim; idem*, "Cultural Revolution as Class War," in *Cultural Revolution*, 3–4, 33, 35, 39.

10. Lewin, "Society, State, and Ideology," 54–59, 72; Vakar, *Taproot*; A. R. Tullock, "The 'Man vs. Machine' Theme in Pilnyak's *Machines and Wolves*," RLT, 8 (1974) 329–39.

11. Fitzpatrick, *Cultural Revolution, passim*.

12. See the works of Fitzpatrick cited above and her *Russian Revolution, 1917–1932* (New York: Oxford University Press, 1982).

13. Tucker, "Does Big Brother Really Exist?," in Irving Howe, ed., *1984 Revisited: Totalitarianism in Our Century* (New York: Harper, 1983) 102.

14. Timasheff, *Great Retreat, passim;* Hindus, *Great Offensive*, 272–73; Starr, *Red and Hot;* Medvedev, *All Stalin's Men*, 12.

15. Hough in Fitzpatrick, *Cultural Revolution*, 248; H. Stein, "Russian Nationality," *Ethos* (Winter 1976); Tucker, *The Soviet Political Mind* (New York: Norton, 1971), 41, 49, 63, 67.

16. Stalin, *Problems of Leninism*, 783, 820.

17. *From Max Weber: Essays in Sociology*, ed. Hans Gerth and C. Wright Mills (New York: Oxford University Press, 1958), 249; Gorchakov, *Istoriya*, 88 (the mock trials); Fueloep-Miller, *Mind and Face*, 140. For the purge trials as ritual see: *The Great Purge Trial*, ed. Robert Tucker and Stephen Cohen (New York: Universal, 1965); Cohen, *Bukharin;* Robert Conquest, *The Great Terror* (Harmondsworth: Penguin, 1968); and Nathan Leites and Elsa Bernaut, *Ritual of Liquidation* (Glencoe: Free Press, 1954).

18. A. F. Zhuravlëv, "Okhranitelnye obryady, svyazannye s padezhom skota, i ikh geograficheskoe rasprostranenie," *Slavyanskii i Balkanskii folklor* (Moscow: Nauka, 1978), 71–94. On the function of "transparency" in revolution, see Lynn Hunt, *Politics, Culture, and Class in the French Revolution* (Berkeley: University of California Press, 1984) 44–46.

19. Timasheff, *Great Retreat*, 173: *Istoriko-revolyutsionyi kalendar, 1939* ed. A. V. Shestakov (Moscow, 1939) 631–49; A. Belyakov, *Iz Moskvy v Ameriku cherez Severnyi Polyus* (Moscow, 1938), 14–15; L. Savelev, *Shturm Zimnego* (Moscow: Shkolnaya Biblioteka, 1939). Komar and Melamid, in "In Search of Religion," relate that reporductions of Ilya Repin's painting of Ivan the Terrible and his son and of Nikolai Ge's Peter the Great and son were used in the 1930s

to illustrate boxes of chocolates. Further documentation in Stites, "Stalin: Utopian or Antiutopian" in J. Held, ed., *The Cult of Power: Dictators in the Twentieth Century* (Boulder: East European Monographs, 1983), 77–94.

20. Kopelev, *Education*, 244.

21. For Stalin as father, see Katerina Clark, *The Soviet Novel: History as Ritual* (Chicago: University of Chicago Press, 1980), 114–35. Vakar, *Taproot*, 79, 81, 86; Stites, "Stalin," 87–88. And for Stalin-as-*tsar-batyushka* among prison inmates: Mandelstam, *Hope against Hope*, 263 and Evgeniya Ginzburg, *Journey into the Whirlwind* (New York: Harvest, 1967), 20, 22, 214, 283.

22. *Tvorchestvo narodov S.S.S.R.*, ed. A. M. Gorky *et al.* (Moscow: Pravda, 1938), 115, 124, and *passim* (see illustrations); Dzhambul, *Kolybelnaya pesnya* (Moscow: Detskaya Literatura, 1938); *New York Times*, November 10, 1942.

23. N. S. Khrushchëv, *The Crimes of the Stalin Era*, ed. Boris Nicolaevsky (New York: New Leader, 1956), p. s–7; Aleksei Stakhanov, *Rasskaz o moei zhizni* (Moscow: Ogiz., 1937), 44–47.

24. Engels, "On Authority," (1872) in Tucker, ed., *The Marx-Engels Reader*, 2 ed. (New York: Norton, 1978), 733; A. M. Arzamastsev, *Kazarmennyi 'Kommunizm'* (Moscow: Mezhdunarodnye otnosheniya, 1974), 19–25; A. I. Volodin, *Utopiya i istoriya* (Moscow: Izd. polit. lit., 1976), *passim*.

25. The samizdat publication *Feniks* quoted in *Grani*, 27/52 (1962) 126. See also Petr Vail and Aleksandr Genis, "Stroiteltsvo utopii," *Grani*, 137 (1985), 157–90. Nekrich and Heller, *Utopia in Power;* and the comic dystopia by Vladimir Voinovich, *Moscow, 2040* (New York: Harcourt-Brace, 1986).

26. For a sharp example of anti-utopianism, see Adam Ulam, "Socialism and Utopia," in Frank Manuel's collection, *Utopias and Utopian Thought* (Boston: Beacon, 1966), 116–34; cf. the Manuels' intelligent speculation about the future of utopia in the concluding chapter of *Utopian Thought in the Western World*.

27. Kopelev, *Education*, ix–xi (qu., ix); Tucker, *Soviet Political Mind*, 133.

28. Bogdanov, "Engineer Menni" in *Red Star*, 204.

29. Boris Kagarlitsky, "The Intelligentsia and the Changes," *New Left Review*, 164 (1987) 5–26.

# Index